Understanding Global Politics

Contemporary international affairs are largely shaped by widely differing thematic issues and actors, such as nation states, international institutions, NGOs and multinational companies. Obtaining a deeper understanding of these multifaceted themes and actors is crucial for developing a genuine understanding of contemporary international affairs. This book provides undergraduate and postgraduate students of global politics and international relations with the necessary knowledge of the forces that shape and dominate our global political, economic and social/cultural environment. The book significantly enhances our understanding of the essentials of contemporary international affairs.

Understanding Global Politics takes a pragmatic approach to international relations, with each chapter written by an expert in his or her respective field:

- Part I provides the historical background that has led to the current state of world affairs. It also provides clear outlines of the major yet often complex theories of international relations.
- Part II is dedicated to the main actors in global politics. It discusses actors such as the most important nation states, the UN, EU, international organisations, NGOs and multinational companies.
- Part III considers important contemporary themes and challenges in global politics, including non-state centered challenges. Chapters focus on international terrorism, energy and climate change issues, religious fundamentalism and demographic changes.

The comprehensive structure of this book makes it particularly viable to students who wish to pursue careers in international organisations, diplomacy, consultancy, the think tank world and the media.

Klaus Larres is the Richard M. Krasno Distinguished Professor in History and International Affairs at the University of North Carolina at Chapel Hill, US. He served as Counselor and Senior Policy Adviser at the German Embassy in Beijing, China. Previously he was Professor at the University of London, UK, Queen's University Belfast and the University of Ulster in Northern Ireland and Johns Hopkins University/SAIS in Washington, DC, US. He held visiting professorships and senior fellowships at Yale, Tsinghua University in Beijing, the German Institute of International and Security Affairs (SWP) in Berlin and the Institute for Advanced Study (IAS) in Princeton, New Jersey. He also held the Henry A. Kissinger Chair at the Library of Congress in Washington, DC. He has published widely on post-1945 global affairs, including several books. In particular, his publications focus on the global Cold War, transatlantic relations in the post-1945 and post-Cold War years and trilateral relations among the US, China and Europe/Germany. Find his website at www.klauslarres.org.

Ruth Wittlinger is Professor in the School of Government and International Affairs at Durham University, UK. She has published extensively on memory and identity in post-unification Germany and Europe. She is the author of the monograph *German National Identity in the Twenty-First Century: A Different Republic After All?* and her research has been published in a number of journals, including *West European Politics*, *Nationalism and Ethnic Politics*, *German Politics*, *German Politics and Society* and *Cooperation and Conflict*. She has held research fellowships at the American Institute for Contemporary German Studies in Washington, DC, and the Hebrew University of Jerusalem. She is currently working on a project which examines the state of the German diaspora in the former Soviet Union, which involves field research in Ukraine, Kazakhstan, Kyrgyzstan, Russia/Western Siberia, Uzbekistan and Tajikistan. In 2018, she became Chair of the International Association for the Study of German Politics.

Understanding Global Politics

Actors and Themes in International Affairs

Edited by Klaus Larres and Ruth Wittlinger

Routledge
Taylor & Francis Group

LONDON AND NEW YORK

First published 2020
by Routledge
2 Park Square, Milton Park, Abingdon, Oxon OX14 4RN

and by Routledge
52 Vanderbilt Avenue, New York, NY 10017

Routledge is an imprint of the Taylor & Francis Group, an informa business

British Library Cataloguing-in-Publication Data
A catalogue record for this book is available from the British Library

Library of Congress Cataloging-in-Publication Data
Names: Larres, Klaus, editor. | Wittlinger, Ruth, 1961– editor.
Title: Understanding global politics : actors and themes in international affairs / edited by Klaus Larres and Ruth Wittlinger.
Description: Abingdon, Oxon ; New York, NY : Routledge, 2019. | Includes bibliographical references and index. |
Identifiers: LCCN 2018048251 (print) | LCCN 2019002317 (ebook) | ISBN 9781315545288 (eBook) | ISBN 9781134818600 (Adobe) | ISBN 9781134818747 (Mobipocket) | ISBN 9781134818679 (ePub) | ISBN 9781138682276 (hardback : alk. paper) | ISBN 9781138682269 (pbk. : alk. paper) | ISBN 9781315545288 (ebk.)
Subjects: LCSH: World politics. | International relations.
Classification: LCC JZ1310 (ebook) | LCC JZ1310 .U53 2019 (print) | DDC 327—dc23
LC record available at https://lccn.loc.gov/2018048251

ISBN: 978-1-138-68227-6 (hbk)
ISBN: 978-1-138-68226-9 (pbk)
ISBN: 978-1-315-54528-8 (ebk)

Typeset in Sabon
by Apex CoVantage, LLC

Contents

Figures

Tables

Contributors

Jutta Bakonyi is Associate Professor in Development and Conflict at Durham University, UK.

Annamarie Bindenagel Šehović is Acting Professor of International Politics at the University of Potsdam, Germany, and Research Fellow at PAIS at the University of Warwick, UK.

Mark K. Cassell is Professor of Political Science at Kent State University, Ohio, US.

Sarah Cohen is Senior Lecturer in Politics at Northumbria University, UK.

John Dumbrell is Emeritus Professor in American Politics at Durham University, UK.

Peter Eltsov is Assistant Professor of International Security Studies at the National Defense University in Washington, DC, US.

Ulf Engel is Professor of African Studies and Global Studies at the University of Leipzig, Germany.

Margit Fauser is Professor of Sociology, Organisation, Migration and Participation at Ruhr-University Bochum, Germany.

Matthew Flinders is Professor of Politics at the University of Sheffield, UK.

Manuel Fröhlich is Professor of International Relations at the University of Trier, Germany.

Marc Geddes is Lecturer in British Politics at the University of Edinburgh, UK.

Rainer Hillebrand is Professor of International Economics at the Fulda University of Applied Sciences, Germany.

Tobias Hof is Privatdozent for Modern and Contemporary History at the Ludwig-Maximilians-University Munich, Germany.

Dianne Kirby is Emeritus Reader in History at Trinity College Dublin, Ireland.

Klaus Larres is the Richard M. Krasno Distinguished Professor of History and International Affairs at the University of North Carolina at Chapel Hill, US.

Yvonne McDermott is Professor of International Criminal Law and International Human Rights Law at Swansea University, UK.

Wayne McLean is Sessional Teacher at Australian National University, Canberra, Australia.

John Mikler is Associate Professor at the University of Sydney, Australia.

Holger Moroff is Lecturer at Leibnitz University in Hanover, Germany, and teaches Political Science at the University of North Carolina at Chapel Hill, US.

Hannah Murphy-Gregory is Lecturer in Politics and International Relations at the University of Tasmania, Australia.

Linda Risso is Senior Research Fellow at the Institute of Historical Research in the School of Advanced Study at the University of London, UK.

Indrajit Roy is Lecturer in Politics at the University of York, UK.

Jonas Schneider is Senior Researcher at the Center for Security Studies (CSS) of the Swiss Federal University of Technology (ETH), Zurich, Switzerland.

Christian Schweiger is Professor of Comparative European Governance Systems at Chemnitz University of Technology, Germany.

Gudrun Wacker is Senior Fellow at the German Institute for International and Security Affairs (SWP), Berlin, Germany.

Christian Wagner is Senior Fellow at the German Institute for International and Security Affairs (SWP), Berlin, Germany.

Ruth Wittlinger is Professor in Politics at Durham University, UK.

Introduction

Global politics is shaped by actors and long-term forces. This book attempts to give room to both. It considers the impact of states, still the most crucial entity in world politics, and a wide variety of public and private organisations. The volume also explores some of the major transnational overarching developments and long-term challenges we are grappling with today. The book does not enter into the almost non-resolvable debate about whether or not world politics is primarily driven and influenced by people or long-term structures, such as demographic or economic developments. Clearly, both actors and themes shape global politics today.

We have assembled experts on the major states and organisations and the largest transnational challenges of our age. While we have attempted to cover the most crucial themes and the most influential actors in global politics, such an endeavour can never hope to be comprehensive. Some readers will quibble with our choice, which has been influenced by the availability of the required expertise and the necessity of keeping the book at a manageable length. We are hopeful, however, that readers will find the chapters invigorating.

Readers of all ages and professions but not least students – tomorrow's leaders – may feel stimulated by our choice of actors and themes. When exploring the engaging topics of the book, the sober, highly readable and well-structured assessments of our contributors will provide much food for thought to anyone interested in global affairs. Readers may take up their lead and think some more about how best to guide our tumultuous, chaotic and overly nationalistic times along more stable, less divisive and perhaps more pragmatic lines. As Shakespeare already knew, this formidable task cannot be attempted by an individual; it has to be a truly common and global enterprise:

> The time is out of joint. O cursèd spite, That ever I was born to set it right! Nay, come, let's go together.[1]

Klaus Larres, Chapel Hill, NC,
and Ruth Wittlinger, Durham, UK, January 2019

Note

1 William Shakespeare, *Hamlet* (Act 1, Scene 5).

Part I

Background

History and theory

Chapter 1

Global politics since 1945

Klaus Larres

It has been quite a rollercoaster. Global politics since 1945 have never been boring though the post–World War II era has constituted a highly dangerous and deeply divided era. There was a short moment of unity and talk about a constructive new world order in the aftermath of the fall of the Berlin Wall in November 1989 and the disintegration of the Soviet Union in late 1991 (Bush and Scowcroft, 1998;

FIGURE 1.1 National flags at the entrance to the UN office in Geneva, Switzerland

Hurst, 1999; Engel, 2018). Altogether, however, the post–Cold War years have been quite unsettling. While East–West divisions have been overcome in geographical and strictly ideological ways, thinking along lines of 'us' and 'them' is alive and kicking. The world is still deeply divided. In terms of politics, religion, race, ethnicity as well as prosperity, demographic trends and, not least, questions of migration and immigration, an unbridgeable gulf seems to exist in many parts of the globe.

The 21st century is also turning increasingly nationalistic. The world has become much more inward looking and self-focused than was the case in the preceding half-century (McCormick, 1995). The forces of globalisation and integration have been on the defensive since at least the second decade of the 21st century. The memory of the violent and destructive consequences of the irresponsibly nationalistic 1930s and 1940s seem to have faded away (Ullrich, 2016). Yet, it was the violence, genocide and wholesale destruction wielded during those dark days that led to the global orientation of the years since 1945.

In our multifaceted and diverse world it is almost impossible to find some overarching developments that are characteristic for the entire era since 1945. Still, a number of long-term features can be identified, some negative and quite disturbing ones as well as several much more positive and visionary factors. The former include the potential of sudden annihilation by nuclear weapons and the ongoing step-by-step environmental destruction of the world as we know it. Other decisive forces of destruction with a long-term legacy have been transnational terrorism, the Iraq War of 2003 and the 'Great Recession' a few years later. Fortunately the post-1945 era has also been characterised by at least two crucial positive aspects: the rise of relative stability and integration in formerly deeply divided regions and the growing and beneficial importance of the rule of law and international institutions in global politics. This chapter elaborates on these aspects before then also outlining some likely trajectories for the future of global politics in the 21st century.

Forces of destruction and annihilation

It was only less than 80 years ago that two atomic bombs destroyed the Japanese cities of Hiroshima and Nagasaki in August 1945. Ever since the nuclear threat, and thus the destruction of the entire planet, has been the ever-present danger that has accompanied world politics since the end of World War II (Rhodes, 1996). Not only the 1962 Cuban Missile Crisis (Fursenko and Naftali, 1998) but also quite a few other accidents and miscommunications brought the world close to a nuclear holocaust. An unexploded nuclear bomb is still buried deep in a field near the small town of Faro in the US state of North Carolina. The B-52 that was carrying two 3- or 4-megaton H-bombs broke up in mid-air and dropped its payload, almost leading to the detonation of the bombs. Only one of the bombs has been recovered (Dobson, 2013; Burr, 2014). Many similar nuclear accidents in the US and elsewhere have become known to the wider public, not least due to the investigative work of journalists and political historians (Schlosser, 2014).

With the growing number of nuclear powers during the Cold War and since, it has become increasingly likely that something might go wrong, be it for political-military or technical reasons or for reasons of miscommunication. In September 1983, for instance, at a time when superpower relations had hit rock bottom, the alarm went off at the secret command centre in Moscow that monitored the country's early warning satellite system. It appeared that the US had launched five nuclear missiles that would hit the Soviet Union within 25 minutes. Duty officer Lieutenant Colonel Stanislav Petrov should have immediately informed his superiors who would have passed on the information to Soviet leader Yuri Andropov and his top military advisers. If he had done so, the Kremlin leaders may well have immediately launched a retaliatory strike, causing a nuclear holocaust in the process (Anthony, 2015).

Petrov hesitated, however. His gut feeling and a number of inexplicable unusual satellite images made him think that this might be a false alarm. Although being in two minds about it, he reported a system malfunction to his superiors rather than an incoming imminent nuclear attack on the Soviet Union. He was right. It later turned out that the satellite system had mistaken the reflection of the sun off the top of clouds as the launch of a number of missiles. With his caution and hesitation based on his gut instinct, Petrov had virtually saved the world, and certainly the US, from nuclear annihilation. 'I was just at the right place at the right time', he later modestly explained. Essentially it had been sheer good luck that a nuclear war between the superpowers had been averted (Chan, 2017).

The UK, France and China developed their nuclear arsenals in the 1950s and 1960s. Israel, which does not admit to having nuclear weapons, managed to obtain its nuclear capacity in late 1966. At present it probably has approximately 80 nuclear bombs (ACA, 2018). Developing countries such as India and Pakistan, as well as North Korea, are the world's latest nuclear armed countries. Already by the late 1990s both India and Pakistan possessed a significant number of powerful 'nukes'. At present they have approximately 130 and 140 nuclear devices, respectively. North Korea managed to achieve nuclear status only recently; by early 2018 it was estimated to have between 15 and 50 atomic bombs (ACA, 2018). The country also claims to have successfully tested for the first time an intercontinental strategic missile in late November 2017; such a missile is essential for its nuclear warheads to reach the continental US (McCurry and Borger, 2017). Whether or not this is correct and whether or not the country already has a warhead that after its launch into space can actually re-enter the earth's atmosphere and then target an American city is anyone's guess. Pyongyang may well need another couple of years to develop such a warhead (Sanger and Broad, 2018a). Iran has serious nuclear ambitions that, however, have been curtailed by the April 2015 framework treaty and a subsequent Joint Comprehensive Plan of Action (Ritter, 2018).[1]

It remains an open question whether in particular Pakistan and North Korea possess the political stability or have the security provisions in place that makes their nuclear deterrent secure and safe. Some of Pakistan's nuclear knowhow, for example, clandestinely found its way to North Korea and contributed to Pyongyang's controversial development of its atomic arsenal. There is some evidence that North Korea has sold chemical weapons to the Syrian government and it cannot be excluded that Pyongyang would also be ready to sell its nuclear knowhow for hard currency (Harris, 2018). There is justified concern that the nuclear proliferation threshold is decreasing. Eventually some of the world's growing number of autocratic and failing states as well as ill-intentioned terror organisations may obtain a real nuclear bomb or perhaps a so-called dirty bomb – one which combines conventional explosives with radioactive material as an 'area denial' weapon against civilians. In the 1970s and early 1980s, however, South Africa, Brazil, Argentina as well as Taiwan, South Korea and Algeria gave up on their fledging nuclear programs (as had Sweden in the 1960s), and Kazakhstan, Ukraine and Belarus disposed of the Soviet nuclear bombs on their territories in the 1990s. Libya agreed to dismantle its nuclear program in 2003–4.

Despite this positive development, there are a number of countries with nuclear ambitions, including perhaps Japan. In the volatile Middle East above all Saudi Arabia, but perhaps also Egypt, is seriously pondering going nuclear (Editorial Board, 2018). Still, the world's largest nuclear arsenals continue to be held by the US and Russia. Washington is estimated to have 6800 nuclear bombs and Moscow is believed to have 7000 nuclear devices, followed by France, China and the UK with 300, 270 and 215 atomic bombs respectively (ACA, 2018). Even more disconcerting is the development of a new nuclear arms race between Russia and the US. Both countries are rapidly modernising their nuclear arsenals (MacFarquhar and Sanger, 2018; Sanger and Broad, 2018b; Hille and Foy, 2018) and have given up on the 1987 Intermediate-Range Nuclear Forces (INF) Treaty, one of the last remaining nuclear arms control agreements of the Cold War era. A more recent phenomenon is the growing importance of cybersecurity and its underlying infrastructure. Having the technical knowhow to fend off growing and increasingly sophisticated cyberattacks on military and civilian computer systems has become essential. Cyberwars with nations such as Russia and China but also North Korea, Iran, Pakistan and many others are a growing possibility (Clarke and Knake, 2010; Kaplan, 2016).

In the years since the end of World War II, the major powers have been involved in a significant number of proxy wars and other military conflicts. They have, however, mostly refrained from large-scale wars with other major powers. The danger of nuclear escalation has simply been too great. Some scholars have even spoken of a 'long peace' (Gaddis, 1986, 1989), though in view of the various vicious wars in Asia, the Middle East and elsewhere, the notion of something like a protracted situation of peace only makes sense with regard to Europe. Many analysts believe that the outbreak of World War III has been prevented (so far) precisely because of the existence of the nuclear threat. This led John Mueller to conclude (tongue-in-cheek) that all countries ought to possess the atomic bomb as this was likely preserving peace on earth (Mueller, 1988, 2009).

Regarding North Korea the opposite is true, however. The escalating rhetoric over Pyongyang's nuclear program during Donald Trump's first year as US president showed perhaps that the horror of a nuclear war and its consequences in terms of radiation and environmental destruction were gradually being downplayed and underestimated. Talk such as 'my [nuclear] button is bigger than yours' was highly irresponsible rhetoric that in connection with the nuclear deterrent had never been used before by the leader of the world's only remaining superpower (Baker and Tackett, 2018). This, too, was a rather disconcerting development, though subsequently the Trump administration had second thoughts and embarked on a more constructive summit and negotiation process with North Korea.

While nuclear war, so far, has been avoided, the world since 1945 has been a ruthless battlefield in many other respects. One of its major victims has been the global environment. Rachel Carson's *Silent Spring* (1962) was among the first accounts that drew attention to the need for protecting our environment. A wider environmental movement emerged in many parts of the world in the course of the 1960s and 1970s. Politically it became identified with the Green Party (Shabecoff, 2003; Doyle, 2005; Doyle et al., 2016). Wars, such as the major ones in Korea, Vietnam and Cambodia, as well as in Afghanistan and Iraq, but also the many smaller civil wars and intra-ethnic conflicts in Africa and Latin America, have also contributed to the devastation of many natural habitats. War has led to the wholesale destruction of vegetation, harvests, prime forests and jungles and the killing of an ever-larger number of wild animals, be it as a consequence of warfare and eroding habitation or as a result of ruthless poaching (Closmann, 2009; Smith, 2017). This sad state of affairs has become a fundamental global problem; it represents a serious challenge for anyone dealing with global affairs in a professional way.

In the early to mid-1970s the Club of Rome warned that natural resources, in particular energy resources – coal, oil and gas – as well as vital living resources such as clean water would soon become very scarce (Meadows et al., 1974). It was right, and in many parts of the world the battle for water, heating material and protection from difficult weather and climate conditions dominate political life and the daily struggle for survival (Sengupta, 2018). In coastal areas, ever-rising water levels, often caused by the melting of glaciers in the Arctic, have turned into a growing problem during the last few decades. Climate change and man-made global warming, as well as the rapid disappearance of animal species, have become a very real fact of life in 21st-century global politics. Only a few decades ago this was merely a niche subject area and largely ignored by mainstream political parties and the wider population (Lynas, 2008; Gore, 2006; Klein, 2015; Sachs, 2015).

The 2015 Paris Climate Change Treaty so far is the most concerted effort to do something about these dangerous developments that threaten the survival as well as the safety and security of almost half of the globe's population. With the notable exception of US President Trump, who in May 2017 withdrew his country from the pact, the important Paris Climate Change Treaty has been signed by all other nations on earth, including war-torn Syria (Allitt, 2014; Klein et al., 2017).

Contrary to what the Club of Rome expected in the 1970s, a revolution in energy production in the US and other Western countries has led to an abundance rather than to the predicted scarcity of oil and gas for industrial and private consumption. The extraction of shale oil, commonly referred to as fracking, has made the US almost energy independent within the last decade (Gold, 2014; Levant, 2014). Energy consumption as such, however, is still growing, despite many attempts to reduce the usage of fossil energy sources by means of the development of solar power and electric and battery powered automobiles. At present an overwhelming number of cars, trucks and of course aeroplanes are still moved by engines fed with fossil fuel (Yergin, 1992; Nye, 1998). The air pollution and the warming of the earth's atmosphere that have accompanied the world's rising use of carbon fuel energy sources, therefore, continues to bedevil both the developed and the developing world. In particular in populous threshold countries, such as China and India, air pollution well exceeds on an almost daily basis the maximum level regarded as safe for people's health (Jacobson, 2012).

The almost near-total dependency of the West on oil from the Middle East that characterised much of the 20th century, however, is a thing of the past. While many Middle Eastern oil producers, such as Saudi Arabia, Iraq, Iran, the United Arab Emirates and Kuwait, are haphazardly – and without much success at present – attempting to diversify their income base away from oil, the repercussions of the fracking revolution in energy production and consumption has not yet become fully felt (Cherif et al., 2016). Still, Washington's decreasing interest in the Middle East (with the exception of continued strong support of Israel), that perhaps began in earnest during the Obama administration and has continued under his successor, is certainly influenced by the diminishing importance of oil in the region. In fact, by 2019 at the latest the US had become the world's leading oil producer and exporter, well ahead of Russia and Saudi Arabia (Tsukimori, 2018). This is a dramatic and entirely unexpected development. Still, the violence and political chaos in the region also plays a role for US disinterest. Ignoring US responsibility for contributing to the creation of these conditions in the first place, administrations from Bush to Obama and Trump became frustrated about their inability to contain the turmoil and gradually began to disengage America from the whole region (Berman, 2014).

Transnational terrorism, war and economic distress

The world since 1945 has seen a tremendous increase of both religious movements, particularly among evangelicals and Islamists, and global terrorism. It is therefore tempting to believe in a causal link between the two. Thus, in the 21st century transnational terrorism has frequently become identified in people's minds with fundamentalist religious developments. For many, Harvard scholar Samuel Huntington's 1993 thesis of a coming 'clash of civilizations' appears to have become true. In fact it is a comparatively recent phenomenon that religious fundamentalism and transnational terrorism have entered into an unholy alliance.

In contemporary global politics terrorism first became a well-known and quite secular phenomenon of Western societies in the 1970s. Left-wing niche groups, such as the Red Brigades in Italy and the Baader-Meinhof gang in West Germany, began attacking establishment figures who they considered as symbols of fascist-leaning oppressive capitalist societies. Their activities culminated in the kidnapping and killing of Italian Prime Minister Aldo Moro and the head of West Germany's employers' association, Hanns Martin Schleyer (Orsini, 2011; Aust, 2009).

Since the 1979 Iranian revolution and the emergence of a great number of fundamentalist Islamist movements in the decades since, transnational terrorism has gradually developed a strongly political and cultural anti-Western direction. Terrorist groups such as Al-Qaeda and a decade later the Islamic State (ISIS) were frequently but not exclusively based in a number of Middle Eastern and African regions and states that had strong links with extreme Islamist movements and their missionary drives (Choueiri, 2010; Hoffman, 2017). When two planes were flown into the twin towers of the World Trade Center in New York City on September 11, 2001, the massive buildings collapsed and were utterly destroyed, with a loss of life of more than 3000. It demonstrated the spreading danger that terrorist organisations from the Middle East were now even able to reach the very heart of the West's foremost power (9/11 Report, 2011).

The events of 9/11 led to a radical and dramatic response. It was not so much the events of that day that changed the world, as was claimed by the George W. Bush administration in Washington, but it was the strong and largely ill-conceived response of the Bush administration that led to a dramatic turning point in Western relations with many countries in the Middle East and elsewhere. It also resulted in a growing fission within the West. While the initial tension between the US and France and Germany, both of whom were strongly opposed to the 2003 Iraq War, was quickly overcome (Dettke, 2009), European suspicion of American unpredictability and disingenuity about the West's shared value system never entirely subsided.

US responsibility for the global financial and economic crisis of the years after 2008 only confirmed the conviction of many EU governments that America had become an irresponsible power (Lewis, 2010; Posner, 2009; Farrell, 2010). During the Trump administration the estrangement between the US and most NATO countries and the member states of the European Union reached unprecedented heights. The emergence of a wide transatlantic value gap that some scholars had already noticed in the context of the Iraq War in the early 2000s (Larres, 2003; Kagan, 2003) now was undisputable. The German chancellor even admitted as much in public when she admonished the freshly elected President Trump that transatlantic cooperation was only possible on the basis of the West's liberal value system. 'Germany and America are connected by values of democracy, freedom and respect for the law and the dignity of man, independent of origin, skin color, religion, gender, sexual orientation or political views', Angela Merkel explained in a statement. She could only 'offer the next President of the United States close cooperation on the basis of these values' (Giacomo, 2016).

Although many, if not most, of the reasons for the rise of religiously driven transnational terrorism lie within the Middle Eastern and Islamic world itself, Western politics have contributed to the deep anger and anti-Western resentment that is a common phenomenon in the Middle East and elsewhere. In particular, the first Gulf War of early 1991 to liberate Kuwait from Iraqi occupation caused much anger. The war preparations saw tens of thousands of US troops deployed in the desert in Saudi Arabia, the home of Islam's two holiest cities, Mecca and Medina. It led Osama bin Laden to turn decisively toward his fundamentalist beliefs and ruthless and aggressive methods. Bin Laden and his fellow violent Jihadists, however, had already been greatly inspired by opposing and contributing to the defeat of the Soviet Union in Afghanistan in the 1980s. Although armed by both Saudi Arabia and the CIA, the *mujahidin* of the 1980s soon turned on the US (Coll, 2004, 2009).

Oil and strategic considerations were crucial for President George H.W. Bush's decision to liberate Kuwait from Saddam Hussein's conquest of the kingdom. Bush believed that potentially Saddam was threatening Saudi Arabia's oil wealth; it could not be excluded, after all, that if the Iraqi dictator was allowed to get away with the occupation of Kuwait, he would feel encouraged to move onto Saudi Arabia next. A number of factors may also have convinced Saddam Hussein that his move into Kuwait would not lead the US to respond with military action (Baker et al., 2006).

Despite the deployment of hugely destructive weapons, the 1991 Gulf War was still a fairly conventional war meant to contain an aggressive autocrat and it was fought for fairly traditional power, political and economic reasons.

The much less successful Iraq War of 2003, however, was decisive for greatly disillusioning the world about both the moral superiority of the West and its capabilities (Pauly, 2017; Weston, 2016; Cerf and Sifry, 2003; Whitney, 2005). It was a missionary war fought under wrong pretenses. The George W. Bush administration hoped to turn Iraq into a democratic, pro-American country whose democracy would then spread throughout the Middle East. It was based on the faulty assumption, repeatedly expressed by leading members of the George W. Bush administration, that Saddam Hussein had cooperated with bin Laden in the 9/11 attacks and still had weapons of mass destruction that he intended to use shortly. It was an illegal war, not sanctioned by the UN. Besides, Iraq was not posing an immediate threat to the US and its allies or neighbours, despite American claims to the contrary. The war also saw the US use of torture and other ruthless methods of interrogation and capture forbidden under international law (ibid.). The 1949 Geneva Convention, which regulates the standards of international law and humanitarian treatment in war, was almost totally ignored by the West's foremost liberal democratic country (Clapham et al., 2018).

The Iraq War not only severely undermined America's global prestige and domestic self-respect, it also utterly destroyed and weakened the country – and caused at least 100,000 Iraqis to die, possibly more. The war also enabled Iraq's arch-rival Iran to step into the resulting geopolitical vacuum in the Middle East. Both countries, after all, had fought a ruthless but inconclusive ten-year-long war in the 1980s for supremacy in the region (Razoux, 2015; Murray and Woods, 2014). The large-scale destruction of Iraq caused the crisis to spread but it is highly unlikely that it led to the brief democratic awakening of the Arab Spring in 2011, though former administration officials have attempted to make this point (Maass, 2013). Instead, as Paul Pillar, a former CIA agent, has argued, 'rather than being inspired by what happened in Iraq after the invasion, Middle Easterners were repelled by it. If the violence, disorder, and breakdown of public services in Iraq were the birth pangs of a new Middle Eastern order, most people in the region wanted nothing of it' (Pillar, 2011).

The resulting counter-revolutions by the region's conservative-autocratic rulers brought much further instability and unspeakable human suffering and great misery to Libya, Syria and Yemen and many neighbouring countries such as Jordan and Lebanon. The latter two found themselves quickly overrun by refugees escaping from war-torn Libya, Syria and Yemen to seek shelter elsewhere. In 2015 the refugees also arrived in huge numbers in Europe (more than a million in Germany alone), hugely straining the social and political fabric of European societies in the process (Alexander, 2017). These developments also gave new nourishment to right-wing nativist and often anti-Semitic and anti-European parties in most EU countries, thus creating a destabilising wave of political populism almost everywhere on this once stable continent (Broening, 2016).

But the humanitarian tragedy of the war in Syria with its complex geopolitical implications has been particularly troubling (Erlich, 2016). The ruthless bombing of civilians and hospitals in Aleppo and eastern Ghouta, just outside Damascus, and of many other population centres, must clearly be classified as war crimes and crimes against humanity. Not only are a plethora of larger and smaller rebel and opposition groups (usually referred to as 'terrorists') fighting against each other and Syrian strongman Assad, but in September 2015 Russia became a warring party. Since then the war has become further inflamed by Moscow's ruthlessly applied air power. Increasingly, Iran, which attempts to expand its growing regional dominance, and also the US (with a pro-Kurdish bent), became militarily engaged (Stein, 2018a). NATO member Turkey also embarked on military action in Syria. Turkish President Erdogan strongly opposed the establishment of a Kurdish state on Turkey's borders and, thus, just in time to create nationalistic fervor in Turkey shortly before imminent elections, found himself in stark confrontation with Washington (Stein, 2018b).

In short, the 2003 Iraq War and its terrible legacy in the Middle East have been responsible for undermining the standing of the US as the global and often benign and enlightened superpower that the world had come to know since 1945. Furthermore, the global and financial overreach of the Bush administration and its loosening of the regulations that governed the behaviour of banks and other financial institutions in the US resulted in the global economic and financial crisis of 2008–2012. From the US the crisis spread to Europe and to many other parts of the world, almost bringing down the globe's entire complex financial framework. Only the enormous printing of money ('quantitative easing') in the US, China, the UK and soon also by the European Central Bank in Frankfurt prevented a wholesale collapse and the repetition of a 1929-style global Great Depression (Hausken and Ncube, 2013).

Instead a 'Great Recession' arrived which was not nearly as calamitous in global terms; yet for the millions of individuals affected, it proved to be almost as heart wrenchingly devastating. It was not only America's European allies whose faith in US leadership in global economic affairs was undermined by the crisis, but China was even more profoundly disappointed, perhaps because Beijing still had an elevated idea of American 'greatness' and competency. The Chinese authorities made US 'excessive consumption and high leverage' responsible for the crisis and admonished Washington to 'speed up domestic adjustment, raise its savings and reduce its trade and fiscal deficits' (*China Digital Times*, 2008). At the height of the financial crisis, Politburo member Wang Qishan, one of only four vice-prime ministers and the country's leading economic expert, told Treasury Secretary Henry Paulson, who at the time was busy putting pressure on Beijing to open up its banking and economic system: 'You were my teacher but look at your system, Hank, we aren't sure we should be learning from you any more' (Paulson, 2015, p. 240).

The legacy of the painful economic, housing and employment crisis of the Great Recession in the US caused a dramatic rise of protective and semi-isolationist sentiments in many parts of the US, particularly in 'fly-over-country' in the Midwest. A new era of nationalism emerged that was directed against anything loosely connected with 'globalisation', including America's rich culture of immigration (Swain, 2004; Green, 2017; King, 2017). Paradoxically this backlash against globalisation and against anyone who seemed to benefit from it – mostly the established elites on the east coast and experts at all levels – resulted in the electoral victory of Donald Trump in November 2016. Russian meddling in the US election campaign may also have played a role. Trump, a billionaire property developer and TV celebrity, was in fact a long-standing though not particularly popular member of the New York upper class. Yet, he managed to sell himself as the voice of the downtrodden and the 'forgotten (white) men'. He made nationalism, selfishness, the building of walls instead of bridges and sheer vulgarity acceptable to many in the US (Green, 2017; Wolf, 2018).

But US nationalism corresponded to a rise of nationalism (or populism at it is often called) in much of the rest of the world. The EU is grappling with this phenomenon, in particular among its eastern members and in the UK. There are also many other countries affected. For instance in Prime Minister Shinzo Abe's Japan, Narendra Modi's India, Recep Erdogan's Turkey, Abdel Fattah el-Sisi's Egypt and not least in Vladimir Putin's Russia and Xi Jinping's China, growing nationalistic forces are at work (Moffitt, 2016; Judis, 2016).

In fact, nationalism has become an influential factor that no leader can afford to ignore if he (still mostly he) wishes to continue holding the mettle of power. Most therefore believe it to be wise to side with the rising nationalistic fervor in their respective countries for their own political objectives and survival in power. Yet, resorting to more hardline nationalistic and selfish politics has enflamed further the forces of nationalism and contributed to even greater divisions within their respective countries. A vicious circle has developed. The 'politics of fear' has become widespread, not least in terms of more repressive domestic behaviour, protectionist economic policies and attempts to close borders and keep immigrants and refugees out (Wodak, 2015; Altheide, 2017). Whether national leaders, often autocrats or those with autocratic sympathies, can actually contain and use the forces of nationalism and manipulate them successfully for their own purposes for any length of time remains to be seen.

This indeed is another recent phenomenon of world politics. The popularity and appeal of autocrats and semi-democratic leaders has increased tremendously. Russian President Putin, in power since 1999, is the role model and a growing number of countries are hopping on the authoritarian bandwagon. China's Xi Jinping began to emphasise the importance of the Communist Party and its doctrines and he managed to persuade its Politburo to do away with the term limit for the country's president (Lee Myers, 2018).

Even inside the democratic and liberal EU new autocratic leaders have emerged. With it the freedom of the press, the judicial system, freedom of expression and religion and many other democratic liberties, including women's dress codes, have come under strong attack. Within the EU this has been the case in Poland, the Czech Republic and above all in Hungary. These countries hardly deserve the label 'democracy' anymore (Hutton, 2018; Bayer, 2017). In many other parts of the world, including in some of the most prosperous countries on earth, basic human rights, including the freedom of the media, have become endangered species (Galston, 2018).

According to the annual Democracy Index of the Economist Intelligence Unit (part of the respected conservative UK magazine *The Economist*), these countries need to be classified as 'flawed democracies'. Already since 2015 the Democracy Index has classified the US (as well as Italy, France and South Korea, for instance) as a flawed democracy (Karlis, 2018). A report by US think tank Freedom House also concluded that the US was no longer a full democracy. The report explained that democracy is confronted with its 'most serious crisis in decades'. To some extent the report blamed the US for this as Washington has 'retreated from its traditional role as both a champion and an exemplar of democracy' (Freedom House, 2018). Even Richard Haass, the respected president of the elite Council on Foreign Relations, concluded that

> not just democracy but the rule of law and respect for civil society and individual liberty are in decline around the world. One reason is that the United States is failing to set an example that many wish to emulate. The U.S. has removed the promotion of democracy and human rights from its foreign policy agenda. Its silence on these issues gives repressive regimes a free pass to crack down. But our increasingly divisive domestic politics are also part of the problem.
>
> (Haass, 2017, 2018)

Stability and global order: the rule of law and international institutions

Yet global politics since 1945 is not all doom and gloom. After all, the often-predicted World War III has not yet occurred. In fact, despite a plethora of wars and military conflicts and plenty of terrorist attacks, the world since 1945 has actually been more peaceful than is commonly perceived. In particular Europe – the continent riven by several major wars between 1871 and 1945 – has become a rather stable and relatively peaceful place. There were exceptions however, such as Moscow's grim determination to clamp down on uprisings against Soviet rule during the Cold War (1953 East Germany, 1956 Hungary, 1968 Czechoslovakia) with some other, more muted, interventions, such as in Polish politics in the early 1980s (Westad, 2017). In the years since 1990, European peace and stability were crudely disturbed by the ruthless civil wars in the former Yugoslavia in the mid-1990s and the Kosovo War in 1999 (Baker, 2015). Russia's annexation of Crimea in March 2014 and its unofficial invasion (now often called 'hybrid warfare') of eastern Ukraine was another ruthless and disturbing development. It rode roughshod over Europe's post–World War II insistence that borders can only be changed by negotiations and agreement but no longer by war (Toal, 2017).

Peace and stability in Europe, coupled with immense prosperity, has been one of the major achievements of the process of European integration that commenced with the European Coal and Steel Community (ECSC; the so-called Schuman Plan), in 1952. Five years later the Rome Treaties were agreed and the creation of the European Economic Community (EEC) occurred on 1 January 1958. The EEC, the ECSC and the European Atomic Energy Commission morphed into the European Communities (EC) in 1967. Eventually, by means of the 1991 Maastricht Treaty, the EC was transformed into the European Union of 28 members, including pre-Brexit UK (Loth, 2015). Due to the June 2016 Brexit referendum, the British conservative government, led by embattled Prime Minister Theresa May, decided that the UK would have to depart the EU by the end of March 2019 (Clarke et al., 2017; Barnett, 2017), though subsequently this deadline was repeatedly postponed.

No parliamentary majority for leaving the EU could be found and British politics descended into unprecedented turmoil and chaos.

Other countries, however, such as Macedonia and Albania and not least the western Balkan region (Serbia, Bosnia-Herzegovina, Montenegro, Kosovo), have the ardent desire to become members of the EU. Quite unrealistically, Ukraine and other Caucasus states such as Georgia are also knocking on the doors of the EU. They all wish to improve their economic fortunes and overcome the divisions of their respective regions. After all, for more than 60 years the EU has proven to be rather good at creating peace and stability as well as prosperity. The full integration of Germany and the establishment of a very close and deep rapprochement between France and Germany, the long-standing arch-enemies of the world prior to 1945, were part and parcel of the successful transformation of an aggressive and war-torn continent into a beacon of democracy and stability (Loth, 2017).

Another major positive development in the world since 1945 is the immense rise of international institutions, treaties and conventions that protect the rule of law. It has led to a largely multilateral world and a more rationally organised global order than had hitherto been the case. This global post-war order is still based on the agreements reached at the July 1944 Bretton Woods conference at the Mount Washington Hotel in New Hampshire. Led by two of the world's most eminent and fiercely antagonistic economists, Britain's John Meynard Keynes and senior US Treasury official Henry Dexter White, the 730 delegates from 44 allied nations managed to agree on establishing a new financial and monetary order. It was based on a fixed exchange rate system and the US dollar as the world's reserve currency. The latter's value was based on gold. They also created a number of international institutions such as the World Bank and the International Monetary Fund (IMF) that in the decades to come proved to be highly important for the West's rising prosperity in the post-1945 world (Conway, 2016; Steil, 2014). The 1944 monetary order, however, was decisively amended in the early 1970s when in the context of the growing influence of more neo-liberal economic convictions the fixed exchange rate order was replaced by a flexible exchange rate system that is still in place today. The link between the dollar and America's gold reserves held at Fort Knox was also dissolved (Cesarano, 2008).

In the wake of the Bretton Woods conference other international organisations and institutions were established, now commonly referred to as the Bretton Woods system. Over the years these organisations and institutions have demonstrated their usefulness and resilience in the wake of successive economic crises that seem to shake the world every few years. As noted, the International Bank for Reconstruction and Development (IBRD, the World Bank) and the International Monetary Fund, but also in a broader sense the 1947 General Agreement on Tariffs and Trade (GATT) and its successor, the World Trade Organisation (WTO, 1995), as well as the Organisation for European Economic Co-operation (OEEC; in 1961 renamed OECD) were the crucial Bretton Woods organisations that helped stabilise the international economic system after World War II (Helleiner, 2016).

In the more recent past, these Western-dominated institutions have been complemented by Asia-based organisations that have been set up under Chinese leadership, such as the Asian Infrastructure Investment Bank (AIIB) – the Asian World Bank as it has often been termed – the BRICS New Development Bank (NDB), as well as the

Silk Road Fund (Ikenberry and Lim, 2017). This clearly indicated not just dissatisfaction with the old post–World War II institutions but also the ambition to replace them or at least provide the world with alternative institutions based in Asia (Dollar, 2015; Dadush, 2014). It also is a sign that economic and monetary power is increasingly shifting toward the Pacific and in particular to China. President Obama's 2011 'pivot to Asia' that emphasised US re-engagement in the region did not delay or stop this development (Campbell, 2016).

After all, since the 1990s China has come into its own and has rapidly risen to be the second most important country in the world in terms of global trade, economics and increasingly global political influence. In fact, Beijing is actively challenging the US for the top position (Shambaugh, 2014; White, 2013). Still, despite China and Asia's rapid rise, at present most world trade is still transatlantic trade, however. More than 40 per cent of all global trade still occurs between the countries (mostly the US and the EU) on both sides of the Atlantic (Hamilton and Quinlan, 2017). The development of a transatlantic trade war and above all a US-Chinese trade war in the course of 2018–19 and the imposition of US tariffs on Chinese and also European steel, aluminum and other products, however, undermines transatlantic unity. Most major companies in the US and the EU are highly dependent for their profit margins on their markets in China.

While in military terms there still is no country on earth that can rival America, although that might be eroding in the Pacific (Haddick, 2014; Heritage Foundation, 2017), in global economic and political-democratic terms, it appears the US is an embattled power, with China being ascendant. This clearly is the view in Beijing. China's 'market authoritarianism', the country's elite has concluded, is the model of the future. 'Disorder in the West', communist official Zhang Weiwei wrote, 'has become a major source of global insecurity and instability' with 'the western model now' encountering 'grave challenges'. He made the distorting influence of money and capital in US elections and politics responsible for this situation (Kynge, 2018). Xi Jinping expressed a similar view of superiority when he explained in 2017 that China was offering 'a new option to other countries and nations who want to speed up their development while preserving their independence' from Western insistence on certain democratic and human rights norms they had to fulfill to obtain Western support (ibid.). Perhaps, as Martin Wolf has argued in the *Financial Times*, 'We are, once again, in an era of competition of systems' – and strategic rivalry – 'between democratic and – strange though it may sound (and indeed is) – communist capitalism' (Wolf, 2018).

In the post-World War II era, the United Nations, established at the San Francisco conference in June 1945, and its many sub-organisations have also demonstrated their usefulness for global stability (and emergency military and humanitarian relief action) (Schlesinger, 2004). The important UN Security Council with its five permanent veto-possessing powers (US, Russia, China, the UK and France) and its temporary ten members, selected on a two-year rotating basis, was paralysed during much of the Cold War. But even during the Cold War both the Security Council and the General Assembly proved to be important debating chambers in which member states could let off steam, talk to each other and, on occasion, hammer out preparatory deals for resolving a number of urgent crises. During the Cuban Missile Crisis, in the course of various great power clashes in the 1960s and 1970s as well as during the run-up to the 2003 Iraq War, the UN proved to be an important instrument. Both vicious East–West clashes and, on occasion, intra-Western disagreements occurred but also constructive cooperation for working out compromise solutions (Malone, 2004; Von Einsiedel et al., 2015; Lowe et al., 2010). Throughout the long war in Syria that began already in 2011, however, and the perhaps even more vicious war in Yemen, the UN proved to be rather ineffective.

UN bodies and UN overseen conventions and norms have also been responsible for making the rule of law an increasingly important criteria in international affairs. This not only applies to human rights, which became an ever-more important part of international relations since the 1975 Helsinki conference. It was this conference that agreed on formally accepting the post-war borders in Europe as defined toward the end of World War II. At Helsinki, the Soviet Union also signed off on the so-called Basket Three that focused on human rights. It soon became a rallying point for the proliferating dissenting movements in the Soviet bloc in the 1980s. It could be argued, therefore, that the Helsinki conference significantly contributed to bringing about the end of the Cold War (Snyder, 2011; Morgan, 2018).

It was under UN auspices that the development occurred of not only the 1949 Geneva Convention referred to earlier but also of the global norm-setting legal mechanisms of the post-war world (Weiss and Davis, 2009; Weiss, 2016). Part of these is the complex court and tribunal system that has emerged from the 1982 treaty of the UN Convention on the Law of the Seas (UNCLOS) (Worster, 2012; Anderson et al., 2016). Among the UN system's most influential body is perhaps the International Criminal Court (ICC) based in The Hague, Netherlands, which is meant to complement national judicial systems; it began working in June 2002. The ICC, viewed with suspicion by the US government, is tasked with prosecuting individuals for war crimes, crimes of genocide and crimes against humanity. In particular, the International Criminal Tribunal for the Former Yugoslavia (ICTY) and the prosecution of figures such as Slobodan Milosevic, Radovan Kradzic and Ratko Mladic became well known (Bosco, 2014; Schabas, 2006, 2017; Clark, 2015).

Compared to much of the Cold War era, the new significance of human rights, environmental politics and the serious international attempts to enforce the rule of law in global affairs, despite the strenuous opposition of authoritarian regimes, have perhaps been the most positive developments in post–Cold War international relations.

The structure of global politics since 1945 and the past as a guide to the future

Global politics since 1945 can usefully be divided into four stages of differing lengths. First is the era of transition from World War II to what came to be called the Cold War. These years between 1943–4 and 1946–7 were much occupied with post-planning activities and the haphazard and ultimately failed attempts to prevent the wholesale collapse of the anti-Hitler alliance. The next and second stage was the Cold War era from c. 1947 to the unification of Germany and Europe and the fall of the Soviet Union in 1990–1.

The Cold War itself can be sub-divided in the years of its greatest dangers and potential instability from the late 1940s to the early 1960s, punctured by a brief period of détente in the aftermath of Stalin's death in March 1953 to the 1955 Geneva Summit conference. The second major Cold War stage was the era of détente and rapprochement between East and West from the mid-1960s to the late 1970s. From the mid to late 1970s this era of détente was slowly undermined by a growing wave of new hardline criticism of the Soviet Union in the US and some European countries. Moscow's 1979 invasion of Afghanistan led to the symbolic termination of superpower détente (détente in Europe, however, continued haphazardly). The final and third major stage of the Cold War in the 1980s initially saw renewed intensive conflict and rearmament in the first few years of the decade and subsequently an era of negotiation and cooperation, once Mikhail Gorbachev had come to power in the Kremlin in 1985.

Following the four and a half decades of Cold War, a much shorter post–Cold War phase of transition of just over 20 years occurred from 1991 to the early 21st century. It was characterised by a growing democratisation of much of the globe and by increasing conflict. This phase can usefully be regarded as the third stage of global politics since 1945. In particular it was punctuated not only by the first Gulf War and the civil wars in the former Yugoslavia but above all by 9/11 and the American wars in Afghanistan and Iraq.

Many scholars have considered the events of 9/11 and the subsequent 'war on terrorism' as a major turning point in international relations. Yet, it was not only 9/11 but also the Great Recession of 2008–2012 that saw the slow beginning of a new transformative period of world history. The current, for the time being, fourth and final stage of global politics since 1945 is characterised by deep and increasing economic, social, cultural, religious and political divisions and, not least, by the re-nationalisation of global politics that gradually began to emerge with the second decade of the 21st century.

In fact, the continued rise of new powers and the shifting of the balance of power in global politics toward Asia and the Pacific, as well as the simultaneous growth of nationalism and protectionism, appear to be the major global characteristics of our age. At the same time, in particular, in the Middle East and Africa but also in part of Asia and Latin America, further turbulence, competition for resources and civil war must be expected. Judging by recent developments, it can be assumed that for a prolonged period of time the US and Europe, once the pillars of democratic stability, are also likely to be more nationalistic and inward-looking, and thus also much less stable and content than hitherto.

An overarching new global order is not on the horizon. Instead, there will be further turmoil and strife. The only stable and lasting factor in current global politics seems to be the expectation of further unpredictability and the continuation of a long transition to a new global order that, however, may never arrive (Falk, 2016; Kissinger, 2014). In fact, ours is a highly precarious and dangerous age. In 10 or 20 years our times may well be referred to as an interwar era during which many chances and opportunities for global peace and stability were thrown away due to sheer incompetence, selfishness and, not least, misapplied bravado and the politics of bias and ego (Bradley, 2018). One can only hope for the return of competency and professionalism to global politics.

Note

1 It is formally called 'Parameters for a Joint Comprehensive Plan of Action Regarding the Islamic Republic of Iran's Nuclear Program', and was agreed between Iran and the so called P5+1 countries (the four permanent members of the UN Security Council, US, Russia, China, the UK, France and Germany) in July 2015. In May 2018, US President Trump announced the unilateral withdrawal of his country from the agreement.

Further reading

Calvocoressi, Peter (2009) *World Politics since 1945*, 9th ed. (Harlow, England: Pearson Longman).

Herring, George C. (2008) *From Colony to Superpower: U.S. Foreign Relations since 1776* (New York/Oxford: Oxford University Press).

Hunt, Michael H. (2016) *The World Transformed: 1945 to the Present*, 2nd ed. (New York/Oxford: Oxford University Press).

Immerman, Richard H. and Petra Goedde (eds.) (2013) *The Oxford Handbook of the Cold War* (New York/Oxford: Oxford University Press).

Keylor, William R. (2009) *A World of Nations: The International Order since 1945*, 2nd ed. (New York/Oxford: Oxford University Press).

Kissinger, Henry (2014) *World Order* (New York: Penguin Books).

Larres, Klaus (ed.) (2009) *The Blackwell Companion to Europe since 1945* (Malden, MA/Oxford: Wiley Blackwell).

McWilliams, Wayne C. and Harry Piotrowski (2009) *The World since 1945: A History of International Relations* (Boulder, CO: Lynne Riener).

Westad, Odd Arne (2017) *The Cold War: A World History* (New York: Basic Books).

Young, John W. and John Kent (2004) *International Relations since 1945* (New York/Oxford: Oxford University Press).

Bibliography

The 9/11 Commission Report: The Attack From Planning to Aftermath. The National Commission on Terrorist Attacks Upon the United States (New York: W.W. Norton, 2011).

ACA, Arms Control Association (2018) 'Nuclear Weapons: Who Has What at a Glance', www.armscontrol.org/factsheets/Nuclearweaponswhohaswhat.

Alexander, Robin (2017) *Die Getriebenen: Merkel und die Fluechtlingspolitik: Report aus dem Innern der Macht* (Muenchen: Siedler Verlag).

Allitt, Patrick (2014) *A Climate of Crisis: America in the Age of Environmentalism* (New York: Penguin Books).

Altheide, David L. (2017) *Terrorism and the Politics of Fear*, 2nd ed. (Lanham, MD: Rowman & Littlefield).

Anderson, David, Alan Boyle, Robin Churchill et al. (2016) *Law of the Sea: UNCLOS as a Living Treaty* (London: British Institute of International Affairs).

Anthony, Peter (2015) *The Man Who Saved The World (movie)*.

Aust, Stefan (2009) *Baader-Meinhof: The Inside Story of the R.A.F.* (Oxford: Oxford University Press).

Baker, Catherine (2015) *The Yugoslav Wars of the 1990s* (Basingstoke: Palgrave Macmillan).

Baker, James A., Lee H. Hamilton et al. (2006) *The Iraq Study Group Report: The Way Forward – A New Approach*, authorized Ed. (New York: Vintage Books).

Baker, Peter and Michael Tackett (2018) 'Trump Says His 'Nuclear Button' Is "Much Bigger" than North Korea's', *New York Times* (January 18).

Barnett, Anthony (2017) *The Lure of Greatness: England's Brexit and America's Trump* (London: Random House).

Bayer, Lili (2017) 'EU Divisions on the Eastern Front', *Politico* (October 10).

Berman, Russell A. (2014) *America's Withdrawal from the Middle East* (Stanford, CA: Hoover Institution Press).

Bosco, David (2014) *Rough Justice: The International Criminal Court in a World of Power Politics* (Oxford: Oxford University Press).

Bradley, Chris (2018) 'How Biases, Politics and Egos Trump Good Strategy', McKinesy.com (January 18), www.mckinsey.com/business-functions/strategy-and-corporate-finance/our-insights/the-strategy-and-corporate-finance-blog/how-biases-politics-and-egos-derail-business-decisions.

Broening, Michael (2016) 'The Rise of Populism in Europe: Can the Center Hold?', *Foreign Affairs* (June 3).

Burr, Bill (2014) *New Details on the 1961 Goldsboro Nuclear Accident.* Briefing Book, National Security Archive Electronic Briefing Book No. 475 (Washington, DC: National Security Archive).

Bush, George H. and Brent Scowcroft (1998) *A World Transformed* (New York: Knopf).

Campbell, Kurt M. (2016) *The Pivot: The Future of American Statecraft in Asia* (New York/Boston: Twelve).

Carson, Rachel (1962) *Silent Spring* (New York: Houghton Mifflin Harcourt).

Cerf, Christopher and Micah L. Sifry (eds.) (2003) *The Iraq War Reader: History, Documents, Opinions* (New York: Touchstone).

Cesarano, Filippo (2008) *Monetary Theory and Bretton Woods: The Construction of an International Monetary Order* (Cambridge: Cambridge University Press).

Chan, Sewell (2017) 'Stanislav Petrov, Soviet Officer Who Helped Avert Nuclear War, Is Dead at 77', *New York Times* (September 18).

Cherif, Reda et al. (2016) *Breaking the Oil Spell* (Washington, DC: IMF).

China Digital Times (2008) 'China Admonishes U.S. Economic Envoy', https://chinadigitaltimes.net/2008/12/china-admonishes-us-economic-envoy/

Choueiri, Yousseff M. (2010) *Islamic Fundamentalism: The Story of Islamist Movements*, 3rd ed. (London: Continuum).

Clapham, Andrew, Paola Gaeta and Marco Sassoli (eds.) (2018) *The 1949 Geneva Conventions: A Commentary* (Oxford: Oxford University Press).

Clark, James Natalya (2015) *International Trials and Reconciliation: Assessing the Impact of the International Criminal Tribunal for the Former Yugoslavia* (London: Routledge).

Clarke, Harold D., Matthew Goodwin and Paul Whiteley (2017) *Brexit: Why Britain Voted to Leave the European Union* (Cambridge: Cambridge University Press).

Clarke, Richard A. and Robert Knake (2010) *Cyber War: The Next Threat to National Security and What to Do about It* (New York: HarperCollins).

Closmann, Charles E. (ed.) (2009) *War and the Environment: Military Destruction in the Modern Age* (College Station: Texas A&M University Press).

Coll, Steve (2004) *Ghost Wars: The Secret History of the CIA, Afghanistan, and Bin Laden, from the Soviet Invasion to September 10, 2001* (New York: Penguin Books).

Coll, Steve (2009) *The Bin Ladens: An Arabian Family in the American Century* (New York: Penguin Books).

Conway, Ed (2016) *The Summit: Bretton Woods, 1944: J.M. Keynes and the Reshaping of the Global Economy* (London/New York: Pegasus Books).

Dadush, Uri (2014) 'The Decline of the Bretton Woods Institutions', *The National Interest* (September 22).

Dettke, Dieter (2009) *Germany Says No: The Iraq War and the Future of German Foreign and Security Policy* (Washington, DC: Woodrow Wilson Center Press).

Dobson, Joel (2013) *The Goldsboro Broken Arrow: The B-52 Crash of January 24, 1961 and its Potential as a Tipping Point for Nuclear War*, 2nd ed. (Lulu Publishing Service).

Dollar, Davie (2015) 'The AIIB and the 'One Belt, One Road', *Brookings* (Summer), www.brookings.edu/opinions/the-aiib-and-the-one-belt-one-road/

Doyle, Timothy (2005) *Environmental Movements in Minority and Majority Worlds* (New Brunswick, NJ: Rutgers University Press).

Doyle, Timothy, Doug McEachern and Sheilyn MacGregor (2016) *Environment and Politics*, 4th ed. (London: Routledge).

Economist Intelligence Unit (2018) *Democracy Index 2018* (London: The Economist).

Editorial Board (2018) 'Will the U.S. Help the Saudis Get a Nuclear Weapon?' *New York Times* (February 25, 2018).

Engel, Jeffrey A. (2018) *When the World Seemed New: George H.W. Bush and the End of the Cold War* (New York: Houghton, Mifflin, Harcourt).

Erlich, Reese (2016) *Inside Syria: The Backstory of Their Civil War and What the World Can Expect* (New York: Prometheus Books).

Falk, Richard (2016) *Power Shift: On the New Global Order* (New York: Zed Books).

Farrell, Greg (2010) *Crash of the Titans: Greed, Hubris, the Fall of Merrill Lynch, and the Near-Collapse of Bank of America* (New York: Crown).

Freedom House (2018) *Democracy in Crisis: Freedom in the Word 2018* (New York: Freedom House), https://freedomhouse.org/report/freedom-world/freedom-world-2018.

Fursenko, Aleksandre and Timothy Naftali (1998) *One Hell of a Gamble: Khrushchev, Castro, and Kennedy, 1958–1964: The Secret History of the Cuban Missile Crisis* (New York: W.W. Norton).

Gaddis, John Lewis (1986) 'The Long Peace: Elements of Stability in the Postwar International System', *International Security* 10(4) (Spring), pp. 99–142.

Gaddis, John Lewis (1989) *The Long Peace: Inquiries into the History of the Cold War* (Oxford: Oxford University Press).

Galston, William A. (2018) 'Trump and the Decline of Democracy', *Wall Street Journal* (January 16).

Giacomo, Carol (2016) 'Angela Merkel's Message to Trump', *New York Times* (November 21).

Gold, Russell (2014) *The Boom: How Fracking Ignited the American Energy Revolution and Changed the World* (New York: Simon & Schuster).

Gore, Al (2006) *An Inconvenient Truth: The Planetary Emergency of Global Warming and What We Can Do about It* (Emmaus, PA: Rodale Press).

Green, Joshua (2017) *Devil's Bargain: Steve Bannon, Donald Trump, and the Storming of the Presidency* (New York: Penguin Books).

Haass, Richard (2017) 'America and the Great Abdication', *The Atlantic* (December 28).

Haass, Richard (2018) 'As U.S. Leadership Dims, the World Is Drifting Away from Democracy', *Axios* (March 1), www.axios.com/us-leadership-dims-world-drifting-from-democracy-1519685722-c4e2f5e7-5065-475a-813e-d4297c00a3fd.html?source=sidebar.

Haddick, Robert (2014) *Fire on the Water: China, America and the Future of the Pacific* (Washington, DC: Naval Institution Press).

Hamilton, Dan and Joseph P. Quinlan (eds.) (2017) *The Transatlantic Economy 2017: Annual Survey of Jobs, Trade and Investment Between the United States and Europe* (Washington, DC: Center for Transatlantic Relations/SAIS).

Harris, Bryan (2018) 'N Korea Sent Chemical Weapons Supplies to Syria, Says Report', *Financial Times* (February 28).

Hausken, Kjell and Mthull Neube (2013) *Quantitative Easing and its Impact in the US, Japan, the UK and Europe* (New York: Springer).

Helleiner, Eric (2016) *Forgotten Foundations of Bretton Woods: International Development and the Making of the Postwar Order* (Ithaca, NY: Cornell University Press).

Heritage Foundation (2017) *2017 Index of U.S. Military Strength: Assessing America's Ability to Provide for the Common Defense* (Washington, DC: Heritage Foundation).

Hille, Kathrin and Henry Foy (2018) 'Russia to Deploy "unstoppable" Nuclear Weapons Says Putin', *Financial Times* (March 1).

Hoffman, Bruce (2017) *Inside Terrorism*, 3rd ed. (New York: Columbia University Press).

Huntington, Samuel P. (1993) 'The Class of Civilizations?', *Foreign Affairs* 72(3) (Summer), pp. 22–49.

Hurst, Steven (1999) *The Foreign Policy of the Bush Administration: In Search of a New World Order* (London: Continuum).

Hutton, Will (2018) 'Beware the Illiberal Alliance of Poland and Hungary, a Grave Threat to the EU', *The Guardian* (January 6).

Ikenberry, G. John and Darren Lim (2017) 'China's Emerging Institutional Statecraft: The Asian Infrastructure Investment Bank and the Prospects for Counter-Hegemony', *Brookings/American German Business Club Berlin*, www.agbc-berlin.de/content/brookings-china%E2%80%99s-emerging-institutional-statecraft.

Jacboson, Mark Z. (2012) *Air Pollution and Global Warming: History, Science, and Solutions*, 2nd ed. (Cambridge: Cambridge University Press).

Judis, John B. (2016) *The Populist Explosion: How the Great Recession Transformed American and European Politics* (New York: Columbia Global Reports).

Kagan, Robert (2003) *Of Paradise and Power: America and Europe in the New World Order* (New York: Knopf).

Kaplan, Fred (2016) *Dark Territory: The Secret History of Cyber War* (New York: Simon & Schuster).

Karlis, Nicole (2018) 'New Report Classifies US as a "flawed democracy"', *Salon* (January 31), www.salon.com/2018/01/31/new-report-classifies-us-as-a-flawed-democracy/

King, Joseph (2017) *Awake: An Introduction to New Nationalism* (New York: New Nationalists).

Kissinger, Henry (2014) *World Order* (New York: Penguin Books).

Klein, Daniel et al. (eds.) (2017) *The Paris Agreement on Climate Change: Analysis and Commentary* (Oxford: Oxford University Press).

Klein, Naomi (2015) *This Changes Everything: Capitalism vs the Climate* (New York: Simon and Schuster).

Kynge, James (2018) 'Xi Jinping Needs Chinese History to be on His Side', *Financial Times* (March 2).

Larres, Klaus (2003) 'Mutual Incomprehension? U.S. German Value Gaps over Iraq and Beyond', *Washington Quarterly* 26(2) (Spring), pp. 23–42.

Lee Myers, Steven (2018) 'With Xi's Power Grab, China Joins New Era of Strongman', *New York Times* (February 26).

Levant, Ezra (2014) *Groundswell: The Case for Fracking* (New York: Random House).

Lewis, Michael (2010) *The Big Short: Inside the Doomsday Machine* (New York: W.W. Norton).

Loth, Wilfried (2015) *Building Europe*: A History of European Unification (Amsterdam/Munich: De Gruyter/Oldenbourg).

Lowe, Vaughan, Adam Roberts, Jennifer Welsh and Dominik Zaum (eds.) (2010) *The United Nations Security Council and War: The Evolution of Thought and Practise since 1945* (Oxford: Oxford University Press).

Lynas, Mark (2008) *Six Degrees: Our Future on a Hotter Planet* (Washington, DC: National Geographic).

Maass, Peter (2013) 'Did the Iraq War Bring the Arab Spring?', *The New Yorker* (April 9).

MacFarquhar and David E Snager (2018) 'Putin's Invincible Missile Is Aimed at U.S. Vulnerabilities', *New York Times* (March 1).

Malone, David M. (2004) *The UN Security Council: From the Cold War to the 21st Century*, new ed. (Boulder, Col.: Lynne Riener).

McCormick, Thomas J. (1995) *America's Half-Century: United States Foreign Policy in the Cold War and After*, 2nd ed. (Baltimore, MA: Johns Hopkins University Press).

McCurry, Justin and Julian Borger (2017) 'North Korea Missile Launch: Regime Says New Rocket Can Hit Anywhere in US', *The Guardian* (November 29).

Meadows, Donella H., et al. (1974) *The Limits of Growth: A Report for the Club of Rome's Project on the Predicament of Mankind*, 2nd ed. (New York: Universe Books).

Moffitt, Benjamin (2016) *The Global Rise of Populism: Performance, Political Style, and Representation* (Standford, CA: Standford University Press).

Morgan, Michael C. (2018) *'The Final Act': The Helsinki Accords and the Transformation of the Cold War* (Princeton: Princeton University Press).

Mueller, John (1988) 'The Essential Irrelevance of Nuclear Weapons: Stability in the Postwar World', *International Security* 13(2) (Fall), pp. 55–79.

Mueller, John (2009) 'Think Again: Nuclear Weapons', *Foreign Policy* (December 18).

Murray, Williamson and Kevin M. Woods (2014) *The Iran-Iraq War: A Military and Strategic History* (Cambridge: Cambridge University Press).

Nye, David E. (1998) *Consuming Power: A Social History of American Energies* (Cambridge, MA: MIT Press).

Orsini, Alessandro (2011) *Anatomy of the Red Brigades: The Religious Mind-Set of Modern Terrorists* (Ithaca, NY: Cornell University Press).

Paulson, Henry M. (2015) *Dealing with China: An Insider Unmasks the New Economic Superpower* (New York/Boston: Twelve).

Pauly, Robert J. (2017) *Strategic Preemption: U.S. Foreign Policy and the Second Iraq War* (London: Routledge).

Pillar, Paul R. (2011) 'The Neocons' Undemocratic Domino', *The National Interest* (August 15).

Posner, Richard A (2009) *A Failure of Capitalism: The Crisis of '08 and the Descent into Depression* (Cambridge, MA: Harvard University Press).

Razoux, Pierre (2015) *The Iran-Iraq War* (Cambridge, MA: Belknap Press).

Rhodes, Richard (1996) *Dark Sun: The Making of the Hydrogen Bomb*, reprint edition (New York: Simon and Schuster).

Ritter, Scott (2018) *Deal of the Century: How the Iranian Nuclear Agreement Was Won, then Lost, and the Possible Consequences* (New York: Clarity).

Sachs, Jeffrey D. (2015) *The Age of Sustainable Development* (New York: Columbia University Press).

Sanger, David E. and William J. Broad (2018a) 'How U.S. Intelligence Agencies Underestimated North Korea', *New York Times* (January 6).

Sanger, David E. and William J. Broad (2018b) 'To Counter Russia, U.S. Signals Nuclear Arms Are Back in a Big Way', *New York Times* (February 4).

Schabas, William A. (2006) *The UN International Criminal Tribunals: The Former Yugoslavia, Rwanda and Sierra Leone* (Cambridge: Cambridge University Press).

Schabas, William A. (2017) *An Introduction to the International Criminal Court*, 5th ed. (Cambridge: Cambridge University Press).

Schlesinger, Stephen C. (2004) *Act of Creation: The Founding of the United Nations* (New York: Basic Books).

Schlosser, Eric (2014) *Command and Control: Nuclear Weapons, the Damascus Accident, and the Illusion of Safety*, reprint edition (New York: Penguin).

Sengupta, Somini (2018) 'Warning Water Crisis, Then Unrest: How Iran Fits an Alarming Pattern', *New York Times* (January 18).

Shabecoff, Philip (2003) *A Fierce Green Fire: An American Environmental Movement*, rev. ed. (Washington, DC: Island Press).

Shambaugh, David (2014) *China Goes Global: The Partial Power* (Oxford: Oxford University Press).

Smith, Gar (ed.) (2017) *War and Environment Reader* (Washington, DC: Just World Books).

Snyder, Sarah B. (2011) *Human Rights Activism and the End of the Cold War: A Transnational History of the Helsinki Negotiations* (Cambridge: Cambridge University Press).

Steil, Benn (2013) *The Battle of Bretton Woods: John Maynard Keynes, Harry Dexter White, and the Making of a New World Order* (Princeton: Princeton University Press).

Steil, Benn (2014) *The Battle of Bretton Woods: John Maynard Keynes, Harry Dexter White, and the Making of a New World Order* (Princeton: Princeton University Press).

Stein, Aaron (2018a) 'Strategic Incoherence in Syria: Why Iran, Russia and Turkey Can't All Get What they Want', *Foreign Affairs* (March 2).

Stein, Aaron (2018b) 'Turkey's Afrin Offensive and America's Future in Syria: Why Washington Should be Eyeing the Exit', *Foreign Affairs* (January 23).

Swain, Carol M (2004) *The New White Nationalism in America: Its Challenge to Integration* (Cambridge: Cambridge University Press).

Toal, Gerard (2017) *Near Abroad: Putin, the West and the Contest over Ukraine and the Caucasus* (Oxford: Oxford University Press).

Tsukimori, Osamu (2018) 'U.S. to Overtake Russia as Top Oil Producer by 2019 at the Latest', *Reuters Press Agency* (February 26).

Ullrich, Volker (2016) *Hitler: Ascent, 1889–1939* (New York, Knopf).

Von Einsiedel, Sebastian, David M. Malone and Bruno Stagno Ugarte (eds.) (2015) *The UN Security Council in the 21st Century* (Boulder, CO: Lynne Rienner).

Weiss, Thomas G. (2016) *The United Nations and Changing World Politics* (London: Routledge).

Weiss, Thomas G. and Sam Davis (eds.) (2009) *The Oxford Handbook on the United Nations* (Oxford: Oxford University Press).

Westad, Odd Arne, *The Cold War: A World History* (New York: Basic Books).

Weston, J. Kael (2016) *The Mirror Test: America at War in Iraq and Afghanistan* (New York: Vintage).

White, Hugh (2013) *China's Choice: Why We Should Share Power* (Oxford: Oxford University Press).

Whitney, Craig R. (2005) *The WMD Mirage: Iraq's Decade of Deception and America's False Premise for War* (New York: Public Affairs).

Wodak, Ruth (2015) *The Politics of Fear: What Right-Wing Populist Discourse Mean* (London: Sage).

Wolf, Martin (2018) 'Xi's Power Grab means China Is Vulnerable to the Whims of One Man', *Financial Times* (February 27).

Wolff, Michael (2018) *Fire and Fury: Inside the Trump White House* (New York: Henry Holt).

Worster, William Thomas (2012) *United Nations Convention on the Law of the Seas*, 2nd ed. (Create Space Independent Publishing Platform).

Yergin, Daniel (1992) *The Prize: The Epic Quest for Oil, Money, and Power* (New York: Simon & Schuster).

Chapter 2

Democracy

Problems and challenges, opportunities and design

Matthew Flinders and Marc Geddes

FIGURE 2.1 The ancient temple of the Parthenon, Acropolis, Athens, Greece

The Acropolis of Athens overlooks the city traditionally known as the birthplace of Western democracy. It is protected as a UNESCO World Heritage Site because of its architectural importance and its historical significance. Among other things, the Acropolis highlights the pinnacle of civilisation and progress during an age of ancient democracy. We draw attention to this impressive site and its buildings not only because it symbolises the enduring idea of democracy – but also because it so aptly symbolises its very fragility. The Acropolis is the site where ancient democracy was born, but it was also a site of military conquest, the demonstration of despotic power and where ancient democracy ended. In this sense, the Acropolis reminds us that democracy is in absolutely no way to be regarded as the 'natural' or 'inevitable' peak of an advanced political society. It is something that has to be continually fought for, practised and defended. And we would urge: now, more than ever.

Perusing any library's section on democracy appears to show us democracy in crisis: from *Why We Hate Politics* (2007) to *The End of Representative Politics* (2015) (and many more in between), all point towards worrying pictures of democratic decline (for a review of this literature, see Ercan and Gagnon, 2014). This chapter attempts to grapple with this literature and its consequences for democracy across the globe and at different levels. The picture we paint is necessarily stark because the challenges that democracies face are significant. However, this chapter is also not one of pure pessimism. Rather, we want to argue that while democracy may well face a number of problems, the fluid modernity (Bauman, 2000) that we inhabit gives rise to a number of opportunities to reinvigorate democratic politics.

In order for us to make our argument, this chapter proceeds in three sections: first, we identify the current trends in democratic politics; second, we summarise the causes and consequences of those trends in terms of the problems we face; and third, we carve out how those consequences might be met in the current political climate through our concluding discussion.

Wither democracy?

We can see the decline of democracy along a range of markers and indices in established democracies. The most obvious trend to highlight is turnout in general elections, which have been in decline across democracies. Peter Mair's analysis in *Ruling the Void* (2013, pp. 17–44) comprehensively assesses the decline in Europe since the 1990s: European citizens are voting less often; they have become more volatile in casting their vote; fewer are identifying with a political party; and, they are less willing to take on party membership and its associated duties and obligations. These shifts are not isolated to Europe. They are indicative of wider declines across the globe, where average voter turnout in elections fell to 70 per cent in the 1990s and to 66 per cent in the period between 2011 and 2015 (International Institute for Democracy and Electoral Assistance, 2016, p. 24). Looking at other indices, we can see that approval ratings of the US Congress have not risen above 21 per cent since May 2011, and have not reached 50 per cent since 2003 (at time of writing) (Gallup, 2017); the average trust in European national governments stands at 31 per cent (European Commission, 2016); and, 40 per cent of citizens in sub-Saharan

Africa have little or no trust in their legislature (Lavallée et al., 2008, p. 5). Worryingly, these problems are set to continue into the future given that young people are increasingly less likely to engage in any form of political activity according to recent studies (e.g. Grasso, 2016).

What these trends reveal is that engagement with established political institutions across the globe is in decline, and affects both newer and older democratic systems. It raises the question as to whether democracy as a form of government will be promoted in future. Some political scientists believe that once countries develop democratic institutions, a robust civil society and a certain level of wealth, democracies generally remain secure. This is known as 'democratic consolidation' (Linz and Stepan, 1996). Even if there is dissatisfaction or distrust in relation to specific institutions, politicians or political parties this does not affect deeper underlying social commitment to the principles and values of democracy. So, consolidated democratic states remain democratic. Indeed, and since 1945, it seemed that nation states were inexorably moving towards democratic forms. This was reinforced by key periods that led to further democratisation: in 1974–5, military rule in Spain, Portugal and Greece came to an end; during the 1980s, Latin American countries democratised; and, following the downfall of the Soviet Union in 1989, many former communist countries transitioned to democracies. Francis Fukuyama (1989) famously asked if this was the 'end of history' and, a short number of years later, Juan J. Linz and Alred Stepan (1996, p. 5) exclaimed that democracy was 'the only game in town'.

However, while approximately 60 per cent of the world's nation states had embraced democracy, Larry Diamond (2008, p. 36) argues that 'celebrations of democracy's triumph are premature' because 'the democratic wave has been slowed by a powerful authoritarian undertow' and that the world has 'slipped into a democratic recession'. More recently, Freedom House (2017) argues that 2017 marks the 11th consecutive year in which there have been more declines in political rights and civil liberties than there have been advances. There are a number of examples that demonstrate this: in Poland, the national-conservative government has enacted a range of policies to limit civil liberties, increase control over public media and reduce powers over the courts (with resulting investigations from the European Commission) (Krastev, 2016); elsewhere, in Hungary, the independence of the judiciary has been undermined and journalists fear to speak out (Marton, 2014). Both examples are part of a wider trend.

There is not only a decline in trust in democratic institutions, but also acquiescence in dismantling those institutions (think also of events in Turkey (Karaveli, 2016) and Venezuela (Corrales, 2015), for example). According to Roberto Stefan Foa and Yascha Mounk (2016), long-established democracies (such as the US or UK) are not immune to those trends. Their data shows *inter alia* a decline in citizens' express support for their political system, a decline in support for key institutions of liberal democracies, and an increasing openness to authoritarian alternatives to democratic rule. While Ronald F. Inglehart (2016) argues that the picture is far more subtle, when placed in the context of other global figures and trends since the 1970s, Foa and Mounk's research is distressing because it implies that citizens are increasingly not only dissatisfied with their democrats but with democracy as a system.

These trends extend to global political institutions – the pertinent focus of this book. Trust in the European Union as a whole, for example, stands at 36 per cent.

Other international organisations face similar deficits, including the World Trade Organisation (Kaldor, 2000) and the International Monetary Fund, which has itself acknowledged that it faces an 'international crisis of legitimacy' (Seabrooke, 2007). This matters because these organisations play an increasing role in the governance of nation states while concomitantly coming under increasing challenge to demonstrate their legitimate democratic credentials (Buchanan and Keohane, 2006; Archibugi and Held, 2011).

Why does it matter? It matters because it paints a picture of growing global disengagement with established and newer democratic institutions. But far more than that, it reveals increasing examples of where institutions are being dismantled that could pave the way for a more authoritarian turn in global politics. It also raises a number of further questions about the causes for this decline of confidence in democracy, to which we now turn.

Challenges to democracy

The aim of this section is to explore a number of the aforementioned challenges in more detail in order to dissect and unpick the underlying drivers. This includes the rise of individualism, the rise of populism and a lack of political literacy. This is clearly not an exhaustive review of the challenges to democracy and other scholars have set out their own thoughts on 'the problem with democracy' (e.g. Flinders, 2016). Rather, this section provides a balance of breadth and depth that facilitates a more focused discussion on the global challenges to democracy and the global challenges to professional students of democracy (professors included) in the next and final section.

Voting alone

The nature of engagement between citizens and political institutions has changed. And, arguably, democratic institutions have not adequately adapted to those changes. A number of commentators have pointed out that civic culture has changed in a way that has given rise to 'critical citizens', or the emergence of new forms of direct, assertive and issue-specific political engagement (Inglehart, 1977; see also Stoker and Evans, 2014). This changed engagement with political institutions is part of broader shifts in society where once solid social reference points that allowed people to make sense of their world and their place within it have been eroded in important ways. In particular, we echo the work of Bauman (2000, 2003) in arguing that traditional social anchorage points have been lost and societal relations have become more transient. This creates challenges for democracy: how to engage citizens in traditional political institutions that are underpinned and legitimised by a *collective* social ethos when individuals are increasingly turning *away* from those collective-orientated social institutions and towards individualised, issue-focused and often non-institutionalised forms of activity and engagement. This is the democratic gap that has emerged between the governors and the governed.

This problem intensifies when we link changes in public engagement to other trends, such as political elites' pursuit of market-focused policy programs. Specifically, the practices of governance, the social system of production, dominant notions of 'value' and collective understandings of citizenship have been altered in such a way that each of these spheres is construed in market terms (Sandel, 2012). This focus on the market since the 1960s has eviscerated traditional liberal democracies, undermined civic culture and exacerbated inequalities (Streeck, 2013; Piketty, 2013). Crucially, market dominance has also changed political culture into a more *individualised* system of market democracy. In this sense, individuals view their interactions with parties and political candidates as they would a retail relationship in which goods and services are bought. The citizen-consumer makes their choice, spends their vote and then waits for the goods to be delivered – almost as if they were a CD or book purchased on Amazon. Democratic politics was never intended to satisfy a world of individualised wants, and when compared to simplistic market assumptions, it will generally fail because democracy is geared to collective outputs. As Gerry Stoker (2006, p. 68) argues, 'many citizens fail to fully appreciate that politics in the end involves the collective imposition of decisions', and that, 'this problem has been compounded by the spread of market-based consumerism and . . . individualism'. It suggests that democracy is no longer something done for the community or for the common good, but has descended to the level of autonomous individuals (Gairdner, 2003). What this highlights is the emergence of a rather 'thin' model of democracy in which the public behave (and are treated) as customers rather than citizens (for a discussion, see Scammell, 2014).

This challenge has taken a uniquely global angle in many respects. Not only in the sense that civic culture is changing across the globe, as the previous section has shown, but also in the sense that market-inspired reforms are taking a global picture. So, for example, the International Monetary Fund has become a global institution that comments across many aspects of national economic policies and sets medium- to long-term objectives and goals, offers a range of training services to civil servants and has, especially in recent years, attempted to restore stability to pre-existing financial markets. This has led one scholar to conclude that, 'its voice carries far in global markets, in national economic policies, and eventually in local and household budgets' (Scholte, 2000). The World Bank and WTO are two other organisations with similar far-reaching effects. Taken together, their agenda includes the introduction of commercial criteria for success, the dismantling of nationalised industries and monopolies, and the reduction of government in industrial or business relations (Pauly, 1999). Reforms instituted by the IMF, the World Bank or the WTO entrench many trends in economic globalisation and, in doing so, further promote marketisation across political institutions under the auspices of 'good governance'. This matters because it encourages new relationships between the public and politics, namely through market mechanisms that we mentioned before. This global dimension enhances the challenge for democrats everywhere because significant questions remain around how to reconcile the predominance and imposition of market-based policies in national economies with a decline in trust and participation in traditional political and democratic institutions. This is especially problematic because these international organisations encourage power from democratic bodies to be taken away (Vibert, 2007). We only need to think of the way in which economic reforms and austerity policies were imposed on a number of European governments since 2007, notably Greece (Blyth, 2013). This has, unsurprisingly, led to dramatic declines in satisfaction with democracy (Armingeon and Guthmann, 2014).

Anti-politics and the resurgence of populism

In 1997, Alan Blinder, economist and academic, asked 'is government too political?' in an article for *Foreign Affairs*. He was not alone in asking this question. Over the past 30 or so years, we have seen a range of politicians and commentators explain that there is too much politics in decision making. These thoughts were part of a wider belief, originating in the work by Anthony Downs (1957) and Kenneth Arrow (1951) among others, that actors – and especially politicians and administrators – are self-interested, utility-maximising agents. In internalising these assumptions, all officials are assumed to seek public office for self-interested motives, which has had debilitating consequences for political trust. For example, Colin Hay (2007, p. 58) suggests that, 'in a context in which even politicians concede that "politics" is something we need rather less of', it is unsurprising that 'public political disaffection and disengagement is rife'.

Consequently, there has been a shift in many countries to limit politicians' competencies and to 'depoliticise' decision making. This echoes trends in marketisation covered earlier because the aim is to shift decision-making powers to non-elected agencies or private sector organisations, veiled in the language of New Public Management (NPM). According to NPM principles, this would increase efficiency and responsiveness for public policy decision, especially because politicians are not to be trusted. However, the persistence of major social and political challenges (migration, employment, climate change, economic (in)security) continues to stimulate questions from the public about what steps *politicians* are taking to deal with those issues. Politicians rarely reply with a developed policy response. Instead, these questions are met with blame avoidance strategies or blame games, which fuels much public frustration and undermines confidence in the capacity of democracy to respond (Hood, 2010). This brings us back to a notion of a global democratic gap that has emerged between governors and the governed.

What has received less attention is the link between blame games and globalisation. This is a critical point. Even the most cursory analysis of the major sociopolitical challenges facing most countries will immediately reveal the global roots of those issues. Even if the issue is not global in terms of the geographic extent of the challenge then the mechanisms through which an effective response can be orchestrated will very often involve international coordination and cooperation. In many ways, the creation of supranational governing units that involve the pooling of resources (and to some extent sovereignty) is an explicit recognition of the limited 'reach' or capacity of nation states. However, the flipside is that the 'reach' of democracy does not seem to have expanded accordingly. It therefore becomes relatively easy to place a whole range of social evils at the door of 'faceless' or 'unaccountable bureaucrats' while at the same time decrying the 'weakness' of national politicians for either delegating powers or refusing to repatriate them in the face of what is interpreted as policy failure. The location of public services and regulatory powers beyond the sphere of (direct) democratic politics has therefore facilitated the emergence of a relatively simple but incredibly powerful populist narrative that is based upon a rejection of globalisation. To some extent it is even forged upon a protectionist model of nationalist populism as a reaction against what is perceived or framed to be the technocratic, globalised, distant, unaccountable, elitist model of contemporary politics.

Although these populist or 'anti-political' parties profess to be intensely democratic and located against the depoliticised modes of governance that have emerge in recent decades, it is possible to suggest that they are just as anti-democratic or democratically problematic as the technocratically inspired and multi-levelled networks of actors they seek to dismantle. Populists are impatient of procedures and unwilling to accept the simple fact that democratic politics tends to be slow, messy and cumbersome – as well as prone to producing suboptimal decisions – because politics (as just pointed out) is about the ability to squeeze collective decisions out of multiple and competing interests and opinions (Stoker, 2006, p. 196).

The emergence of populist parties and candidates across liberal democracies (and their successes, such as Donald Trump's presidential election victory in the US or the inroads made by the National Front in France) highlights at least three central challenges for democracy. First, populism's grip on the public's imagination reminds us of low levels of political literacy and political processes. Perhaps populism would not be so compelling if the public more clearly appreciated the need for compromise in a globalised world. This has arguably been exacerbated in recent times in a changing media and political information landscape to which we return in the next subsection. Second, populism is arguably tied to a belief that it is possible to take the politics out of democracy, thereby sweeping away the need for the compromises and constraints of politics. Populists often offer simplistic interpretations of problems and simplistic solutions to those problems, and make a virtue out of their simplicity: immigration control is 'the answer' to changing societies; economic protectionism is 'the answer' to changing patterns of economic organisation. Mainstream political parties have found it difficult to respond to this because many acknowledge (and indeed have to work through) the complexity of political problems in an age of global interdependence.

A third facet, which returns us to the opening of this subsection, is the belief that politics is no longer seen as the art of the possible. Established politicians themselves have abdicated responsibility for politics in a number of significant ways, which means that their perceived abilities to change and impact current challenges has been diminished. Populist parties have capitalised on this, as Peter Mair (2013, p. 4) notes:

> a simple populist strategy – employing the rhetoric of 'the people' as a means of underlining the radical break with past styles of government . . . gelled perfectly well with the tenets of what were then seen as newly emerging school of governance and the idea that . . . any attempts on the part of government to intervene will be ineffective.

The danger that populism represents can be seen in the decline of democratic institutions in some states, such as the examples of Poland and Hungary cited in the previous section. These authoritarian turns have become difficult to counter in recent times because of their incremental and barely noticeable nature. So, a significant challenge or theme that democrats face is how to combat populist rhetoric and behaviour. This is especially important given that the overtures made by many far-right populists is to the detriment of global institutions – and, indeed, to globalisation itself. Donald Trump (2016), for example, has commented that 'globalisation has made the financial elite who donate to politicians very, very wealthy . . . but it has left millions of our workers with nothing but poverty and heartache'. Elsewhere, Marine Le Pen, leader of France's National Front, has called for an end to the tyranny of globalisation and, in the event of a future election victory, promises to take France out of the eurozone (Front National, 2017). In the UK, we have seen the direct consequences of this with the withdrawal of the country from a 27 member-state union. These trends are suggesting that, increasingly, populists are utilising globalisation and global governance institutions and actors as a lightning rod for disengaged publics to divide people, indicating the uniquely *global* challenges to democracy.

Staying informed

Distrust in institutions extends beyond political and democratic ones. Accusations are now also brought against journalists and the media for supposedly distorting truths, exaggerating claims made by established elites and downplaying the views that run counter to elite attitudes. This growth of distrust in the media represents a huge challenge for democrats because mainstream media outlets are the single most important channels by which political ideas travel. It is often in such environments where populist groups are able to flourish and maintain support. *The Atlantic* (Frum, 2017) cites one such example: on 27 November 2016, Donald Trump tweeted that he had in fact 'won the popular vote if you deduct the millions of people who voted illegally'. If true, this would arguably be the biggest instance of electoral fraud in US history. And while Trump has left his comments unsubstantiated, it was also perceived as factual. For example, a YouGov survey found that by 1 December 2016, 43 per cent of Republicans accepted the claim that millions of people had voted illegally. The phenomenon, described variously as 'fake news' or 'alternative facts', is becoming an increasing problem for the accurate dissemination of information in a democracy because it disrupts the traditional ways by which the public receive, digest and engage with politics.

This is compounded in no small way by the continued rise and prevalence of the internet. It is not difficult to see why the internet was lauded as a way to build global democracy because it could allow for instant communication across the planet. However, and at the same time, the internet and wider technological changes have thrown up fundamental challenges. For example, there is a danger of creating echo chambers on a range of digital platforms including Facebook or Twitter. Social media platforms allow individuals to choose with whom they engage, and so almost all information – including political information and news – comes from friends, colleagues and family on Facebook or the people that users follow on Twitter. There are debates over the extent to which this limits the exposure of different forms of news and knowledge that the public relies on to engage with politics (e.g. Colleoni et al., 2014), but, regardless of the extent of this effect, it throws up a crucial challenge to democrats to ensure their messages are received (and undistorted, at that).

The internet has wider effects that challenge democracy today, and it is important to note the influence of global companies at this point. Organisations such as Google and Facebook have become very important political actors in that they mediate news as well as provide information on politics. Google, for example, now regularly attempts to predict phrases in search engines, and makes suggestions based on other users' behaviour. While the extent to which Google plays a role in democracies is far from clear, some research (e.g. Epstein and Robertson, 2015) suggests that there is something called a 'search engine manipulation effect' (SEME). Findings suggest that search-rank results could affect voting patterns. These trends are significant, yet policymakers have not yet begun to think about their consequences despite growing calls and questions about regulatory frameworks or algorithmic transparency. Ultimately, this challenge cuts across national boundaries given the multinational nature of these technological companies, raising yet further questions about the impact on global democratic trends.

This discussion implies that technological changes have not led to an enlightened citizenry but one that is exposed to huge swathes of information while, simultaneously, being increasingly more niche about the information it receives. The final added problem is that the growth of tweets, status updates, ability to sign petitions, etc., brings with it an increased emphasis on democratic voice and choice. However, as Andrew Dobson (2014, p. 2) points out, this can come at a cost: 'Although much prized in daily conversation, good listening has been almost completely ignored in political conversation, and particularly in the form we know as democracy'. He suggests that, 'speaking has garnered the lion's share of attention, both in terms of the skills to be developed and the ways in which we should understand what improving it might entail'. Dobson's argument is that a listening democracy would be a far better democracy because it would be more responsive. This links us back to the previous two subsections in multiple ways. The growth of democratic voice is in no small part down to changes to the technological landscape. However, it is also a wider cultural shift that we have noted earlier whereby it is assumed that individual preferences are more important than anything else. The idea of democracy as a *collective* endeavour has been lost, and so it is no surprise to see a growth of many, many voices shouting for competing and contradictory ideas in democratic spaces. Meanwhile, fewer and fewer people are *listening* because it goes against the principle idea of the autonomy or even sovereignty of the individual that dominant, neo-liberal ideas are encouraging in democratic culture.

We have argued in this section that public attitudes have changed significantly because of what appears to be a cultural shift towards individualism and the primacy of the market. Market-logic brings with it a set of assumptions about rational behaviour that rarely presents individuals in a positive light or being capable of selfless behaviours; it also offers little in terms of understanding the role of democracy in terms of the collective pooling of resources in order to combat shared risks. The 'Logic of the Market' and what might be termed 'the Logic of Democracy' are therefore arguably opposed. As Sir Bernard Crick's seminal *In Defence of Politics* (2013 [1962]) illustrated with great verve and wit, the institutions of democratic politics were intended to act as a counterweight to potentially negative and vicious market forces and instabilities. A global example of this would be the global financial crisis of 2007–8, which resulted from a democratic failure to regulate financial markets. Though only one example, it shows that debates and issues around the past, present and future of democracy have a global reverberation. This has been the core of our argument that we now wish to summarise more directly in our conclusion.

Conclusion: the global reverberation and (re)designing for democracy

This chapter has examined the state of democracy. It has outlined a number of problems and challenges, many of which are core features of the existing literature. The focus of this concluding section is to make a slightly more novel and provocative contribution to this literature through a focus on three issues. The first is on what might be termed the global politics of democracy and, more specifically, on *the global politics of national democratic politics*. This aims to highlight the existence of very different causal linkages and relationships that deserve further analysis. The second issue is a focus on what we term 'the nexus' or 'nexus politics'. It draws attention away from the common problems, issues and themes that have dominated the analysis of democratic change in recent decades and towards a focus on the *intersection* between many of those themes and issues. The third and final issue is what might be termed 'a twist', or 'a hook' or 'a barb' in the sense of a plea to political and social scientists to consider a quite fundamental shift in their approach to the analysis of democracy towards a more solution-focused and design-infused mode of inquiry. Rephrased, it could be said that the three core themes of this section are the *matrix*, the *nexus* and the *promise*. We make no attempt to engage with these themes in any great detail but simply offer them as topics that seem to us to offer great intellectual traction and leverage in terms of understanding both 'democratic politics as theory' and 'democratic politics as practice'.

In order to open up an under-acknowledged field of inquiry, we draw on the work of Bauman (2000, 2003), whose focus on the changing nature of human bonds has been instructive. Human bonds or connections are at one and the same time necessary enablers in life but simultaneously can also be limiting. They have altered in terms of form, texture and substance as a result of technological advances that fit with a broader meta-narrative concerning fluidity and mutating form. At one level, people are connected as never before through the power of a smartphone that can transmit pictures, videos and messages to a global audience at almost no cost. People have more (Facebook) friends than ever and emojis provide for demonstrative expression at the touch of a key. Dating apps (e.g. Tinder and Grindr) provide a range of opportunities for personal interactions with like-minded individuals with no emotional commitment or long-term obligations. Relationships can therefore be traversed and navigated without investment, and connections can be disconnected at the touch of a key. Modern life has taken on a technologically facilitated sense of semi-detachment from traditional emotional or relationship expectations. As Bauman (2003) argued, semi-detached couples stay together only long enough to enjoy the fun but not long enough to create complex emotional bonds. It is the personal equivalent of the economic model of the gig economy in terms of being low commitment, temporary, highly fluid, etc. – the employer and employee do not stay together long enough to create any legal responsibilities. The Tinder generation and the gig economy flow into this chapter's focus on the changing civic culture and a predilection – notably amongst the young – for political relationships that are similarly non-existent, fleeting, short-term and instrumental. The challenge from this perspective is simply that such relationships may become the expected way that *all* relationships (political, interpersonal, economic, etc.) are approached. Taking this a step further, it may become normal never to risk investing in collective endeavours or forging deeper emotional relationships or even understand why such an approach to the art of life may offer far deeper value and satisfaction. The loss of solid social anchorage points provides a slightly oblique and unconventional way of thinking about democracy in the 21st century, yet also one that offers a clear connection to the three themes that form the pillars of our concluding focus.

The notion of *the matrix* relates to the existence of both vertical and horizontal relationships between democracy and globalisation. The horizontal dimension relates to a relatively well known pool of scholarship on the democratisation of global governance (e.g. Stephenson and Dryzek, 2014). This offers a general focus on the upscaling of democratic structures, values, procedures and relationships to the global level in order to close the democratic 'gap' that appears to have emerged. Democratisation, then, not of the nation state but of global affairs more broadly (Erman, 2012; Kuyper, 2014). It is in this vein that democratic theorists have argued that global democracy is increasingly important and a justified pursuit. John Dryzek (2011, p. 213), for example, has identified three justifications: first, global democracy is instrumental to the achievement of global justice over issues such as climate change; second, democracies are particularly good kinds of systems for solving complex collective problems; and third, it is intrinsically valued and thereby crucial to ensure the legitimacy of global institutions, including the WTO, IMF and World Bank. This logic has led to more specific proposals such as calls for a global parliament (Falk and Strauss, 2000), the creation of cosmopolitan institutions (Held, 1995; Archibugi, 2008), building stronger links between domestic and international structures (Keohane et al., 2009), global political parties (Patomäki, 2011), deliberative systems (Dryzek, 2009) or democratic global constitutionalism (Peters, 2009), among others.

There is a second, more vertical dimension to *the matrix* that has received less attention and that is the global reverberation at the national level. By this, we simply mean the negative externalities caused by globalisation in terms of creating exactly those democratic frustrations that have been so effectively utilised by populist nationalist parties in recent years. This vertical focus directs our attention to the many different layers and levels at which governments operate (multi-level governance). This has, according to Peters and Pierre (2004), created a Faustian bargain. While increased multi-levelled structures provide new problem-solving capacities, they also come at the cost of reducing democratic procedures and blurring lines of accountability. As the rise in anti-establishment populist parties has risen, it seems that this bargain was not worth paying.

The intersection – or *the nexus* – encourages us to re-think understandings of contemporary anti-political sentiment for the simple reason that, in reality, very little of this sentiment is actually *anti*-political. Very few groups, protestors or politicians are arguing that politics and democracy are in some way unnecessary. Behind the 'anti-political' demands of veiled protestors is actually a more positive demand for a different form of 'doing' politics. What is lacking, however, is a tangible linkage or nexus between the demands of what are generally fairly fluid, bottom-up explosions of democratic energy and the capacity of generally bureaucratic and inflexible top-down structures of democratic politics. It is at the nexus between these two forms that global democratic theories and innovations may offer great potential to create new structures in new spheres.

This brings us to a final focus, namely the importance of the social and political sciences. If anti-politics is actually a social demand to 'do politics differently', then surely it is for the social and political sciences to play a role in designing and testing new democratic innovations. This is not a new argument. As long as 60 years ago, C. Wright Mills wrote *The Sociological Imagination* (1959), in which he outlined the importance of understanding both a 'trap', i.e. social trends and pressures that make it increasingly hard for individuals to understand their place in the world (forerunning Bauman's arguments (2000, 2003)), and a 'promise'. It is this promise of the social sciences that exists to help make sense of the world and promote the public understanding of society and politics. One question for the future is therefore whether these disciplines can, at last, begin to deliver just a little of this promise by focusing upon designing *for* democracy and how exactly we might 'do' politics differently. This seems to be the biggest challenge of all.

It is with the final thought of hope, possibility and opportunity that we want to end this chapter, and specifically we want to turn back to the Acropolis. While the buildings may be damaged and under constant renovation projects, they are still standing. The Parthenon remains a towering example over the ancient city of Athens, and the ideas that it represents will, we hope, continue to endure.

Further reading

Archibugi, Daniele and David Held (2011) 'Cosmopolitan Democracy: Paths and Agents', *Ethics and International Affairs* 25(4), pp. 433–461.

Dryzek, John S. (2006) *Deliberative Global Politics* (Cambridge: Polity Press).

Ercan, Selen and Jean-Paul Gagnon (2014) 'The Crisis of Democracy: Which crisis? Which democracy?', *Democratic Theory* 1(2), pp. 1–10.

Flinders, Matthew (2012) *Defending Politics* (Oxford: Oxford University Press).

Hay, Colin (2007) *Why We Hate Politics* (Cambridge: Polity Press).

Held, David (1995) *Democracy and the Global Order* (Cambridge: Polity Press).

Mair, Peter (2013) *Ruling the Void: The Hollowing Out of Western Democracy* (London: Verso).

Scammell, Margaret (2014) *Consumer Democracy: The Marketing of Politics* (Cambridge: Cambridge University Press).

Stoker, Gerry (2006) *Why Politics Matters* (Basingstoke: Palgrave Macmillan).

Bibliography

Archibugi, Daniele (2008) *The Global Commonwealth of Citizens: Toward Cosmopolitan Democracy* (Princeton, NJ: Princeton University Press).

Archibugi, Daniele and David Held (2011) 'Cosmopolitan Democracy: Paths and Agents', *Ethics and International Affairs* 25(4), pp. 433–461.

Armingeon, Klaus and Kai Guthmann (2014) 'Democracy in Crisis? The Declining Support for National Democracy in European Countries, 2007–11', *European Journal of Political Research* 53(3), pp. 423–442.

Arrow, Kenneth (1951) *Social Choice and Individual Values* (New York: Wiley).

Bauman, Zygmunt (2000) *Liquid Modernity* (Cambridge: Polity Press).

Bauman, Zygmunt (2003) *Liquid Love* (Cambridge: Polity Press).

Blinder, Alan S. (1997) 'Is Government Too Political', *Foreign Affairs* 76(6), pp. 115–126.

Blyth, Mark (2013) *Austerity: The History of a Dangerous Idea* (Oxford: Oxford University Press).

Buchanan, Allen and Robert O. Keohane (2006) 'The Legitimacy of Global Governance Institutions', *Ethics and International Affairs* 20(4), pp. 405–437.

Colleoni, Elanor, Alessandro Rozza and Adam Arvidsson (2014) 'Echo Chamber or Public Sphere? Predicting Political Orientation and Measuring Political Homophily in Twitter Using Big Data', *Journal of Communication* 64(2), pp. 317–332.

Corrales, Javier (2015) 'Autocratic Legalism in Venezuela', *Journal of Democracy* 26(2), pp. 37–51.

Crick, Bernard (2013 [1962]) *In Defence of Politics* (London: Bloomsbury Academic).

Diamond, Larry (2008) 'The Democratic Rollback: The Resurgence of the Predatory State', *Foreign Affairs* 87(2), pp. 36–48.

Dobson, Andrew (2014) *Listening for Democracy* (Oxford: Oxford University Press).

Downs, Anthony (1957) *An Economic Theory of Democracy* (New York: Harper Collins).

Dryzek, John (2011) 'Global Democratization: Soup, Society, or System?', *Ethics and International Affairs* 25(2), pp. 211–234.

Dryzek, John S. (2009) 'Democratization as Deliberative Capacity Building', *Comparative Political Studies* 42(11), pp. 1379–1402.

Epstein, Robert and Ronald E. Robertson (2015) 'The Search Engine Manipulation Effect (SEME) and Its Possible Impact on the Outcomes of Elections', *Proceedings of the National Academy of Sciences of the United States of America* 112(33), pp. E4512–E4521.

Ercan, Selen and Jean-Paul Gagnon (2014) 'The Crisis of Democracy: Which Crisis? Which Democracy?', *Democratic Theory* 1(2), pp. 1–10.

Erman, Eva (2012) 'In Search of Democratic Agency in Deliberative Governance' *European Journal of International Relations* 19(4), pp. 847–868.

European Commission (2016) *Standard Barometer 86* (Brussels: European Commission).

Falk, Richard and Andrew Strauss (2000) 'On the Creation of a Global Peoples Assembly: Legitimacy and the Power of Popular Sovereignty', *Stanford Journal of International Law* 36(2), pp. 191–219.

Flinders, M. (2016) 'The Problem With Democracy', *Parliamentary Affairs* 69(1), pp. 181–203.

Foa, Roberto Stefan and Yascha Mounk (2016) 'The Democratic Disconnect', *Journal of Democracy* 27(3), pp. 5–17.

Freedom House (2017) *Freedom in the World 2017* (Washington, DC: Freedom House).

Front National (2017) *144 Engagements Présidentiels* (Nanterre: Front National).

Frum, David (2017) 'How to Build an Autocracy', *The Atlantic* (March Issue), www.theatlantic.com/magazine/archive/2017/03/how-to-build-an-autocracy/513872/ (accessed February 23, 2017).

Fukuyama, Francis (1989) 'The End of History?', *National Interest* (Summer), pp. 3–18.

Gairdner, William D. (2003) 'From Democracy to Hyper-Democracy', *Humanitas* 16(1), pp. 74–89.

Gallup (2017) 'Congress and the Public', www.gallup.com/poll/1600/congress-public.aspx (last accessed February 23, 2017).

Grasso, Maria (2016) *Generations, Political Participation and Social Change in Western Europe* (London: Routledge).

Hay, Colin (2007) *Why We Hate Politics* (Cambridge: Polity Press).

Held, David (1995) *Democracy and the Global Order* (Cambridge: Polity Press).

Held, David and Anthony McGrew (2007) *Globalization/Anti-Globalization: Beyond the Great Divide*, 2nd ed. (Cambridge: Polity Press).

Hood, Christopher (2010) *The Blame Game: Spin, Bureaucracy, and Self-preservation in Government* (Princeton, NJ: Princeton University Press).

Inglehart, Ronald (1977) *The Silent Revolution: Changing Values and Political Styles among Western Publics* (Princeton, NJ: Princeton University Press).

Inglehart, Ronald F. (2016) 'How Much Should We Worry?', *Journal of Democracy* 27(3), pp. 18–23.

International Institute for Democracy and Electoral Assistance (2016) *Voter Turnout Trends Around the World* (Stockholm: IDEA).

Kaldor, Mary (2000) 'Civilising' Globalisation? The Implications of the 'battle in Seattle', *Millenium* 29(1), pp. 105–114.

Karaveli, Halil (2016) 'Erdogan's Journey: Conservatism and Authoritarianism in Turkey', *Foreign Affairs* 95(6), pp. 121–131.

Keohane, Robert O., Stephen Macedo and Andrew Moravcsik (2009) 'Democracy-Enhancing Multilateralism', *International Organisation* 63(1), pp. 7–23.

Krastev, Ivan (2016) 'The Unravelling of the Post-1989 Order', *Journal of Democracy* 27(4), pp. 5–15.

Kuyper, Jonathan W. (2014) 'Global Democratisation and International Regime Complexity', *European Journal of International Relations* 30(3), pp. 620–646.

Lavallée, Emmanuelle, Mireille Razafindrakoto and François Roubaud (2008) *Corruption and Trust in Political Institutions in Sub-Saharan Africa*, Working Paper No.102, Afrobarometer.

Linz, Juan J. and Alfred Stepan (1996) *Problems of Democratic Transition and Consolidation* (Baltimore: John Hopkins University).

Mair, Peter (2013) *Ruling the Void: The Hollowing Out of Western Democracy* (London: Verso).

Marton, Kati (2014) 'Hungary's Authoritarian Descent', *The New York Times*, published on 14 November, www.nytimes.com/2014/11/04/opinion/hungarys-authoritarian-descent.html?_r=0 (accessed February 23, 2017).

Patomäki, Katarina Sehm (2011) 'Towards Global Political Parties', *Ethics and Global Politics* 4(2), pp. 81–102.

Pauly, Louis W. (1999) 'Good Governance and Bad Policy: The Perils of International Organisational Overextension', *Review of International Political Economy* 6(4), pp. 401–424.

Peters, Anne (2009) 'Dual Democracy', in Jan Klabers, Anne Peters and Geir Ulfstein (eds.) *The Constitutionalization of International Law* (Oxford: Oxford University Press), pp. 263–240.

Peters, B Guy and Jon Pierre (2004) 'Multi-Level Governance and Democracy: A Faustian Bargain?', in Matthew Flinders and Ian Bache (eds.) *Multi-Level Governance* (Oxford: Oxford University Press).

Piketty, Thomas (2013) *Capital in the Twenty-First Century* (Harvard: Harvard University Press).

Sandel, Michael (2012) *What Money Can't Buy: The Moral Limits of Markets* (London: Penguin).

Scammell, Margaret (2014) *Consumer Democracy: The Marketing of Politics* (Cambridge: Cambridge University Press).

Scholte, Jan Aart (2000) ' "In the Foothills": Relations Between the IMF and Civil Society', in Richard A. Higgott, Geoffrey R.D. Underhill and Andreas Bieler (eds.) *Non-State Actors and Authority in the Global System* (London: Routledge), pp. 256–273.

Seabrooke, Leonard (2007) 'Legitimacy Gaps in the World Economy: Explaining the Sources of the IMF's Legitimacy Crisis', *International Politics* 44(2), pp. 250–268.

Stephenson, Hayley and John S. Dryzek (2014) *Democratizing Global Climate Governance* (Cambridge: Cambridge University Press).

Stoker, Gerry (2006) *Why Politics Matters: Making Democracy Work* (Basingstoke: Palgrave Macmillan).

Stoker, Gerry and Mark Evans (2014) 'The Democracy-Politics Paradox: The Dynamics of Political Alienation', *Democratic Theory* 1(2), pp. 26–36.

Streeck, Wolfgang (2013) *Politics in an Age of Austerity* (Cambridge: Polity Press).

Tomey, Simon (2015) *The End of Representative Politics* (Cambridge: Polity Press).

Trump, Donald (2016) 'Declaring America's Economic Independence', speech delivered on 28 June.

Vibert, Frank (2007) *The Rise of the Unelected: Democracy and the New Separation of Powers* (Cambridge: Cambridge University Press).

Wright Mills, Charles (1959) *The Sociological Imagination* (Oxford: Oxford University Press).

Chapter 3

The global economy and the Great Recession

Mark K. Cassell

FIGURE 3.1 Bull and Bear statues outside the Frankfurt Stock Exchange, Germany

The 2008 financial crisis that triggered the Great Recession was the worst economic crisis since the Great Depression. Within a span of seven months, from March to September 2008, eight major US financial institutions failed – Bear Stearns, Indy-Mac, Fannie Mae, Freddie Mac, Lehman Brothers, AIG, Washington Mutual and Wachovia – six of them in September alone. More than 20 European banks across ten countries also took heavy losses and were forced to be rescued by their governments. The value of global assets dropped $50 trillion in 2008 (Loser, 2009). Robert Solow (2009) put the loss in more personal terms: 'A population that thought in 2007 that they had $64 trillion with which to plan their lives discovered in 2008 that they had lost 20 percent of that' (para. 23). The International Monetary Fund (IMF) estimated banks and other investment houses had lost more than $4 trillion in asset value. McKinsey Global Institute estimated global aggregate losses of $27 trillion or roughly 50 per cent of global economic output. And, as in the early years of the Great Depression, the contagion spread from Wall Street to European banks and then to the 'real economy' throughout the world.

Solid companies with little connection to Wall Street were threatened with bankruptcy because of steep declines in commodity prices and a tightening of credit. As Verick and Islam (2010) note, the crisis-induced credit crunch literally 'strangled the real economy and trade flows' (p. 5). During the first ten months of the Great Recession, economic output, global trade and global equity values all grew faster than they had in the first ten months of the Great Depression (Drezner, 2014). Some refer to the period as the 'Great Trade Collapse' (Shelburne, 2010). The collapse of global trade from 2008 to 2009 was the largest decline in 40 years and one of the quickest. World trade volumes fell 14 per cent from December 2008 to February 2009. In short, by nearly all measures, at the end of 2007, the global economy was headed toward another Great Depression. Financial indicators at the start were worse than at the start of the Great Depression. But Great Depression 2.0 never happened.

The economy rebounded after 2008. Global governing institutions prevented another depression (Dresner, 2014). Despite predictions, cooperation among advanced industrialised countries increased during and after the crisis. The G20 supplemented the G7/G8 as the focus of global governance, coordinating monetary and fiscal policies. Other global financial bodies expanded membership and authority. The Basel Committee on Banking Supervision enlarged its membership from 13 to 27 advanced industrialised states. Basel III upgraded the Basel II standards to prevent bank failures (Braithwaite, 2012). The Financial Stability Board's authority was increased; the Financial Action Task Force on Money Laundering added China, India and South Korea; and even the International Monetary Fund (IMF) and the World Bank expanded the power and influence of advanced developing countries like China and the BRIC economies. Concomitant with the governing changes, IMF and World Bank policies shifted, recognising capital controls, for example, as a legitimate policy tool – a 'stunning reversal' to the bank and fund's previous orthodoxy (Rodrik and Varoufakis, 2010). As Deeg and O'Sullivan (2009) note, the crisis 'led not only to a renewed level of involvement by governments . . . but also a breathtaking expansion in the scope of their role in the economy' (p. 742). Global governing institutions increased coordination and cooperation, maintained liquidity and capital flows, implemented lasting regulatory changes and kept global markets open; all of which helped to maintain the liberal economic order in the face of a financial crisis worse than the Great Depression.

Although the initial drop in global output and trade was steeper than in the 1930s, the rebound was much more robust. Four years after the start of the Great Recession, global industrial output was nearly 10 per cent higher than when the recession began. Economic growth declined by .59 per cent in 2009 but was followed by 5.22 per cent growth in 2010 and 3.95 per cent in 2011. Compare that to 1930 when global economic growth shrunk 3 per cent and then 4 per cent in the next two years. In fact, growth rates between 2010 and 2012 were similar to growth rates in the decade that preceded the Great Recession. Social measures such as global poverty also improved despite the Great Recession, in large part because poorer countries had access to global markets (Drezner and McNamara, 2013).

In contrast to the Great Depression, cross-border trade flows did not dry up after the 2008 crisis. In the midst of the Depression, countries turned inward and put up trade walls. Eichengreen (2016) notes that four years after the 1929 stock market crash, trade flows were 25 per cent below pre-crisis levels. Yet four years after the Great Recession, trade flows were more than 5 per cent higher than their pre-crisis levels. Drezner points out that global trade since 2008 has been more robust than even postwar recoveries.

Finally, perhaps the biggest contrast to the Great Depression is that the Great Recession did not lead to unravelling of international security and order, and increased political conflict. The Institute for Economics and Peace reported in 2012 that the average level of peacefulness in 2012 was about the same as in 2007 (Institute for Economics and Peace, 2012). Cooperation and coordination among countries increased, particularly around fiscal and regulatory policies.

This is not to suggest that the Great Recession did not cause enormous pain and suffering. High unemployment, poverty and inequality continued years after the recession officially ended. The human toll of the recession is reflected in the large number people who lost retirement savings (McFall, 2011), workers who lost jobs (Segal, 2009), and of course the extraordinary number of foreclosed homes and boarded up properties that dotted the urban landscape of America's cities. In my home town of Cleveland, Ohio, the epicentre of the foreclosure crisis, entire neighbourhoods were wiped out (Kotlowitz, 2009).

Yet, what is surprising about the Great Recession is that it did not follow the course it was on and become another Great Depression. Policymakers working within global governing institutions looked back at the experience of the Great Depression and took deliberate steps to avoid a repeat. National and global governing institutions changed course. Advanced industrial countries with strong capitalist systems approved large public expenditures and kept interest rates low in order to maintain their financial systems. Even countries like the US, despite a long-standing commitment to supply-side monetary policy rather than fiscal policy, embraced Keynesianism, passing one of the largest fiscal stimulus packages in history. Internationally, countries coordinated with each other to enact policies that maintained liquidity in the global economy, avoid protectionism and improve regulation of the global financial system.

What explains the Great Recession and the policy response? What can the experience of the Great Recession – the period prior to and after the crisis – teach us about international affairs? Popular understanding of the Great Recession is that it was a failure of epic proportions; a combination of casino capitalism gone wild coupled with incompetent government. While popular books,[1] movies,[2] and podcasts[3] describe plenty of casino capitalism and government failure, the Great Recession offers International Political Economy (IPE) scholars a chance to think about a more nuanced story; one that focuses on systemic factors that maintain the status quo and what contributes to change in the status quo.

This chapter introduces the Great Recession and compares how Political Economy (PE) and IPE scholars make sense of the recession. Following this introduction, the next section sets the context with a brief summary of the recession. The third section discusses how PE scholars think about the recession and the financial crisis that triggered it. Finally, the fourth section turns to how IPE scholars view the Great Recession.

What was 'great' about the Great Recession?

The Great Recession, like all recessions, was characterised by decline in economic activity and contraction of the business cycle for two or more quarters. According to the National Bureau of Economic Research (NBER), the recession in the US lasted from December 2007 to June 2009, making it the longest recession since World War II. Globally, the recession started in the third quarter of 2008 and continued through the first quarter of 2009 (NBER, 2017).

Two factors account for why the Great Recession was more severe than previous post-war recessions and more similar to the Great Depression. The first is that the recession was born out of a financial crisis that reduced availability of credit throughout the economy. As Charles Kindleberger (2000), in his seminal work *Manias, Panics and Crashes*, notes, 'Most economies are mostly healthy, but on occasion, an economy can be infected with one or another economic virus' (p. 220). The economic virus that made the 2007 recession so severe was a loss of trust in financial markets and the seizing up of capital markets. Large lenders had placed highly leveraged, complex, secretive bets on the US housing market, particularly the market for the riskiest borrowers, known as the subprime mortgage market. When the housing bubble burst, banks and investment houses experienced unprecedented losses and bankruptcies. Because bets by banks were financed with loans from other financial institutions, losses in the US housing market triggered a cascade of bankruptcies across financial firms, creating a credit crunch (Krugman, 2009). Widespread uncertainty over the extent of losses meant that financial firms were unwilling to extend credit even for short periods of time to consumers, firms, governments and especially other banks. Indeed, financial firms were calling in loans to boost their capital reserves and remain solvent.

The crisis quickly spilled over to Main Street when economically solid companies with little connection to Wall Street were threatened with bankruptcy because they could no longer get even short-term credit. As Verick and Islam (2010) note, the crisis-induced credit crunch literally 'strangled the real economy and trade flows' (p. 5). Homeowners who had purchased variable rate mortgages suddenly faced rising interest rates at the very moment their home values were plummeting (Hurd and Rohwedder, 2010). When the bubble burst, economic actors questioned the value of assets used as collateral and demanded higher premiums. Banks and investment houses questioned their balance sheets and those of their business partners. The entire financial system froze. And businesses across many sectors of the economy either struggled to get financing or paid a significant premium (Gosling and Eisner, 2013). The downward spiral was reminiscent of the early 1930s: as firms and homeowners went into bankruptcy because they could not roll over their debt, the demand for products including housing declined which, in turn, drove down the value of assets used as collateral, leading to further losses and bankruptcies (Krugman, 2009).

The freezing up of capital markets also depressed global trade. Schelburne (2010, p. 12) notes 10 to 50 per cent of trade depends on bank financing. When global capital markets froze and bank financing for trade evaporated, creditors were no longer willing to finance international trade. Declines in trade underscore another factor that set the Great Recession apart from previous post-war recessions: its global scope.

Post-war recessions in the US, Asia, or Latin America were typically constrained to a single country or region. Global capital markets had become extremely interconnected by 2007. The US financial crisis quickly spread into other parts of the world through what is known as contagion and helped turn a US recession into a global recession. The process occurred in several phases (Roubini and Mihm, 2011).

The first phase was a global banking crisis. It was not just US banks and investment houses that gambled on the US subprime housing market. Icelandic, German, Irish and Spanish banks also sought to get in on the action. In mid-2007, the *New York Times* reported that 'funds and banks around the world have taken hits because they purchased bonds or risk related to bonds, backed by bad home loans' (Anderson and Timmons, 2007). Germany, a country known for its risk-averse culture, suffered enormous losses. Surprisingly, the largest bank losses occurred among the 12 state-owned *Landesbanken* whose post–World War II mission was to serve as house banks to state governments, provide credit for regional economic development and state infrastructure projects and support local publicly owned savings banks. Yet by the 1990s and 2000s *Landesbanken* had ventured well beyond that mission, setting up offices in Dublin, Ireland, and elsewhere from which they placed highly leveraged bets on the US housing market. The results were devastating. Although they comprised only approximately 21 per cent of German banking assets prior to the crisis, the state-owned banks accounted for 41 per cent of the countries' losses. Similar stories played out in Iceland where the entire banking system collapsed after Iceland's three largest private banks – Kaupthing, Landsbanki and Glitnir – went into default as a result of bets on US housing markets. Unfortunately, the global fallout from the collapse of that market did not stop with a banking crisis.

As financial institutions around the world took heavy losses, governments were forced to step in for fear (justifiably) the collapse would harm the entire economy. Governments dealt with failing banks by nationalising them through conservatorship, encouraging mergers or shutting them down. All options were costly. The German government set aside EUR 480 billion (approximately $550 billion) in 2010 to cover the losses, twice the country's federal budget at the time. The UK, Spain, Italy and Cyprus were also forced to spend billions to bail out banks and pay depositors. As governments sought to stabilise financial systems, uncertainty grew among creditors over government ability to cover debts. A global banking crisis morphed into a sovereign debt crisis. Poorer countries like Greece, Spain, Ireland and Portugal were unable to raise capital on private markets and were thus forced to borrow from other eurozone countries, the European Central Bank and the International Monetary Fund. In exchange, these parties demanded that governments adopt austerity measures such as privatising utilities, cutting public spending and pensions, and raising taxes. These had the perverse effect of further weakening economies, increasing unemployment and raising deficits (Blyth, 2015).

Finally, as wealthier countries began to stagnate, demand for exports fell and trade collapsed (Francois and Woerz, 2009). The prices of some goods fell much more than others, which meant some sectors (consumer durables and machinery) suffered more. Agricultural products experienced the smallest price declines, while oil and minerals experienced the largest. Consequently, energy exporters like Russia and other former Soviet states were particularly hard hit. Export-based economies in developing countries like China, India and Singapore also suffered from declines in global demand for goods. Not all countries suffered. Governments with significant wealth funds or international reserves were able to absorb much of the decline in trade and global economic activity (Arestis et al., 2014).

In short, the recession that started in 2007 was, according to the IMF, the worst global recession since the 1930s. The Great Recession was different because it was not limited to a single sector. Instead, the crisis that triggered the recession threatened to choke off credit, the lifeblood of the entire economy. The recession was also global in scope. When America sneezed, the world caught the flu. Because of the interconnectedness of global capital markets, the US financial crisis quickly became a global financial crisis, a sovereign-debt crisis and a full-scale global recession.

Political economic debates surrounding the Great Recession

PE scholars devote considerable effort to the roots of the Great Recession. Their explanations draw heavily on market failure, including information asymmetries, monopolist behaviour, externalities, conflicts of interest, regulatory arbitrage and fraud (Posner, 2011; Cline, 2014).

Housing bubble

Political economists argue the most proximate cause of the recession was a decline in housing prices after a long climb, known as the housing bubble (Zandi, 2009; Cline, 2014. Between 1998 and 2006 the price of the typical American home increased by 124 per cent ('CSI: credit crunch', 2008) even as incomes for most Americans remained flat (Steverman and Bogoslaw, 2008). The decades-long upward trajectory encouraged individuals (even those with poor credit or low to moderate incomes) to take out home loans or finance consumer spending through second mortgages secured by price appreciation. Home equity 'extractions' doubled from $627 billion in 2001 to $1,428 billion in 2005 as the housing bubble reached a crescendo, a total of nearly $5 trillion over the period (Greenspan and Kennedy, 2008). The fever also spilled into other assets: stock prices, for instance, doubled in the five years 2003–2007 (Solow, 2009).

Creditors and investors, including governments, pension funds and sovereign wealth funds, were eager to meet the demand for mortgage loans. Record low-interest rates, the collapse of the dot-com bubble in 2001 and the enormous trade surpluses in countries like China created a 'Giant Pool of Money' in search of safe, high-yield investments. Investment banks connected investors to the US mortgage market; earning enormous fees for each stage of the mortgage supply chain. Wall Street introduced riskier mortgage products, such as adjustable rate mortgages (ARMs), interest only loans and low down payment loans. Mortgage loans were no longer held by the originating institution but sold to another institution or to the Federal National Mortgage Association (Fannie Mae),[4] which packaged them into mortgage-backed securities (MBS). In what Schwartz (2009) calls 'global arbitrage', Wall Street firms packaged and sold MBS securities and other products to investors hungry to get in on the high returns of the housing market without buying actual houses in places like Cleveland.

By 2003, demand for mortgages by qualified lenders who met traditional underwriting criteria was exhausted. To satisfy the Global Pool of Money's insatiable demand for mortgages, Wall Street targeted low-income or poor-credit borrowers, expanding the sale of so-called subprime mortgages, which applied looser underwriting standards. Subprime loan applications de-emphasised income and assets, required lower down payments and, in the most egregious cases, verified no income, job or assets, known as NINJA mortgages.

Prime and subprime loans were packaged into securities which were, in turn, purchased by investors. Loose underwriting standards made subprime loans especially vulnerable to shifts in the market. As Jarsulic (2012) writes, 'Like a juiced-up baseball player deprived of steroids, the performance of nonprime loans was bound to falter once rapid house price appreciation came to an end' (p. xiv). Subprime loans defaulted in record numbers and in record time, and the securities backed by subprime loans also left investors with major losses. Gorton (2009) notes that losses in subprime MBS coupled with opacity of the new innovations undercut confidence in the financial system.

Financial innovations

Housing bubbles have occurred without causing recessions. But PE scholars argue that this time, complex financial innovations that began in the 1990s created a time bomb (Farlow, 2013 Rajan, 2005; Wolfe, 2014; Financial Crisis Inquiry Commission, 2011; Jarsulic, 2012). Innovations included mortgages bundled into collateralised debt obligations (CDO), forms of credit insurance called credit default swaps (CDS) and derivatives which are indirect bets – securities whose value derives from one or more underlying assets. The billionaire investor Warren Buffett famously referred to derivatives as 'Financial Weapons of Mass Destruction' because of their potential to destabilise markets.

The innovations grew exponentially during the 2000s. CDOs grew from $20 billion in 2004 to $180 billion in 2008. Derivatives grew to over $680 trillion by 2008. And credit default swaps, insurance or bets against loss which barely existed in 1998, grew to over $50 trillion in face value by 2008 (Johnson and Kwak, 2011).

Advocates argued that despite their complexity, the innovations reduced overall risk. Alan Greenspan and others believed that innovation spread risks out across layers of players such that the failure of a few would be ironed out by the large numbers. But as Andrew Marlow (2013) writes, 'the financial innovations used to link together the bits of financial fabric are sometimes complex and opaque, such that the more interconnected an individual player is, the harder it is to predict the impact of that player's failure on the whole system' (p. 72). Instead of reducing risk, financial innovations created the condition for fraud, bad judgment and market collapse, fulfilling Buffett's definition.

The negative impact of investments in CDOs and derivatives was magnified by leverage, the debt used to purchase assets like MBS (Solow, 2009; Farlow, 2013). In the past, banks leveraged investments at 10–1, meaning a $1000 investment could be made with $100. Depositors (covered by deposit insurance) typically provided the stable base of funding. If the investment earned 10 per cent, leverage turned the $100 investment into a $100 net profit rather than a $10 profit: a $1100 return minus the $900 borrowed. While leverage magnifies returns, the reverse also holds. Leverage magnifies losses.

In the lead-up to the crisis, investment banks like Lehman Brothers and Bear Stearns reached for 30–1 leverage and sometimes more; meaning a $300 million bet could be made with a mere $10 million. Moreover, investment banks relied on commercial paper and short terms rather than deposits for their investment. They were thus far more vulnerable to seizing up in markets when their housing bets failed, since short-term loans had to be repaid and did not enjoy protection from the federal government, as deposits do. Further increasing riskiness of leveraging was widespread use of off–balance sheet vehicles to avoid regulatory capital requirements, making investment houses look less leveraged than they actually were (Cline, 2010, p. 288).

Regulatory failure

PE scholars cite insufficient or inefficient regulation as a major factor contributing to the financial crisis. Barth (2009) notes 'it was quite obvious that a housing bubble was forming and that insufficient regulatory actions were taken to limit its growth and magnitude while there was still time' (p. 292). Regulation of subprime lending was fragmented across many federal and state regulators and about half of subprime mortgages were originated by companies with no federal supervision at all.

Regulatory problems were twofold. First, deregulation unleashed a torrent of new products and actors. The post-war regulatory structure that oversaw the financial system for more than 40 years began to be dismantled by Congress in the 1980s (Hoffmann and Cassell, 2010; Arestis and Karakitsos, 2014; and Gosling and Eisner, 2013). The Depository Institutions Deregulation and Monetary Control Act repealed limits on interest rates depository institutions could offer on deposits. Two years later the Garn-St Germain Act broadened the types of loans and investments that thrifts could make and gave banks and thrifts broader scope in the mortgage market. The act allowed banks and thrifts to issue interest-only, balloon-payment and adjustable-rate mortgages (ARMs), even where state laws forbade them. Finally, the Gramm-Leach-Bliley (GLB) Act, signed by President Bill Clinton in 1999, effectively removed previous separation between lightly regulated Wall Street investment banks and heavily regulated depository banks. GLB thus put investment banks like Bear Stearns and Lehmann Brothers into direct competition with commercial banks, creating a regulatory race to the bottom. In short, dismantling New Deal regulatory architecture had the intended effect of generating enormous growth and innovation in the finance and credit industry. Much of that growth occurred with little government oversight.

Secondly, with the introduction of new financial actors and new financial products, government regulation failed to adjust to the new reality (Johnson and Kwak, 2011). As Gosling and Eisner (2013) note, 'little effort was devoted to creating a new regulatory structure' to replace the one that had been dismantled (p. 203). Weak regulation, in turn, triggered immense growth in new financial products. At the very moment need for regulation was greatest, US regulatory capacity was at its lowest. This phenomenon was not limited to the US.

National governments, central banks and international bodies also failed to hold financial firms accountable. Financial liberalisation encouraged banks to grow beyond national borders, creating opportunities but also a financial contagion that spread market disturbances from one country to the next. Without effective oversight and regulatory controls, global financial interdependence led to global volatility and instability. As banks conducted business across borders – for example, a small German *Landesbank* opening offices in Dublin, Ireland – national and European-level regulators lacked the will and capacity to oversee their activities (Müller, 2010). As Johnson and Kwak (2011) note, the failure to regulate 'made possible a decade-long financial frenzy that ultimately created the worst financial crisis and deepest recession the world has endured since World War II' (p. 29).

PE scholars cite a number of other factors as causes of the Great Recession, including income inequality and stagnant wages (Arestis and Karakitsos, 2014; Gosling and Eisner, 2013); policies that promote homeownership, particularly among poor and minority communities; conflicts of interest among credit rating agencies that failed to accurately assess the quality of financial products; and finally, monetary policy that set interest rates artificially low, promoting risk taking and greater debt (Cline, 2010).

While PE scholars differ in how they view the crisis, each represents a different type of market failure or market distortion which generated excessive risk taking and a financial bubble. Kindleberger (2000) points out that financial mania is triggered by innovations that generate overtrading and bubbles. The new financial products unleashed by deregulations and global demand sparked excessive optimism and herd behaviour partly because of the belief that such products decreased overall systemic risk, reflecting lack of information and transparency about underlying risks. As Gillian Tett (2009) writes, 'the CDS market turned into a vast, opaque spider web of deals' (p. 226).

Although these perspectives are valuable, they say relatively little about political and systemic instabilities that produce such market failures, why they are allowed to continue and the conditions under which policies might change. Much of the PE scholarship is also heavily focused on the US experience. It has an implicit assumption that as long as we correct market failures and distortions, the global financial system will work. In that sense, the causes identified by political economists share a similar ontological perspective that eclipses systemic understandings of the Great Recession. As Brigitte Young (2016) notes, 'Mainstream financial academics, chief economists at central banks . . . as well as national finance ministers . . . circumvent any discussion about systematic instabilities of finance, and instead focused on market failure as the culprit for financial instabilities' (p. 145). The next section turns to debates among IPE scholars.

IPE debates surrounding the Great Recession

IPE scholarship on the Great Recession applies a range of perspectives that looks broadly at systemic factors that contributed to the recession and how the recession, in turn, transformed the global financial system. A comprehensive examination of the IPE contributions is beyond the scope of this chapter. Instead, the following highlights some key insights and questions examined by IPE scholars.

Benjamin Cohen and Eric Helleiner note that IPE scholars – who specialise in systemic understandings of governments and markets – largely failed to anticipate the crisis (Helleiner, 2011; Drezner and McNamara, 2013). Cohen (2009) argues they had a 'dismal' record anticipating the crisis, comparing the failure to international relations scholars' failure to predict the collapse of the Soviet Union. Drezner and Cohen argue that IPE's reliance on an open economy approach (OEA), which Cohen describes as 'reductionist', impeded ability to predict the crisis. The OEA begins with a set of utility-maximising assumptions about preferences of economic and political actors and then maps those preferences within each country. Domestic institutions, such as type of electoral system or regime type, aggregate preferences of economic and political actors thereby generating a set of foreign policies for each country. Finally, OEA analyses how different foreign economic policies interact to generate global policy outcomes (Lake, 2009; Drezner McNamara, 2013, p. 156). OEA privileges domestic interests and institutions as the source of an economic actor's preferences. While much of the work in IPE applies OEA to effectively model national structure-induced equilibriums, its emphasis on domestic institutions and interests limits the ability to understand how systemic processes like financial contagion affect national economic policies and how the interaction of domestic and systemic levels reinforce each other or contribute to change. Drezner and McNamara (2013) note, 'By bracketing the international systemic elements . . . and excluding power and social dynamics in favour of economic analysis of preferences . . . IPE has severely limited our ability to understand and interpret both the political sources and impact of phenomena like the 2008 financial crisis' (p. 156). But criticism of the field is overstated. IPE scholarship provides considerable theoretical and empirical insight into factors that shaped the Great Recession.[5]

One group of IPE scholars takes an inside-out approach to understanding the recession and global finance. These scholars open the black box of global finance, focusing attention on the practices, products, institutions and rules that shape global financial markets (Mackenzie, 2005). Kapstein's (2006) work, for example, challenges common understandings of financial innovation and risk. His work details how firms used CDS contracts to reduce capital requirements, increase leverage and shift risk to sellers of insurance like AIG. Kapstein's analysis of the 'financial risk environment' demonstrated how the opacity of derivatives increased risk among financial institutions and warned of a possible future crisis involving 'collapse of a trillion-dollar institution, with myriad tentacles of complex financial engagements reaching deeply into firms, markets, and households' (p. 148).

Other IPE scholarship analysed global regulatory mechanisms that triggered the recession. Susan Strange (2001) called attention to dangers of delegating regulatory authority to private actors who set international standards and the lack of transparency of derivative trading in over-the-counter markets. Blyth's (2003) work examined decisions and assumptions by Basel II regulators, finding regulators deferred too heavily to banks' own internal risk models to evaluate risks from derivatives and other products. Best (2007) and Bryan and Rafferty (2014) also focus attention on the dangers of derivatives and the inability to accurately assess an institution's risk. Langley's (2006) work describes the mechanisms of securitisation and how they transformed mortgages into financial products that could be spread overseas.

A further strand of IPE scholarship takes an 'outside-in' approach, examining the role of global interests, power and ideas in shaping the regulatory landscape. Rather than focus on state-centred patterns of regulation, these scholars point to the influence of state and private actors in influencing transnational governance regimes that combine public and private regulation (Deeg and O'Sullivan, 2009; Abdelal, 2009). Johnson and Kwak (2011) note the growing capture of international policymaking processes by powerful market players organised in transnational lobby groups. Work by Drezner (2014) and Schwarz (2009) emphasises America's market power in shaping the global governance of finance. And work by Underhill and Zhang (2008) highlights how financial regulatory practices are particularly susceptible to regulatory capture by private interests. They point to the complexity of the global financial system, prevalence of revolving doors between regulators and the finance industry, heightened mobility of financial capital and regulator independence from domestic politics. Still, other IPE work points to the growing significance of private standards and self-regulation in a sector where traditional nation state boundaries are weakened (LiPuma and Lee, 2004).

IPE scholars in the constructivist tradition point to the power that ideas have in shaping the global financial landscape (Jessop et al., 2016). Ideas and beliefs matter because they define and frame the problems of any global financial order. Over time ideas and beliefs become institutionalised into bodies like the IMF, Federal Reserve or European Union. IPE scholars point to several ideas that were particularly important in creating conditions for the Great Recession (Blyth, 2003; Best, 2007; Mackenzie, 2005). First, the belief that financial innovations like derivatives and new forms of securitisation reduce systemic risk helped fuel the housing bubble. Second, within the global financial order, IPE scholars point to the Washington Consensus as accepted wisdom prior to the crisis. The Washington Consensus is that open, lightly regulated, internationally integrated financial markets provide the best engine for global economic growth (Simmons et al., 2006). Finally, the efficient market hypothesis (EMH) that an asset's prices always fully reflect the full amount of information became institutionalised within regulatory agencies like the Federal Reserve. EMH implies that regulation is unnecessary since all information about any financial asset is encapsulated in its price. IPE scholars note these ideas were powerful because they framed the debate over regulatory oversight and provided a justification for allowing private actors to police themselves even when scholars or policymakers voiced concerns about risks of new financial products. The combination of these three ideas blinded US policymakers to systemic problems that caused the Great Recession.

Tsingou (2006) also shows how these ideas were widespread within the transnational policy community of experts, technical officials and private actors who dominated international regulatory debates before the crisis. The beliefs of national European regulators, the European Central Bank, the IMF and the European Union promoted the pre-crisis global order of financial politics in which policies facilitated the liberalisation of monetary and financial flows (Kirshner, 2003). Reinhart and Rogoff (2011) also show that ideational context fuelled excessive optimism within financial markets. Sinclair's (2008) work focuses on the role of ideas, arguing that failure of credit rating agencies to adequately assess risks of financial products is linked to the social construction of knowledge that underlies credit ratings. Specifically, he argues that static and ahistorical thinking is privileged in the rating process.

Work by scholars like Jabko (2012) emphasise a 'strategic constructivism' to argue that it is not just ideas that matter but effective use of ideas by policy actors. Jabko shows how bureaucrats in the European Commission used ideas to successfully foster market liberalisation. Abdelal (2009) focuses on French statesmen as policy actors who created and spread 'new scripts' – formal and informal written rules and new understandings of markets – that shaped global finance. Similarly, Posner (2009) illustrates how the spread of stock exchanges in Europe was a function of European bureaucrats' success in shaping political discourse.

Finally, IPE scholarship considers the somewhat surprising ability of the Global Financial Order (GFO) to adapt in response to the global financial crisis. Scholars suggest a shared sense of crisis spurred cooperation (Kahler and Lake, 2013; Lavelle, 2013). Others suggest that governing institutions worked because policymakers had learned from past mistakes (Davis and Pelc, 2016). Drezner (2014) and Drezner and McNamara (2013) suggest that ability of the GFO to adjust was a function of the interplay of ideas and power. GFOs are analogous to international regimes in which power is allocated to particular policy subsystems[6] that often enjoy a policy monopoly. Conflict is minimal because relatively few actors are involved, issues lack public saliency and decision is often narrow in scope (Thurber, 1991). The policy monopoly, in turn, is based on a particular idea.

An open economy approach within IPE works in times of stability when systemic factors can be held constant. However, during a crisis, the original ideas on which a GFO is founded no longer provide adequate answers and the process shifts from the subsystem to the macro political level, revealing the underpinnings of the system. New actors and interests are introduced and old ideas are challenged, opening possibilities for new strategies and templates. The global financial crisis shook the GFO. While US power in the global economy remained, Japan's and Europe's power was weakened and replaced by China. Rather than challenge global governing structures and imposing a 'Beijing Consensus', China largely supported the rules of global governance by 2013 and took steps toward bolstering the Washington Consensus. Drezner writes, 'There wasn't a second Great Depression in 2008 because the United States and China were both able and willing to help' (p. 183).

Conclusion

So what can someone interested in global affairs learn from the Great Recession? One insight is that financial markets, left to themselves, will likely fail. The assumption that greater financialisation contributes to stability and reduces risk was dramatically disproven by the Great Recession. A second insight: all market failures and distortions are not the same, nor are they independent of one another. PE scholars demonstrated how market failures, such as asymmetric information about derivative risks helped fuel the housing bubble. Alternatively, the lack of a new regulatory structure to accommodate new financial products promoted the financial industry, while their products created blind spots and a failure to understand the systemic risks at stake. Broadly speaking, the PE literature underscores that regulatory oversight is often most needed at the very moment it is politically most difficult to achieve. This insight points to systemic issues addressed by IPE scholars.

The interplay of power, ideas and institutions creates the conditions for global recession. The political power of private financial actors increased as finance's share of the global economy grew. Liberalisation of financial markets was promoted by global institutions like the IMF and World Bank and accepted by national regulators. Belief in the Washington Consensus, efficient market hypothesis and austerity as the means to growth legitimised the power of financial actors and governments' hands-off policy toward regulating new financial products. But the story told by IPE scholars is not all pessimistic.

IPE scholars show that global governing institutions worked. The crisis did not become another global depression. Countries coordinated to keep markets open and liquidity flowing. At the same time, they improved the global regulatory infrastructure. That process continues through today. The European Union's member states, for instance, agreed to a European-wide regulatory and resolution system for its largest banks. And European-wide deposit insurance may also emerge, suggesting that interest in global cooperation has not entirely faded in the years after the crisis. Although IPE scholars apply different theoretical and empirical perspectives to understanding the Great Recession, their central insight is that while markets matter, political and social systems within which markets are embedded may matter a lot more.

Notes

1 Two particularly popular books are Michael Lewis' (2011) *Big Short* and Andrew Ross Sorkin's (2009) *Too Big to Fail*.
2 Three particularly good movies on this are *Inside Job*, *The Big Short* and *Margin Call*.

3 Two podcasts that do an excellent job of describing the financial crisis are (1) Ira Glass, Adam Davidson and Alex Blumberg, 'Bad Bank', NPR: *This American Life*, February 27, 2009; and (2) Ira Glass, Adam Davidson and Alex Blumberg, 'The Giant Pool of Money', NPR: *This American Life*, May 9, 2009. One podcast is 'The Giant Pool of Money' produced by the radio show *This American Life*.

4 The Federal National Mortgage Association (FNMA) is a government-sponsored enterprise created to expand the secondary mortgage market by securitizing mortgages in the form of mortgage-backed securities (MBS). This allows lenders to reinvest their assets into more lending, thereby increasing the number of lenders in the mortgage market by reducing reliance on local savings and loan associations (or 'thrifts'). Its competitor is the Federal Home Loan Mortgage Corporation (FHLMC), known as Freddie Mac.

5 For several excellent surveys of the IPE literature on the Great Recession, see Deeg and O'Sullivan review article (2009) and Helleiner (2011). For an account of national responses to the recession across a range of countries, see Savona et al. (2011).

6 Policy subsystems refers to networks of legislatures, interest groups, beneficiaries and agencies with responsibility for setting policy in an issue area. Actors in this system are relatively closed off.

Further reading

Blustein, Paul (2016) *Laid Low: Inside the Crisis that Overwhelmed Europe and the IMF* (Waterloo, ON: CIGI Press).

Blyth, Mark (2015) *Austerity: The History of a Dangerous Idea* (Oxford: Oxford University Press).

Drezner, Daniel W. (2014) *The System Worked: How the World Stopped Another Great Depression* (New York: Oxford University Press).

Epstein, Rachel A. (2017) *Banking on Markets: The Transformation of Bank-State Ties in Europe and Beyond* (New York, NY: Oxford University Press).

Farlow, Andrew. (2013) *Crash and Beyond: Causes and Consequences of the Global Financial Crisis* (Oxford: Oxford University Press).

Helleiner, Eric. (2011) 'Understanding the 2007–2008 Global Financial Crisis: Lessons for Scholars of International Political Economy', *Annual Review of Political Science* 14(1), pp. 67–87.

Johnson, Simon and James Kwak (2011) *13 Bankers: The Wall Street Takeover and the Next Financial Meltdown* (New York, NY: Vintage Books).

Lewis, Michael. (2011) *The Big Short* (New York, NY: W.W. Norton).

Stiglitz, Joseph E. (2010) *Freefall: America, Free Markets, and the Sinking of the World Economy* (New York: W.W. Norton).

Wolf, Martin (2014) *The Shifts and the Shocks: What We've Learned – and Have Still to Learn – From the Financial Crisis* (London: Penguin Press).

Bibliography

Abdelal, Rawi (2009) *Capital Rules: The Construction of Global Finance* (Cambridge, MA: Harvard University Press).

Anderson, Jenny and Heather Timmons (2007) 'Why a U.S. Subprime Mortgage Crisis Is Felt Around the World', *The New York Times*, 31 August, p. C1.

Arestis, Philip and Elias Karakitsos (2014) 'Current Crisis in the US and Economic Policy Implications', in P. Arestis, R. Sobreira and J.L. Oreiro (eds.) *Assessment of the Global Impact of the Financial Crisis* (New York: Palgrave Macmillan), pp. 12–35.

Arestis, Philip, Rogerio Sobreira and Jose Luis Oreiro (2014) 'Introduction', in Philip Arestis, Rogerio Sobreira and Jose Luis Oreiro (eds.) *Assessment of the Global Impact of the Financial Crisis* (New York: Palgrave Macmillan), pp. 1–11.

Barth, James (2009) *The Rise and Fall of the U.S. Mortgage and Credit Markets: A Comprehensive Analysis of the Market Meltdown* (Hoboken, NJ: Wiley).

Best, Jacqueline (2007) *The Limits of Transparency: Ambiguity and the History of International Finance* (Ithaca: Cornell University Press).

Blyth, Mark (2003) 'The Political Power of Financial Ideas', in Jonathan Kirshner (ed.) *Monetary Orders: Ambiguous Economics, Ubiquitous Politics* (Ithaca: Cornell University Press), pp. 339–359.

Blyth, Mark (2015) *Austerity: The History of a Dangerous Idea* (Oxford: Oxford University Press).

Böfinger, Peter, Wolfgang Franz, Bert Rürup, Beatrice Di Mauro and Wolfgang Wiegand (2008) *Das Deutsche Finanzsystem Effizienz Steigern – Stabilität Erhöhen* (Wiesbaden: Sachverständigenrat Zur Begutachtung der Gesamtwirtschaftlichen Entwicklung Statistisches Bundesamt).

Braithwaite, Tom (2012) 'Enforcement of Basel III Should Be Focus', *Financial Times* (1 October), www.ft.com/content/ada55f5a-0bcc-11e2-b8d8-00144feabdc0.

Bryan, Dick and Michael Rafferty (2014) *Capitalism with Derivatives: A Political Economy of Financial Derivatives, Capital and Class* (Houndmills, Basingstoke, Hampshire: Palgrave Macmillan).

Cline, William R. (2014) *Financial Globalization, Economic Growth, and the Crisis of 2007–09* (Washington, DC: Peterson Institute for International Economics).

Cohen, Benjamin J. (2009) 'A Grave Case of Myopia', *International Interactions* 35(4), pp. 436–444.

Cohen, Benjamin J. (2012) 'CSI: Credit Crunch', *The Economist (US)* (19 October).

Davis, Christina L. and Krzysztof Pelc J. (2016) 'Cooperation in Hard Times', *Journal of Conflict Resolution* 61(2), pp. 398–429, doi:10.1177/0022002715595699.

Deeg, Richard and Mary O'Sullivan A. (2009) 'The Political Economy of Global Finance Capital', *World Politics* 61(4), pp. 731–763, doi:10.1017/s0043887109990116.

Deeg, Richard and Elliot Posner (2016) 'Durability and Change in Financial Systems', *Oxford Handbooks Online*, doi:10.1093/oxfordhb/9780199662814.013.26.

Drezner, Daniel W. (2014) *The System Worked: How the World Stopped Another Great Depression* (New York: Oxford University Press).

Drezner, Daniel W. and Kathleen R. McNamara (2013) 'International Political Economy, Global Financial Orders and the 2008 Financial Crisis', *Perspectives on Politics* 11(1), pp. 155–166, doi:10.1017/s1537592712003660.

Eichengreen, Barry J. (2016) *Hall of Mirrors: The Great Depression, the Great Recession, and the Uses- and Misuses- of History* (New York: Oxford University Press).

Farlow, Andrew (2013) *Crash and Beyond: Causes and Consequences of the Global Financial Crisis* (Oxford: Oxford University Press).

The Financial Crisis Inquiry Commission (2011) *The Financial Crisis Inquiry Report: Final Report of the National Commission on the Causes of the Financial and Economic Crisis in the United States* (Washington, DC: Government Printing Office).

Francois, Joseph and Julia Woerz (2009) 'The Big Drop: Trade and the Great Recession', http://voxeu.org/article/big-drop-trade-and-great-recession.

Gorton, Gary (2009) 'The Subprime Panic', *European Financial Management* 15(1), pp. 10–46, doi:10.1111/j.1468-036x.2008.00473.x.

Gosling, James J. and Marc Allen Eisner (2013) *Economics, Politics, and American Public Policy* (Armonk, NY: Sharpe).

Greenspan, Alan and James Kennedy (2008) 'Sources and Uses of Equity Extracted From Homes', *Oxford Review of Economic Policy* 24(1), https://academic.oup.com/oxrep/article-abstract/24/1/120/479131/Sources-and-uses-of-equity-extracted-from-homes.

Helleiner, Eric (2011) 'Understanding the 2007–2008 Global Financial Crisis: Lessons for Scholars of International Political Economy', *Annual Review of Political Science* 14(1), pp. 67–87.

Hoffmann, Susan M. and Mark K. Cassell (2010) *Mission Expansion in the Federal Home Loan Bank System* (Albany, NY: SUNY Press).

Hurd, Michael D. and Susann Rohwedder (2010) *Effects of the Financial Crisis and Great Recession on American Households* (Cambridge, MA: National Bureau of Economic Research).

Institute for Economics and Peace (2012) 'Global Peace Index 2012', http://economicsand peace.org/

Jabko, Nicolas (2012) *Playing the Market: A Political Strategy for Uniting Europe, 1985–2005* (Ithaca, NY: Cornell University Press).

Jarsulic, Marc (2012) *Anatomy of a Financial Crisis: A Real Estate Bubble, Runaway Credit Markets, and Regulatory Failure* (Basingstoke: Palgrave Macmillan).

Jessop, Bob, Brigitte Young and Christoph Scherrer (eds.) (2016) *Financial Cultures and Crisis Dynamics* (New York, NY: Routledge).

Johnson, Simon and James Kwak (2011) *13 Bankers: The Wall Street Takeover and the Next Financial Meltdown* (New York, NY: Vintage Books).

Kahler, Miles and David A. Lake (2013) *Politics in the New Hard Times* (Ithaca, NY: Cornell University Press).

Kapstein, Ethan (2006) 'Architects of Stability?' in Claudio Borio, Gianni Toniolo and Piet Clement (eds.) *The Past and Future of Central Bank Cooperation* (Cambridge: Cambridge University Press), pp. 115–152.

Kindleberger, Charles P. (2000) *Manias, Panics, and Crashes: A History of Financial Crisis* (New York: Wiley).

Kirshner, Jonathan (2003) 'Explaining Choices about Money', in Jonathan Kirshner (ed.) *Monetary Orders: Ambiguous Economics, Ubiquitous Politics* (Ithaca, NY: Cornell University Press), pp. 260–280.

Kotlowitz, Alex (2009) 'All Boarded Up', *New York Times Magazine* (March 8), pp. 28–32.

Krugman, Paul (2009) *The Return of Depression Economics and the Crisis of 2008* (New York: W.W. Norton).

Lake, David A. (2009) 'Open Economy Politics: A Critical Review', *The Review of International Organizations* 4(3), pp. 219–244, doi:10.1007/s11558-009-9060-y.

Langley, Paul (2006) 'Securitising Suburbia: The Transformation of Anglo-American Mortgage Finance', *Competition & Change* 10(3), pp. 283–299, doi:10.1179/102452906x114384.

Lavelle, Kathryn C. (2013) 'Bailing Out Capitalism', *Current History* 112(757), pp. 304–310.

Lewis, Michael (2011) *The Big Short* (New York: W.W. Norton).

LiPuma, Edward and Benjamin Lee (2004) *Financial Derivatives and the Globalization of Risk* (Durham, NC: Duke University Press).

Loser, Claudio (2009) 'Global Financial Turmoil and Emerging Market Economies', *Asian Development Bank* 1(2).

Mackenzie, Donald (2005) 'Opening the Black Boxes of Global Finance', *Review of International Political Economy* 12(4), pp. 555–576, doi:10.1080/09692290500240222.

McFall, Brooke H. (2011) 'Crash and Wait? The Impact of the Great Recession on Retirement Planning of Older Americans', *American Economic Review* 101(3), pp. 40–44.

Müller, Leo (2010) *Bank-Räuber* (Berlin, Germany: Ullstein Buchverlag).

NBER (2017) 'US Business Cycle Expansions and Contractions', www.nber.org/cycles.html.

Posner, Elliot (2009) *The Origins of Europe's New Stock Markets* (Cambridge, MA: Harvard University Press).

Posner, Richard A. (2011) *A Failure of Capitalism: The Crisis of '08 and the Descent into Depression* (Cambridge, MA: Harvard University Press).

Rajan, Raghuram G. (2005) *Has Financial Development Made the World Riskier?* (Cambridge, MA: National Bureau of Economic Research).

Reinhart, Carmen M. and Kenneth S. Rogoff (2011) *This Time Is Different: Eight Centuries of Financial Folly* (Princeton: Princeton University Press).

Rodrik, Dani and Yanis Varoufakis (2010) 'The End of an Era in Finance' (March 11), www.project-syndicate.org/commentary/the-end-of-an-era-in-finance.

Roubini, Nouriel and Stephan Mihm (2011) *Crisis Economics a Crash Course in the Future of Finance* (London: Penguin Books).

Savona, Paolo, John J. Kirton and Chiara Oldani (2011) *Global Financial Crisis: Global Impact and Solutions* (Burlington, VT: Ashgate).

Schelburne, Robert C. (2010) *The Global Financial Crisis and Its Impact on Trade: The World and European Emerging Economies* (New York: United Nations UNECE Discussion Paper, Working paper No. 2010.2).

Schwartz, Herman M. (2009) *Subprime Nation: American Power, Global Capital, and the Housing Bubble* (Ithaca: Cornell University Press).

Segal, David (2009) 'Enter the Recession's Waiting Room', *The New York Times* (27 September), p. BU1.

Simmons, Beth A., Frank Dobbin and Geoffrey Garrett (2006) 'Introduction: The International Diffusion of Liberalism', *International Organization* 60(4), pp. 781–810, doi:10.1017/s0020818306060267.

Sinclair, Timothy J. (2008) *The New Masters of Capital: American Bond Rating Agencies and the Politics of Creditworthiness* (Ithaca: Cornell University Press).

Steverman, Ben and David Bogoslaw (2008) 'The Financial Crisis Blame Game', *BusinessWeek* (October 18).

Strange, Susan (2001) *Mad Money: When Markets Outgrow Governments* (Ann Arbor: University of Michigan Press).

Solow, Robert (2009) 'How to Understand the Disaster', *The New York Review of Books* (May 14).

Sorkin, Andrew R. (2009) *Too Big to Fail* (New York: Viking Adult).

Tett, Gillian (2009) *Fool's Gold: How the Bold Dream of a Small Tribe at J.P. Morgan was Corrupted by Wall Street Greed and Unleashed a Catastrophe* (New York: Free Press).

Thurber, James A. (1991) *Dynamics of Policy Subsystems in American Politics* (Washington, DC: American University, Center for Congressional and Presidential Studies).

Tsingou, Eleni (2006) 'The Governance of OTC Derivatives Markets', in Peter Mooslechner, Helene Schuberth and Beat Weber (eds.) *The Political Economy of Financial Market Regulation: The Dynamics of Inclusion and Exclusion* (Cheltenham: Edward Elgar), pp. 168–190.

Underhill, Geoffrey R. and Xiaoke Zhang (2008) 'Setting the Rules: Private Power, Political Underpinnings, and Legitimacy in Global Monetary and Financial Governance', *International Affairs* 84(3), pp. 535–554, doi:10.1111/j.1468-2346.2008.00723.x.

Verick, Sher and Iyanatul Islam (2010) 'The Great Recession of 2008–2009: Causes, Consequences and Policy Responses', Working Paper No. 4934, www.ilo.org/employment/Whatwedo/Publications/working-papers/WCMS_174964/lang – en/index.htm.

Wolf, Martin (2014) *Shifts and the Shocks: How the Financial Crisis Has Changed Our Future* (New York: Penguin Books).

Young, Brigitte (2016) 'Financial Stability and Technological Fixes as Imaginaries Across Phases of Capitalism', in Bob Jessop, Christoph Scherrer and Brigitte Young (eds.) *Financial Cultures and Crisis Dynamics* (New York, NY: Routledge), pp. 145–161.

Zandi, Mark (2009) 'The Economic Impact of the American Recovery and Reinvestment Act', [Web Log Post] (21 January). Moody's.com.

Chapter 4

Theorising global politics

Wayne McLean

What value does theory have in a world where multiple actors, across several levels of global politics, act in increasingly complex ways? Furthermore, in an age where news and data are freely available from an increasing number of sources, where is the value in complicated theoretical frameworks that have often been inaccurate and provided few clear answers? One response to such criticism is that disregarding theory entirely is impossible, because almost all interpretations of politics are built upon some existing organisational principles of information. Hence, people use political theories, consciously or not, in almost every analysis of politics. This means identifying theory is essential to political analysis, as it allows scholars and observers to understand the 'lens' an author is using to make their claims, thereby providing important context to their arguments (Walt, 1998, p. 29). In fact, political claims, in the absence of a rigid frame of reference, are problematic, because criticisms and analytical counterpoints risk becoming mere polemics. Perhaps more importantly, scholarly contributions have decreased reusability in the future if not grounded in theory. In contrast, when analysis *is* placed within a solid theoretical framework, scholars can build upon the wider methodological programs to further the political science research agenda.

The value of theory and the perils of ignoring it are visible in analysis around the presidency of Donald J. Trump. At an immediate level, the day-to-day drama of the US administration provides a plethora of data and information, but the media, in general, takes an agency-driven position in its descriptions by providing an intense focus on individual decision making (see Lawrence and Boydstun, 2017). While entertaining, a narrow analytical focus can be problematic, as it results in a great deal of the broader context being neglected. In contrast, analysis grounded in theory allows richer descriptions and more useful outputs and prescriptions. For example, better understandings are found when we ground analysis of Trump and his unexpected emergence in the work of scholars such as Paul Kennedy, whose *The Rise and Fall of Great Powers* (1989) argued that strong powers faced a difficult task in balancing their domestic concerns with their external military commitments. Per his hypothesis, the UK, France and Spain suffered decline in ways that mirror the experience of the US, where military overreach creates financial strain, which in turn leads to a polarisation of domestic debates about ways to maintain empires. When applied to a more recent instance, his theory can be used to test hypothesis against the emerging isolationist 'America First' doctrine promoted by Trump (Landler and Parker, 2016) that has proposed a 10 per cent increase in military spending (Taylor et al., 2017), despite the fact it spends more than its next eight military competitors combined (U.S. Defense Spending Compared to Other Countries, 2017).

Similarly, testing theory against the Trump presidency sometimes reveals paradoxical rhetoric that often aligns with those deeply against his agenda, including left-leaning politicians such as Bernie Sanders. So, while Sanders' and Trump's positions differ on social justice, Anatol Lieven (2016, p. 8) has made the claim that their policies towards foreign policy isolationism and economic nationalism are quite similar. In this instance, an organisational framework of analysis (i.e. a theory) elicits a differing, yet informative, interpretation of the current political environment in the US. Elsewhere, theory focused on public discourse has suggested that Trump's rise was assisted by information warfare from adversaries including Russia and China, who see no point challenging the US in military terms, but do see currency in disrupting the cultural and institutional hegemony of the US via means including social media and propaganda (Paul and Matthews, 2016, pp. 1–16).

Value from theory is also available when exploring prominent conflicts such as those in Syria during the 2010s. For instance, realists, whose framework places power and interests first, have argued that Syria is largely the result of geopolitical clashes and resource competition. Using the realist theoretical framework, conflict in Syria (and the rest of the Middle East) is a result of power competitions stemming from its pivotal position between Asia, Europe and Africa (see Mead, 2014; Aras and Yorulmazlar, 2017). In contrast, adherents of the 'new' security frameworks, such as those put forward by Barry Buzan et al. (1998), have argued it is essential to move beyond the political and military focus, and encompass environmental and social issues. Under this type of analysis, severe drought in the Middle East during 2006–10 displaced millions of people and disturbed food supply chains. This was instrumental in causing conflict in Syria, and should therefore be assigned equal weighting with political- and military-based assessments (Greenwood, 2014, pp. 140–156). In this instance, by invoking different theoretical frameworks, different interpretations of the forces driving conflict are revealed and these provide alternatives to the prominence of analysis focused on extremism and terrorism. Importantly, both approaches are credible, and by locating each in theory clearly, different drivers of radicalism and conflict are revealed, thereby providing more comprehensive long-term prescriptions and insights to policy planners.

Despite these advantages, some scholars, such as David Lake, have been critical of the way theory has been used in global political assessments. For instance, Lake (2011, p. 1) argued that the use of the so-called canonical works of global politics – those by Waltz, Keohane, Wendt – are rarely used appropriately, and instead have become simple demarcation points to stake out theoretical ground. This is visible in the 2012 survey of academics, which found an even split between the use of theoretic approaches: 22 per cent used a constructivist position, while 21 per cent and 16 per cent used liberal and realist positions, respectively (Avey et al., 2012). By doing so he claims scholars of global politics 'lose subtlety [and] sophistication' and promote a form of sectarianism that often devolves into 'theological wars and crusades' (Lake, 2011, p. 1). Jack Snyder (2004, p. 54) also finds the use of theory in the field challenging, stating it 'can sometimes become intellectual window dressing for simplistic worldviews'. Despite these challenges, the use of key theoretical paradigms remains an essential element of global political analysis, and this next section provides an overview of what constitutes a theory, followed by a description of the main paradigms and their central ideas.

Defining theory and theories of global politics

There is no single definition of theory, but in general theories are frameworks designed to provide satisfactory explanations of what caused a certain phenomenon (Van Evera, 1997, p. 15). Put simply, theories provide a clear way to frame cause and effect. For James Dougherty and Robert Pfaltzgraff, theory is 'systematic reflection on phenomena, designed to explain them and to show how they are related to each other in a meaningful, intelligent pattern, instead of being merely random items in an incoherent universe' (in Sterling-Folker, 2006, p. 5). More broadly, Steven van Evera (1997, p. 17) has attempted to outline a set of generalised qualities that makes for good theory. For him good theories have (1) explanatory power that allows a complex set of facts to be tied together by a simple set of conditions; (2) 'satisfaction' where they provide a credible narrative to a diverse set of political events; (3) clear framing; (4) are falsifiable (i.e. not tautological); (5) they explain important phenomena; and (6) they have prescriptive richness. For him, a theory possessing these attributes will provide an important framework to understand the 'raw' data of politics interactions.

Overall the study of global politics consists of a variety of theoretical approaches where progress and advancement is achieved by the aggregation of 'different theories with common elements' (Elman and Elman, 2003, p. 47). And while a wide range of theoretical positions exist in global politics, three tend to dominate the literature: realism, liberalism and constructivism. A fourth, critical theory (which groups together a wide set of diverse viewpoints), has also emerged and contests many of the fundamental claims in these three. Though frequently pitched as adversarial in nature, a better way to understand the usefulness of these theories is again by metaphor. Each can be seen as a different pair of 'glasses' to observe phenomena, with each enabling a different focus or allowing a new or differing explanation. Despite their differences, the three most prominent theories (realism, liberalism and constructivism) all rely on a core assumption: that the international system is anarchic and that there is no overarching body to police international affairs. This makes the international environment one distinctly different from domestic politics, where, to use Max Weber's phrase, the state has a 'monopoly on violence' thereby allowing it to enforce laws with a high degree of consistency. In contrast, the international environment lacks a single unified entity capable of coercion by force, and adherence to laws and rules in the international sphere is therefore less rigid than in domestic affairs. Instead a combination of military, economic, ideational and societal variables are the strongest determinates of political outcomes.

This generalised anarchic political environment creates a paradox known as the *security dilemma*. The paradox of the security dilemma is that even if states do not seek conflict, there are perverse incentives to maximise their own security. Consequently, within an anarchic environment, the only way to obtain security is through *self-help*. This line of thought lies at the heart of the three main theoretical approaches in global politics, but each has a differing prescription of how to approach the security dilemma and to what extent states are truly alone in the international political arena.

Realism is the most pessimistic of the main theoretical approaches: it emphasises the role of the state and views conflict stemming from the security dilemma as largely inevitable and as something to be managed rather than avoided. For realists, international engagement will also be driven by the pursuit of power, and altruistic outcomes are unlikely given the propensity for human selfishness and incentives in the international structure to treat all global political engagement as potentially hostile. Liberalism has challenged these pessimistic assertions and its scholars have instead argued that there are various mechanisms (such as trade, democracy and shared values) that can be used to mitigate effects of the security dilemma. Constructivism contests the epistemologies taken as fact by realists and liberals. Their argument is that if one accepts that all political relationships are the result of social constructions rather than objective facts, then one can effectively rebuild the political environment by the construction of norms or shared understandings.

Realism

Realism is the oldest and most persistent of theoretical approaches, and it still dictates a great deal of policy formulation in military and security thinking. Its central proposition is that states are self-interested and that their primary interest is the extension or maintenance of power and, therefore, security. Realism, in its classical form, is often traced back to *History of the Peloponnesian War* by Thucydides, where the powerful Athenians rejected appeals to justice and morality by the weaker Melians to stay neutral: their only offer was one between death or slavery, leading to the famous claim that 'the strong do what they can and the weak suffer what they must'. Realists have also drawn heavily on the ideas of the 15th-century political theorist Thomas Hobbes and the notion of the 'state of nature' where a world without a strong, central and powerful actor (a sovereign) was 'unpleasant, brutish and short'. Hobbes' prescription was that humans should surrender their individual liberties to a sovereign power, whereby they gained security and therefore the ability to establish a more 'civil' society.

Hobbes' idea of humans as brutish remains central to those who emphasise the role of security in global politics. This included the highly influential Hans Morgenthau, who claimed that global politics had certain objective laws – namely that humans desired to dominate other – and that these remained unchanged and therefore central to all political activity (Morgenthau, 1967). From this position, issues such as morality and the individual preferences of leaders and decision makers are ultimately secondary, because when politics is distilled down to its core, politics is primarily concerned with power and domination. Most importantly, if one accepts this pessimistic premise, a rational theory framework can be built using scientific objective principles, which then allows policymakers to make 'prudent' policy decisions based on the unprejudiced theory.

While often viewed as crude to popular audiences, realism was the driving force behind many foreign and security policy decisions throughout the 20th century. For instance, the US policy of containment was grounded in realist thought, with its architect, George Kennan, rejecting 'idealist' approaches to foreign policy (i.e. values driven engagement that hoped to shift the ideas of Soviet leaders) in favour of 'counterforce' (see Kennan, 1947). Such thinking was a substantial force behind US actions during the Cold War including military activity in Cuba, Korea and Vietnam. Henry Kissinger's pursuit of détente with China in 1972 also demonstrated the influence of realism and 'realpolitik', with the US viewing improved Chinese relations as a useful tool to balance against the Soviets, despite Beijing's ideological position clashing with the US.

This highly rationalised approach to power and foreign policy, where ethical and moral considerations were largely cast aside in favour of pragmatism, reached its apex in the literature after the publication of Kenneth Waltz's book *Theory of International Politics* (1979). Within he formulated the influential theory of structural realism. This theory expanded on Morgenthau's of states as rational actors, viewing states as not only pragmatic but also as undifferentiated or 'like' units. It argued that the domestic conditions of the state were largely irrelevant, and essentially disregarded the role of ideology and culture within borders. Instead, all states, whether run by despots or pacifists, would, in the end, act in a similar (rational) manner. Under this model, it was the structure of the international system that dictated conditions of stability or volatility. The structural model of a 'bipolar' system, where two great powers dominated was the most stable because in a 'balanced' system, intentions and capacities were clear to the other side. In contrast, a multipolar system was undesirable and inherently unstable, as this systemic condition incentivised revisions of power through mechanisms including alliance posturing and arms races.

Realism's influence waned in the later part of the 20th century, but theorists such as John Mearsheimer have remained prominent voices for realists. Mearsheimer's pessimistic *Tragedy of Great Power Politics* (Mearsheimer, 2001) presented an 'offensive' interpretation of Waltz's structural realism, where actors always sought to maximise their power viewing the quest for regional hegemony as the only way to truly ensure security. If one excepts this hypothesis, then the long-term pattern of conflict between great powers is inevitable (hence the 'tragedy'), meaning policy practitioners should always use this worst-case assumption when formulating security policy.

Even though realism regained some popularity to describe the rise of Chinese power during the 2000s, its wider decline as a theoretical framework was driven by the end of the Cold War and failure of any of its main voices to anticipate the collapse of the Soviet Union, despite it being the primary focus of leading intellectuals in the field. Scholars, such as Richard Ned Lebow (1994), were highly critical of this failure, claiming that this real-world test demonstrated realism's lack of explanatory power. Elsewhere, John Gaddis Lewis claimed the failure to anticipate the major changes in global politics during the late 1980s was the equivalent of a 'methodological passing of ships in the night' (1992, p. 52). He argued that a preference for using the methods grounded in classical science had created a narrowness in the theory of realism which cast aside 'narrative, analogy, paradox, irony, intuition, imagination' (Gaddis, 1992, p. 58). In short, realism's assumed self-importance and disregard of a wide range of variables, such as ideas and culture, had contributed to it being blind to one of the major political events of the 20th century.

Newer variations have attempt to redress these shortcomings, including neoclassical realism, which incorporated both structural and domestic variables. Neoclassical realism argued that while states generally follow structural logic, domestic-level variables, especially within democracies, can prevent states from acting in the way that structural realists predict (see Rose, 1998). By doing so, it attempted to answer some of the criticisms of the post–Cold War world and especially the use of the Waltzian 'black box' model, where domestic factors were largely disregarded. Hence, under the neoclassical realist interpretation of the fall of the Soviet Union, Moscow's economic and military capabilities were clearly declining, but domestic conditions did not facilitate an immediate shift in policy. Consequently, it took the removal of the 'old' thinkers and domestic guardians of ideas to facilitate political change in line with their decreasing material capacity (Brooks and Wohlforth, 2001). Randall Schweller has also used this neoclassical approach to explain outliers in state behaviour, such as the hesitance of the US to enter major conflicts. For example, the sinking of the *Lusitania* and the bombing of Pearl Harbor were catalysts for US entry into World Wars I and II, respectively, and Schweller argued that shocks 'allowed' leaders to mobilise the internal resources of the state to correspond with the material realities of the international system. Consequently, one of neoclassical realism's central claims is that changing ideas 'let' structural corrections occur, rather than 'making' things happen (Schweller, 1998, p. 6).

Liberalism

Realism's primary theoretical competitor has been liberalism. Liberalism initially emerged as a theory that challenged the absolutist view of the human condition by Hobbes and the perceived amoralism of political realism. While early liberals such as John Locke argued that certain commonalities with Hobbes' philosophy existed, including the belief that humans are primarily self-interested, he rejected the blunt objectivism of Hobbes, believing that humans could move beyond a simple survivalist position. He asserted that the human mind was a *tabula rasa* (blank slate) capable of prioritising cooperation, rather than possessed with Hobbes' brutish *a priori* set of instincts obsessed with power and dominance.

Locke's work still informs a great deal of today's liberal theory, but Immanuel Kant's work has had the greatest legacy for global political theorists. Kant developed a set of ideas around *idealism*, including the belief that a stateless global society could lead to universal values ('cosmopolitan rights') and a utopian 'perpetual peace'. Kant's influence was particularly pronounced in the earlier part of the 20th century where academics and policymakers sought to explain the reasons for the bloody conflicts of World War I. For example, Kantian logic is visible in Woodrow Wilson's 'Fourteen Points': a broad statement designed to outline the architecture of the post-World War I order. Wilson's points advocated for 'open covenants of peace' with the longer-term goal of creating an international environment based on free trade, democracy, multilateral agreements and respect for self-determination.

In more recent times, liberalism and its variations were revitalised by the end of the Cold War and the proliferation of democracies facilitated a scholarly return to Kantian logic. Michael Doyle was one of the most prominent scholars in this area after a reassessment of his earlier work, specifically in his 1983 article *Kant, Liberal Legacies and Foreign Affairs*. Within this theoretical proposition, he argued that 'zones of peace' were inextricably linked to democratic processes. Furthermore, he argued that should the US decline in terms of relative power, the 'liberal legacy' should provide stability through a transition rather than conflict, pointing to the transfer of hegemony between the UK and the US. A second, and perhaps more important claim was made, too: that 'constitutionally secure liberal states have yet to engage in war with one another' (Doyle, 1983, p. 213). By doing so he started a body of work around the notion of 'democratic peace theory', which asserted that no two democracies had gone to war with one another, thereby providing a strong empirically testable theory in a field dominated by qualitative assessments.

Liberalism's main sub-branch is neo-liberalism. Like realists, neo-liberals recognise the state as the prime actor in international affairs and that the security dilemma is unlikely to be fully ameliorated. Instead, neo-liberals argued the potential for conflict can be mitigated through trade and deep interstate engagement. Joseph Nye and Robert Keohane's *Power and Interdependence* is the canonical book in the field (Keohane and Nye, 1973). This claimed that by opening multiple channels via institutions, the realist notion of military primacy in international affairs could be challenged. Keohane and Nye later retreated from some of the concepts of complex interdependence after criticism from Stanley Michalak that their position on realism was crude and therefore an attack on a straw man (Griffiths et al., 2009, p. 108) but Keohane refined many of the core elements of his neo-liberalism in *After Hegemony* (Keohane, 1984). Within, he still challenged the core realist assumption of relative gains and articulated how states can make rational choices to maximise their position, where cooperative approaches can benefit many parties. The larger thesis was that political economic orders worked best when shaped around global regimes, as they created incentives across a range of actors, including small states, middle powers and hegemons. Thus, neo-liberalism emphasises the idea that common interests can result in absolute gains for states and that institutions and regimes are increasingly important actors in global politics.

But liberalism also suffered a set of unique and unexpected challenges that emerged near the end of the 20th century. Of note was the fetishisation of Francis Fukuyama's 1989 *End of History* thesis by hawkish US liberals. Fukuyama argued that the collapse of the Soviet Union meant a Kantian utopia was potentially achievable given that the key ideological competitor to liberalism – communism – was dead. His central claim was that the end of the Cold War resulted in 'the total exhaustion of viable systematic alternatives to Western liberalism' (Fukuyama, 1989, p. 3). Yet, liberalism's primacy, and the belief that it would universally be adopted, was soon challenged by resistance to US activities in Somalia, Serbia and by the emergence of unanticipated ideational competitors – including Islamic radicalism – who all rejected political liberalism. In order to 'convince' these outliers, an aggressive form of liberalism that quickly became known as neo-conservatism emerged. This used Fukuyama's ideas as a way to push for actions that would allow US hegemony in perpetuity, in order to sustain what George W. Bush called the 'global democratic revolution' (Barbash, 2003).

Constructivism and critical theory

The failure to democratise and 'liberalise' states such as Iraq by force helped accelerate the third major theoretical program in global politics: social constructivism. This challenged the rationalist positions of the existing global political theories, and was spearheaded by Alexander Wendt (1992 p. 394), who rejected the concept of anarchy having any pre-existing 'logic'. A logical objective approach to global politics was the accepted approach during neo-liberal and neo-realist debates of the 1980s, with debate largely focused on whether anarchic structures could result in cooperation or not (see Nye Jr, 1988). Instead, Wendt argued that anarchy has no objective structure, and that when international political structures did emerge, they were contingent on both 'identity and interest' of the states involved (p. 396).

This position was quickly popularised, assisted by the dearth of rationalist explanations for the end of the Cold War. More specifically, Wendt's *Social Theory of International Politics* (1999) argued that the collapse of the Soviet Union was simply not the result of material factors as realists would assert, or attributable to institutions and trade, as liberal theories suggested. Rather, Wendt argued that a sociological explanation possessed greater explanatory power and that events in the USSR could be explained as a 'breakdown of consensus about identity commitments' (Wendt, 1999, p. 420). Hence, the Soviet view of their place in the anarchic system was rapidly changed because of the 'new thinking' of the Gorbachev regime, who made the relatively simple calculation that a foreign policy based on realist thinking was fuelling an unaffordable level of defence spending. By adopting a new security position more favourable to the liberal order, Wendt claimed that the Cold War ended almost overnight via the creation of a new 'social kind' (Wendt, 1999, p. 76). In making this claim, he challenged the aforementioned rational 'logic of anarchy' and instead reasoned that anarchy was socially constructed and that by simply having elites change ideas, the way that state approached the self-help international environment would also change (Wendt, 1999, p. 375). This interpretivist position, where political outcomes were not necessarily isomorphic with the seemingly objective world, quickly became a popular way to address questions where rationalist positions had failed.[1] In turn, this empowered theoretical scholars, by giving them an active role in effecting change, where scholarship could be an agent for change, as it could shape and promote positive norms.

Martha Finnemore and Sikkink further articulated the way in which such norms could be actualised in their influential article 'International Norm Dynamics and Political Change' (1998). Their model started with so-called norm entrepreneurs who emerged to pitch an idea of ideational change. If a state or actor adapted a norm, it enhanced its legitimacy, leading to it being taken on by others states and actors, thereby starting a 'norm cascade'. Eventually a tipping point is reached where the norm was internalised, and therefore became an integral part of the political order. A useful analogy of internalised norms is that of stop signs or a traffic light, which are regulated, but whose purpose or task is rarely questioned, yet have a significant existential impact on the real world.

In the following decade, the R2P (responsibility to protect) doctrine became a real-world test of Finnemore and Sikkink's thesis, and tested the ability of actors to promote norms in the international community and facilitate change in the behaviour of actors. This push followed the failure of the international community to intervene in atrocities in Rwanda, Somalia, Kosovo and Bosnia, despite the wider systemic conditions of peace and stability. In the instance of R2P, an ad hoc commission, the International Commission on Intervention and State Sovereignty (ICISS), acted as the norm entrepreneur by arguing that sovereignty was a responsivity and that gross human rights abuses were not protected by the existing norms built around sovereignty and non-interference (Weiss et al., 2010). This led to the R2P being broadly accepted within the United Nations and international community, and it was later invoked around interventions in Libya, Yemen and Sudan, although debates continue about its effectiveness (see Hehir, 2016).

One key criticism is that norms with good intentions can be hijacked by immediate state interests, most notably when the US used the emerging intervention norm in an attempt to legitimise its occupation of Iraq, beginning in 2003 (see Moses et al., 2011). Here, George W. Bush used the language of 'responsibility' around Iraq without explicitly invoking R2P doctrine (Chandler, 2004, pp. 59–81). Similarly, Russia exploited the intervention norm when it used R2P as an excuse for military actions in Georgia during 2008. More recently, Moscow has used similar arguments to justify actions in Ukraine and Syria. Another deeper criticism is from critical theorists who sometimes equate norm construction with neo-colonialism. This includes Ray Bush et al. (2011) who claimed that R2P is simply 'imperialist intervention [that] uses the language of humanitarianism' (p. 358).

A number of sub-theories draw on the ideas of constructivism including securitisation (see Buzan et al., 1998). Securitisation positioned itself as a paradigmatic bridge between neorealist and constructivist viewpoints into a rigorous framework. This gained popularity in the aftermath of 9/11, when the main theoretical approaches struggled to understand how a small group of people, with few material capabilities, managed to retool the security and foreign policy of one of the most powerful actors in history (Buzan, 2006, pp. 1102–1118). While Wendt's constructivism successfully addressed how states could reframe anarchy, securitisation addressed how ideational threats, such as Al-Qaeda and its ideology, were internalised and acted on by large bureaucratic structures. A critical element within securitisation is the idea of 'speech acts', which explained the rapid elevation of issues, such as terrorism, into the global political discourse. One popular example is George Bush's 'Axis of Evil' speech in 2002, which was an enabling and framing device for the ultimately abstract concept of a 'war on terror'. By utilising public fears and sentiment in the aftermath of the 9/11 attacks, this 'speech act' enabled a radical shift in US foreign policy priorities, leading to US involvement in two major conflicts and doubling of the defence budget between 2001 and 2003 (Plumer, 2013).

Despite these apparent analytical benefits, constructivism has its share of methodological critics, including Dale Copeland (2000), Stefano Guzzini and Anna

Leander (2005) and Brent Steele, 2007. For example, Copeland highlights how constructivism has problems providing useful prescriptions of future intentions given its uncertainty around the genesis of political action (p. 210). Guzzini and Leander claim the generalised constructivist concept of 'politics' is contradictory: if states formulate their own image of international politics, they argue it is problematic to assume that they have a unified vision of what constitutes political engagement and polity itself (p. 90). Sterling-Folker follows a similar line of critique, arguing that constructivism is largely a revision of neo-liberalism, relying on the same ontology and arguments around social advancement, with constructivism's role being to conceptualise fringe arguments that remain 'unexplored' by liberal theory (p. 100).

These types of broader criticisms are addressed under the range of frameworks generally described as critical theory. They are 'critical' because they challenge the fundamental ontological and epistemological presuppositions used by realism and liberalism (and to a lesser extent constructivism). They do so by questioning the emphasis on the state, and existing political norms. Instead, they assert that variables such as the context of history and the power embedded in knowledge itself are central to understanding the very concept of politics and what constitutes the political. This includes Marxism, where authors including Robert Cox (1981, p. 129), have argued that 'critical theory is directed to the social and political complex as a whole rather than to the separate parts' and is critical of the 'problem-solving' approach of realism. Instead, he states that critical theory's role is to take a holistic position, where all assumptions, including supposed objective truths, should be challenged. For Cox, doing so allows the incorporation of a wider range of social and political complexities, which can be a 'guide to strategic action for bringing about an alternative order' (p. 130). This sits in contrast to theories such as realism and liberalism, which simply 'sustain the existing order' (p. 130).

Other variants of critical theory include post-structuralism, which also questioned the fundamental assumptions of politics, led by scholars such as Michel Foucault, Jacques Derrida and Jean Baudrillard. Post-structuralism argued that the concept of power was much more complex than the existing paradigms acknowledged, being multifaceted, and is deeply embedded within our understandings of truth and knowledge, with Foucault (1966) challenging the basis of political knowledge, which was built around historiographies constructed around the works of a few Western thinkers, including Kant and Locke.

Elsewhere, feminist perspectives emerged as part of the critical movement, viewing the dominance of white European males in the literature as its own type of hegemonic institutionalised power, which marginalised myriad of important contributions. For example, Ann Tickner has argued that the so-called objectivity of realists is in fact constructed around a masculinised discourse of power, hierarchy, control and warfare. This makes the academic study of international politics hostile towards women and resistant to any actors who are not participants in the simplistic 'vocabulary of power' (Tickner, 1988, p. 429). Consequently, for her an 'ungendered, or human, discourse becomes possible only when women are adequately represented in the discipline' (Tickner, 1988, p. 438). Jacqui True has extended this to argue that the masculine representation of conflict that stresses the role of 'traditional' war obscures a great deal of important phenomenon. For her, the persistence of masculine narratives in global political theories 'disaggregates' women and the role of sexual violence in conflict. Hence, violence against women does not simply occur in a vacuum, or in specific instances of conflict, but instead is part of a sustained set of injustices that continue within what the traditional literature would call a time of 'peace' (True, 2012, p. 19).

Conclusion

In conclusion, when engaging with global political theory, it quickly becomes apparent there are many contrasting debates, of which this chapter has only briefly covered. And each theoretical approach has a bewildering array of variants and sub-theories that could fill a lifetime of scholarship. This can prove daunting to those new to global politics. Nonetheless, understanding theory and its place remains central to the study of global politics, because, as argued at the outset of this chapter, in the absence of theory, political analysis that seek to make an important claim is at best a polemic, and at worst propaganda. Perhaps more importantly, the value of theory is clear in the nascent political competitions dominating global politics towards the end of the 2010s.

For example, much of the realist literature on Soviet–US relations can be revived and applied to the rise of China and the potential re-emergence of a bipolar international system. Likewise, the weakening of the EU as evidenced by Brexit and the Greek financial crisis was predicted by many realists in the 1990s. For them, the EU, at its core, was a security mechanism tasked with balancing against the USSR and constraining German power and is intrinsically linked to the US security presence (see Wohlforth and Zubok, 2017). Should US power retrench, they predict new security dilemmas emerging, as states such as Germany might 'normalise' their militaries or seek nuclear deterrents (Kühn and Volpe, 2017). Liberalism, too, remains valuable and there are strong arguments that the 'peaceful' rise of China is attributable to the extensive system of interconnected trade and that despite substantial political differences conflict remains unlikely (Zhao and Liu, 2010, pp. 1–23). Under this reading, the prospect of war is limited because Beijing is deeply invested in the liberal economic order set up by the US after World War II. Finally, postmodern approaches are proving valuable in the emerging 'post-truth' era (Davies, 2016), where increasing political entropy because of technology and access to information is providing political constituents with a variety of alternative realities to inhabit.

Consequently, the theorising of global politics remains an important pursuit, given almost all knowledge builds on a loose theoretical knowledge, whether explicit or not. Clearly, global politics is a complex combination of political, economic and social factors, and without an organisational framework for analysis, extracting explanations around phenomena is increasingly difficult but necessary. Perhaps the way forward, as Hansen et al. (2013, p. 420) suggest, is to focus on 'turning points' to guide and further specific theories rather than continuing the competitive approaches outlined here. Regardless, even if existing theories are at an impasse, they remain central and important tools to the wider study of global politics.

Note

1 For a discussion of the turn towards 'intersubjective understandings' and the application of sociological concepts into the global political scholarship in the 1990s, see Finnemore (1996).

Further reading

Cox, R.W. (1981) 'Social Forces, States and World Orders: Beyond International Relations Theory', *Millennium* 10(2), pp. 126–155.

Elman, C. and M.F. Elman (2003) *Progress in International Relations Theory: Appraising the Field* (Cambridge, MA: MIT Press).

George, A.L. and A. Bennett (2005) *Case Studies and Theory Development in the Social Sciences* (Cambridge, MA: MIT Press).

Gaddis, J.L. (1992) 'International Relations Theory and the End of the Cold War', *International Security* 17(3), pp. 5–58.

Hansen, L., T. Dunne and C. Wight (2013) 'The End of International Relations Theory?' *European Journal of International Relations* 19(3), pp. 405–425.

Snyder, J. (2004) 'One World, Rival Theories', *Foreign Policy* (145), 52.

Sterling-Folker, J.A. (2006) *Making Sense of International Relations Theory* (Boulder, CO: Lynne Rienner Publishers).

Van Evera, S. (1997) *Guide to Methods for Students of Political Science* (Ithaca, NY: Cornell University Press).

Walt, S.M. (1998) 'International Relations: One World, Many Theories', *Foreign Policy* (110), pp. 29–46.

Bibliography

Aras, B. and Yorulmazlar, E. (2017) 'Mideast Geopolitics: The Struggle for a New Order', *Middle East Policy* 24(2), pp. 57–69.

Avey, P., M.C. Desch, J.D. Long, D. Maliniak, S. Peterson and M.J. Tierney (2012) 'The Ivory Tower Survey', *Foreign Policy*.

Barbash, F. (2003) 'Bush: Iraq Part of "Global Democratic Revolution"', *Washington Post*, www.washingtonpost.com/wp-dyn/articles/A7991-2003Nov6.html (accessed June 29, 2017).

Brooks, S.G. and W.C. Wohlforth (2001) 'Power, Globalization, and the End of the Cold War: Reevaluating a Landmark Case for Ideas', *International Security* 25(3), pp. 5–53.

Bush, R., G. Martiniello, and C. Mercer (2011) 'Humanitarian Imperialism', *Review of African Political Economy* 38(129), pp. 357–365.

Buzan, B. (2006) 'Will the "Global War on Terrorism" Be the New Cold War?' *International Affairs* 82(6), pp. 1101–1118.

Buzan, B., O. Wæver, and J. Wilde, de (1998) *Security: A New Framework for Analysis* (London: Lynne Rienner Publishers).

Chandler, D. (2004) 'The Responsibility to Protect? Imposing the "Liberal Peace"', *International Peacekeeping* 11(1), pp. 59–81.

Copeland, D.C. (2000) 'Review: The Constructivist Challenge to Structural Realism: A Review Essay', *International Security* 25(2), pp. 187–212.

Cox, R.W. (1981) 'Social Forces, States and World Orders: Beyond International Relations Theory', *Millennium* 10(2), pp. 126–155.

Davies, W. (2016) 'The Age of Post-Truth Politics', *The New York Times* (24 August).

Doyle, M.W. (1983) 'Kant, Liberal Legacies, and Foreign Affairs', *Philosophy & Public Affairs* 12(3), pp. 205–235.

Elman, C. and M.F. Elman (2003) *Progress in International Relations Theory: Appraising the Field* (Cambridge: MIT Press).

Finnemore, M. (1996) 'Norms, Culture, and World Politics: Insights from Sociology's Institutionalism', *International Organization* 50(2), pp. 325–347.

Finnemore, M. and K. Sikkink (1998) 'International Norm Dynamics and Political Change', *International Organization* 52(4), pp. 887–917.

Foucault, M. (1966) *Les mots et les choses: Une archéologie des sciences humaines* (Paris: Gallimard).

Fukuyama, F. (1989) 'The End of History?' *The National Interest* (16), pp. 3–18.

Gaddis, J.L. (1992) 'International Relations Theory and the End of the Cold War', *International Security* 17(3), pp. 5–58.

Greenwood, S. (2014) 'Water Insecurity, Climate Change and Governance in the Arab World', *Middle East Policy* 21(2), pp. 140–156.

Griffiths, M., S.C. Roach, and M.S. Solomon (2009) *Fifty Key Thinkers in International Relations*, 2nd ed. (London: Routledge).

Guzzini, S. and A. Leander (eds.) (2005) *Constructivism and International Relations: Alexander Wendt and His Critics* (London: Routledge).

Hansen, L., T. Dunne and C. Wight (2013) 'The End of International Relations Theory?' *European Journal of International Relations* 19(3), pp. 405–425.

Hehir, A. (2016) 'Assessing the Influence of the Responsibility to Protect on the UN Security Council During the Arab Spring', *Cooperation and Conflict* 51(2), pp. 166–183.

Kennan, G.F. (1947) 'The Sources of Soviet Conduct', *Foreign Affairs* 25(4), pp. 566–582.

Kennedy, P. (1989) *The Rise and Fall of the Great Powers*, 1st ed. (New York: Vintage).

Keohane, R.O. (1984) *After Hegemony: Cooperation and Discord in the World Political Economy* (Princeton, NJ: Princeton University Press).

Keohane, R.O. and J.S. Nye (1973) 'Power and Interdependence', *Survival: Global Politics and Strategy* 15(4), 158.

Kühn, U. and T. Volpe (2017) 'Keine Atombombe, Bitte', *Foreign Affairs* (July/August 2017).

Lake, D.A. (2011) 'Why "isms" Are Evil: Theory, Epistemology, and Academic Sects as Impediments to Understanding and Progress', *International Studies Quarterly* 55(2), pp. 465–480.

Landler, M. and A. Parker (2016) 'Donald Trump, Laying Out Foreign Policy, Promises Coherence', *The New York Times* (27 April).

Lawrence, R.G. and A.E. Boydstun (2017) 'What We Should Really Be Asking About Media Attention to Trump', *Political Communication* 34(1), pp. 150–153.

Lebow, R.N. (1994) 'The Long Peace, the End of the Cold War, and the Failure of Realism', *International Organization* 48(2), pp. 249–277.

Lieven, A. (2016) 'Clinton and Trump: Two Faces of American Nationalism', *Survival* 58(5), pp. 7–22.

Mead, W.R. (2014) 'The Return of Geopolitics: The Revenge of the Revisionist Powers', *Foreign Affairs* 93, p. 69.

Mearsheimer, J.J. (2001) *The Tragedy of Great Power Politics* (New York, NY: W.W. Norton).

Morgenthau, H.J. (1967) *Politics Among Nations: The Struggle for Power and Peace* (New York: Knopf).

Moses, J., B. Bahador, and T. Wright (2011) 'The Iraq War and the Responsibility to Protect: Uses, Abuses and Consequences for the Future of Humanitarian Intervention', *Journal of Intervention and Statebuilding* 5(4), pp. 347–367.

Nye Jr, J.S. (1988) 'Neorealism and Neoliberalism', *World Politics: A Quarterly Journal of International Relations*, pp. 235–251.

Paul, C. and M. Matthews (2016) *The Russian 'Firehose of Falsehood' Propaganda Model: Why It Might Work and Options to Counter It* (Santa Monica, CA: RAND Corporation).

Plumer, B. (2013) 'America's Staggering Defense Budget, in Charts', *Washington Post* (7 January).

Rose, G. (1998) 'Neoclassical Realism and Theories of Foreign Policy', *World Politics* 51(1), pp. 144–172.

Schweller, R. (1998) *Deadly Imbalances: Tripolarity and Hitler's Strategy of World Conquest* (New York, NY: Columbia University Press).

Snyder, J. (2004) 'One World, Rival Theories', *Foreign Policy*, (145), 52.

Steele, B.J. (2007) 'Liberal-Idealism: A Constructivist Critique', *International Studies Review* 9(1), pp. 23–52.

Sterling-Folker, J.A. (2006) *Making Sense of International Relations Theory* (Boulder, CO: Lynne Rienner Publishers).

Taylor, J., D. Kurtzleben and S. Horsley (2017) 'Trump Unveils "Hard Power" Budget That Boosts Military Spending', *NPR.org*, www.npr.org/2017/03/16/520305293/trump-to-unveil-hard-power-budget-that-boosts-military-spending (accessed August 31, 2017).

Tickner, J.A. (1988) 'Hans Morgenthau's Principles of Political Realism: A Feminist Reformulation', *Millennium* 17(3), pp. 429–440.

True, J. (2012) *The Political Economy of Violence against Women* (Oxford: Oxford University Press).

U.S. Defense Spending Compared to Other Countries (2017) *Peter G. Peterson Foundation*, www.pgpf.org/chart-archive/0053_defense-comparison (accessed August 31, 2017).

Van Evera, S. (1997) *Guide to Methods for Students of Political Science* (Ithaca, NY: Cornell University Press).

Walt, S.M. (1998) 'International Relations: One World, Many Theories', *Foreign Policy* (110), pp. 29–46.

Weiss, T.G., R. Thakur, and J.G. Ruggie (2010) *Global Governance and the UN: An Unfinished Journey* (Indiana: Indiana University Press).

Wendt, A. (1992) 'Anarchy is What States Make of It: The Social Construction of Power Politics', *International Organization* 46(2), pp. 391–425.

Wendt, A. (1999) *Social Theory of International Politics* (Cambridge, UK: Cambridge University Press).

Wohlforth, W.C. and V.M. Zubok (2017) 'An Abiding Antagonism: Realism, Idealism and the Mirage of Western – Russian Partnership After the Cold War', *International Politics* 54(4), pp. 405–419.

Zhao, Q. and G. Liu (2010) 'Managing the Challenges of Complex Interdependence: China and the United States in the Era of Globalization', *Asian Politics & Policy* 2(1), pp. 1–23.

Part II

Global actors

Chapter 5

The US

John Dumbrell

Since the end of World War II, the United States of America has, by various competing definitions of global power, consistently been the world's most powerful nation. The US has faced numerous economic challenges – including Asian competition, sluggish domestic productivity and the financial crash of 2007–9; yet the US remains the world's pre-eminent economy. The US has benefited from, as well as being sometimes discomforted by, its capacity for technological innovation, its position as custodian of the global free market system and by its relatively flexible

FIGURE 5.1 Capitol Building, Washington, DC, US

labour markets. During the presidency of Barack Obama (2009–17), the US defence budget was cut significantly as a result both of deliberate policy decisions (notably in connection with the contraction of US military presence in the Middle East and Afghanistan) and of the failure of the federal government to agree on viable overall spending budgets. However, in 2014, US military spending accounted for roughly 34 per cent of the world's total. The figure for China was 12 per cent, with Russia at 4.8 per cent (SIPRI, 2015).

The US also possesses formidable 'soft power', that combination of appeal and attraction – from Hollywood to leading universities – which helps shape global preferences and terms of understanding in ways that are conducive to American interests (Nye, 2004). As Josef Joffe wrote in 2006, even as President George W. Bush (2001–9) was widely perceived as having overextended the US in the Middle East: 'If we liken the games played by nations to poker, and the various sources of power to chips, then the United States commands the biggest pile on the table' (2006, p. 127). The decade or so since Joffe made this comment has witnessed problems, new doubts and many more criticisms of America's foreign policy leaders; yet Joffe's verdict on the stakes of international power still broadly holds.

Despite its global eminence, post-1945 America has faced significant reversals, including the defeat in Vietnam and the vicious backfire associated with the 2003 invasion of Iraq. Even at the height of its international reach, the US was never able to dictate global outcomes with much confidence. The Sputnik launch of 1957 sparked a national panic about the march of militarised science and technology in the Soviet Union. The oil crisis of the early 1970s seemed to indicate the limits of America's ability to act as a stabiliser of the non-communist international economic system. The end of the Cold War and the collapse of the Soviet Union represented major victories for the US and for its prevailing ideology of liberal, democratic capitalism. Charles Krauthammer (1990/91) coined the term 'unipolar moment' to describe the geopolitical position in which America found itself in the early 1990s. For Krauthammer, the US needed to recognise that it *had* decisively won the Cold War and to act as victors act. Yet the US in the immediate post–Cold War years often appeared uneasy with its victory. George Kennan, the veteran theorist of US Cold War strategy, wrote in 1993 that the onset of a world 'devoid of anything that could be seen as a major great-power enemy' presented the US 'with a problem for which few of us are prepared' (Kennan, 1993, p. 180).

Bill Clinton (US president, 1993–2001) struggled, with varying degrees of success, to impart a consistent sense of direction to a US foreign policy without Kennan's great-power rival. The 9/11 terror attacks of 2001 brought a new sharpness to national foreign policy direction, now shaped around President George W. Bush's global war on terror. Before long, however, reversals and policy stagnation in Iraq had, along with the global rise of China, led to new intimations of US international decline. By the second decade of the 21st century, the nation was faced by prominent evidence of domestic self-doubt. In March 2010, the Gallup organisation reported that 79 per cent of Americans were 'dissatisfied with the way things are going' (Heale, 2011, p. 261). In the same year, Pew Center polling (2013) indicated that a plurality of US public opinion considered (wrongly) that China had overtaken the US as the world's leading economic power. Donald Trump's 2016 presidential campaign was predicated on the assumption that America had somehow slid from 'greatness' and needed to be made 'great again'.

The point of the foregoing paragraphs has been to indicate the long-standing nature of gaps between the reality of American global reach – always in the post-1945 context considerable, but never unchallenged nor omnipotent – and continual perceptions of decline, decay and global shrinkage. As will become apparent, the US is currently in the process of adjusting to a world of rising powers and indeed of long-term terror threats. Such adjustment requires a combination of national will – expressed through a variety of democratic political institutions – and flexible presidential leadership. We turn now to a consideration of competing foreign policy outlooks in the contemporary US before considering the foreign policy impact and legacy of Barack Obama. The chapter will conclude with a brief discussion of the possible impact of the Trump presidency.

Foreign policy outlooks

It is tempting to trace all competing contemporary American foreign policy philosophies and outlooks to the onset and early history of the global war on terror. Of course, typologies of ideas about the American global purpose reach far further back. US foreign policy advocates are typically described as being split between 'realists' (concerned to maximise the US geopolitical sway) and 'idealists' (concerned to promote democratic capitalist values). American 'exceptionalism' is often understood in terms of the elite American commitment to uniting the pursuit of 'interest' with the promotion of 'values' (see Nielsen, ed., 2000). David Milne (2015) has reinterpreted the history of US thinking on foreign policy by distinguishing between 'artists' and 'scientists'. Where artists (like George Kennan) rely on intuition and creativity, scientists (like Paul Wolfowitz, deputy secretary of defence, 2001–5) see the world as malleable and define diplomacy as a science. Possibly the most influential typology with a long-term perspective is that attempted by Walter Russell Mead (2002). According to Mead, the leading US foreign policy traditions may be associated with Thomas Jefferson (US president, 1801–9), Andrew Jackson (president, 1829–37) and Woodrow Wilson (president, 1913–21), as well as with Alexander Hamilton (US treasury secretary, 1789–95). Where Jeffersonians are cautious about international commitments, Jacksonians identify with populist nationalism and are always keen to defend narrowly defined American interests. Wilsonians are internationalist democracy promoters, while Hamiltonians emphasise economic interests.

At crucial junctures in US history, debate over the preferred global directions thus tends to hark back to earlier positions. For example, in the 1990s, Presidents George H.W. Bush (1989–93) and Bill Clinton were variously urged to make the most of America's 'unipolar moment' by enhancing and consolidating the US military pre-eminence; to embrace new, non-military and values-oriented agendas; to retrench even to the point of adopting a new isolationism; and to develop a foreign policy geared towards improving America's economic competitiveness (see Dumbrell, 1997, p. 162; Crabb et al., 2001). The war on terror recast these debates about US international purpose, with divisions opening up between cautious, pragmatic approaches to waging the war on the one hand, and, on the other, more ideological programs for remaking a world without terror. For the purposes of contemporary analysis, we will consider six major contemporary tendencies in US foreign policy thinking: neo-conservatism, pragmatic Republicanism, neo-Hamiltonianism, Obamaism, assertive internationalism and neo-Jacksonianism.

Somewhere between an intellectual movement, a persuasion and a network, neo-conservatism has become a recognisable force – despite the leftist origins of many of its early exponents – within the Republican Party. Neo-conservative views on foreign policy combine a strong commitment to US global primacy, including military primacy, with a sense that a malleable world may be attuned to liberal capitalist values as a result of elite directed action from Washington. Within contemporary neo-conservatism – sometimes labelled 'Wilsonianism with boots' – there is a strong commitment to American exceptionalism, the idea that the US has a unique historic destiny, rooted in 'freedom' and the commitment to democratic values. Neo-conservatives are prepared to give history a shove, pushing and enticing other nations towards the liberal capitalist path. According to Robert Kagan and William Kristol (2000): 'it is precisely because American foreign policy is infused with an unusually high degree of morality that other nations find they have less to fear from its otherwise daunting power' (p. 13). Neo-conservatives have had significant policy impact, notably in connection with the 2003 invasion of Iraq, a project that was strongly sponsored within the George W. Bush administration by second-tier appointees such as Paul Wolfowitz, Douglas Feith (under secretary at the Pentagon) and Lewis Libby (chief of staff to Vice President Richard Cheney) (Halper and Clarke, 2004).

Set against neo-conservative forces within the Republican Party is what might be described as the pragmatic Republican tradition. Associated with figures such as President Dwight Eisenhower (1953–61) and Brent Scowcroft (national security adviser to President George H.W. Bush), pragmatic Republicans value caution, internationalism and the circumspect pursuit of the American interest. Pragmatic Republicanism may be associated with the elder President Bush's cautious approach to the collapse of Soviet power in the late 1980s and early 1990s (declining to 'dance on the Berlin Wall'). Within the elder Bush's administration, pragmatism tended to win out over neo-conservative projects such as the 1992 Defense Planning Guidance – a blueprint for enhanced US military primacy at the time of the 'unipolar moment'. Colin Powell, the younger President Bush's first secretary of state and in-house doubter concerning the direction of policy towards Iraq, may be identified with the pragmatic Republican tradition following 9/11. The tradition was reflected in the policy statements of Mitt Romney, Republican presidential candidate in 2012. It was abandoned in the 2016 campaign of Donald Trump.

Neo-Hamiltonianism in recent American history was best exemplified in the foreign policy of President Bill Clinton and his administration's commitment to free trade and economic globalisation. In his February 1993 American University address, Clinton promised to ride the 'bucking bronco' of globalisation – constantly securing new free trade deals, embracing 'constant innovation'. The US was to be both the facilitator of global free trade and itself 'like a big corporation competing in the global marketplace'. For Clinton (and his national security advisers Tony Lake and Sandy Berger), the emergence of a global free trade order was linked to the securing of international peace: 'Just as neighbors who raise each others' barns are less likely to become arsonists, people who raise each others' living standards through commerce are less likely to become combatants' (Dumbrell, 2009, pp. 46, 168). By the end of the Bill Clinton administration, such hopes for an economics-led 'democratic peace' were, at least to some extent, already being undermined by the rising threat of global Islamist terror. The rise of populist ('neo-Jacksonian') critiques of globalised free trade in the 21st century further undermined Bill Clinton's intellectual free trade legacy. Hillary Clinton, in her 2016 presidential campaign, actually compromised her earlier adherence to this legacy by opposing new trade deals being negotiated by the Obama administration (Krugman, 2016).

Barack Obama himself broadly supported a free trade agenda. He was concerned to cast US international commitments within a multilateral framework, easing the US into a global order in which America was not overexposed. As will become evident in the following section of this chapter, disputes within the Obama administration tended to revolve around 'ideals' (notably democracy-promotion and the concern not to be on the 'wrong side' of history) versus pragmatic realism. Such disputes were most often resolved in favour of Obama's keen, pragmatic awareness of the costs of risk-taking, with 'costs' here being defined as economic and political/ electoral as well as lives. Obama on occasion even asserted his respect for the pragmatic Republican tradition.

Obama's foreign policy bore the imprint of post-Iraq invasion caution. The president preferred covert action, notably drone strikes against terrorist targets, to overt military action. The ensuing foreign policy (which we may term 'Obamaism') has thus been interpreted as one of strategic restraint and retrenchment (including a shift in regional prioritisation towards the Far East) and 'leading from behind'. Two contemporary commentators, Colin Dueck and Derek Chollet, offer contrasting insights into the essence of Obamaism. For Dueck: 'Obama's primary and overarching emphasis on strategic retrenchment, international accommodation, and domestic priorities has allowed multiple security threats to germinate overseas in ways that already hold very dangerous consequences for American interests' (Dueck, 2015, p. 102). Contrast this with Chollet:

> Balance has defined Obama's foreign policy approach in multiple ways: balance between America's interests and values; balance between priorities at home and abroad; balance between our goals in different regions; balance between our priorities when seeking a certain outcome; balance between the responsibility we would assume and that we expected of others; balance among the tools of defense, diplomacy and development we use to solve problems.
>
> (2016, p. 216)

My next category for inclusion in a list of contemporary foreign policy outlooks is 'assertive internationalism' and is identified particularly with those elite Democrats who tended to see Obama as too cautious – as a president who had, in effect, 'over-learned' the lessons of Iraq. In the context of intra-Obama administration policy debates, 'assertive internationalism' embodied both 'idealist' commitments to democracy-promotion and the more general perception that, especially in connection with the use of military power, Obama was excessively risk-averse (Mann, 2012). Hillary Clinton tended, certainly as Obama's first term secretary of state, publicly to reinforce rather than even obliquely criticise Obamaism. On leaving office, however, she became more obviously critical. For example, in August 2014, she described Obama's failure to arm 'moderate' rebels in Syria as leaving a security vacuum which was filled by Islamic extremism.

Mark Landler sees the differences between Obama and Hillary Clinton as less ideological than temperamental, generational and cultural. Thus Hillary Clinton, far closer to the US military than was Obama, exhibits what Landler calls a 'steel-belted pragmatism', rooted in experiences going back to the Cold War (Landler, 2016, pp. xvi, xix, xxii). In her 2016 presidential campaign, Hillary Clinton tended to cast herself as wishing to accelerate action begun under Obama, rather than as in any way criticising her predecessor. However, the tone of some of her remarks suggested that her version of post-Obama 'assertive internationalism' was unlikely to embrace much 'leading from behind': 'If America doesn't lead we leave a vacuum – and that will either cause chaos, or other countries will rush in to fill the void' (*New York Times*, 23 March and 27 April 2016).

The 'neo-Jacksonianism' – unilateralist in security policy, protectionist in trade – of Donald Trump's 2016 presidential campaign harked back to the foreign policy debates of the early post–Cold War years. In the 1992 Republican nomination campaign, Pat Buchanan attacked the very concept of foreign aid, opposed the North American Free Trade Agreement and argued that President George H.W. Bush should never have fought the 1991 Gulf War. On the Democratic side, 'globosceptic' Jerry Brown offered a leftist version of the so-called new populism – thus to some degree anticipating the Democratic nomination campaign of Bernie Sanders in 2016. Jerry Brown agreed with Buchanan on US participation in the Gulf War and held that not 'a penny' should be given in foreign aid until 'every small farmer, businessman and family' in America was relieved of debt (Schneider, 1997, p. 29).

For the Republicans in 2016, Trump developed a free-wheeling foreign policy agenda, rooted in anti-globalisation, anti-immigration and a strong commitment to the kind of 'America First' sentiments which had opposed US entry into World War II. Islamic radicalism would be 'hit hard' (presumably by unilateral action) wherever it appeared. Trump promised to get 'out of the nation-building business'. US commitment to the North Atlantic Treaty Organisation would be contingent on NATO allies paying their dues. As for international free trade: 'We will no longer surrender this country or its people to the false song of globalization' (*The Guardian*, 23 April 2016). China was effectively threatened with a trade war. Distressed by what they saw as Donald Trump's commitments to a kind of new, populist unilateralism-shading-into-isolationism, some leading neo-conservatives (such as Robert Kagan and Max Boot) in 2016 endorsed Hillary Clinton's 'assertive internationalism' over the Republican candidate's neo-Jacksonianism (*The American Conservative*, 19 August 2016).

Obama

The commitment to multilateralism (while not completely shutting off the prospect of unilateral action); strategic retrenchment; the shift towards the Far East in terms of preferred policy prioritisation; the preference for covert rather than overt military action; the keeping alive of an 'idealist' agenda (including democracy-promotion and the commitment to leading international efforts to tackle climate change); a keen pragmatic awareness of 'costs'; leading from behind: these features of Obama's foreign policy outlook emerge from our earlier discussion of 'Obamaism'. Obama inherited from President George W. Bush wars in Afghanistan and Iraq, as well as a near-collapsing global financial system. This inheritance melded with Obama's personal understanding of the scope and limits of American international power to produce important tensions and countercurrents in US relations with the rest of the world following the presidential election of 2008. These tensions and counter-currents will continue to influence the trajectory of US foreign policy in years to come. When does strategic restraint become a failure of leadership? How exactly *can* a country (especially when that country is the United States) 'lead from behind'? When does caution become paralysing inaction? What degree of terrorist threat is to be regarded as 'normal'? What is the price of choosing one set of regional 'strategic priorities' over another set?

The tensions set in motion by Obama's clear recognition of limits and by his general strategic outlook were vividly illustrated in a series of early policy speeches, as well as in reports of policy battles within the administration. At a press conference in January 2009, Obama emphasised that US power had to come to terms both with international cultural differences and with shifting international conditions: 'other countries have different cultures, different perspectives, and are coming out of different histories'. The US should lead 'by example' – not, he implied, by coercion (Murray, 2013, p. 150). Obama dismissed 'goals that are beyond what can be achieved at a reasonable cost'. 'Each program must be weighed in the light of a broader consideration: the need to maintain balance in and among national programs' (Mandelbaum, 2010, p. 2). Obama's Prague address of April 2009 presented the US as sponsor of global nuclear disarmament. His Cairo speech of June 2009 held out the prospect of a new understanding between the US and the leaders of Muslim countries. His Nobel Peace Prize speech delivered towards the end of 2009 emphasised that he retained the right to use necessary military force to protect vital US interests, and to do so unilaterally where necessary (Dueck, 2015, pp. 35, 59, 151). In May 2012, Obama advanced a version of American exceptionalist thinking: 'I see an American century because no other nation seeks the role we play in global affairs, and no other nation can play the role we play'. Yet he also emphasised that America's exceptional international mission to lead was not compromised by 'the rise of peaceful, responsible emerging powers'. Obama welcomed such rising powers, because 'when more nations step up and contribute to peace and security, that doesn't undermine American power, it enhances it' (Stepak and Whitlock, 2012, p. 54). In May 2014, Obama told West Point graduates that the question facing the US was 'not whether America will lead, but how we will lead'. Military force would be used for the protection of 'core interests'. Obama's 2016 State of the Union address returned to the 'big question' of how to safeguard national security without becoming dangerously overextended: 'how to keep America safe and strong without either isolating ourselves or trying to nation-build everywhere there's a problem' (White House website).

In David Milne's terms, President Obama was a diplomatic 'artist'. He was not a 'scientist' who believed that the application of reason (and indeed measured coercion) could predictably shift the world in a direction consonant with America's geostrategic interests (Milne, 2015, pp. 457–513). Barack Obama's case-by-case pragmatism was only to some degree offset by his fear of being on the 'wrong side' of history – notably in relation to the Arab Spring, the upsurge in democratic protest in the Muslim world which began in Tunisia in December 2010. Obama's stock question in relation to foreign policy debates was 'can we afford it?' In general terms, Obama's elite foreign policy process seemed reasonably successful in adjudicating disputes. President Obama had two highly visible and activist secretaries of state in Hillary Clinton and John Kerry. However, policymaking was fairly intensively centralised. Tom Donilon, who replaced James Jones as national security adviser in 2010, commented that Obama's process mirrored that put in place by Brent Scowcroft under President Bush Senior (Sanger, 2013, p. 430; Lizza, 2011, p. 4).

The State Department tended to operate at one remove from key policy debates, with Hillary Clinton, for example, not being centrally involved in policy development for Iraq and Iran. Key figures on the national security council staff (such as Samantha Power, later US ambassador to the United Nations, and Michael McFaul, later US ambassador to Russia) emerged quite early as proponents of 'idealist' positions on democracy-promotion and humanitarian intervention. They tended, in the first Obama term, to be opposed by the more 'realist' (more narrowly interests-oriented) positions defended by Donilon (Mann, 2012, pp. 167–170).

Despite the relative coherence of the foreign policy process – adjudication of disputes was far less messy under Obama than under many of his predecessors – intra-administration disagreements did regularly surface. Their nature, essentially debates around cost-conscious realism versus liberal activism, tells us much about the trajectory and preoccupations of contemporary US foreign policy. Much of 2009 was taken up with very public debates about the commitment to Afghanistan, with Defence Secretary Robert Gates and Hillary Clinton arguing for a 'surge' in troop commitments – a position opposed by Vice President Joe Biden. Obama's adjudication involved sending fewer troops than demanded by the US military while simultaneously setting an eventual date for a US military exit. US action against the crumbling Gaddafi regime in Libya in 2011 was strongly advocated by Samantha Power and Susan Rice, US ambassador to the UN. Obama approved the humanitarian multilateral initiative in terms which suggested his wider concerns and doubts about the entire direction of his foreign policy: 'If we don't act, if we put brakes on this thing, it will have consequences for US credibility and leadership, consequences for the Arab Spring, and consequences for the international community' (Sanger, 2013, p. 345).

Significant fissures and tensions within the administration also developed over the war in Syria. In September 2013, Obama made an abortive effort to seek congressional authorisation for military action against the Assad regime in Syria, now implicated in the use of chemical weapons. The whole initiative was pushed into abeyance as a result of an intervention by Moscow in the dispute over monitoring and control of chemical weapons. The episode revealed an administration in some disarray. Secretary Kerry, for example, was effectively humiliated by the Obama's equivocation about taking decisive action against the Syrian transgression of a presidentially defined 'red line' on the use of chemical weapons (Chollet, 2016, pp. 1–26; Milbank, 2013).

It is beyond the remit of this chapter to provide a detailed evaluation of Obama's foreign policy. However, a broad audit of key Obama successes and failures will permit some insight into the condition of America's engagement with the world as the Trump administration took office.

The Obama administration's response to the Arab Spring uprisings was disjointed and confused. Such confusion reflected the inherent difficulty of managing US interests in a region whose dynamics were intensely complex and which was still recovering from the backlash to the 2003 invasion of Iraq. The Libyan intervention of 2011 failed to produce either democratisation or stability following the fall of General Gaddafi. Obama's policy towards Syria veered between the ineffectual and the quixotic. Russia took the opportunity of disorder in Syria to revive its status as a major regional power in the Middle East. In Ukraine, Russia effectively challenged the US-led international order to offer more than symbolic resistance to its interventions into Ukraine. Despite the imposition of multilateral sanctions, Russia annexed Crimea (formerly part of Ukraine) in 2014. Progress on North Korean nuclear weapons was stalled as the administration settled for a policy of 'strategic patience'.

On the positive side, an exit from Iraq was effected, though agreements with Baghdad over residual US force retentions were not achieved. The US eased itself away from Afghanistan, opting for a 'good enough' solution there (effectively abandoning any hope of establishing Afghanistan as a democratic, stable and functioning state). The 'pivot' (or rebalancing) towards Asia represented a clear, intellectually defensible adjustment to shifting global conditions. The consequences of increasing regional strategic competition with China and the implications of this new US prioritisation remain unclear and will preoccupy post-Obama policymakers. The new rapprochement with Cuba, announced in December 2014, drew a line under decades of policy stasis and failure. The Paris Agreement on climate change (December 2015), with its important breakthroughs in international cooperation on this issue, was at least to some degree the product of US multilateral diplomacy.

The Iranian nuclear deal (the July 2015 Joint Comprehensive Plan of Action, following the interim agreement of 2013) incited intense partisan opposition both in the US and in Iran. It offered a solution to short-term crisis and a way forward for future regional diplomacy, not of course without many possible pitfalls (Hurst, 2017). According to some of his critics, Obama was the slave of public opinion, forever opting for 'median' public opinion preferences on foreign policy options and failing to provide real leadership (Nasr, 2013, pp. 11–13). Such judgments take insufficient account of the impact on US (and indeed on US elite) opinion of the failures of massive American military intervention in the Middle East in 2003. Robert Gates put the point with characteristic clarity, in 2011: 'In my opinion, any future defense secretary who advises the president to again send a big American army into Asia or into the Middle East or Africa should 'have his head examined', as General MacArthur so delicately put it' (Mann, 2012, p. 288). Inhibitions on large troop commitments do not last forever; General Douglas MacArthur did not live long enough to witness the escalation of commitment to Vietnam in 1965. However, a failure by Obama to recognise the impact of the failed invasion would have been the greatest failure of all.

One of the promises made by Obama in 2008–9 was to move the US in a post-partisan direction. Such moves did not materialise. The US system remains submerged in a swamp of political partisanship and polarisation. Such polarisation, intensely observable in the 2016 presidential election campaigns, has been attributed to factors ranging from shifting patterns of population distribution to the emergence of highly ideological media and communications on television, radio and the internet (see Dumbrell, 2013; Bishop, 2008). The gerrymandering of House of Representatives constituencies has encouraged the emergence of many safe seats and thus of ideological extremism in congressional primary contests. The rise of neo-Jacksonianism in the Trump campaign of 2016 was paralleled by many anti-elite, anti-globalisation movements across the world. Obama was assisted by the ability of presidents to exploit presidential prerogatives in foreign policy. He ran a very 'presidentialist' operation, for example invoking questionable interpretations of executive war powers in connection with the 2011 Libyan action (Ackerman, 2011). It is also the case that elite polarisation in foreign policy, at least under Obama, tended to be somewhat less intense than its counterpart in the domestic arena. Jeffrey Bader, who served on Obama's national security staff as a China specialist, wrote in 2012: 'the extreme polarization that marked domestic politics in the Obama years was absent from foreign policy' (p. 141). Obama was thus able to exploit cross-cutting cleavages in the US Congress, where dovish Democrats sometimes voted alongside what John Kerry called the forces of 'armchair isolationism' within the Republican Party (Douhat, 2013).

Conclusion

Part of President Obama's strategic legacy consisted of the provision of a clear sense of strategic direction: essentially towards a shift towards multilateral engagement and towards a particular focus on economic and strategic priorities in the Far East. In some respects, Obama's foreign policy showed quite high levels of continuity with that of the preceding administration (George W. Bush's second administration, 2005–9, rather than the more unilateralist and interventionist presidential administration of 2001–5). The exit from Iraq took place probably very much as it would have done had George W. Bush still been in office. The rebalancing towards Asia was foreshadowed by policy developments after 2005. By the same token, Obama – for example in relation to the Iranian nuclear deal – also took the US in new directions. Obama's particular combination of continuity and change, however, left unanswered many of the key questions raised in the preceding section of this chapter. How committed is the US to the maintenance of primacy in the Middle East? What are the implications of the Asian rebalancing for the US commitment to European defence? Is the US really and permanently out of the business of nation-building? Under exactly what conditions would a future US administration undertake large-scale military intervention?

The election of a neo-Jacksonian foreign policy president, Donald Trump, in November 2016, represented not only a sharp break from Obama's legacy but also, at least potentially, an existential threat to the internationalist assumptions which have (albeit at times rather uncertainly) guided US foreign policy since 1945. Less an 'isolationist' than a self-conscious foreign policy insurgent, Trump presented himself as an enemy of multilateral international organisations, a global free trade sceptic, a nativist opponent of mass immigration, a procedural authoritarian and a believer in (preferably unilateral) military responses to threats to US security. No longer did it appear axiomatic to the US foreign policy leadership that US security depended on secure, cooperative alliance structures which Washington was prepared to sustain and foster across the globe. The integrating purpose of the new foreign policy look would be 'America First'. Rather than 'indispensable nation', America, in Trumpian rhetoric, is the hapless victim of global free-riding.

The impact of Trump's foreign policy insurgency is impossible to predict. At one level, it might be argued that what is likely to emerge is a re-setting of the foreign policy compass after the Obama years of retrenchment. Such periods of retrenchment have, historically, tended to give way to periods of 'maximal' assertions of power (see Sestanovich, 2014). Trump's presidency may be interpreted as likely to involve such cyclical 'maximalism'. Much speculation at the start of Trump's presidency centred on the extent to which the rhetoric of the 2016 campaign was likely to be translated into actual policy. Although the foreign policy presidency is less inhibited by constitutional checks and balances than its domestic equivalent, presidential leadership in foreign policy is certainly not free of constraint. The global system (including the logic of great power competition), the foreign policy bureaucracy (with its inherent scepticism about the wisdom of rapid intellectual shifts in how the US should view the world) and the sheer explosive unpredictability of global developments all militate against self-conscious revolutions in foreign policy led by insurgent presidents. Indeed, Robert Jervis in late 2016 argued that the Trump presidency represented something of an idealised laboratory experiment in structure and agency problems within international relations theory (Jervis, 2016; Walt, 2016). It is also worth emphasising that, at least at present, neo-Jacksonianism seems a great distance from establishing itself as a new national consensus on how the US should interact with the rest of the world.

The rise of neo-Jacksonianism to levels surpassing those seen in the immediate post–Cold War years, nevertheless, clearly has massively important policy implications, not least in respect of trade policy. The US is still the world's pre-eminent power and is likely to remain so for the foreseeable future. Future agendas include the need to continue to develop a relationship of cooperation (where possible) and competition (where not) with China. The Trump administration's apparent willingness to countenance a trade war with Beijing raises the stakes to intensely hazardous levels. The US will have to continue to come to terms with a world of ascending middle powers, continuing terrorist threats and a revanchist and expansionist (though still very economically vulnerable) Russia. To quote Joseph Nye (2015, pp. 126–127): 'Now, with slightly less preponderance and a much more complex world, the United States will need to make smart strategic choices both at home and abroad if it wishes to maintain its position'. To risk stating the obvious, it might be added that making such 'smart' strategic choices is far from easy in the current domestic political environment.

Further reading

Clinton, Hillary Rodham (2014) *Hard Choices: A Memoir* (London: Simon and Schuster).

Haass, Richard N. (2013) *Foreign Policy Begins at Home: The Case for Putting America's House in Order* (New York: Basic Books).

Ikenberry, G. John (2011) *Liberal Leviathan: The Origins, Crisis, and Transformation of the American World Order* (Princeton: Princeton University Press).

Indyk, Martin S., Kenneth G. Lieberthal and Michael E. O'Hanlon (2012) *Bending History: Barack Obama's Foreign Policy* (Washington, DC: Brookings Institution).

Kupchan, Charles (2012) *No-One's World: The West, the Rising Rest, and the Coming Global Turn* (New York: Oxford University Press).

Quinn, Adam (2011) 'The Art of Declining Politely: Obama's Prudent Presidency and the Waning of American Power', *International Affairs* 87, pp. 803–824.

Singh, Robert (2012) *Barack Obama's Post-American Foreign Policy: The Limits of Engagement* (London: Bloomsbury Academic).

Zakaria, Fareed (2011) *The Post-American World*, 2nd ed. (New York: W.W. Norton).

Bibliography

Ackerman, Bruce (2011) 'Legal Acrobatics, Illegal War', *New York Times* (20 June).

Bader, Jeffrey A. (2012) *Obama and China's Rise: An Insider's Account of America's Asia Strategy* (Washington, DC: Brookings Institution).

Bishop, Bill (with Cushing, Robert W.) (2008) *The Big Sort: Why the Clustering of Like-Minded Americans is Tearing Us Apart* (New York: Houghton Mifflin).

Chollet, Derek (2016) *The Long Game: How Obama Defied Washington and Redefined America's Role in the World* (New York: PublicAffairs).

Crabb, Cecil V., Leila Sariedinne and Glenn J. Antizzo (2001) *Charting a New Course: Alternative Approaches to America's Post-Cold War Foreign Policy* (Baton Rouge: Louisiana State University Press).

Douhat, Ross (2013) 'What Hath Rand Paul Wrought?', *New York Times*, 9 March.

Dueck, Colin (2015) *The Obama Doctrine: American Grand Strategy Today* (New York: Oxford University Press).

Dumbrell, John (1997) *American Foreign Policy: Carter to Clinton* (London: Macmillan).

Dumbrell, John (2009) *Clinton's Foreign Policy: Between the Bushes* (London: Routledge).

Dumbrell, John (ed.) (2013) *Issues in American Politics: Polarized Politics in the Age of Obama* (London: Routledge).

Halper, Stefan and Jonathan Clarke (2004) *America Alone: The Neoconservatives and the Global Order* (Cambridge: Cambridge University Press).

Heale, Michael J. (2011) *Contemporary America: Power, Dependency, and Globalization since 1980* (Chichester, UK: Wiley-Blackwell).

Hurst, Steven (2017) 'Obama and Iran', in John Dumbrell and Edward Ashbee (eds.) *The Obama Presidency and the Politics of Change* (New York: Palgrave), pp. 289–306.

Jervis, Robert J. (2016) 'Introductory Essay: President Trump and IR Theory', https://issforum .org/ISSF/PDF/Policy-Roundtable-1-5B.pdf (accessed December 3, 2016).

Joffe, Josef (2006) *Uberpower: The Imperial Temptation of America* (New York: W.W. Norton).

Kagan, Robert and William Kristol (2000) 'Introduction', in I. Kagan and Kristol (eds.) *Present Dangers: Crisis and Opportunity in American Foreign and Defense Policy* (San Francisco: Encounter Books), pp. 2–11.

Kennan, George F. (1993) *Around the Cragged Hill: A Personal Political Philosophy* (New York: W.W. Norton).

Krauthammer, Charles (1990/1), 'The Unipolar Moment', *Foreign Affairs* 70, pp. 23–33.

Krugman, Paul (2016) 'Clinton and CAFTA' (Central American Free Trade Agreement), *New York Times* (21 March).

Landler, Mark (2016) *Alter Egos: Hillary Clinton, Barack Obama and the Twilight Struggle over American Power* (London: W.H. Allen).

Lizza, Ryan (2011) 'The Consequentialist: How the Arab Spring Remade Obama's Foreign Policy', *The New Yorker* (2 May).

Mandelbaum, Michael (2010) *The Frugal Superpower: America's Global Power in a Cash-Strapped Era* (New York: Public Affairs).

Mann, James (2012) *The Obamians: The Struggle Inside the White House to Redefine American Power* (London: Penguin Books).

Mead, Walter Russell (2002) *Special Providence: American Foreign Policy and How it Changed the World* (New York: Taylor and Francis).

Milbank, Dana (2013) 'Obama's Syria Muddle', *Washington Post* (10 September).

Milne, David (2015) *Worldmaking: The Art and Science of American Diplomacy* (New York: Farrar, Straus and Giroux).

Murray, Donette (2013) 'Military Action But Not as We Know It', *Contemporary Politics* 19, pp. 141–163.

Nasr, Vali (2013) *The Dispensable Nation: American Foreign Policy in Retreat* (New York: Doubleday).

Nielsen, Jonathan M. (ed.) (2000) *Paths Not Taken: Speculations on American Foreign Policy and Diplomatic History: Interests, Ideals, and Power* (Westport, Connecticut: Praeger).

Nye, Joseph S. (2004) *Soft Power: The Means to Success in World Politics* (New York: PublicAffairs).

Nye, Joseph S. (2015) *Is The American Century Over?* (Cambridge: Polity Press).

Pew Research Center (2013) www.pew-globalorg/2013/07/18/worlds-leading-economic-power/ (accessed January 25, 2016).

Sanger, David E. (2013) *Confront and Conceal: Obama's Secret Wars and the Surprising Use of American Power* (New York: Crown Paperbacks).

Schneider, William (1997) 'The New Isolationism', in Lieber, Robert J. (ed.) *Eagle Adrift: American Foreign Policy at the End of the Century* (New York: Longman), pp. 27–40.

Sestanovich, Stephen (2014) *Maximalist: America in the World from Truman to Obama* (New York: Knopf).

SIPRI (Stockholm International Peace Research Institute) (2015) http://books.sipri.org/files/FS/SIPRIFS1504.pdf (accessed March 17, 2015).

Stepak, Amir and Rachel Whitlark (2012) 'The Battle Over America's Foreign Policy Doctrine', *Survival* 54, pp. 48–65.

Walt, Stephen M. (2016) 'The Donald versus "The Blob"', http://issforum.org/ISSF/PDF/Policy-Roundtable-1-5B.pdf (accessed December 4, 2016).

White House Website (Obama) (28 May 2014 and 13 January 2016).

Chapter 6

The People's Republic of China

Gudrun Wacker

Since its founding on October 1, 1949, the People's Republic of China (PRC) has undergone fundamental changes in its perception of global politics and the international system, in the role it has been playing at the international stage and with respect to the domestic actors that are involved in foreign policy decision making. China went through a long phase of (self-)isolation and remained a suspicious and

FIGURE 6.1 Beijing Financial District, China

passive international actor after being admitted into the United Nations in 1971. Even when its global economic weight increased during the 1990s and early 2000s and it had become deeply integrated in all major international organisations and institutions, its leaders pursued a predominantly reactive and risk-averse foreign policy. While China's growing economic activities around the world and the global financial crisis in 2008–9 pulled and pushed it into a more prominent position, it only reluctantly and selectively became more proactive. Under the leadership of Xi Jinping, who took office in 2012–13, we have been seeing a China that has the ambition to actively shape global politics, or at least parts of it.

What has remained unchanged in the PRC's foreign policy and engagement with the world over the last seven decades is that above all Beijing has been following and serving domestic priorities or 'core national interests'. Notable among them are maintaining the rule of the Communist Party and safeguarding the sovereignty and territorial integrity of the country. Another constant has been the 'Five Principles of Peaceful Coexistence' developed in 1954. But while they are still quoted in official statements today, their usage has changed over time due to domestic and international transformations. In general, seemingly fixed formulations and slogans used in the official Chinese diplomatic language undergo modifications in meaning and always have to be contextualised.

China outside the international system: isolation and self-isolation

In 1949, the armed forces of the Communist Party (CCP) won the civil war in China and forced the Nationalist Army and the Kuomintang (KMT) government under Chiang Kai-shek to flee to the island of Taiwan. When the PRC was officially founded, only a small number of countries in the world granted diplomatic recognition to the new state. The Republic of China (ROC) on Taiwan, which claimed to represent all of China and aspired to 'recover' the Mainland, had held the Permanent Seat in the Security Council of the United Nations (UN) since 1945 and enjoyed continued diplomatic recognition, at least by major Western countries. Thus, in the first three decades of its existence, the PRC was a poor and isolated socialist country, and its role in the world and footprint in global politics was marginal at best.

In 1954, India's foreign minister and China's prime minister worked out the Five Principles of Peaceful Coexistence, namely, mutual respect for each other's territorial integrity and sovereignty, mutual non-aggression, mutual non-interference in each other's internal affairs, equality and cooperation for mutual benefit, and peaceful coexistence (Panda, 2014). These principles were officially adopted at the Bandung Conference in 1955, where 29 Asian and African countries came together to improve solidarity and cooperation among developing countries, many of them still colonies at that time.[1] The Five Principles of Peaceful Coexistence are one of the few constants guiding China's foreign policy over the decades – until today. They are frequently cited by Chinese leaders.

To counterbalance the Soviet Union, the US set up a 'strategic triangle' (Levine, 1989; Ross, 1993; Goh, 2005) composed of the US, the USSR and China. This was possible because the relationship between Beijing and Moscow had deteriorated in the late 1950s for political and ideological reasons, leading to a deep split in the early 1960s and even culminating in a brief military conflict between the two former socialist 'brothers' in 1969. During the 1970s, the US, under President Nixon and his National Security Adviser Henry Kissinger, set up relations with the PRC. Washington gave up its opposition to China's accession to the United Nations, and it became a member in 1971, replacing the ROC, including in the Security Council.

Despite the warming relationship with the US and the diplomatic recognition by Western countries like Japan and major European states, China's (self-)isolation remained pretty much in place during the 1970s: domestically, the Cultural Revolution was still underway. At the time, China's leader Mao Zedong saw the world divided into three different layers ('three worlds theory') with the US and the Soviet Union as the first layer (superpowers or hegemons); Europe, Canada, Australia and Japan the second; and developing countries in Asia, Africa and Latin America as the third (Kim, 1980; Gillespie, 2004, pp. 123ff.). In Mao's thinking, another World War between the two hegemonic powers was inevitable. And while the PRC never formally joined the Non-Aligned Movement or the Group of 77 (G77), China saw itself as part of the Third World of developing nations. Moreover, as a revolutionary country, it supported communist and rebel forces in Southeast Asia during the 1960s and until the mid-1970s.

Having inherited the ROC's permanent seat in the Security Council of the UN, the PRC joined other organisations affiliated with the UN. However, it remained a quite passive member, usually abstaining in UNSC votes, and it stayed out of other international organisations and institutions (Kim, 1999, pp. 45ff.). The principle of self-reliance and a reluctance to be bound by international rules and regulations were still guiding Beijing's demeanour at the global stage. For the same reason, China did not seek formal alliances with other countries.[2]

The need for a peaceful international environment: 'keeping a low profile'

With the death of Mao Zedong in 1976 and the purge of the 'Gang of Four', marking the official end of the Cultural Revolution, a new period began for China. In late 1978, at the third Plenary Session of the 11th Central Committee, the CCP under the leadership of Deng Xiaoping started the era of 'Reform and Opening-up'. No master plan existed for the reform process and it was controversial within the Party what its scope and final outcome should be. It started out with land reforms in the agricultural sector and a limited opening of China's economy to the outside world by establishing so-called Special Economic Zones in some of China's coastal provinces. The entire reform period since 1979 was characterised by a series of experiments. It was an approach of trial and error, or, as Deng Xiaoping famously described it with a Chinese proverb, as 'crossing the river while feeling the stones'.

In parallel to the process of domestic reforms and gradual economic opening to the outside world, China cautiously and step by step underwent a process of integrating itself in the international system during the 1980s. It joined the international financial institutions like World Bank and International Monetary Fund and started to accept international funding for development projects. In 1986, it applied for membership in the General Agreement on Tariffs and Trade (GATT; later renamed the World Trade Organisation, WTO). In 1992 it acceded to the Non-Proliferation Treaty (NPT) as a nuclear weapon state[3] and later joined most regimes for nuclear, biological and chemical weapons. China had been actively involved in negotiating the UN Convention on the Law of the Sea (UNCLOS), but only ratified it in 1996, albeit with specifications on certain provisions of the Convention (United Nations Division for Ocean Affairs and the Law of the Sea, 2013). In the same year, the PRC – after conducting a final series nuclear tests – signed the Comprehensive Test Ban Treaty (CTBT), but to date has not ratified it.

Moreover, China signed the two major UN Human Rights covenants on economic, social and cultural rights (in 1997) and on political and civil rights (in 1998) (Foot, 2000). However, until the time of this writing, the PRC has only ratified the first covenant (in 2001) (United Nations Treaty Collection), but not the second one on civil and political rights, arguing that more time was needed for making the necessary modifications in China's domestic laws. By the end of the 1990s the PRC had become a member of practically every international institution, organisation and association, culminating in its accession to the World Trade Organisation (WTO) in 2001.

Behind this international outreach in the 1990s stood a general belief that conditions for China's development and modernisation could be improved by normalising diplomatic relations with important neighbours (such as Singapore, Indonesia and South Korea) and by getting access to international as well as regional organisations. This was seen as contributing to the creation of a 'peaceful international environment'. But it was also motivated by concrete domestic as well as international events. The industrialised countries in the West responded to the decision of China's leaders to end the student demonstrations on Tian'anmen Square by military force in June 1989 with condemnation and sanctions. In light of the transformation processes going on at the time in the Soviet Union and in the entire Eastern bloc, China had mutated overnight from a forerunner of socialist reform to a dinosaur ('*Tyrannosaurus leniniensis*' as Steven I. Levine famously put it; Levine, 1992). Therefore, China saw the need to overcome international criticism and isolation (at least by the West) following Tian'anmen. As a first step, in November 1990, the PRC abstained in the vote on Resolution 678 which set an ultimatum for Iraq to withdraw its forces from Kuwait, despite its usual aversion to the interference in internal affairs of other countries. In the early 1990s China also participated for the first time in a UN-led peacekeeping mission (Wang, 1999, pp. 76ff.).

The transformation of the Soviet Union, which ultimately led to its breaking up into independent states, came as a shock for China's leaders (Zhang, 1994). In the immediate aftermath of these events, it was unclear whether the last big socialist country would continue on the path of reform and opening up. Ultimately, it was Deng Xiaoping himself with his 'southern journey' in early 1992 who gave the crucial signal that China would stay on a course of economic reform. But the fate of the Soviet Union serves as a negative model for the leaders of the PRC until today, confirming how dangerous reforms of the political system can be.

Observing the downfall of the Soviet Union and Russia's situation afterwards also explains at least in part China's mistrust towards the West, most notably towards the US, whose goal is suspected to be regime change (by 'peaceful evolution') and the containment of China. In response to developments in the 1980s, Tian'anmen and the end of the Cold War guidelines, usually ascribed to Deng Xiaoping himself, were developed for China's posture at the international stage. Consisting of 24 Chinese characters,[4] these guidelines are usually summed up in the phrase 'keep a low profile' (*taoguang yanghui*). For the next two decades, this formula provided the general recipe for China's foreign policy and approach to global politics with the main goal of avoiding confrontation or conflict, especially with the US. In the post–Cold War period, the Five Principles of Peaceful Coexistence were used predominantly to fend off interference in the internal affairs of other countries, including China.

The 1990s also saw a systematic effort of the PRC to reform and modernise its armed forces. Witnessing US military operations and high-tech warfare in the Gulf War (1990–1) made China's leaders realise how backward and antiquated its own military was. This realisation resulted in a process of professionalising the People's Liberation Army and upgrading its equipment, with the focus on air and naval capabilities. In the same decade, the concept of 'comprehensive national power' was developed, which goes beyond military capabilities to include economic, political, technical and ideational resources.

Ever since the end of the Cold War, Chinese leaders and academics had proclaimed that the world had become or was going to be a multi-polar one. The Chinese concept remained slightly vague, since it oscillated between multi-polarity either being a fact already, or being an ongoing process that needed active support, or being a demand for a post-hegemonial world. Also, the number of poles in this new global set-up varied based on different assessments of national strength. But it is safe to assume that China saw itself as one of the poles or at least as on the way to become one.

With a permanent seat in the UN Security Council and its membership in the NPT as a recognised nuclear weapon state, the PRC had achieved the highest possible credentials at the global *political* stage. By acceding to the WTO in 2001, China completed the process of integration into the international economic institutions. With unprecedented GDP growth rates, China improved its economic position in the world considerably over two and a half decades. In 1990, China's economy held the 11th rank behind the US, Japan, the biggest European countries, Canada and Brazil; by the year 2000, it had moved up to the 6th rank, and by 2011 it had overtaken Japan and became number 2. It also became the biggest emitter of greenhouse gases in 2007, one of the biggest oil importers and the biggest consumer of aluminum, copper, lead, nickel, tin, zinc, iron ore, coal, wheat, rice, palm oil, cotton and rubber (Griswold, 2007). In order to satisfy its growing demands, China started to increase its economic activities all over the world, including in Africa, Asia and Latin America.

In light of these developments it became much harder to 'keep a low profile'. The growing international economic weight sparked debates about China's position and future role in the world. Within the PRC, Zheng Bijian, former vice-president of the Central Party School, promoted the theory of China's 'peaceful rise' (*heping jueqi*) in the early 2000s (Zheng, 2005; Glaser and Medeiros, 2007). A few years later, then Deputy Secretary of State Robert Zoellick publicly called on China to become a 'responsible stakeholder', arguing that it had a responsibility to 'strengthen the international system that enabled its success' (Zoellick, 2005).

Despite such suggestions which were widely and controversially discussed among academic circles inside China, Beijing's leaders remained cautious and continued to argue that the PRC was still a developing and poor country in terms of per capita GDP. In order to achieve the goal of modernising the economy and building a 'moderately prosperous society', a peaceful international environment was still a necessity. Thus, 'keeping a low profile' (*taoguang yanghui*) was still accepted and cited as the general guideline for China's demeanour at the global stage. However, the Chinese leadership had to acknowledge the fact that China was now not only much more visible in the world, but it also had interests everywhere and therefore had to become more actively engaged in international affairs (Chen and Wang, 2011).

This selectively stronger engagement was expressed with the words 'make some achievements' (*you suo zuowei*) which were then added to Deng's original guidelines. The remaining reluctance to strive for a bigger footprint in the world reflects China's double identity or self-perception – as a developing country and as a regional or even great power at the same time. As the biggest developing country, China would have hesitated to join the G7/8 which it considered a 'club of the rich', even if it had been officially invited. For the same reason the idea of BRIC, consisting of Brazil, Russia, India and China,[5] looked much more appealing: despite the political/ideological differences between the four countries, they all shared certain interests in having a bigger say in global (mainly economic) affairs. The formation of BRIC(S) was one of the signs of China becoming more proactive, albeit not by itself.

In contrast, the idea of a 'Group of Two' suggesting that the US and China sort of co-managed global affairs, which was put forward by former national security adviser Zbigniew Brzezinski (Brzezinski, 2009) did not fall on fertile ground in China. Many academics saw it as a 'trap' (Guo and Guo, 2010, p. 7) to lure China into spending resources on issues that were not really in its interest. These resources would then not be available for China's national development anymore.

From the early 2000s onward, China started to invest more in improving its image in the world, to counter what it perceived to be an unfounded 'China Threat Theory', especially among its neighbours. The enormous economic success combined with military modernisation had nurtured fears in the region and beyond of a coercive or even aggressive China. Public diplomacy and soft power efforts worldwide can be seen in the establishment of Confucius Institutes in many countries (Paradise, 2009) and official support for Chinese state media like CCTV, Xinhua News Agency or China Daily to establish a strong presence abroad (Shi, 2013). The rhetoric of 'win-win' was introduced to suggest that cooperation with China was beneficial to all sides involved (even though 'win-win' did not necessarily mean equal benefits). And while the political and academic elite in the country would still argue that China does not provide a model for development to be emulated by others, it considerably stepped up economic (mainly focusing on energy and natural resources) activities and developmental aid, mostly in the form of soft loans, in Asia, Africa and Latin America (Zhou and Hou, 2017).

The fact that China hosted the 2008 Olympic Games in Beijing as well as the 2010 World Expo in Shanghai clearly demonstrated from the Chinese perspective that the country had finally 'arrived' in the international community as an equal partner and wanted to be recognised as such. Both events provided opportunities to showcase its achievements in terms of modernisation (Lee, 2016, p. 106). These mega-events coincided with the global financial crisis, which pulled China into a new position at the global stage. The upgrading of the G20 from ministers of finance to head of states level with China and other emerging countries as full members indicated a shift in the global distribution of power. In other areas of global politics/governance like fighting climate change or preventing the proliferation of weapons of mass destruction it had also become clear that there could be no sustainable solution if China's cooperation could not be ensured. And without China's rapid economic development, the global balance sheet on fighting poverty would look a lot worse than it did.

Thanks to an unprecedented stimulus program, China overcame the ramifications of the financial crisis astonishingly fast. The crisis itself was interpreted in China (as elsewhere) as a proof of the failure of the Western capitalist system (Breslin, 2012). Both boosted China's self-confidence, even though it was clear that China itself needed to get prepared for slowing growth rates if it wanted to switch to a more sustainable economic path.

With respect to political and social stability, China's leaders remained concerned about external interferences and support for unrest at home: the so-called colour revolutions in some post-Soviet states (Georgia in 2003, Ukraine in 2004 and Kyrgyzstan in 2005) (Wilson, 2009) and later the events during and after the Arab Spring (2010–11) (Poulain et al., 2014) re-fuelled earlier fears of a 'peaceful evolution'.

A new era of activism: 'striving for achievement'

The leadership change in 2012–13 from Hu Jintao and Wen Jiabao to Xi Jinping brought with it profound changes and an acceleration of pre-existing trends in Chinese politics, domestically as well as at the global stage. Xi Jinping managed to become 'core leader'[6] of the Communist Party within his first four years in power, and his style of leadership was strikingly different from previous generations of leaders. He has concentrated power in his own hands and is personally heading the newly established State Security Committee as well as all important 'Leading Small Groups',[7] several of them focusing on foreign policy. His overall vision for China was encapsulated in the 'China Dream'.[8] This dream and Xi's idea of a great 'national rejuvenation' (Xi, 2012) also have a foreign policy and global dimension and foresee a stronger and more proactive role of China in the world. While this is not a total break from his predecessors, it means that under Xi Jinping, China's profile in global politics has increased and proactive efforts have accelerated. Beijing no longer confines itself on criticising the existing international order as unfair, but has launched its own concepts and initiatives. In other words, it has started to 'strive for achievement' (*fenfa youwei*) (Yan, 2014) and the formula of 'keeping a low profile', which had become less and less credible, has quietly disappeared from official statements in the era of Xi Jinping.

The incoming leadership also put forward new ideas for the relationship with the US. When he visited Washington, DC as vice president in February 2012, Xi

Jinping suggested a 'new type of major power relations' – a concept to prevent conflict between the established power (US) and the emerging or rising power (China), or in other words to avoid the Thucydides trap (Allison, 2015). This 'new type' of relationship, as suggested by Xi, was supposed to be guided by some basic principles, namely no conflict and no confrontation, mutual respect, including for 'core national interests' and mutually beneficial cooperation (Li and Xu, 2014). The concept can be interpreted as a response to the 'rebalancing' or 'pivot to Asia' launched by the US under the presidency of Barack Obama. The 'pivot' had largely been perceived in China as an effort of containment and strategic encirclement. In contrast to the idea of a 'G2' described earlier, the 'new type' aimed more at avoiding a negative spiral in Sino-US relations. This time, critical voices in the US spoke of the Chinese concept as a 'trap' (Erickson and Liff, 2014).

The argument that China is a developing country or, to be more precise, the biggest developing country in the world, is still used in certain contexts, but the question whether China is rising or not seems to have been settled: it has risen and is stepping up its presence and visibility at the global level. However, China remains selective with respect to the areas where it is taking on more responsibility. This is mainly due to the fact that its identity is still in flux and oscillating between developing country and great power; in other words, China has 'multiple layers' of identity (Summers, 2014, p. 1) and thus is playing different roles in different contexts and at different levels.

It has become popular to argue that China is a revisionist power that aims at undermining the Western-dominated international institutions and is creating alternative structures – 'shadow' or 'parallel' institutions which will ultimately challenge the established international order (Rudolf et al., 2014) However, if we take a closer look at China's new activism at the regional and global stage, it is questionable whether the term 'revisionist' is an appropriate description. We can discern three trends that are going on in parallel (Ekman, 2016).

First, China is increasing its engagement in existing institutions and formats (e.g. UN, G20), using them to raise China's international profile. Second, it has been trying to revive existing but stagnating or withering organisations (e.g. the Conference on Interaction and Confidence Building in Asia, or CICA). And third, it has been creating new forums and institutions, in which China can play a decisive, but not necessarily *the* dominating role. The Shanghai Cooperation Organisation, founded in 2001, is the earliest example for an organisation co-founded by China. The New Development Bank (NDB) of the BRICS countries was launched in 2014, and the Asian Infrastructure Investment Bank (AIIB) took up its work in 2015. While this third category is largely seen as a challenge to the established order, China presents these formats as complementary to existing ones and as filling gaps that would otherwise not be filled. For example, the AIIB and NDB are supposed to address the need for enormous investments in infrastructure in Asia and in emerging or developing countries outside of Asia. While it is fairly obvious that the creation of these new financial institutions was in part motivated by the unwillingness of their Western-dominated counterparts to reform and adjust to new economic (and political) realities in the world, it is important to understand that there is a difference between reforming the global order on the one hand, and eroding or replacing it, on the other.

In China's case, we see a specific mix of status quo and reformist/revisionist elements in its global politics. It should also be noted that the international institutions founded after World War II have themselves undergone changes, so they don't represent a fixed system that cannot evolve or be adapted. Since China has benefited enormously from globalisation and has therefore a huge stake in the existing economic and financial institutions, it is unlikely that it pursues the goal of undermining or destroying these same institutions. Rather, the goal is modifying them in a way that gives China a greater say in their norms, standards and rules. With its permanent seat in the Security Council of the UN and the veto power that comes with it, China's stance on Security Council reform has been rather conservative and status quo oriented. More active Chinese efforts to actually *shape* international norms and standards can be observed in relatively new, and as of now unregulated fields, such as cyberspace or outer space (Chen, 2016).

Generally, there are three manifestations of China's new activism at the global stage:

- Commitment to make more contributions to global commons (UN peacekeeping, UN development goals, climate change)
- 'Host diplomacy' and upgrading of international dialogue formats (CICA, Xiangshan Forum, APEC, G20, World Internet Conference)
- Own initiatives, most prominently the Silk Road initiatives ('Belt and Road Initiative' BRI or OBOR), Asia Infrastructure Investment Bank (AIIB) and BRICS Development Bank ('New Development Bank')

The language in China's foreign policy has notably changed over the last years: not only has the doctrine of 'keeping a low profile' disappeared from official discourse, but Chinese politicians and academics speak quite openly of a 'leading' (*yinling*) role for China in several areas of global politics and of a 'great power diplomacy with Chinese characteristics' (Wang, 2017, p. 1). The fact that Chinese investment, economic activities and the number of citizens working all over the world have been on the rise provides one of the major drivers behind this stronger international engagement. Given this new context, even the time-honoured principle of non-interference (one of the Five Principles of Peaceful Coexistence) has come under scrutiny (Duchâtel et al., 2014).

Stronger commitment

Since the year 2000, China has continually raised its financial contribution to the UN budget, and with nearly 8 per cent in 2016–18 it has become the third biggest contributor behind the US and Japan – on par with the UK and France (Fontaine and Rapp-Hooper, 2016; Jiang and Wang, 2015).

Already in 2008, China had put the 'Peace Ark', a modern hospital ship, into commission. The ship has since conducted various missions to provide medical services to residents in other countries; it participated in disaster relief missions, for example in 2013 after the Philippines had been struck by a typhoon; and in 2014 it was one of three Chinese ships taking part in the multination RIMPAC exercise organised by the US (Mizokami, 2014). In 2009, the first training facility for peacekeeping was opened near Beijing, which included offering training people from other countries (China Daily, 2009).

But under Xi Jinping, Beijing has stepped up peacekeeping activities and financial/material contributions even more: in his speech at the 70th General Assembly of the UN in September 2015, President Xi underlined China's commitment to peacekeeping with concrete promises. He announced that China would build up a permanent stand-by peacekeeping force of 8000 troops and promised US$100 million to the African Union to build an immediate response unit. At a special summit on peacekeeping convened by US President Obama on the same occasion, Xi pledged a helicopter squad for peacekeeping operations in Africa and declared that China would train 5000 peacekeepers from other countries (Perlez, 2015). According to media reports, China also aspired to head the UN Department of Peacekeeping Operations (Lynch, 2016), but the position was filled with a French national once again – France has held this position since 1996 (United Nations Secretary-General, 2017). This last example shows that China expects that more Chinese nationals will be chosen for leading positions in international organisations and institutions.

On climate change, the PRC had for a long time refused to sign up to any internationally binding agreement or legally binding goals to reduce carbon dioxide emissions. Though a signatory to the Kyoto Protocol in 1997, China (like India) had joined as a developing country and was thus exempted from mandatory reductions. Two main arguments were brought forward by Beijing when a follow-up to the Kyoto Protocol was being negotiated: first, that emissions should be calculated on a per capita basis, and second, that the accumulated emissions over time should be taken into consideration.

In the run-up to the climate summit in Copenhagen in 2009, China and the US had basically gone into a game of mutual blame, with each side demanding the other side to move first. However, faced with serious environmental problems within China and the need to diversify its energy sources, the country has become one of the champions in developing renewable energy resources. And with a changed attitude in the White House under President Obama, both sides reached an agreement in which they pledged to cooperate and work towards an international protocol or legal instrument on climate change (The White House, 2014). Without such a breakthrough at the bilateral level, the Paris Agreement on climate change would have been much harder, if not impossible, to reach. Both sides used the eve of the G20 summit in Hangzhou in September 2009 to announce that their respective countries would ratify the accord (Phillips et al., 2016). The US withdrawal from the Paris Agreement under President Donald Trump has not changed China's commitment to the climate pact (Bendix, 2017).

Higher regional and global profile

China taking over the presidency of the G20 and hosting the summit in September 2016 is only one example of the 'host diplomacy' which has become a feature of China's efforts to raise its regional and global profile and to demonstrate its willingness to play a constructive international role.

Another example of 'host diplomacy' was the summit of the so far little-known Conference on Interaction and Confidence Building in Asia (CICA), which had originally been initiated by Kazakhstan's President Nursultan Nazarbaev in the early 1990s and has a broad and diverse membership of mainly Asian, but also some Middle Eastern countries. The gathering was held in Shanghai in June 2014. China not only organised the summit, but Xi Jinping gave a speech in which he proposed a new security concept for Asia and argued that Asian countries should take security in the region into their own hands (Xi Jinping, 2014).

Beijing also upgraded the Xiangshan Forum, a conference on security organised by the China Association for Military Science. It had been initiated in 2006 as a track 2 event and took place bi-annually. In 2014, it was expanded in scope and transformed into a track 1.5 event (including officials) and from that year on has been held on an annual basis. It seems quite clear that China tries to develop this conference format into an equivalent of the Shangri-La Dialogue, which has been organised annually in Singapore since 2002.

Worth mentioning is the World Internet Conference or Wuzhen Summit, which has been held annually since 2014 in Zhejiang province. At the 2015 conference, Xi Jinping himself delivered the opening speech and promoted the concept of 'cyber sovereignty' (Xi, 2015). Internet and cyberspace are areas where China tries to actively shape the rules of the game, insisting that the sovereign rights of a country apply here as well.

While China has hosted international events before, such occasions are now more systematically used to unveil new ideas and initiatives. For example, on the eve of the summit of the Asia-Pacific Economic Cooperation (APEC) in November 2014, Xi Jinping announced the US$40 billion Silk Road Fund China. At the summit itself Xi spoke of fulfilling the 'Asia-Pacific dream', and the host country also promoted the idea of an APEC-wide Free Trade Agreement (Wang, 2014). This idea of a Free Trade Agreement of the Asia-Pacific (FTAAP) was also in response to the Trans-Pacific Partnership (TPP), the FTA that was negotiated at the time between the US and 11 Pacific Rim states, but without China.

A new grand initiative

Arguably the most far-reaching and potentially most influential initiative was launched by China's leader in 2013. During his visit to Central Asia in September 2013, Xi Jinping announced the 'Silk Road Economic Belt'. A month later when speaking to the Indonesian parliament, he propagated a '21st Century Maritime Silk Road'. What became first known as 'One Belt, One Road', or OBOR, has since been officially renamed into the 'Belt and Road Initiative'. Behind it is the idea of connecting Asia, Europe and parts of Africa by building economic corridors with a focus on infrastructure construction (ports, railroads, roads, pipelines, energy grids, telecommunication lines).

China presents OBOR as an initiative, not as a strategy, since it is rather open in terms of participating countries and projects. A first more concrete description of the idea was laid out by a joint document of three government institutions in 2015 under the title 'Vision and Actions on Jointly Building Silk Road

Economic Belt and 21st-Century Maritime Silk Road' (National Development and Reform Commission et al., 2015).

As an important instrument for funding such projects, China – in addition to the Silk Road Fund – announced the establishment of a new development bank, namely the Asian Infrastructure Investment Bank (AIIB). The bank was formally established with 57 founding members in December 2015 and started operating in January 2016. Among the bigger states in the world, only the US and Japan remained suspicious of the bank and decided not to join. So far, the AIIB has been mainly co-financing projects with the World Bank, the Asian Development Bank and the European Bank for Reconstruction and Development (Elen, 2017).

With OBOR, China managed for the first time to bring a slogan into the world that has been taken up in the political and economic discourse of other countries, and the initiative has the potential to change the geo-economic landscape over time (Ferdinand, 2016, p. 951). Previous Chinese efforts to promote concepts or ideas and to influence the international discourse, like the 'harmonious world' of former president and leader of the CCP Hu Jintao, have been less successful. OBOR, despite or because of its vagueness, seems to offer the prospect of tangible and beneficial results for all parties involved. Despite the major Belt and Road summit that took place in Beijing in May 2017 and was attended by the leaders of 28 countries, including a US delegation, at this point it is way too early to tell whether the initiative will fulfil the expectations it has created.

Conclusion: China has risen, but is it ready to lead?

The PRC has undergone a huge transformation in its attitude towards and its role in global politics since the 1950s. Starting out as a fairly isolated country with no representation in the UN during the 1950s and 60s, it became a suspicious and rather passive member of the international community in the 1970s. Only with the advent of the reform period in the early 1980s, China started to cautiously seek membership in international institutions. This process of integrating itself accelerated during the 1990s and early 2000s, but China still presented itself as a poor developing country, not ready to shoulder more international responsibilities. This attitude became less and less credible and tenable in light of the unprecedented economic development and modernisation in the two decades after the end of the Cold War. Hosting the Olympic Games and the World Expo signalled China's ambition to be accepted as an equal partner by Western industrialised countries, and the global financial crisis pulled it into assuming a more proactive role at the global stage. The willingness to not only criticise the existing order as unfair, but also to actively contribute more to shaping the rules of the game became more pronounced under the leadership of Xi Jinping.

It is not predetermined what China's higher ambitions and bigger footprint in global politics mean for the future international order. A rules-based order is not necessarily negated or challenged by China – after all, much of its economic and political success was made possible by this very order. But from the Chinese perspective, different sets of rules can apply at different levels or in different regions of the world. The global financial crisis was seen as proof that the recipes of an international system dominated by the capitalist West no longer work and that new approaches were needed to address the complexities of the world today. That China now sees itself in a position to make constructive contributions here can be concluded from a new formula, the 'China approach' (*Zhongguo fang'an*)[9] which has been introduced into the official Chinese vocabulary by Xi Jinping in 2016.

The election of Donald Trump as the 45th president of the United States has added to the list of uncertainties the world is facing, raising questions as to the future of the 'Western' liberal and rules-based order. Although it is too early to tell what the impact of the Trump presidency will be over the next years, a few assumptions are safe to make. The US (at least at the federal level) will no longer be a partner in fighting climate change; the Transpacific Partnership (TPP), now named CPTPP, will have to cope without US participation; and human rights and democratic values will not be a very high priority on an agenda entitled 'America First'.

All of this provides another pull factor for China to take over more global responsibility. Given the prospect of the US pursuing a protectionist and anti-globalisation agenda, China's leadership has at least rhetorically signalled its willingness and readiness to step in and to step up its global profile as the defender of globalisation and free trade (Xi, 2017). But whether China can provide across-the-board global leadership in the future will not only depend on how it will be able to cope with the domestic challenges the country is facing – economic, social and demographic to name a few – but also on the acceptance of the 'China approach' by other countries.

Notes

1 The Bandung Conference prepared the ground for the Non-Aligned Movement (Panda, 2014).
2 The only formal ally of China remains North Korea. Both countries signed a Treaty of Friendship, Cooperation and Mutual Assistance in 1961.
3 China had conducted a first successful nuclear test in October 1964. It acceded to the NPT in the same year as France.
4 Usually, the 24 characters are translated as follows: 'Observe calmly; secure our position; cope with affairs calmly; hide our capacities and bide our time; be good at maintaining a low profile; and never claim leadership'.
5 The grouping was originally invented by Goldman Sachs in 2001, forecasting that these were four emerging economies. The idea was taken up by the countries themselves and their leaders held a first meeting in 2006 during the G8 Outreach Summit in St Petersburg. They held their first separate summit in 2009. South Africa joined in 2011 and the acronym was changed to BRICS accordingly. For detailed information on BRICS, see BRICS Information Centre at www.brics.utoronto.ca/.
6 The 6th Plenary Session of the 18th CPC Central Committee included the formulation of Xi Jinping as the 'core' in its official Communiqué (Xinhua News, 2016).
7 'Leading Small Groups' are coordinating bodies in which representatives from different Party and State agencies participate (Lawrence and Martin, 2013, p. 14).
8 Actually, the Chinese *Zhongguo meng* can be translated as 'China dream' or 'Chinese dream'. But since 'Chinese dream' immediately evokes the American dream, the translation 'China dream' seems more appropriate. There has been a debate within China on the question whether the China dream is also the dream of individual Chinese people.

9 *Zhongguo fang'an* can also be translated as China's 'plan'. It has been translated as 'solution' (Kelly, 2017) – and Chinese official media have used this term – but that seems too strong and ambitious.

Further reading

Buzan, Barry and Rosemary Foot (eds.) (2004) *Does China Matter? A Reassessment* (London and New York: Routledge).

Cabestan, Jean-Pierre (ed.) (2016) 'Special Issue: What Kind of International Order Does China Want? Between Reformism and Revisionism', *China Perspectives* 2016(2) (Hong Kong).

Economy, Elizabeth and Michel Oksenberg (eds.) (1999) *China Joins the World. Progress and Prospects* (New York: Council on Foreign Relations Press).

Foot, Rosemary (ed.) (2013) *China across the Divide: The Domestic and Global in Politics and Society* (Oxford: Oxford University Press).

Goh, Evelyn (2013) *The Struggle for Order: Hegemony, Hierarchy and Transition in Post-Cold War East Asia* (Oxford: Oxford University Press).

Kim, Samuel S. (1979) *China, the United Nations, and World Order* (Princeton, NJ: Princeton University Press).

Kim, Samuel S. (1998) *China and the World. Chinese Foreign Policy Faces the New Millennium*, 4th ed. (Boulder, CO: Westview Press).

Shambaugh, David (2011) 'Coping with a Conflicted China', *The Washington Quarterly* 34(1), pp. 7–27.

Shambaugh, David (2013) *China Goes Global. The Partial Power* (Oxford: Oxford University Press).

Summers, Tim (2014) *China's Global Personality*, June 2014 (London: Chatham House Asia Programme), www.chathamhouse.org/sites/files/chathamhouse/field/field_document/20140617ChinaGlobalPersonalitySummers.pdf (accessed April 12, 2017).

Bibliography

Allison, Graham (2015) 'The Thucydides Trap: Are the U.S. and China Headed for War?', *The Atlantic* (September 24), www.theatlantic.com/international/archive/2015/09/united-states-china-war-thucydides-trap/406756/.

Bendix, Aria (2017) 'The Global Reaction to Trump's Climate Change Decision', *The Atlantic* (June 1), www.theatlantic.com/news/archive/2017/06/the-global-reaction-to-trumps-climate-change-decision/528777/ (accessed June 13, 2017).

Breslin, Shaun (2012) 'Paradigm(s) Shifting? Responding to China's Response to the Global Financial Crisis', in Wyn Grant and Graham K. Wilson (eds.) *The Consequences of the Global Financial Crisis: The Rhetoric of Reform and Regulation* (Oxford: Oxford University Press), pp. 226–246.

Brzezinski, Zbigniew (2009) 'The Group of Two that Could Change the World', *Financial Times* (January 13), www.ft.com/content/d99369b8-e178-11dd-afa0-0000779fd2ac (accessed June 14, 2017).

Chen, Dingding and Wang, Jianwei (2011) 'Lying Low No More? China's New Thinking on the *Tao Guang Yang Hui* Strategy', *China: An International Journal* 9(2), pp. 195–216.

Chen, Zheng (2016) 'China's Domestic Debate on Global Governance', *The Diplomat* (November 23).

China Daily (2009) 'China Opens 1st Peacekeeping Training Center' (June 25), www.china daily.com.cn/china/2009-06/25/content_8324367.htm (accessed June 14, 2017).

Duchâtel, Mathieu, Oliver Bräuner and Zhou Hang (2014) 'Protecting China's Overseas Interests. The Slow Shift Away from Non-Interference', SIPRI Policy Paper No. 41, June (Stockholm: SIPRI), http://books.sipri.org/files/PP/SIPRIPP41.pdf (accessed June 14, 2017).

Ekman, Alice (2016) 'China's Multilateralism: Higher Ambitions', EUISS Issue Alert 2, www.iss.europa.eu/uploads/media/Alert_2_China.pdf (accessed June 14, 2017).

Elen, Maurits (2017) 'AIIB Official: Regional Integration Creates Much Richer ASEAN', *The Diplomat* (April 7), http://thediplomat.com/2017/04/aiib-official-regional-integration-creates-much-richer-asean/ (accessed June 14, 2017).

Erickson, Andrew S. and Adam P. Liff (2014) 'Not-So Empty Talk. The Danger of China's "New Type of Great-Power Relations" Slogan', *Foreign Affairs* 9(October), www.foreignaffairs.com/articles/china/2014-10-09/not-so-empty-talk (accessed June 14, 2017).

Ferdinand, Peter (2016) 'Westward ho – the China Dream and 'one belt, one road': Chinese Foreign Policy under Xi Jinping', *International Affairs* 92(4), pp. 941–957.

Fontaine, Richard and Mira Rapp-Hooper (2016) 'How China Sees World Order', *The National Interest* (May–June), http://nationalinterest.org/feature/how-china-sees-world-order-15846 (accessed June 14, 2017).

Foot, Rosemary (2000) *Rights Beyond Borders: The Global Community and the Struggle over Human Rights in China* (Oxford: Oxford University Press).

Gillespie, Sandra (2004) 'Diplomacy on a South-South Dimension: The Legacy of Mao's Three-Worlds Theory and the Evolution of Sino-African Relation', in Hannah Slavik (ed.) *Intercultural Communication and Diplomacy* (Malta and Geneva: DiploFoundation), pp. 109–130, www.diplomacy.edu/sites/default/files/IC%20and%20Diplomacy%20%28FINAL%29_Part8.pdf (accessed June 14, 2017).

Glaser, Bonnie S. and Evan S. Medeiros (2007) 'The Changing Ecology of Foreign Policy-Making in China: The Ascension and Demise of the Theory of China's "Peaceful Rise"', *China Quarterly* 190(June 2007), pp. 291–310.

Goh, Evelyn (2005) 'Nixon, Kissinger, and the "Soviet Card" in the U.S. Opening to China, 1971–1974', *Diplomatic History* 29(3) (June 2005), pp. 475–502.

Griswold, Daniel (2007) 'The Competition for World Resources: China's Demand for Commodities', Speech February 8 (Washington, DC: CATO Institute), www.cato.org/publications/speeches/competition-world-resources-chinas-demand-commodities (accessed June 14, 2017).

Guo, Baogang and Guo Sujian (2010) 'Introduction: Thirty Years of China-U.S. Relations: Reappraisal and Reassessment', in Guo Baogang and Guo Sujian (eds.) *Thirty Years of China-U.S. Relations* (Lanham: Rowman and Littlefield Publishers), pp. 1–17.

Jiang, Hezi and Qingyun Wang (2015) 'Nation to Contribute More to UN Budgets', *China Daily* (December 25), http://english.gov.cn/news/top_news/2015/12/25/content_281475260295906.htm (accessed June 14, 2017).

Kelly, David (2017) 'The "China Solution": Beijing Responds to Trump', *The Interpreter* (February 17) (Sydney: Lowy Institute), www.lowyinstitute.org/the-interpreter/china-solution-beijing-responds-trump (accessed June 14, 2017).

Kim, Samuel S. (1980) 'Mao Zedong and China's Changing World View', in C. Hsiung and S.S. Kim (eds.) *China in the Global Community* (New York: Praeger), pp. 16–39.

Kim, Samuel S. (1999) 'China and the United Nations', in Elizabeth Economy and Michel Oksenberg (eds.) *China Joins the World: Progress and Prospects* (New York: Council on Foreign Relations Press), pp. 42–89.

Lawrence, Susan V. and Michael F. Martin (2013) *Understanding China's Political System*, CRS Report for Congress 7–5700 (March 20) (Washington, DC: Congressional Research Service), https://fas.org/sgp/crs/row/R41007.pdf (accessed June 14, 2017).

Lee, Paul S.N. (2016) 'The Rise of China and Its Contest for Discursive Power', *Global Media and China* 1(1–2), pp. 102–120, http://journals.sagepub.com/doi/pdf/10.1177/2059436416650549 (accessed June 1, 2017).

Levine, S.I. (1989) 'Chinese Foreign Policy in the Strategic Triangle', in J.T. Dreyer and I.J. Kim (eds.) *Chinese Defence and Foreign Policy* (New York: Paragon House), pp. 63–86.

Levine, Steven I. (1992) 'China's Global Role', *Problems of Communism* (May–June), pp. 145–151, www.unz.org/Pub/ProblemsCommunism-1992may-00145 (accessed June 14, 2017).

Li, Cheng and Lucy Xu (2014) 'Chinese Enthusiasm and American Cynicism Over the "New Type of Great Power Relations"', Brookings China-US Focus (December 4), www.brookings.edu/research/opinions/2014/12/05-chinese-pessimism-american-cynicism-great-power-li-xu (accessed June 14, 2017).

Lynch, Colum (2016) 'China Eyes Ending Western Grip on Top UN Jobs With Greater Control over Blue Helmets', *Foreign Policy* (October 2), http://foreignpolicy.com/2016/10/02/china-eyes-ending-western-grip-on-top-u-n-jobs-with-greater-control-over-blue-helmets/ (accessed June 14, 2017).

Mizokami, Kyle (2014) 'Peace Ark: Onboard China's Hospital Ship', *USNI News* (July 23), https://news.usni.org/2014/07/23/peace-ark-onboard-chinas-hospital-ship (accessed June 14, 2017).

National Development and Reform Commission and Ministry of Foreign Affairs and Ministry of Commerce of the People's Republic of China (2015) *Vision and Actions on Jointly Building Silk Road Economic Belt and 21st-Century Maritime Silk Road* (March 28), http://en.ndrc.gov.cn/newsrelease/201503/t20150330_669367.html (accessed June 14, 2017).

Panda, Ankit (2014) 'Reflecting on China's Five Principles, 60 Years Later', *The Diplomat* (June 26), http://thediplomat.com/2014/06/reflecting-on-chinas-five-principles-60-years-later/ (accessed May 4, 2017).

Paradise, James F. (2009) 'China and International Harmony: The Role of Confucius Institutes in Bolstering China's Soft Power', *Asian Survey* 49 (July/August)(4), pp. 647–669.

Perlez, Jane (2015) 'China Surprises U.N. With $100 Million and Thousands of Troops for Peacekeeping', *The New York Times* (September 28), www.nytimes.com/interactive/projects/cp/reporters-notebook/xi-jinping-visit/china-surprisesu-n-with-100-million-and-thousands-of-troops-for-peacekeeping (accessed April 4, 2017).

Phillips, Tom, Fiona Harvey and Alan Yuhas (2016) 'Breakthrough as US and China Agree to Ratify Paris Climate Deal', *The Guardian* (September 3), www.theguardian.com/environment/2016/sep/03/breakthrough-us-china-agree-ratify-paris-climate-change-deal (accessed June 14, 2017).

Poulain, Ann-Sophie, Christl De Landtsheer and Lieuwe Kalkhoven (2014) 'The Arabic Spring in the Eyes of Chinese Political Leaders: A Critical Discourse Analysis of Chinese Political Rhetoric', *Politics, Culture and Socialization* 1, pp. 82–100.

Ross, Robert (ed.) (1993) *China, the United States, and the Soviet Union: Tripolarity and Policy Making in the Cold War* (New York: M.E. Sharpe).

Rudolf, Moritz et al. (2014) 'Chinas Schatten-Außenpolitik: Parallelstrukturen fordern die internationale Ordnung heraus', *China Monitor* 18(23 September) (Berlin: MERICS), www.merics.org/fileadmin/templates/download/china-monitor/China_Monitor_No_18.pdf (accessed June 1, 2017)

Shi, Li (2013) 'Propagating China to the World: China's "Public Diplomacy through Media" Strategy in the Age of Globalization', *gnovis*, April 26, 2013, www.gnovisjournal.org/2013/04/26/propagating-china-to-the-world-chinas-public-diplomacy-through-media-strategy-in-the-age-of-globalization/ (accessed June 1, 2017).

Summers, Tim (2014) *China's Global Personality*, Research Paper, June (London: Chatham House Asia Programme), www.chathamhouse.org/sites/files/chathamhouse/field/field_document/20140617ChinaGlobalPersonalitySummers.pdf (accessed April 12, 2017).

United Nations Division for Ocean Affairs and the Law of the Sea (2013) 'Declaration and Statements – China', www.un.org/depts/los/convention_agreements/convention_declarations.htm#China%20Upon%20ratification (accessed April 18, 2017).

United Nations Secretary General (2017) 'Mr. Jean-Pierre Lacroix of France – Under-Secretary-General for Peacekeeping Operations', Statements, February 14, www.un.org/sg/en/content/sg/personnel-appointments/2017-02-14/mr-jean-pierre-lacroix-france-under-secretary-general (accessed May 4, 2017).

United Nations Treaty Collection, 'Chapter IV Human Rights – 3. International Covenant on Economic, Social and Cultural Rights', https://treaties.un.org/Pages/ViewDetails.aspx-?src=IND&mtdsg_no=IV-3&chapter=4&clang=_en (accessed May 4, 2017).

United Nations Treaty Collection, 'Chapter IV Human Rights – 4. International Covenant on Civil and Political Rights', https://treaties.un.org/Pages/ViewDetails.aspx?src=IND&mtdsg_no=IV-4&chapter=4&clang=_en (accessed May 4, 2017).

Wang Jianwei (1999) 'Managing Conflict: Chinese Perspectives on Multilateral Diplomacy and Collective Security', in Yong Deng and Fei-Ling Wang (eds.) *In the Eyes of the Dragon: China Views the World* (Lanham: Rowman and Littlefield Publishers), pp. 73–96.

Wang Xiangwei (2014) 'Towards a New Order, Xi Jinping Touts Asia-Pacific Dream', *South China Morning Post* (November 17), www.scmp.com/news/china/article/1641627/towards-new-order-xi-jinping-touts-asia-pacific-dream (accessed June 14, 2017).

Wang Yi (2017) 'Zhongguo tese daguo waijiao gongjian kaituo zhi nian'/'China's Diplomacy in 2016: Blazing New Paths and Making New Progress', *Guoji Wenti Yanjiu* 1, pp. 1–10.

The White House Office of the Press Secretary (2014) 'U.S.–China Joint Announcement on Climate Change', Beijing, November 12, https://obamawhitehouse.archives.gov/the-press-office/2014/11/11/us-china-joint-announcement-climate-change (accessed June 14, 2017).

Wilson, Jeanne L. (2009) 'Coloured Revolutions: The View from Moscow and Beijing', *Journal of Communist Studies and Transition Politics* 25(2–3), pp. 369–395.

Xi Jinping (2012) 'Achieving Rejuvenation Is the Dream of the Chinese People', in Xi Jinping (ed.) *The Governance of China* (Beijing: Foreign Languages Press), pp. 37–39.

Xi Jinping (2014) 'New Approach for Asian Security Cooperation' (speech held on May 21) in Xi Jinping (ed.) *The Governance of China* (Beijing: Foreign Languages Press), pp. 389–386.

Xi Jinping (2015) 'Remarks by H.E. Xi Jinping President of the People's Republic of China at the Opening Ceremony of the Second World Internet Conference' (December 16), www.fmprc.cn/mfa_eng/wjdt_665385/zyjh_665391/t1327570.shtml (accessed June 13, 2017).

Xi Jinping (2017) 'Jointly Shoulder Responsibility of Our Times, Promote Global Growth', Keynote Speech at the Opening Session of the World Economic Forum in Davos (January 17), https://america.cgtn.com/2017/01/17/full-text-of-xi-jinping-keynote-at-the-world-economic-forum (accessed June 14, 2017).

Xinhua News (2016) 'CPC Central Committee with Xi as "core" leads China to Centenary Goals' (October 28), http://news.xinhuanet.com/english/2016-10/28/c_135785846.htm (accessed June 14, 2017).

Yan Xuetong (2014) 'From Keeping a Low Profile to Striving for Achievement', *The Chinese Journal of International Politics* 7(2) (Summer), pp. 153–184.

Zhang Jialin (1994) *China's Response to the Downfall of Communism in Eastern Europe and the Soviet Union* (Stanford: Hoover Institution on War, Revolution and Peace).

Zheng Bijian (2005) 'China's "Peaceful Rise" to Great-Power Status', *Foreign Affairs* 84 (September/October) 5, www.foreignaffairs.com/articles/asia/2005-09-01/chinas-peaceful-rise-great-power-status (accessed June 1, 2017).

Zhou Hong and Hou Xiong (eds.) (2017) *China's Foreign Aid. Sixty Years in Retrospect* (Singapore: Springer).

Zoellick, Robert B. (2005) 'Whither China: From Membership to Responsibility? Remarks to National Committee on U.S.-China Relations', *New York City* (September 21) (Washington, DC: US Department of State), https://2001-2009.state.gov/s/d/former/zoellick/rem/53682.htm (accessed June 14, 2017).

Chapter 7

Russia's resurgent political identity

Peter Eltsov

Since the collapse of the Soviet Union, American presidents have persuaded them-selves that the successor of the USSR, the Russian Federation, is little more than a 'weak regional power', as Barack Obama declared in March 2014 after the annex-ation of Crimea, with scant ability to alter global trends. It is long past time to acknowledge that these assessments have been wrong. Today, Russia's resurgent

FIGURE 7.1 Russian President Vladimir Putin and Metropolitanv Panteleimon of Yaroslavl and Rostov at the Kremlin in Moscow, Russia

imperial might is visible worldwide – especially in the Middle East and Europe, but also since Russia's interference in the 2016 US presidential election in the Americas.

It is also long past time to figure out a long-term strategy for dealing with a resurgent, autocratic Russia – one that harks back to February of 1946, when American diplomat George Kennan sent from Moscow to Washington what came to be known as the Long Telegram. It was an approximately 5000-word text that offered a profound explanation of Soviet Russia and provided simple yet wise advice on dealing with this difficult-to-understand and in many ways frightening society. In light of the current anti-Russian hysteria in the media, what is badly needed is, in effect, a new and sober explanation of Russia, showing the essential elements of this society, where Russia is headed and how the West can work with Russia not only under Putin but also under his successors.

The best current policy is a combination of strategic patience and realpolitik that acknowledges that harsh truth about today's Russia. It is not, as presently constituted, going to become a democracy, not under Vladimir Putin or even his successor, whoever that might be (not even if the Kremlin's young opponent Alexy Navalny were to become president). While the US needs to stand for its interests and allies, it must also realise that it is useless and counterproductive to ostracise Russia over its aggressive behaviour and autocratic policies. That is only a recipe for exacerbating what has already become a new Cold War, one that may be even more dangerous than the original due to the existence of several hegemonic powers and unpredictable non-state actors.

This new Cold War has an ideological side: a struggle between globalised liberalism and nationalistic authoritarianism. The US needs to work hard at keeping this war cold and not hot. FDR worked with Stalin because he had to do so. The same must go today for Washington's approach to Vladimir Putin and whoever follows him. Sanctions (except for individual ones under the Magnitsky Act) are unlikely to bring desired results. Conversely, they are likely to create more anti-American sentiments both in Russia and Europe. Pushing Russia into a corner will only aggravate the already brewing 'Weimar syndrome' – a burning sense of defeat and humiliation after Soviet Union's defeat in Cold War I – alienating not only the Kremlin but the Russian people. As occurred in post–World War I Germany, when a sense of national injustice over the treaty of Versailles and weakness and chaos in the Weimar government precipitated a right-wing reaction and ultimately the rise of the Nazis, the post–Cold War backlash in Russia was fired by a nationalistic sense of injury.

The bleak underlying reality of US–Russia relations today is that there is much support for an authoritarian regime inside Russia. Russia can become a democracy arguably only if the very composition of the country changes – in other words, if it disintegrates into various constituent states. There are many reasons for this grim assessment, and they require a close examination of Russian history, starting with the tripartite dictum 'Orthodoxy, Autocracy, Nationality', formulated in 1832 by then Minister of Public Education Sergey Uvarov as an antithesis to the famous motto of the French revolution: 'Liberté, Égalité, Fraternité'.

The first two traits in Uvarov's triad are fairly straightforward. Church was an innate part of the state under czars. 'To weaken people's faith', wrote Uvarov, 'is like depriving them of their blood and tearing out their hearts'. The minister meant, of course, exclusively the Russian Orthodox Church, while ignoring all other religions practiced in the empire. Autocracy, according to Uvarov, was likewise the 'main condition for the political existence of Russia in its current form', the 'cornerstone', on which 'the Russian colossus' rested (Uvarov, 2014a, pp. 104–105).

The third trait in Uvarov's triad – *narodnost'* – is more ambiguous. The word 'nationality' does not render it properly. Deriving from *narod* (Russian: a folk, a people), it can be explained as the necessity by Russians to maintain and cherish their language, traditions, history and values. 'Nothing but the Russian spirit is the source of our state foundation, that keystone, on which the throne and the altar firmly stand', writes Uvarov in a report to Nicholas I on Slavic nationalist movements (Uvarov, 2014b, p. 80). *Narodnost'*, to Uvarov, is all about the leading role of the titular nationality – the Russians – in all planes of imperial existence.

This chapter extends Uvarov's dictum to eight pillars that help to explain Russia's political culture over centuries.

Pillar 1: autocracy

Intellectuals and politicians in the West fail to understand that autocracy in Russia is still more natural than democracy, both among the elites and the ordinary people, and this has deep cultural roots (Berdiaev, 1946; Karamzin, 1959, 1991; Keenan, 1986; Pipes, 1974; Yanov, 1981). Consider the view of Fyodor Dostoevsky, who is seen around the world as a writer who plumbed the depths of Russia's soul. Shortly before his death, Dostoevsky wrote in his diary: 'To the people the Czar is the incarnation of themselves, their whole ideology, their hopes and beliefs . . . there is in Russia no creative, protective and leading force other than this live organic bond of the people with their Czar, from which everything is derived' (Dostoevsky 1954, pp. 1032–1033).

Today, many in Russia, including its top public intellectuals, agree with Dostoevsky, only their 'czar' has become Vladimir Putin. 'I believe that the restoration of monarchy, either formally or informally, is the only choice for Russia, since it is the only way to restore the sanctity of the supreme power', said pro-Kremlin political scientist Stanislav Belkovsky in 2005 (www.apn.ru/news/article6389.htm). Even in the 1990s, the period seen as the acme of post-Soviet democratic fervor, Russia's democrats under the guidance of Boris Yeltsin had plans to restore monarchy.

Most recently, Natalya Poklonskaya, a deputy of the Russian parliament and a former attorney general of annexed Crimea, has tried to forbid the forthcoming Russian film *Matilda*, which narrates a story of love between young Nicholas II and Russian ballerina Matilda Kseshinskaya. Poklonskaya has even threatened to file criminal charges against the director of the film, Aleksei Uchitel, for the alleged public defamation of Russia's ruler Nicholas II.

Czarist nostalgia permeates the highest echelons of power. Putin's favourite Russian philosophers are Konstantin Leontiev (1831–1891) and Ivan Ilyin (1883–1954). Both are very popular in modern Russia. Ilyin's remains were even brought back from Switzerland to be reburied in Moscow under the personal patronage of the Russian president. Both Leontiev and Ilyin were fascinated with autocracy. In a magisterial work, *Byzantinism and Slavdom*, Leontiev professed that 'neither a Polish revolt not a peasant rebellion could cause Russia as much damage as could be caused by a very peaceful, very lawful constitution' (Leontiev, 1885, Vol. 1, pp. 100–101). Just like Uvarov, Leontiev believed that the foundation of Russia was in the sacred union of the people, the czar and the Orthodox Church.

Half a century later, Ivan Ilyin became mesmerised with fascism. In 1933, in an essay titled 'National Socialism: A New Spirit', Ilyin compared democracy with writer's block and said that Hitler gave Europe a huge favour by saving it from Bolshevism. 'While Mussolini leads Europe and Hitler leads Germany, European culture gets a break', wrote Ilyin (1933, p. 2). Even after the war, when the atrocities of the Nazis became publicly known, Ilyin called fascism a complex and multifaceted phenomenon, within which 'one finds elements of health and illness, old and new, protections and destruction' (Ilyin, 1956: Vol. 1, p. 70). At that time, Ilyin expressed solidarity with Francisco Franco and Antonio Salazar, wishing that Russia be ruled by a dictator when Bolshevism ends – a wish that came true under the leadership of Vladimir Putin.

The key point of these developments is simple yet politically crucial: autocracy has been and still is so important in Russian culture that it would be almost more honest, if the Kremlin reinstated monarchy officially. With the exception of Boris Yeltsin's election as the first president of Russia in June of 1991, it is autocracy – either czarist or Soviet – that has always provided Russia with a mechanism for the transfer of power. For the world, this way Russia would be more predictable as the heirs to the throne would be known.

Pillar 2: exceptionalism

Vladimir Putin has called American exceptionalism a dangerous ideology. In an op-ed published by the *New York Times* on September 11, 2013, Putin addressed the American people and blamed the US government for maintaining the ideology of exceptionalism. 'It is extremely dangerous to encourage people to see themselves as exceptional, whatever the motivation', wrote Putin.

> There are big countries and small countries, rich and poor, those with long democratic traditions and those still finding their way to democracy. Their policies differ, too. We are all different, but when we ask for the Lord's blessings, we must not forget that God created us equal.
>
> (Putin, 2013)

Putin was being disingenuous in the extreme. In reality, Russia's elites are convinced of Russia's own exceptional and messianic role in history. Moreover, today, as never before, Russia's elites are merging all forms of Russian exceptionalism: Moscow the Third Rome (Stremoukhoff, 1953; Toumanov, 1955; Poe, 2001; Østbø, 2016), Slavophilia (Walicki, 1975; Rabow-Edling, 2006; Engelstein, 2009), Soviet Socialism (Lewin, 2005; Suny, 2010), Eurasianism (Laruelle, 2008; Laruelle and Akcali, 2015; Bassin and Pozo, 2017) and most recently the Russian World (Laruelle, 2015) – a concept that is meant to unite the Russian speaking people living outside of Russia in the countries of the former Soviet Union. The Russian people support this nationalist revival. According to the 2017 Levada poll, 64 per cent of the respondents in Moscow believe in the special mission of the Russian people. For comparison, in 1992 only 13 per cent of the Muscovites answered this question positively (www.bbc.com/russian/media-42454795).

Obviously, Russia is not unique in producing ideologies of exceptionalism and messianism. The US has a particularly strong tradition of exceptionalism (Roberts and DiCuirci, 2013; Lechner, 2017). However, there are fundamental differences between these two types of exceptionalism. First, American exceptionalism is based on liberalism and individualism, while Russian exceptionalism promotes authoritarianism and collectivism. Second, American exceptionalism no longer justifies annexations of foreign lands while Russian exceptionalism does. Most importantly, for the first time in its history, Russian exceptionalism has combined all of its expressions from the two seemingly irreconcilable yet in reality complementary ideologies: czarism and communism. A great symbolic example of this paradoxical continuity is the reestablishment by the Kremlin of the order of 'The Hero of Labor' that was previously called 'The Hero of Socialist Labor'. The golden Soviet star of the new order is the same, yet instead of the hammer and sickle it is now embossed with the double-headed eagle – a symbol of the Russian Empire.

The reality is that today, yet again, Russia has an imperial ideology that purports to provide a global alternative to liberalism. The ideology can be defined as enlightened autocracy that combines the traits of fascism, socialism, nationalism, imperialism and Orthodox Christianity. This ideology is much in line with what Russian philosopher Alexander Dugin calls the Fourth Political Theory, the first three being liberalism, socialism and fascism. Dugin suggests removing materialist and atheistic features from socialism and racist and nationalist aspects from fascism, thus creating a new authoritarian alternative to liberalism (Dugin, 2012).

Following this ideology, today Russia seeks to execute full-scale revenge after the defeat in the Cold War. 'To create a new image of Russia . . . means to participate in the ongoing remaking of the world and to execute velvet revenge after the defeat of our country in the Third World War, the Cold War', wrote Piotr Shchedrovitsky and Efim Ostrovsky (1999) in a polemical piece, published prior to the new confrontation between Russia and the West.

Pillar 3: expansionism

The Russian writer Alexander Prokhanov says that the annexation of Crimea by Russia marked the rebirth of the Russian Empire. The Russian state, according to Prokhanov, is 'imperial in a sense that it is a symphony, it is a union of spaces, it is a union of peoples, cultures, faiths and languages' (http://discussio.ru/politics/proxanov-krym-i-donbass-eto-vozrozhdenie-imperii). Prokhanov is right in the sense that given her size and multi-ethnic composition, Russia, in its current borders, can exist only as an empire: with a highly centralised autocratic government and a perpetual tendency for expansion. The only other option is territorial fragmentation in the manner experienced by other empires: British, Ottoman or Austro-Hungarian.

Russia has not reconciled with its past (LeDonne, 1996; Plokhy, 2017). The resurgent imperial models – such as recently reinvented Eurasianism and the Russian world – transcend the borders of the Russian federation, justifying territorial expansion. If Crimea is Russia, Eastern Ukraine, Belarus, Kazakhstan, Moldova and even the Baltic states could be Russia as well. Neither the Russian people nor the Russian government know exactly what Russia is geographically.

A popular Russian TV commentator, Sergey Kurginyan, says that the purpose of his life is to bring back the USSR (https://pozneronline.ru/2009/05/5541/). Commentator Mikhail Leontiev (reportedly one of Putin's favourites) says Russia should conquer the three Baltic states (http://www.geopolitika.lt/?artc=2981). Aleksey Pushkov, the head of the Foreign Affairs Committee at the State Duma, threatens Ukraine with a full-scale war if the US supplies Ukraine with arms (http://zn.ua/WORLD/pushkov-ugrozhaet-evrope-voynoy-esli-ssha-vooruzhit-ukrainu-bbc-166575_.html). Dmitry Rogozin, Russia's deputy prime minister, whose duty is to oversee Russia's defence industry, bluntly states that wherever the Russian people shed their blood and sweat, they have a full right to reclaim these lands (Rogozin, 2006, p. 33).

There is even evidence that the Kremlin has interest in the ideas of German reactionary thinkers associated with Nazism – such as Friedrich Ratzel (1897, 1901–1902), Karl Haushoffer (1925, 1935, 1939) and Carl Schmitt (1922, 1933, 1950). One of the pro-Kremlin ideologues, Alexander Filippov (2006), does not even hide his fascination with Carl Schmitt, discussing the ideas of the latter in a volume that includes the writings by Vladimir Putin and Dmitry Medvedev. Filippov pays particular attention to Schmitt's definition of sovereignty through the ability of a leader to announce the state of emergency, the notorious German concept of *ausnahmezustand*, which was used to justify Hilter's advent to power (Schmitt, 1922). Filippov does not mention Schmitt's whole-hearted endorsement of Nazism.

Shortly before the collapse of the Soviet Union, Alexander Solzhenitsyn, the Nobel Prize–winning author, best known for the writings that exposed the horrors of the Soviet labour system, included Ukraine, Belarus and most of Kazakhstan (Southern Siberia, in Solzhenitsyn's words) into his definition of Russia (Solzhenitsyn, 1990, 1991). It is known that Vladimir Putin has great respect for the writer. What if this plan is on the mind of Russia's leader?

Pillar 4: historical primordialism

Today, the issue of the beginning of Russia's history – when and where it started – has become especially political (Plokhy, 2006). For example, Russia's military actions in Ukraine are directly affected by the question of who owns the historical legacy of Kyivan Rus, a state that existed between the 9th and 13th centuries AD. Russians call Kyiv 'the mother of Russian cities' and Kyivan Rus 'the cradle of Russian civilization'. Prince Vladimir (958–1015), who baptised Kyivans into Orthodox Christianity, is seen in Russia as the spiritual father of the nation, while both the Ukrainian language and identity are considered late and artificially created phenomena.

Many distinguished Russian intellectuals have embraced this one-sided and deeply nationalistic version of history. 'All the talk of a separate Ukrainian people existing since something like the ninth century and possessing its own non-Russian language is recently invented falsehood', stated bluntly Alexander Solzhenitsyn (1991, p. 14). The Russian government forcefully promotes this version of history. On 4 November 2014, at a meeting with young historians, Vladimir Putin spoke of ancient Rus as the first Russian state (https://www.youtube.com/watch?v=JsqaZ6wB9d0&t=428s). In summer of 2015, the 1000-year anniversary of the death of Prince Vladimir was celebrated in Moscow on grand scale with Putin throwing a gala reception for several hundred guests in the Kremlin. On the same occasion, Moscow authorities decided to erect a giant statue of Prince Vladimir, while Russia's Ministry of Education and Science, together with the Russian Orthodox Church and one of Moscow's universities, sponsored a conference with a provocative title 'Prince Vladimir: The Roots of Wisdom, the Lessons of Statehood, and the Principles of Spirituality'.

Even a more frightening aspect of the abuse of history in Russia is the revitalisation of 'the Aryan Question'. 'Our fatherland has a great past. A branch of the Aryan tribe came down from the Carpathian mountains, peacefully settled the Great Russian Plain and Siberia (the coldest part of the planet), reached the Pacific Ocean, founded Fort Ross, absorbed the best from the most lavish cultures of Byzantium, Europe, and Asia, defeated the most terrifying enemy of humankind, Nazism, and opened the road to space', writes Viacheslav Nikonov, a high-profile member of the Russian parliament on the website of the Russian parliament, the State Duma (https://echo.msk.ru/blog/ym4/1299092-echo/). Notably, Nikonov happens to be a grandson of Viacheslav Molotov, Stalin's foreign minister, who is best known for signing a treaty with Hitler's foreign minister, Joachim von Ribbentrop, that divided Eastern Europe into the spheres of influence laying grounds for World War II. Ribbentrop stood trial at Nuremberg and was hanged for war crimes. Molotov lived until 1986, never expressing any remorse about his role in launching the war.

There are numerous historical examples that demonstrate vividly that aggressive interference of the state into the writing of history – when only one version is taken as the correct one – sparks nationalist fervor that, in turn, leads to war. Russia's current meddling with the past is frightening at the least.

Pillar 5: worship of the military past

The worship of its military past is a defining trait of Russian national consciousness (Carleton, 2017). 'Those who come to us sword in hand will die by the sword. On that Russia stands and forever will we stand', says Prince Alexander Nevsky after the battle with the Teutonic knights in a 1938 film directed by Sergey Eisenstein with a score by Sergey Prokofiev. There is no historical evidence that the prince of Novgorod ever said these words. However, they became proverbial, illustrating Russia's iron will to defeat its enemies. At the historic parade on the Red Square on 7 November 1941, when Nazi troops were approaching Moscow, Joseph Stalin evoked Alexander Nevsky as an example of patriotism.

Three historic themes are particularly important to the Russian military psyche: the Mongols, Napoleon and Nazism. It was Russia, according to its mainstream historians, that saved the world from each of these evils, almost single-handedly. President Putin has revived and strengthened this narrative, and it is a keystone of his popularity. Even the Soviet propaganda did not rely so heavily on its military history.

For example, today Russian children read of Russia's victory over Napoleon, but this reading is largely inaccurate. Clearly, other nations that participated in the defeat of Napoleon's army – particularly Spain and the UK – deserve equal recognition (Fraser, 2008; Muir, 1996). While in exile on the Island of Saint Helena, Napoleon confessed that it was the war in Spain that was 'the first cause of the misfortune of France' (Alison, 1835–1842, p. 607). Conversely, Russia's government is of an opinion that Russia not only defeated Napoleon on its territory but that it liberated the rest of Europe. At the 200-year anniversary of the battle of Borodino that took place near Moscow in 1812, the then-prime minister Putin stated that Russia's resistance to Napoleon not only changed the course of Napoleon's Russian adventure but also played a decisive role in the liberation of Europe. 'It was here that the fate of Europe and the future of its peoples were decided', said Putin (https://www.you tube.com/watch?v=B4kTFXp5FqA).

World War II is by far the most important part of the Russian military narrative. However, Russia has not reconciled with its role in it. Having divided Eastern Europe on par with Nazi Germany in 1939, the Soviet Union holds full responsibility for launching this war (Snyder, 2010). Under Mikhail Gorbachev, the Soviet authorities, for the first time, admitted this dark side of their history. However, the current Russian government reversed the interpretation and made it the key element of resurgent Russian nationalism. Russia's minister of culture, Vladimir Medinsky, calls the infamous German-Soviet Military Parade in Brest-Litovsk, which on 22 September 1939 marked the division of Poland between Hitler and Stalin, 'an official withdrawal of German troops under the supervision of Soviet officers' (https://pozneronline.ru/2012/11/3580/). Defending his minister, Vladimir Putin says that the Nazi-Soviet Pact 'made sense in terms of guaranteeing the Soviet Union's security' (https://www.youtube.com/watch?v=QBtGKScm-10). Putin also implicitly claims that Nazi Germany could be defeated by Russia alone – even without former Soviet republics, such as Ukraine (https://www.youtube.com/watch?v=K 0FJge8nDxM). Notably, Joseph Stalin, who led the Soviet Union through the war, held a very different opinion. According to Nikita Khrushchev (2004–2007: Vol. 1, pp. 638–639), among his inner circle, Stalin 'stated bluntly that if the United States had not helped', the Soviet Union would have lost. Khrushchev, who himself had leading positions in the Soviet government during World War II, agreed with Stalin's interpretation.

Today, as never before, the dogmatised and perverted narratives of Russia's wars are used by the Russian government to consolidate the people against the imagined enemy, the West, led by the US. The alleged desire of the West to partition Russia is presented by the Russian government as the main national security threat, thus diverting the attention of Russian citizens from their potential concerns with their own government.

Pillar 6: glorification of suffering

Westerners are often mystified by the willingness of Russians to accept the primacy of the state in their lives, and the extent to which even opponents of the regime accept their alienation from the political process. Russian fatalism is expressed the best in one uniquely Russian form of disenfranchisement – the tradition of holy foolishness (*yurodstvo*). Although this phenomenon existed and exists in other cultures, in Russia it has played a role so important that it can be seen as a foundational principle for the formation of both the Russian national character and the Russian political system (Panchenko, 1984; Thompson, 1987; Lunde, 1995; Ivanov, 2005; Hunt and Kobets, 2011).

Holy fools are ascetics who play the madman in public, yet in most cases they are mentally healthy. In fact, some holy fools are highly intelligent people. Panchenko even uses the word 'intelligentsia' when describing them (Panchenko, 1984). Holy foolishness is a tradition that spans hundreds of years and is fully revived today in examples of seemingly outrageous protests like the songs of Pussy Riot and performance acts by Piotr Pavlensky. Pavlensky is known for a series of bizarre performances such as sewing his mouth in support of Pussy Riot, lying naked wrapped in barbed wire in front of the Legislative Assembly in St Petersburg and nailing his testicles to the stone pavement in front of Lenin's Mausoleum on the Red Square. More recently, on 9 November 2015, Pavlenksy set fire to the entrance door to the notorious Lubyanka building (the headquarters of the KGB and the FSB) – an act of performance titled 'Threat'. Finally, on 16 October 2017, Pavlensky set the entrance of the Bank of France on the Place de la Bastille in Paris on fire. Calling his act 'Lighting', Pavlensky said it was aimed to commemorate the Paris Commune – a revolutionary government which took over Paris for 72 days in the spring of 1871.

It is much of the Russian literature, music and art that teaches the Russian people to carry their cross, finding happiness in suffering and preventing Russia from changing its political system. In Dostoevsky's *Crime and Punishment*, the murderer Rodion Raskolnikov and the prostitute Sonya Marmeladova find peace and love in a Siberian prison camp. In a famous final scene, Raskolnikov falls at Sonya's feet, cries and embraces her knees. Dostoevsky narrates: 'They wanted to speak, but could not; tears stood in their eyes. They were both pale and thin; but those sick pale faces were bright with the dawn of a new future, of a full resurrection into a new life. They were renewed by love; the heart of each held infinite sources of life for the heart of the other' (Dostoevsky, 1917, p. 557).

President Putin himself praises this tradition of suffering, which supposedly elevates Russians above Westerners spiritually. In January 2013, he poked fun at Americans for their materialism, ridiculing Scarlett O'Hara's famous line from *Gone with the Wind*: 'I will never be hungry again'. 'Take Scarlett O'Hara from "Gone with the Wind" for instance. She says "I'll never be hungry again"', he told an interviewer. 'This is the most important thing for her. Russians have different, far loftier ambitions, more of a spiritual kind; it is more about your relationship with God. We have different visions of life'. 'The Russian people have other tasks', said Putin, 'There is something moving beyond the horizon; something spiritual; something connected to God' (https://www.youtube.com/watch?v=DBhoNz66L8E).

In other words, the Russian people, according to Putin, will endure any hardships, such as economic sanctions and war – and, certainly, political disenfranchisement. Putin appears to have read his people correctly, at least for the time being and with regards to a significant part of population. Many Russians indeed are fatalistic about their lot, conceiving of and engaging in politics in a demonstratively hands-off manner.

Pillar 7: orthodoxy

Since the fall of the Soviet Union, the Russian Orthodox Church has regained its role in the cultural and political life of Russia (Burgess, 2017; Mitrofanova, 2005). Today, the Russian Church has a direct influence on the decision making of the Russian state. The church has helped Putin's government to consolidate power, to adopt anti-liberal policies and even to expand Moscow's sphere back into the former Soviet bloc. Accordingly, thanks to his conservative policies – especially, the anti-gay legislation and the decriminalisation of domestic violence – Putin has gained the reputation of a 'Lion of Christianity' among Christian fundamentalists in the West, such as Bryan Fischer or Franklin Graham in the US.

The concept of 'Holy Rus' is particularly illustrative (Aksakov, 1864; Cherniavsky, 1958; Likhachev, 1992). This concept was widely used in Russian literature, including the works of Alexander Pushkin, Nikolai Gogol and Fyodor Dostoevsky. It was also visualised in the paintings of Russian artist Mikhail Nesterov (1862–1942), who joined the Union of the Russian People (URP), a radical nationalist and monarchist organisation best known for instigating brutal pogroms against Jews in the Russian Empire (Klier and Lambroza, 1992; Strickland, 2013). After the fall of the Soviet Union, the idea of Holy Rus is being used by Russia's public figures, most frequently by the official representatives of the Russian Orthodox Church.

Some recent developments show how frightening the political implications of this concept are. After a visit to Ukraine in 2009, the Russian Patriarch Kirill published a book *Holy Rus: Together or Apart*, in which he stated bluntly that 'Holy Rus' comprised not only Russia but both Ukraine and Belarus (Kirill, 2009). In 2010, during a visit to Moldova, Patriarch Kirill went further by including Moldova (an Orthodox but not Slavic post-Soviet state) into this notion. 'Holy Rus', said Kirill, 'is neither an ethnic, nor a political, nor a linguistic idea. It is a spiritual idea. When we pray with our brothers and sisters from Moldova, we do not see any difference. We are one people under God'. Kirill ended his statement with an explicitly political endorsement: 'Today, we are praying for Moldova, for the prosperity of the Moldovan people, and that the political orientation of Moldova would facilitate the preservation of the unity of Holy Rus' (www.patriarchia.ru/db/text/1254808.html). Evidently, what Kirill meant is that politically Moldova needs to stay in Moscow's orbit.

Among the reasons for the annexation of Crimea by Russia, Putin named the alleged sacredness of Khersones, an extinct Crimean city, which, according to Putin, is as sacred to the Russians as the Temple Mount in Jerusalem to Jews and Muslims. In a speech on the occasion of the annexation of Crimea by Russia delivered on 18

March 2014, Putin said: 'Everything in Crimea speaks of our shared history and pride. This is the location of ancient Khersones, where Prince Vladimir was baptized. His spiritual feat of adopting Orthodoxy predetermined the overall basis of the culture, civilization and human values that unite the peoples of Russia, Ukraine, and Belarus' (http://en.kremlin.ru/events/president/news/20603).

The choosing of Khersones as a symbol of Russian nationhood is an example of the blatant abuse of religion for political purposes, which could not be further from the truth. Khersones was founded by Greek colonists around the 6th century BCE and, for the most part of its history, was part of the Greco-Roman world (Khapaev and Zolotarev, 2008). For some period of time, between the 10th and 13th centuries, it may have fallen under the control of Kyivan princes, but historians still argue when and how this happened (Beliaev, 2009). When in 1773 Catherine the Great brought Crimea into Russia's imperial orbit, the city no longer existed. It had gone extinct by the end of the 15th century.

The conclusion is grim. Today, the Russian Orthodox Church actively interferes in Russia's politics, including Russia's military operations. In this context, the war in Ukraine can even be seen – at least, to an extent – as a religious war.

Pillar 8: the nationalities issue

Under free and fair elections, Russia would lose some of its territories or fully disintegrate. The main reason for this is that Russia's shared national identity does not encompass its entire population. The Russian state – czarist, Soviet and post-Soviet – failed to create a national identity that would be shared by all of its citizens (Kappeler, 1992; Martin, 2001; Sulashkin, 2008; Kolstø and Blakkisrud, 2016). This means that a significant segment of the population in Russia (about 20 per cent, or 30 million) may not have allegiance to the Russian state. Moreover, owing to the Soviet administrative reforms that followed the Leninist principle of national self-determination, these people have their own autonomous republics: Tatarstan, Chechnya, Ingushetia, Bashkortostan, Buryatia, and such. As the Chechen insurgency of the turn of the 21st century shows (Galeotti, 2014), these republics pose a threat to Russia's territorial integrity – a 'time-bomb' or an 'atomic bomb' underneath Russia, according to Vladimir Putin (https://www.youtube.com/watch?v=5K va3HjoTeM; https://www.youtube.com/watch?v=Rg-D7okfj2c).

The demographics are not very encouraging for ethnic Russians either. There are some stunning studies that predict that by 2050 ethnic Russians will represent only one half of the population of Russia (Laruelle, 2016). Under free elections, Russia may even experience regional separatism from ethnic Russians living in resource-rich areas. After the fall of the Russian Empire in 1917, there were attempts to create independent states in Siberia, the Far East, the Urals and Kuban. After the fall of the Soviet Union in 1991, there were talks of Russian separatism in the Urals and Siberia. The Kremlin knows if the control of the central government weakens, Russia thus may experience separatism both from her ethnically Russian and non-Russian populations that will eventually lead to the collapse of the new-old Russian Empire. This is the reason why the Russian government has recently outlawed any attempts of separatism, criminalising even public discussions on the issue.

This being said, it is likely that Russia will either lose some of its autonomous regions or disintegrate within the next two or three generations. Some empires take decades to collapse, some centuries. In a sense, the beginning of the end of the Russian Empire was the abdication of the throne by Czar Nicholas II in 1917. After a bloody civil war, the Bolsheviks managed to resuscitate the empire for 70-odd years under a different ideological umbrella. Today, the Russian government is doing the same, trying to create a seemingly unthinkable symbiosis of Romanov's and Leninist Russia. However, due to its demographics and nationalities issues – especially, owing to the Leninist administrative reforms that resulted in the creation of autonomous republics for non-Russian ethnic groups within Russia – the new-old Russian Empire is doomed. The disintegration of former Yugoslavia provides a grim yet illuminating example of how it will happen: Josip Broz Tito introduced administrative divisions in a way very similar to that of the Soviet governments. Evidently, it is impossible to determine when exactly the Russian Empire will cease to exist. Yet it is highly unlikely that it will outlive the Soviet Union.

Why America needs to work with Russia

In his inaugural address, President Donald Trump spoke these words: 'We will seek friendship and good will with the nations of the world – but we do so with the understanding that it is the right of all nations to put their own interests first. We do not seek to impose our way of life on anyone, but rather to let it shine as an example for everyone to follow' (https://www.whitehouse.gov/briefings-statements/the-inaugural-address/). If implemented, this political philosophy would mark a major change in American foreign policy. It would put an end to humanitarian interventionism and democracy promotion, marking a concession that democracy cannot not be planted everywhere by force.

Trump's words are reminiscent of the advice given by George Kennan, who pointed out in the Long Telegram how important it was for America to deal with its own internal problems first. Kennan asserted that every measure to 'solve the internal problems of our own society' would be 'a diplomatic victory over Moscow worth a thousand diplomatic notes and joint communiqués' (Kennan, 1969, p. 708). As the last presidential elections show, today US society is divided as it has not been since the time of the civil rights and anti-war movements in the 1960s. So, the US needs to take this advice very seriously. With regards to Russia, this means that the US should drop any strategy that is aimed at turning Russia into a democracy. Since the 16th century, Russia has been an autocratic empire with a deeply messianic and expansionist identity. Vladimir Putin did not create the new Russia that is currently demonised in the West. Putin returned Russia to doing business as usual.

The world has been able to deal with such a Russia for more than 500 years, occasionally even prevailing over it in war. Likewise, the best strategy for now is to accept it. While defending their interests and deterring Russia, the US, EU and NATO should even work with it in the directions where they can: for example, in military operations against ISIS. Eventually the new-old Russian Empire will cease to exist. Putin is right that by creating ethnically defined territorial divisions within Russia, Lenin laid a time bomb underneath it.

The only way to prevail in the current Cold War is to win the hearts and minds of the Russian people. Given the history of the last quarter of a century marked by failed humanitarian interventionism and the rise of anti-Americanism throughout the world, it is not an easy task. Yet one thing is clear. Economic sanctions will not help: the examples of Iran, Cuba and North Korea demonstrate this vividly. Cold War I was won not because of sanctions but because the Russian people, including some individuals in the highest echelons of the Soviet government, lost faith in their ideology, turning their aspirations towards the West. The only sanctions that should stay in place are those that are imposed on individuals (such as prescribed by the Magnitsky Act). It would even make sense to extend these sanctions on the families of these individuals, prohibiting their children, wives, cousins and parents-in-law to live, study and own properties in the West.

First and foremost, the US needs to talk to and work with the Russian leadership on a regular basis. Good personal relations between the US and Russian presidents would be an asset. Leo Tolstoy famously wrote that leaders of genius are those who penetrate the meaning of history and the will of their people. In spite of revolutionaries such as Vladimir Lenin and reformers such as Mikhail Gorbachev, Russia has so far miraculously and consistently resuscitated its imperial self. Whether we like it or not, Vladimir Putin, in the view of his numerous supporters, is the ideal leader – the one who, according to them, penetrated the meaning of history and understood their will. Taking this into account, the US must foster direct and open lines of communication with Russia's leadership and political elites on a regular basis. This approach is not an appeasement; it is realpolitik. The US and EU need a strategy that would balance between strategic patience and offensive realism, using quid pro quo deals on a regular basis.

Acknowledgements and disclaimer

This chapter is a short version of the author's forthcoming book. The author is thankful to Michael Hirsh, Klaus Larres and Amanda Lindsey. The views expressed in this chapter are those of the author and do not reflect the official policy or position of the National Defense University, the Department of Defense or the US government.

Further reading

Bassin, Mark and Gonzallo Pozo (eds.) (2017) *The Politics of Eurasianism: Identity, Popular Culture and Russia's Foreign Policy* (London: Lanham).
Berdiaev, N.A. (1946) *The Russian Idea* (New York: Macmillan).
Burgess, John P. (2017) *Holy Rus: The Rebirth of Orthodoxy in the New Russia* (New Haven: Yale University Press).
Carleton, Gregory (2017) *Russia: The Story of War* (Cambridge: The Belknap Press of Harvard University Press).
Clover, Charles (2017) *Black Wind, White Snow: The Rise of Russia's New Nationalism* (New Haven: Yale University Press).

Dugin, Alexander (2012) *The Fourth Political Theory*. With the introduction by Alain Soral (London: Arktos Media Ltd.).

Hunt, Priscilla and Svitlana Kobets (eds.) (2011) *Holy Foolishness in Russia: New Perspectives*. (Bloomington: Slavica Publishers).

Kappeler, Andreas (2001) *The Russian Empire: A Multiethnic History*, translated by Alfred Clayton (London: Routledge).

Keenan, Edward (1986) 'Muscovite Political Folkways', *Russian Review* 45(2), pp. 115–181.

Kolstø, Pål and Helge Blakkisrud (ed.) (2016) *The New Russian Nationalism: Imperialism, Ethnicity, and Authoritarianism* (Edinburgh: Edinburgh University Press).

Laruelle, Marlène (2008) *Russian Eurasianism: An Ideology of Empire* (Washington, DC: Woodrow Wilson Center Press).

Laruelle, Marlène and Emel Akcali (eds.) (2015) *Eurasianism and the European Far Right: Reshaping the Europe-Russia Relationship* (London: Lanham).

Laruelle, Marlène and Jean Radvanyi (2018) *Understanding Russia: The Challenges of Tranformation* (Lanham, Maryland: Rowman & Littlefield).

Leatherbarrow, William and Derek Offord (eds.) (2010) *A History of Russian Thought*. (Cambridge: Cambridge University Press).

Lucas, Edward (2014) *The New Cold War: Putin's Russia and Threat to the West* (New York: Palgrave Macmillan).

Martin, Terry (2001) *The Affirmative Action Empire: Nations and Nationalism in the Soviet Union, 1923–1939* (Ithaca: Cornell University Press).

Østbø, Jardar (2016) *The New Third Rome: Readings of a Russian Nationalist Myth* (Stuttgart: ibidem-Verlag).

Perrie, Maureen, Dominic Lieven, and R.G. Suny (eds.) (2006) *The Cambridge History of Russia*. In 3 volumes (Cambridge: Cambridge University Press).

Pipes, Richard (1974) *Russia under the Old Regime* (New York: Scribner).

Pipes, Richard (1994) *Russia under the Bolshevik Regime* (New York: Alfred Knopf).

Plokhy, Serhii (2006) *The Origins of the Slavic Nations: Premodern Identities of Russia, Ukraine, and Belarus* (Cambridge: Cambridge University Press).

Plokhy, Serhii (2017) *Lost Kingdom: The Quest for Empire and the Making of the Russian Nation* (New York: Basic Books).

Poe, Marshall (2001) 'Moscow, the Third Rome: The Origins and Transformations of a "Pivotal Moment"', in *Jahrbücher für Geschichte Osteuropas* (Neue Folge, Bd. 29, H. 3), pp. 412–429.

Solzhenitsyn, A.I. (1991) *Rebuilding Russia: Reflections and Tentative Proposals*. Translated and annotated by Alexis Klimoff (New York: Farrar, Straus, and Giroux).

Suny, Ronald G. (2010) *The Soviet Experiment: Russia, the USSR, and the Successor States*, 2nd ed. (Oxford: Oxford University Press).

Thompson, Ewa M. (1987) *Understanding Russia: The Holy Fool in Russian Culture* (Lanham: University Press of America).

Walicki, Andrzej (2015) *The Flow of Ideas: Russian Thought from the Enlightenment to the Religious-Philosophical Renaissance*. Translated by Jolanta Kozak and Hilda Andrews-Rusiecka; Editorial Work by Cain Elliott (Frankfurt am Main: Peter Lang) [(2005) *Zarys myśli rosyjskiej od oświecenia do renesansu religijno-filozoficznego* (Kraków: Wydawnictwo Uniwersytetu Jagiellońskiego)].

Bibliography

Aksakov, Ivan (1864) 'Gde ogranicheskaia sila Rossii', *Den* 1864(40), October 3, pp. 1–4.

Alison, Archibald, Sir (1835–1842) *History of Europe from the Commencement of the French Revolution in 1789 to the Restoration of the Bourbons in 1815*. In 10 volumes (Edinburgh: W. Blackwood and Sons).

Bassin, Mark and Gonzallo Pozo (eds.) (2017) *The Politics of Eurasianism: Identity, Popular Culture and Russia's Foreign Policy* (London: Lanham).

Beliaev, S.A. (ed.) (2009) *Ocherki po Istorii Khristianskogo Khersonesa* (Sankt-Peterburg: Aliteia).

Berdiaev, N.A. (1946) *Russkaia ideia: osnovnye problemy russkoi mysli XIX veka in nachala XX veka* (Parizh: YMCA); translation by R.M. French. (1947) *The Russian Idea* (New York: Macmillan).

Burgess, John P. (2017) *Holy Rus: The Rebirth of Orthodoxy in the New Russia* (New Haven: Yale University Press).

Carleton, Gregory (2017) *Russia: The Story of War* (Cambridge: The Belknap Press of Harvard University Press).

Cherniavsky, Michael (1958) ' "Holy Russia": The Study of the History of an Idea', *The American Historical Review* 63(3), pp. 617–637.

Dostoevsky, F.M. (1917) *Crime and Punishment*. Translated by Constance Garnett (New York: Collier and Son).

Dostoevsky, F.M. (1954) *The Diary of a Writer*. Translated and annotated by Boris Brasol (New York: George Braziller).

Dugin, Alexander (2012) *The Fourth Political Theory*. With the introduction by Alain Soral (London: Arktos).

Engelstein, Laura (2009) *Slavophile Empire: Imperial Russia's Illiberal Path* (Ithaca: Cornell University Press).

Filippov, Alexander (2006) 'Suverenitet kak politicheskii vybor', in N. Garadja (ed.) *Suverenitet: sbornik* (Moskva: Evropa), pp. 173–200.

Fraser, Ronald (2008) *Napoleon's Cursed War: Popular Resistance in the Spanish Peninsular War, 1808–1814* (London: Verso).

Galeotti, Mark (2014) *Russia's Wars in Chechnya, 1994–2009* (Oxford: Osprey Pub Co.).

Haushofer, Karl (1925) *Geographie und Weltmacht: eine Einführung in die Geopolitik* (Berlin: Grunewald, K. Vowinckel).

Haushofer, Karl (1935) *Geopolitische Grundlagen* (Berlin. Industrieverlag Spaeth & Linde).

Haushofer, Karl (1939) *Grenzen in ihrer Geographischen und politischen Bedeutung*. 2nd revised ed. (Heidelberg: K. Vowinckel).

Hunt, Priscilla and Svitlana Kobets (eds.) (2011) *Holy Foolishness in Russia: New Perspectives* (Bloomington: Slavica Publishers).

Ilyin, I.A. (1933) 'National-Socialism: A New Spirit', *Vozrozhdenie*. Paris, May 17, 1933, p. 2.

Ilyin, I.A. (1956) 'O Fashizme', in I.A. Ilyin (ed.) *Nashi zadachi: statii 1948–1954* (Parizh: Izdatelstvo obshche-voennogo soiuza, Vol. 1), pp. 70–72.

Ivanov, S.A. (2005) *Blazhennye Pokhaby: Kulturnaia Istoriia Yurodstva* (Moskva: Yazyki Slavianskikh Kultur).

Kappeler, Andreas (1992) *Russland als Vielvölkerreich: Entstehung, Geschichte, Zerfall* (München: Beck) [(2001) *The Russian Empire: A Multiethnic History*, translated by Alfred Clayton (London: Routledge)].

Karamzin, N.M. (1959) *Memoir on Ancient and Modern Russia*. A translation and analysis by Richard Pipes (Cambridge: Harvard University Press).

Karamzin, N.M. (1991) *Zapiska o drevnei i novoi Rossii v ee politicheskom i grazhdanskom otnoshenii. Predislovie, podgotovlenie teksta, primechaniia Yu. S. Pivovarova* (Moskva: Nauka).

Keenan, Edward (1986) 'Muscovite Political Folkways', *Russian Review* 45(2), pp. 115–181.

Kennan, George (1969) 'The Chargé in the Soviet Union (Kennan) to the Secretary of State', *Foreign Relations of the United States, 1946, Vol. VI, Eastern Europe, The Soviet Union* (Washington, DC: Government Printing House), pp. 696–709.

Khapaev, V.V. and M.I. Zolotarev (2008) *Khersones Tavricheskii v Mirovoi Istorii: Istoricheskie Ocherki* (Simferopol: Biznes-Inform).

Khrushchev, N.S. (2004–2007) *Memoirs of Nikita Khrushchev*, ed. Sergei Khrushchev, translated by George Shriver. In 3 volumes (University Park: Pennsylvania State University).

Kirill, the Patriarch of Russia (2009) *Sviataia Rus – Vmeste ili Vroz?* (Moskva: Danilov Muzhskoi Monastyr).

Klier, John D. and Shlomo Lambroza (eds.) (1992) *Pogroms: Anti-Jewish Violence in Modern Russian History* (Cambridge: Cambridge University Press).

Kolstø, Pål and Helge Blakkisrud (ed.) (2016) *The New Russian Nationalism: Imperialism, Ethnicity, and Authoritarianism* (Edinburgh: Edinburgh University Press).

Laruelle, Marlène (2008) *Russian Eurasianism: An Ideology of Empire* (Washington, DC: Woodrow Wilson Center Press).

Laruelle, Marlène (2015) *The 'Russian World': Russia's Soft Power and Geopolitical Imagination* (Washington, DC: Center on Global Interests).

Laruelle, Marlène (2016) 'How Islam Will Change Russia', *The Jamestown Foundation*, https://jamestown.org/program/marlene-laruelle-how-islam-will-change-russia/

Laruelle, Marlène and Emel Akcali (eds.) (2015) *Eurasianism and the European Far Right: Reshaping the Europe-Russia Relationship* (London: Lanham).

Lechner, Frank J. (2017) *The American Exception.* In 2 volumes (New York: Palgrave Macmillan).

LeDonne, John P. (1996) *The Russian Empire and the World, 1700–1917: The Geopolitics of Expansion and Containment* (Oxford: Oxford University Press).

Leontiev, K.N. (1885) 'Vizantizm i slavianstvo', in K.N. Leontiev (ed.) *Vostok, Rossiya, i Slavianstvo* (Moskva: Tipo-Litografiia I.N. Kushnera i Ko), Vol. 1, pp. 81–193.

Lewin, Moshe. (2005) *The Soviet Century* (London: Verso).

Likhachev, D.S. (1992) 'Sviataia Rus', in *Zhizneopisaniia Dostopamiatnykh Liudei Zemli Russkoi: X–XX vv* (Moskva: Moskovskii Rabochii), pp. 6–7.

Lunde, Ingunn (ed.) (1995) *The Holy Fool in Byzantium and Russia: Papers Presented at a Symposium Arranged by the Norwegian Committee of Byzantine Studies, 28 August 1993 at the University of Bergen* (Bergen: Universitetet i Bergen, Russisk Institut).

Martin, Terry (2001) *The Affirmative Action Empire: Nations and Nationalism in the Soviet Union, 1923–1939* (Ithaca: Cornell University Press).

Mitrofanova, Anastasia V. (2005) *The Politicization of Russian Orthodoxy: Actors and Ideas.* With a foreword by William C. Gay (Stuttgart: ibidem-Verlag).

Muir, Rory (1996) *Britain and the Defeat of Napoleon, 1807–1815* (New Haven: Yale University Press).

Østbø, Jardar (2016) *The New Third Rome: Readings of a Russian Nationalist Myth* (Stuttgart: ibidem-Verlag).

Ostrovsky, Efim and Pyotr Shchedrovitsky (1999) 'Rossia strana kotoroi ne bylo', *Soobshchenie*, http://soob.ru/n/1999/1/5/0; www.shkp.ru/lib/publications/71/print.

Panchenko, A.M. (1984) 'Smekh kak Zrelishche', in D.S. Likhachev, A.M. Pancheno, and N.V. Ponyrko. *Smekh v Drevnei Rusi* (Leningrad: Nauka), pp. 74–153; Translated as 'Laughter as Spectacle: Holy Foolishness in Old Russia', in P. Hund and S. Kobets (eds.) (2011) *Holy Foolishness in Russia: New Perspectives* (Bloomington: Slavica Publishers), pp. 41–147.

Pipes, Richard (1974) *Russia under the Old Regime* (New York: Scribner).

Plokhy, Serhii (2006) *The Origins of the Slavic Nations: Premodern Identities of Russia, Ukraine, and Belarus* (Cambridge: Cambridge University Press).

Plokhy, Serhii (2017) *Lost Kingdom: The Quest for Empire and the Making of the Russian Nation* (New York: Basic Books).

Poe, Marshall (2001) 'Moscow, the Third Rome: The Origins and Transformations of a "Pivotal Moment', in *Jahrbücher für Geschichte Osteuropas* (Neue Folge, Bd. 29, H. 3), pp. 412–429.

Putin, V.V. (2013) 'A Plea for Caution from Russia', *New York Times* (September 12, 1913), A31.

Rabow-Edling, Susanna (2006) *Slavophile Thought and the Politics of Cultural Nationalism* (Albany: State University of New York Press).

Ratzel, Friedrich (1897) *Politische Geographie* (München und Leipzig: R. Oldenbourg).

Ratzel, Friedrich (1901–1902) *Die Erde und das Leben: Eine vergleichende Erdkunde*. In 2 volumes (Leipzig un Wien: Bibliographisches Institut).

Roberts, Timothy and Lindsay DiCuirci (eds.) (2013) *American Exceptionalism*. In 4 volumes (London: Pickering and Chatto).

Rogozin, Dmitrii (2006) *Vrag naroda* (Moskva: Algoritm).

Schmitt, Carl (1922) *Politische Theologie: vier Kapitel zur Lehre von der Souveränität* (München und Leipzig: Duncker und Humblot) [(1985) *Political Theology: Four Chapters on the Concept of Sovereignty*. Translated by George Schwab (Cambridge: MIT Press)].

Schmitt, Carl (1933) *Der Begriff des Politischen* (Hamburg: Hanseatische Verlagsanstalt) [(1976) *The Concept of the Political*. Translation, introduction, and notes by George Schwab; with comments on Schmitt's essay by Leo Strauss (New Brunswick: Rutgers University Press)].

Schmitt, Carl (1950) *Der Nomos der Erde im Völkerrecht des Jus Publicum Europaeum* (Köln: Greven) [(2003) *The Nomos of the Earth in the International Law of the Jus Publicum Europaeum*. Translated and annotated by G.L. Ulmen (New York: Telos Press)].

Snyder, Timothy (2010) *Bloodlands: Europe between Hitler and Stalin* (New York: Basic Books).

Solzhenitsyn, A.I. (1990) *Kak nam obustroit Rossiiu: posilnye soobrazheniia* (Leningrad: Sovetskii pisatel).

Solzhenitsyn, A.I. (1991) *Rebuilding Russia: Reflections and Tentative Proposals*. Translated and annotated by Alexis Klimoff (New York: Farrar, Straus, and Giroux).

Stremoooukhoff, Dimitri (1953) 'Moscow the Third Rome: Sources of the Doctrine', *Speculum*. 28(1), pp. 84–101.

Strickland, John (2013) *The Making of Holy Russia: The Orthodox Church and Russian Nationalism before the Revolution* (Jordanville: Trinity Publications).

Sulashkin, S.S. (ed.) (2008) *Natsionalnaa identichnost Rossii i demograficheskii krizis: materialy II Vserossiiskoi nauchnoi konferentsii*. Moskva, 15 noiabria 2007 goda (Moskva: Nauchnyi ekspert).

Suny, Ronald G. (2010) *The Soviet Experiment: Russia, the USSR, and the Successor States*, 2nd ed. (Oxford: Oxford University Press).

Thompson, Ewa M. (1987) *Understanding Russia: The Holy Fool in Russian Culture* (Lanham: University Press of America).

Toumanoff, Cyril (1955) 'Moscow the Third Rome: Genesis and Significance of a Politico-Religious Idea', *The Catholic Historical Review* 40(4), pp. 411–447.

Uvarov, Sergey (2014a) 'O nekotorykh obshchikh nachalakh, mogushchikh sluzhit rukovodstvom pri upravlenii ministerstvom narodnogo prosveshcheniia', in Sost., pred., i comment. V.B. Trofimovoi, *Gosudarstvennye Osnovy* (Moskva: Institut Russkoi Tsivilizatsii), pp. 102–107.

Uvarov, Sergey (2014b) 'Doklad Imperatoru Nikolaiu I o Slavianstve', in Sost., pred., i comment. V.B. Trofimovoi, *Gosudarstvennye Osnovy* (Moskva: Institut Russkoi Tsivilizatsii), pp. 76–85.

Walicki, Andrzej (1975) *The Slavophile Controversy: History of a Conservative Utopia in Nineteenth Century Russian Thought*. Translated by Hilda Andrews-Rusiecka (Oxford: Clarendon Press) [(1964) *W kręgu konserwatywnej utopii: struktura i przemiany rosyjskiego słowianofilstwa* (Warszawa: Naukowe)].

Yanov, Alexander (1981) *The Origins of Autocracy: Ivan the Terrible in Russian History* (Berkeley: University of California Press).

Chapter 8

India[1]

Christian Wagner

The Indian Union belongs to the group of emerging and rising powers whose claims for greater representation and responsibility seem to shake up the post–World War II international order. Indian decision makers have always derived their global ambitions from their country's size, its international contributions and historic achievements. India's importance for global politics results from a number of factors.

First, with more than 1.3 billion people (2016) India is the second largest country with approximately one-sixth of the world population. Forecasts predict that India

FIGURE 8.1 Chhatrapati Shivaji Terminus railway station in Mumbai, India

will overtake China by 2030 (United Nations, 2015, p. 4). Hence, any solution in global policy areas such as climate, environment and energy will not succeed without India.

Second, despite all progress in the reduction of poverty in recent decades, India still has the largest number of poor people. In 2013, 224 million Indians lived below the poverty line of US$1.90 a day. Hence, India houses one in three of the poor worldwide (World Bank, 2016, p. 40). This means that the global fight against poverty, as laid out in the United Nations Sustainable Development Goals (SDG), will only succeed if decisive progress is achieved in India.

Third, India's liberalisation after 1991 has led to the rise of its middle class. The size of the middle class is a controversial issue with figures ranging from 50 to 150 million people. More recent studies have estimated the Indian middle class with 5 to 10 per cent of the population (Kharas, 2010; Meyer and Birdsall, 2012). But even the size of 65 to 130 million makes India's middle class an important factor in the global economy and for multinational companies both as consumer and service providers.

Finally, India perceives itself as the fastest growing democracy and G20 economy. With GDP growth rates of 7 per cent, India is going to surpass China, which has reduced its growth projections intentionally to lower levels. Prime Minister Modi's 'Make in India' campaign has underlined India's ambition to become a major manufacturing hub for the global economy.

But India's global aspirations are facing various challenges. First, its ambitions to become a growth engine of the global economy are hampered by the increasing discourse on protectionism in many developed countries. The success of India's aspirations depends on a liberal economic order which is increasingly challenged. Second, so far the Indian state has hardly been able to allocate adequate resources and capacities in order to pursue its self-proclaimed ambitions. This mismatch between global power ambitions and middle power resources is not only visible with regard to the development problems on the national level but it is also leaving its mark on the foreign policy. In order to shed some light on the prospects and limitations, the first part will deal with India's ideas for the international order and global politics. The second part will look at some foreign policy instruments. The third part will analyse India's behaviour in selected global governance institutions and regimes.

Ideas and interests

From the beginning, India's foreign policy was shaped by the anti-colonial and anti-imperialist discourse of the Indian National Congress when it achieved independence from Great Britain in August 1947. India was facing severe socio-economic challenges after independence and the partition with Pakistan. But India's first Prime Minister, Jawaharlal Nehru, who became the main architect for the country's foreign policy, also had a strong international outlook. He saw his country as one of the leading powers that would shape the international system after World War II along with the US, the Soviet Union and China (Nehru, 1946, p. 535). So Indian foreign policy was shaped both by national interests with regard to development and security and by the quest for great power status and the support of anti-colonial movements in other parts of the world.

Nehru pursued an independent foreign policy and sought collaboration in newly established international organisations in order to achieve these goals. India became a founding member of the United Nations in 1945 when the country was still under British rule. In spring 1947, even before independence, the Indian interim government held the first Asian Relations Conference that sought to increase Asia's role in international politics. In December 1947, Nehru decided to bring the Kashmir conflict that had erupted with Pakistan in October 1947 to the United Nations and he suggested the idea of a plebiscite to end the conflict.

India's interest in establishing global institutions became also visible in the economic sphere. India belonged to the 23 original signatories of the General Agreement on Tariffs and Trade (GATT), which established a global regime for trade in 1948. But domestically, the Indian government opted for a policy of import substitution so that the country's share in global trade declined in the following decades. India's 'mixed economy' resulted in only modest growth rates of an average of 3.5 per cent until 1991, which was not enough to overcome the problems of underdevelopment.

In the 1950s, the Indian government supported various anti-colonial movements in Africa and other parts of Asia in their anti-colonial struggle. The most decisive bilateral relationship was with China, which also had far reaching implications for India's foreign policy. Nehru had a strong interest in cooperating with China in order to increase Asia's role in international affairs. Nehru also tried to bring the new communist regime in China back to the international arena. In 1954, the treaty with China on Tibet laid out the five principles of peaceful coexistence (Panchsheel) that became the normative guideline for India's foreign policy: mutual respect for territorial integrity and sovereignty, non-aggression, non-interference in internal affairs, equality and mutual benefit and peaceful coexistence.

Nehru also became one of the main architects of the Non-Alignment Movement (NAM) that was established in 1961. Although the organisation failed to overcome the East–West antagonism, it underlined India's aspiration for a different global order.

India's great power ambitions were also pursued by Nehru's successors. In 1974, Prime Minister Indira Gandhi, Nehru's daughter who took office in 1966, decided for India's first nuclear test. Her main motivation was to seek recognition for India's global aspirations and to underline the country's technological capacities. Security concerns were of lesser importance since Pakistan had been defeated in the war in 1971. In the 1970s, India became one of the main representatives of the developing countries in the United Nations and was one of the main protagonists to promote a New International Economic Order (NIEO).

India's balance of payment crisis in 1991 brought an end to the mixed economy. The new government of Narasimha Rao initiated an economic liberalisation that paved India's way into the global economy. India became an attractive partner in the era of globalisation with rising inflows of foreign direct investments and high economic growth rates.

India's global ambitions have adapted to the new international constellations after 1991. Indian prime ministers have underlined the global ambitions of their country for instance by the quest to be 'one pole' in a future multipolar world order. The new international constellations have also increased India's attractiveness and the country has entered several strategic partnership agreements for instance with the US, Japan, France, Germany and the European Union (EU). One of the most important international agreements was the civilian nuclear deal with the US in 2005 that ended India's isolation in the nuclear field (Mistry, 2014).

India also became a founding member of the World Trade Organisation (WTO) that replaced the GATT and a member of the G20 which consists of the 20 most important global economies. The primacy of trade and economic ties with the industrial countries over balance of power politics was at the heart of the 'Manmohan doctrine' of Prime Minister Manmohan Singh, who headed the government of the United Progressive Alliance under the leadership of the Congress Party from 2004 to 2014 (Mohan, 2005). India also joined Brazil, Russia, China and South Africa to establish BRICS in 2009 as a new platform to pursue its interest on the global level (Saran and Rubin, 2013).

In 2015, Prime Minister Modi from the Bharatiya Janata Party (BJP) underlined again his country's global ambitions with his demand that India should be a leading power with a strong economy as its main foundation and not just a balancing force (Tellis, 2016, p. 3). With regard to influence in Asia, Foreign Secretary Jaishankar wanted India to be on par with China and the US (Jaishankar, 2015). He also laid out that India's 'foreign policy is dominated by the quest for capital, resources, technology, capabilities and best practices' (Jaishankar, 2016a).

The brief overview shows that Indian decision makers always had a clear understanding of their country being a great power and having a special role on the global level. They tried to position India in the international order despite the limited resources at their disposal. Since 1991, all prime ministers have tried to increase India's weight in the global economy both to initiate development at home and to strengthen their country's international position. Despite India's growing economic interdependence, its foreign policy is still guided by concepts of sovereignty and strategic autonomy, which can also be seen as synonyms for its great power aspirations (Khilnani et al., 2014; Bajpaj et al., 2014).

As for India's relations with China and Pakistan, Nehru's trust in multilateral institutions and diplomacy did not pay out. The UN resolutions on Kashmir did not bring a durable solution for the conflict and India's defeat in the border war of 1962 ended Nehru's hope for a closer collaboration with China.

Instruments

Nehru may have been an idealist on the international level but he was also able to pursue realist policies, especially concerning India's smaller neighbours in South Asia. A system of treaties and secret agreements gave India enormous influence in the Himalayan kingdoms and helped to safeguard its security interests vis-à-vis China.

But on the global level, India's weak economic foundation has limited its foreign policy options. Nehru's decision to pursue a mixed economy with the focus on import substitution in order to overcome underdevelopment was economically ineffective. Indira Gandhi and her son and successor Rajiv Gandhi already started economic reforms in the 1980s but it took the balance of payment crisis in summer 1991 to initiate a liberalisation that followed the strategies of the East Asian Tiger economies with the emphasis on integration into the global economy.

But despite high growth rates, which have even surpassed China in recent years, the benefits, for instance the achievements of its software and information technology, have hardly trickled down to the average Indian family. The country's rank on the Human Development Index (HDI) has shown only marginal improvement over the last 20 years. In 1993, India was ranked 135th, and it still ranked 130th in 2015. The middle class has expanded and India is now in the group of lower middle income countries. The per capita incomes have risen from US$350 (1991) to US$1600 (2015) (World Bank, no year). But inequality has also increased and India is still by far the poorest and most underdeveloped country of the BRIC group (Drèze and Sen, 2013, p. 66). The Indian state is still not able to penetrate its society and to extract the necessary resources for development (Tellis, 2016, p. 11). Hence India's tax to GDP ratio is only 16.6 per cent, which is much lower compared to other emerging economies and the OECD world (Sikarwar, 2016).

The limited state resources also have a negative impact on foreign policy. This is most obvious with regard to the small number of Indian diplomats. India's diplomatic corps consists of 912 diplomats of which one-third is posted in India, and the remaining two-thirds are posted in one of the 172 diplomatic missions abroad (Ministry of External Affairs, 2016, p. 337). The size of India's diplomatic service is similar to countries like Singapore and New Zealand, which have different international aspirations. The small human resource base and the weak economic foundation have led to weak delivery on the domestic as well as international level. Foreign policymakers have highlighted the problems of this weak delivery that has hampered time and again the outcome of India's international ambitions (The Hindu, 2004). Since several years, the government has initiated reforms in order to increase the capacities of the Foreign Service (Jacob, 2015).

Despite its weaknesses, the size of India's economy is also seen as an asset and an opportunity in the global competition. Its high GDP growth rates have attracted multinational companies and foreign direct investment. Institutional reforms initiated by the Modi government have improved India's position in the Ease of Doing Business Index from rank 130 to 100 in 2018. But India's manufacturing sector, which is meant to lead Prime Minister Modi's 'Make in India' campaign, has been stagnating since many years. The manufacturing share of the GDP was 16.2 per cent in 2015–16, which was even slightly below the level of 16.4 per cent in 1989–90 (Puri, 2017, p. 4). The industry lacks a skilled workforce in many areas, which also limits the country's attraction for international investors (Nageswaran and Natarajan, 2017, p. 18).

Since decades, India is one of the biggest beneficiaries of international development assistance (ODA). But it is much lesser known that India has also been a donor country since more than 50 years. Already in 1964, the Indian Technical and Economic Cooperation (ITEC) was established as the main instrument of India's goal to increase South–South collaboration. India has signed the Paris declaration of the Development Assistance Committee (DAC) of the Organisation for Economic

Co-operation and Development (OECD) as recipient but not as donor. From the view of Indian governments this would imply restrictions of national sovereignty that are not compatible with their international self-image. The bulk of the ITEC are scholarships and capacity building programs in various fields ranging from language courses to renewable energy.

The programs aim at bureaucrats, scholars, politicians and members of the armed forces from other developing countries. ITEC has probably contributed to India's leading role as a representative of the developing countries in international organisations. Until 2006–7 there were as many as 40,000 participants in these activities (Agarwal, 2007, p. 9). In 2013–14, India offered 8000 slots for the ITEC program (Ministry of External Affairs, 2014, p. 127). On the basis of these figures it can be calculated that more than 50,000 persons from developing countries have participated in these programs over the last 50 years. Moreover, India also gives financial support to other developing countries through grants and loans. But because the economic development lags behind China, India's financial assistance is much lower. Hence, the Indian government is not in a position to finance similar large-scale infrastructure projects like the Belt and Road Initiative (BRI) by China.

India has the second largest standing army with 1.2 million soldiers. India has two major territorial conflicts with its neighbours. The dispute with Pakistan over Kashmir was the reason for three (1947–8, 1965, 1999) of the four wars (1971) between the two countries so far (Ganguly, 2002; Cohen, 2013). The relationship between India and China is marred by the dispute over the border demarcation. The conflict escalated in 1962 when China defeated India in a short border war. Beyond these conflicts, India does not lay claim on other territories or maritime waters beyond its jurisdiction. Since 1974, India is a nuclear power and has developed its own nuclear deterrence outside the Non-Proliferation Treaty (NPT) (discussed later). India has never been part of a military alliance which is regarded as a restriction of national sovereignty. India is rapidly modernising its armed forces and was the largest importer of weapons even overtaking China and Pakistan between 2011 and 2015 (Fleurant et al., 2016, p. 6). Despite the extensive modernisation of its armed forces, the share of military expenditure in India's GDP has been between 2.5 to 3.0 per cent for many years.

In recent years, Indian governments have become increasingly concerned about China's encroachment in the Indian Ocean by port investments in Myanmar, Bangladesh, Sri Lanka and Pakistan. Indian security experts fear an encirclement by this 'String of Pearls' of Chinese posts. Since the late 1990s, Indian governments have promoted the concept of 'extended neighbourhood' as their zone of influence which ranges from East Africa to the Pacific Ocean (Scott, 2009; Mohan, 2012; Wadhwa, 2014). The government of Manmohan Singh has promoted India as a 'net security provider' in the Indian Ocean and the Modi government has increased economic, political and military cooperation with island states such as the Maldives, Mauritius and the Seychelles. The Indian navy has been enlarged in order to increase its power projection capabilities (Ladwig, 2010; Joshi, 2015; Jaishankar, 2016b).

Since the 1990s, India has also discovered soft power as a tool for foreign policy. In the global context, the Indian diaspora is a very important political and economic asset. The presence of two million Indians in the US, mostly highly skilled and affluent above the American average, has contributed to the improved relationship between the two countries. The presence of seven million Indian migrant workers in the Gulf who are vulnerable to regional crises poses new challenges for the evacuation capacities of the Indian armed forces as demonstrated in the Gulf War (1990), in Libya (2011) and in Yemen (2015). India has also invested in cultural institutions and programs in order to counter the growing Chinese presence. But India does not use its soft power resources for instance to promote its democracy as a model (Mohan, 2007; Muni, 2009; Wagner, 2009) but rather to gain a positive international image in the global competition for investment opportunities.

Institutions

Politics

India has always been a strong promoter of the United Nations. In 1950, the US offered India to join the UN Security Council (UNSC) as a permanent member and the Soviet Union repeated this offer in 1955. But Nehru refused both of these offers because he saw the entry of China to the UN as a much more important priority than his country getting a permanent seat in the UNSC (Harder, 2015, p. 12). In 1971, China finally became a member of the UNSC and increased its international position. Because India perceives itself to be on par with China and in order to underline its global aspirations, it has made persistent claims for a permanent seat in the UNSC since then. The Indian army has contributed to international peace and security since the 1960s and has become one of the largest contributors of armed personnel for UN peacekeeping missions.

In June 2015, Prime Minister Modi justified India's demand for a permanent seat with its demographic size and the complaint that the institution that was established after World War II did no longer reflect the international constellations of the 21st century (The Economic Times, 2015). So far, India stood 18 times as a candidate for a non-permanent seat but was only elected seven times to the Security Council, the last time for the period from 2010 to 2012. Although India is often seen as a representative of the developing countries, it does not have the support of regional organisations when it comes to the elections of non-permanent members (Mishra, 2012, p. 199). India has formed together with Germany, Japan and Brazil the Group of 4 (G4) in order to pursue a reform of the United Nations, which would also include an enlarged Security Council.

Even if the prospects of a UNSC reform may seem remote, India's global role has increased in recent years. One indicator is the growing number of strategic partnership agreements. India signed its first agreement of this kind in 1998 with France and has entered into probably more than 30 strategic partnership agreements since then. The MEA conceded that there is no official list and no indicators for strategic partners (Haidar, 2017). But despite the symbolic nature of the instrument, it indicates the aspirations of two countries for closer collaboration even if the signatures are not always followed by concrete programs. But India's strategic partnership agreements with the US, Japan, Germany, France, the UK, the European Union (EU) and many others developed countries indicate that they see India as an important partner in bilateral and global affairs.

Security

India has always refused to join the Non-Proliferation Treaty (NPT) that came into force in 1970, since it could only join the treaty as a non-nuclear weapon state. But this was not acceptable with India's international aspirations and its quest for equality with China. In direct reaction to India's test in 1974, the developed countries set up the Nuclear Suppliers Group (NSG) that enforced various sanctions against India's nuclear program, which also hampered the technological development. India's second tests in 1998 were followed by new sanctions.

In India, there is a strong national consensus against the NPT, which has established a 'nuclear apartheid' between the 'nuclear haves' and 'have nots'. But this remains an exclusive perspective in the international context because the NPT regime has one of the highest numbers of followers. Despite its opposition to the NPT, India has never pursued a policy of nuclear proliferation. After the tests in 1998, Indian politicians made it clear that India is following the main principles of the NPT even if the country is not willing to join the treaty in its present form.

The Indo-US nuclear agreement of 2005 brought an end to India's isolated position. The agreement pursued several goals. On the global level, India's involvement was meant to strengthen the non-proliferation regime. On the regional level, it promoted the collaboration between India and the US, especially vis-à-vis China. On the bilateral level, the agreement opened the door for multinational companies to set up new nuclear power plants, which should help to overcome India's energy shortage that is regarded as a major impediment for its economic development. India also aims for a membership in other multilateral export control regimes. Although China was blocking India's entry to the NSG because of geo-strategic considerations vis-à-vis Pakistan, India became a member of the Missile Technology Control Regime (MTCR) in 2016. India's efforts to join the Australia Group and the Wassenaar Arrangement underline its commitments to strengthen international arms control regimes.

India's biggest security concern is the fight against terrorism. India has been confronted with different terrorist groups for many years. The most serious challenge are attacks of religious militant groups, many of which are operating from Pakistan with the support of the Pakistani security agencies. Already in 1996, India took up the initiative for a Comprehensive Convention on International Terrorism (CCIT) in the United Nations (Ministry of External Affairs, 2016, p. xxi). India has supported all international efforts after 2001 and has reinforced the UN Global Counter Terrorism Strategy in 2006. During the period when India was an elected member in the UNSC between 2010 and 2012, the counterterrorism committee passed a resolution for zero tolerance against terrorists, for instance by not providing them safe havens (Kumar, 2012).

Economics

India has always endeavoured to increase its position in multilateral forums. In 2008–9, India successfully increased its weight in the World Bank and the International Monetary Fund (IMF). But these changes are still not implemented because the US Congress has not approved them so far. Much more important for India's global ambitions was the elevation to the G20. The finance ministers and central bank executives had initiated the new grouping after the Asian financial crisis in the late 1990s. In the context of the global financial crisis of 2008–9, the status of the G20 was enhanced and it has become the main platform for the heads of states of the 20 most important global economies.

In 2015, Prime Minister Modi declared that India will increase its share in global trade from 2.1 to 3.5 per cent and that it will double its exports to US\$900 billion by 2020 (Puri, 2017, pp. 6, 7). Although India is still not a very big player in the global economy despite economic liberalisation, export promotion and foreign direct investments, it has been very successful in pursuing its interests in the context of the World Trade Organisation (WTO). India has expanded its capacities and has forged a successful alliance with Brazil and China (Hopewell, 2015). India is regarded as a difficult negotiating partner by the developed countries. For many years, Indian and Western negotiators blamed each other for being 'moralising', 'instructive' and 'arrogant'. In international forums, the developed countries regard India as a 'naysayer' (Narlikar, 2011), 'agreement averse' (Cohen, 2002) or as a 'contrarian loner' (Perkovich, 2003).

In 2008, the Doha Round failed because of the opposition from India and China. In 2013, the Indian government refused its consent to the 'Bali Package' of the Doha Round because of regulations for the food security programs. The Indian government had passed a new food security bill in the same year which affected 75 per cent of the rural households and 50 per cent of the urban households. Prime Minister Modi, who took office in May 2014, made it clear that he was not willing to sacrifice food security and the interests of the poor for a trade pact (The Hindu, 2014). His government entered into separate negotiations with the US and was granted special concessions for its food security program, so that India finally gave its consent to the 'Bali Package' in November 2014 (Mehra, 2014).

Climate change

Although India has still a relatively small manufacturing sector, it is already the third largest emitter of greenhouse gases worldwide, after the US and China. Environmental damage and the pollution of air and water pose serious challenges to large parts of the population. In recent years, air pollution levels in Indian cities have become worse than in China and may diminish the life expectancy of 50 per cent of the population (Aggarwal, 2015, 2016). In 2008, the Indian government passed a national action plan to tackle the repercussions of climate change. India is heavily investing in renewable energies and the Modi government has started new programs, for instance for 'Smart Cities' and a cleaning of the Ganges River. But in the context of its 'Make in India' campaign with a focus on the manufacturing sector, the Modi government has also weakened environmental regulations in favour of economic development.

On the international level, Indian governments have always promoted the principle of 'common but differentiated responsibilities and respective capacities' (CBDR-RC) in international climate negotiations. For India, the developed countries are the main polluters and therefore have the major responsibility to tackle climate change. India's per capita CO_2 emissions were 1.6 (2013), which was much below the global average of 4.9 (World Bank, no year).

India has slowly changed its negotiation position in international regimes in recent years. In October 2015, India declared its Intended Nationally Determined Contribution (INDC) for the climate negotiations and agreed to reduce emission intensity and to enlarge the share of renewable energies. India did not block the Paris negotiations in 2015 but rather contributed to the consensus. Although it emphasised again the CBDR-RC principle, India did also accept the 1.5 degree goal of the Paris declaration and the review of national targets every five years, among other things (Byravan and Rajan, 2015; Rajamani, 2015).

Conclusions: India's gradual rise

India can be regarded as one of the main beneficiaries of the new international constellations after the end of the Cold War. Since then, India has experienced a gradual rise in different areas of international politics. Even if India's ambitions for a permanent seat in the UNSC will not materialise in the foreseeable future, it should not be overlooked that the increasing number of strategic partnership agreements indicate that many P5 members, developed countries and emerging powers want India to play a more important political role in global politics.

In the field of international security, the civilian nuclear agreement with the US has freed India from its isolated position and brought it closer to the NPT. Moreover, the deal opened the way for similar agreement for nuclear cooperation with other countries. Geo-strategically, the nuclear agreement bolstered the bilateral relations between the oldest and the largest democracy. From the US perspective, the support of India's rise is seen as an antidote against a more assertive China in the long term. But even China, India's long-time rival, has recognised that New Delhi will play a more important political role in global politics. In 2017, the White Paper of the Chinese government explicitly mentioned India as one of the major powers (State Council Information Office of the People's Republic of China, 2017). Despite their regional rivalries, both countries will enhance their collaboration in global institutions like BRICS and in regional organisations like the Shanghai Cooperation Organisation (SCO), which India joined together with Pakistan in 2017. Economically, increasing FDIs, Modi's 'Make in India' campaign and his success to improve India international ranking for doing business underline the government's commitments to integrate India in the global value chains. Being part of the G20 also emphasises the importance for India's economy for the global trade and financial system.

India's global ambitions are facing different challenges. First, it is not without irony that India, which has always been critical towards the liberal economic order before 1991, has benefitted from it afterwards. But recent technological developments, like increasing automatisation, and the new debate on protectionism, may thwart India's efforts to increase its role in the global economy. Hence, India should become a protagonist of the present liberal order and its multilateral institutions

(Puri, 2017, p. 5; Nayyar, 2017). But domestically, this will be a tightrope walk for every government because there has always been opposition against globalisation, both from the left parties and right-wing groups that are close to the ruling BJP. Second, despite all the improvements that the country has seen since 1991, India's global ambitions continue to suffer from the mismatch between the rhetorical claims and the resources and instruments available for pursuing its interests. Global aspirations are a costly endeavour with regard to human capacities, material resources and financial capabilities. Hence, it will remain an uphill task for all governments in New Delhi in the foreseeable future to push reforms at the domestic and the international level at the same time.

Note

1 The author thanks Claudius Engeling for his input to this chapter.

Further reading

Bajpai, Kanti, Saira Basit and V. Krishnappa (eds.) (2014) *India's Grand Strategy. History, Theory, Cases* (London/New Delhi: Routledge).
Ganguly, Sumit (2016) *Engaging the World. Indian Foreign Policy since 1947* (New Delhi: Oxford University Press).
Karnad, Bharat (2015) *Why India Is Not a Great Power (Yet)* (Oxford: Oxford University Press).
Khilnani, Sunil, Rajiv Kumar, Pratap Bhanu Mehta, Prakash Menon, Nandan Nilekani, Srinath Raghavan, Shyam Saran and Siddharth Varadarajan (2014) *Nonalignment 2.0. A Foreign and Strategic Policy for India in the Twenty-First Century* (New Delhi: Penguin Publications).
Malone, David M., C. Raja Mohan and Srinath Raghavan (eds.) (2015) *The Oxford Handbook on Indian Foreign Policy* (Oxford: Oxford University Press).
Mohan, Raja C. (2015) *Modi s World – Extending India's Sphere of Influence* (New Delhi: Harper Collins India).
Ogden, Chris (2014) *Indian Foreign Policy* (Cambridge: Polity Press).
Sikri, Rajiv (2013) *Challenge and Strategy. Rethinking India's Foreign Policy* (New Delhi, India: SAGE Publications India).

Bibliography

Aggarwal, Mayank (2015) 'Air Pollution in India Cutting 660 Million Lives Short by 3 Years' (February 21) www.livemint.com/Politics/lLrXlGTwTIQZ8DfydLSiQJ/Air-pollution-in-India-cutting-660-million-lives-short-by-3.html?utm_source=copy (accessed February 21, 2015).
Aggarwal, Mayank (2016) 'Indians Exposed to Higher Levels of Pollutants than Chinese: Study' (February 23), www.livemint.com/Politics/rDDvszborXdZWYQt9U5ioK/Indians-exposed-to-higher-levels-of-pollutants-than-Chinese.html (accessed February 23, 2016).
Agrawal, Subhash (2007) *Emerging Donors in International Development Assistance: The India Case* (International *Development* Research Centre (IDRC)).

Bajpai, Kanti, Saira Basit and V. Krishnappa (eds.) (2014) *India's Grand Strategy. History, Theory, Cases* (London/New Delhi: Routledge).

Byravan, Sujatha and Sudhir Chella Rajan (2015) 'At Paris, Something for Everyone', *The Hindu* (December 15), www.thehindu.com/opinion/op-ed/paris-agreement-at-paris-some thing-for-everyone/article7987957.ece (accessed December 15, 2015).

Cohen, Stephen P. (2002) *India. Emerging Power* (Washington, D.C.: The Brookings Institution).

Cohen, Stephen P. (2013) *Shooting for a Century: The India-Pakistan Conundrum* (Washington, DC: Brookings Institution Press).

Drèze, Jean and Amartya Sen (2013) *An Uncertain Glory. India and Its Contradictions* (London: Penguin Books).

The Economic Times (2015) 'India Deserves UNSC Permanent Membership, Says PM Narendra Modi' (June 8), http://economictimes.indiatimes.com/news/politics-and-nation/india-deserves-unsc-permanent-membership-says-pm-narendra-modi/articleshow/4757 8554.cms?prtpage=1 (accessed January 18, 2016).

Fleurant, Aude, Sam Perlo-Freeman, Pieter D. Wezeman and Siemon T. Wezeman (2016) 'Trends in International Arms Transfers 2015' (February) (Stockholm: SIPRI Fact Sheet), http://books.sipri.org/files/FS/SIPRIFS1602.pdf (accessed May 31, 2016).

Ganguly, Sumit (2002) *Conflict Unending. India-Pakistan Tensions since 1947* (Oxford: Oxford University Press).

Haidar, Suhasini (2017) 'Strategic Partners' Are Now Dime a Dozen', *The Hindu* (January 12), www.thehindu.com/news/national/%E2%80%98Strategic-partners%E2%80%99-are-now-dime-a-dozen/article17024245.ece (accessed January 12, 2017).

Harder, A. (2015) 'Not at the Cost of China: New Evidence Regarding US Proposals to Nehru for Joining the United Nations Security Council', Working Paper # 76, The Cold War International History Project (Washington, DC: Woodrow Wilson International Center for Scholars), www.wilsoncenter.org/publication/not-the-cost-china-india-and-the-united-nations-security-council-1950.

The Hindu (2004) 'Implementation of Foreign Policy Weak: Saran' (September 15), www.the hindu.com/2004/09/15/stories/2004091505161100.htm (accessed September 15, 2004).

The Hindu (2014) 'India Not Blocking Rule-Based Global Trade: Narendra Modi' (September 9), www.thehindu.com/news/national/india-not-blocking-rulebased-global-trade-narendra-modi/article6394311.ece (accessed September 9, 2014).

Hopewell, Kristen (2015) 'Different Paths to Power: The Rise of Brazil, India and China at the World Trade Organization', *Review of International Political Economy* 22(2), pp. 311–338.

Jacob, Happymon (2015) 'Brick and Mortar of Foreign Policy', *The Hindu* (June 12), www.thehindu.com/opinion/lead/brick-and-mortar-of-foreign-policy/article7306310.ece (accessed June 12, 2015).

Jaishankar, Dhruva (2016b) 'India's Military Diplomacy', in Sushant Singh and Pushan Das (eds.) *Defence Primer. India at 75* (New Delhi: Observer Research Foundation), pp. 18–24.

Jaishankar, S. (2015) 'India, the United States and China', *IISS-Fullerton Lecture* (July 20), www.iiss.org/en/events/events/archive/2015-f463/july-636f/fullerton-lecture-jaishankar-f64e (accessed February 28, 2017).

Jaishankar, S. (2016a) 'Opening Keynote: Aligning Business and Strategic Goals', *Gateway House* (June 13), www.gateway house.in/keynote-address-by-foreign-secretary-jaishan kar-at/ (accessed June 20, 2016).

Joshi, Shashank (2015) *Indian Power Projection. Ambitions, Arms and Influence*, Whitehall Papers 85 (London: Royal United Services Institute (RUSI)).

Kharas, Homi (2010) *The Emerging Middle Class in Developing Countries* (Paris: OECD Development Centre).

Khilnani, Sunil, Rajiv Kumar, Pratap Bhanu Mehta, Prakash Menon, Nandan Nilekani, Srinath Raghavan, Shyam Saran and Siddharth Varadarajan (2014) *Nonalignment 2.0. A Foreign and Strategic Policy for India in the Twenty First Century* (New Delhi: Penguin Publications).

Kumar, Keerthi Sampath (2012) *India's Past Year at the UN Security Council*, IDSA Comments (February 7) (New-Delhi: The Institute for Defense Studies and Analyses (IDSA)).

Ladwig, Walter III (2010) 'India and Military Power Projection. Will the Land of Gandhi Become a Conventional Great Power?', *Asian Survey* 50(6), pp. 1162–1183.

Mehra, Puja (2014) 'India-U.S. Deal Paves the Way for Global Trade Pact', *The Hindu* (November 13), www.thehindu.com/news/national/us-resolve-impasse-over-food-security-issues-at-wto/article6594065.ece (accessed February 23, 2016).

Meyer, Christian and Nancy Birdsall (2012) *New Estimates of India's Middle Class, Technical Note* (Washington, DC: Peterson Institute for International Economics, Center for Global Development).

Ministry of External Affairs (2014) *Annual Report 2013–2014* (New Delhi: Dolphin Printo-Graphics).

Ministry of External Affairs (2016) *Annual Report 2015–2016* (New Delhi: Dolphin Printo-Graphics).

Mishra, Saurabh (2012) 'India Amidst Increased Activity in the Security Council: A Few Observations', *Strategic Analysis* 36(2), pp. 198–205.

Mistry, Dinshaw (2014) *The US-India Nuclear Agreement: Diplomacy and Domestic Politics* (New Delhi: Cambridge University Press).

Mohan, Raja C. (2005) 'The Manmohan Doctrine', *The Daily Times* (February 28), www.dailytimes.com.pk/default.asp?page=story_28-2-2005_pg3_5 (accessed March 1, 2005).

Mohan, Raja C. (2007) 'Balancing Interests and Values. India's Struggle with Democracy Promotion', *The Washington Quarterly* 30(3), pp. 99–115.

Mohan, Raja C. (2012) *Samudra Manthan. Sino-Indian Rivalry in the Indo-Pacific* (Washington, D.C.: Carnegie Endowment for International Peace).

Muni, S.D. (2009) *India's Foreign Policy: The Democracy Dimension (With Special Reference to Neighbours)* (Delhi: Foundation Books).

Nageswaran, Anantha, V. and Gulzar Natarajan (2017) *Can India Grow? Challenges, Opportunities, and the Way Forward* (New Delhi: Carnegie Endowment for International Peace).

Narlikar, Amrita (2011) 'Is India a Responsible Great Power?' *Third World Quarterly* 32(9), pp. 1607–1621.

Nayyar, Dhiraj (2017) 'India's Asian integration strategy, East Asia Forum. Economics, Politics and Public Policy in East Asia and the Pacific', *East Asian Forum* (March 7), www.eastasiaforum.org.

Nehru, Jawaharlal (1946) *The Discovery of India* (Calcutta: Signet Press).

Perkovich, George (2003) 'Is India a Major Power?', *The Washington Quarterly* 27(1), pp. 129–144.

Puri, Hardeep Singh (2017) *India's Trade Policy Dilemma and the Role of Domestic Reform* (New Delhi: Carnegie Endowment for International Peace).

Rajamani, Lavanya (2015) 'Paris Triumph. The Climate Agreement Strikes a Fine Balance between Ambition, Differentiation and Finance', *The Indian Express* (December 16), http://indianexpress.com/article/opinion/columns/united-nations-paris-cliamte-agreement-triumph/ (accessed December 16, 2015).

Saran, Samir and Daniel Rubin (2013) 'BRICS and Mortar for India's Global Role', *The Hindu* (March 26), www.thehindu.com/opinion/op-ed/brics-and-mortar-for-indias-global-role/article4548094.ece (accessed March 27, 2013).

Scott, David (2009) 'India's "Extended Neighborhood" Concept: Power Projection for a Rising Power', *India Review* 8(2), pp. 107–143.

Sikarwar, Deepshikha (2016) 'Eco Survey 2016: Raise Taxpayers to GDP Ratio, Not Exemption Threshold', *The Economic Times* (February 27), http://economictimes.indiatimes.com/news/economy/policy/eco-survey-2016-raise-taxpayers-to-gdp-ratio-not-exemption-threshold/printarticle/51153610.cms (accessed February 28, 2016).

State Council Information Office of the People's Republic of China (2017) *China's Policies on Asia-Pacific Security Cooperation*, 1st ed. (Beijing: Foreign Language Press).

Tellis, Ashley J. (2016) *India as a Leading Power* (Washington, DC: Carnegie Endowment for International Peace). United Nations (2015) *World Population Prospects. The 2015 Revision, Key Findings and Advance Tables*, Working Paper No. ESA/P/WP.241 (New York: Department of Economic and Social Affairs, Population Division).

Wadhwa, Anil (2014) 'India's Extended Neighbourhood: Prospects and Challenges', Keynote Address at 6th IISS-MEA Dialogue on 'India's Extended Neighbourhood: Prospects and Challenges', March 4, (New-Delhi: Institute for Defence Studies and Analyses), www.idsa.in/keyspeeches/6thIISSMEADialogue_secretaryeast (accessed July 18, 2016).

Wagner, Christian (2009) *Promotion of Democracy and Foreign Policy in India*, SWP Research Paper 13/October (Berlin: Stiftung Wissenschaft und Politik).

World Bank (2016) *Poverty and Shared Prosperity 2016: Taking on Inequality* (Washington, DC: World Bank).

World Bank (no year) 'CO2 Emissions (Metric Tons Per Capita)', http://data.worldbank.org/indicator/EN.ATM.CO2E.PC (accessed March 1, 2017).

World Bank (no year) 'GNI Per Capita, Atlas Method (current US$)', http://data.worldbank.org/indicator/NY.GNP.PCAP.CD?locations=IN (accessed March 1, 2017).

Chapter 9

The European Union

Christian Schweiger

The European Union has undergone fundamental and dramatic internal and external changes throughout the past decade which have put its long-term future in doubt. Intergovernmental decision making in the European Council has gradually turned into an ineffective joint decision-making trap. This is the result of the growing diversity of national interests in the wake of successive enlargements. The EU

FIGURE 9.1 European flags outside the Berlaymont building in Brussels, Belgium

was therefore ill prepared for the major internal and external policy challenges it has been facing in recent years. Amongst these challenges were the eurozone sovereign debt crisis, Ukraine, Syria and the refugee crisis. With the UK's Brexit decision, the EU now even faces the unprecedented exit of a member state.

The progressively more obvious mismatch between political ambition and reality has undermined public trust in the EU's problem-solving capability. As EU institutions and policies have become more publicly scrutinised than in the past, citizens consider the way the EU operates increasingly as ineffective, technocratic and not sufficiently focused on addressing the concerns in their daily lives. Sixty years from the signing of the Treaty of Rome, which created the institutional foundations for the EU as we know it today, the EU is facing its most existential crisis. The crisis could ultimately lead to its demise if member states do not find the political determination to resolve the deepening legitimacy problem and reverse the growing trend towards the re-nationalisation of politics.

The decline of the permissive consensus: the EU's growing legitimacy problem

At no point since its onset has the process of institutionalised European integration been accompanied by substantial levels of public enthusiasm. Citizens have in principle always recognised the need for more collective action to tackle common problems. At the same time, the appetite for the transfer of political sovereignty to the EU institutional level remained limited. Up until the late 1980s public support for the creation of a political union was still relatively strong, with between 70 and just over 90 per cent of citizens in the then-nine member states supporting the notion of a 'United States of Europe' (European Commission, 1987, p. 27). This was effectively the honeymoon period of the integration process, which has been widely described as the era during which it was carried by a 'permissive consensus' (Hooghe and Marks, 2009, p. 5). Under the permissive consensus the general public had sufficient trust in political elites to make the right decisions on their behalf. Demands for direct participatory mechanisms consequently remained limited. The neofunctionalist school of European integration theory assumed that this trust would result in the gradual transfer of public loyalties towards the supranational institutional institutions, such as the Commission or the European Parliament. It was believed that this process of political spillover would ultimately result in the full harmonisation of political decision making (Haas, 1968, p. 317). Over time it however became clear that the generally elitist and remote decision-making processes of the European Community failed to inspire enthusiasm amongst the general public. The initially steady public support for the Community was grounded in rational utilitarianism rather than passionate cultural affection. The EC hence possessed formal legitimacy but struggled to build social legitimacy, in the form of lasting normative support for its values (Weiler, 1999, p. 180). In practice this meant that citizens considered the Community to be beneficial as long as it produced increasing returns in the form of effective collective policy solutions. This was reflected by the steadfast and growing public support for Community membership up until the early

1990s. Before the foundation of the European Union under the Maastricht Treaty, the average public support amongst member states for Community membership was steadily rising, from a modest 50 per cent in 1981 to just over 70 per cent in 1990 (European Commission, 1998, p. 18).

The existence of the permissive consensus was evident by the lack of public interest in direct participatory mechanisms. Most prominently this was shown in the low levels of public interest in the work of the European Parliament. At the time of election to the European Parliament in 1979 only two member states recorded majority public support in favour of a more important role for the EP (Ireland and Luxembourg, with 56 and 53 per cent, respectively). In the remaining seven member states, the general public remained openly indifferent to the EP, with only between 24 and 40 per cent of citizens advocating a more important role for the parliament in the future (European Commission, 1979, p. 19).

This was also reflected in the relatively low voter turnout during European Parliament elections. Even at the first European Parliament election in June 1979, average voter turnout only stood at just 61.9 per cent and subsequently continued to fall (European Parliament, 2017).

Maastricht became the turning point which marked the onset of the decline of the permissive consensus. Support for EU membership declined noticeably after the agonising and controversial public discussions that surrounded the ratification of the treaty in many member states. The gap between those that considered membership of the newly founded European Union to be beneficial and those that rated membership as non-beneficial narrowed substantially after 1992. In the late 1980s, over 60 per cent of the population in the member states on average had considered membership as beneficial. By 1992, this figure had dropped to less than 50 per cent and reached 40 per cent in 1996 (European Commission, 1998, p. 20). This showed that under the institutional setting of Maastricht the EU was starting to develop a serious legitimacy problem.

The decline of the permissive consensus in the EU had its roots in the combination of the growing public uneasiness with the ever more complex multi-level governance setting of the EU and the increasingly obvious constraints in the Council to produce effective policy solutions. The EU hence became squeezed between the new public focus on what is considered to be a profound democratic deficit in its decision-making architecture and its inability to tackle mounting internal and external challenges effectively. The tendency to 'muddle through' internal and external challenges manifested itself in frequently inconsistent policy decisions and the blurring of responsibilities for these decisions (Richardson, 2015, p. 26). The new euroscepticism, which emerged in the 1990s, however did not yet pose a systemic challenge to the EU. It remained on the level of what has been classified as 'inside' euroscepticism (Bruter, 2012, p. 26). This means that public scrutiny concentrated on specific policy areas and institutional developments without fundamentally challenging the purpose of European integration as such. This was nevertheless problematic as the EU's member states collectively turned out to be unable to address neither the democratic deficit problem, nor the lack of effective policymaking. This paved the way for an increasingly constrained consensus which ultimately risks turning into what has already been termed as a permanent 'constraining dissensus' (Hooghe and Marks, 2009, p. 6). This term refers to the growing gap between the priorities of the general public and those of the EU's political agenda determined by political elites. A lasting dissensus would ultimately fundamental question the purpose of the EU's existence.

The Council as an increasingly ineffective joint decision trap

Fritz W. Scharpf has pointed out that the EU lacks collective solidarity because member state governments are permanently forced to compromise on their national interests in what he branded as the 'joint decision trap' of the Council (Scharpf, 1988, p. 265). The result is the tendency to produce 'sub-optimal' supranational policies which fail to resolve major challenges (Scharpf, 1988, p. 271). Scharpf also points towards the obvious tendency of the joint decision trap to produce predominantly deregulatory policies in the area of market liberalisation, while positive policy harmonisation tends to remain limited (Scharpf, 1999). In most countries, except for the UK, the EU has therefore been perceived as a deregulatory force which is weak on the development of integrated policies. This perception of the EU as a force for negative integration has been augmented further under the adverse conditions of the eurozone sovereign debt crisis. The crisis in the eurozone had its origins in the collapse of parts of the financial industry in the US in 2008. The US crisis resulted from the reckless lending practices of financial service providers which had insufficient liquidity, which became known as the subprime loan crisis. The ripple effects of the sudden shortfall in liquidity swiftly spilt over towards European banks and caused a three-dimensional (economic, banking and budgetary) crisis in affected member states (Stiglitz, 2010).

The EU responded to the crisis by determining positive integrative targets under the Europe 2020 Strategy in the areas of education and training, research and development, environmental sustainability and poverty reduction (European Commission, 2010). These targets have, however, been overshadowed by the prioritisation of budgetary austerity in the coordinative policy cycle of the Annual Semester, which has been in operation since 2011. Under the Annual Semester the European Commission has prioritised budgetary solidity in its overall priorities published every autumn, which member states must implement as part of their budgetary national Stability and Convergence Programmes and macroeconomic National Reform Programmes (European Commission, 2017).

This occurred in response to German government's drive to turn the eurozone into a stability union and to expand the principle of balanced budgets to the rest of the EU through the 2013 Fiscal Compact, which was eventually implemented by 25 member states (Schweiger, 2014). The dwindling policy autonomy of national governments and the substantially expanded autonomous role of the Commission to act as the supervisor and enforcer of policy targets under the eurozone six pack governance mechanisms and the Europe 2020 Strategy Annual Semester has intensified public demands for greater democratic scrutiny. The reality of decision making in the EU under crisis conditions has however been one of ever-more remote elite-level decision making. This mode of governance, which has been branded as 'intensive transgovernmentalism' (Wallace and Reh, 2015, p. 109) or 'EU2' (Giddens, 2014,

p. 6), is characterised by policymaking in selected circles of individual member states and EU institutions. The collective consultation of all member states in the Council and also the European Parliament is neglected in the process. Intensive transgovernmentalism has frequently been applied under Germany's leadership. After some initial hesitation, German Chancellor Angela Merkel accepted the need for Germany to act as the 'hegemonic stabilizer' (Bulmer and Paterson, 2013, p. 1397) with the purpose of leading the EU out of the eurozone crisis. Merkel favoured swift decision making over democratic scrutiny in her desire to stabilise the eurozone and to restore dwindling market confidence. This resulted in the reverse qualified majority rule under the Fiscal Compact, which gives the Commission the exclusive right to initiate an excessive deficit procedure against eurozone countries without having to consult the Council. An unresolved excessive deficit of more than 60 per cent of the GDP will then automatically lead to financial penalties of up to 0.1 per cent of a country's GDP, if the other member states in the Council do not stop the procedure through by qualified majority or the European Court of Justice fails to confirm it (European Council, 2012). Under the strengthened eurozone governance framework the Commission and the European Central Bank also obtained an autonomous role, in cooperation with the IMF and the European Central Bank, as the enforcing agent of structural reforms under the pillar of the so-called troika.

The troika directly negotiates structural reforms with countries which are receiving financial support under the newly founded temporary European Financial Stability Facility (EFSF) and the now permanent eurozone financial support mechanism, the European Stability Mechanism (ESM). The troika practically operates outside of any democratic scrutiny on the level of technocratic elite decision making. This shows that under the German-led post-crisis policy architecture in the eurozone and the EU functional policy management has received substantial priority over ensuring that processes of multi-level democratic accountability are adhered to (Wessels, 2013, p. 202). Economic governance in the EU has hence turned into 'a technocratic and non-political field of action' which is governed by a small group of unelected bodies that claim to derive their legitimacy through democratic expertise (Giannone, 2015, p. 104). The technocratic and market-orientated approach towards resolving the eurozone crisis has had a threefold negative effect on the EU: firstly, it has profoundly undermined public trust in the EU, which is perceived as being ever more remote from the daily concerns of ordinary people. Secondly, solidarity amongst member states has dwindled substantially as an overall trend towards the renationalisation of politics is taking hold in across the EU. Thirdly, although Chancellor Merkel aspired to tie member states closer together through the various interlinked mechanisms of policy coordination, the EU today resembles ever more that of a disunion, with various internal political and economic cleavages having emerged (Hayward, 2012, p. 10).

Since the onset of the eurozone crisis, trust in the EU's governance has sharply declined. Before the crisis on average around 50 per cent of citizens across the EU would express trust in the EU and its institutions. Since 2009 this figure has dropped steadily to between 31 and currently 36 per cent (European Commission, 2016, p. 14). At the same time, those who consider the EU as very positive achievement are now in the minority. In 2006 on average 50 per cent of citizens in the member states had a very positive perception of the EU. Currently only 35 per cent of citizens across the 28 member states express such a positive view, while 38 per cent express a neutral and 25 per cent a 'totally negative view' (ibid., p. 15). This is the reflection of grave public concerns about the lack of democratic accountability in the way the EU reaches decisions and determines policies. A clear majority disagrees with the notion that citizens' voices count in the EU and this majority grew to over 60 per cent during the peak of the eurozone crisis between 2009 and 2013. In the latest Eurobarometer conducted in the autumn of 2016, the majority of citizens in 19 member states considered their voice not to count in the EU. In seven countries this figure reached as high as 70 per cent (Czech Republic, Spain, Italy, Latvia, Estonia, Cyprus and Greece). Only in nine member states (Sweden, Denmark, Netherlands, Belgium, Finland, Austria, Germany, Croatia and Luxembourg) a majority of citizens expressed the view that their voice counts in the EU's policy process (ibid., pp. 17–18). Hardening public scepticism towards the EU's 'experimentalist' governance approach in trying to tackle major challenges, such as the eurozone crisis, is reflected by these figures as the approach lacks solidarity and vision beyond technocratic functionality (Sabel and Zeitlin, 2008, p. 280). The eurozone crisis has been widely considered as an 'existential threat' to the future of the EU (Dyson, 2017, p. 65). This is not simply because of the economic instability it created but mostly due to the deepening internal division it has revealed. The division runs most obviously between the public and political elites but at closer examination also profoundly between the member states.

Increasing internal differentiation under crisis conditions

The eurozone crisis has revealed a deep-seated cleavage between the richer economies of Northern Europe, the transition economies in East-Central Europe and the crisis economies in Southeastern Europe. The group of economically stronger economies in the North led by Germany moved into the position of creditors under the EFSF and the ESM arrangements. The crisis economies of Ireland, Spain, Portugal and Cyprus at least temporarily turned into debtor countries. In the case of the Greece the creditor-debtor relationship has become permanent and has already resulted in a profound rift between the interests of the socially ailing Greek society and the elite-level EU political agenda (Sepos, 2016, p. 51; Laffan, 2017, p. 144). In East-Central Europe these developments have initiated a trend towards 'democratic backsliding', most noticeably in Hungary and Poland (Agh, 2016, p. 121). This is the result of the combination between 'national resistance' towards the notion of the eurozone as a transfer union and the negative external circumstances under deepening economic and political crisis conditions (Haughton, 2017, p. 258). The divergence of national interests in the eurozone are also reflected in the political core-periphery division of the Single Market governance. The Single Market is now divided into the ever more deeply integrated eurozone (as a result of the six pack governance mechanisms, the ESM and most recently the Banking Union), the associated semi-periphery of aspiring eurozone members represented in the Euro Plus Pact (predominantly in East-Central and Southern Europe) and a detached outside periphery. The latter was originally confined to the UK and the Czech Republic.

More recently the outside periphery group has grown because of increasingly euro-sceptic and nationalist political developments in Hungary and Poland (Schweiger, 2015, p. 107).

The divisions that emerged during the eurozone crisis were deepened even further during the subsequent migration crisis, which peaked in the summer of 2015. The combination of the eurozone crisis and subsequent migration crisis played a major role in the decision of the British public to leave the EU. The decision to hold a second public referendum on EU membership in the UK after the initial referendum in 1975 resulted to a large extent from the mounting pressure from within Prime Minister David Cameron's Conservative Party to renegotiate British membership terms. The Thatcherite eurosceptic wing of the Conservatives were alarmed by what they perceived as the German-led drive towards deeper political integration in response to the eurozone crisis (Allen, 2013, p. 110; McGowan and Phinnemore, 2017, p. 79). Cameron tried to appease the eurosceptics by demanding clear red lines from what he characterised as Merkel's 'one-size-fits-all' approach towards integration (Cameron, 2013). Cameron's renegotiation demands concentrated on legal opt-outs from the principle of ever closer union, which reflected the prime British concern that the deeper policy integration in the eurozone could spill over towards the imposition of a new binding regulatory framework for the financial industry in the whole of the Single Market. British eurosceptics hence were predominantly concerned that such developments could substantially weaken the competitive advantage of their economy in the area of financial liberalisation (Schweiger, 2016, p. 68). This explains why Cameron deliberately vetoed the inclusion of the Fiscal Compact into the EU Treaty Structure. Another major British concern which was also widely reflected in the public debate leading up to the referendum referred to the principle of the freedom of movement of EU citizens within the Single Market. The alleged abuse of the British welfare system by EU migrants, especially from East-Central and South-eastern Europe, had been successfully exploited as a vote winning theme by the UK Independence Party (UKIP) during the 2014 European Parliament election. Under pressure from rising poll ratings for UKIP, Cameron prioritised safeguards against alleged welfare migration from other EU member states in his renegotiation strategy for the UK's EU membership. Cameron won substantial concessions in the negotiations with the rest of the EU on the revision of British membership terms, amongst them the right to limit welfare payments to EU migrants for four years after their first arrival in the UK (European Council, 2016). The referendum was nevertheless overshadowed by the issues of sovereign border controls and immigration. Both Conservative eurosceptics in favour of leaving the EU, such as the prominent *Vote Leave* campaign leader Boris Johnson, and also UKIP, spearheaded by its leader Nigel Farage, convinced a majority of the British public that staying inside the EU would result in the inability to effectively control migration coming to the UK from inside and outside the EU (Gutteridge, 2016). The slim majority of 52 per cent of the British people who voted in favour of leaving the EU therefore did so mainly because of concerns about the persistent loss of sovereignty inside the Union. As Boris Johnson put it: 'The jailer has accidentally left the door of the jail open and people can see the sunlit and beyond' (Riley-Smith, 2016). This view was backed up by the analysis of the referendum outcome conducted by Lord Ashcroft Polls. The analysis showed that the top two reasons for Brexit amongst Leave voters were firstly the principle that decisions about the UK should be taken in the UK and secondly that voting to leave offered the best chance for the UK to regain control over immigration and its own borders (Lord Ashcroft Polls, 2016).

Since the onset of the migration crisis this has also been a major concern of the countries in East-Central Europe (ECE). Despite their internal differences, the Viségrad group of countries in ECE is standing united in its opposition against the introduction of compulsory refugee quotas, which German Chancellor Merkel tried to impose on the EU in response to the mounting wave of refugees and migrants in the summer of 2015. Even the more liberal social democratic governments in the Czech Republic and Slovakia supported a joint Viségrad initiative to categorically rule out the introduction of mandatory permanent refugee quotas. This was mainly driven by Hungary and Poland (Visegrád Group, 2015, p. 3). The background to this is the persistent gap in the levels of economic development and social cohesion in the ECE member states, especially in rural areas. Immigration is therefore a contentious political issue which tends to boost support for far-right extremist parties (Göncz, 2013, p. 174).

The economic and social differentiation of the ECE region is also the background to the recent tendency towards democratic backsliding. It has been pointed out that the transition process in the ECE region is standing on fragile ground, not only in economic terms but particularly politically. The thin levels of Europeanisation (Agh, 2013, p. 38) offer a fertile breeding ground for the new agenda of economic nationalism and political illiberalism under the adverse external crisis environment in the EU. Hungary's autocratic prime minister, Viktor Orbán, presented the ideological framework for this trend when he brought up the concept of the 'illiberal state' in 2014. He has since been promoting this as a new mode of governance for the countries in the region (Mahony, 2014).

Orbán connects this with an economic nationalist perspective which rejects outside interference in his country's economic affairs (Orbán, 2013). Orbán puts the concept of the illiberal state in clear contrast to the values promoted by the EU, which he has frequently compared to the Stalinist Soviet Union. In his 2017 annual address to the Hungarian nation, Orbán compared the recent surge in populism in Europe and the US with the struggle against Soviet Union oppression during the Cold War and in particular the Hungarian uprising in 1956:

> There has been an uprising by those who are not usually asked, whose voices are not usually heard . . . whose mouths have been gagged in the name of political correctness; who were promised a share of the profits of the global economy and global governance. . . . They demanded the return of the world in which they once felt at home: the wide and diverse world of nations.
>
> (Orbán, 2017)

Orbán followed up his rhetoric with concrete political decisions which have resulted in enhanced state influence on the media and the limitation of the ability of the parliament and the constitutional court to scrutinise government policies. This has been replicated by the eurosceptic and populist centre-right Justice and Law government in Poland under Prime Minister Beata Szydlo, who takes a similar approach to that of Orbán. Like Orbán, Szydlo has engaged in a war of words with the European Commission over the domestic constitutional reform agenda her government is implementing in Poland (Rae, 2017). Szydlo has adopted a hard line against what she perceives as unjustified interference of the EU into her country's domestic affairs: 'The Rule of Law Opinion, as it is, is just an opinion will not impact in any way the decisions we make in Poland' (Kokoszynski, 2016). In spite of positive trends in the economic transition of many of the ECE countries before the onset of the global financial crisis in 2008, the region is still considered to be part of the EU's economic periphery. This is due to persistently low wage cultures, high levels of economic poverty and the tendency of particularly younger people to migrate to other EU member states to make a living. If the recent trend of economic and political renationalisation in Hungary and Poland spreads to other countries, the ECE region risks even deeper peripheralisation and substantial loss of influence on the EU's political agenda (Agh, 2014, p. 36).

The EU's internal differentiation consequently runs across multiple economic and political dividing lines, which are closely interconnected. The UK has traditionally been a special case which is characterised by exceptionalism in terms of a persistent 'profound discomfort with the concept and realities of integration' (George, 1998; McGowan and Phinnemore, 2017, p. 80). The Brexit decision therefore was not only favoured by the particular circumstances of the EU's lingering internal and external crises but to a large extent also the result of the deep-seated and growing British discomfort with the concept of ever closer institutionalised European integration. The multiple core-periphery divides amongst the remaining 27 member states predominantly stem from persistent economic and social cleavages, which have started to spill over into the political arena.

The EU's fragmented external relations capabilities

The mismatch between the EU's lack of capabilities to tackle political challenges jointly is even more obvious in the area of external relations. The EU's external environment has become progressively more unstable since the end of the Cold War. As a result, member states were confronted with successive foreign policy challenges. These range from the collapse of the former Yugoslavia, the mounting threat of global terrorism in the wake of 9/11, the challenge of managing a growing migration stream to the military conflicts in Afghanistan, Iraq, Libya and the ongoing civil war in Syria under the circumstances of worsening relations with Russia. In all these cases, the EU's response has turned out to be fractured by strongly diverging national interests. Despite the gradual build up of its capabilities in this area, the EU external relations consequently remain disjointed and resemble more that of a disunion than of a united international organisation (Domiguez, 2016, p. 528). National ownership of common strategies, such as the European Neighbourhood Policy (ENP), remains weak as member state governments continue to prioritise the pursuit of their national foreign policy interests. The ENP was aimed at creating an area of freedom, security and stability around the EU's external borders but has failed to achieve this because of growing instability in Northern Africa, the Middle East and the Eastern neighbourhood. The EU's diplomatic engagement with autocratic regimes in these regions under the ENP was aimed at putting a normative soft power approach into practice by instilling economic and political reform towards good governance based on conditional financial, economic and political support through bilateral privileged partnership agreements (Smith, 2005, p. 763).

The failure to push the participating countries towards good governance became obvious in the growing political instability in these regions, which was the result of at least partial public uprisings against autocratic regimes during the 2010–12 Arab Spring and the 2013–14 Ukraine crisis. Individual EU member states selectively engaged in resolving these crises with only limited effect, such as the semi-permanent ceasefire in Ukraine and overthrow of the Gaddafi regime in Libya after military intervention led by the UK, France and the US in 2011. Collectively the EU has been accused of making matters worse by on the one hand legitimising an 'authoritarian ring of friends' through the ENP (Grant, 2011) and on the other hand increasing the risk of political instability in the partnership countries through the persistent drive towards democratisation (Börzel and Hüllen, 2014, p. 1041). Overall the collective institutional representation of the EU remained weak as the group of larger member states (Germany, France, the UK and Poland) formed shifting leadership alliances to initiate the diplomatic or military initiatives. Against the background of the persistence of diverging national interests, Catherine Ashton and Federica Mogherini, the two EU High Representatives for Foreign and Security appointed so far, have struggled to coordinate national foreign policy interests and to achieve an effective collective representation for the EU.

The EU's persistent preference for soft power in the form of diplomatic efforts and economic relations (Smith and Steffenson, 2011, p. 428) stems not only from the failure of member states to overcome their national differences but also the widespread adversity towards prioritising investment in military capabilities. The accusation made by former US Defence Secretary Robert Gates that the EU displays an adversity to military risk (Gates, 2011) refers to the failure of the majority of EU member states (except for the UK, Greece, Estonia and Poland) to spend the minimum 2 per cent of their annual GDP on defence. This minimum level reflects a political commitment that was agreed at the 2014 NATO summit in Wales (NATO, 2017).

Under lingering economic crisis conditions, EU member states are unlikely to aspire to meet the spending targets. There is therefore the real risk that the EU's continuing failure to engage in military burden-sharing will clash with the new realism in American foreign policy under President Donald Trump, who has demanded that EU member states should pay for NATO if they want to keep it in operation (Jacobs, 2016). The long-standing rift in transatlantic relations, which opened during the disagreements over the 2003 military intervention in Iraq, could therefore grow even wider in the future and poses an existential threat to the future of NATO.

Conclusion: from European Union towards permanent disunion?

The future of the EU remains uncertain if the internal economic and political differentiation deepens under the remnants of the lingering effects of the financial crisis and the subsequent eurozone sovereign debt crisis. The EU only has a viable future if national leaders find the resolve to act determinately and in the spirit of solidarity to collectively overcome the vast array of challenges facing the member states. If the rift between the economic and social developments of the EU's core and the peripheries grows further it is likely that the currently still limited trend towards the renationalisation of politics may turn into a systemic crisis. Ultimately a persistent systemic crisis could lead to the breakup of the eurozone and the Single Market.

One the positive side one can currently detect a glimpse of light at the long dark tunnel of crises which the EU has travelled through throughout the past decade. As much as Brexit poses a major challenge for the remaining 27 member states, it also offers an opportunity to regroup and reinstill purpose and vision into the European project. The recent election of Emmanuel Macron as the new president of France could signify the end of the populist wave in the EU and offer the chance for the renewal of the Franco-German leadership partnership after the 2017 German federal election. The UK's exit from the EU in principle offers Berlin and Paris the chance to develop a new agenda aimed at deeper political cooperation amongst the remaining members. The trend towards ever deeper disunion amongst the member states of the EU can be reversed if EU members manage to develop an inclusive agenda which emerges because of the widespread consensus amongst the variety of national interests.

For too long EU member states have lacked the collective will to engage in effective joint policy management and instead muddled themselves through from crisis to crisis (Webber, 2017, p. 355). For the EU to survive as a regional organisation with global clout, it needs to develop democratically accountable decision-making procedures which result in both effective and purposeful policy joint solutions for the present and future multidimensional challenges.

Further reading

Baker, David and Pauline Schnapper (2015) *Britain and the Crisis of the European Union* (Basingstoke: Palgrave MacMillan).

Bulmer, Simon and William E. Paterson (2013) 'Germany as the EU's Reluctant Hegemon? Of Economic Strength and Political Constraints', *Journal of European Public Policy* 20(10), pp. 1387–1405.

Champeau, Serge et al. (2015) *The Future of Europe: Democracy, Legitimacy and Justice After the Euro Crisis* (London and New York: Rowan and Littlefield).

Demetriou, Kyriakos N. (2015) *The European Union in Crisis: Explorations in Representation and Democratic Legitimacy* (Berlin: Springer).

Dinan, Desmond Neill Nugent and William E. Paterson (eds.) (2017) *The European Union in Crisis* (London: Palgrave).

Giddens, Anthony (2014) *Turbulent and Mighty Continent: What Future for Europe?* (Cambridge: Polity).

Hayward, Jack and Rüdiger Wurzel (eds.) (2012) *European Disunion: Between Sovereignty and Solidarity* (Basingstoke: Palgrave MacMillan).

Leuffen, Dirk, Berthold Rittberger and Frank Schimmelfennig (2013) *Differentiated Integration: Explaining Variation in the European Union* (Basingstoke: Palgrave MacMillan).

Magone, José M., Brigid Laffan and Christian Schweiger (eds.) (2016) *Core-periphery Relations in the European Union* (Abingdon: Routledge).

Rodrigues, Maria Joao and Eleni Xiarchogiannopoulou (eds.) (2014) *The Eurozone Crisis and the Transformation of EU Governance* (Farnham: Ashgate).

Schweiger, Christian (2016) *Exploring the EU's Legitimacy Crisis: The Dark Heart of Europe* (Cheltenham: Edward Elgar).

Wallace, Helen, Mark A. Pollack and Alasdair R. Young (eds.) (2014) *Policy-Making in the European Union* (Oxford: University Press).

Witzleb, Normann, Alfonso Martinez Arranz and Pascaline Winand (eds.) (2015) *The European Union and Global Engagement: Institutions, Policies and Challenges* (Cheltenham: Edward Elgar).

Bibliography

Agh, Attila (2013) *Progress Report on the New Member States: 20 Years of Social & Political Developments* (Budapest: College of Communication and Business).

Agh, Attila (2014) 'Ten Years of Catching up Story in the European Union: Differentiated Integration and Multilevel Governance in ECE', in Attila Agh, Tamas Kaiser and Beata Koller (eds.) *10 Years After: Multi-level Governance and Differentiated Integration in the EU* (Budapest: Blue Ribbon Research Centre), pp. 31–61.

Agh, Attila (2016) 'The Increasing Core-Periphery Divide and New Member States: Diverging from the European Union's Mainstream Developments', in José Magone, Brigid Laffan and Christian Schweiger (eds.) *Core-Periphery Relations in the European Union* (Oxon: Routledge), pp. 117–129.

Allen, David (2013) 'The United Kingdom: Towards Isolation and a Parting of the Ways?', in Simon Bulmer and Christian Lequesne (eds.) *The Member States of the European Union*, 2nd ed. (Oxford: University Press), pp. 108–133.

Börzel, Tanja A. and Vera van Hüllen (2014) 'One Voice, One Message, but Conflicting Goals: Cohesiveness and Consistency in the European Neighbourhood Policy', *Journal of European Public Policy* 21(7), pp. 1033–1049.

Bruter, Michael (2012) 'The Difficulty Emergence of a European People', in Jack Hayward and Rüdiger Wurzel (eds.) *European Disunion: Between Sovereignty and Solidarity* (Basingstoke: Palgrave MacMillan), pp. 17–31.

Cameron, David (2013) 'EU Speech at Bloomberg' (23 January), www.gov.uk/government/speeches/eu-speech-at-bloomberg.

Dominguez, Roberto (2016) 'The EU Governance System of External Relations', *Journal of Contemporary European Research* 12(1), pp. 518–531.

Dyson, Kenneth (2017) 'Playing for High Stakes: The Eurozone Crisis', in Desmond Dinan, Neill Nugent and William E. Paterson (eds.) *The European Union in Crisis* (London: Palgrave), pp. 54–76.

European Commission (1979) *Eurobarometer: After the Election of the European Parliament*, No. 12, December, http://ec.europa.eu/COMMFrontOffice/PublicOpinion/index.cfm/ResultDoc/download/DocumentKy/62785.

European Commission (1987) *Eurobarometer: Public Opinion in the European Community 1957–1987*, http://ec.europa.eu/COMMFrontOffice/PublicOpinion/index.cfm/ResultDoc/download/DocumentKy/58266.

European Commission (1998) *Standard Eurobarometer 49* (September), http://ec.europa.eu/COMMFrontOffice/PublicOpinion/index.cfm/ResultDoc/download/DocumentKy/62920.

European Commission (2010) *Communication from the Commission: Europe 2020 – A Strategy for Smart, Sustainable and Inclusive Growth*, COM(2010) 2020 final, http://eur-lex.europa.eu/LexUriServ/LexUriServ.do?uri=COM:2010:2020:FIN:EN:PDF.

European Commission (2016) *Standard Eurobarometer 86 Autumn 2016: First Results*, http://ec.europa.eu/commfrontoffice/publicopinion//includes/images/mimetype/pdf1.gif.

European Commission (2017) *European Semester: Setting the Priorities*, https://ec.europa.eu/info/strategy/european-semester/european-semester-timeline/setting-priorities_en.

European Council (2012) *Treaty on Stability, Coordination and Governance in the Economic and Monetary Union* (1 February), www.consilium.europa.eu/european-council/pdf/Tre aty-on-Stability-Coordination-and-Governance-TSCG/

European Council (2016) *A New Settlement for the United Kingdom Within the European Union*, 2016/C 69 I/01) (18–19 February), http://eur-lex.europa.eu/legal-content/EN/ TXT/?uri=OJ%3AJOC_2016_069_I_0001.

European Parliament (2017) *European Parliament Elections Turnout*, www.europarl.europa. eu/elections2014-results/en/turnout.html.

Gates, Robert (2011) 'The Security and Defense Agenda (Future of NATO)', Speech by US sec retary of defense, Brussels, Belgium, 10 June, http://blogs.wsj.com/washwire/2011/06/10/ transcript-of-defense-secretary-gatess-speech-on-natos-future/

George, Stephen (1998) *An Awkward Partner: Britain in the European Community* (Oxford: University Press).

Giannone, Diego (2015) 'Suspending Democracy? The Governance of the EU's Political and Economic Crisis as a Process of Neoliberal Restructuring', in Kyriakos N. Demetriou (ed.) *The European Union in Crisis: Explorations in Representation and Democratic Legiti macy* (London: Springer), pp. 101–122.

Giddens, Anthony (2014) *Turbulent and Mighty Continent: What Future for Europe?* (Cam bridge: Polity).

Göncz, Borbála (2013) 'A Persistent East-West Divide? The Effect of the Crisis on People's Perceptions of the European Union', in Attila Agh and Lázló Vass (eds.) *European Futures: The Perspective of the New Member States in the New Europe* (Budapest: College of Communication and Business), pp. 171–210.

Grant, Charles (2011) 'A New Neighbourhood Policy for the EU' (March), www.cer.org. uk/sites/default/files/publications/attachments/pdf/2011/pb_grant_neighbourhood_ 11march11-170.pdf.

Gutteridge, Nick (2016) 'Farage Warns Cameron "Don't Abandon our Borders to Brussels" as EU Plots Asylum Power Grab' (7 March), www.express.co.uk/news/uk/650404/EU-ref erendum-Brexit-Brussels-immigration-power-grab-migrants-refugees-Britain-UK-asylum.

Haas, Ernst B. (1968) *The Uniting of Europe: Political, Social and Economic Forces 1950– 1957*, 2nd ed. (Stanford: University Press).

Haughton, Tim (2017) 'Central and Eastern Europe: The Sacrifice of Solidarity, the Dis comforts of Diversity, and the Vexations of Vulnerabilities', in Desmond Dinan, Neill Nugent and William E. Paterson (eds.) *The European Union in Crisis* (London: Palgrave), pp. 253–269.

Hayward, Jack (2012) 'Union without Consensus', in Jack Hayward and Rüdiger Wurzel (eds.) *European Disunion: Between Sovereignty and Solidarity* (Basingstoke: Palgrave), pp. 5–16.

Hooghe, Liesbet and Gary Marks (2009) 'A Postfunctionalist Theory of European Integra tion: From Permissive Consensus to Constraining Consensus', *British Journal of Political Science* 39(1), pp. 1–23.

Jacobs, Ben (2016) 'Donald Trump Reiterates He Will Only Help NATO Countries that Pay "Fair Share"', *The Guardian* (28 July), www.theguardian.com/us-news/2016/jul/27/don ald-trump-nato-isolationist.

Kokoszynski, Krzysztof (2016) 'Poland shrugs off EU warning', *EURACTIV* (3 June), https:// www.euractiv.com/section/justice-home-affairs/news/poland-shrugs-off-eu-warning/

Laffan, Brigid (2017) 'The Eurozone in Crisis: Core-Periphery Dynamics', in Desmond Dinan, Neill Nugent and William E. Paterson (eds.) *The European Union in Crisis* (Lon don: Palgrave), pp. 131–148.

Lord Ashcroft Polls (2016) *How the United Kingdom Voted on Thursday . . . And Why* (24 June), http://lordashcroftpolls.com/2016/06/how-the-united-kingdom-voted-and-why/

Mahony, Honor (2014) 'Orban Wants to Build "Illiberal State"', *Euobserver* (28 July), https://euobserver.com/political/125128.

McGowan, Lee and David Phinnemore (2017) 'The UK: Membership in Crisis', in Desmond Dinan, Neill Nugent and William E. Paterson (eds.) *The European Union in Crisis* (London: Palgrave), pp. 77–99.

NATO (2017) *Defence Expenditure of NATO Countries (2009–2016)* (13 March), www.nato.int/cps/eu/natohq/news_142152.htm.

Orbán, Viktor (2013) *Prime Minister Viktor Orbán State of the Nation Speech* (25 February), Budapest, http://2010-2014.kormany.hu/en/prime-minister-s-office/the-prime-ministers-speeches/prime-minister-viktor-orban-s-state-of-the-nation-speech.

Orban, Viktor (2017) *Prime Minister Viktor Orbán State of the Nation Address* (14 February), www.kormany.hu/en/the-prime-minister/the-prime-minister-s-speeches/prime-minister-viktor-orban-s-state-of-the-nation-address-20170214.

Rae, Gavin (2017) 'Poland's Conservative Nationalism and a Multi-Speed Europe' (22 March), www.socialeurope.eu/2017/03/polands-conservative-nationalism-multi-speed-europe/

Richardson, Jeremy (2015) 'The EU as a Policy-Making State: A Policy System Like Any Other?' in Jeremy Richardson and Sonia Mazey (eds.) *European Union: Power and Policy-Making*, 2nd ed. (Abingdon: Routledge), pp. 3–32.

Riley-Smith (2016) 'Boris Johnson: Leaving the EU Would Be Like 'Prisoner Escaping Jail', 6 March, www.telegraph.co.uk/news/newstopics/eureferendum/12184958/EU-referendum-Boris-Johnson-outlines-case-for-Brexit-on-Andrew-Marr-Show-live-updates.html.

Sabel, Charles F. and Jonathan Zeitlin (2008) 'Learning From Difference: The New Architecture of Experimentalist Governance in the EU', *European Law Journal* 14(3), pp. 271–327.

Scharpf, Fritz W. (1988) 'The Joint Decision Trap: Lessons from German Federalism and European Integration', *Public Administration* 66(Autumn), pp. 239–278.

Scharpf, Fritz W. (1999) *Governing in Europe: Effective and Democratic?* (Oxford: University Press).

Schweiger, Christian (2014) 'The EU-25 Fiscal Compact: Differentiated Spillover Effects under Crisis Conditions', *Perspectives on European Politics and Society* special issue 'The Effects of the Eurozone Sovereign Debt Crisis: Differentiated Integration Between the Centre and the New Peripheries EU' 15(3), pp. 293–304.

Schweiger, Christian (2015) 'The CEE Countries' First Decade of EU Membership: From Policy-Takers towards Agenda-Setters?, *Problemy polityki społecznej – Problems of Social Policy* 31(4), pp. 99–118.

Schweiger, Christian (2016) 'National Interests and Differentiated Integration in the EU Under Crisis Conditions', in José M. Magone, Brigid Laffan and Christian Schweiger (eds.) *Core-periphery Relations in the European Union: Power and Conflict in a Dualist Political Economy* (London and New York: Routledge), pp. 59–71.

Sepos, Angelos (2016) 'The Centre-Periphery Divide in the Euro Crisis: A Theoretical Approach', in José M. Magone, Brigid Laffan and Christian Schweiger (eds.) *Core-Periphery Relations in the European Union: Power and Conflict in a Dualist Political Economy* (London and New York: Routledge), pp. 35–57.

Smith, Karen E. (2005) 'The Outsiders: The European Neighbourhood Policy', *International Affairs* 81(4), pp. 757–773.

Smith, Michael and Rebecca Steffenson (2011) 'The EU and the United States', in Christopher Hill and Michael Smith (eds.) *International Relations and the European Union* (Oxford: University Press), pp. 404–434.

Stiglitz, Joseph (2010) *Freefall: Free Markets and the Sinking of the Global Economy* (London: Penguin).

Visegrád Group (2015) 'Joint Statement of the Heads of Governments of the Visegrád Group of Countries, Prague', 4 September, www.visegradgroup.eu/calendar/20150904-v4-joint.

Wallace, Helen and Christine Reh (2015) 'An Institutional Anatomy and Five Policy Modes', in Hellen Wallace, Mark A. Pollack and Alasdair R. Young (eds.) *Policy-Making in the European Union* (Oxford: University Press), pp. 72–114.

Webber, Douglas (2017) 'Can the EU Survive?', in Desmond Dinan, Neill Nugent and William E. Paterson (eds.) *The European Union in Crisis* (London: Palgrave), pp. 336–357.

Weiler, J.H.H. (1999) *The Constitution Europe: 'Do the New Clothes Have an Emperor?' and Other Essays on European Integration* (Cambridge: University Press).

Wessels, Wolfgang (2012) 'National Parliaments and the EP in Multi-Tier Governance: In Search for an Optimal Multi-Level Parliamentary Architecture', European Parliament Directorate General for Internal Policies, *Challenges of Multi-Tier Governance in the European Union: Effectiveness, Efficiency and Legitimacy, Compendium of Notes*, www.europarl.europa.eu/RegData/etudes/etudes/join/2013/474438/IPOL-AFCO_ET(2013)474438_EN.pdf.

Chapter 10

Germany

Ruth Wittlinger

Germany has come a long way since the end of World War II. From a country that had to admit military and moral surrender in 1945 and that was divided during the Cold War, it is now a country that does economically well and is politically stable. During the Cold War, West Germany's international role was very much determined by the pressures of the bipolar world and its geopolitical position within it but

FIGURE 10.1 German Chancellor Angela Merkel

also by the restrictions imposed by the Western Allies. Furthermore, the scope of West German foreign policy was significantly restricted by the memory of the Nazi past and the norms and values which had emerged after 1945 in opposition to this period. The public and political discourse was very much shaped by this memory and (West) Germany's foreign policy as well as its international role more generally were influenced by it.

The key question was what role a united Germany would play in the post–Cold War order. Would John Mearsheimer be right with the prediction he put forward in his essay 'Back to the Future: Instability in Europe after the Cold War', published in 1990, and Germany would seek nuclear weapons in order to overcome its insecurity and vulnerable position in the centre of Europe and 'raise its military status to a level commensurate with its economic status' (p. 36)? Or would it continue in the foreign policy traditions of the Bonn Republic (1949–90), which had emerged during the Cold War and which were characterised by modesty and a 'culture of restraint'? According to Markovits and Reich, it was an 'ideology of smallness' that prevented Germany from acknowledging its centrality to the new order. In their view, Germany was 'once again in an unenviable predicament. It is damned if it acts in a way commensurate with its structural power, and it is damned if it stays aloof and acts small' (1997, p. 7).

In order to understand the role Germany is playing in global politics in the 21st century, it is necessary to trace the main developments and debates that accompanied Germany's change from a defeated nation in 1945 to a successful and stable united country which plays an increasingly prominent role again in global affairs. After examining the way the Nazi past shaped West Germany's development in terms of policy and discourse, this chapter will discuss the importance of the European dimension for Germany's journey from international pariah to internationally recognised partner and ally. It will then look at Germany's foreign policy identity in more general terms and consider how Germany's self-understanding and participation in international affairs has changed since unification.

The presence of the past: Germany's international role after 1945

Since there is no identity without memory, there is no doubt that the identity of every country is shaped by its past. After 1945, this became particularly obvious in (West) Germany (Frei, 1997; Fulbrook, 1999; Kansteiner, 2006; Langenbacher, 2010; Maier, 1998; Niven, 2002; Pearce, 2008; Wittlinger, 2010). The Nazi past provided what has been described as the 'basic narrative' of the Federal Republic (Schwab-Trapp, 2003), which was very much an antithesis of the Third Reich in terms of institutions, policies and discourses. (West) Germany's international role was also very much determined by its Nazi past and the collective memory of that past. The international community as well as (West) Germany itself evaluated policy as well as discourse very much through the lens of the Nazi past. Germany's political history after 1945 was thus strongly characterised by attempts to overcome this past. The main aims of West Germany's foreign policy were rehabilitation and re-gaining the trust of the international community as well as ensuring security against the Soviet threat.

The collective memory of the Nazi past thus had a very clear effect on West Germany's foreign policy identity after 1945 (Berger, 1996). (West) Germany was a state that appeared to have moved beyond nationalist self-interest and that was keen to be integrated into supranational as well as international institutions and organisations. It was very reluctant to express its national interest explicitly, although arguably this reluctance actually *was* in its national interest. Generally speaking, the notion of the nation was tainted in post-1945 (West) Germany and European integration provided Germans who struggled with an identification with the German nation with a welcome way out (Wittlinger, 2010). The Federal Republic had developed a postnational identity and its conduct in international affairs was characterised by a strong commitment to multilateralism.

The stark reality of German division was also an obvious reminder of its past. As a saying ascribed to the French writer François Mauriac – 'I love Germany so much that I am glad there are two of them' – makes abundantly clear, European neighbours felt quite comfortable with the existence of two German states. In view of Germany's history of military aggression and the Holocaust in the first half of the 20th century, the division of Germany was by and large considered a fair punishment.

The prospect of unification that arose after the fall of the Berlin Wall in 1989 made Germany's European neighbours nervous. In fact, even many West Germans were not overly enthusiastic about unification and the prospect of a different, united Germany. The rather unassuming Bonn Republic, which had played a relatively modest role in international affairs and which relied heavily on the US for security, had served its people well. Domestically, there was no desire for that to change through German unification. The Federal Republic was described as having gone from 'total war' in the first half of the 20th century to 'total peace' in the second part of the 20th century (Baumann and Hellmann, 2001), that is, from an obsession with power (Machtbesessenheit) to an oblivion of power (Machtvergessenheit) (Schwarz, 1985) and the international community as well as the Germans themselves were very comfortable with this.

As German political elites repeatedly emphasised in the run-up to unification and in the early 1990s, the 'Berlin Republic' – and many people were even reluctant to use this term since it suggested change (Brunssen, 2005) – was to continue in the foreign policy traditions of the Bonn Republic. Even though this by and large reassured those members of the international community which had feared a 'Fourth Reich', it soon became apparent that pressure for change came from the external environment, especially the US, which expected its European allies to share the burden of their defence. Already in 1989, President George H.W. Bush had hinted at expectations that Germany should play a more prominent role in international affairs when he invited Germany to be 'partners in leadership'.

Whereas the post-unification Kohl governments persisted in emphasising the continuity of Germany's international role, a different tone started to emerge with the red-green coalition which came to power in 1998. Chancellor Gerhard Schröder in particular emphasised the impact of generational change brought about by his government which, in his view, also impacted on Germany's international role. In the context of the events in Kosovo; for example, he expressed the view that 'Germany's role in the world had changed' and that it now carried more responsibility also for the fate of other peoples. This 'new German responsibility' was to be expected after the end of the Cold War and German unity, according to Schröder (1999a).

From a European Germany to a German Europe?

European integration was crucial for West Germany's upward trajectory in the post-war period. Not only did it allow West Germany to prosper economically, maybe even more importantly, it provided a forum through which the Bonn Republic could regain international trust and confidence. A West Germany which was tightly integrated into a strong Western Europe was clearly also in the interests of its allies since it offered what Wilfried Loth termed 'double containment' (1984). A strong anti-communist Western Europe not only helped to stand up to the Soviet threat, it also helped to control the Germans.

In addition to the economic and political benefits, European integration also provided West Germans with a layer for collective identification which went beyond the much discredited German nation. An identification with Europe rather than Germany also accommodated the reality of German division. A European identity provided West Germans with a forward-looking approach which seemed to have left behind the narrowness of the nation state. Accordingly, there was a broad consensus in society as well as among political elites in favour of European integration even if West Germany did not necessarily benefit from it directly and immediately in material terms. This 'permissive consensus' or 'tacit approval' lasted for much of the lifetime of the Bonn Republic and was characterised by a lack of any significant eurosceptic opposition at the level of political elites. European integration had become the raison d'état of the Federal Republic (Karama, in Müller-Brandeck-Bocquet, 2003, p. 47).

The European policy of political elites, just like Germany's foreign policy in more general terms, was characterised by a strong commitment to multilateralism and a reluctance to exercise leadership unless it was in tandem with France (Paterson, 2003, p. 207), displaying what came to be described as a 'leadership avoidance complex' (Paterson, 2003, p. 211).

Unsurprisingly, Germany's European neighbours acted with concern over the prospect of unification. After all, the division of Germany had come to be regarded 'as a prerequisite for stability in Europe' (Steininger, 2001, p. 20). Particularly, UK Prime Minister Margaret Thatcher vehemently opposed the idea of a united Germany, fearing the domination of the 'German giant' (1995, p. 798) or the 'German juggernaut' (1995, p. 797). The French response to the prospect of German unification, however, was that France would agree to German unification provided that a united Germany would be more closely integrated into the European framework. At the time, Chancellor Helmut Kohl described German and European unity as 'two sides of the same coin' and even a 'question of war and peace' (Banchoff, 1997).

The Maastricht Treaty, or more precisely, the Treaty on European Union, emerged from this desire to integrate united Germany more closely into Europe. Significantly, however, the Maastricht Treaty can be seen as a major turning point in Germany's policy towards Europe and as indicating the end of Germany's Europeanism by default (Schweiger, 2007, p. 61). Even though German political elites and the public were still by and large in favour of European integration, a more pragmatic and less idealist approach started to emerge more clearly under the leadership of the red-green coalition of Chancellor Schröder, which came to power in 1998. In contrast to Kohl, Schröder did not hesitate to express Germany's national interest more openly, particularly regarding budgetary issues. Shortly after being elected, he announced in an interview that Germany was not prepared to fund compromises in the EU anymore (1999b). More significantly, however, Schröder 'did away with this fiction of the European interest being the same as the German interest. You can talk of the German national interest in a much more relaxed way today. The time was ripe for this and he acknowledged it' (Biedenkopf, quoted in Karp, 2006, p. 76).

Nevertheless, Germany under the red-green coalition (1998–2005) continued to support European initiatives. At the same time, it made sure however that Germany would be protected from potential negative side effects of these initiatives. In the context of Eastern enlargement, for example, Schröder ensured that the vulnerable German labour market would be protected from a sudden influx of workers from the new Eastern European member states by negotiating a transitional period which delayed their access to the German labour market (Paterson, 2010; Wood, 2004).

In spite of the realism that was setting in in European matters around the turn of the millennium, Germany has remained committed to Europe. Even though there might have been reason to question the suitability of particular German policies, for example, its emphasis on austerity in the aftermath of the global financial crisis in 2007–8 and the subsequent eurozone crisis (Bulmer, 2014), the commitment of Angela Merkel's governments to the European idea has never really been called into question. She tried to give the European idea a new rationale and provide the European project with some visionary input that went beyond the question of 'war and peace', which had been very much at the heart of the previous generation of political leaders which still had a living memory of World War II. Even though in her view Europe would remain the concept for peace in the 21st century, that would not suffice for current generations. According to Merkel, the commonalities of EU member states were to be seen in shared values such as freedom, justice, democracy, the rule of law and a respect for human rights and it was the common understanding of these values that held Europe together internally (Merkel, 2006). Borrowing an image of the former President of the European Commission, Jacques Delors, in her first speech to the European Parliament during Germany's EU presidency, Merkel identified the 'soul of Europe' to be 'tolerance' (2007).

Particularly during difficult economic circumstances, Merkel has shown, however, that she does not hesitate to put Germany's economic interests first, for example in 2008 when she prioritised the protection of jobs in Germany's heavy industry over environmental concerns and the EU's agenda to pass emission regulations. Timothy Garton Ash's comment indicates the novelty character of a German chancellor explicitly putting German interests first: 'It's nothing new that France and Britain are behaving like France and Britain. . . . What's new is that Germany is now behaving like France and Britain' (2009). The fact that Germany had become a lot more reluctant to finance initiatives which might have been in the broader European interest but came at significant expense to Germany as the dominant creditor economy that would carry the largest burden was particularly obvious in the eurozone crisis and Germany's insistence on solutions based on austerity (Hall, 2012; Galpin, 2015; Hillebrand, 2015; Oppermann, 2012).

This has been accompanied by Germany losing its, at least since 1945, traditional tendency to 'punch below its weight'. As Paterson has pointed out, the eurozone crisis turned out to be the tipping point for classic German Europeanism, pushing Germany 'somewhat reluctantly centre stage to become Europe's reluctant hegemon' (2011, p. 57) with Germany's long-serving Chancellor Angela Merkel having become the 'decider' of Europe (Faiola and Kirchner, 2017). Whether it welcomes this development or not, the balance of power in the European Union is likely to further tip in Germany's favour with the UK leaving the EU. The next section will look at the way Germany's role has evolved on the international stage.

Beyond the European Union: Germany's role in the post–Cold War order

During the lifetime of the Bonn Republic, a foreign policy consensus emerged which helped to turn West Germany from a defeated and divided nation into a reliable and trusted ally of the Western bloc. Just like on the European stage, throughout the lifetime of the Bonn Republic, West Germany was very reluctant to express any kind of nationalism, even its national interest, in the international arena openly and explicitly (Wittlinger, 2010).

The main pillars of the foreign policy consensus that emerged in West Germany after 1945 included a clear Western orientation (Westpolitik) which was later complemented by a constructive policy towards the East (Ostpolitik), a strong commitment to multilateralism, as evidenced through membership of European institutions as well as NATO. Rather than leaning towards one or the other, like other countries in Europe, Germany managed to balance its European and Atlanticist commitments and maintain equidistance to Paris and Washington (Webber, 2001). A deeply entrenched antimilitarism was a further crucial characteristic of (West) Germany after 1945 in terms of policy as well as attitudes in society at large (Berger, 1998). It was complemented by a renunciation of power politics, even though Germany eventually gained 'soft power', prompting Henry Kissinger to describe the Bonn Republic as economically a giant but politically a dwarf (Crawshaw, 2004, p. 175). In more general terms and in line with its conduct in European affairs, West Germany's foreign policy was characterised by modesty, self-limitation and a 'culture of restraint' (Baumann and Hellmann, 2001). This consensus remained by and large intact throughout the lifetime of the Bonn Republic and provided the basis for the trust that the international community was prepared to offer Germany once again.

In the 1990s, it became increasingly difficult, however, not to break with the foreign policy consensus that had developed between 1949 and 1990. The challenges that emerged in the post–Cold War world made it difficult for Germany to continue in the low-profile role it had fostered internationally during the Cold War. It became clear that in particular the US was getting worried that Europe in general and Germany in particular – in spite of their prosperity – were free-riding when it came to security matters. The Gulf War in 1991 and the Balkan conflicts throughout the 1990s made it blatantly obvious that only the US had the military capabilities and the necessary network to solve the crises. The US became increasingly irritated since Europe was growing 'financial muscle' but still required 'American leadership to preserve its unprecedented peace and prosperity' (Pond, 1999, p. 205).

Becoming 'partners in leadership', as US President George H.W. Bush had suggested in May 1989, clearly came with a new set of responsibilities and duties for Germany. In the context of 'burden-sharing', Germany came increasingly under pressure to contribute to peace-making and peacekeeping missions in line with its size and importance. This constituted a clear challenge to the so called Kohl Doctrine, which prescribed that German soldiers should not be deployed where the Wehrmacht had been during World War II (Zehfuss, 2002, p. 129). Already in 1993, UN General Secretary Boutros Boutros-Ghali suggested that it was wrong to think that the international community resented the deployment of German soldiers (quoted in Schöllgen, 2004, p. 74). Schröder pointed out in his memoirs that it was not really understood in Germany at the time that German unification had resulted in more extensive international responsibilities. In his view this had been largely accepted abroad, but the German population still needed to be convinced (2006).

The awareness that united Germany would probably be unable to continue in the parochial tradition of the Bonn Republic had started to set in among political elites in the 1990s. Five years after German unification, Federal President Roman Herzog, for example, suggested in a speech to the German Council on Foreign Relations (Deutsche Gesellschaft für auswärtige Politik) that German foreign policy had entered a new phase which was characterised by its 'globalisation' (1995). As Adrian Hyde-Price has pointed out, however, crucially, this meant that two key pillars of traditional German foreign policy became increasingly incompatible. Germany's strong commitment to multilateralism, which suggested participation, was increasingly at odds with its post-1945 antimilitarism, which made it difficult to mobilise support for the use of military force from the German left's own ranks as well as society at large (2003).

In addition to the widespread lack of support for the use of force, there were also constitutional constraints on German military involvement. Although the Bundeswehr had contributed to humanitarian missions of the UN in the past, it was traditionally an army whose main task was national defence. Any military missions outside of NATO territory had therefore always been contentious. A ruling of the Federal Constitutional Court in 1994 clarified the situation, however, by deciding that German participation in out-of-area military missions was compatible with the German constitution provided that it took place within a multilateral framework and had the backing of the German parliament (Wittlinger, 2010).

Somewhat surprisingly, a more emancipated and also more participatory approach which also included the use of military force started under the red-green coalition from 1998 onwards (Crawford, 2007). In his government declaration in November 1998, Gerhard Schröder spoke of 'the confidence of a grown up nation' which did not need to feel either superior or inferior towards others but which faced up to its history and the responsibility arising from it and in spite of its preparedness to engage with it, looked towards the future. After numerous, at times very emotional discussions which nearly tore the parties in government as well as their coalition apart, the German Bundestag voted overwhelmingly in favour of an involvement of the Bundeswehr in the Kosovo war (Wittlinger, 2010). Chancellor Schröder later suggested that the Kosovo war had made Germany's responsibility brutally clear. The end of the postwar period had come and there was no way Germany could continue to claim a special status: 'We had to fulfil our obligations towards our allies. Ducking away was not possible' (2006, p. 85).

Schröder's promise of 'unconditional solidarity' in the wake of the terrorist attacks on the World Trade Center in New York and the Pentagon in Washington, DC, and the subsequent decision of the German Federal Security Council to support the international coalition against terror provided further evidence of united Germany's attempt to take on more responsibility in global affairs. In his memoirs, Schröder described the change to Germany's international role that had been triggered by unification as follows:

We have to accept: After the epochal changes since autumn 1989 Germany has regained its full sovereignty. With that it has also taken on new duties which our allies remind us of. We have no right to complain about that. Rather, we should be pleased about the fact that since the epochal changes of 1989, we have become equal partners in the community of nations.

(2006, p. 180)

Germany's emancipation and its behaviour as an equal partner became even more apparent in the run-up to the Iraq War (Dettke, 2009). We will never know for sure whether Schröder's no to Iraq was based on his convictions or whether it was a strategic electoral consideration to mobilise the still deeply entrenched 'no more war' strand in German society. The decision not to support its most important ally in the postwar period by refusing to join the war in Iraq does illustrate very clearly however the emancipation of Germany as a sovereign country. Schröder left no doubt about this when he stressed in this context that questions regarding the German nation were decided in Berlin and nowhere else (Bundestag, 2002).

The Kosovo war, the war against Afghanistan and also the Schröder government's refusal to join the war in Iraq were thus the key events which showed a clear reorientation of the foreign policy of the Berlin Republic and freed it – at least to a large extent – from the constraints of the Bonn Republic (Wittlinger and Larose, 2007).The Schröder governments thus presided over the period during which the most significant changes were made to German foreign policy. Frank-Walter Steinmeier, the Social Democratic Foreign Secretary in Angela Merkel's government coalition that came to power in 2005, acknowledged that German foreign policy had undergone a considerable reorientation in the 15 years since unification. According to Steinmeier, Germany had found a new role in the post–Cold War order: 'Our value in foreign affairs is not determined any more by our role as the (last) outpost of the western world. That is why we have to see to it ourselves how we can influence developments beyond our borders according to our wishes' (2005).

Whether the world is ready for a return of German leadership is a different matter, however. The ambiguity felt at the prospect of an enhanced role for Germany in international matters is expressed in an article in the *Washington Post* when its author suggests that 'Germany's richly deserved 60-year holiday from leadership abroad is ending sooner than many here would like' (8 October, 2006).

Speeches made by leading German politicians at the Munich Security Conference in 2014 suggest that the debate about Germany's role in the world is not yet settled, however (see also Hellmann et al., 2015). As Gale Mattox has pointed out, German President Joachim Gauck, Foreign Minister Frank-Walter Steinmeier and Defence Minister Ursula von der Leyen all argued in favour of an enhanced and more engaged international role for Germany (2015). Whether Germany is actually becoming more engaged is a different matter. As *The Economist* suggested in the context of the Munich Security Conference four years later, 'Germany remains reluctant to pull its weight in the world' offering 'much rhetoric and little action' (2018).

Conclusion

Germany has experienced a significant reorientation in its foreign policy and its international role since unification in 1990. Although it is still strongly committed to multilateralism and favours diplomacy over the use of military force in conflict resolution, on occasion it is now prepared and has the constitutional provisions to employ military force. Nevertheless, debates about Germany's place in the post–Cold War world continue suggesting that this place is not quite clearly defined yet. On the one hand there are still suggestions that Germany is 'punching below its weight' and on the other hand, it is depicted as dominant, particularly within the EU. Angela Merkel's cautious and consensus-seeking leadership and Germany's strong economic performance have contributed to an image of Germany as a stable and successful country, even though – as in the context of its trade surplus – this success is sometimes considered to be at the expense of others. Merkel has not only been described as the 'decider' of Europe but it was also suggested that – in view of President Trump's erratic behaviour and leadership – Merkel should become 'the leader of the free world'.

Germany is still very committed to European integration, even though an identification with Europe is not as important anymore as a kind of ersatz identity. By and large, Germans seem to have found their way back to identifying with the German nation (Götz, 2016). And even though German political elites and society at large continue to be pro-integrationist, this is complemented by a clearer and less reluctant articulation of German interests. For the first time since 1949, however, the federal elections to the Bundestag in 2017 returned a sizeable group of parliamentarians to the chamber – the Alternative für Deutschland (Alternative for Germany) – which started off as a eurosceptic party and then turned into an anti-establishment, openly nationalist and xenophobic far-right populist party.

These changes have taken place against the background of the very different geopolitical environment of the post–Cold War period. Since 1990, Western Europe and Germany, in particular, have become strategically significantly less important for the US. Especially since the advent to power of Donald Trump, Germany has given up trying to appear to maintain equidistance between the EU and the US. Angela Merkel has come down firmly on the side of Europe. She made it very clear that she thought Europe would now have to look after its own affairs rather than looking to the US for help and guidance. This approach is also reflected in the coalition agreement between the Christian Democratic Union, the Christian Social Union and the Social Democratic Party of Germany of 2018, which articulates two main aims for Germany's position within Europe and vis-à-vis the US: to 'remain transatlantic' but to 'become more European' (Koalitionsvertrag, 2018, p. 144).

Further reading

Colvin, Sarah (ed.) (2017) *The Routledge Handbook of German Politics & Culture* (London: Routledge).

Crawford, Beverly (2007) *Power and German Foreign Policy: Embedded Hegemony in Europe* (Basingstoke: Palgrave Macmillan).

Larres, Klaus and Ruth Wittlinger (2018) *A Fragile Friendship: German-American Relations in the 21st Century*. Special Issue of *German Politics*.

Lemke, Christiane and Helga Welsh (2018) *Remapping Germany: Politics and Policies in a Changing World* (Lanham, MD: Rowman & Littlefield).

Maull, Hans (2006) (ed.) *Germany's Power* (Basingstoke: Palgrave).

Mushaben, Joyce Marie (2017) *Becoming Madam Chancellor: Angela Merkel and the Berlin Republic* (Cambridge: Cambridge University Press).

Oppermann, Kai (2012) 'National Role Conceptions, Domestic Constraints and the New "Normalcy" in German Foreign Policy: The Eurozone Crisis, Libya and Beyond', *German Politics* 21(4), pp. 502–519.

Padgett, Stephen and William E. Paterson (2014) *Developments in German Politics 4* (Basingstoke: Palgrave).

Roberts, Geoffrey (2016) *German Politics Today* (Manchester: Manchester University Press).

Wittlinger, Ruth (2010) *German National Identity in the Twenty-First Century: A Different Republic After All?* (Basingstoke: Palgrave).

Wittlinger, Ruth (2013) 'Shaking Off the Past? The New Germany in the New Europe', in Eric Langenbacher, Bill Niven and Ruth Wittlinger (eds.) *Dynamics of Memory and Identity in Contemporary Europe* (New York: Berghahn).

Bibliography

Banchoff, Thomas (1997) 'German Policy Toward the European Union: The Effects of Historical Memory', *German Politics* 6(1), pp. 60–76.

Baumann, Rainer and Gunther Hellmann (2001) 'Germany and the Use of Military Force: "Total War", the "Culture of Restraint" and the Quest for Normality', *German Politics* 10(1), pp. 61–82.

Berger, Thomas U. (1996) 'Norms, Identity and National Security in Germany and Japan' in Peter J. Katzenstein (ed.) *The Culture of National Security: Norms and Identity in World Politics* (New York: Columbia University Press), pp. 317–356.

Berger, Thomas U. (1998) *Cultures of Antimilitarism: National Security in Germany and Japan* (Baltimore: Johns Hopkins University Press).

Brunssen, Frank (2005) *Das neue Selbstverständnis der Berliner Republik* (Würzburg: Königshausen & Neumann).

Bulmer, Simon (2014) 'Germany and the Eurozone Crisis: Between Hegemony and Domestic Politics', *West European Politics* 37(6), pp. 1244–1263.

Bundestag, Plenarprotokoll, 253. Sitzung, 13 September 2002, see also Plenarprotokoll, 32. Sitzung, 14 March 2003.

Crawford, Beverly (2007) *Power and German Foreign Policy: Embedded Hegemony in Europe* (Basingstoke: Palgrave Macmillan).

Crawshaw, Steve (2004) *Easier Fatherland: Germany and the Twenty-First Century* (London: Continuum).

Dettle, Dieter (2009) *Germany Says 'No': The Iraq War and the Future of German Foreign and Security Policy* (Baltimore: Johns Hopkins University Press).

The Economist (2018) 'Germany Remains Reluctant to Pull its Weight in the World' (19 February), www.economist.com/blogs/kaffeeklatsch/2018/02/happily-vegetarian.

Faiola, Anthony (2016) 'Angela Merkel Congratulates Trump – Kind of'. *The Washington Post* (9 November), www.washingtonpost.com/news/worldviews/wp/2016/11/09/angela-merkel-congratulates-donald-trump-kind-of/?utm_term=.7112369bd150.

Faiola, Anthony and Stephanie Kirchner (2017) 'Trump Set to Meet Merkel, "Europe's Decider", After Frosty Start to Relations', *The Washington Post* (9 November), www.washingtonpost.com/world/trump-set-to-meet-merkel-europes-decider-after-frosty-start-to-relations/2017/03/13/7912a5a0–07f7–11e7-bd19-fd3afa0f7e2a_story.html?utm_term=.a8b9b07a1325.

Frei, Norbert (1997) *Vergangenheitspolitik: Die Anfänge der Bundesrepublik und die NS-Vergangenheit* (Munich: Beck Verlag).

Fulbrook, Mary (1999) *German National Identity After the Holocaust* (Cambridge: Blackwell).

Galpin, Charlotte (2015) 'Has Germany "Fallen out of Love" with Europe? The Eurozone Crisis and the "Normalization" of Germany's European Identity', *German Politics and Society* 33(1–2), pp. 25–41.

Garton Ash, Timothy (2009) 'One Great Power Will Be Absent from the London G20 Summit', *The Guardian* (26 March).

Götz, Irene (2016) 'The Rediscovery of "the National" in the 1990s – Contexts, New Cultural Forms and Practices in Reunified Germany', *Nations and Nationalism* 22(4), pp. 820–823.

Hall, Peter A. (2012) 'The Economics and Politics of the Euro Crisis', *German Politics* 21(4), pp. 355–371.

Hellmann, Gunther, Daniel Jacobi and Ursula Stark Urrestarazu (eds.) (2015) *'Früher, entschiedener und substantieller'? Die neue Debatte über Deutschlands Außenpolitik*. Sonderheft der Zeitschrift für Außen- und Sicherheitspolitik. Sonderheft 6 (Cologne: Springer VS).

Herzog, Roman (1999) Speech, Berlin (13 March).

Hillebrand, Rainer (2015) 'Germany and its Eurozone Crisis Policy: The Impact of the Country's Ordoliberal Heritage', *German Politics and Society* 33(1–2), pp. 6–24.

Hyde-Price, Adrian (2003) 'Foreign and Security Policy', in Stephen Padgett, William E. Paterson and Gordon Smith (eds.) *Developments in German Politics* (Basingstoke: Palgrave Macmillan), pp. 184–205.

Kansteiner, Wulf (2006) 'Losing the War, Winning the Memory Battle: The Legacy of Nazism, World War II, and the Holocaust in the Federal Republic of Germany' in Richard Ned Lebow, Wulf Kansteiner and Claudio Fogu (eds.) *The Politics and Memory in Postwar Europe* (Durham, NC: Duke University Press), pp. 102–146.

Karp, Regina (2006) 'The New German Foreign Policy Consensus', *The Washington Quarterly* 29(1), pp. 61–82.

Koalitionsvertrag zwischen CDU, CSU und SPD (2018) *Ein neuer Aufbruch für Europa. Eine neue Dynamik für Deutschland. Ein neuer Zusammenhalt für unser Land.* www.cdu.de/system/tdf/media/dokumente/koalitionsvertrag_2018.pdf?file=1.

Langenbacher, Eric (2010) 'Still the Unmasterable Past? The Impact of History and Memory in the Federal Republic of Germany', *German Politics* 19(1), pp. 24–40.

Loth, Wilfried (1984) 'Die doppelte Eindämmung. Überlegungen zur Genesis des Kalten Krieges 1945–1947', *Historische Zeitschrift* 238, pp. 611–631.

Maier, Charles S. (1998) *The Unmasterable Past: History, Holocaust, and German National Identity* (Cambridge, MA: Harvard University Press).

Markovits, Andrei S. and Simon Reich (1997) *The German Predicament: Memory and Power in the New Europe* (Ithaca: Cornell University Press).

Mattox, Gale (2015) 'Two Steps Forward, One Step Back: Germany Rethinks its Security Policy', American Institute for Contemporary German Studies (30 June), www.aicgs.org/publication/two-steps-forward-one-step-back/#_ftn5.

Mearsheimer, John J. (1990) 'Back to the Future: Instability in Europe after the Cold War', *International Security* 15(1), pp. 5–56.

Maull, Hans (2006) (ed.) *Germany's Uncertain Power* (Basingstoke: Palgrave).

Merkel, Angela (2006) Regierungserklaerung (14 December 2006).

Merkel, Angela (2007) Speech to the European Parliament during Germany's EU Presidency (17 January 2007).

Müller-Brandeck-Bocquet, Gisela (2003) 'Die Europapolitik des vereinten Deutschland', in Wichard Woyke (ed.) *Neue deutsche Außenpolitik* (Schwalbach: Wochenschau Verlag), pp. 47–73.

Niven, Bill (2002) *Facing the Nazi Past: United Germany and the Legacy of the Third Reich* (London: Routledge).

Paterson, William E. (2003) 'Germany and Europe', in Stephen Padgett, William E. Paterson and Gordon Smith (eds.) *Developments in German Politics* (Basingstoke: Palgrave Macmillan), pp. 206–226.

Paterson, William E. (2010) 'Does Germany Still Have a European Vocation?' *German Politics* 19(1), pp. 41–52.

Paterson, William E. (2011) 'The Reluctant Hegemon? Germany Moves Centre Stage in the European Union', *Journal of Common Market Studies: Annual Review* 49, pp. 57–75.

Pearce, Caroline (2008) *Contemporary Germany and the Nazi Legacy: Remembrance, Politics and the Dialectics of Normality* (Basingstoke: Palgrave Macmillan).

Pond, Elizabeth (1999) *The Rebirth of Europe* (Washington, DC: Brookings Institution Press).

Schöllgen, Gregor (2004) *Der Auftritt. Deutschlands Rückkehr auf die Weltbühne* (Berlin: Ullstein).

Schröder, Gerhard (1998) Regierungserklärung (10 November 1998).

Schröder, Gerhard (1999a) *Erklärung der Bundesregierung zum Stand der Deutschen Einheit* (19 April).

Schröder, Gerhard (1999b) Interview, *Der Spiegel*, no. 1, 4 January 1999, p. 44.

Schröder, Gerhard (2006) *Entscheidungen. Mein Leben in der Politik* (Hamburg: Hoffmann und Campe).

Schwab-Trapp, Michael (2003) 'Der Nationalsozialismus im öffentlichen Diskurs über militärische Gewalt', in Wolfgang Bergem (ed.) *Die NS-Diktatur im deutschen Erinnerungsdiskurs* (Opladen: Leske & Budrich), pp. 171–185.

Schwarz, Hans Peter (1985) *Die gezähmten Deutschen. Von der Machtversessenheit zur Machtvergessenheit* (Stuttgart: Deutsche Verlags-Anstalt).

Schweiger, Christian (2007) *Britain, German and the European Union* (Basingstoke: Palgrave Macmillan).

Steininger, Rolf (2001) 'The German Question, 1945–1995', in Klaus Larres (ed.) *Germany since Unification*, 2nd ed. (Basingstoke: Palgrave), pp. 9–32.

Steinmeier, Frank-Walter, Speech (23 November 2005).

Thatcher, Margaret (1995) *The Downing Street Years* (London: HarperCollins).

The Washington Post (8 October 2006).

Webber, Douglas (2001) 'Introduction: German European and Foreign Policy Before and After Unification', *German Politics* 10(1), pp. 1–18.

Wittlinger, Ruth (2010) *German National Identity in the Twenty-First Century: A Different Republic After All?* (Basingstoke: Palgrave).

Wittlinger, Ruth and Martin Larose (2007) 'No Future for Germany's Past? Collective Memory and German Foreign Policy', *German Politics* 16(4), pp. 481–495.

Wood, Steve (2004) *Germany and East-Central Europe: Political Economic and Sociocultural Relations in the Era of EU Enlargement* (Farnham: Ashgate).

Zehfuss, Maja ((2002) *Constructivism in International Relations: The Politics of Reality* (Cambridge: Cambridge University Press).

Chapter 11

The United Nations

Manuel Fröhlich

The United Nations represents the most universal attempt at world organisation in the history of international affairs. Founded in 1945, its structures, principles and procedures are still tied to the experience and challenges of World War II and the post-war planning of the anti-axis powers that, already in 1942, had assembled

FIGURE 11.1 Security Council meeting at the United Nations in New York, US

under the name of 'United Nations'. Out of a war-alliance emerged an international organisation with nearly 200 member states and a broad range of activities. Looking back at more than seven decades of its existence, the organisation has undergone a number of substantial transformations with regard to the polity of the UN system, the politics that rule its dynamics as well as the policies adopted and pursued by the UN and its member states. The United Nations, with all its achievements and failures, can also be seen as mirroring central features of international affairs at large.

The idea of world organisation

The question on how to further peace and avoid war is a recurring theme in the history of ideas and political philosophy (cf. Hinsley, 1963; Fröhlich 2010, 2017). In modern times, the literary genre of peace plans or peace proposals emerged and offered a series of quite detailed blueprints that stemmed from a number of common convictions regarding the nature of interaction between states and peoples as well as the construction of structures to avoid human suffering. Starting with Erasmus of Rotterdam and his 'Querela Pacis' in 1517, the arguments for world organisation are closely tied to a description of the ultimate benefits of peaceful coexistence and cooperation instead of a state of continuous war. Already in Erasmus' plea we can find the insight that world organisation is mainly a challenge of managing diversity and plurality – of states, peoples, religions and ideologies. The experience of Europe's wars of religion had called into questions the ordering principle of Universitas Christiana from medieval times which no longer provided sufficient stability and orientation in international affairs. World organisation thus was not a given, it had to be created. William Penn's 'Essay towards the Present and Future Peace of Europe, by the Establishment of an European Dyet, Parliament, or Estates' from 1693 as well as the Abbé de Saint-Pierre's 'Projet pour rendre la paix perpetuelle en Europe' from 1713 already detail a number of institutional features and legal provisions that account for a system of collective security and the rule of law in international relations.

One of the basic assumptions of these plans was the 'domestic analogy', i.e. that the strategy for the pacification of relations between states is essentially the same as the one for pacification of relations between individuals in a given state (cf. Bull, 1995). This strategy includes the establishment of a monopoly on the use of force, the rule of law as well as the possibility of sanctions in order to uphold the status quo created by a social contract among the members of a given community. In order to account for the differences in size and power among states, both Penn and Saint-Pierre discuss several institutional ideas of creating a plenary organ and voting procedure for all member states. Notwithstanding the basic analogy to the pacification within states, most peace plans did not argue for a simple transfer of this model that would lead to a world state. The protection of the social contract, the constitution and political sovereignty that citizen had already established within their respective states thus emerged as one crucial element of world organisation. At the same time, the tension between (national) sovereignty and (international) cooperation, intensified by discrepancies in power and wealth, was already apparent in these peace plans and would in fact remain with the project of world organisation until today (cf. Mazower, 2012).

The most influential blueprint for world organisation can be seen in Kant's essay 'Perpetual Peace' from 1795 (Kant, 1984; cf. Gerhardt, 1995). Apart from its rich impact in the history of ideas, Kant's essay served as a philosophical roadmap inspiring both the experiments of the League of Nations after World War I and the United Nations after World War II. Kant's essay was in fact structured in the fashion of contemporary peace agreements offering a set of preliminary and definitive articles that contained the negative and positive conditions for peace. Among the negative conditions one can find a plea for the replacement of standing armies with small militias and the prohibition to violently interfere in the constitution of another state. The three definite articles, on the other hand, offered a triad of measures to comprehensively limit the possibilities of war:

The first article ('The civil constitution of every nation shall be republican') underlined the fact that efforts for international peace have to start with domestic politics. Republican states in which those who actually have to fight will have the power to decide on matters of war and peace, have an inclination to avoid war. This argument laid the basis for the manifold research on the 'democratic peace' (cf. Brown and Lynn-Jones, 1996). The second definite article ('The rights of nations shall be based on a federation of free states') provided the groundwork for what later would be called international organisations. Kant does not give too much detail on structure and procedure of such a federation but drafts a permanent mechanism to reconcile the actions of member states, avoid war and sanction possible aggressors if the rules of the federation are violated. Kant's construction does not stop there: in his third definite article ('Cosmopolitan right shall be limited to the conditions of universal hospitality') he introduced yet another level of pacification. Apart from national constitutions and international laws or treaties, the effort for world organisation also has to address and incorporate the notion of laws and rights that directly originate with the individual – irrespective of his or her nationality. Behind this argument one can see the classical liberal idea of universal human rights. There is a direct line between Kant's ideas and the institutional efforts to bring about world peace after the World Wars of the 20th century. In the case of the League of Nations, one can even argue that the post-war order envisioned by US President Woodrow Wilson was directly influenced by Kant's text which, in his earlier life as an academic, he had studied intensively. The common assumptions of a system of collective security and shared norms of law and conflict resolution, despite the failure of the League, resurfaced in the form of the United Nations and its Charter in 1945.

The structure of the United Nations

The first experiment of creating a world structure for peace, for a number of reasons, was not able to stop the outbreak of World War II (cf. Housden, 2012). This failure of the League also led to a challenge of its underlying assumptions: the idea of collective security, the rule of law, the appeal to reason and trust in international affairs as well as the sanctity of international treaties and the positive dynamics of international law were seen as expressions of so called idealist thinking in international relations that had to give way to a more 'realist' way of looking at the world (cf. Wilson and Long, 1995). The debate between these schools of thought thus became the first grand debate in international relations (cf. Jackson and Sorensen, 2015).

With its efforts to learn from the failure of the League but at the same time re-start the project for a universal world organisation, the United Nations, which was founded as a war-time alliance, aimed for a more robust structure for peace. Idealist concepts and realist experiences can be detected in one of the main documents preceding the United Nations, the Atlantic Charter from August 1941. In this document, the prime minister of the UK and the president of the US sketched a vision for a post-war order. The eighth principle that they proclaimed calls for 'the establishment of a wider and permanent system of general security' and global disarmament 'for realistic as well as spiritual reasons'.

The preamble to the Charter of the United Nations, signed at the founding conference on 26 June 1945 in San Francisco, spells out the determination 'to save succeeding generations from the scourge of war, which twice in our lifetime has brought untold sorrow to mankind'. The Charter, therefore, does not only contain procedural rules of an international organisation. It also codifies central rules of international law and international relations that have become the accepted aspiration and norm of state behaviour. One fundamental feature of the order thus established is the general prohibition of the use of force spelled out in article 2 (4) of the Charter. The UN took a decisive step in curtailing what was long regarded as the ultimate expression of state sovereignty, the 'right' to go to war. The decision on the rightfulness of using force, under the Charter, was now subject to multilateral deliberation in the UN Security Council, the executive organ holding the main responsibility for the maintenance of international peace and security. Only the Council can order the use of force 'in the common interest' (preamble). The only other exception from the general prohibition of force is individual or collective self-defence 'if an armed attack occurs' (article 51). While these efforts set new international standards, article 2 (7) also protects each member's freedom to decide and act upon 'matters which are essentially within the domestic jurisdiction of any state'. The perennial tensions between international organisation and national sovereignty thus also permeate the structure of the United Nations. Although the Charter focuses on the maintenance of international peace and security, its conception of peace also encompasses the development of friendly relations among states, the promotion of economic, social and cultural cooperation as well as the protection of fundamental rights of individuals.

The organisational structure of the United Nations mirrors a triad that is present in nearly all international organisations since the first administrative unions were created in the 19th century (cf. Archer, 2015 and the overview in Weiss and Daws, 2018). Echoing the creation by common will and assembly of state parties, we find a plenary organ, the General Assembly, which today encompasses 193 member states. The General Assembly has a broad thematic mandate to deal with all the aspects of the world organisation. It can issue resolutions, establish programs and committees, call for inquires or assign budgetary resources. Its decisions are, however, not directly binding to member states.

The more executive organ of the United Nations is the Security Council with a membership of five permanent (US, Russia, China, the UK and France) and ten non-permanent members elected by the General Assembly on a regional basis. The permanent members of the Council hold special veto rights, i.e. they can use their single vote to block a resolution that a majority of at least nine members of the Council would have favoured. The privileges of the permanent members can be linked to what US President Franklin D. Roosevelt conceptualised as the 'policemen' of the world that held a special part in the defeat of the axis powers and would henceforth take on a special responsibility for securing the peace. Chapter VII of the UN Charter gives the Council special instruments to deal with threats and breaches of the peace that range from recommendations and non-military sanctions to the use of force under article 42.

Resolutions of the Council, in contrast to those of the Assembly, are directly binding to member states. Although the Charter details some plans for the common management of military contingents, military action basically has to rely on contributions of member states that make their resources available to the UN. Echoing the wider concept of peace depicted earlier, the UN not only has a Security Council but a Social and Economic Council as well as (since 2005 in its present form) a Human Rights Council (the UN Trusteeship Council which dealt with former colonial territories is inoperative since the independence of Palau in 1994). These specialised councils work on their own procedure and agenda. They cooperate with the General Assembly but also with a number of specialised agencies and programs whose work, as well as that of the International Court of Justice (another main organ of the UN), is beyond the scope of this chapter.

The third basic pillar of the UN organisational structure is the UN Secretariat, compromising a core staff of roughly 40,000 international civil servants working worldwide for the United Nations (cf. Fröhlich, 2008a; Gordenker, 2010). The Secretariat is headed by the Secretary-General, who is appointed by the Assembly on a recommendation by the Security Council. The Secretary-General is more than 'the chief administrative officer' (Article 97) of the UN. The Charter also bestows him with vague but potentially large and important political powers. The scope of the office can also be illustrated in the fact that Roosevelt, for a time, floated the idea of calling this officer the 'World's Moderator'. Chapter XV of the Charter establishes the Secretary-General as a manager of three parallel tasks (cf. Fröhlich, 2008a): the office-holder is supposed to work as a manager of administration, running the organisation (article 97), as a manager of conflict, providing good offices and leading peace mission (articles 98 and 99) as well as a manager of ideas (article 100) charged with upholding and updating the values and vision of the Charter. This comparatively strong personal mandate is also a contrast to the League. But all Charter provisions basically provide a loose structure whose use and performance is heavily dependent upon a variety of dynamics and influences that need to be contextualised (cf. Fröhlich and Williams, 2018).

Understanding the United Nations

To speak of 'the' United Nations is a problematic generalisation that can lead to theoretical and even practical misunderstandings. In order to grasp the dynamics of the UN more precisely, a set of triadic distinctions is useful.

The first triad borrows from a general distinction in the study of international organisations that Clive Archer (2015) introduced. In this perspective, international organisations (not only the UN) can play three different roles as instrument, arena or actor. Thus, the UN can be used as an instrument of its most powerful member states (for example in the Security Council). It may also function as place of deliberation and cooperation among its members (as for example in debates of the General Assembly) or it may act as an actor in its own right (epitomised by initiatives and actions of the Secretary-General or the international civil service at large). These roles are not tied to specific organs and may mix and overlap but they offer a first useful clarification to specify what is actually meant by reference to 'the' United Nations in a given situation.

The second triad, which goes back to a distinction by Inis Claude Jr. (1996), is also helpful in that context. Claude distinguished the 'first' from the 'second' UN. The former would comprise the member states of the organisation while the latter would look at its officials and staff. Thomas Weiss and others have extended this perspective and introduced the concept of a 'third' UN that consists of experts, consultants, academics and representatives of civil society that work in 'parallel' to the 'first' and 'second' UN (Weiss et al., 2009). This last form of the UN gained importance due to the rise of non-governmental organisations in international affairs as well as new structures of public-private cooperation.

These triadic distinctions already offer more precise terms to not only understand the UN as an organisation but also its actions, its successes and failures. Broadly speaking, these roles of the UN can also be linked to different theories of international relations: looking at the UN as a function of national interests of great powers would accord to a (neo-)realist perspective, emphasising its forum-like quality as a hub of cooperation matches fundamental assumptions of liberal/institutionalist thinking whereas the actions of the 'second' UN would concur with basic tenets of constructivist thinking (especially when an actor like the Secretary-General has more ideational than material resources available to him). Employing these distinctions also has a practical value since it is important for attributing agency as well as political responsibility.

A further triadic distinction tries to take a closer look at how the UN operates (cf. Fröhlich, 2008b). In order to illustrate this point, the metaphor of three table games in a casino may give some orientation: The basic idea is that UN action or inaction is tied to the performance at three different tables that, in order to allow for 'successful' UN action, have to be 'won' simultaneously. So winning at each table is a necessary but not a sufficient condition for success. The rules of the game, the required skills and resources as well as the stakes are different for each table: the first table is the 'legal' table, the second one the 'political' and the third one the 'ethical' table. Successful UN action would ideally have a sound legal basis in general international law or the Charter specifically. This alone, however, does not suffice. In order for UN action to be realised, political majorities have to be generated. And even if legal basis and political majority are in place, this does not automatically mean that a given UN action would be compatible with the high ethical standards and aspirations of the Charter. While lawfulness of action is the winning argument at the first table, political support counts at the second and ethical soundness at the third table. In order to exemplify this metaphor with a case, we can think of the

UN's action in the face of the unfolding genocide in Rwanda (cf. Melvern, 2000; Independent Inquiry, 2000). Both the first and the second table, in the eyes of the Security Council members, precluded action: member states did not see the necessary legal basis for intervening in a domestic situation and there was no majority for a resolution to use the powers available to the Council.

While one could argue that the eventual inaction of the Council followed the rules of the game, the existence of table three accounts for the discontent with the action by the UN in Rwanda. Legal arguments and political majorities cannot supersede ethical arguments which, in turn, do not necessarily provide legal justification or generate political support. The case of Rwanda, with catastrophic results, is also illustrative of the importance of the first triadic sets that we introduced: the independent investigation into 'the' UN's role differentiated responsibility regarding the Secretary-General, international civil servants, members of the Council or the membership at large. Going beyond the example of Rwanda, the three triadic distinctions can be helpful to look at the achievements and failures, the benefits and deficits of the work of the UN in international relations.

The work of the United Nations

The work of the UN can broadly be separated into the three areas of security, development and human rights (cf. Weiss et al., 2016). Maintaining international peace and security is the core task of the UN under the Charter. The work of the UN in this field has, however, only seldom followed strictly the provisions of Chapter VII. Two situations are generally seen to be matching the original Charter vision of collective security: The first one occurred when the UN engaged into an armed intervention on the Korean peninsula in May 1950 after North Korea invaded South Korea. The situation, at first glance, seems to be matching the foundational Charter model of one state attacking another and the UN coming to the help against the aggressor. The UN thus became a part of the Korean War but there are some particularities of that first implementation of collective security. The necessary resolution of the Security Council was taken when the Soviet Union chose to be absent because it protested the presence of the Republic of China on the Council. It quickly returned and, given its support for the North, threatened a veto on any further council action. This is when the General Assembly, in a remarkable move, self-legitimised itself to make recommendations on peace and security by a two-thirds majority of its members when the Council was blocked.

In contrast to today, where the African and Asian countries constitute the largest member groups, back in the 1950s there was still a solid majority of 'Western' countries in the Assembly from the European and Latin American regional groups. The second particularity of the Korean case was that the military force under the UN flag was in fact predominantly American and did certainly not work under the auspices of the military staff committee that the Charter created as a meeting point of representatives from the permanent members in order to conduct and advise on military matters. So this first test of collective security action is a special case that also foreshadowed the blockade that hampered the UN during the Cold War.

The second situation that is often cited as a rather close realisation of the collective security idea of the Charter is the Council's reaction to Iraq's invasion of Kuwait in 1990 by mandating 'Operation Desert Storm' that restored the territorial integrity and sovereignty of Kuwait. This action to protect one member state of the United Nations against aggression from its neighbour was facilitated by the end of bloc-power confrontation at the end of the Cold War. During the tensions between East and West, the Council was not able to deal with a lot of crises. In this situation, the peace and security work of the UN partly moved to the General Assembly and the office of the Secretary-General whose incumbent, Dag Hammarskjöld, was especially successful in innovating new procedures for the maintenance of international peace and security that the Charter did not explicitly mention (cf. Fröhlich, 2008a).

The best case in point here is the development of peacekeeping operations as a central tool of the UN's work. These missions evolved from a precedent during the Suez crisis in 1956 in order to separate warring parties and de-escalate a conflict (Fröhlich, 2014). The first peacekeeping mission was mandated not by the Security Council (with France and the UK, being part of the crisis, ready to veto any measure against their interests) but by the General Assembly. Without a mandate of the Council (who alone can use the tools of Chapter VII), the central principles of peacekeeping included the necessary consent of the parties involved, the imperative to act impartially and the limitation to the use of force by lightly armed 'blue helmets' only in self-defence. Such a peacekeeping mission would thus not be concerned with peace enforcement but rather work as an additional instrument of mediation, reconciliation and the peaceful settlement of disputes in the sense of Chapter VI of the Charter. This is why the characterisation of these missions as working under 'Chapter VI and a half' is a fitting term.

From this precedent in the 1950s developed a core activity of the UN – especially after the end of the Cold War when the Security Council also reclaimed its position in setting up and mandating missions. While there were only 18 missions between 1945 and 1990, the total count has now has passed 70 operations. Just after the 70th anniversary of the organisation, there were about 100,000 soldiers serving in 16 missions around the globe. These operations also have changed in many ways (cf. Bellamy and Williams, 2010): they are primarily deployed in intra-state (rather than inter-state) conflicts and work on an increasing number of tasks that nowadays can range from security sector reform to electoral assistance and even transitional administration of countries such as Kosovo and East Timor before their independence. This is why they often are no longer described as peacekeeping missions but rather as peace operations – underlining the fact that they work in a spectrum that Secretary-General Boutros-Ghali, in his 1992 'Agenda for Peace', described as ranging from peacemaking through peacekeeping to peacebuilding. The latter encompasses all activities that help sustain peace in a given country. The enlargement of tasks also coincided with a transformation of the classical principles of peacekeeping.

At present a great number of Council missions have Chapter VII powers not only for self-defence but also for defence of the mission goals or the protection of civilians (i.a. a consequence of the Rwanda experience sketched earlier). Peace operations also play an important role in stabilising fragile states or even engage in counterterrorism activities. Once again, the tension between international organisation and national sovereignty is marked by these new developments. Going beyond the operational level of peace missions, the UN is also engaged in efforts to find new ways of how to respond to mass atrocities, genocide, crimes against humanity or ethnic cleansing. Following up on the experience of Rwanda, Kosovo and East Timor, the concept of a 'responsibility to protect' (cf. ICISS, 2001; Bellamy, 2009; Fröhlich, 2016) that falls upon the international community when national authorities are not willing or able to protect their citizens has sparked off a lot of debate and controversy. UN-mandated action in Libya in 2011 and prolonged inaction in the case of Syria are two concrete manifestations of the evolution and contestation of this new norm.

In the field of development work, the UN has created a series of instruments and programs to further not only national development but also the welfare of individual people. While efforts at reconstruction and humanitarian aid were the focus right after World War II, the process of decolonialisation brought the needs and support of newly independent countries on the agenda. Early efforts at technical assistance paved the way to more institutionalised structures, most notably the UN Conference for Trade and Development (UNCTAD) in 1964 and the more operational United Nations Development Programme in 1965 (see Stokke, 2009). Several concepts for modernisation and economic change tried to address especially the problems of the least developed countries. The work of the UN soon went beyond structural programs that focused solely on economic growth to addressing broader social, political and cultural questions of development.

The UN also started to tackle structural causes of inequality and poverty in a long-term perspective while expanding its work on emergency, disaster and crisis response in a short-term perspective. Notable agencies in this context are the UN High Commissioner for Human Rights (UNHCR) and the Office for the Coordination of Humanitarian Affairs (OCHA). The broad range of activities from poverty reduction to questions of crisis prevention, democratic governance or environmental sustainability is accompanied by new conceptual tools that focus on people rather than states.

The publication of the first Human Development report by UNDP in 1990 ushered in a new understanding of interdependent aspects of human development beyond econometric factors. Following up on these transformations, the proclamation of the Millennium Development Goals (MDGs) by the General Assembly in the year 2000 marked a new era for development activities of the world organisation. Member states had accepted eight development goals – from halving the number of people living in conditions of absolute poverty, an increase in access to basic school education to the fight against global pandemics or the improvement of maternal health. The target date for the realisation of these goals was 2015. When the target date was reached, the progress was remarkable but also mixed, with strong improvements in some parts of the globe but persistent problems in other areas (cf. United Nations, 2015). As a follow-up to the MDGs, the General Assembly agreed upon a continuation and reorientation of these efforts in the form of 17 Sustainable Development Goals (SDGs) with a new target date in 2030. Common to this new set of goals is a more pronounced emphasis on ecological aspects of development. This ties in with the fact that the UN, starting with the foundation of the UN Environmental Program (UNEP) in 1972, has become a central platform for combating climate change.

The example of climate change is a good illustration of how the UN works on new challenges for the international community in conceptual and operational terms. Starting with the 1992 Earth Summit in Rio that helped to create a consensus on challenges in the realm of environmental policies, the United Nations Framework Convention on Climate Change (UNFCCC) was adopted with the aim of monitoring pledges and progress for limiting the emission of greenhouse gas. Big milestones were reached with the 1997 Kyoto and 2015 Paris Agreements. Another major aspect of the UN's work in this field is scientific research, standard-setting and data generation which, in the field of climate change, is primarily done by the intergovernmental Panel on Climate Change (IPCC), established by the General Assembly in 1988, whose work was awarded (together with other actors) the Nobel Peace Prize in 2007. Progress in consensus-building and the establishment of standards and norms does, however, stand in contrast to problems in the implementation and effective realisation of the agreed policies. This, once again, partly has to do with the fact that treaties and resolutions oftentimes are phrased as recommendations rather than binding obligations with the necessary sanctions. Effective implementation is in any case dependent upon decentralised efforts by each and every member state. The overall tension between international organisation and national sovereignty once again stands out as a recurring feature of the work of the United Nations. This also holds true for the third main area of the world organisations efforts.

The UN's work in the realm of human rights starts with the preparation of the Universal Declaration of Human Rights (cf. Morsink, 2000) that was drafted by a special commission under the aegis of the Economic and Social Council. Its adoption in 1948 by the General Assembly was a consequence of the catastrophic experience of human suffering and the denial of human rights during totalitarianism and the war that reinforced a common conviction in the importance of human rights. The formula of the Atlantic Charter that wanted to safeguard 'freedom from fear and want' (an echo of Roosevelt's State of the Union address in 1941) built a bridge between classical liberal rights and economic and social rights that, under the increasing influence of the East–West conflict, became weakened. This is one reason why the next two important documents that complement the Universal Declaration to an International Bill of Rights were focused thematically.

The International Covenant on Civil and Political Rights as well as its twin document, the International Covenant on Economic, Social and Cultural Rights, were adopted by the UN in 1966 and entered into force in 1976. This cumulative Bill of Rights is also extended by a series of thematic treaties and covenants from children's rights to those of migrant workers, etc. The Convention on the Elimination of All Forms of Discrimination against Women (CEDAW) is another milestone in this context. It is also illustrative of the working procedures employed by the UN: the Convention established a separate organ to monitor the implementation of women's rights that works with regular reports from member states. Once again, the implementation is decentralised. States can, however, accept more binding obligations in optional protocols to such treaties. They do, at the same time, also make use of such addenda in order to opt out of certain provisions or express reservations. Even after the end of the Cold War, human rights policy at the United Nations remains heavily contested: states show different priorities in either political or economic rights. They argue for and against the inclusion of group rights instead of only individual rights or doubt the universality of rights that allegedly threaten religious convictions or cultural heritage. The World Conference on Human Rights in Vienna 1993, against this background, underlined the indivisibility and universality of human rights. Recent developments in the so-called war against terror and connected infringements of human rights as well as nationalistic policies have again raised controversies about the nature and range of human rights policy.

Conclusion

The United Nations remains the primary manifestation of the project and problems of world organisation. Its relevance is based on a series of accomplishments but also on the fact that its shortcomings and failures mirror situational and structural problems of world politics. This representation of shifting power dynamics and the changing agenda of international affairs, rather inevitably, has resulted in continuous calls for reform of the world body and its practices. The reform of the Charter is tied to high procedural requirements: two-thirds of the member states in the General Assembly have to adopt a reform proposal that only enters into effect when two-thirds actually ratify this adoption – including the permanent members of the Security Council whose veto thus practically extends to questions of substantial reform.

Although the Charter has not been changed often, the organisation, which still holds the same name and basic structure as in 1945, has dramatically changed in the past seven decades: the number of members has increased from 50 to 193, the geographical and political groups in the Assembly have shifted, the budget has reached record heights (with the separate budget for peacekeeping operations actually being higher than the regular budget), a myriad of committees and institutions was created and the main organs of the UN have, through practice and precedent, taken on new responsibilities and roles. But this overall expansion does not mirror a linear enlargement of the UN's resources, capacity and influence in world affairs. There are persistent tensions within the membership of which the ongoing debate between sovereigntists and interventionists is only one illustration. Member states who, by force of their number in the General Assembly, can decide on UN action are not necessarily concurring with the relatively small group of states that finance the bulk of the budget to pay for these measures. And those who vote or pay for certain measures may also not be the same as those who actually take on the largest responsibility in implementing these measures.

Questions of agency and authority, of legitimacy and representativeness as well as inclusion and effectiveness are getting more and more attention. This is most visibly apparent in the now decades-long debate on a reform of the Security Council, which is being portrayed as being outdated as well as potentially illegitimate and in need of new members or at least new working methods. The impact of globalisation on the UN has been ambivalent. On the one hand, it has underlined the central position of the UN as 'the' global organisation in and of the world. On the other hand, it has come under pressure for being too slow and too cumbersome to allow for the management of multiple crisis situations. As a consequence, various formats of club governance and incidental returns to unilateral policies have evolved. The rise of new global actors, widening disparities around the globe as well as multiple challenges to multilateral diplomacy and indeed a liberal international order present a formidable challenge to the UN which, once again, in its successes and setbacks is indicative of central features of international affairs.

Further reading

Chesterman, Simon, Ian Johnstone and David M. Malone (eds.) (2016) *Law and Practice of the United Nations*, 2nd ed. (Oxford and New York: Oxford University Press).

Einsiedel, Sebastian von, David M. Malone and Bruno Stagno Ugarte (eds.) (2016) *The UN Security Council in the 21st Century* (Boulder and London: Lynne Rienner).

Fröhlich, Manuel (2008) *Political Ethics and the United Nations. Dag Hammarskjöld as Secretary-General* (London and New York: Routledge).

Fröhlich, Manuel and Abiodun Williams (eds.) (2018) *The UN Secretary-General and the Security Council. A Dynamic Relationship* (Oxford: Oxford University Press).

Jolly, Richard, Louis Emmerij and Thomas G. Weiss (2009) *UN Ideas that Changed the World* (Bloomington and Indianapolis: Indiana University Press).

Karns, Margaret P., Karen A. Mingst and Kendall W. Stiles (2015) *International Organizations. The Politics and Processes of Global Governance*, 3rd ed. (Boulder and London: Lynne Rienner).

Schlesinger, Stephen C. (2003) *Act of Creation. The Founding of the United Nations* (Boulder: Westview Press).

Urquhart, Brian (1987) *A Life in Peace and War* (New York and London: W.W. Norton).

Weiss, Thomas G. and Sam Daws (eds.) (2018) *The Oxford Handbook on the United Nations*, 2nd ed. (Oxford: Oxford University Press).

Weiss, Thomas G. (2018) *Would the World Be Better Without the UN?* (Cambridge: Polity Press).

Bibliography

Archer, Clive (2015) *International Organizations*, 4th ed. (Third Abingdon and New York: Routledge).

Bellamy, Alex J. (2009) *Responsibility to Protect. The Global Effort to End Mass Atrocities* (Cambridge: Polity Press).

Bellamy, Alex J. and Paul D. Williams (2010) *Understanding Peacekeeping* (Cambridge and Malden: Polity Press).

Brown, Michael E., Sean M. Lynn-Jones and Steven E. Miller (eds.) (1996) *Debating the Democratic Peace* (Cambridge: The MIT Press).

Bull, Hedley (1995) 'Society and Anarchy in International Relations (1966)', in James Der Derian (ed.) *International Theory. Critical Investigations* (Basingstoke: Macmillan), pp. 75–94.

Claude, Inis Jr (1996) 'Peace and Security: Prospective Roles for the Two United Nations', *Global Governance* 2(3), pp. 289–298.

Fröhlich, Manuel (2008a) *Political Ethics and the United Nations. Dag Hammarskjöld as Secretary-General* (London and New York: Routledge).

Fröhlich, Manuel (2008b) 'UN Studies: Eckpunkte eines Programms zur Beschäftigung mit der Institution und den Aufgaben der Weltorganisation', in Manuel Fröhlich (ed.) *UN Studies. Umrisse eines Lehr- und Forschungsfeldes* (Baden-Baden: Nomos), pp. 9–32.

Fröhlich, Manuel (2010) 'Organizations, Rise of International', in Nigel J. Young (ed.) *The Oxford International Encyclopedia of Peace* (Oxford: Oxford University Press), pp. 297–392.

Fröhlich, Manuel (2014) ' "The Suez Story": Dag Hammarskjöld, the United Nations and the Creation of UN Peacekeeping', in Carsten Stahn and Henning Melber (eds.) *Peace Diplomacy, Global Justice and International Agency. Rethinking Human Security and Ethics in the Spirit of Dag Hammarskjöld* (Cambridge: Cambridge University Press), pp. 305–340.

Fröhlich, Manuel (2016) 'The Responsibility to Protect: Foundation, Transformation and Application of an Emerging Norm', in Fabian Klose (ed.) *The Emergence of Humanitarian Intervention. Concepts and Practice from the Nineteenth to the Twenty-First Centuries* (Cambridge and New York: Cambridge University Press), pp. 299–330.

Fröhlich, Manuel (2017) 'Politische Philosophie der Internationalen Beziehungen', in Frank Sauer and Carlo Masala (eds.) *Handbuch Internationale Beziehungen*, 2nd ed. (Wiesbaden: Springer VS), pp. 3–19.

Fröhlich, Manuel and Abiodun Williams (eds.) (2018) *The UN Secretary-General and the Security Council. A dynamic Relationship* (Oxford: Oxford University Press).

Gerhardt, Volker (1995) *Immanuel Kants Entwurf 'Zum ewigen Frieden'. Eine Theorie der Politik* (Darmstadt: Wissenschaftliche Buchgesellschaft).

Gordenker, Leon (2010) *The UN Secretary-General and Secretariat*, 2nd ed. (Abingdon and New York: Routledge).

Hinsley, F.H. (1963) *Power and the Pursuit of Peace* (Cambridge: Cambridge University Press).

Housden, Martyn (2012) *The League of Nations and the Organization of Peace* (London: Longman).

ICISS (2001) *The Responsibility to Protect. Report of the International Commission on Intervention and State Sovereignty* (Ottawa: International Development Research Centre).

Independent Inquiry (2000) *Report of the Independent Inquiry into the Actions of the United Nations During the 1994 Genocide in Rwanda*, UN Doc. S/1999/1257.

Jackson, Robert and Georg Sørensen (2015) *Introduction to International Relations. Theories and Approaches* (Oxford and New York: Oxford University Press).

Kant, Immanuel (1984) *Perpetual Peace and Other Essays* (Indianapolis and Cambridge: Hacket Publishing).

Mazower, Mark (2012) *Governing the World* (New York: The Penguin Press).

Melvern, Linda (2000) *A People Betrayed. The Role of the West in Rwanda's Genocide* (London: Zed Books).

Morsink, Johannes (2000) *The Universal Declaration of Human Rights. Origins, Drafting, and Intent* (Philadelphia: University of Pennsylvania Press).

Stokke, Olav (2009) *The UN and Development. From Aid to Cooperation* (Bloomington and Indianapolis: Indiana University Press).

United Nations (2015) *The Millennium Development Goals Report 2015* (New York: United Nations).

Weiss, Thomas G., Tatiana Carayannis and Richard Jolly (2009) 'The "Third" United Nations', *Global Governance* 15(1), pp. 123–142.

Weiss, Thomas G. and Sam Daws (eds.) (2018) *The Oxford Handbook on the United Nations*, 2nd ed. (Oxford: Oxford University Press).

Weiss, Thomas G., David P. Forsythe, Roger A. Coate, and Kelly-Kate Pease (2016) *The United Nations and Changing World Politics* (New York: Westview Press).

Wilson, Peter C. and David Long (eds.) (1995) *Thinkers of the Twenty Years' Crisis: Inter-War Idealism Reassessed* (Oxford: Oxford University Press).

Chapter 12

The North Atlantic Treaty Organisation

Linda Risso

The North Atlantic Treaty Organisation is a defensive military alliance built on the idea of an Atlantic community of values, ideals and shared history. NATO is also a political forum in which consensus is consolidated on a daily basis, as the Alliance could not aspire to respond to an attack if its members did not have a shared vision of the Alliance's mission and remit.

FIGURE 12.1 NATO soldiers arrive at the scene of a suicide car bomb attack in Kabul, Afghanistan

Based on the principles of the Atlantic Charter of 1941, the Washington Treaty was signed in April 1949 and its text has never been amended. It is only 14 articles long and it was negotiated and signed at record speed. In the emerging geopolitical tensions of the early Cold War, it was urgent for the West to come together to defend territorial integrity, democracy and market economy from a possible attack led by the Soviet Union. This could only be achieved by ensuring a clear and long-lasting commitment of the US to the defence of Western Europe. Without the American help, Europe was not in a position to put up any credible defence against what many feared to be an imminent Soviet invasion. The Washington Treaty was therefore as much about protecting Western Europe as about keeping the Americans tied to the Continent. The third factor was the need to keep balance and create consensus within Western Europe. The lessons of the two World Wars had demonstrated the need to create a forum in which countries could talk about common security concerns and in which any potential disagreement and tension could be solved before it escalated into open conflict (Kaplan, 2007).

NATO: aims and scope

NATO's decision-making procedure is straightforward: in peacetime, the member states work together on common procurement policies, Alliance-wide infrastructure projects and joint military exercises. All members contribute to the NATO budget, and pledge to meet an agreed percentage of the national defence budgets to make sure that, in case of an attack, the Alliance is in a position to respond quickly and effectively. Yet, the national governments retain full sovereignty and control over their own military forces and foreign policies at all times. All decisions are taken by the North Atlantic Council, in which all members have a vote.

The overarching mission of the Alliance is captured by article 2, which mandates political and economic cooperation, and by article 5, which enshrines the principle of mutual military defence. Article 5 is the one most often associated with NATO. It defines the Alliance's defensive nature and its commitment to a common security strategy. The aim of the Alliance, as enshrined in article 5, is to defend its members by deterring an attack through the idea that any attempt to undermine the territorial integrity and stability of one member would be seen as an attack on NATO as a whole.

The article's wording is crucial to understand why the Washington Treaty was agreed so quickly and why other attempts, for example by the European Union, to produce common foreign and security policies are instead so problematic. While membership of the Alliance entails that all members subscribe to a common overarching strategic concept, article 5 does not force its members to take military action in defence of one of the other members. In case of an attack, each national government can decide the extent, time and modality of its own action. The 'response' of each member can range from direct military action in coordination with other members, including for example the use of nuclear weapons, to a mere operational support action. National governments retain full sovereignty. This is radically different from the European Union, which envisages truly common foreign and security policies (Drent, 2015; Webber and Hyde-Price, 2016).

It should also not be forgotten that the Washington Treaty limits the scope of the Alliance to the defence of Western Europe and North America. It excludes areas beyond its members' borders, including – during the Cold War era – colonial territories. The decision to limit the scope of the Alliance in this way was due to the fact that members had competing colonial and strategic interests beyond the European theatre and any military action 'out-of-area' would likely jeopardise the political consensus within the North Atlantic Council. As explained later, it was only after the end of the Cold War that NATO started to engage beyond its own borders, the first example being the Balkan crises of the 1990s.

An effective military response could not be possible without strong political cohesion and leadership within the North Atlantic Council. Thus, the provisions of article 5 are strictly connected to article 2, which builds on the idea of an Atlantic Community. It aims to strengthen economic, political and cultural ties among the NATO members (Mariano, 2010; Aubourg et al., 2008).

Political consensus is essential to fulfil the military mission of the Alliance. If NATO is divided, it is difficult to imagine it having the resolve to carry out a full-scale military response or to stand firmly behind the use of nuclear weapons. A politically fragmented Alliance would make its deterrent value hollow. Hence, since its inception NATO and the national governments have spent considerable effort to foster consensus within the Council via the weekly Permanent Representatives' meetings as well as the Foreign and Defence Ministries meetings and the bi-annual Heads of State Summits.

Article 4, which was not widely known during the Cold War, has attracted attention in recent decades (Mayer, 2014). It gives members the right to request consultation whenever their territorial integrity, political independence or security are threatened. 'Consultation' can vary from informal exchange of information, advice and expertise up to official Council meetings. Article 4 complements article 2 and is aimed at strengthening political consensus and at providing support for members that feel under threat. The article has been invoked relatively often in recent years. Turkey did so in 2003, about concerns on its southern border as a result of the on-going conflict in Iraq. Turkey also invoked article 4 twice in 2012 after incidents on the Syrian border, and once more in 2015 after terrorist attacks in Istanbul. Poland invoked article 4 in March 2014 following increasing tensions in Ukraine. While in all cases no decision was taken, political consultations allowed members to share security concerns and to foster political consensus on the issues raised. This is an essential precondition in case of future military action in response to heightened tensions on the NATO borders.

The history of the Alliance shows that political cohesion was easier to achieve during the Cold War, when NATO had a specific and well-defined mission: to protect Western Europe from Soviet aggression. The Soviet Union incarnated the antitheses of what the Atlantic Community stood for: communism, totalitarianism and atheism. Anticommunism and fear of a Soviet attack provided strong glue that held the Alliance together (Risso, 2014). NATO has been less successful in maintaining political cohesion after 9/11 when new concepts of security, a series of enlargements and the re-definition of what constitutes a threat have undermined the image of a shared community of values and a common sense of purpose (Sloan, 2016; Mayer, 2014).

The new Strategic Concepts (1991, 1999, 2010) have broadened the Alliance's remit so to include tasks like crisis management, human rights protection and disaster relief. NATO's scope is now so broadly defined and its tools so varied that, potentially and given the right circumstances, NATO could act anywhere in any scenario at any time. Since the end of the Cold War, NATO has been involved in several operations as different as disaster relief in the aftermath of Hurricane Katrina, military operations in the Balkans in the 1990s, anti-piracy action in the Gulf of Aden and Operation Sea Guardian, which patrols the Mediterranean Sea in cooperation with Frontex (the European Border and Coast Guard Agency).

Despite the number of operations, NATO's political cohesion and shared sense of purpose are volatile. Operation Unified Protector is a case in point. In March 2011, NATO agreed to patrol the no-fly zone in Libya as part of the United Nations Resolution 1973. NATO's air campaign took advantage of the extensive partnership agreements with Jordan, Qatar and the UAE. Yet, Unified Protector exposed rifts within the North Atlantic Council and the lack of appetite for military engagement. Three months after the Council had given the go-ahead, only eight of the 28 members were participating in the operation, with some governments hinting that the Alliance was overstepping its mandate. Angela Merkel's German government joined Russia, China, Brazil and India abstaining from a vote on the UN resolution that sanctioned the use of force in Libya. It was a blow to the political cohesion of the Alliance (Dyson, 2014). This resulted in an acrimonious exchange between the German Foreign Ministry and US Defence Secretary Robert Gates (Birnbaum, 2011).

The recurring debate regarding the national military budgets is another example of the Alliance's seemingly fragile consensus. The discussion has been particularly bitter since the economic crisis of 2008 and has often jeopardised the Alliance's cohesion.

In order to understand the significance of this issue it is essential to distinguish between direct and indirect contributions, on top of which come the national defence budgets. All members make direct contributions according to an agreed cost-sharing formula based on gross national income. Direct contributions pay, for example, for the integrated command structure as well as the running costs of the NATO headquarters. Members also make indirect contributions when they volunteer equipment or troops to a military operation approved by the North Atlantic Council.

In addition to direct and indirect contributions, NATO members attempt to coordinate their defence budgets to make sure that all nations contribute proportionally and fairly. Today, only a handful of countries meet the 2 per cent target agreed at the Wales Summit in 2014. The US contributes the largest share, close to 3.6 per cent of its gross domestic product (NATO Public Diplomacy Division, 2017). At this point, only four other countries fulfil the 2 per cent pledge: Greece, the UK, Estonia and Poland. The remaining members do not meet the target, although they have at least reversed the declining trend that had characterised the last decade and some have indeed increased their defence budgets (NATO Public Diplomacy Division, 2017).

The 2 per cent pledge has often been an object of criticism as it defines the 'input', the amount of money spent, but not the kind and quality of its 'output', in other words, how the money is spent. The 2 per cent figure is a political yardstick to measure the members' commitment to the Alliance and to the joint defence effort rather than a long-term plan to make the Alliance stronger and more resilient (Techau, 2015). Further evidence of this is the fact that NATO does not define what can be included in the national defence budgets, which remain fully under governments' control. This means that national governments are free to decide what to include in their budget and what to leave out. NATO would like members to invest in weapon modernisation, joint procurement programs and training. Yet, members may decide to meet the figures in other ways. Most of Greece's defence budget, for example, goes into salaries and pensions, which do not enhance Greece's military readiness and effective contribution to the Alliance's defence capability. In a similar vein, since 2015 the UK includes veterans' pensions as part of the defence budget (Strategic Defence and Security Review, 2010).

NATO's strategic concepts through time

The size of the budget, joint training exercises and common procurement policies would not go very far if NATO did not have a vision of how to use them in case of an attack. Since 1949, NATO has produced six documents – known as 'Strategic Concepts' – to guide its action in times of peace, crisis and war. Each Strategic Concept is accompanied by additional classified documents setting out specific military measures. In addition – and as discussed later in this chapter – documents like the Report on Non-Military Cooperation (December 1956), the Harmel Report (December 1967), the Ottawa Declaration (1974) and the London Declaration (1990) have offered political guidance and placed the Strategic Concepts within a wider political framework.

During the Cold War, territorial defence and deterrence consistently characterised the Alliance's posture, with various degrees of attention paid to diplomatic dialogue and détente, depending on the changing nature of the geopolitical tensions. NATO's first Strategic Concept, DC 6/1, dates back to January 1950. According to DC 6/1, the primary purpose of the Alliance was to deter aggression and, if this failed, to respond collectively to an attack against one or more of its members (Heuser, 1999).

The first Strategic Concept introduced the concept of complementarity between members. This means that each member's contribution to the Alliance's defence should be in proportion to its capacity – defined as economic, industrial, geographical and military. Members are encouraged to put their resources and expertise to the service of the Alliance. Sharing resources and expertise makes NATO stronger and more resilient as individual countries do not need to 'do everything' and to invest massively in air, sea and land forces. As members of the Alliance, they are part of a wider defence framework in which neighbouring countries can support and step in by contributing their own defence structures for the benefit of all members. The complementarity principle still stands today.

Only six months after DC 6/1 was approved, the Korean War forced the Alliance to give greater consideration to the effectiveness of its military structures and to the actual strength of its military forces. In December 1952, the North Atlantic Council approved the Second Strategic Concept, which foresaw the establishment of an integrated military force under a centralised command. General Dwight D. Eisenhower became NATO's first Supreme Allied Commander, Europe (SACEUR). The European Regional Planning Groups established in 1950 merged into one Atlantic Ocean Regional Planning Group led by Allied Command Atlantic (SACLANT), thus making collective defence more efficient and effective. These structural changes took place just before NATO's first enlargement to Greece and Turkey, which brought the borders of the Alliance much closer to the USSR and the Middle East.

The document also enshrined the concept of a 'forward strategy', which meant that the Alliance would resist an attack in Europe as far to the east as possible so to spare the devastation of Western Europe and to prevent prolonged Soviet occupation. This decision raised the delicate issue of Germany's role in the defence of Western Europe, which was solved only in 1955 when the Federal Republic of Germany joined the Alliance (Risso, 2007).

The Second Strategic Concept also expanded upon its predecessor in terms of the nature of its nuclear deterrent. According to the document, NATO would respond to an attack with 'all types of weapons', thus including nuclear weapons. At the time, Western European governments found it difficult to divert resources away from the reconstruction effort on to defence and rearmament. It soon became clear that the rearmament goals set at the Lisbon meeting of 1952 were too ambitious and unrealistic. In an attempt to bridge the gap and to make NATO's deterrence capability credible, President Dwight D. Eisenhower increased the American, and therefore the Alliance's, dependency on nuclear weapons (NSC 162/2). The 'New Look' policy offered the advantage of greater military effectiveness without the need to spend disproportionately more on conventional defence.

The US, Canada and the UK advocated massive retaliation because they thought it reduced force requirements and, as a consequence, defence expenditures. But agreement was not widespread and many members, particularly in continental Europe, were opposed to the idea of massive retaliation and feared 'annihilation by mistake'. A degree of flexibility was therefore introduced and the use of conventional weapons and strategy was retained to deal with small and well-defined aggressions (MC14/2 and MC 48/2, 1957).

The discussion about 'massive retaliation' opens a window on the limits of NATO as a cohesive Alliance and on the role of the US as an equal partner. Precisely because the Alliance is not a mere extension of US foreign policy, it has always been problematic to integrate nuclear weapons into NATO's strategy. Who should have control of these weapons? Where should they be stationed? What should their target be? What kind of Command and Control (C2) structure would be put in place? The issue of political control of nuclear weapons has never been entirely solved by the Alliance. The Standing Group in Washington can issue the decision but ultimately it is only the governments of the nuclear-capable members that decide. Yet, the other members demand to have a say on such a crucial decision (Pedlow, 2010).

There are two more considerations worth making about the Alliance's strategy in the Cold War. NATO did not accept the concept of a limited war with the Soviet Union. It was assumed that if a conflict with the USSR did start, it had to lead to the fall of one of the two superpowers. Second, although NATO's remit was limited to Western Europe and North America, NATO internal reports produced during the Cold War acknowledged the destabilising impact of Soviet political and economic activities outside the NATO area on the Alliance's own political cohesion and stability. The importance of out-of-area crises became increasingly central to East–West relations and was aptly exploited by the Soviet Union. This was particularly relevant in the context of the Suez crisis and the crushing of the Hungarian uprising by the Soviet Union in 1956.

Diverging views about massive retaliation and nuclear weapons as well as about how to respond to the infiltration of international communism in Africa and Southeast Asia created divisions within the North Atlantic Council and undermined the political cohesion of the Alliance as a whole. Hence, while hardening its military and strategic stance, the Alliance took measures to reinforce its political cohesion. In December 1956, the Report of the Committee of Three on Non-Military Cooperation in NATO – also known as the Three Wise Men Report – recommended more robust political consultation mechanisms on all aspects relating to East–West relations, including areas outside the Alliance's scope.

As it is often the case with NATO policies, no sooner was the ink dry on the Second Strategic Concept than international developments forced a re-think of the very idea of massive retaliation and nuclear weapons. The Soviets developed intercontinental ballistic missile capabilities and expanded their own nuclear and chemical weapon arsenal. They were able to hit targets on America soil. Western European leaders doubted that any American president would sacrifice an American city to save a European one. The Second Berlin Crisis (1961) and the Cuban Missile Crisis (1962) reinforced these doubts as it became clear that a localised and well-defined crisis could not be solved with nuclear weapons.

The Third Strategic Concept (MC 14/3) was eventually approved in 1968, after the withdrawal of France from the integrated military command, the relocation of NATO HQs to Brussels and the publication of the Harmel Report. MC 14/3 put forward two important principles: flexible response and escalation. Flexible response meant that the US and NATO allies could draw on a variety of tools, from conventional weapons to full-scale nuclear response. Flexible response was designed to 'prevent the potential aggressor from predicting with confidence NATO's specific response to aggression', thus producing an 'unacceptable degree of risk' in the enemy's mind (NATO MC 14/3). The Alliance's members could choose between 'direct defence' (same level at which the enemy chose to fight) and 'deliberate escalation' (steep rise of defence measures up to and including nuclear weapons). The Third Strategic Concept, and accompanying documents, remained valid until the end of the Cold War despite the shifting nature of détente in the 1970s and 1980s.

MC 14/3 should be read along with the Harmel Report, which envisaged a dual-track approach to Western security: political cohesion and military cooperation. At a time of détente in Europe, the Harmel Report advocated the need to maintain adequate and modern defence capabilities while seeking a relaxation of tensions in East–West relations through diplomatic dialogue, cultural exchange and trade agreements. Crucially, it was argued that precisely because NATO was engaged in dialogue with the East, it had to maintain a strong deterrence value so to be able to negotiate a possible disarmament. This was a conundrum, difficult to explain to NATO's own public, who often took to the street to express dismay about NATO's military build-up (Ziemann, 2007).

In the immediate post–Cold War years, after the collapse of the Soviet Union and the Warsaw Pact, it was not at all clear whether NATO should and could survive. The period between 1989 and 1991 was characterised by hectic diplomatic dialogue and cooperation with ex-Warsaw Pact members. NATO Secretary General Manfred Wörner acted as a catalyst in the dialogue with the East and engaged in partnership agreements and enlargement talks much earlier than the European Union (Wörner, 1994).

In 1991 and again in 1999, NATO issued two Strategic Concepts that advocated a broader approach to security.[1] Collective defence remained of course the central aim of the Alliance but NATO sought to improve the security and stability of Europe as a whole through partnership agreements and political and military cooperation with countries beyond its borders. Some of these partnership agreements, particularly those with Ukraine and Georgia, created tensions with Moscow, which claimed NATO was trying to encircle Russia (Asmus, 2010).

The 1999 Strategic Concept put forward a broad and all-encompassing definition of security which recognised the importance of political, economic, social and environmental cooperation. It committed the Alliance to common defence as well as peace and stability of the wider Euro-Atlantic area, which was broadly defined but which clearly extended beyond the border of the Alliance itself. New challenges like terrorism, ethnic conflict, human rights abuses, political instability, economic fragility and the spread of nuclear, biological and chemical weapons were identified as the new threats, although the protection of the members' territorial integrity remained the core task. While political consultation, deterrence and defence continued to be central, new tasks like crisis management and peacekeeping found their place in the list.

It is, however, undeniable that the disappearance of the Soviet Union deprived NATO of its own raison d'être. Public support for the Alliance decreased in the 1990s and appetite for military engagement was at an all time low, as demonstrated by the protests and criticism met by NATO when it engaged in the Balkans (Mandelbaum, 1999; Everts and Isernia, 2001).

The 9/11 terrorist attacks mark a watershed in the Alliance's history. It was the first time that a member invoked article 5 and that the mutual defence clause was applied. The Alliance's military thinking, strategies and resources became geared towards the fight against terrorism, non-state actors and the spread of weapons of mass destruction. In the new security environment, NATO engaged well beyond its region and the most prominent example of this renewed engagement is the UN-mandated International Security Assistance Force (ISAF) in Afghanistan.

In the 2010 Strategic Concept, NATO continues to be described as 'a unique community of values committed to the principles of individual liberty, democracy, human rights and the rule of law'. Today, the Alliance's core tasks include collective defence, crisis management and cooperative security. Threats to its security include the proliferation of ballistic missiles and nuclear weapons as well as terrorism, cyberattacks and natural disasters. Crucially, the new Strategic Concept confers NATO a much more proactive role in world affairs. NATO now aims to actively promote international security through political and military cooperation. Examples include participating in disarmament and non-proliferation efforts led by other organisations like the UN and the EU. In addition, NATO itself takes a proactive role through the membership application process and by creating partnership agreements in the broad sense of the term. Not surprisingly then, as mentioned earlier, in recent decades NATO has been busier than ever and its recent operations are as different as disaster relief in the aftermath of Hurricane Katrina, direct military operations in the Balkans and Afghanistan, police and military training in Iraq and the patrolling of the Gulf of Aden to prevent piracy (Mayer, 2014).

Sharing of military and technical expertise, intelligence and infrastructure

As it has been argued earlier, the Alliance is primarily a political forum. The meetings of the North Atlantic Council, in the form of the weekly meetings of the Permanent Representatives and the meetings of foreign and defence ministers at the NATO headquarters, provide permanent channels of consultation and cooperation. The bi-annual Heads of Government Summits offer leadership and long-term guidance. There is of course also a tight network of committees and ad hoc working groups that provide guidance on specific policies and regional problems according to expertise required.

Military expertise is naturally an important item on the agenda. All members must agree on the general lines set out by the Strategic Concepts and classified military guidelines. They must also know how to put them into practice. In order for the Alliance to be able to act as one in a conflict, common weapon procurement policies and weapon standardisation programs are updated regularly. Joint military training exercises and language programs are now part of the national armies' training. Infrastructure has also been crucial. Airports, railways and roads, radio broadcasting networks, telecommunications and energy supplies at national levels have to keep in mind the needs of the Alliance as a whole. Standardisation is necessary to produce an alliance-wide infrastructure. In fact, NATO's needs and standards play a pivotal role in the planning of key infrastructure projects at national levels, more than the public realises and one would wonder whether much of the anti-EU front regarding infringement of national prerogatives is missing a point (Turchetti, 2012).

An important, yet not declassified, aspect of NATO's role in promoting cooperation is intelligence. During the Cold War, NATO did not carry out its own intelligence gathering operations. The NATO Special Committee (AC/46) acted as a clearing-house for intelligence matters. Its documents are not – and will not be – declassified, but we know that this part of NATO cooperation and exchange of expertise is crucial, particularly in helping countries with less developed intelligence communities to catch up with their counterparts.

In recent years, NATO has strengthened its intelligence gathering and intelligence sharing capabilities. The Joint Intelligence, Surveillance and Reconnaissance (JISR) brings together data and information gathered through projects such as NATO's Alliance Ground Surveillance system or NATO AWACS aircrafts as well as a wide variety of national assets from the space, air, land and maritime domains.

At the Warsaw Summit in 2016, NATO approved the use of Boeing E-3 Sentry AWACS ('Sentry' Airborne Warning and Control System) surveillance planes to provide information and intelligence to the Global Coalition to counter ISIL from Turkish and international airspace. Both surveillance and reconnaissance include visual observation (from soldiers on the ground) and electronic observation (for example from satellites, unmanned aircraft systems, ground sensors and maritime vessels), which are then analysed, turning information into intelligence. The Initial Operational Capability (IOC) launched in February 2016 represents a significant achievement, enabling better connectivity between NATO and Allies' capabilities.

The degree of intelligence sharing within NATO should not however be overestimated. It is well known that NATO's walls are not watertight and that in the Cold War – as well as today – it was assumed that the information circulated in Brussels would soon find its way to desks in Moscow and elsewhere. Key intelligence partners, like the UK, US and Canada, continue to privilege their own partnership through separate bi- and tri-lateral exchanges. Nevertheless, the Special Committee does play an important role in bridging the gap in terms of expertise and methods, if not of content, between the most advanced members and the newcomers (Lefebvre, 2003).

Since the Cold War, NATO has developed its own scientific expertise. The Science Committee (SCOM) was launched in 1958. It initially concerned itself with pure science and particularly theoretical physics; later it specialised on military applications. The Science Committee has a rather tortuous history and it has failed to act as catalyst for high-level research, as many of its promoters had hoped. Yet, it did play an important role in fostering scientists' mobility by putting in place grant and fellowship schemes (Krige, 2008; Fenstad, 2009). In 2006, the CCMS merged with the Science Committee in the new NATO Science for Peace and Security program (SPS or AC/328).

In response to increasing environmental concerns, in 1969 President Richard Nixon proposed the creation of the Committee on the Challenges of Modern Society (CCMS). The CCMS did not produce its own research but it brought together scientists and specialists to examine well-define environmental and social problems like oil spills, car safety, work motivation and so on. The aim of the CCMS was to show that the alliance was more than tanks and bombs and that it understood the concerns of its people. At the same time, Nixon was looking for a way to move the East–West dialogue on a non-ideological territory and the environment seemed the best bet. The CCMS's work and proceedings were fully open and transparent and non-NATO members were often asked to contribute to pilot studies. The Soviet Union itself took part in the discussion on oil spills, for example (Macekura, 2011; Risso, 2016).

The Science Committee and the CCMS allowed NATO to claim in the early post–Cold War years that the Alliance had already developed a more complex definition of security and stability, which included environmental protection and disaster relief. Secretary General Manfred Wörner and his successors could point confidently to a sound track record that went back to the late 1950s. In 1990–1, Wörner could argue successfully that even if the Warsaw Pact had been disbanded, the Alliance had all the instruments and expertise to respond to any kind of threat old and new.

New century, new challenges

The debate about the role of the Alliance in the post–Cold War era is now 25 years old but the fundamental choice remains the same. To put it in the colourful words of Senator Richard Lugar, for many years up to the invasion of Crimea in 2014,

NATO needed to go 'out-of area or out of business'. NATO did so in two ways. It expanded its membership and it engaged in military operations beyond the European and North Atlantic theatres.

Between 1999 and 2009, NATO accepted 12 new members and it is currently in the process of admitting Montenegro. In addition, over the past two decades, NATO launched the Partnership for Peace (PfP) program, which consists of a series of bilateral agreements based on individual circumstances and security concerns. Other programs like the Mediterranean Dialogue and the more recent Istanbul Cooperation Initiative and the Gulf Cooperation Council allow the Alliance to engage on the volatile Southern Flank (Yost, 2014). Over the past ten years, NATO has also established cooperation with Japan, Colombia, New Zealand and Australia (Yonah, 2015). All these measures taken together mean that NATO is now actively engaged across the world in a new form of 'cooperative security', which operates through a network of partners capable of serving as security providers in their respective regions (Rynning, 2014).

In the post-9/11 era, the North Atlantic Council sees NATO's own security as dependent on the peace, stability and good governance of its periphery as well as further afield. NATO must therefore engage with partners around the world. Cooperation includes political consultation on security issues, contributions to NATO-led missions, counterterrorism, counterproliferation of WMDs, cyberwarfare, energy security and civil emergency planning.

The crisis in Ukraine has brought NATO's focus back on to territorial defence and the European theatre. The occupation of Crimea and the military confrontation in the Donbass region have reignited the fear of an aggressive Russia. The new NATO members on the Eastern Flank, and particularly the Baltic Republics, have been the target of cyberattacks and of social media trolling aimed at destabilising the countries from within. A combination of conventional military strategy with cyberwarfare that interferes with the infrastructure networks could open the door to a Russian invasion.

NATO has strengthened its military presence in the East with four battalions stationed in Poland and the Baltic Republics on a rotational basis as well as a brigade in the Black Sea region to support Romania and Bulgaria. The NATO Response Force created in 2002 is now enhanced by the creation of a 'spearhead force', known as the Very High Readiness Joint Task Force (VJTF). The new measures aim to allow NATO to respond quickly and effectively to crises and attacks on its borders (Lasconjarias, 2014).

'Hybrid warfare' – a mixture of propaganda, subversion, espionage, cyberwarfare and the use of irregular military force ('little green men') – presents new challenges. In the Baltic Republics' case, for example, hybrid warfare could involve attempts to incite ethnic and regional tensions, or to spread panic and misinformation so to undermine the political stability of the country from within. Hybrid warfare poses unique problems in terms of attribution (where did the attack come from? was it government-sponsored?) and of threshold (is the attack serious enough to trigger article 5 and to demand an Alliance-wide response?). What might count locally as an intolerable assault on the Baltic states' sovereignty may not be seen in Brussels as an 'attack' for article 5 purposes. Much NATO effort is now going into ensuring that it can respond, militarily and politically, to appeals for help. All the strength of the world's mightiest military alliance will not amount to much if its members cannot agree when an aggressor has actually stepped over the line.

At the Warsaw Summit (July 2016), cyberwarfare was recognised as a new operational domain of warfare, along with air, sea and land. This means that for the first time unconventional warfare opens the possibility of a conventional military response. Yet, the issue of attribution and threshold outlined earlier remain open. It is still unclear how the Alliance would respond and the North Atlantic Council will take the decision on a case-by-case basis.

A shared vision of security and new forms of cooperation based on complementarity and division of labour have led to closer links with the European Union. In the 1990s, the key aim of the enhanced cooperation between the two organisations originated from the need to accommodate European ambitions for greater autonomy in security and defence. Today, NATO and the EU face common challenges like terrorism, cyberwarfare and mass migration.

In December 2016, NATO and the EU agreed on a series of more than 40 measures to advance how the two organisations work together – including on countering hybrid threats, cyber defence and making their common neighbourhood more stable and secure. On cyber defence, NATO and the EU have strengthened their mutual participation in exercises and foster research, training and information sharing. The cooperation builds upon the Joint Declaration at the Warsaw Summit, whereby the two organisations step up cooperation in areas like maritime security and border control. NATO and the EU are integral parts of the Atlantic Community. With the uncertainty the West faces today, this is more important than ever.

Conclusion

NATO is approaching its 70th anniversary. Over the past decades, the Alliance demonstrated a remarkable ability to adapt to rapidly changing geopolitical and strategic circumstances. After the fall of the Berlin Wall, NATO reshaped its own mission and responded to the challenges of the post–Cold War environment by adopting a new definition of security, which allowed it to engage in new areas and well beyond its traditional geographical scope.

This transformation did not come without costs: enlargements and engagement in military operations exposed the fragile political cohesion within the North Atlantic Council. Different visions of the Alliance's role and of what constitutes security meant that behind the scenes, the Council was often divided between those members who were eager to engage to secure peace and stability through military action and those who were reluctant to use military force.

Since 2014, a resurgent Russia has brought the focus back on the European theatre and on more traditional notions of military defence. The Baltic Republics have been keen to see the Alliance strengthen its military capability. Yet, while territorial defence is back on the agenda, it is clear that NATO must continue to engage in peace and security beyond its borders. The refugee crisis across the Mediterranean Sea and via Turkey and Greece has put pressure on the Southern Flank. At the same time, cyber defence has forced NATO to develop its own cyber defence capabilities.

This happens at a time in which transatlantic unity, which has been underpinning the Alliance since its foundation, is under strain. President Trump has been critical of NATO and made US participation dependent on the European members increasing their contribution to the Alliance's defence capabilities.

As this chapter goes to press, NATO is about to face multiple challenges as serious as those it faced in 1989–91. Its survival will depend on the extent to which political cohesion will be strengthened within the Council.

Note

1   Rather unhelpfully, both documents have the same title and only differ by the date: the Alliance Strategic Concept – 1991 and the Alliance Strategic Concept – 1999. Companion documents are, respectively, 'Directive for Military Implementation of the Alliance's Strategic Concept' (MC 400), 12 December 1991; and 'MC Guidance for the Military Implementation of the Alliance Strategy' (MC 400/2), 12 February 2003. Both documents are classified.

Further reading

Asmus Ronald D (2002) *Opening NATO's Door: How the Alliance Remade Itself for a New Era* (New York: Columbia University Press).

Hallams, Ellen, Luca Ratti and Benjamin Zyla (eds.) (2013) *NATO Beyond 9/11: The Transformation of the Atlantic Alliance* (Basingstoke: Palgrave Macmillan).

Kaplan Lawrence, S. (2004) *NATO Divided, NATO United: The Evolution of and Alliance* (Westport: Praeger).

Mayer, Sebastian (ed.) (2014) *NATO's Post-Cold War Politics: The Changing Provision of Security* (Basingstoke: Palgrave Macmillan).

Medcalf, Jennifer (2005) *NATO: A Beginner's Guide* (Oxford: Oneword Publications).

Risso, Linda (2014) *Propaganda and Intelligence in the Cold War: The NATO Information Service* (London: Routledge).

Sloan, Stanley (2016) *The Defense of the West: NATO, The European Union and the Transatlantic Bargain* (Manchester: MUP).

Thies, Wallace J. (2009) *Why NATO Endures* (Cambridge: CUP).

Yonah, Alexander and Richard Prosen (eds.) (2015) *NATO: From Regional to Global Security Provider* (Lanham: Lexington Books).

Yost, David S. (2007) *NATO and International Organizations* (Rome: NATO Defense College).

Yost, David S. (2014) *NATO's Balancing Act* (Washington, DC: United States Institute of Peace).

Bibliography

Asmus, Ronald D. (2010) *A Little War that Shook the World: Georgia, Russia and the Future of the West* (New York: Palgrave).

Aubourg, Valerie, Gerard Bossuat and Giles Scott Smith (eds.) (2008) *European Community, Atlantic Community?* (Paris: Soleb).

Birnbaum, Michael (2011) 'Gates Rebukes European Allies in Farewell Speech', *The Washington Post* (10 June).

Drent, Margriet (2015) 'EU-NATO Relations in Crisis Management Operations: The Price of Informality', in Galantino, Maria Grazia and Freire, Maria Raquel (eds.) *Managing Crises, Making Peace: Towards a Strategic EU Vision for Security and Defence* (Basingstoke: Palgrave), pp. 91–110.

Dyson, Tom (2014) 'German Defence Policy under the Second Merkel Chancellorship', *German Politics* 23(4), pp. 460–476.

Everts Philip P. and Pierangelo Isernia (eds.) (2001) *Public Opinion and the International Use of Force* (London: Routledge).

Fenstad, Jen Erik (2009) 'NATO and Science', *European Review* 17(3–4), pp. 487–497.

Heuser, Beatrice (1999) *The Bomb: Nuclear Weapons in their Historical, Strategic and Ethical Context* (London: Longman).

HM Government (2015) *National Security Strategy and Strategic Defence and Security Review 2015. A Secure and Prosperous United Kingdom.* Cm 9161, http://ow.ly/6Dwh 30daDXb (accessed June 30, 2017).

Kamp, Karl-Heinz (2014) 'From Wales to Warsaw: NATO's Future beyond the Ukraine Crisis', *American Foreign Policy Interests* 36(6), pp. 361–365.

Kaplan, Lawrence S. (2007) *NATO 1948: The Birth of the Transatlantic Alliance* (Lanham: Rowman & Littlefield).

Krige, John (2008) *American Hegemony and the Postwar Reconstruction of Science in Europe* (Cambridge, MA: MIT Press).

Lasconjarias, Guillaume (2014) 'NATO's Posture after the Wales Summit', *AIA Working Papers* 14/15.

Lefebvre, Stéphane (2003) 'The Difficulties and Dilemmas of International Intelligence Cooperation', *International Journal of Intelligence and Counterintelligence* 16(4), pp. 527–542.

Macekura, Stephen (2011) 'The Limits of the Global Community: The Nixon Administration and Global Environmental Politics', *Cold War History* 11(4), pp. 489–518.

Mandelbaum, Michael (1999) 'A Prefect Failure: NATO's War against Yugoslavia', *Foreign Affairs* 78(5), pp. 2–8.

Mariano, Marco (2010) *Defining the Atlantic Community: Culture, Intellectuals, and Policies in the Mid-Twentieth Century* (London: Routledge).

Mayer, Sebastian (ed.) (2014) *NATO's Post-Cold War Politics: The Changing Provision of Security* (Basingstoke: Palgrave Macmillan).

NATO Public Diplomacy Division (2017) *Defence Expenditure of NATO Countries (2009–2016)* (Brussels: NATO).

North Atlantic Council (1956) *Report of the Committee of Three on Non-Military Cooperation in NATO* (Brussels: North Atlantic Treaty Organization, Information Service).

North Atlantic Council (1967) *Report of the Council on the Future Tasks of the Alliance (Harmel Report)* (Brussels: North Atlantic Treaty Organization, Information Service).

North Atlantic Council (1990) *NATO's Declaration on a Transformed North Atlantic Alliance*, www.nato.int/cps/en/natolive/official_texts_23693.htm (accessed June 30, 2017).

North Atlantic Council (1991) *NATO Strategic Concept 1991*, www.nato.int/cps/en/natolive/official_texts_23847.htm (accessed June 30, 2017).

North Atlantic Council (1999) *NATO Strategic Concept 1999*, www.nato.int/cps/en/natolive/official_texts_27433.htm (accessed June 30, 2017).

North Atlantic Council (2010) *Strategic Concept: For the Defence and Security of The Members of the North Atlantic Treaty Organisation* (Short title: 'Active Engagement, Modern Defence'), www.nato.int/lisbon2010/strategic-concept-2010-eng.pdf (accessed June 30, 2017).

North Atlantic Military Committee (1954) *The Most Effective Pattern of NATO Military Strength for the Next Five Years* (MC 48).

North Atlantic Military Committee (1957) *Overall Strategic Concept for the Defence of the NATO Area* (MC 14/2).

North Atlantic Military Committee (1968) *NATO's Third Strategic Concept: Overall Strategic Concept for the Defence of the North Atlantic Treaty Organization Area* (MC 14/3).

North Atlantic Military Committee (1969) *Measures to Implement the Strategic Concept for the Defence of the NATO Area* (MC 48/3).

Pedlow, Gregory W. (2010) *The Evolution of NATO's Command Structure, 1951–2009.* NATO Unclassified, http://tinyurl.com/ydd8fxgu (accessed June 30, 2017).

Risso, Linda (2007) '"Enlightening Public Opinion": A Study of NATO's Information Policies Between 1949 and 1959 Based On Recently Declassified Documents', *Cold War History* 7(1), pp. 45–74.

Risso, Linda (2016) 'NATO and the Environment: The Committee on the Challenges of Modern Society', *Contemporary European History* 25(3), pp. 505–535.

Rynning, Stan (2014) 'The Geography of Atlantic Peace: NATO 25 Years After the Fall of the Berlin Wall', *International Affairs* 90(6), pp. 1383–1401.

Techau, Jan (2015) *The Politics of 2%. NATO and the Security Vacuum in Europe* (Washington, DC: Carnegie Endowment for International Peace).

Turchetti, Simone (2012) 'Sword, Shield and Buoys: A History of the NATO Sub-Committee on Oceanographic Research, 1959–1973' *Centaurus* 54(3), pp. 205–231.

Webber, Mark and Adrian Hyde-Price (eds.) (2016) *Theorising NATO: New Perspectives on the Atlantic Alliance* (Abingdon: Routledge).

Wörner, Manfred (1994) 'Shaping the Alliance for the Future' *NATO Review* (February).

Yonah, Alexander and Richard Prosen (eds.) (2015) *NATO: From Regional to Global Security Provider* (Lanham: Lexington Books).

Yost, David S. (1999) *NATO Transformed: The Alliance's New Roles in International Security* (Washington, DC: United States Institute of Peace).

Ziemann, Benjamin (ed.) (2007) *Peace Movements in Western Europe, Japan and the USA during the Cold War* (Essen: Klartext).

Chapter 13

IMF and World Bank

Rainer Hillebrand

In the post-1945 international economic and monetary order, three international institutions have played a key role (Kahler, 2016; Stiglitz, 2002): the General Agreement on Tariffs and Trade, which later became the World Trade Organisation (WTO), the International Monetary Fund (IMF) and the World Bank.[1] While the WTO is concerned with trade in goods and services as well as intellectual property

FIGURE 13.1 Former US President Barack Obama talks with Christine Lagarde, managing director of the International Monetary Fund, at the White House, Washington, DC, US

rights, the IMF and World Bank focus on the international monetary and financial system. Their central goal is to foster macroeconomic stability, economic development and poverty reduction. Both sister organisations were established at the UN Monetary and Financial Conference in Bretton Woods, US, in 1944, where representatives from 44 countries convened under US and UK leadership in order to agree on a post-war economic and monetary order.

In essence, the Bretton Woods system was conceived of as a response to the economically and politically disastrous interwar years which were, in many countries, characterised by the Great Depression, unemployment, impoverishment and political extremism. Governments at the time compounded the economic downturn by pursuing 'beggar-thy-neighbour' policies, including the imposition of high tariffs, competitive currency devaluations and mercantilist price and wage deflation. Instead of agreeing to policies internationally, each government tried to protect its domestic industries at the expense of imports in an attempt to safeguard national wealth and jobs. Consequently, cross-border trade and capital flows plummeted, and economic conditions deteriorated further. The Bretton Woods idea was therefore to guarantee open markets and free trade, to establish fixed but adjustable exchange rates and to help countries develop towards full employment (Babb and Kentikelenis, 2017).

In this economic order, the Bretton Woods sisters had specific areas of responsibility (Rajan, 2008; Reinhart and Trebesch, 2016). The IMF was established to maintain the system of stable exchange rates, where currencies were basically pegged to the US dollar, which, in turn, was convertible into gold. More specifically, the IMF had to (1) monitor national policies and discourage actions, such as competitive devaluations, which would undermine international economic stability; and (2), in a (potential) balance-of-payment crisis, provide short-term funds to countries with insufficient foreign currency reserves, thereby enabling them to undertake necessary reforms while defending or slowly adjusting the fixed parity (Eichengreen and Woods, 2016). In contrast to the IMF's original short-term macroeconomic orientation, the World Bank was created as a development agency, preoccupied with reconstruction and long-term growth primarily in war-torn countries. It provided assistance for investment projects when domestic savings were insufficient and access to international private capital was non-existent owing to market imperfections (Clemens and Kremer, 2016).

Since 1945 the global political and economic environment has changed substantially, and so have the two organisations. With decolonisation after World War II and the collapse of the Soviet system in the early 1990s, membership soared up to its current 189 members, almost universal coverage. In the global economy, Western dominance has decreased, with new growth poles emerging, for instance, the so-called BRICS countries. Simultaneously, globalisation and political liberalisation, especially in finance, have made countries more interconnected and exposed to spillovers. While in the post-war years the lack of private funding was a major bottleneck for investment, diverse international capital markets have now developed, thus arguably curtailing the need for public capital provision (Ravallion, 2016). A major change occurred when the Bretton Woods fixed exchange rate system collapsed in 1971–3, ridding the IMF of its original purpose. With floating currencies, balance-of-payment crises in industrialised countries became less prevalent, whereas sovereign debt and banking crises in the developing world – and since 2008 in Europe – emerged, posing more severe challenges to crisis solution (Reinhart and Trebesch, 2016). Further, in the 1970s the dominant post-war economic policy paradigm shifted from market-sceptical Keynesianism to the neo-liberal Washington Consensus of market supremacy. This, in turn, came under fire in the wake of the 1990s Asian and the more recent global financial crisis.

Despite these fundamental changes, the Bretton Woods sisters continue to play a major role in international economics (Krugman, 1998; Nissan, 2015). At the same time, their efficacy and legitimacy as global organisations is questioned (Eichengreen and Woods, 2016; Global Exchange, 2015; Meltzer, 2005; Reinhart and Trebesch, 2016). Against this background, this chapter offers an analytical introduction to the two organisations and their policies. It is organised as follows: the next two sections look at the IMF's and the World Bank's governance, objectives and instruments, respectively. Based on these separate status-quo analyses, major criticisms and future challenges are discussed for both organisations together. The chapter ends with a short conclusion and suggestions for further reading.

The IMF: governance, objectives and instruments

Despite various reforms, the institutional set-up of the IMF still largely reflects the economic and political dominance of the West. Thus, the IMF is headquartered in Washington, DC, and the managing director traditionally comes from a Western European country with US approval (Weisbrot and Johnston, 2016). Even though each member country is represented in the Board of Governors, voting power in this shareholder body varies with the so-called quota. This is denominated in Special Drawing Rights (SDR), the IMF's unit of account, and based on a country's relative global economic weight measured primarily by GDP and economic openness. The quota also informs a country's financial contribution (membership fee) and its access to IMF loans in times of crisis (discussed later in the chapter). In contrast to the UN principle of 'one nation, one vote', the weighted IMF system gives relatively more voice to rich countries, rather than populous lower income countries.

With the latest quota reform in 2016, the US managed to keep the biggest vote share by far with 16.52 per cent, followed now by China and Japan with about 6 per cent each and major European economies ranging between 4 and 5.4 per cent. The five biggest European economies still control about two times the aggregate votes of the BRICS countries, despite only having approximately 60 per cent of their aggregate GDP (Vestergaard and Wade, 2015). While for most decisions, majority suffices, IMF charter amendments and the quinquennial quota reviews require an 85 per-cent supermajority, giving the US and some Europeans combined veto power. Similarly, the eight biggest members are also over-represented in the IMF's Executive Board: they send a national representative each, while the remaining 181 countries are clustered in 16 (mainly) regional constituencies which elect one delegate per group (IMF, 2017).

With the end of the Bretton Woods exchange rate system, the IMF's central objective changed 'from the maintenance of stable exchange rates to the maintenance of stable economic and financial conditions broadly defined' (Eichengreen and Woods, 2016, p. 39). Stability (i.e. the absence of crises) does not only benefit individual countries but also protects others from contagion. Moreover, it facilitates the cross-border exchange of goods and capital, which, in turn, is conducive to sustained economic growth. In pursuit of this overarching objective, the IMF promotes international cooperation and engages in the prevention and management of international financial crises. In principle, the IMF represents a multilateral, rule-based approach to dealing with international financial and monetary concerns in contrast to a system that would primarily rely on market mechanisms and/or unilateral action by some powerful countries.

At the instrumental level, the IMF predominantly engages in surveillance, capacity development and lending.

Surveillance

As for surveillance, the IMF regularly carries out the bilateral Article-IV consultations, which are mandatory for members (IMF, 2016b): in collaboration with relevant national stakeholders IMF economists review a country's policies and its economic performance. Furthermore, voluntary assessments are conducted at the behest of members, for example concerning the stability of national financial markets (Poole, 2015). At the multilateral level, the organisation oversees developments in capital markets and the world economy more generally. The findings are published regularly in the *World Economic Outlook*, the *Global Financial Stability Report* and the *Fiscal Monitor*, among others. With its reports, the IMF intends to identify risks and possible country-to-country spillovers. If needed, policy reforms are advised in order to restore stability and minimise the exposure to dangers.

By publishing standardised information and analyses the IMF supplies a global public good, which would be difficult and costly to provide nationally (Meltzer, 2003). For individual countries it proves almost impossible to systematically gather information outside their jurisdiction. Local authorities are more likely to convey sensitive information to an international organisation than to other governments or market actors such as rating agencies (Eichengreen and Woods, 2016). Given the complicated nature of financial risks, elected politicians with a restricted time horizon have little incentive to consider foreign developments or the long-term impact of their policies on other countries. In contrast, an international organisation is perceived of as more impartial and it is less myopic owing to the lack of electoral constraints. Given its accumulated expertise, it is capable of compiling information comprehensively and drawing lessons from it. This could result in better informed policies and investment decisions, leading to improved market allocation and system stability (Meltzer, 2003). Thus, public scrutiny might pressurise governments to adopt stability-oriented policies, and private investors could overcome information asymmetries relative to borrowers more readily so that irrational panic and uninformed herd behaviour become less probable.

While there is a convincing rationale for IMF surveillance, the practical implementation is imperfect. A prominent example is the IMF's failure to foresee recent financial crises in the US and Europe. Partly, the economics discipline per se is to blame, since it suffers from 'knowledge gaps around the interaction between the macroeconomy and the financial sector ("macrofinancial" linkages)' (Poole, 2015, p. 87).[2] However, part of the problem lies within the IMF itself. Informational 'silos' impede the pooling of knowledge across departments and the identification of vulnerabilities (IEO, 2011). Publications sometimes lack clarity, consequently impairing the quality of information. The most serious issue relates to the surveillance bias that favours more powerful members. According to the IMF's Independent Evaluation Office, self-censorship among IMF staff results in 'limits as to how critical they could be regarding the policies of the largest shareholders' (IEO, 2011, p. 20). Moreover, powerful members manage to have unsolicited passages in IMF reports deleted far more often than developing nations (Eichengreen and Woods, 2016). While the IMF has started to address some of the internal shortcomings, the lack of evenhandedness is still an issue that is closely linked to the unresolved Western-dominated governance structure.

Capacity development

Besides surveillance, the IMF promotes capacity development. In particular, it provides technical assistance and training to member countries in order to strengthen staff skills and build up institutional capacities (IMF, 2016c). In principle, the IMF is well equipped to offer capacity development. There are economies of scale and learning curve effects in the design and supply of training programs and the accumulation of technical expertise. Accordingly, governments – especially from poorer countries – get more value for money when resorting to internationally available know-how. Moreover, cross-country experiences foster policy learning and transfer (Dolowitz and Marsh, 2000). Indeed, the IMF can field-test its programs in different countries and channel them to others. In doing so, it has the advantage of being independent from domestic vested interests (Rajan, 2008). However, reality is different: in order to be successful capacity development needs to be made-to-measure, considering local conditions and constraints. In fact, reform blueprints developed in Washington, DC, are too often tailored to the interests of powerful shareholders rather than to a receiving country's circumstances.

Lending

The arguably most important IMF instrument is lending. By granting loans to member countries in balance-of-payment difficulties, the IMF acts as a quasi-lender-of-last-resort (Meltzer, 2003; Reinhart and Trebesch, 2016). Basically, a member country without adequate international reserves or access to affordable private capital can borrow from the IMF, thus receiving breathing space to 'restore conditions for strong economic growth' (IMF, 2016d). Typically, loan agreements are up to four years with final maturity of ten years. They can amount to a multiple of between two and six of a country's quota, depending on the specific program. In the eurozone crisis, however, these so-called access limits have been surpassed drastically to a factor of up to 30 (Reinhart and Trebesch, 2016). While advanced and emerging nations are charged market-related interest rates, low-income countries can borrow on concessional terms, currently at zero per cent. For countries with a heavy debt burden, the IMF runs debt relief programs in cooperation with the World Bank, for instance the Heavily Indebted Poor Country (HIPC) Initiative or the Multilateral Debt Relief Initiative (MDRI) (IMF, 2016f).

IMF lending is funded through various sources. The most important one is quotas, i.e. the paid-in capital by IMF members, currently amounting to 477 billion SDR (approximately $642 billion). In addition, the IMF can temporarily borrow through multilateral agreements with member countries (another 460.5 billion SDR). Subsidised concessional lending and debt relief programs are funded through bilateral contributions by richer member countries and IMF profits, for instance from gold sales (IMF, 2016e). Overall, the IMF has massively boosted its lending capacity since the global financial crisis, primarily as lending demands have increased significantly and the ongoing crisis requires larger liquidity firewalls to appease financial markets and protect countries from collapse and contagion.

In order to safeguard loan repayment and avoid moral hazard – a situation where countries run into problems relatively insouciantly, knowing that there will be a fairly pain-free bail-out – IMF loans are subject to conditionality. In most cases, this takes the form of ex-post conditionality: in so-called Stand-By Arrangements, for example, the IMF agrees with the borrowing country a specific set of macroeconomic and structural reforms that are supposed to guarantee recovery, growth and poverty reduction (Dreher, 2004). Financial assistance is then disbursed in phased instalments subject to compliance with program stipulations. Conditionality constitutes a strong link between lending and surveillance. In principle, the IMF cannot coerce its members to adopt the policies it advises based on surveillance. However, when a country requires financial assistance it can use conditionality as a lever to make countries implement the recommended reforms.

Theoretically, the existence of an emergency lender is pertinent to the stability of the international monetary system, just as a country's central bank acts as lender-of-last-resort in a national financial crisis. Rather than defaulting in an unorderly way and/or resorting to destructive measures, a country short of liquidity can access emergency funds, while simultaneously adjusting its policies and/or realigning its currency. Further, IMF loans can catalyse private capital inflows as they signal a country's efforts to avoid default (van der Veer and de Jong, 2013). However, since the breakdown of the Bretton Woods pegged exchange rate order, reality has been different. Instead of temporary lending for balance-of-payment crises the IMF has primarily been concerned with more systemic crises such as the 1980s debt crises in Latin America and Africa, the Asian and transition country banking and economic crises in the 1990s and the eurozone crisis since 2009. These shifts coincide with changes in IMF lending patterns (Reinhart and Trebesch, 2016): while median loan volumes amounted to less than 2 per cent of borrowers' GDP when currency crises dominated, the size doubled to approximately 4 per cent thereafter, even reaching between 10.7 and 15.8 per cent in Europe post-2008. Similarly, average program duration increased, and consecutive loan arrangements have led to serial lending in several Latin American and African countries, with uninterrupted spells of IMF loaning of up to 30 years. Instead of assisting illiquid but fundamentally solvent countries as originally intended, the IMF has thus partly come to replace private debtors in countries with deficient debt sustainability.

This alteration in IMF practice has serious implications. For one, the IMF actually starts being involved in long-term aid, the World Bank's traditional domain. Moreover, when loans can be easily renewed countries are enticed to over-borrow and evergreen their debt. Through lending into insolvency or arrears the IMF jeopardises its traditional status as most senior creditor, for example, as in Greece in mid-2015. Similarly, financial assistance to (practically) insolvent countries blurs the important distinction between illiquidity and insolvency. Consecutive liquidity loans might protract eventually unavoidable debt restructuring and – owing to moral hazard – implicitly encourage private investors to continue (co-)lending for too long, assuming that the IMF will bail them out (Eichengreen and Woods, 2016). What is more, IMF lending gains a bad reputation of being associated with insolvency. Illiquid but solvent countries, for which the IMF was intended as a short-term port of call, then risk being stigmatised as insolvent when taking up an IMF loan, with negative consequences for their access to private capital markets. Thus, the IMF loses its function as a quasi-lender-of-last-resort, thereby putting financial market stability at risk.

The World Bank: governance, objectives and instruments

To a large extent, World Bank governance resembles that of the IMF. The bank is also located in Washington, DC, and its president has traditionally been a Westerner. Voting power in the Board of Governors depends largely on shares in the capital stock. Once again, the US is the largest shareholder with 16.45 per cent, next to Japan and China with 7.11 and 4.59 per cent, respectively (World Bank, 2017a).[3] The US and certain country coalitions have blocking power concerning statute amendments which require an 85 per-cent supermajority. Day-to-day business – including loan and guarantee approvals, borrowing and financial decisions – is carried out by the board of directors, which is made up of 25 executive directors. The six largest shareholders – the US, Japan, Germany, France, the UK and China – appoint an executive director each, while the other member countries are grouped in constituencies which are represented by an elected director. In March 2017, advanced countries had voting power of at least 51 per cent.

There are, however, also important differences between the Bretton Woods sisters. Thus, World Bank membership is contingent on IMF membership (the opposite is not the case). While the IMF has approximately 2700 members of staff primarily situated in the headquarters, the World Bank is almost four times as big and maintains more than 130 national offices which facilitate access to up-to-date local information (IMF, 2016a; World Bank, 2017b). In contrast to the monolithic IMF, the World Bank is made up of five separate but related subsidiaries with different purposes (discussed later in the chapter). While the IMF is essentially unique as a global provider of last-resort liquidity – the European Stability Mechanism, the Chiang-Mai Initiative and the BRICS Contingency Reserve Arrangement have a limited regional focus and/or have not yet been put to the test (Desai and Vreeland, 2014) – the World Bank is just one, albeit the biggest among several development banks.[4]

The World Bank's central objective is the eradication of poverty, explicitly defined as ending 'extreme poverty by decreasing the percentage of people living on less than $1.90 a day to no more than 3%' of the world population and promoting 'shared prosperity by fostering the income growth of the bottom 40% for every country' by 2030 (World Bank, 2017b). While the original goal was reconstruction in war-torn countries in Europe and Japan with insufficient access to private capital[5] (Rajan, 2008), the emphasis is now on development and growth in Asia, Africa and Latin America. Addressing poverty and inequality is a global public good that benefits all countries in two ways (Clemens and Kremer, 2016): first, the well-being of citizens with altruistic preferences increases when the world becomes a fairer place. Second, many poverty-stricken countries feature political, ecological, social and economic conditions that potentially prompt externalities for richer nations in the form of terrorism, crime, ecological degradation, pandemics and migration. Consequently, poverty eradication is in the self-interest of more advanced countries.

Still, the question arises as to why development aid is – at least in parts – delegated to an international organisation rather than being shaped by donor countries individually. The latter allows governments to focus on specific regions and projects, for instance in pursuit of business for the domestic export industry (so-called tied aid) or as a diplomatic bargaining chip (Ravallion, 2016). An international organisation, however, offers different advantages (Clemens and Kremer, 2016). Owing to economies of scale, negotiations over aid agreements become less costly and donors increase their bargaining power relative to developing countries. Money can be allocated more efficiently on a global scale, disregarding particular countries' or local constituencies' special interests. As a public good, poverty eradication is subject to free-riding: since no country can be excluded from its benefits, 'not donating' (while still gaining) becomes a viable option. If too many countries free-ride, the global aid level will be inefficiently low. In this case, an international organisation can help coordinate donations and exert more pressure on individual countries to comply, for example, through transparency.

Similar to the IMF, the World Bank's key instruments comprise financing and the provision of information, technical assistance and advice. Whereas the IMF focuses on macro-critical areas, the World Bank is generally concerned with longer-term growth-enhancing projects, structural policies and government programs.

Financing

The type of financial support alters with the particular World Bank subsidiary. The International Bank for Reconstruction and Development (IBRD), the core unit created in 1944, funds public investment projects concerning physical and social infrastructure in creditworthy lower and middle-income countries (Investment Project Financing) (World Bank, 2017c). Further, it undertakes policy-based lending, which has grown massively since the 1980s (Chang, 2006). This includes contributing to government programs run by developing countries themselves ('Program for Results') and providing non-earmarked budget support for structural policies that fight poverty and inequality sustainably, for example by diversifying the economy or improving the investment climate (Development Policy Financing). Loan periods usually range from five to ten years and interest rates are 'ostensibly close to market terms' (Clemens and Kremer, 2016, p. 54). In contrast, the International Development Association (IDA), launched in 1960, subsidises public investment projects and policy programs in the least developed countries and those at 'risk of debt distress', with a concentration on 'primary education, basic health services, clean water and sanitation, environmental safeguards, business climate improvements, infrastructure and institutional reforms' (IDA, 2017). Financial support predominantly takes the form of concessional loans, so-called credits, which currently carry zero or very low interest and have a maturity of 25 to 38 years. Countries in debt distress are eligible for grants (IDA, 2017). IDA also runs debt relief programs in collaboration with the IMF.[6]

In 2016, the World Bank as a whole had lending commitments of $45.9 billion (World Bank, 2017d), financial volumes substantially smaller than the IMF's. The World Bank has several sources for funding. The IBRD predominantly issues bonds in world capital markets. Owing to its AAA ratings, it can borrow relatively inexpensively and lend at favourable terms, with the margin adding to profits. These are, in turn, partly redirected to finance IDA activities. The lion's share of IDA funding stems from donating governments which replenish funds every three years. In addition, the World Bank holds so-called Trust Funds on behalf of non-governmental and public donors, which pursue specific pre-determined goals such as fighting AIDS or malaria or promoting child vaccinations (Clemens and Kremer, 2016).

Policy-based World Bank lending contains conditionality, usually complementing IMF conditions (Dreher, 2004). By stipulating conditions for prior action (pre-loan approval) or, subsequently, for the disbursement of further tranches (tranche-release conditions), the World Bank intends to improve aid effectiveness while at the same time ensuring that borrowers use the resources as agreed, including repayment. Conditions refer specifically to the funded program or policy and/or, more generally, to the macroeconomic and institutional environment (World Bank, 2005). The latter typically entails structural adjustment measures such as the reduction of budget deficits through tax increases and/or spending cuts, foreign debt restructuring, currency devaluations and – more long-term – privatisation, liberalisation and institutional policies (Hernandez, 2016). Similar to the IMF, the World Bank can use conditionality to make a recipient country adopt its policy advice.

At a theoretical level, it is contestable whether a public financer is still required in a world where capital is relatively abundant and finance has lost its critical role as development bottleneck (Rajan, 2008; Ravallion, 2016).[7] A substantial part of World Bank lending, for instance, goes to middle-income countries such as China or Brazil; countries which have access to financial markets or even their own resources to fund poverty reduction independently. However, World Bank lending is still important in that it can fill in where private investors are not willing to wait for uncertain, long-term returns or national governments underinvest because the benefits are (partly) accrued by political opponents and/or neighbouring countries. For instance, the World Bank can help supply regional or global public goods where national solutions fall short, including cross-border climate protection or the containment of pandemics such as Ebola. In addition, World Bank engagement can provide a positive signal to private actors who might neglect certain projects or regions owing to a lack of trustworthy local information; the World Bank can consequently act as a catalyst for private investment. From a public choice perspective, however, World Bank lending can also be deficient (Rajan, 2008). In the absence of competitive pressures and with staff being interested in boosting the number of deals and loan volumes in order to raise their significance, World Bank investment decisions might be taken less diligently than those by private investors who bear the full risk of default.

Provision of information, technical assistance and advice

In any case, the World Bank's influence has reached far beyond its direct financial involvement in more than 12,800 development projects carried out since 1947 (World Bank, 2017b). In fact, in the field of development policy the World Bank is the most significant supplier of information, technical assistance and policy advice, thus shaping the international aid scene (Gavin and Rodrik, 1995). In cooperation with member countries the World Bank collects and analyses data that is published freely, including the influential *World Development Report* and the *Doing Business* report on regulation (Besley, 2015). Further, the World Bank offers 'professional technical advice that supports legal, policy, management, governance and other reforms needed for a country's development goal' (World Bank, 2017c) and it helps governments devise and implement development strategies. Moreover, the World Bank assumes the role of an agenda-setter in international development policy in that it organises conferences, coordinates negotiations between donors and recipients and has its staff publish scholarly work. Finally, the World Bank promotes ideas via acting as a reservoir for human resources when staff members, who embraced World Bank culture, become high-ranking government officials in their home countries (Clemens and Kremer, 2016).

Similar to the IMF, the World Bank's activities in research, analysis and policy advice address economic problems inherent in the 'production' of knowledge, which are essential ingredients for the skill-intensive field of development policy (Ravallion, 2016). An international organisation can realise economies of scale resulting from the pooling of resources for information gathering, the conceptual design of development policies and the build-up of technical assistance capacities. In contrast, individual donors have little incentive to document their experiences and share them with others, given the public-good character of knowledge. With its global reach, the World Bank is – at least theoretically – in a position to compare projects and programs implemented in different national and local contexts, thus providing benchmarks and critical success factors. What is more, an international organisation with its nationally diverse staff is usually perceived of as more independent and trustworthy than national donor agencies so that legitimacy and reliability of information and policy advice increases. This enables the World Bank, just like the IMF (Stubbs et al., 2016), to act as a leader or aid catalyst that other donors follow.

While the World Bank's significance has shifted from mere lending to knowledge provision – as reflected in former World Bank president Wolfensohn's idea of a 'knowledge bank' in contrast to the 'lending bank' (Ravallion, 2016, p. 78) – there are ongoing shortcomings regarding knowledge production (Babb and Kentikele-nis, 2017). Admittedly, since 2010 the World Bank publishes more data, but some relevant information pertaining to the Bank's own loan programs is still withheld (Ravallion, 2016). As in the IMF, information 'silos' hinder the exchange of information across units and therefore impair its quality. At times, research output is 'sugarcoated' pre-publication in order not to upset major World Bank shareholders; a fact that possibly triggers 'preemptive obedience' regarding research questions and results. The role of powerful stakeholders also impinges on the World Bank's impartiality and legitimacy and therefore the trustworthiness of its knowledge creation and policy advice (Clemens and Kremer, 2016). Eventually, even though policy advice has become far more country-centred in recent years, 'one-size-fits-all' proposals are sometimes still made, thus ignoring local context and consequently rendering World Bank support either ineffectual or even detrimental to the goal of poverty reduction.

Challenges and criticisms

Since their inception, both IMF and World Bank have undergone significant changes and they continue to be under pressure in the aftermath of the Great Recession. While their principal objectives – macroeconomic (financial) stability, development and growth, equality and poverty eradication – remain largely uncontested, current challenges notably concern the two organisations' specific policy instruments, their governance structure and, most recently, their rule-based multilateralist approach.

For decades, IMF and World Bank policies have been heavily criticised. Given the ongoing existence of economic crises, underdevelopment, poverty and inequality, both organisations are blamed for having missed their goals, at least partly (Stiglitz, 2002; Rajan, 2008). Where poverty reduction has been most impressive – in East Asia and in particular in China – governments pursued state-centred development policies rather than the market-liberal IMF and World Bank recipes. Some studies suggest that World Bank, and especially IMF lending, may have very little or even negative effects on economic growth in recipient countries (Butkiewicz and Yanik-kaya, 2004). One concern is that IMF lending is usually accompanied with requirements for spending cuts which reduce aggregate demand and economic growth. At times, loans might sustain corrupt regimes through the availability of relatively unaccountable, external resources (Birchler et al., 2016). Another issue stems from serial lending which keeps developing countries reliant on public loans rather than encouraging debt sustainability and economic independence (Reinhart and Trebesch, 2016). The burden of adjustment is unilaterally imposed on borrowing countries while surplus countries are generally spared adjustment pressures (Nissan, 2015). Criticism also concerns the convergence of both organisations' policy remits. Instead of distinguishing between short-term balance-of-payment crises (IMF) and long-term development (World Bank) both organisations have increasingly engaged in so-called structural adjustment (Dreher, 2004). This blurs responsibilities and reduces competition of ideas and policies between World Bank and IMF. The IMF, in particular, is said to engage in 'mission creep' beyond its core competence so that policy advice often lacks adequate expertise (Stiglitz, 2002).

The most severe policy criticism has focused on conditionality (Babb and Kentikelenis, 2017; Blanton et al., 2015). According to this, IMF and World Bank have imposed neo-liberal policies on borrowing countries via 'one-size-fits-all' structural adjustment programs. These follow the Washington Consensus, a set of reforms ranging from far-reaching privatisation, deregulation, liberalisation to currency devaluations and austerity. Even the pace and sequence of reforms is dictated (Stiglitz, 2002). While intended to create growth, these policies are criticised for their detrimental effects on the environment, social structure, democratic set-up and culture of the recipient country as well as the ignorance of country circumstances. Local governments often lack ownership of the reform programs and support from their electorate. Indeed, many critics perceive of conditionality as a veil for major shareholders' vested interests and US hegemony (Dreher and Sturm, 2012; Cardim de Carvalho, 2016). The apex of conditionality-based interference occurred during the Asian crisis in the late 1990s when crisis countries were almost micro-managed (Feldstein, 1998). Since then the Bretton Woods sisters have streamlined conditionality by imposing fewer and more targeted conditions (World Bank, 2005). As regards content, the focus has broadened to include the institutional framework and human development rather than simple output growth (sometimes called the Post-Washington Consensus). More specifically, seemingly anti-neo-liberal policies such as social spending and cross-border capital controls have become acceptable when they benefit the poor or support recovery. However, criticism remains and some of the changes are labelled as 'window dressing', with the neo-liberal market paradigm still intact (Kentikelenis et al., 2016; Güven, 2012).

Closely related to these criticisms is the issue of governance. As outlined earlier, the Bretton Woods sisters are still dominated by the West, despite recent institutional reforms (Vestergaard and Wade, 2015). Consequently, major emerging economies continue to be under-represented relative to their share in global GDP. This governance bias has important repercussions for the two organisations' effectiveness. First, it undermines their impartiality, accountability and legitimacy – key resources required for exerting 'soft power' in the form of policy advice and knowledge when hard financial and coercive powers are limited (Eichengreen and Woods, 2016). Second, major emerging countries have responded to their misrepresentation by establishing alternative mechanisms (Reisen, 2015; Vestergaard and Wade, 2015). Following the Asian crisis, for instance, some emerging nations started accumulating foreign exchange reserves as an individual insurance against financial crises. The BRICS countries founded the New Development Bank, plus the Contingent Reserve Arrangement as a reserve fund for balance-of-payment crises (Langhammer, 2014). Some countries such as China, Brazil and India provide other developing nations with large-scale aid unilaterally (Desai and Vreeland, 2014).[8]

While new global actors potentially threaten the IMF and World Bank's standing externally, recent political trends challenge the multilateral system from within. In international trade, bilateral and regional agreements already seem to dominate at the expense of WTO-based multilateral trade talks (Vestergaard and Wade, 2015). In major Western democracies, a political shift is under way towards protectionism and economic nationalism, currently most obvious in the US and UK. In other European countries right-of-centre political parties or movements also put pressure on mainstream governments to pursue more inward-looking policies. Anti-globalisation protests in the developed world are not new, as evident from the existence of NGOs such as Occupy Wall Street or ATTAC and the protests against G7/8/20 and IMF/World Bank meetings. However, globalisation resistance now also comes from the political right and has in some cases assumed governmental power. These relatively recent developments question what IMF and World Bank represent most fundamentally: globalisation and multilateralism (Woods, 2007).

Multilateralism of the Bretton Woods type does not automatically imply an equal or fair power distribution. Both organisations provide ample evidence for political dominance by a few countries. Hence, the US and others used IMF and World Bank resources during the Cold War to keep developing countries in their political orbit. There is empirical evidence that US-friendly governments – in particular those of political interest, for example, owing to a temporary seat in the UN Security Council – receive loans more easily relative to political foes of the US such as Iran (Clemens and Kremer, 2016). At the same time, developing countries benefiting from Bretton Woods loans seem to 'vote more frequently in line with the average G7 country' in the UN General Assembly (Dreher and Sturm, 2012, p. 387). However, multilateralism is still a (if not *the* most) useful cooperative tool to govern global relations, especially the provision of public goods such as macroeconomic stability, poverty eradication, climate protection and anti-corruption. In a multilateral system, international organisations offer a place for dialogue, coordination and collaboration and a tool to respond to international crises systematically. They help overcome free-riding and exploit economies of scale, and their staff – freed from local interests – can produce relatively impartial analysis and advice (Rajan, 2008). All of this is particularly important for medium and smaller countries. If intergovernmental fora such as the G20 or G7/8 gained power at the expense of the Bretton Woods organisations, relatively marginal countries would be disadvantaged even more, losing access to information, crises solution and power-sharing completely.

Conclusion

The Bretton Woods sisters look back on more than 70 years as key organisations in the global economic regime. Both provide financial resources, alongside information, expertise and policy advice. Their influence, however, extends beyond official instruments, since they serve as guide for national governments, other international actors and private capital. Major shifts in the political economy – the independence of former European colonies, the end of both the Bretton Woods exchange rate system and the Cold War, the emergence of new global players, the intensification of globalisation and the massive increase in cross-border capital flows – have required both organisations to adapt.

Even more change will be unavoidable, if the IMF and World Bank are to remain as central elements of the pro-globalisation, multilateral economic order. Clinging to Western-centric policy approaches, conditionality and governance will result in the continuous emergence of competing power blocs and, consequently, the marginalisation of the Bretton Woods system. While some competition might help pressurise the West to adapt, the downside could be a 'race to the bottom' of global standards. As can already be observed, some new donors have a 'no strings attached' approach: they offer financial support independent of typical (Western) liberal values in the fields of human rights, democracy, the rule of law, environmental and social protection. Hence, authoritarian and corrupt regimes' power increases as they can 'shop' for funds and development aid that best suit their needs, possibly at the expense of these values.

The challenge for the dominant IMF and World Bank stakeholders will thus be twofold. On the one hand, they have to transfer more power to newly emerging economies in order to keep them in the multilateral system and thus sustain basic Bretton Woods principles. On the other hand, the Western democracies in particular have to ensure that the socio-economic situation of their electorates is not eroded. Otherwise, populism might grow, undermining the multilateral consensus of the last decades. Unless these issues are addressed, the ideals of multilateralism and open economies could vanish, with detrimental consequences for economic development worldwide.

Acknowledgements

I gratefully acknowledge the help of the editors as well as Dietmar Hillebrand, Harold Jones and Deema Kaneff. The chapter is dedicated to Kristin Jakob.

Notes

1 In this chapter, the term World Bank is used instead of the formally correct 'World Bank Group'.
2 The OECD and European Commission, among others, also failed to predict these events (Poole, 2015).
3 These figures refer to the Board of Governors of the International Bank for Reconstruction and Development (IBRD), the core organisation of the World Bank. Governance for other World Bank subsidiaries varies slightly.
4 Others include the Inter-American Development Bank, the Asian Development Bank and the newly established, China-dominated Asian Infrastructure Investment Bank (AIIB).
5 Access to private capital was limited owing to capital market imperfections, for instance information asymmetries, moral hazard, herding and irrational behaviour (Clemens and Kremer, 2016).
6 Other World Bank subsidiaries promote private sector engagement in economic development and poverty reduction. For example, the International Finance Corporation (IFC) supports commercial investment projects while the Multilateral Investment Guarantee Agency (MIGA) and the International Centre for Settlement of Investment Disputes (ICSID) are concerned with private foreign direct investment in developing countries.
7 In 2012, the World Bank provided as little as '5 percent of the aggregate private capital flow to developing countries' (Ravallion, 2016, p. 78).
8 China, for instance, founded the Asian Infrastructure Investment Bank (AIIB) and funds infrastructure investment abroad with its 'Silk Road Fund'.

Further reading

There are numerous publications on the IMF and World Bank. Particularly useful are the monographs by Woods (2007) and Stiglitz (2002). Bird (2007) provides an overview of the IMF, Dreher (2004) focuses on conditionality. Reinhart and Trebesch (2016), Eichengreen and Woods (2016), Clemens and Kremer (2016) and Ravallion (2016) all constitute up-to-date scholarly assessments of the IMF and World Bank. Some future scenarios for multilateral organisations are presented in Kahler (2016).

Several reform proposals have been discussed over the years, for instance the report of the International Financial Institution Advisory Commission (2000) to the US Congress (the so-called Meltzer Commission) and the report of the Commission of Experts of the President of the United Nations General Assembly on Reforms of the International Monetary and Financial System (the so-called Stiglitz report) (Stiglitz et al., 2010).

The IMF (www.imf.org) and World Bank (www.worldbank.org) both sustain valuable websites, providing research and comprehensive data sets. For an up-to-date critical review of IMF and World Bank policies from a civil society perspective, the UK-based website www.brettonwoodsproject.org is very useful.

Bibliography

Babb, Sarah L. and Alexander E. Kentikelenis (2017) 'International Financial Institutions as Agents of Neoliberalism' to appear in D. Cahill, M. Cooper and M. Konings (eds.) *The SAGE Handbook of Neoliberalism* (Thousand Oaks: Sage).

Besley, Timothy (2015) 'Law, Regulation, and the Business Climate: The Nature and Influence of the World Bank Doing Business Project', *Journal of Economic Perspectives* 29(3), pp. 99–120.

Birchler, Kassandra, Sophia Limpach and Katharina Michaelowa (2016) 'Aid Modalities Matter: The Impact of Different World Bank and IMF Programs on Democratization in Developing Countries', *International Studies Quarterly* 60, pp. 427–439.

Bird, Graham (2007) 'The IMF: A Bird's Eye View of its Role and Operations', *Journal of Economic Surveys* 21(4), pp. 683–745.

Blanton, Robert G., Blanton, Shannon L. and Dursun Peksen (2015) 'The Impact of IMF and World Bank Programs on Labor Rights', *Political Research Quarterly* 68(2), pp. 324–336.

Butkiewicz, James L. and Halit Yanikkaya (2004) 'The Effects of IMF and World Bank Lending on Long-Run Economic Growth: An Empirical Analysis', *World Development* 33(3), pp. 371–391.

Cardim de Carvalho, Fernando J. (2016) 'Back to Original Mission', *Development and Cooperation* 2016/03, www.dandc.eu/en/article/why-emerging-markets-deserve-more-say-imf (accessed March 17, 2017).

Chang, Ha-Joon (2006) 'Policy Space in Historical Perspective with Special Reference to Trade and Industrial Policies', *Economic and Political Weekly* 41(7), pp. 627–633.

Clemens, Michael and Michael Kremer (2016) 'The New Role for the World Bank', *Journal of Economic Perspectives* 30(1), pp. 53–76.

Desai, Raj and James Vreeland (2014) 'What the New Bank of BRICS Is All About', *Washington Post* 17 July 2014, www.washingtonpost.com/news/monkey-cage/wp/2014/07/17/what-the-new-bank-of-brics-is-all-about/?utm_term=.bdd246651f50 (accessed March 7, 2017)

Dolowitz, David and David Marsh (2000) 'Learning from Abroad: The Role of Policy Transfer in Contemporary Policy-Making', *Governance* 13(1), pp. 5–24.

Dreher, Axel (2004) 'A Public Choice Perspective of IMF and World Bank Lending and Conditionality', *Governance* 119, pp. 445–464.

Dreher, Axel and Jan-Egbert Sturm (2012) 'Do the IMF and the World Bank Influence Voting in the UN General Assembly?' *Public Choice* 151, pp. 363–397.

Eichengreen, Barry and Ngaire Woods (2016) 'The IMF's Unmet Challenges', *Journal of Economic Perspectives* 30(1), pp. 29–52.

Feldstein, Martin (1998) 'Refocusing the IMF', *Foreign Affairs* 77(2), pp. 20–33.

Gavin, Michael and Dani Rodrik (1995) 'The World Bank in Historical Perspective', *American Economic Review* 85(2), pp. 329–334.

Global Exchange (2015) 'Top Ten Reasons to Oppose the IMF', www.globalexchange.org/sites/default/files/IMFTopTen.pdf (accessed February 28, 2017).

Güven, Ali Burak (2012) 'The IMF, the World Bank, and the Global Economic Crisis: Exploring Paradigm Continuity', *Development and Change* 43(4), pp. 869–898.

Hernandez, Diego (2016) 'Are "New" Donors Challenging World Bank Conditionality?' *AidData Working Paper* 19 (January 2016), http://aiddata.org/sites/default/files/wps19_are_new_donors_challenging_world_bank_conditionality.pdf (accessed March 7, 2017).

IDA (2017) 'Financing', http://ida.worldbank.org/financing/ida-financing (accessed March 7, 2017).

IEO (2011) 'IMF Performance in the Run-up to the Financial and Economic Crisis: IMF Surveillance in 2004–07', Evaluation Report, www.ieo-imf.org/ieo/files/completedevaluations/Crisis-%20Main%20Report%20(without%20Moises%20Signature).pdf (accessed March 1, 2017).

IMF (2016a) 'The IMF at a Glance', www.imf.org/en/About/Factsheets/IMF-at-a-Glance (accessed March 1, 2017).

IMF (2016b) 'IMF Surveillance', www.imf.org/external/np/exr/facts/surv.htm (accessed March 1, 2017).

IMF (2016c) 'Capacity Development: Technical Assistance and Training', www.imf.org/external/np/exr/facts/tech.htm (accessed March 1, 2017)

IMF (2016d) 'IMF Lending', www.imf.org/en/About/Factsheets/IMF-Lending (accessed March 1, 2017).

IMF (2016e) 'Where the IMF Gets Its Money', www.imf.org/en/About/Factsheets/Where-the-IMF-Gets-Its-Money (accessed March 1, 2017).

IMF (2016f) 'Debt Relief Under the Heavily Indebted Poor Countries (HIPC) Initiative', www.imf.org/external/np/exr/facts/hipc.htm (accessed March 1, 2017).

IMF (2017) 'IMF Executive Directors and Voting Power', www.imf.org/external/np/sec/memdir/eds.aspx (accessed March 1, 2017).

International Financial Institution Advisory Commission (2000) *Report to US Congress on Reform of the Development Banks and the International Finance Regime* (Washington, DC: International Financial Institution Advisory Commission).

Kahler, Miles (2016) 'The Global Economic Multilaterals: Will Eighty Years Be Enough?' *Global Governance* 22, pp. 1–9.

Kentikelenis, Alexander E., Thomas H. Stubbs and Lawrence P. King (2016) 'IMF Conditionality and Development Policy Space, 1985–2014', *Review of International Political Economy* 23(4), pp. 543–582.

Krugman, Paul (1998) 'The Indispensible I.M.F.', *New York Times* (May 15), www.nytimes.com/1998/05/15/opinion/the-indispensable-imf.html (accessed February 28, 2017).

Langhammer, Rolf J. (2014) 'Die BRICS-Entwicklungsbank – ein Fonds, aber noch keine Bank', *Wirtschaftsdienst* 94(8), pp. 530–531.

Meltzer, Allan H. (2003) 'The Future of the IMF and World Bank: Panel Discussion', *American Economic Review (Papers and Proceedings)* 93(2), pp. 46–48.

Meltzer, Allan H. (2005) 'New Mandates for the IMF and World Bank: Panel Discussion', *Cato Journal* 25(1), pp. 13–16.

Nissan, Sargon (2015) 'As Obituaries Are Written for the World Bank, the IMF Is Set to Become Indispensible', *Financial Times Beyondbrics* (May 11), http://blogs.ft.com/beyond-brics/author/sargonnissan/ (accessed February 28, 2017)

Poole, Emily (2015) 'The IMF's 'Surveillance': How Has It Changed since the Global Financial Crisis?' *Reserve Bank of Australia Bulletin* (March Quarter), www.rba.gov.au/publications/bulletin/2015/mar/pdf/bu-0315-9.pdf (accessed February 28, 2017)

Rajan, Raghuram G. (2008) 'The Future of the IMF and World Bank', *American Economic Review (Papers and Proceedings)* 98(2), pp. 110–115.

Ravallion, Martin (2016) 'The World Bank: Why It Is Still Needed and Why It Still Disappoints', *Journal of Economic Perspectives* 30(1), pp. 77–94.

Reinhart, Carmen M. and Christoph Trebesch (2016) 'The International Monetary Fund: 70 Years of Reinvention', *Journal of Economic Perspectives* 30(1), pp. 3–28.

Reisen, Helmut (2015) 'Die Entwicklungsbanken der Schwellenländer und die multilaterale Finanzarchitektur', *Wirtschaftsdienst* 95(4), pp. 274–279.

Stiglitz, Joseph E. (2002) *Globalization and Its Discontents* (New York: W.W. Norton).

Stiglitz, Joseph E. et al. (2010) *The Stiglitz Report: Reforming the International Monetary and Financial Systems in the Wake of the Global Crisis* (New York: The New Press).

Stubbs, Thomas H., Alexander E. Kentikelenis and Lawrence P. King (2016) 'Catalyzing Aid? The IMF and Donor Behavior in Aid Allocation', *World Development* 78, pp. 511–528.

Van der Veer, Koen J.M. and Eelke de Jong (2013) 'IMF-Supported Programmes: Stimulating Capital to Non-Defaulting Countries', *The World Economy* 36(4), pp. 375–395.

Vestergaard, Jakob and Robert H. Wade (2015) 'Still in the Woods: Gridlock in the IMF and the World Bank Puts Multilateralism at Risk', *Global Policy* 6(1), pp. 1–12.

Weisbrot, Mark and Jake Johnston (2016) 'Voting Share Reform at the IMF: Will It Make a Difference?' *Center For Economic and Policy Research* (April 2016), http://cepr.net/images/stories/reports/IMF-voting-shares-2016-04.pdf (accessed March 5, 2017).

Woods, Ngaire (2007) *The Globalizers: The IMF, the World Bank, and Their Borrowers, Cornell Studies in Money* (Ithaca: Cornell University Press).

World Bank (2005) 'Review of World Bank Conditionality', http://siteresources.worldbank.org/PROJECTS/Resources/40940-1114615847489/ConditionalityFinalDCpaperDC9-9-05.pdf (accessed March 6, 2017).

World Bank (2017a) 'Voting Powers', www.worldbank.org/en/about/leadership/votingpowers (accessed March 6, 2017).

World Bank (2017b) 'What We Do', www.worldbank.org/en/about/what-we-do (accessed March 6, 2017).

World Bank (2017c) 'Products and Services', www.worldbank.org/en/projects-operations/products-and-services#IPF (accessed March 7, 2017).

World Bank (2017d) 'Projects & Operations', http://projects.worldbank.org/ (accessed March 7, 2017).

Chapter 14

Non-governmental organisations

Hannah Murphy-Gregory

Non-governmental organisations (NGOs), also variously known as interest groups, non-profits, pressure groups, civil society groups or even simply associations, are omnipresent actors in 21st-century global politics. Yet it was only in the latter decades of the 20th century that the roles and contributions of NGOs in the global context were recognised by international relations scholars. According to Boli and

FIGURE 14.1 NGO staff implementing an AIDS/HIV awareness campaign in Mozambique

Thomas (1999), NGOs and their networks have existed in the international arena for well over a century but their numbers have since grown exponentially. In 1909, they calculate that 176 NGOs operated internationally (Boli and Thomas, 1999). By 2014, the Union of International Associations (2015), a dedicated research institute on international organisations, determined that 25,035 NGOs (including federations, universal membership groups, intercontinental and regionally oriented groups, organisations emanating from places, persons and bodies, plus internationally oriented national organisations) were active participants in global politics, especially in the issue areas of human rights, aid, economic justice and environmental conservation.

To explain the proliferation of NGOs at the international level, scholars point to advances in information and communications technology and the growing affordability of international travel in recent decades (Chatfield et al., 1997; Cohen and Rai, 2000; Ruhlman, 2015). But the increased size and diversity of NGOs operating globally is also due to the growing number of transnational policy issues that require a degree of governance beyond the nation state (Reinicke, 1998; Della Porta and Tarrow, 2005; Alaimo, 2016). For example, public health crises, the global financial system, oceans management, climate change, international trade and the Antarctic region are all areas where some form of global governance is viewed as essential to help address collective action problems. In turn, the presence of international organisations promotes NGO activity because most organisations allow for formal and/or informal input from NGOs subject to various accreditation processes. For example, a key factor in understanding the increasing numbers of NGOs engaged with trade policy in recent decades is the 1995 advent of the World Trade Organisation (WTO), an institution with a wide ranging mandate and more effective regulatory and judicial processes than the General Agreement on Tariffs and Trade (GATT), which preceded it (Murphy, 2010). Similarly, the 2015 international climate change conference in Paris saw a plethora of NGOs involved in public advocacy and behind-the-scenes lobbying of governmental delegations (Green, 2016). Indeed, UN Secretary-General Ban Ki-moon told NGOs at the meeting in Paris that 'no government, no international organization, can do its work properly without active engagement and support from civil society' (UN News Centre, 2015).

In spite of their burgeoning numbers and compared with other participants in global politics such as governments and corporations, NGOs are often under-resourced and lack formal authority on the global stage. As such, a primary question for international relations scholars that continues to guide research on NGOs is: how do 'small, overworked and under-funded NGOs with little formal authority manage to oversee changes in the practices of nation-states and international organisations?' (Willetts, 1982, p. 24). This chapter demonstrates that NGOs are prolific contributors to global politics, undertaking a variety of governance roles from agenda-setting and policy formulation through to implementation. They do so through advocacy campaigns, participation at global institutions alongside governments and even monitoring the compliance of other actors with international agreements. The chapter unpacks the various understandings of NGOs as a category of actor and examines the key approaches that are used to address their roles in global politics. The final section discusses the opportunities and challenges facing NGOs as participants in global politics, including their representativeness and accountability.

What are NGOs?

The term 'NGO' denotes an organisation that is voluntary in participation, not-for-profit in orientation and not seeking elected office. NGOs are therefore viewed as distinct from governments, political parties and business actors. In the scholarly literature, NGOs are understood as consisting of 'durable, bounded, voluntary relationships among individuals' (Weiss and Gordenker, 1996, p. 18) and as 'private, voluntary, nonprofit, groups whose primary aim is to influence publicly some form of social change' (Khagram et al., 2002, p. 6). In this regard, Tvedt (1998, p. 2) views NGOs as the embodiment of a kind of 'organised altruism' and as symbols of societal responsibility and global morality in an increasingly fragmented post-modern world polity. Prominent examples of NGOs active in the global political arena include ActionAid, Amnesty International, the Bill and Melinda Gates Foundation, Bird Life International, CARE International, the Catholic Agency for Overseas Development, Climate Action Network International, Fairtrade International, Greenpeace International, the International Committee of the Red Cross (ICRC), the International Trade Union Confederation, Médecins Sans Frontières, Oxfam International, Save the Children, Transparency International, Wikileaks, World Vision and the World Wildlife Fund (WWF), among the many thousands calculated to be active in global politics (see Union of International Associations, 2015).

The various classifications of NGOs shed light on the broad goals and activities of NGOs. Weiss and Gordenker (1996, p. 20) state that NGOs are formal organisations that engage in 'sovereignty-free' behaviour and aspire to be self-governing. However, these authors further make the distinction between government-organised NGOs (GONGOs), such as those set up by governments in the former Soviet bloc, quasi-NGOs (QUANGOs) such as the ICRC, and donor-organised NGOs (DON-GOs), for example, those established by the United Nations (UN) to serve particular purposes (Weiss and Gordenker, 1996, pp. 20–21). Additional labels for NGOs include business-organised NGOs (BONGOs), religious NGOs (RINGOs) and environmental NGOs (ENGOs) (see Weiss and Gordenker, 1996).

Others have categorised NGOs according to their broad issue focus. O'Brien et al. (2000), for instance, distinguish the activities of environmental, gender equity and labour NGOs. Additional labels include aid or development NGOs (Fisher, 1998) and human rights NGOs (Bob, 2009). Complicating matters however is the growing phenomenon of NGOs from differing issue areas joining together in common campaigns or activities. The fair trade movement for example involves a complex array of NGOs from those primarily concerned with the working conditions of producers in developing countries to those seeking to ensure the environmental sustainability of production processes (Hutchens, 2011).

NGOs are also frequently distinguished according to the geographical extent of their operations, with scholars pointing to differences between small-scale local NGOs, national-level NGOs, international NGOs and confederations of international NGOs (Boli and Thomas, 1999; Khagram et al., 2002). International NGOs such as Oxfam International are generally considered to have superior influence, finances and thus autonomy compared to local or national NGOs, though many international NGOs possess links to nationally based affiliate organisations. The NGO Greenpeace, for instance, comprises Greenpeace International in Amsterdam, a presence in more than 55 countries, and 2.8 million supporters worldwide that finance the organisation (Greenpeace International, 2016).

Another method to address the diversity in the NGO sector is to classify organisations according to the nature of their goals. Salmen and Eaves (1989), for example, outline five categories of NGOs along a public/private continuum from those pursuing public interest goals (such as environmental conservation) to those perceived as serving their own interests such as business groups or trade unions. But in reality, all groups represent some mixture of private and public interest goals (Sell and Prakash, 2004), even if an NGO's private interest is simply organisational survival. In this vein, Tvedt (1998, p. 12) states that typologies and acronyms of NGOs such as those listed earlier are problematic; they highlight some aspects while downplaying others, are culturally and politically loaded and none manage to capture the dynamism of the NGO sector. Consequently, Tvedt (1998, p. 16) states that the term NGO should be utilised as a common denominator that underlies the variation in the NGO sector because, as Willetts (1996, p. 62) has stated, '[t]here is no such thing as a typical NGO' (1996, p. 62).

From the 1990s onwards, the term 'global civil society', said to be an arena of activity distinct from governments and markets, has increasingly been used as an umbrella term to describe the NGO sector in its entirety (Florini, 2000; Keane, 2003; Brysk, 2005; Chandler and Baker, 2005; Germain and Kenny, 2005; Kaldor et al., 2012; Buckley, 2013). Global civil society is often cast as a sphere in which NGOs pursue moral or principled causes, such as human rights, environmental conservation and economic justice, seeking to hold governments and corporations to account for their activities and violations (Klotz, 1995; Wapner, 1995; Keck and Sikkink, 1998; Price, 1998). Others, however, contend that global civil society participants may pursue objectives that relate to either 'reinforcing or altering existing rules, norms and/or deeper social structures' (Scholte et al., 1999; Keane, 2003; Sell and Prakash, 2004). Accordingly, business associations seeking to maintain the neo-liberal economic order, and even terrorist groups pursuing 'uncivil' goals (see Kahler, 2009), should not strictly be excluded from the category, though it has become commonplace in the global politics literature to do so.

NGOs fulfil many functions in the global political arena. They have widely varying policy agendas, orientations and goals and seek to influence varying domestic and international policy forums and international organisations in differing ways. For example, NGOs play a significant role in monitoring the compliance of states with respect to international law, treaties and regimes. Alternatively, some NGOs, particularly those that promote economic development in less developed nations, may undertake their own projects and policy implementation. Others, such as Greenpeace and Amnesty International, are significant in the area of issue advocacy and public education through alternative sources of media or attracting the mainstream media by way of 'publicity stunts'. Many NGOs actively, but often not exclusively, engage in insider politics, lobbying elected representatives and bureaucrats at international organisations behind the scenes (Della Porta and Tarrow, 2005; Reinalda, 2011). To capture the varied political activities of NGOs, Alger (1997, pp. 261–268) outlines five categories of what he terms transnational social movement activity: creating and mobilising global networks, participating in multilateral political arenas, facilitating inter-state cooperation, acting within states and enhancing public participation. Similarly, in discussing the functions of environmental NGOs in regime formation, Ringius (1997, pp. 63–65) outlines four hypotheses about the role of NGOs in international regime development: public opinion mobilisation, transnational coalition building, compliance monitoring and advocating protection of the environment. While these activities relate specifically to Global Environmental Governance, they are typical of the functions and activities in which NGOs are engaged in across all global political issues.

Perspectives on NGOs

Despite their wide-ranging activities and proliferating numbers, in general terms, international relations scholars have been slow to acknowledge the significance of NGOs and their networks in global politics. In the 1970s, the seminal work of Keohane and Nye and their collaborators on 'transnational relations' and 'interdependence' sought to challenge the peripheral status accorded to NGOs and other non-state actors in international relations. In attempting to initiate a liberal, pluralistic framework for understanding world politics, Keohane and Nye (1972, 1977), along with Samuel Huntington (1973) and James Rosenau (1980), contended that non-state actors operating in the global sphere, including labour unions, multinational corporations, religious organisations and revolutionary movements, are significant if they participate autonomously (from governments) in political relationships in global politics. The work of Keohane and Nye and their colleagues initiated ongoing discussion about the impact of non-state actors in international politics. As part of the burgeoning focus on the role of ideas and normative values in global politics, it led to the literature on international regimes (Krasner, 1982; Young, 1982), epistemic communities (Haas, 1992, 2016) and, of course, NGOs in global politics.

A number of theoretical approaches have been adopted to understand the varied roles of NGOs in global affairs. Chief among these are institutional perspectives, constructivist perspectives, global social movement perspectives and critical perspectives. Though they share common concerns across key issue areas, each perspective focuses on different aspects of NGO activity. Drawing upon Keohane and Nye's early foray into the area, institutional approaches examine NGO contributions to global governance at various global institutions. Social constructivists highlight the moral entrepreneurship of NGOs via their strategic use of information through transnational campaigns that pressure states and corporations to alter their transgressive behaviour. A third perspective is the critical, neo-Gramscian approach that examines the counter-hegemonic potential of NGOs, often warning that NGO networks, rather than serving to advance progressive economic, social and environmental change, may instead reflect existing neo-liberal power structures. A fourth perspective has grown from political sociology: the global social movement approach views NGOs as a component of global social movements and explores how such movements are created and maintained and how they develop, disseminate and diffuse normative values. In the following, through a brief overview and illustration of some key scholarly contributions to the field, the insights of each major perspective on NGOs in global politics are discussed. The final section reviews the opportunities and challenges associated with NGO contributions to global politics.

Institutional approaches to NGOs in global politics, sometimes referred to as governance or global public policy approaches, seek to evaluate how, and with what impact, NGOs contribute to international policymaking. Typically, these accounts perceive that the institutional arrangements, decision-making processes and informal practices of international institutions condition interactions among NGOs and other actors and thus structure the way in which NGOs attempt to realise their goals in global politics (Fox and Brown, 1998; O'Brien et al., 2000; Keohane and Nye, 2001; Murphy, 2010). In this regard, the increasing authority of international institutions has provided 'a fulcrum for the formation of alliances of different state and nonstate actors' (Della Porta and Tarrow, 2005, p. 236), and such interactions evolve as global policy problems become increasingly complex (Reinicke, 1998; O'Brien et al., 2000; Reinicke et al., 2000; Boehmer-Christiansen and Kellow, 2003; Reinalda, 2011). Reinicke (2000), for instance, argues that 'global public policy networks' comprising loose alliances of international organisations, governments, business and NGOs are emerging in order to manage knowledge, correct market and intergovernmental failures and broaden participation in global governance (see also Hulme and Edwards, 1997; Bob, 2005; DeMars and Dijkzeul, 2015). As Keohane and Nye (1977) contend in *Power and Interdependence*, increasing international interdependence promotes trans-governmental coalition-building and political bargaining that in turn provides for the growth of non-state actors in global politics. The high-profile work of the United Nations and European Union (for example, in the areas of economic development, human rights and environmental conservation) has fostered the growth of NGOs and activists in these issue areas (Willetts, 1996).

One notable example of the manner in which international institutions promote NGO activity is the growing number of NGO parallel or counter-summits. International meetings of NGOs, such as the World Social Forum (WSF), are often staged to coincide with the formal meetings of international institutions. The first WSF meeting in 2001 shadowed the annual World Business Forum in Davos, Switzerland, aiming to highlight those excluded from this high-profile meeting. The WSF has since evolved into a venue for exploring alternatives to neo-liberal globalisation (Pianta and Silva, 2003; Smith and Karides, 2007). Other parallel summits have shadowed meetings of the World Bank, IMF and various UN conferences. In essence, high-profile international meetings provide a platform for media attention for NGOs, even where they are excluded from the formal meeting itself. Parallel summits are said to be beneficial for NGO advocacy because they build links between NGOs, enhance knowledge of policy issues, allow NGOs to formulate and propose alternative solutions to international or global problems and attract media coverage (Pianta, 2001).

Social constructivist scholars, rather than emphasising how international institutions structure NGO activity, highlight the independent agency of NGOs in 'reconstructing' national interests and impacting decision making in global politics (Klotz, 1995; Wapner, 1996; Keck and Sikkink, 1998; Khagram et al., 2002; Joachim, 2007; Klotz and Lynch, 2014; Haas, 2016). In doing so, social constructivists view NGOs as 'norm entrepreneurs' who pursue 'principled issue' causes. A prominent strand of this literature is dedicated to understanding how NGOs work together in transnational advocacy networks (TANS) in order to challenge human rights violations perpetrated by nation states (Keck and Sikkink, 1998). For example, Audie Klotz (1995) examines the anti-apartheid NGOs that worked to spread the US civil rights movement to South Africa, which she argues ultimately contributed to the fall of apartheid in that country. In the security arena, to understand how NGOs persuaded governments to ban landmines, Richard Price (1998) explores the roles of NGOs in issue generation, moral persuasion, network development and 'norm grafting'. And in the environmental policy arena, Paul Wapner (1996) highlights that NGOs can successfully target the environmentally harmful practices of corporations by disseminating normative values that affect the behaviour of larger collectivities throughout the world. By employing consumer activism tactics to alert consumers to undesirable corporate behaviour, such as boycotts and sensationalist media stunts, NGOs may promote widespread changes in the behaviour of multinational corporations and even whole societies. In other words, NGOs can provide 'governance without government', an enduring theme within the literature on NGOs and other non-state actors (Rosenau and Czempiel, 1992; Wapner, 1996; Haufler et al., 1999).

In their landmark book *Activists Beyond Borders*, Keck and Sikkink (1998) employ case studies from both the human rights and environmental areas to develop their 'boomerang' model, describing the ways in which NGO networks may shape nation state behaviour. The model explains how local NGOs reach beyond their own undemocratic governments to alert international NGOs of human rights abuses or environmental degradation. International NGOs then 'return' the boomerang by generating international consensus and global condemnation of a government, thereby pressuring a recalcitrant government to amend its behaviour (Keck and Sikkink, 1998, p. 12). As Keck and Sikkink (1998, p. 147) explain, access to, and strategic use of, information is a key asset as it allows NGOs to provide alternative and legitimate sources of information.

Neo-Gramscian scholars and other critical theorists also make important contributions to the literature on NGOs in global politics. Rather than emphasising the progressive possibilities of NGO agency in global politics or the opportunities or constraints posed by international institutions, they warn that NGOs may be co-opted into global neo-liberal structures that will limit their potential to promote economic equality and environmental sustainability (Goodman, 2002; Laxer and Halperin, 2003; Starr, 2005; McBride and Teeple, 2011; Starr et al., 2011; Buckley, 2013; Lindio-McGovern, 2013). As such, critical theorists often differentiate between professional NGOs and grassroots organisations perceived to be more authentic. They focus on, for example, anti-globalisation protests, workers' rights and other attempts to resist neo-liberalism. From this perspective, the primary concern is the counter-hegemonic potential (or otherwise) of transnational NGO activism.

From a critical, Gramsci-inspired perspective, writers such as McMichael (2000), Smith and Karides (2007), Wilkinson and Clapp (2010) and Starr (2011) question the capacity of international economic institutions such as the WTO, World Bank and International Monetary Fund – as well as national level economic regulators in the post-financial crisis period – to ever deliver equitable policy outcomes given the dominance of elite interests in global economic governance. For McMichael (2000,

p. 466) the WTO, for example, is a flawed institution dominated by business interests and powerful states seeking to advance capitalism and thus should be seen as part of 'the corporate attempt to secure global market rule, framed by a pervasive discourse of neoliberalism'. Consequently, critical scholars are cautious about the impact of greater NGO participation within these institutions. In this respect, large professional NGOs are often viewed as embodying global structural inequalities between the North and South (Hudock, 2001). Instead, critical scholars often advocate a different strategy for promoting global economic equality: the merging of local autonomy with global norms, to be pursued transnationally through a global civil society and locally through the defence of grassroots autonomy (Goodman, 2002; Bronfenbrenner, 2007; Klein, 2008; Pallas, 2013).

Global sociologists view the intensification of NGO advocacy as the growth or 'scaling up' of domestic social movements beyond the nation state (Alger, 1997; Chatfield et al., 1997; Guidry et al., 2000; Della Porta and Tarrow, 2005; McDonald, 2006; Tarrow, 2011; Della Porta, 2013). In identifying the factors that support the growth of global social movements, writers such as Bandy and Smith (2005), della Porta (2013) and Kaldor and Selchow (2015) examine the stability and maintenance of social movements often led by NGOs, with a focus on the linkages within, and sustenance of, global social movement activism. Global social movement scholars tend to recognise the cleavages within the NGO sector, particularly in regard to wealth divides between activists from developed countries and those from developing nations. Bandy and Smith (2005, p. 13) also find for example, that differences between groups of different sizes and types, as well as those spanning class differences, may be problematic for maintaining effective NGO coalitions in the global arena.

In sum, the various perspectives on NGOs attempt to define the capacities and parameters of NGO agency in the global political environment, albeit with differing emphases on structural constraints in the form of international institutions or even the entire neo-liberal order. There is however overlap between these key perspectives. A common thread underlying each approach is an understanding that NGOs often seek to advance progressive values in the areas of social, economic and environmental justice; work in complex networked arrangements; take account of opportunity structures in the institutional environment; and use information strategically to further their campaign goals.

Conclusion

In practice, the NGO label is a misnomer because it implies that NGOs are separate to, or outside of, the process of governance (Hirst and Thompson, 1999, pp. 276–277). But as this chapter emphasises, NGOs are playing increasingly visible roles in global politics. Indeed, international organisations are likely beneficiaries of an active NGO presence in their policy arenas because it may boost their legitimacy, foster acceptance of international agreements and contribute to policy development, implementation and evaluation (Reinalda and Verbeek, 1998; Betsill and Corell, 2008; Murphy, 2010; Abbott and Snidal, 2013; Dany, 2013). In a normative sense, NGO advocacy in global politics is also frequently said to have a moral benefit, as well as serve a functional benefit or opportunity for policymaking. NGO advocacy may provide marginalised people with a crucial link to international policy domains in circumstances where representation by their own governments is not possible due to varying domestic political contexts. In this regard, one of the key benefits of NGO participation in global politics is said to be that NGOs help overcome the 'democratic deficit' which occurs at the global level of governance whereby national governments, rather than citizens, are the chief participants (Steffek et al., 2008). Further, compared with business interests, social justice, economic equality and environmental conservation concerns typically represented by NGOs, are said to be under-represented in global governance processes (Wilkinson and Hughes, 2002; Clapp and Fuchs, 2009; Tallberg, 2013). Scholte et al. (1999, p. 111) explain that NGOs offer international organisations alternative channels for stakeholder input, provide useful and timely information, stimulate debate, provide alternative proposals and serve as agents of civic education. Consequently, Kathryn Sikkink (2002, p. 316) contends that 'NGOs and networks are informal, asymmetrical, and ad hoc antidotes to domestic and international representational imperfections'.

Whilst NGO input is welcomed by many scholars, critics emphasise the importance of NGOs' own accountability, representativeness and transparency, particularly toward those whom they claim to represent (Walker, 1994; Kellow, 2000; Robertson and Kellow, 2001; Bob, 2005; Mallaby, 2009). In regard to environmental advocacy, Walker (1994, p. 675) states for instance, exactly 'who has the authority to act in the name of rainforests and dolphins, is . . . difficult to specify'. Mallaby's (2009) well known account questioning the democratic virtues of 'media-savvy Western activists' in Uganda, poses critical questions about the beneficiaries of NGO advocacy in developing nations. Indeed, in the absence of a democratic blockage – such as that underpinning Keck and Sikkink's (1998) 'boomerang' model – NGOs' endeavours to pressure a state or international organisation have been said to amount to 'representation without taxation' (Kellow, 2001, p. 69). This is because governments, rather than NGOs, are accountable for decision making at this level and NGOs may not necessarily endure the impacts of their policy contributions. Furthermore, NGOs are not usually responsible for the implementation of internationally agreed policy decisions at the national level of governance. The challenge of evaluating NGOs' claims of representativeness, transparency and accountability may be compounded where an NGO possesses a complex organisational structure (Willetts, 1996, p. 60). Despite this, the core mission of groups such as Transparency International is squarely aimed at promoting the transparency and accountability of all political organisations, including NGOs. Since the mid-2000s, cognisant of these challenges for the NGO sector, a growing number of scholars are turning their attention not just to the roles played by NGOs, but also the important issues of NGO legitimacy, representativeness and accountability in the context of global policymaking and NGO activities in developing nations (see Jordan and Tuijl, 2006; Steffek et al., 2008; Makuwira, 2014; DeMars and Dijkzeul, 2015).

To conclude, over the last century, NGOs have become important sources of civic participation in global politics. As the chapter demonstrates, NGO are avid contributors to key issue-areas including human rights, economic development, the environment and contesting neo-liberal globalisation. The growth of the NGO sector internationally is linked to the growth of global governance and global policy institutions in recent decades, which serve as draw cards for NGO advocacy, as well as advances in communications technology and more affordable international travel. The various perspectives on NGOs in global politics – including social constructivist, institutional, critical and global social movement approaches – attempt to delineate the limits and possibilities of NGO agency in a global system where nation states monopolise formal authority and resources. Whilst NGO contributions to global governance have grown in recent decades, critics highlight that NGOs, particularly, large professional groups based in the Global North, may replicate inequalities in global politics in terms of funding, influence and access to international institutions. As such, recent scholarly attention in the field highlights the issues of accountability, transparency and representativeness as they affect NGOs themselves. Despite these challenges, NGOs appear assured to continue their presence in global politics and most international organisations rely on their contributions, whatever form these take, to enhance the legitimacy of global policymaking.

Further reading

Betsill, Michele Merrell and Elisabeth Corell (2008) *NGO Diplomacy: The Influence of Non-governmental Organizations in International Environmental Negotiations* (Cambridge, MA: MIT Press).

Bob, Clifford (2005) *The Marketing of Rebellion: Insurgents, Media, and International Activism* (New York, NY: Cambridge University Press).

Dany, Charlotte (2013) *Global Governance and NGO Participation: Shaping the Information Society in the United Nations* (London; New York: Routledge).

DeMars, William E. and Dennis Dijkzeul (2015) *The NGO Challenge for International Relations Theory* (Abingdon, Oxon; New York, NY: Routledge).

Keck, Margaret E. and Kathryn Sikkink (1998) *Activists Beyond Borders: Advocacy Networks in International Politics* (Ithaca, NY: Cornell University Press).

Kellow, Aynsley and Hannah Murphy-Gregory (2018) *Research Handbook on NGOs* (Cheltenham, UK: Edward Elgar).

Mallaby, Sebastian (2009) 'NGOs: Fighting Poverty, Hurting the Poor', *Foreign Policy* 144 (September–October), pp. 50–58.

Reinalda, Bob (2011) *The Ashgate Research Companion to Non-State Actors* (Farnham, Surrey/Burlington, VT: Ashgate).

Steffek, Jens, Claudia Kissling and Patrizia Nanz (2008) *Civil Society Participation in European and Global Governance: A Cure for the Democratic Deficit?* (Basingstoke England/ New York: Palgrave Macmillan).

Willetts, Peter (2011) *Non-Governmental Organizations in World Politics: The Construction of Global Governance* (Abingdon, Oxon: Routledge).

Bibliography

Abbott, Kenneth W., and Duncan Snidal (2013) 'Taking Responsive Regulation Transnational: Strategies for International Organizations', *Regulation and Governance* 7(1), pp. 95–113.

Alaimo, Salvatore P. (2016) 'Who's Managing Whom? Attempting to Tame the Beast of Globalization through the Management of International Organizations', *Public Administration Review* 76(5), pp. 827–829.

Alger, Chadwick F. (1997) 'Transnational Social Movements, World Politics and Global Governance' in Charles Chatfield, Ron Pagnucco, and Jackie Smith (eds.) *Transnational Social Movements and Global Politics: Solidarity Beyond the State* (Syracuse, NY: Syracuse University Press), pp. 260–278.

Bandy, J. and J. Smith (2005) *Coalitions Across Borders: Transnational Protest and the Neoliberal Order* (Lanham, MD.: Rowman and Littlefield).

Betsill, Michele Merrell and Elisabeth Corell (2008) *NGO Diplomacy: The Influence of Nongovernmental Organizations in International Environmental Negotiations* (Cambridge, MA: MIT Press).

Bob, Clifford (2005) *The Marketing of Rebellion: Insurgents, Media, and International Activism* (New York, NY: Cambridge University Press).

Bob, Clifford (2009) *The International Struggle for New Human Rights* (Philadelphia: University of Pennsylvania Press).

Boehmer-Christiansen, Sonja and Aynsley Kellow (2003) *International Environmental Policy Interests and the Failure of the Kyoto Process* (Cheltenham, UK: Edward Elgar).

Boli, John and George M. Thomas (1999) *Constructing World Culture: International Nongovernmental Organizations Since 1875* (Stanford, CA: Stanford University Press).

Bronfenbrenner, Kate (2007) *Global Unions Challenging Transnational Capital Through Cross-Border Campaigns*, Frank W Pierce Memorial Lectureship and Conference Series No 13 (Ithaca, NY: ILR/Cornell University Press).

Brysk, Alison (2005) *Human Rights and Private Wrongs: Constructing Global Civil Society* (New York: Routledge).

Buckley, Karen M. (2013) *Global Civil Society and Transversal Hegemony: The Globalization-Contestation Nexus* (Abingdon, Oxon: Routledge).

Chandler, David, and Gideon Baker (2005) *Global Civil Society: Contested Futures* (London/New York: Routledge).

Chatfield, Charles, Ron Pagnucco and Jackie Smith (1997) *Transnational Social Movements and Global Politics: Solidarity Beyond the State* (Syracuse, NY: Syracuse University Press).

Clapp, Jennifer and Doris A. Fuchs (2009) *Corporate Power in Global Agrifood Governance* (Cambridge, MA: MIT Press).

Cohen, Robin and Shirin Rai (2000) *Global Social Movements* (London/New Brunswick, NJ: Athlone Press).

Dany, Charlotte (2013) *Global Governance and NGO Participation: Shaping the Information Society in the United Nations* (London/New York: Routledge).

Della Porta, Donatella (2013) *Can Democracy be Saved? Participation, Deliberation and Social Movements* (Cambridge: Polity).

Della Porta, Donatella and Sidney G. Tarrow (2005) *Transnational Protest and Global Activism* (Lanham, MD: Rowman and Littlefield).

DeMars, William E. and Dennis Dijkzeul (2015) *The NGO Challenge for International Relations Theory* (Abingdon, Oxon/New York, NY: Routledge).

Fisher, Julie (1998) *Nongovernments: NGOs and the Political Development of the Third World* (West Hartford, CT: Kumarian Press).

Florini, Ann (2000) *The Third Force: The Rise of Transnational Civil Society.* (Washington, DC: Japan Center for International Exchange and Carnegie Endowment for International Peace).

Fox, Jonathan and David L. Brown (1998) *The Struggle for Accountability: The World Bank, NGOs, and Grassroots Movements* (Cambridge, MA: MIT Press).

Germain, Randall D. and Michael Kenny (2005) *The Idea of Global Civil Society: Politics and Ethics in a Globalizing Era* (London; New York: Routledge).

Goodman, John (2002) *Protest and Globalisation: Prospects for Transnational Solidarity* (Annandale: Pluto Press).

Green, Duncan (2016) 'How Civil Society and Others Achieved the Paris Climate Agreement' (26 April), http://blogs.worldbank.org/publicsphere/how-civil-society-and-others-achieved-paris-climate-agreement.

Greenpeace International (2016) 'About Greenpeace', www.greenpeace.org/international/en/about/.

Guidry, John A., Michael D. Kennedy and Mayer N. Zald (2000) *Globalizations and Social Movements Culture, Power, and the Transnational Public Sphere* (Ann Arbor: University of Michigan Press).

Haas, Peter M. (1992) 'Epistemic Communities and International Policy Coordination', *International Organization* 46(1), pp. 1–35.

Haas, Peter M. (2016) *Epistemic Communities, Constructivism, and International Environmental Politics* (London/New York: Routledge).

Haufler, Virginia, Tony Porter and A. Claire Cutler (1999) *Private Authority and International Affairs* (Albany: State University of New York Press).

Hirst, Paul Q. and Grahame Thompson (1999) *Globalization in Question: The International Economy and the Possibilities of Governance* (Cambridge, UK/Malden, MA: Polity).

Hudock, Ann (2001) *NGOs and Civil Society: Democracy by Proxy?* (Malden, MA: Polity Press).

Hulme, David and Michael Edwards (1997) *NGOs, States and Donors: Too Close for Comfort?* (New York: St. Martin's Press in association with Save the Children).

Huntington, Samuel P. (1973) 'Transnational Organizations in World Politics', *World Politics* 25(3), pp. 334–368.

Hutchens, Anna (2011) 'Playing Games of Governance: How and Why Fair Trade Pioneers Evade Corporate Capture', *Regulation and Governance* 5(2), pp. 221–240.

Joachim, Jutta M. (2007) *Agenda Setting, the UN, and NGOs: Gender Violence and Reproductive Rights* (Washington, DC: Georgetown University Press).

Jordan, Lisa and Peter van Tuijl (2006) *NGO Accountability: Politics, Principles and Innovations* (London/Sterling, VA: Earthscan).

Kahler, Miles (2009) *Networked Politics: Agency, Power, and Governance* (Ithaca: Cornell University Press).

Kaldor, Mary, Henrietta L. Moore and Sabine Selchow (2012) *Global Civil Society 2012: Ten Years of Critical Reflection* (Basingstoke: Palgrave Macmillan).

Kaldor, Mary and Sabine Selchow (2015) *Subterranean Politics in Europe* (Houndmills, Basingstoke, Hampshire: Palgrave Macmillan).

Keane, John (2003) *Global Civil Society?* (Cambridge: Cambridge University Press).

Keck, Margaret E. and Kathryn Sikkink (1998) *Activists Beyond Borders: Advocacy Networks in International Politics* (Ithaca, NY: Cornell University Press).

Kellow, Aynsley (2000) 'Norms, Interests and Environmental NGOs: The Limits of Cosmopolitanism', *Environmental Politics* 9(3), pp. 1–22.

Kellow, Aynsley (2001) 'The Constitution of International Civil Society', in Charles Sampford and Tom Round (eds.) *Beyond the Republic: Meeting the Global Challenges to Constitutionalism* (Annandale, NSW: Federation Press), pp. 68–77.

Keohane, Robert O. and Joseph S. Nye (1972) *Transnational Relations and World Politics* (Cambridge, MA: Harvard University Press).

Keohane, Robert O. and Joseph S. Nye (1977) *Power and Interdependence: World Politics in Transition* (Boston: Little, Brown).

Keohane, Robert O. and Joseph S. Nye (2001) *Power and Interdependence* (New York/London: Longman).

Khagram, Sanjeev, James V. Riker and Kathryn Sikkink (2002) *Restructuring World Politics: Transnational Social Movements, Networks, and Norms* (Minneapolis: University of Minnesota Press).

Klein, Naomi (2008) *The Shock Doctrine: The Rise of Disaster Capitalism* (London: Penguin).

Klotz, Audie (1995) *Norms in International Relations: The Struggle Against Apartheid* (Ithaca: Cornell University Press).

Klotz, Audie and Cecelia M. Lynch (2014) *Strategies for Research in Constructivist International Relations* (London; New York: Routledge).

Krasner, Stephen (1982) 'Structural Causes and Regime Consequences: Regimes as Intervening Variables', *International Organization* 36(2), pp. 185–205.

Laxer, Gordon and Sandra Halperin (2003) *Global Civil Society and its Limits* (Basingstoke: Palgrave Macmillan).

Lindio-McGovern, Ligaya (2013) *Globalization, Labor Export and Resistance: A Study of Filipino Migrant Domestic Workers in Global Cities* (Abingdon, Oxon/New York: Routledge).

Makuwira, Jonathan J. (2014) *Non-Governmental Development Organizations and the Poverty Reduction Agenda: The Moral Crusaders* (London/New York: Routledge).

Mallaby, Sebastian (2009) 'NGOs: Fighting Poverty, Hurting the Poor', *Foreign Policy* (144), pp. 50–58.

McBride, Stephen and Gary Teeple (2011) *Relations of Global Power: Neoliberal Order and Disorder* (Toronto: University of Toronto Press).

McDonald, Kevin (2006) *Global Movements: Action and Culture* (Malden, MA/Oxford: Blackwell Pub.).

McMichael, Philip (2000) 'Sleepless since Seattle: What Is the WTO about?', *Review of International Political Economy* 7(3), pp. 466–474.

Murphy, Hannah (2010) *The Making of International Trade Policy: NGOs, Agenda-Setting and the WTO* (Cheltenham, UK/Northampton, MA: Edward Elgar).

O'Brien, Robert, Ann Marie Goetz, Jan Aart Scholte and Marc Williams (2000) *Contesting Global Governance: Multilateral Economic Institutions and Global Social Movements* (Cambridge: Cambridge University Press).

Pallas, Chris (2013) *Transnational Civil Society and the World Bank: Investigating Civil Society's Potential to Democratize Global Governance* (Houndmills/Basingstoke/Hampshire/New York, NY: Palgrave Macmillan).

Pianta, Mario (2001) 'Parallel Summits of Global Civil Society' in H. Anheier, M. Glasius and M. Kaldor (eds.) *Global Civil Society Yearbook 2001* (Oxford: Oxford University Press), pp. 169–194.

Pianta, Mario and Federico Silva (2003) 'Parallel Summits of Global Civil Society: An Update', in M. Kaldor, H. Anheier and M. Glasius (eds.) *Global Civil Society Yearbook 2003* (Oxford: Oxford University Press), pp. 387–394.

Price, Richard (1998) 'Reversing the Gun Sights: Transnational Civil Society Targets Land Mines', *International Organization* 52(3), pp. 613–634.

Reinalda, Bob (2011) *The Ashgate Research Companion to Non-State Actors* (Farnham, Surrey/Burlington, VT: Ashgate).

Reinalda, Bob and Bertjan Verbeek (1998) *Autonomous Policy Making by International Organizations* (London/New York: Routledge).

Reinicke, Wolfgang H. (1998) *Global Public Policy: Governing Without Government?* (Washington, DC: Brookings Institution Press).

Reinicke, Wolfgang (2000) 'The Other World Wide Web: Global Public Policy Networks', *Foreign Policy* 117, pp. 44–57.

Reinicke, Wolfgang H., Francis Mading Deng and Jan Martin Witte (2000) *Critical Choices: The United Nations, Networks, and the Future of Global Governance* (Ottawa: International Development Research Centre).

Ringius, Lasse (1997) 'Environmental NGOs and Regime Change: The Case of Ocean Dumping of Radioactive Waste', *European Journal of International Relations* 3(1), pp. 61–104.

Robertson, David and Aynsley Kellow (2001) *Globalization, Environment Risk Assessment and the WTO* (Cheltenham, UK: Edward Elgar).

Rosenau, James N. (1980) *The Study of Global Interdependence: Essays on the Transnationalization of World Affairs* (London: Frances Pinter).

Rosenau, James N. and Ernst Otto Czempiel (1992) *Governance Without Government: Order and Change in World Politics* (Cambridge/England/New York: Cambridge University Press).

Ruhlman, Molly A. (2015) *Who Participates in Global Governance? States, Bureaucracies, and NGOs in the United Nations* (London/New York, NY: Routledge).

Salmen, Lawrence F. and Paige A. Eaves (1989) *World Bank Work with Nongovernmental Organizations*. Washington, DC, http://documents.worldbank.org/curated/en/245371468763474225/World-Bank-work-with-nongovernmental-organizations.

Scholte, Jan Aart, Robert O'Brien and Marc Williams (1999) 'The WTO and Civil Society', *Journal of World Trade* 33(1), pp. 107–123.

Sell, Susan K., and Aseem Prakash (2004) 'Using Ideas Strategically: The Contest Between Business and NGO Networks in Intellectual Property Rights', *International Studies Quarterly* 48(1), pp. 143–175.

Sikkink, Kathryn (2002) 'Restructuring World Politics: The Limits and Asymmetries of Soft Power', in S. Khagram, J.V. Riker, and K. Sikkink (eds.) *Restructuring World Politics. Transnational Social Movements, Networks, and Norms* (Minneapolis: University of Minnesota Press), pp. 301–317.

Smith, Jackie and Marina Karides (2007) *Global Democracy and the World Social Forums* (London: Routledge).

Starr, Amory (2005) *Global Revolt: A Guide to the Movements Against Globalization* (London: Zed Books).

Starr, Amory, Luis A. Fernandez and Christian Scholl (2011) *Shutting Down the Streets: Political Violence and Social Control in the Global Era* (New York: New York University Press).

Steffek, Jens, Claudia Kissling and Patrizia Nanz (2008) *Civil Society Participation in European and Global Governance: A Cure for the Democratic Deficit?* (Basingstoke England; New York: Palgrave Macmillan).

Tallberg, Jonas (2013) *The Opening up of International Organizations: Transnational Access in Global Governance* (Cambridge: Cambridge University Press).

Tarrow, Sidney G. (2011) *Power in Movement: Social Movements and Contentious Politics* (Cambridge; New York: Cambridge University Press).

Tvedt, Terje (1998) *Angels of Mercy or Development Diplomats? NGOs and Foreign Aid* (Asmara, Eritrea: Africa World Press).

UN News Centre (2015) 'UN Chief Calls on Civil Society to Keep Governments Accountable on Climate Commitments' (10 December), www.un.org/sustainabledevelopment/blog/2015/12/un-chief-calls-on-civil-society-to-keep-governments-accountable-on-climate-commitments/.

Union of International Associations (2015) 'Yearbook of International Organizations 2015–2016: Guide to Global Civil Society Networks', in Union of International Associations (ed.) *Yearbook of International Associations, Vol. 5: Statistics, Visualizations and Patterns* (Leiden, The Netherlands: Koninklijke Brill), pp. 1–25.

Walker, R.B.J. (1994) 'Social Movements/World Politics', *Millennium: Journal of International Studies* 23(3), pp. 669–700.

Wapner, Paul (1995) 'Politics Beyond the State: Environmental Activism and World Civic Politics', *World Politics* 47(3), pp. 311–340.

Wapner, Paul Kevin (1996) *Environmental Activism and World Civic Politics* (Albany: State University of New York Press).

Weiss, Thomas G. and Leon Gordenker (1996) *NGOs, the UN, and Global Governance* (Boulder, CO: Lynee Rienner).

Wilkinson, Rorden and Jennifer Clapp (2010) *Global Governance, Poverty and Inequality* (London/New York: Routledge).

Wilkinson, Rorden and Stephen Hughes (2002) *Global Governance: Critical Perspectives.* (London/New York: Routledge).

Willetts, Peter (1982) *Pressure Groups in the Global System: The Transnational Relations of Issue-Orientated Non-Governmental Organizations* (London: Pinter).

Willetts, Peter (1996) *'The Conscience of the World': The Influence of Non-Governmental Organisations in the UN System* (Washington, DC: Brookings Institution).

Young, Oran R. (1982) *Resource Regimes: Natural Resources and Social Institutions* (Berkeley: University of California Press).

Chapter 15

Regional organisations

Ulf Engel

With the end of the Cold War the number of regional organisations (ROs) has increased manifold, mainly in what constitutes the Global South (Mansfield and Milner, 1999). This has prompted extensive academic debate about the nature of these organisations and their place in contemporary processes of globalisation. The total number of ROs is difficult to gauge, as this is a very dynamic field and there are few institutions that take regular stock. The Union of International Associations' 'Yearbook of International Organizations' currently 'includes detailed information

FIGURE 15.1 Participants take part in an African Union meeting in Algiers, Algeria

on over 38,000 active and 32,000 dormant international organizations from 300 countries and territories – including inter-governmental (IGOs) and international non-governmental organizations (INGOs)'. Each year, it is claimed, another 1200 new organisations are added to the yearbook.[1] However, the UN Secretary-General, in his annual report on cooperation between the United Nations and ROs, singles out just 26 major ROs that actively participate in the work of the United Nations, ranging from the African Union to the Organization for the Prohibition of Chemical Weapons (UN-Secretary General, 2016).

Just to get an impression of the regional origin and functional scope of ROs, European ROs include, among many others, the European Economic Community (established in 1957) that later became the European Union (EU, 1993), the European Free Trade Association (EFTA, 1960), the European Patent Organisation (EPO, 1977), the European Science Foundation (ESF, 1974) and the European Space Agency (ESA, 1975), but also the Nordic Investment Bank (NIB, 1976) or the Visegrád Group (V4, 1991). Prominent transatlantic ROs are, of course, the North Atlantic Treaty Organisation (NATO, 1949), and also the Organisation for Security and Co-operation in Europe (OSCE, 1975) and the South Atlantic Peace and Cooperation Zone (ZPCAS, 1986).

What has dominated the debate over the last 20 years most is the revival of already existing and the founding of new ROs in the Global South (though some claim that this development has already peaked; see Malamud and Gardini, 2012). In Africa this includes the African Union (which was succeeding the Organisation of African Unity, OAU, in 2001) and its officially recognised eight partnering regional economic communities (RECs): the Community of Sahel-Saharan States (CENSAD, 1998), the Common Market for Eastern and Southern Africa (COMESA, 1994), the East African Community (EAC, 1967 to 1977, revived in 2000), the Economic Community of Central African States (ECCAS, 1981), the Economic Community of West African States (ECOWAS, 1975), the Intergovernmental Authority on Development (IGAD, 1986) at the Horn of Africa, the Southern African Development Community (SADC, 1979 and revised 1992) and the Arab Maghreb Union (UMA, 1989).

In Asia, prominent ROs include the Asian Development Bank (ADB, 1996), the Association of Southeast Asian Nations (ASEAN, 1967) and the Mekong River Commission (MRC, 1995). In the Arab world, the Gulf Cooperation Council (GCC, 1981) is noteworthy. Important Eurasian ROs include the Collective Security Treaty Organization (CSTO, 1992), the Commonwealth of Independent States (CIS, 1991) and the Shanghai Cooperation Organisation (SCO, 1996). And in the Americas, and apart from the Organization of American States (OAS, 1948), the Southern Common Market (Mercado Común del Sur, Mercosur, 1991), the Andean Community of Nations (ACN, 1969/1996), the Caribbean Community (CARICOM, 1973) and the Bolivarian Alliance for the Americas (ALBA, 2004) were established. In addition, there are Indian Ocean ROs, such as the Indian Ocean Commission (COI, 1982), and Arctic ones such as the Arctic Council (1996). In the Pacific Ocean, the Australia, New Zealand, United States Security Treaty (ANZUS, 1951) has to be named, as well as the Pacific Islands Forum (1971, with a change of name in 1991).

In political science this trend of geographic mushrooming and functional proliferation of ROs has mainly been conceptualised in terms of – a rather actor-less – diffusion theory that seeks to explain how ideas or social models travel (see Jetschke and Lenz, 2013; Jetschke and Murray, 2012; but also see Acharya, 2004). In the following, some necessary definitions will be developed as regards regions and regionalisms. This will be followed in the next part of the chapter by a brief discussion of the place of regions and regional cooperation in current processes of globalisation. In the third part of the chapter the theoretical debate about regions will be recalled with a focus on the 'new regionalisms' paradigm and the recent calls for 'comparative regionalism'. The fourth part then looks at practices of regional cooperation, mainly drawing on examples from the African continent. This is followed by a conclusion.

Regional organisations are a geographically defined sub-type of international organisations (IOs), i.e. bureaucratic forms of authority that '(1) classify the world, creating categories of problems, actors, and action; (2) fix meanings in the social world; and (3) articulate and diffuse new norms and rules' (Barnett and Finnemore, 2004, p. 31). In this sense they are also territorialised subsets of inter-governmental organisations in which regional interstate cooperation leads to the construction of region-wide interstate regimes in different fields (Hurrell, 2007, p. 128). The academic debate about ROs addresses processes of regionalisation, i.e. societal integration, and often undirected forms of economic and political integration (see Schultz et al., 2001). ROs are linked to dynamics of regionalism, understood as cross-national (or cross-community) interaction and interdependence (Söderbaum, 2004a, p. 16). Often, they go hand in hand with the development of regional awareness and identity, i.e. the construction of different forms of cognitive regionalism (Hurrell, 2007, p. 128; see also Hettne and Söderbaum, 2000). While the focus of academic debate has mainly been on the role of single ROs in these processes, more recent contributions to this field have highlighted the need to also look into how different ROs and regionalisms increasingly interact with each other, i.e. to empirically reconstruct and conceptualise practices of inter-regionalism (see Söderbaum and Van Langenhove, 2006; Hänggi et al., 2006; Baert et al., 2014; De Lombaerde et al., 2015).

Some, but certainly not all, of the authors contributing to this field take a social constructivist position that allows them to problematise the constructed nature of 'regions'. Thus, Hurrell (1995, p. 38) highlights that '[t]here are no "natural" regions, and definitions of "region" and indicators of "regionness" vary according to the particular problem or question under investigation'. Accordingly, regions, regionalisms and ROs can be studied as 'containers for culture and for value diversity; poles and powers; one level in a system of multi-level governance; and/or harbingers of change and possible transformation' (Hurrell, 2007, p. 136).

The role of regional organisations in processes of globalisation

Academic reasoning that is more profoundly influenced by the 'spatial turn' in the humanities and social sciences considers ROs as a particular form of spatialisation of certain social fields under the global condition, i.e. the historic transformation to modern conditions of globalisation(s) during the period between 1840 and 1880 (see Robinson, 1990; Geyer and Bright, 1995). ROs are discussed as a specific *spatial format* – a vision of an ideal spatial organisation of interests, and in this sense a political project – that usually is contested by competing visions of order and hence somehow 'negotiated'. The attempt to establish a certain spatial format or projects – nation state, empire, commodity chain, to give other examples – eventually leads to the establishment of a concrete, tangible, material *spatial order*.[2] In this respect, ROs constitute a form of spatial reterritorialisation that states (but also actors beyond the state) engage in, mainly to regain sovereignty that has been lost in processes of deterritorialisation through, for instance, the movement of refugees across borders, the impact of climate change, the mobility of capital or the flow of goods and services (on the theoretical foundations see Brenner, 1999; Acharya, 2002; Agnew, 2005).

With the contested making of a 'new world order' after the end of the Cold War (Sørensen, 2006; Chaturvedi and Painter, 2007), and related shifts from bipolarity to a brief period of US hegemony in the 2000s to increasing levels of multi-polarity, regionalism(s) has (have) been discussed in their theoretical and practical relation to what usually is conceived of as 'globalisation' (see Gamble and Payne, 1996; Mittelman, 1996; Hettne, 1999, 2005). Reflecting on the 'relationship between the one world of the international system and the many worlds of the different regionalisms', Hurrell (2007, p. 131) has developed four arguments to explain the attractiveness of regionalism: first, he claims, for countries of the Global South 'the region is the most appropriate and viable level to reconcile the changing and intensifying pressures of global capitalist competition on the one hand with the need for political regulation and management on the other'. Second, he holds that for this group of countries 'it is easier to negotiate "deep integration" and the sorts of profoundly intrusive rules needed to manage globalisation at the regional rather than the global level'. Third, Hurrell finds that regionalism also – 'given that value and societal consensus are likely to be bigger and the practical problems of governance beyond the state more manageable at that level' – for many developing countries, 'can be part of a process of controlled or negotiated integration into the global economy'. And, fourth, in particular for countries from the Global North, regionalism 'offers a favourable level at which to recast the 1945-bargain between market liberalization on the one hand and social protection on the other'.

Regionalisms, and the establishment of ROs, thus can be interpreted as 'sovereignty boosting practices' of states in the Global South (Söderbaum, 2004b, 2015). Regionalisms also 'embody a political rationality' (Engel et al., 2016, p. 5): actors 'are making contingent, case-specific choices with regard to the scale or spatiality that they utilise to achieve certain purposes, such as security, the provision of public goods, etc. (with Revel, 1996 this can be called *jeux d'échelles*, i.e. a play of scales)'.

Sometimes these sovereignty boosting strategies may work against the international system and established universal norms, as the debate about impunity of sitting African heads of state and government in cases of gross human rights violations has shown. At the recent 28th summit of the African Union, held on 30–31 January 2017 in Addis Ababa, Ethiopia, it was decided that African member states of the Rome Statute should withdraw from the International Criminal Court (ICC), because it allegedly has been turned into an 'imperialist' and 'racist' instrument of Western states to harass African leaders. Rather, related cases of genocide, crimes against humanity and war crimes should be referred to the African Court on Human and Peoples' Rights – after the term of office has expired, and not while the leader is still in office (see Pana Press, 2017).

Theoretical debates on epistemology and periodisation

The academic debate about regionalisms somewhat took off in the 1940s, mainly in political science. Controversial academic debates, firstly, were held about the 'right' epistemological way to study the nature and development of regionalisms and, secondly, about the periodisation and, implicitly, the historic profoundness of regionalisms. Traditional rational choice-based international relations approaches towards the study of regionalisms, for instance, have highlighted regional security cooperation with an emphasis on states facing a security dilemma which therefore engage in defence cooperation to minimise opportunity costs (Waltz, 1979). In addition, (neo-)functionalist approaches have stressed how states enter regional groupings as a result of functional spill-over effects (Mitrany, 1948) and engage in political projects (Haas, 1958). Furthermore, inter-governmentalist approaches have emphasised region-building as a consequence of conscious decisions and as a result of negotiations (Moravcsik, 1991).

All these approaches are based on most often implicit meta-theoretical premises, including methodological nationalism, i.e. the exclusive privileging of states as units of analysis (see Brenner, 1999). They are embedded in modernisation theory, i.e. the existence of societies modelled along the 'European' way is – often only implicitly – seen as the prerequisite for regional integration. And they also share a distorted understanding of key terms. The 'region', for instance, is equated with 'regionalisation'; the focus is on political and economic organisations as well as on results, rather than on processes. This orthodoxy has not only been criticised because of its underlying methodological nationalism, but also because of its conceptual eurocentrism (Engel et al., 2016, pp. 2, 6): a contingent experience of regional integration in post–World War II Western Europe, which ultimately has led to the European Union, has been taken as the yardstick and role model for regional integration per se. Regional integration theories worldwide seem to follow a linear European model which assumes that market integration develops in five consecutive and interdependent stages: (1) from a Free Trade Area (FTA) based on the removal of tariff and non-tariff barriers to trade, to (2) a Customs Union with a common external tariff, to (3) a Common Market characterised by the free movement of goods, labour, capital and people, to (4) an Economic and Monetary Union defined by a united monetary and fiscal policy through a central authority, and, finally, to (5) a political union in which all separate national institutions are submersed (for a stunning recent example see Baldwin, 2012).

In contrast, new approaches to the study of regionalisms outside the EU have developed a focus on empirical cases of informal regionalisms, non-state regionalisms and dynamic regionalisms. Against the backdrop of the post–Cold War rise of regionalisms (in general Breslin et al., 2002; Söderbaum and Shaw, 2003) in Africa (see Bøås et al., 1999; Grant and Söderbaum, 2003), Asia (see Beeson, 2007,

2012; Dent, 2008; Frost, 2008; Thomas, 2009) and Latin America (see Cason, 2011; Dabène, 2009; Gomez-Mera, 2013; Riggirozzi and Tussie, 2012), a group of scholars originally based in Gothenburg, Sweden, proclaimed a new paradigm (see Väyrynen, 2003) – the New Regionalism Approach (NRA). It is said to be reflective, process-oriented, multi-dimensional (beyond politics and economics), and often based in new, critical or heterodox International Political Economy (i.e. based on the writings of Canadian political scientist Robert W. Cox – see, for instance, Cox, 1981, 1996).

The NRA school has rather successfully framed a dichotomy between an 'old regionalism' and a 'new regionalism', based on a temporal distinction between post–World War II and post–Cold War dynamics, a geographical distinction between Europe and the Global South, and differences in number, scope and diversity of regionalisms (i.e. narrow versus broad). In addition, the NRA highlighted the social making of new regions, thus almost invoking a spatial turn dimension (which it however did not systematically develop). It also juxtaposed a theoretical (neo-)functionalism versus NRA dimension (Söderbaum, 2004a). Inspired by Bisley (2007), one could think of six distinct, though sometimes overlapping, phases in the development of the NRA argument, starting in the late-1990s when the 'new regionalisms' were identified as something that was driving radical social change (see Hettne, 1999; Söderbaum and Shaw, 2003). Roughly at the same time authors somewhat located the 'new regionalisms' in what they conceived to be 'globalisation' (seen as a single mainly economic process, see Fawcett and Hurrell, 1995; Gamble and Payne, 1996). This was different from the following third phase when this relationship was actually theorised (see Breslin and Hook, 2002; Hurrell, 1995). In the late 2000s authors tried a more substantially empirical grounding of the 'new regionalisms' (see Söderbaum and Taylor, 2008).

The fifth phase, beginning in the early 2010s, saw a consolidation of the 'new regionalisms' as an academic field, characterised by both forms of the institutionalisation of a particular knowledge order, for instance through the editing of 'companions' (Shaw et al., 2011), but also the transfer back to European Studies of insights gained on 'new regionalisms' outside of Europe (Sbragia and Söderbaum, 2010). A sixth phase may have started in response to the previous phases, in which authors tried to go beyond the limits of the NRA, on the basis of consequently treating the 'new regionalisms' debate as a particular discourse formation. Part of the critique of the paradigm is that the 'new regionalisms' debate is said to not really have transcended methodological nationalism: first, at least the empirical recognition of 'new regionalisms' beyond the state is not matched at the level of theorising and, second, despite acknowledging the culturally constructed character of regions, most often they are still equated with the states constituting the region (see Engel et al., 2016, pp. 1–10).

In the late 2000s the notion of a 'comparative regionalism' came up as successor to the 'new regionalism' paradigm (Söderbaum, 2016, p. 31). Although De Lombaerde et al. (2010, p. 731) claim '[d]espite a growing number of specific comparisons of selected aspects of regionalism . . . in selected regions, there is no systematic debate relating to the fundamentals of comparison'. There was also very little exchange on the topic between disciplines, such as political science and economics (ibid., p. 733). However, some serious efforts have been undertaken since to conceptually develop this line of research more thoroughly (Warleigh-Lack, 2008; Acharya, 2012; Börzel, 2013; Börzel and Risse, 2016; Söderbaum, 2015; Fioramonti, 2012b; Fioramonti and Mattheis, 2015; Solingen, 2015). However, substantial empirical contributions are few and far between (for an exception see Mattheis, 2015 on Mercosur and SADC).

On the question of periodisation of regionalisms, basically two competing meta-narratives have been offered, one starting with the League of Nations in the 1920s and the other beginning with the post–World War II situation (from a global history perspective, one might even go back to the Congress of Vienna, 1814–15, on this question). Developing a *longue durée* argument, the Italian political scientist Mario Telò (2017, p. 67) argues that between 1900 and 2016 four 'epochs' of regionalism can be identified (similar Fawcett, 2005). The first one stretched from World War I to the economic crisis of 1929–36 and was characterised by authoritarian and hierarchical regionalisms, such as the British Commonwealth. The second period started with World War II and included the bipolar world order that emerged afterwards.

Regionalisms were framed by US hegemony and multilateral institutions (1950s–1980s), including NATO and ASEAN as key proponents. The third phase began with the relative decline of the US after a short period of US hegemony, the collapse of the USSR (1991) and what was perceived as 'the globalisation wave'. This period is referred to by Telò (2017) as the third 'belle époche', including new regionalisms such as ASEAN, Mercosur, SADC and the African Union. The current epoch started with the global economic crisis (2007–8), fragmentation and the emergence of a multipolar structure. It is characterised by competitive regionalism and inter-regionalism, trade with allies, instrumental regionalism and securitisation. According to Telò, examples are the Eurasian community as well as the Transatlantic Trade and Investment Partnership (TTIP).

In contrast, the Gothenburg-based political scientist Fredrik Söderbaum (2016, p. 31) proposes a periodisation that commences with post–World War II developments. The first stage is characterised by what Söderbaum calls a particular 'world order context' that is based on how the Cold War played out in Europe, by bipolarity and post-colonialism in the Global South. The links between national, regional and global governance are described as regional integration beyond the nation state (in Europe), on the one hand, and advancing development and nation-building (in the 'developing world') on the other. The actors are organised sector specific; regionalisms are formal and state-led through ROs. Still according to Söderbaum the second phase started with the end of the Cold War – 'globalisation' and 'neo-liberalism' are the catch words.

The various forms of multilateralisms are seen as unstable and the nation state is said to be transforming. Regionalisms are seen as 'resisting', 'taming' or 'advancing' economic globalisation. These regionalisms are multi-sectoral or specialised. Söderbaum pitches state actors against non-state actors; regionalisms are seen to be different from processes of regionalisation; and emphasis is on formal versus informal regionalisms. Lately, Söderbaum holds, a multipolar or 'multiplex' world order has arisen in the 2000s that is influenced by the 'war on terror' and the 2007–8 global financial crisis, but also the rise of the BRICS (Brazil, Russia, India, China and – as of 2010 – South Africa) and other so-called emerging powers. In this most recent phase regional governance has become part of multi-layered forms of global governance. Söderbaum emphasises that the actors now mainly involve state as well as non-state players grouped in formal and informal forms of organisation in growing number of sectors.

Regional African practices

In this section the emphasis will be on three concrete examples from Africa for the ordering effects of the practices of ROs as well as their place in the global order. The first example concerns the negotiation of the continental order during the transition from the Organisation of African Unity (OAU) to the African Union in 1999–2002; the second example is about the creation of distinct regional architectures in concrete policy fields, in this case the African Peace and Security Architecture and the African Governance Architecture, respectively; and the third example refers to inter-regionalism by way of international partnerships the African Union has entered into with the United Nations and the European Union.

First, the establishment of the African Union in 2001 as a supranational organisation with little delegation of sovereignty by its member states to the newly created AU Commission was a political compromise between different positions advocated by alliances of OAU member states. Conventional wisdom has it that in these negotiations 'minimalists', such as South Africa under president Thabo Mbeki or Nigeria under Olusegun Obasanjo, were trying to fight off the position of maximalists, such as Gaddafi's Libya (Tieku, 2004). Based on a re-reading of the discussions, Witt (2013) has developed a more nuanced argument. She claims that in fact three different positions were at stake: a 'defence union', a 'people's union' and a 'manager-states' union'.

The first vision was introduced by Libya and supported by member states such as Chad, Ghana, Liberia, Mali, Malawi, Senegal and Sudan. This group regarded 'globalisation' as a hostile environment and followed a pan-Africanist impetus with the aim of creating the 'United States of Africa', without borders and complete transfer of sovereignty of member states. The nature of integration and unity of the African (continent and/or people) has in fact always been on the table, though the timing – gradual incrementalism or accelerated implementation – has been highly contested (see van Walraven, 1999). In fact, Gaddafi pushed the African Union in 2009 to adopt a 'roadmap' for the implementation of the 'United States of Africa' by 2017 – a project that was more or less buried after Gaddafi's death in 2011 (Engel, 2013, pp. 188–194).

The second position on the nature of the future African Union was held by member such as South Africa and Ghana (and later on also by the AU Commission and the Pan-African Parliament) and was in favour of a 'people's union' that would focus on outcome-orientation and democratic participation. The 'manager-states' union', as propagated by heavyweights such as Nigeria, Uganda, Senegal, Egypt and Ethiopia put member states as the only drivers of African integration at centre stage (Witt, 2013). As a result of the compromise that led to the establishment of the African Union, the OAU was transformed into a supranational body with little de facto sovereignty – though in practice the AU Commission has developed strong agency of its own (Engel, 2013, 2016).

Second, in contrast to its predecessor, the OAU that mainly had to deal with decolonisation and apartheid, the African Union is focusing on the various ongoing violent conflicts, terrorism and violent extremism as well as cases of unconstitutional changes of government (UCG, that is, coups d'etats, debates about constitutionally not foreseen additional presidential terms of offices and electoral violence). Based on the same principles as its predecessor – mainly 'the sovereign equality and interdependence among Member States' and 'non-interference by any Member State in the internal affairs of another' – the African Union has quite innovatively also introduced the 'right of the Union to intervene in a Member State pursuant to a decision of the Assembly in respect of grave circumstances, namely war crimes, genocide and crimes against humanity' (OAU, 2000, § 4 [a, d, g-h]). In order to address the current peace and security challenges, the African Union has detailed a complex African Peace and Security Architecture (APSA) and an African Governance Architecture (AGA), respectively. The former is made up of a Peace and Security Council (PSC), a Continental Early Warning System (CEWS), the African Standby Force (ASF), the Panel of the Wise and the Peace Fund (see African Union, 2002). These institutions and related procedures are currently being implemented rather successfully, though often quite cumbersome (Engel, 2016). They also create the need for policy harmonisation and coordination between the African Union on the one hand and the regional economic communities (RECs) on the other. The emerging division of labour between a continental and eight officially recognised regional ROs still remains work-in-progress and, in practice refers to many inter-regional challenges.

In addition, the African Union has embarked on the implementation of a complementary African Governance Architecture (African Union, 2007). It is based on universal values and principles of democracy and respect for human rights and it also promotes the principles of the rule of law, constitutional order, regular free and fair elections, independence of the judiciary, etc. However, ratification of the Charter took five years and revealed a growing split between liberal and illiberal AU member states when it comes to embracing democratic values and principles. As of 1 April 2016, a total of 24 AU member states had ratified and deposited the legal instruments, while eight member states still had not signed and a total of 30 member states had not ratified the Charter. Integrating the two architectures at the level of the AU Commission, between the Commission and member states, and within the RECs remains a complex challenge (Engel, 2016).

Third, the African Union engages in a 'sovereignty-boosting' form of inter-regionalism by forging international partnerships with the United Nations and the European Union in the area of peace and security (here and in the following Engel, 2018a, 2018b). Apart from the important funding role of the UN and EU for peace-support operations in Africa (on which the Union is heavily depending), in both cases a strong network of institutional ties has been developed, leading to closer policy coordination and capacity-building on the part of the African Union. Since 2006 annual consultations are held between the AU PSC and the UN Security Council; an ad hoc Working Group on Conflict Prevention and Resolution in Africa has been established; bi-annual desk-to-desk meetings have been introduced;

in 2009 an AU Permanent Observer Mission to the UN was established and the following year a Joint Task Force on Peace and Security was set up.

The UN Office to the African Union was opened in 2010. And since 2014 regularly updated Joint UN-AU Frameworks for an Enhanced Partnership in Peace and Security are guiding the cooperation. The partnership with the European Union is based on the 2007 Joint Africa-Europe Strategy (JAES) and Plan of Action. Institutionally, it includes regular meetings at the level of summits, ministerial, between the Commissions ('college-to-college'), PSC to Political and Security Committee, EU Military Committee to AU Military Staff Committee and Joint Africa Expert Groups (JAEGs). Despite ongoing disagreement on a number of issues – such as the lack of African representation at the UNSC, political contradictions at operational level (for instance about the interventions in Libya, 2011 or Mali, 2013), as well as the concrete policy agendas of the P3 (i.e. France, the UK and the US) which at times have been in stark contrast to African interests – these partnerships are seen by the African Union as a necessary and helpful way of increasing the continental body's room for manoeuvre. As the Union expects more support for African ownership and priority setting, the AU/UN partnership should be based on the following principles: 'flexible and innovative application of the principle of subsidiarity', 'mutual respect and adherence to the principle of comparative advantage' as well as the development of a 'division of labour underpinned by complementarity' (AUC Chairperson, 2012, §§ 94–97).

Conclusion

ROs have clearly made an imprint on regional and global affairs, across many social fields. Their number and relevance has increased after the end of the Cold War. In the academic debate about RO some challenges remain, most importantly with regard to the place and functioning of ROs in current processes of globalisation, their periodisation over the last 200 years and the parameters for the comparative study of regionalisms. Empirically there still is a need for detailed studies about the exact workings of inter-regionalism, the reconstruction of the national interests of their member states and related decision-making processes. The actorness of ROs is evident, but still needs to be further investigated, both vis-à-vis respective member states, but also other ROs. And, finally, there is also space to analyse in greater detail the professionalisation, institutionalisation and organisational learning of ROs as well as related processes of cultural transfers from one RO to the other.

Notes

1 See www.uia.org/yearbook (accessed May 5, 2019). The yearbook is published by Brill Academic Publishers (Brill: Leiden, Boston).
2 See the research agenda of the Collaborative Research Group 1199, 'Processes of Spatialization under the Global Condition', at Leipzig University in Germany. http://research.uni-leipzig.de/~sfb1199/index.php?id=7 (accessed May 5, 2019).

Further reading

Bach, Daniel (2016) *Regionalism in Africa. Genealogies, Institutions and Trans-State Networks* (Oxon: Routledge).

Börzel, Tanja and Thomas Risse (eds.) (2016) *The Oxford Handbook of Comparative Regionalism* (Oxford: Oxford University Press).

Engel, Ulf et al. (eds.) (2016) *The New Politics of Regionalism. Perspectives from Africa, Latin America and Asia-Pacific* (London/New York: Routledge).

Fawcett, Lousie and Andrew Hurrell (eds.) (1995) *Regionalism in World Politics* (Oxford: Oxford University Press).

Fioramonti, Lorenzo (ed.) (2012a) *Regions and Crises: New Challenges for Contemporary Regionalisms* (Basingstoke: Palgrave).

Fioramonti, Lorenzo (ed.) (2012b) *Regionalism in a Changing World: Comparative Perspectives in the New Global Order* (London: Routledge).

Katzenstein, Peter J. (2005) *A World of Regions: Asia and Europe in the American Imperium* (Ithaca, NY: Cornell University Press).

Shaw, Timothy M., J. Andrew Grant and Scarlet Cornelissen (eds.) (2011) *The Ashgate Research Companion to Regionalisms* (Farnham/Burlington, VT: Ashgate).

Söderbaum, Fredrik (2015) *Rethinking Regionalism* (Basingstoke: Palgrave Macmillan).

Bibliography

Acharya, Amitav (2002) 'Regionalism and the Emerging World Orders: Sovereignty, Autonomy, Identity', in Shaun Breslin et al. (eds.) *New Regionalism in the Global Political Economy. Theories and Cases* (London: Routledge), pp. 20–32.

Acharya, Amitav (2004) 'How Ideas Spread: Whose Norms Matter? Norm Localization and Institutional Change in Asian Regionalism', *International Organization* 58(2), pp. 239–275.

Acharya, Amitav (2012) 'Comparative Regionalism: A Field Whose Time Has Come?', *International Spectator* 47(1), pp. 3–15.

African Union (2002) *Protocol Relating to the Establishment of the Peace and Security Council* (Durban: African Union).

African Union (2007) *African Charter on Democracy, Elections and Governance* (Addis Ababa: African Union).

Agnew, John (2005) 'Sovereignty Regimes: Territoriality and State Authority in Contemporary World Politics', *Annals of the Association of American Geographers* 95(2), pp. 437–461.

AUC Chairperson (2012) *Report of the Chairperson of the Commission on the Partnership Between the African Union and the United Nations on Peace and Security. Towards Greater Political Coherence.* Tabled at the 307th PSC meeting held in Addis Ababa, Ethiopia, 9 January. PSC/PR/2. (CCCVII) (Addis Ababa: African Union), §§ 94–97.

Bach, Daniel (1999) 'Regionalism & Globalization in Sub-Saharan Africa. Revisiting a Paradigm' in Daniel Bach (ed.) *Regionalisation in Africa: Integration and Disintegration* (Oxford: James Currey), pp. 1–13.

Baert, Francis, Tiziana Scaramagli and Fredrik Söderbaum (eds.) (2014) *Intersecting Interregionalism: Regions, Global Governance and the EU* (Dordrecht: Springer).

Barnett, Michael and Martha Finnemore (2004) *Rules for the World. International Organizations in Global Politics* (Ithaca NY/London: Cornell University Press).

Baldwin, Richard (2012) 'Sequencing Asian Regionalism: Theory and Lessons from Europe', *Journal of Economic Integration* 27(1), pp. 1–32.

Beeson, Marc (2007) *Regionalism and Globalization in East Asia: Politics, Security and Economic Development* (Basingstoke: Palgrave).

Beeson, Marc (ed.) (2012) *Routledge Handbook of Asian Regionalism* (London: Routledge).

Bisley, Nick (2007) *Rethinking Globalization* (London: Palgrave Macmillan).

Bøås, Morton, Marianne H. Marchand and Timothy M. Shaw (1999) 'The Political Economy of New Regionalims', *Third World Quarterly* 20(5), pp. 897–910.

Börzel, Tanja A. (2013) 'Comparative Regionalism: European Integration and Beyond', in Walter Carlsnaes, Thomas Risse and Beth Simmons (eds.) *Handbook of International Relations* (London: Sage), pp. 503–530.

Brenner, Neil (1999) 'Beyond State-Centrism? Space, Territoriality, and Geographical Scale in Globalization Studies', *Theory and Society* 28(1), pp. 39–78.

Breslin, Shaun et al. (eds.) (2002) *New Regionalisms in the Global Political Economy* (London: Routledge).

Cason, Jeffrey W. (2011) *The Political Economy of Integration: The Experience of Mercosur* (Abingdon: Routledge).

Chaturvedi, Sanjay and Joe Painter (2007) 'Whose World, Whose Order? Spatiality, Geopolitics and the Limits of the World Order Concept', *Cooperation and Conflict* 42(2), pp. 375–395.

Cox, Robert W. (1981) 'Social Forces, States and World Orders: Beyond International Relations Theory', *Millennium: Journal of International Studies* 10(2), pp. 126–155.

Cox, Robert W. (1996) *Approaches to World Order* (Cambridge: Cambridge University Press).

Dabène, Olivier (2009) *The Politics of Regional Integration in Latin America* (Basingstoke: Palgrave Macmillan).

De Lombaerde, Philippe, Fredrik Söderbaum, Luk van Langenhive and Francis Baert (2010) 'The Problem of Comparison in Comparative Regionalism', *Review of International Studies* 36, pp. 731–753.

De Lombaerde, Philippe, Fredrik Söderbaum and Jens-Uwe Wunderlich (2015) 'Interregionalism', in Knut E. Jorgensen et al. (eds.) *The SAGE Handbook of European Foreign Policy*, volume 2 (London: Sage), pp. 750–761.

Dent, Christopher M. (2008) *East Asian Regionalism* (Abingdon, Oxon: Routledge).

Engel, Ulf (2013) 'The Changing Role of the AU Commission in Inter-African Relations – The Case of APSA and AGA', in John W. Harbeson and Donald Rothchild (eds.) *Africa in World Politics. Engaging a Changing Global Order*, 5th ed. (Boulder, CO: Westview Press), pp. 186–206.

Engel, Ulf (2016) 'The African Union's Peace and Security Architecture. From Aspiration to Operationalization', in John W. Harbeson and Donald Rothchild (eds.) *Africa in World Politics. Constructing Political and Economic Order*, 6th ed. (Boulder, CO: Westview Press), pp. 262–282.

Engel, Ulf (2018a) 'The African Union and the United Nations: Crafting International Partnerships in the Field of Peace and Security', in T. Karbo and T. Murithi (eds.) *The African Union: Autocracy, Diplomacy and Peacebuilding in Africa* (London, New York: I.B. Tauris), pp. 265–281.

Engel, Ulf (2018b) 'An Emerging Inter-regional Peace and Security Partnership: The African Union and the European Union', in S. Aris, A. Snetkov and A. Wenger (eds.) *Interorganizational Relations in International Security. Cooperation and Competition* (London: Routledge), pp. 170–187.

Engel, Ulf et al. (eds.) (2016) 'Introduction. The Challenge of Emerging Regionalisms Outside Europe', in Ulf Engel et al. (eds.) *The New Politics of Regionalism. Perspectives from Africa, Latin America and Asia-Pacific* (London/New York: Routledge), pp. 1–15.

Fawcett, Louise (2005) 'Regionalism from an Historical Perspective', in Mary Farrell, Björn Hettne and Luk van Langenhove (eds.) *Global Politics of Regionalism: An Introduction* (London, Ann Arbor, MI: Pluto Press), pp. 21–37.

Fioramonti, Lorenzo and Frank Mattheis (2015) 'Is Africa Really Following Europe? An Integrated Framework for Comparative Regionalism', *Journal of Common Market Studies* 54(3), pp. 674–690.

Frost, Ellen L. (2008) *Asia's New Regionalisms* (Boulder, CO: Lynne Riener).

Gamble, Andew and Anthony Payne (eds.) (1996) *Regionalism and World Order* (Basingstoke: Macmillan).

Geyer, Michael and Charles Bright (1995) 'World History in a Global Age', *The American Historical Review* 100(4), pp. 1034–1060.

Gómez-Mera, Laura (2013) *Power and Regionalism in Latin America* (Notre Dame, IN: University of Notre Dame Press).

Grant, J. Andrew and Fredrik Söderbaum, F. (eds.) (2003) *The New Regionalism in Africa* (Aldershot: Ashgate).

Haas, Ernst B. (1958) *The Uniting of Europe* (London: Stevens and Sons).

Hänggi, Heiner, Ralf Roloff and Jürgen Rüland (eds.) (2006) *Interregionalism and International Relations* (Abingdon: Routledge).

Hettne, Björn (1999) 'Globalization and the New Regionalism: The Second Great Transformation', in Björn Hettne, András Inotai and Oswaldo Sunkel (eds.) *Globalism and the New Regionalism* (Basingstoke: Palgrave Macmillan), pp. 1–24.

Hettne, Björn (2005) 'Reconstructing World Order', in Mary Farrell, Björn Hettne and Luk Van Langenhove (eds.) *Global Politics of Regionalism* (London: Pluto Press), pp. 269–286.

Hettne, Björn and Fredrik Söderbaum (2000) 'Theorising the Rise of Regionness', *New Political Economy* 5(3), pp. 457–474.

Hurrell, Andrew (1995) 'Regionalism in Theoretical Perspective', in Louise Fawcett and Andrew Hurrell (eds.) *Regionalism in World Politics* (Oxford: Oxford University Press), pp. 37–73.

Hurrell, Andrew (2007) 'One World? Many Worlds? The Place of Regions in the Study of International Society', *International Affairs* 83(1), pp. 127–146.

Jetschke, Antje and Tobias Lenz (2013) 'Does Regionalism Diffuse? A New Research Agenda for the Study of Regional Organizations', *Journal of European Public Policy* 20(4), pp. 626–637.

Jetschke, Antje and Philomena Murray (2012) 'Diffusing Regional Integration: The EU and Southeast Asia', *West European Politics* 35(1), pp. 174–191.

Malamud, Andrés and Gian Luca Gardini (2012) 'Has Regionalism Peaked? The Latin American Quagmire and its Lessons', *International Spectator* 47(1), pp. 116–133.

Mansfield, Edward D. and Helen V. Milner (1999) 'The New Wave of Regionalism', *International Organization* 53(3), pp. 589–627.

Mattheis, Frank (2015) *New Regionalism in the South: Mercosur and SADC in a Comparative and Interregional Perspective* (Leipzig: Leipziger Universitätsverlag).

Mitrany, David (1948) 'The Functional Approach to World Organization', *International Affairs* 24(3), pp. 350–363.

Mittelman, James H. (1996) 'Rethinking the "New Regionalism" in the Context of Globalization', *Global Governance* 2(2), pp. 189–213.

Moravcsik, Andrew (1991) 'Negotiating the Single European Act: National Interests and Conventional Statecraft in the European Community', *International Organization* 45(1), pp. 19–56.

OAU (2000) *Constitutive Act of the African Union* (Lomé: Organisation of African Unity).

PANA Press (2017) '28th Summit of the African Union Addis Ababa Ethiopia', 22–31 January 2017, http://www.panapress.com/pana-dossier-6-UA-lang2-index.html (accessed May 1, 2017).

Revel, Jacques (1996) *Jeux d'échelles. La micro-analyse à l'expérience* (Paris: Gallimard).

Riggirozzi, Pia and Diana Tussie (eds.) (2012) *The Rise of Post-Hegemonic Regionalism: The Case of Latin America* (Dordrecht: Springer).

Robinson, Richard (1990) 'Mapping the Global Condition: Globalization as the Central Concept', *Theory, Culture & Society* 7(2), pp. 15–30.

Sbragia, Alberta and Fredrik Söderbaum (2010) 'EU-Studies and the "New Regionalism": What can be Gained from Dialogue?' *Journal of European Integration* 32, pp. 563–582.

Schultz, Michael, Fredrik Söderbaum and Joakim Öjendal (2001) 'Introduction: A Framework for Understanding Regionalization', in Michael Schultz, Fredrik Söderbaum and Joakim Öjenda (eds.) *Regionalization in a Globalizing World* (London: Zed Books), pp. 1–17.

Shaw, Tinothy M., J. Andrew Grant and Scarlett Cornelissen (2011) 'Introduction and Overview: The Study of New Regionalism(s) at the Start of the Second Decade of the Twenty-First Century', in Timothy M. Shaw, J. Andrew Grant and Scarlet Cornelissen (eds.) *The Ashgate Research Companion to Regionalisms* (Farnham, Burlington, VT: Ashgate), pp. 3–30.

Söderbaum, Fredrik (2004a) *The Political Economy of Regionalisms. The Case of Southern Africa* (Basingstoke, New York: Palgrave MacMillan).

Söderbaum, Fredrik (2004b) 'Modes of Regional Governance in Africa: Neoliberalism, Sovereignty Boosting, and Shadow Networks', *Global Governance* 10(4), pp. 419–436.

Söderbaum, Fredrik (2015) *Rethinking Regionalism* (Basingstoke: Palgrave Macmillan).

Söderbaum, Fredrik (2016) 'Old, New and Comparative Regionalism. The History and Scholarly Development of the Field' in Tanja Börzel and Thomas Risse (eds.) *The Oxford Handbook of Comparative Regionalism* (Oxford: Oxford University Press), pp. 16–37.

Söderbaum, Fredrik and Timothy M. Shaw (eds.) (2003) *Theories of New Regionalism: A Palgrave Reader* (Basingstoke, New York: Palgrave Macmillan).

Söderbaum, Fredrik and Ian Taylor (eds.) 2008. *Afro-Regions: The Dynamics of Cross-Border Micro-Regionalism in Africa* (Uppsala: Nordiska Afrikainstitutet).

Söderbaum, Fredrik and Luk Van Langenhove (eds.) (2006) *The EU as a Global Player: The Politics of Interregionalism* (London: Routledge).

Solingen, Etel (2015) *Comparative Regionalism. Economics and Security* (London: Routledge).

Sørensen, Georg (2006) 'What Kind of World Order? The International System in the New Millennium', *Cooperation and Conflict* 41(2), pp. 343–363.

Telò, Mario (eds.) (1999) *European Union and New Regionalism. Regional Actors and Global Governance in a Post-hegemonic Era* (Aldershot: Ashgate).

Telò, Mario (2017) *Regionalism in Hard Times. Competitive and Post-Liberal Trends in Europe, Asia, Africa, and the Americas* (Abingdon: Routledge).

Thomas, Nicholas (ed.) (2009) *Governance and Regionalism in Asia* (Oxon: Routledge).

Tieku, Thomas K. (2004) 'Explaining the Clash and Accommodation of Interests of Major Actors in the Creation of the African Union', *African Affairs* 103(411), pp. 249–267.

UN Secretary-General (2016) *Cooperation Between the United Nations and Regional and Other Organizations* (=A/71/160 and S/2016/621) (New York: United Nations).

Van Walraven, Klaas (1999) *Dreams of Power: The Role of the Organization of African Unity in the Politics of Africa 1963–1993* (Aldershot: Ashgate).

Väyrynen, Raimo (2003) 'Regionalism: Old and New', *International Studies Review* 5(1), pp. 25–51.

Waltz, Kenneth (1979) *Theory of International Politics* (New York: McGraw-Hill).

Warleigh-Lack, Alex (2008) 'Studying Regionalisation Comparatively: A Conceptual Framework' in Andrew F. Cooper, Christopher W.H. Hughes and P. de Lombaerde (eds.) *Regionalisation and Global Governance. The Taming of Globalisation?* (Abingdon/New York: Routledge), pp. 43–60.

Warleigh-Lack, Alex, Nick Robinson and Ben Rosamund (eds.) (2011) *New Regionalism and the European Union. Dialogues, Comparisons and New Research Directions* (London/New York: Routledge).

Witt, Antonia (2013) 'The African Union and Contested Political Order(s)', in Joao Gomes Porto and Ulf Engel (eds.) *Towards an African Peace and Security Regime. Continental Embeddedness, Transnational Linkages, Strategic Relevance* (Farnham/Burlington: Ashgate), pp. 11–30.

Chapter 16

Multinational businesses

John Mikler

Corporations are among the most powerful political actors on the planet, and we are often told that the size and scope of their operations mean the world is increasingly 'ruled' by them (e.g. Korten, 2015). This view is often expressed with negative sentiments, to the extent that Micklethwait and Wooldridge say they are portrayed

FIGURE 16.1 Shopping signs of major international brands at a Prague shopping centre, Czech Republic

as 'the dark lords of globalisation' (2003, p. 168). This is because at the heart of debates about globalisation is the question of the extent to which the demise of states' sovereignty is being caused by global neo-liberal market deregulation, and the rise of market actors in the form of multinational businesses that are no longer bound by national territories. Much of the literature therefore considers the extent to which states are constrained to function, rather than govern, in a more passive, market-facilitating role with the interests they serve corporate rather than those of their citizens. The extent to which global markets, and multinational businesses as key actors in them, are now 'in charge' is therefore an important consideration in contemporary debates about actors and agendas in global politics.

As an introduction to these debates, in the first section of this chapter multinational businesses are defined. Given the size and scope of their operations, arguments are then presented for why they should be conceived as controlling, rather than competing in markets. This suggests that they are increasingly political rather than market actors. As political actors, in the second section it is shown that their power is multifaceted, encompassing instrumental-relational, structural and discursive aspects. The point made is that the political power of multinational businesses vis-à-vis states is not a straightforward matter, because while they rival states, they also share authority with them. In the third section, it is demonstrated that while multinational businesses' interests transcend states' territorial boundaries, it also remains very much the case that they are not placeless entities. There is a tension between their multinational operations and their national identities that suggests a need to re-territorialise their power in relation to their home states in particular. Therefore, in the final section the case is made for why institutional diversity in the practice of capitalism between states remains salient despite the rise of multinational businesses.

The conclusion reached is that both powerful states and their corporations still matter, rather than a focus on the importance of one versus the other. It is the intersection of the interests of both, and how they reconcile their interests, that should be at the heart of any contemporary political analysis of the impact of multinational businesses on global politics.

Defining multinational businesses

In 1970 there were just 7000 multinational businesses, which is to say parent firms associated with foreign affiliates beyond the borders of their home states (Clapp, 2005). There are now over 100,000 with nearly 900,000 foreign affiliates (UNCTAD, 2011). Whether conceived as multinational corporations (MNCs), transnational corporations (TNCs) or multinational enterprises (MNEs), a global dimension to almost all the world's major corporations is now taken for granted. MNCs are defined as such because they invest, produce and sell their products and services in more than one national jurisdiction. Seeing them as TNCs goes beyond them operating in several jurisdictions to passing through/across borders as if these were irrelevant. The MNE term, most often used in the international business and management literature, encompasses aspects of both in the sense that modern business involves the management of supply chains and coordinating networks of operations across several national jurisdictions. Global MNEs are regarded, somewhat tautologically, as those which operate on a global scale. There is no clear definition of what this means, but one is that these are corporations with at least 20 per cent of their sales in each of at least three continental markets (*Financial Times*, no date).

In all cases the result is at least a regional, if not purely global, conception of their operations, with this increasingly the norm as they come to operate 'as if the entire world (or major regions of it) were a single entity' (Levitt, 1983, p. 92). The implications for global politics are apparent, one of which is that state sovereignty is weakened because no individual government has jurisdiction over all the activities of any multinational business. Even if they were to agree to share sovereignty to regulate corporate activity, which is highly challenging as evidenced by the case of the European Union (EU) as perhaps the only example of this 'working' in practice, in the absence of global government nothing less than global governance is required. If this does not eventuate, the alternative is an economically interconnected world dominated by multinational businesses' interests in which states must accept the reality that, in the words of Friedman 'your economy grows and your politics shrinks' (2000, p. 105). Hence the arguments that globalisation tends to produce a convergence on a neo-liberal form of the state.

This has led to the argument that market forces, expressed through multinational businesses as 'market actors', now tend to define global politics. If this is the case, it is not a matter of market competition but market control. Multinational businesses tend to control the markets for their products and services to the extent that by the end of the 20th century no more than five corporations controlled each of the world's major industries, with around a third of these having one corporation accounting for more than 40 per cent of global sales (Nolan et al., 2002). There may be over 100,000 multinational businesses, but the reality is that very few of these dominate the global economy. As Crouch (2011, p. 49) observes, there has been a 'corporate takeover of the market', the result of which is that the visible hand of the state has not been replaced by the invisible hand of Adam Smith's market forces, but by a visible handful of corporations.

A basic measure of their size is given by their annual revenues. In 2015, the Fortune Global 500 companies, a list compiled on the basis of annual revenues, together had sales totalling US$31.2 trillion (Fortune, 2015). Given that the size of the global economy was estimated to be US$73.5 trillion in the same year (World Bank, 2016), it could be argued that through the networks they control and the supply chains they coordinate, they effectively accounted for nearly half of it. In fact, the 20 most global corporations on the basis of their foreign assets have sales greater than the combined gross domestic product of the bottom 138 states, while some of them are as large as middle income or emerging states like Algeria and Portugal. However, a comparison with national expenditure is probably more accurate because a state's budget is analogous to a corporation's sales, these being an indicator of how much it has spent on purchasing labour, resources, investments, goods, advertising, corporate image-making, lobbying, consultants and so on in order to produce a desired surplus. In short, corporate sales are an indicator of organisational budget, rather like a state's budget. On this basis, the 20 most global corporations' sales are greater than the combined expenditure of the bottom 166 states, while several are as large as many of the top 30 states – e.g. Exxon Mobil's sales of US$390 billion in 2013 were greater than South Korea's government expenditure of US$273 billion (UNCTAD, 2014; IMF, 2015).

In addition to rivalling the world's major states on the basis of such measures, it is noteworthy that in the same year the United Nations had a budget of US$5.1 billion (United Nations, 2012) while the World Trade Organisation, which describes itself as 'the only global international organisation dealing with the rules of trade between nations', had a budget of just US$210 million (WTO, 2016).[1] Therefore, some multinational businesses are much larger than not only many of the world's most powerful states, but also the international organisations that are so much more often the focus of analysis by international relations scholars.

Theorising the political power of multinational businesses

The political, as opposed to market, power of multinational businesses is not simply a function of their size. It is multifaceted and debates about it are inseparable from the master concept of our time, globalisation. Conceptualising globalisation has been characterised by Martell (2007) as occurring in three broad, and sequential, 'waves' since the end of the Cold War: the globalists, sceptics and transformationalists. These waves suggest different conceptions of the power relationships between states and non-state actors, including multinational businesses.

The globalists of the late 1980s and early 1990s stressed the retreat of the state. All the other implications of globalisation – political, social, cultural, etc. – were seen as flowing from a belief that markets were increasingly 'the masters over the governments of states' (Strange, 1996, p. 4). In other words, market forces, whether 'free' or dominated by multinational businesses as previously suggested, dictate the political choices open to states regardless of what their governments might like to do, or what their citizens may desire. As they need to attract and retain globally mobile finance and productive investment, the implication is that states are less able to effectively regulate globally mobile corporations, having sacrificed the right to do so on the altar of globally integrated markets. Ultimately, state sovereignty is so undermined that the only regulatory functions left for governments are those which support markets. The globalists did not see this as a matter of opinion, nor necessarily a matter of politically left versus right ideology, but as a *structural* reality. Multinational businesses that straddle the globe with the prime goal of maximising their material returns, and bearing allegiance to no one except their shareholders, were seen as taking political control of the policies and strategies of states which are dependent on them for the economic benefits they can confer or take elsewhere.

Since the 1990s, many authors have taken issue with this viewpoint. The sceptics countered it by conceiving of globalisation as more a discourse, or idea, that is largely what states make of it. As such, states remain key actors, with global politics still best understood as a function of political agency in relations between states. In particular, the sceptics say that it is a fallacy to suggest all states are weakened by the globalisation of the world economy, and the opposite may be the case for some. This is because the 'globalization consensus' (Wade, 2010) that markets and market forces are, and should, be in charge of national destinies may serve the interests of economically powerful states. Through it they are able to promote the notion that there are undeniable 'forces' of globalisation in order that their flagship corporations may more easily access cheap factors of production worldwide and sell their products in new markets. In other words, it serves their interests to promote the international interests of their multinational businesses. This may seem like a contradiction in terms, but as will be shown in the following section to the extent that there is something popularly termed globalisation underway, it is often driven by multinational businesses that are more national and regional in their orientations rather than global. They therefore potentially serve to internationalise the economic interests of the states from which they hail, which act to ensure they are free to do so.

The transformationalists recognise the changes being wrought by globalisation, and therefore do not dismiss these as easily as the sceptics, yet they do not see states as increasingly irrelevant so much as their political agency is being reconstructed. They share the concerns of the sceptics, in that they reject what Hay and Marsh term the 'globaloney' (2000, p. 6) of the globalists, but in recognising that states remain central actors in international politics they do not dismiss the idea of the increasing importance of non-state actors either. They therefore paint a complex picture of global politics, one key aspect of which is the recognition that states' political agency relies on them sharing their sovereignty with each other in order to retain it, as well as with private actors such as multinational businesses. This means that sometimes states embrace neo-liberal deregulatory reforms if this is in their interests, such as when they are economically powerful and are the headquarters to powerful multinational businesses. But this is one of a range of policy paths that states may choose to pursue. As such, the transformationalists can be seen as occupying a complex middle ground between the globalists and the sceptics.

The ongoing debate about conceptualising globalisation suggests that theorising the role, and therefore power, of multinational businesses is not at all straightforward. Drawing on a wealth of literature analysing the nature of power, Fuchs (2007) suggests that there are three broad aspects of the power corporations wield in respect of states: instrumental, structural and discursive. Corporations possess instrumental power in the sense that there are direct and observable relationships of power between the two. In relational terms, what one does affects the other, and as corporations have grown in size and transnationality, their instrumental power to achieve their ends has increased accordingly. Rather like traditional perspectives of power in international relations more generally, where the relative power of states determines their position in the international system and their ability to act in their interest, so the increased resources at the disposal of multinational businesses through their market power enhances their ability to lobby in pursuit of their desired ends. If states desire to maximise their power, while multinational businesses desire to maximise their profits, then their ability to achieve these ends depends on their relative positions and relations with one another.

The problem with a focus purely on relational forms of power is that it does not lend itself to an in-depth understanding of the interests and actions of corporations versus states. Structural conceptions do so to a greater degree by emphasising agenda-setting power, which multinational businesses certainly possess because their global economic dominance puts them in a 'privileged position' to get what they want before they need to ask for it (Tienhaara, 2014, p. 166; see also Lindblom, 1977). In simpler terms, their size and domination of global markets mean they can get what they want without needing to lobby for it. In this regard, it is the transnationality of their operations that is said to be the main reason they rival states, and thereby influence states' policy agendas.

For example, Margaret Thatcher's 'TINA' dictum of the 1980s – that There Is No Alternative to the free market – led to states *handing* power to corporations via deregulatory reforms and the privatisation of formerly public services in the belief that this was 'inevitable'. States came to see their fortunes as dependent on satisfying corporate interests, because not giving multinational businesses what they wanted risked them locating their operations elsewhere. This is why it is often said that the structural power of multinational businesses has the propensity to produce a 'race to the bottom': a competitive bidding down of salaries, conditions and standards by states. In general, their control of 'pivotal networks and resources' (Fuchs, 2007, p. 59) both within and across states' borders means multinational businesses are able to influence political agendas to the extent that their interests come to be seen as synonymous with states' national interests.

Discursive power is perhaps the most nuanced, and the hardest to observe. It involves the power of ideas, and the way in which 'some definitions of issues are organised into politics while other definitions are organised out' (Hajer, 1997 quoted in Fuchs, 2007, p. 60). This is not just on the basis of structural power, but on the basis of what is perceived as legitimate in the eyes of governments and the public. It has to do with achieving ends by influencing, shaping or determining the wants of others. As Elbra (2014) puts it, 'interests do not need to be pursued if they can be created', and essentially through the creation of 'truths' multinational businesses can promote the 'projection of a particular set of interests as the general interest' (Levy and Newell, 2002, p. 87; see also Clapp and Fuchs, 2009). For example, it is striking that democratically elected governments are now judged on their ability to attain and retain credit ratings that are determined by private ratings agencies, that international standards are a matter for private business associations to determine through the International Organisation for Standardisation, and that corporate social responsibility is now widely accepted to be as important as making profits. It is certainly the case that the instrumental and structural power of multinational businesses has facilitated this, but their discursive power has led them to be perceived as legitimately entitled to make such claims.

The complexity of theorising corporate power suggests that it is problematic to purely understand multinational businesses in terms of their size, sales and resulting market power. Rather than the more classical liberal vision of the firm as a mechanism of profit, multinational businesses are now often seen as either self-regulators or solvers of environmental and social problems, not just nationally but globally. To begin to comprehend why this is the case, one needs to see their power in three dimensions, and recognising the links between these dimensions – e.g. the discursive power of multinational businesses enhances their instrumental and structural power, and vice versa. Having said this, discursive power is the 'prize' multinational businesses ultimately seek precisely because it is the hardest to observe. When they possess it, it establishes their legitimacy and thereby private authority over global political processes and agendas. It does so because they do not just have to rely on their size, nor their structural ability to influence states' policymaking processes, but can manipulate and condition society into accepting their desires and ends as *right*.

Multinational, but not placeless, businesses

The question of the places where they do so remains relevant too. While it may seem obvious to say that their size, transnationality and efforts to dominate discourses puts them in a position to make rules for the world, the reality is that they rule some parts of it more than others. In this regard, it has been noted that despite more than 60 years of the global liberalisation of world markets, it remains the case that rich, industrialised states dominate international investment and production, and are the source of 70 to 90 per cent of all foreign direct investment (Chang, 2008, p. 32). More accurately, it is the corporations from these states that do so. The FT Global 500, a list of the largest corporations in the world on the basis of their stock market capitalisation, are responsible for at least 80 per cent of the world's stock of FDI, and around 70 per cent of world trade (Rugman, 2000; see also Bryant and Bailey, 1997).

In fact, whatever the measure used – annual revenues, stock market capitalisation or a composite index of factors – around 80 per cent of the world's top 500 corporations are headquartered in just ten states. These are the economically powerful industrialised states of North America, Western Europe and East Asia. The same geopolitical patterns are observable for those headquartered in emerging market economies for which again ten states account for over 80 per cent of the top 500 emerging market multinational businesses. As the US alone accounts for nearly half the headquarters of established multinational businesses, so China does for those of a younger vintage (Financial Times, 2016; Fortune, 2015; Forbes Global, 2000, 2015).

It therefore seems that rather than stressing the transnationality of multinational businesses, it is important to note the way in which they reflect geopolitical patterns of power. It may no longer be as true as it once was that 'a statistical profile for the current corporation indicates that it is predominantly Anglo-American' (Harrod, 2006, pp. 27–28), but it remains the case that the headquarters of the world's largest corporations are like a map of global economic power, hence the close correlation between the national economic and corporate data. In addition to this being evident for their headquarters, measures of corporations' transnationality show them to be less global than often held to be the case. One such measure is UNCTAD's Transnationality Index (TNI). It calculates corporations' transnationality as the arithmetic mean of three ratios: foreign assets to total assets; foreign sales to total sales; and foreign employment to total employment. According to UNCTAD (2014), the average TNI of the world's 100 most transnational corporations on the basis of their foreign assets is 60 per cent.[2] Although on average they have more of their interests and operations abroad than at home, and while some corporations are indeed highly transnational, many that one might have expected to be are not. For example, the world's largest retailer, Walmart, has a TNI of only 36 per cent. This is not to say that its impact on global markets is irrelevant, and nor should its impact in particular states such as China where many of its products are manufactured be ignored. However, Walmart is clearly an American company. Furthermore, a corporation's TNI may overstate its transnationality as the aggregate data used to calculate it may considerably abstract from the actual geographical spread of its operations. Many are more accurately regional than global in their operations and interests. For example, Rugman and Verbeke (2009) demonstrate that *only nine* of the top 500 multinational businesses have sales in so many regions that they may be regarded as global, while 320 of them still derive 80 per cent of their sales from their home region. Of the others for which they have data, 25 are more accurately defined as bi-national or bi-regional on the basis of their sales.

Therefore, even the most multinational businesses are not as global as one might think. The trend towards greater globality is also not as rapid as often popularly asserted. The average TNI for the world's top 100 most transnational MNCs grew from 52 to 60 between 1993 and 2014 (Dicken, 2007 and UNCTAD, 2014).[3] At this rate, it will be another 30 to 40 years before their average TNI reaches 75 per cent. Secondly, global trends mask national specificities. For example, the average TNI of the 22 US firms in the world's 100 most transnational corporations is just 50, meaning that the multinational businesses headquartered in the world's most economically powerful state retain half their sales, assets and employment at home. By comparison, the 16 corporations from the UK, which has the second most number of corporations in the top 100, have an average TNI of 71 (UNCTAD, 2014). Such differences suggest something American and British about the profile of these corporations as opposed to their 'globality'. Thirdly, while the trend towards greater transnationality has been steady, albeit gradual, it is by no means irreversible. As the opportunities for efficiencies/exploitation shrink with the development of the states in which these companies have invested, and as the cost of oil and carbon emissions ultimately must be factored into corporate strategic decision making, multinational strategies may become less attractive (see e.g. Anon, 2011). This may at least produce a rationalisation of global supply chains, even if it does not involve a wholesale consolidation of operations in corporations' home states.

Perhaps most tellingly, corporate ownership and control has long been recognised as remaining very much national rather transnational, diffused or whatever other descriptor one may like to choose. Wade's declaration over two decades ago that 'in Japanese companies foreign directors are as rare as British sumo wrestlers' (1996, p. 79) remains applicable today. On the one hand, there is evidence of increasing diversity in board members' nationalities, so that according to Staples (2007) three quarters of the 80 largest multinational businesses had at least one non-national board member in 2005 by comparison to around a third in 1993. On the other hand, he also finds that no more than 25 per cent of the board members of these companies are comprised of non-nationals (i.e. those of a nationality different to the corporation's headquarters), and that for only 10 per cent of them were the majority of board members non-nationals. Furthermore, he finds the main way that boards become more globalised is through mergers and acquisitions, not because of their global sales and production interests. He concludes that 'like a wide but shallow lake, board globalisation does not yet reach very deep' (Staples, 2007, p. 317).

Varieties of Capitalism

These observations are important, because rather than placeless entities, they suggest multinational businesses remain institutionally embedded in their home states. Markets are increasingly global, but the corporations that compete in them are less so, and therefore the limited or varying degrees to which businesses are multinational suggests national institutions remain salient for understanding state-business relations, and variations in capitalist relations of production between states.

The comparative capitalism literature is considerable, and has burgeoned since the 1990s. Of particular relevance to the study of corporations specifically, Hall and Soskice (2001) proposed a firm (rather than state) centred Varieties of Capitalism (VOC) approach. Their desire was to 'to bring firms back into the centre of the analysis of comparative capitalism', in recognition that firms are 'the crucial actors in a capitalist economy' (Hall and Soskice, 2001, pp. 2, 6). In observing that all firms must 'solve' coordination problems to succeed, they then went further than other studies of comparative capitalism to categorise capitalist states as tending towards liberal market economies (LMEs) versus coordinated market economies (CMEs). Putting it simply, LME-based corporations prefer to coordinate their activities via market competition whereas CME-based corporations prefer more non-market cooperative relationships to coordinate their activities, including with the state. The US is usually taken to be the archetypal LME, others of which include Anglo-Saxon countries like the UK, Canada, Australia, New Zealand and Ireland. Many European states are CMEs. Some, such as Italy and France, occupy more ambiguous positions, though the latter has long been characterised as a *dirigiste* state in the sense that elites within the bureaucracy perform a steering function in respect of the national economy. East Asian industrialised and industrialising states such as Japan, South Korea and China are often said to possess 'Asian' forms of capitalism that share CME attributes with continental European countries (see e.g. Walter and Zhang, 2012; Nölke, 2013).

Although the VOC approach has been the subject of sustained attack for its dualistic categorisation of states, it has come to be a dominant starting point for studying the strategic preferences of nationally embedded corporations. The rationale for the simplifying assumptions underlying the VOC approach's categories is that states possess sub-national institutional complementarities and therefore can be considered not just as discreet cases, but as belonging to coherent and enduring categories. That states in each of these two categories tend to have more in common with each other than across the categories has been borne out by multiple studies which have demonstrated that even if there has been a 'slide' towards more liberal forms of capitalism worldwide, if anything the *gap* between states has widened along with a clustering around the two categories proposed by the VOC approach (see e.g. Hall and Gingerich, 2009). This is because public and private actors 'inhabit' institutional structures at any given point in time that they cannot easily change. They certainly can over time, and indeed act purposively to do so along the lines of the three conceptions of power previously outlined, but they do so path dependently. As such, it is easier for LMEs to become more liberal than CMEs, and it is preferable for institutional complementarities that have served states and their corporations well to be reinforced in the face of international challenges, rather than abandoned.

While it is an oversimplification to say that firms of the same nationality are identical, national characteristics nevertheless predominate such that corporations of the same nationality, as with their home states, have more in common with each other than those of different nationalities. For example:

- There are closer state-business relations in CMEs versus a preference for the separation of the state and markets in LMEs. Therefore, a preference for market-based solutions in LMEs is the case, versus a partnership approach and acceptance of a greater coordinating function on the part of the state in CMEs.
- There is a resulting priority for markets as organisers of economic activity in LMEs, in both the product and financial spheres, versus markets as one among a variety of mechanisms for organising economic activity in CMEs on a more relational, cooperative basis. Therefore, there is a greater willingness on the part of corporations to accommodate higher levels of state intervention in markets by comparison to LME-based firms.
- LME-based firms may be conceived of as networks of contracts with significant power invested in management. They act on market signals to make profits in the short term and pay dividends to shareholders. A CME-based firm is best conceived as a collective (Germany) or community (Japan) that acts to enhance its reputation through close relational ties with stakeholders. Therefore, a stronger role for senior office holders as drivers of strategic change is the case for LME-based firms, by comparison to overall corporate culture that is not necessarily driven from the 'top' in CME-based firms.
- There is a preference for non-price competition via product innovation in established industries in CMEs via incremental technological change, versus price competition in established industries in LMEs. Radical technological change is favoured in new industries in LMEs. This suggests that incremental steps in mature industries are most likely to be driven by CME-based firms in the absence of market and regulatory signals, whereas LME-based firms will resist this until new industries become materially viable.

This is neither an exhaustive list, nor an unproblematic one, but it serves to make the point that there are nationally differentiated institutional constructions of corporate strategic interests. These may also produce global effects as multinational businesses do not just control the global markets for their products, but also 'export' the institutional basis for their relationships with states and their societies as they operate beyond their headquarters. This is why despite having global strategies, multinational businesses display a range of national and regional identities, rather than a singular global identity. Studies such as Kahancová (2007) demonstrate the existence of corporate organisational inertia, as routines which have supported growth and legitimacy in corporations' home states tend to be retained where possible when they invest in others. Rather than some disembodied, transnational form of capitalism being spread by multinational businesses which is essentially in opposition to states, because they are adapted to particular and differentiated national business systems that pertain in their home states they seek to operate in a similar manner elsewhere. Indeed, their ability to do so may be critical to sustaining competitiveness in institutional contexts with which they are initially unfamiliar (see e.g. Kelly and Amburgey, 1991; Miller and Chen, 1994; Xia et al., 2009).

The extent to which this happens is the question. Yet if multinational businesses remain nationally embedded in states the support of which they depend on for their ongoing viability, then it follows that states themselves are in turn dependent on multinational businesses in supporting their national interests. It is anything but inevitable that as states and multinational businesses share political power in world affairs, they must operate according to one variety of capitalism or another. To the extent they do, this reflects the dominance or otherwise of the states from which they hail.

Conclusion

The global economy is not predominantly characterised by small, entrepreneurial firms adrift on a sea of competitive market forces. Rather, large multinational businesses moderate and are potentially in a position to make market conditions in their interests. The choices they make affect the fortunes of states as a result of their political power, which they exercise instrumentally, structurally and discursively. Yet they do not so much rival states, as they also reflect their power. Headquartered in the world's most economically powerful industrialised states and the major emerging market economies, they potentially serve each other's interests. The political power they possess is therefore not just a function of their market dominance, but also a reflection of the power of their home states. Therefore 'to focus on the study of the global activities of the corporation means to study the point of entry rather than the source of its power and activity' (Harrod, 2006, p. 34). In other words, there is the reality of a more economically interconnected world, and multinational businesses are the actors that help make it so, but the sources of their power are substantially the home bases from which they wield it.

As such, neo-liberal globalisation and the power of markets and market actors it suggests is not an inevitable outcome. For economically powerful states and those emerging to challenge them, there is nothing inevitable about the role played by multinational businesses in their national economies, nor in the global economy. Today, in the aftermath of the global financial crisis, the Brexit vote in the UK, the rise of nationalism in Europe and the election of the Trump administration in the US, free market capitalism and globalisation are being questioned much as communism was three decades ago. Just as the fall of the Berlin Wall and the end of the Cold War produced an expectation of the inevitability of convergence on a neo-liberal form of the state, where markets and corporations as the dominant actors in them were 'in charge', it seems intuitively reasonable to think that the first two decades of the 21st century may end with an impetus for movement in the opposite direction. There is even the possibility that powerful states and the international organisations to which they belong may increasingly become masters over their multinational businesses, or at least attempt to be so in an effort to ensure they more explicitly serve each other's interests rather than seeming to oppose them.

Notes

1 Its 2013 consolidated budget of CHF197,203,900 converted at a 2013 yearly average of CHF1=US$1.079397 using www.usforex.com/forex-tools/historical-rate-tools/yearly-average-rates.
2 This calculation treats the top 100 corporations as a group, calculating their transnationality based on the sum of their assets, sales and employment.
3 This calculation again treats the top 100 corporations as a group, calculating their transnationality based on the sum of their assets, sales and employment.

Further reading

Culpepper, P.D. (2011) *Quiet Politics and Business Power: Corporate Control in Europe and Japan* (Cambridge: Cambridge University Press).
Cutler, A.C., V. Haufler and T. Porter (eds.) (1999a) *Private Authority and International Affairs* (Albany: State University of New York Press).
Dicken, P. (2015) *Global Shift: Mapping the Changing Contours of the World Economy*, 7th ed. (New York: The Guilford Press).
Fuchs, D. (2007) *Business Power in Global Governance* (Boulder: Lynne Rienner Publishers).
May, C. (ed.) (2006) *Global Corporate Power* (Boulder: Lynne Rienner Publishers).
Micklethwait, J. and A. Wooldridge (2003) *The Company: A Short History of a Revolutionary Idea* (London: Phoenix).
Mikler, J. (2018) *The Political Power of Global Corporations* (Cambridge: Polity Press).
Mikler, J. (ed.) (2013) *The Handbook of Global Companies* (Oxford: Wiley Blackwell).
Nölke, A. (ed.) (2013) *Multinational Corporations from Emerging Markets Economies: State Capitalism 3.0* (Houndmills Basingstoke: Palgrave Macmillan).
Rugman, A. (ed.) (2009) *The Oxford Handbook of International Business*, 2nd ed. (Oxford: Oxford University Press).
Walter, A. and X. Zhang (eds.) (2012) *East Asian Capitalism: Diversity, Continuity and Change* (Oxford: Oxford University Press).
Wilks, S. (2013) *The Political Power of the Business Corporation* (Cheltenham: Edward Elgar).

Bibliography

Anon (2011) 'The Dwindling Allure of Building Factories Offshore', *The Economist*, 12 May, www.economist.com/node/18682182?story_id=18682182 (accessed May 25, 2011).
Bryant, R.L. and S. Bailey (1997) *Third World Political Ecology* (London: Routledge).
Chang, H. (2008) *Bad Samaritans: The Myth of Free Trade and the Secret History of Capitalism* (New York: Bloomsbury Press).
Clapp, J. (2005) 'Transnational Corporations and Global Environmental Governance', in P. Dauvergne (ed.) *Handbook of Global Environmental Politics* (Cheltenham: Edward Elgar).
Clapp, J. and D. Fuchs (2009) 'Agrifood Corporations, Global Governance and Sustainability: A Framework for Analysis', in J. Clapp and D. Fuchs (eds.) *Corporate Power in Global Agrifood Governance* (Cambridge: MIT Press).
Crouch, C. (2011) *The Strange Non-Death of Neoliberalism* (Cambridge: Polity Press).
Dicken, P. (2007) *Global Shift: Mapping the Changing Contours of the World Economy*, 5th ed. (London: Sage Publications).

Elbra, A. (2014) 'Interests Need Not be Pursued if they can be Created: Private Governance in African Gold Mining', *Business and Politics* 16(2), pp. 247–266.

Financial Times (2016) *FT Global 500 2015*, www.ft.com/ft500 (accessed June 5, 2016).

Financial Times (no date) *Definition of Global Multinational Enterprises*, http://lexicon. ft.com/Term?term=global-multinational-enterprises (accessed October 28, 2016).

Forbes Global 2000 (2015) *The World's Biggest Public Companies*, www.forbes.com/ global2000/list/ (accessed November 11, 2015).

Fortune (2015) *Fortune Global 500*, http://fortune.com/global500/ (accessed November 11, 2015).

Friedman, T. (2000) *The Lexus and the Olive Tree*, revised ed. (London: Harper Collins).

Fuchs, D. (2007) *Business Power in Global Governance* (Boulder: Lynne Rienner Publishers).

Hajer, M. (1997) *The Politics of Environmental Discourse: Ecological Modernization and the Policy Process* (Oxford: Clarendon).

Hall, P.A. and D.W. Gingerich (2009) 'Varieties of Capitalism and Institutional Complementarities in the Political Economy', *British Journal of Political Science* 39(3), pp. 449–482.

Hall, P.A. and D. Soskice (2001) 'An Introduction to Varieties of Capitalism', in P.A. Hall and D. Soskice (eds.) *Varieties of Capitalism: The Institutional Foundations of Comparative Advantage* (Oxford: Oxford University Press).

Harrod, J. (2006) 'The Century of the Corporation', in C. May (ed.) *Global Corporate Power* (Boulder: Lynne Rienner Publishers).

Hay, C. and D. Marsh (2000) 'Introduction: Demystifying Globalization', in C. Hay and D. Marsh (eds.) *Demystifying Globalization* (Houndmills Basingstoke: Palgrave Macmillan).

IMF (2015) *World Economic Outlook Database: April 2015Edition*, www.imf.org/external/ pubs/ft/weo/2015/01/weodata/index.aspx (accessed January 12, 2016).

Kahancová, M. (2007) *Corporate Values in Local Contexts: Work Systems and Workers' Welfare in Western and Eastern Europe*, Max Planck Institute for the Study of Societies, MPIfG Working Paper 07/1.

Kelly, D. and T.L. Amburgey (1991) 'Organizational Inertia and Momentum: A Dynamic Model of Strategic Change', *Academy of Management Journal* 34(3), pp. 591–612.

Korten, D. (2015) *When Corporations Rule the World*, 3rd ed. (Oakland: Berrett-Koehler Publishers).

Levitt, T. (1983) 'The Globalization of Markets', *Harvard Business Review* 61(3), pp. 92–102.

Levy, D.L. and P.J. Newell (2002) 'Business Strategy and International Environmental Governance: Towards a Neo-Gramscian Synthesis', *Global Environmental Politics* 2(4), pp. 84–101.

Lindblom, C. (1977) *Politics and Markets* (New York: Basic).

Martell, L. (2007) 'The Third Wave in Globalization Theory', *International Studies Review* 9(2), pp. 173–196.

Micklethwait, J. and A. Wooldridge (2003) *The Company: A Short History of a Revolutionary Idea* (London: Phoenix).

Miller, D. and M.J. Chen (1994) 'Sources and Consequences of Competitive Inertia: A Study of the US Airline Industry', *Administrative Science Quarterly* 39(1), pp. 1–23.

Nolan, P., D. Sutherland and J. Zhang (2002) 'The Challenge of the Global Business Revolution', *Contributions to Political Economy* 21(1), pp. 91–110.

Nölke, A. (ed.) (2013) *Multinational Corporations from Emerging Markets Economies: State Capitalism 3.0* (Houndmills Basingstoke: Palgrave Macmillan).

Rugman, A. (2000) *The End of Globalization* (London: Random House Business Books).

Rugman, A. and A. Verbeke (2009) 'Location, Competitiveness, and the Multinational Enterprise', in A. Rugman (ed.) *The Oxford Handbook of International Business*, 2nd ed. (Oxford: Oxford University Press).

Staples, C.L. (2007) 'Board Globalisation in the World's Largest TNCs 1993-2005', *Corporate Governance* 15(2), pp. 311–321.

Strange, S. (1996) *The Retreat of the State: The Diffusion of Power in the World Economy* (Cambridge: Cambridge University Press).

Tienhaara, K. (2014) 'Corporations: Business and Industrial Influence', in P.G. Harris (ed.) *Routledge Handbook of Global Environmental Politics* (Abingdon: Routledge).

UNCTAD (2011) *World Investment Report 2011*, Web Table 34: Number of Parent Corporations and Foreign Affiliates, by Region and Economy 2010, http://unctad.org/Sections/dite_dir/docs/WIR11_web%20tab%2034.pdf (accessed July 20, 2015).

UNCTAD (2014) *World Investment Report 2014*, Web Table 28: The World's Top 100 Non-Financial TNCs, Ranked by Foreign Assets 2013, http://unctad.org/Sections/dite_dir/docs/WIR2014/WIR14_tab28.xls (accessed October 20, 2015).

United Nations (2012) *Regular Budget 2012–2013*, www.un.org/en/hq/dm/pdfs/oppba/Regular%20Budget.pdf (accessed March 9, 2016).

Wade, R. (1996) 'Globalisation and its Limits: Reports of the Death of the National Economy Are Greatly Exaggerated', in S. Berger and R. Dore (eds.) *National Diversity and Global Capitalism* (Ithaca: Cornell University Press).

Wade, R. (2010) 'Is the Globalization Consensus Dead?', *Antipode* 41(1), pp. 141–165.

Walter, A. and X. Zhang (eds.) (2012) *East Asian Capitalism: Diversity, Continuity and Change* (Oxford: Oxford University Press).

World Bank (2016) *Gross Domestic Product 2015*, World Development Indicator Database, 11 October, http://databank.worldbank.org/data/download/GDP.pdf (accessed November 1, 2016).

WTO (2016) 'WTO Secretariat Budget for 2013–14', *The WTO: Secretariat and Budget*, www.wto.org/english/thewto_e/secre_e/budget_e.htm (accessed January 15, 2016).

Xia, J., K. Boal and D. Delios (2009) 'When Experience Meets National Institutional Environmental Change: Foreign Entry Attempts of US Firms in the Central and Eastern European Region', *Strategic Management Journal* 30(12), pp. 1286–1309.

Part III

Transnational challenges

Chapter 17

Global environmental politics

Sustainable development, climate change and the energy dilemma

Sarah Cohen

FIGURE 17.1 Flooding caused by Hurricane Sandy in New York City, US

Humans have always utilised the Earth's resources to sustain life. Whilst many have an idealised view of the past, the negative impacts of human development have long been evident resulting in consequences such as the loss of species, minerals and pollution. However, the advent of mass industrialisation in the 19th century exacerbated many of these damaging effects. The 20th century saw exponential population growth and continued rapid expansion of industry. Over this period the detrimental impact of human development on the environment became even more apparent. Concerns about pollution and resource scarcity in the 1960s and 1970s led to debates about the 'environment' becoming truly multidisciplinary encompassing, but not restricted to, politics, philosophy, law, geography, economics and the natural sciences.

This chapter focuses on the relationship between global environmental politics and environmental problems. It explores how this relationship has evolved over the last 50 years, the period in which the environment has been recognised as a distinct policy area and when there has been acceptance that many environmental problems are not just of local, or even national, concern. The recognition that the negative impacts of human development are transnational has created some unique challenges for politics and the question of how to find ways to address *global* environmental problems has occupied the attention of scholars and policymakers alike.

Global environmental politics is conventionally understood to have evolved over the past 50 years. There have been major debates about the nature and extent of environmental problems, which actors should be charged with dealing with them and how they should tackle them. Initially there was a clash of ideas between those advocating dealing with environmental problems by limiting economic and population growth and those who questioned whether such drastic action was really needed. When governments accepted that they needed to do something about environmental problems this largely meant individual states creating departments and developing regulation. With this 'traditional nation state' approach, if problems crossed borders, states would create bilateral agreements. However, it was increasingly recognised that this approach would not work because the problems were often global in nature requiring greater international cooperation. These challenges needed a different approach and the answer lay in the concept of *sustainable development* which defined much of the debate in the latter part of the 20th century. Sustainable development recognised the link between economic growth and environmental degradation and advocated involving new actors and finding new mechanisms to facilitate sustainable growth which would alleviate global poverty and inequality.

Sustainable development emerged alongside the changes in the role of government associated with the growth of neo-liberal ideology after the 1980s. Scholars have described these changes in debates about governance which were taking place within nation states, and at international and subnational levels of government (Rhodes, 1997; Rosenau, 1992; Hooghe and Marks, 2001; Finkelstein, 1995). By the end of the 20th century the term Global Environmental Governance (GEG) became prominent and, despite some variation in usage, is now widely used to describe the change in approach to governing global environmental problems (Dauvergne and Clapp, 2016; Biermann and Pattberg, 2008). The GEG narrative of increasing actors (state and non-state) and more informal and networked solutions with overlapping tools provides an effective framework for understanding the development of global environmental politics. More recently, as scientific evidence has increased, there has also been a shift from general concerns about pollution and resource scarcity towards a new focus on the huge challenges posed by climate change (Dauvergne and Clapp, 2016). The attempts to address climate change have resulted in renewed attention on the relationship between economic development and energy needs which highlight many of the tensions from the earlier sustainable development debates; and how to resolve issues of growth and individual nation state goals with global long-term interests.

This chapter provides insight into the progress made in how global environmental problems have been addressed by reviewing three areas: the development of sustainable development, the problem of climate change and the energy dilemma. In each area it is claimed that there has been a shift from a traditional nation state government approach with standard command and control tools towards GEG with more international agreements, more actors and different ways to implement the necessary changes. However, assessment of these claims shows that we remain a long way from finding successful ways to address global environmental problems and tensions continue between the industrialised West, which has benefitted from unsustainable growth practices, and developing nations, which still seek their own path to economic development. GEG has led to the inclusion of more actors but this has largely meant greater private sector involvement and the focus for solutions on supporting innovation and new technology. The narrowness of this approach fails to recognise the complex relationship between humankind and the planet and enables the continued dominance of the industrialised West over the Global South.

Sustainable development

In 1962 Rachael Carson's *Silent Spring* detailed the growing scientific evidence which helped draw political and public attention of the detrimental impact of human activity on the environment. Concerns about pollution inspired the environmental movement and drew a political response as governments began to recognise the environment as a policy area in its own right. The initial reactions saw the introduction of legislation primarily to address pollution concerns (clean air, water and pesticide use) and institutional changes (1970 saw the first UK Department of the Environment and the establishment of the US Environmental Protection Agency). Environmental pressure groups formed such as Friends of the Earth (1969), Greenpeace (1971) and explicitly 'green' political parties were established around the world. The emergence of the zero growth school of thought, typified by Paul Ehrlich's (1968) *The Population Bomb* and Meadows et al. (1972) *The Limits to Growth* fuelled a wider debate on how environmental problems were to be dealt with by an industrial society.

The most enduring contribution to this debate was Garrett Hardin's (1968) article 'The Tragedy of the Commons', which provided a widely accepted argument for why technological solutions were not sufficient for certain types of problems as they lead to free riding and overuse of resources. Hardin's main concern was population growth but he recognised other 'no technical solution problems' including pollution. Hardin identified the reasons why individual decision making and self-interest are unlikely to result in optimum outcomes for society even in the face of pressing evidence. The problem is market failure, notably of negative externalities, which mean that private costs are less than social costs (Pigou, 1920). Hardin argues that the answer lies in regulation to coerce and, controversially, to recognise that there is a necessity to limit the freedom to choose. The solution advocated by environmental economists was to internalise the environmental costs of production and consumption, namely waste and pollution, in order for the market to work more effectively (Baumol and Oates, 1975).

In the natural sciences, ecologists turned their attention to improving the understanding of complex ecosystems. Resulting knowledge of sustainable yields and carrying capacity helped identify the limits of the Earth's resources to support life. The recognition of which underpinned the 1980 World Conservation Strategy which introduced the concept of sustainable development (IUCN, 1980). The 1987 World Commission on Environment and Development (WCED) publication *Our Common Future* (commonly known as the Brundtland Report) provided the most influential definition of sustainable development as 'development that meets the needs of the present without compromising the ability of future generations to meet their own needs' (WCED, 1987, p. 43). The task the WCED undertook was to formulate 'a global agenda for change' (ibid., p. ix) and to find ways to address environmental concerns to ensure that everyone had the opportunity for prosperity and security.

The Brundtland Report acknowledged that economic growth brings the risk of environmental damage and accepted that there were limits to growth as determined by the planet's capacity to sustain human development. However, it also argued that economic growth was necessary because it was the key to alleviating poverty and so should not be limited but rather needed to be managed and delivering sustainable development would require a change in approach by governments. The Brundtland Report argued for a framework of international agreements, nation state cooperation, stronger local government and greater public participation to integrate economic and environmental concerns (WCED, 1987, pp. 63–64).

The concept of sustainable development was further established at the 1992 the UN Conference on Environment and Development (the Earth Summit) in Rio which marked a milestone in obtaining international agreement with delegates committing to deliver sustainable development through the Agenda 21 program. This required nation states to devise their own national and local action plans, identifying policies and processes to achieve sustainable development. The Rio Earth Summit also agreed on 27 principles to deliver sustainable development (United Nations, 1992). As a normative concept sustainable development, as defined by the Brundtland Report and the Rio Earth Summit, provided a framework for addressing global environmental problems and the inequalities between the North and South through sustainable economic growth. It was also a more palatable way forward which helped its wide acceptance by Western governments, business and (some) environmentalists and citizens. However, the Rio Earth Summit also sparked further debate about what sustainable development really meant as it became clear that as a concept it could be interpreted in many different ways. Economists distinguished a spectrum from weak to strong sustainability, differentiated by disagreements over how much attention should be paid to environmental capital as special in its own right and whether the environment's role was an adjunct to economic growth or more fundamental precondition to economic and social wellbeing (Pearce, 1993, pp. 15–19).

The concept of sustainable development is also criticised as being anthropocentric, human-centred, with an argument that growth should be measured in qualitative terms with equal value awarded to human and non-human life (Dobson, 2007). The attempts to classify the interpretations of sustainable development highlight different approaches to measuring growth, but also philosophical differences, which reveal diverse perspectives on the environment's role for society and policymaking (Baker, 2006, p. 28).

The spirit of governance can be seen in the early sustainable development debates, particularly in respect of recognising the need to include actors beyond the formal state and that operate at different spatial levels to address global challenges. However, the wider economic and political environment has influenced the development of this new approach. The neo-liberal ideology of the 1980s conflicted with traditional nation state interventions to dealing with environmental problems with resistance to solutions that affected the market and imposed additional costs to business. Sustainable development, as defined by the Brundtland Report, found synergies between the economy, environmental and social objectives rather than arguing for limits to growth. This provided support for Ecological Modernisation (EM) Theory, which argued that economic and environmental goals could be achieved together and called for changes in state-market relations to deal with the environmental crisis (Mol, 1996; Mol and Janicke, 2009). EM emphasised exploring new policy measures, integrating environmental policy into areas which previously neglected the environment and, importantly, the innovation and diffusion of new technology which is environmentally friendly and more efficient, thereby solving environmental problems and benefitting business (Gouldson and Murphy, 1996). The approach advocated by EM has influenced the sustainable development agenda, for example, the EU has a commitment to sustainable development in its rhetoric but in practice this has been implemented through an EM approach based on the principle of environmental policy integration (Baker, 2007).

International agreements have played a key role in leading the way to address global environmental problems, with the UN central to the commitment to deliver sustainable development (Baker, 2006, p. 54). The core themes from Brundtland and Rio have been reinforced in other international agreements from the Millennium Development Goals in 2000, the 2002 World Summit on Sustainable Development (Rio+10), the World Bank's *Inclusive Green Growth* (2012) and the UN's 2030 Agenda for Sustainable Development (2015). Such agreements have largely sought to establish formal targets and, influenced by EM, there is a continued focus on new technology as key to delivering sustainable development. There are criticisms of the progress made. Even the UN recognises that more needs to be done to deliver the goals of sustainable development (United Nations, 2002). The Millennium Ecosystem Assessment (2005) found that the degradation to ecosystems has continued since 1960. International agreements are negotiated by nation states and many times efforts have been thwarted by powerful state players who defend their own interests which undermine solutions for global environmental problems.

Addressing the collective action challenges identified by Hardin (1968) remains a key issue for GEG. The recent UN 2015 Agenda promised to deliver sustainability through a 'revitalised global partnership' with 17 Sustainable Development Goals (SDG) and 169 targets. There is some hope that this 'novel approach' of global governance by goal setting may succeed (Biermann et al., 2017). In 2016, for the first time, the World Bank's World Development Indicators included reference to the UN's global goal to promote sustainability and the SDGs. However, the implementation of agreements remains at national and subnational levels. The use of regulation continues and, whilst increased participation of citizens is encouraged, it is the relationship with industry which is key as governments have turned towards using voluntary agreements and market-based solutions such as eco-taxes and trading schemes to promote improvements in environmental protection. Questions remain as to whether this approach will succeed in delivering sustainable development (Paterson, 2009).

Climate change

Knowledge of our climate and how it is influenced by greenhouse gases (GHG) goes back over 200 years to the mid-19th century debates culminating with John Tyndall's 1859 paper which laid the basis for understanding the greenhouse effect (in Hulme, 2009). In the 20th century scientists looking to explain the fluctuations in Earth's temperature, particularly in the post-industrial period, pointed to the increased GHG being the cause of temperature rises. As concerns grew, in 1988 the UN's Environment Program (UNEP), together with the World Meteorological Organisation, formed the Intergovernmental Panel on Climate Change (IPCC). The main aim of the IPCC was to review and assess the scientific research and publish the evidence with the goal of finding solutions for what most scientists concluded was a man-made problem. The first report of the IPCC in 1990 confirmed the link between human activity and climate change. With scientific evidence mounting it was recognised that this global problem needed a global solution and international cooperation became the focus of attention. In 1992 over 150 countries signed up to the United Nations Framework Convention on Climate Change at the Rio Earth Summit. Key to the agreement was the principle of 'common but differentiated responsibility' which acknowledged that, whilst everyone has responsibility to protect the environment, the industrialised countries had gained their economic growth through methods which had resulted in high GHG emissions and the resulting negative consequences. Developing countries would need support to grow in a more sustainable manner. The Precautionary Principle, which states that scientific uncertainty cannot be used to stop measures to prevent environmental degradation, was also important given the nature of scientific uncertainty about the causes and particularly the likely impacts of climate change. This uncertainty has contributed to the continued opposition to any solutions which suggest that there should be limits to economic growth.

After Rio, international negotiations continued with regular Conferences of the Parties (COP) and in 1997 the Kyoto Protocol (COP3) saw developed countries agree to reduce their GHG emissions by 5.2 per cent against a 1990 baseline. However, negotiations were difficult and many criticised the final agreement as weak. The US refused to ratify the treaty. Russia and Australia also delayed (Kyoto was not implemented until 2004, when Russia signed to meet the threshold to enact it). After 2000, increased scientific knowledge led to more consensus on the cause of the problem, namely human activity, which was reflected in the IPCC reports of 2001 and 2007. Other events, such as the devastation caused by Hurricane Katrina 2005, saw climate change recognised beyond the scientific community. In 2006 Al Gore's *An Inconvenient Truth* reached a wide audience and in the UK the Stern Review (2006) highlighted the economic cost of taking action later rather than sooner. In 2006 the IPCC and Al Gore shared the Nobel Peace Prize for raising awareness of climate change and in 2007 climate change was high on the agenda for discussion for political and business leaders at the World Economic Forum (Davos) in Switzerland.

Although 2006 appeared to mark a turning point in recognition of climate change, actions did not follow. Hopes were high that the 2009 Copenhagen Climate Conference would result in a framework to mitigate climate change post-2012. However, in the end the outcome was disappointing. Despite widespread acceptance of the evidence, questions remained about who was responsible and crucially who should pay. China as a 'developing country' had not been part of the 1997 Kyoto agreement, but by 2009 was the biggest emitter of GHG. The US never ratified Kyoto and was second biggest GHG producer. However, some countries, particularly low-lying countries such as Bangladesh and the Maldives, were beginning to see the impact of climate change. They demanded action and wanted those who had caused the problems to pay. When world leaders arrived in Copenhagen, there was no agreement to sign. It was left to the US President Barack Obama and Chinese Premier Wen Jiabao to broker a deal to rescue the talks (Giddens, 2011, pp. 190–192).

Agreements were reached to limit global temperature increases to no more than 2 degrees Celsius above pre-industrial levels and to reduce emissions. However, there was no legally binding commitment. Progress continued slowly; the Cancun (2010) and Durban (2011) Climate Conferences reaffirmed commitments to reduce emissions and support developing countries. However, the turning point came at the Paris Climate Conference (2015) which at last saw a legally binding agreement reached. With the US and China on board, targets were set to limit warming to below 2 degrees Celsius with financial arrangements in place to support developing countries and a more rigorous monitoring of progress. The most significant success was that the treaty was quickly ratified by the required 55 per cent of countries for it to enter into force before the end of 2016.

Alongside the UN, the European Union has taken a lead on addressing climate change. From the early commitment to reducing CO_2 emissions in 1991, the EU has recognised the challenge of agreeing to reductions and finding ways to achieve them together with its obligation to developing countries (Giddens, 2011, p. 195). The first EU Climate Change Program in 2000 worked with a variety of stakeholders including member states, industry and environment groups to find ways to implement the Kyoto targets to reduce emissions. The second program in 2005 continued this work and in 2010 Directorate-General for Climate Action was created. The two main tools for action have been the setting and monitoring of emission targets and schemes encouraging innovation, particularly around energy efficiency (Giddens, 2011, p. 195).

In 2005 the European Emissions Trading Scheme (ETS) was established, which became the world's biggest carbon trading scheme (Stern, 2009). This market-based initiative set overall caps for emissions and companies that signed up were allocated a specific allowance for each tonne of carbon released. If they limited their carbon emissions they could trade their allowances; if they exceeded them they had to buy more allowances. Some success can be claimed as it introduced regulation, via a market, to carbon emissions, a previously unregulated commodity and, by setting upper limits, provides a way to meet climate change targets through introducing price created incentives and costs to produce the necessary outcomes. However, the scheme has been beset by problems and behavioural change has been limited, not least because too low a price was set with too many allowances available (Stern, 2009). Debates about reform of the EU ETS scheme continue (Grosjean et al., 2016). Despite the flaws, reformed versions of trading schemes remain part of the strategy to tackle climate change.

The 21st century has seen increased acceptance by politicians, businesses and citizens that climate change is a challenge for humankind. However, there remain debates about who is to blame and scepticism about some of the predicted catastrophic consequences (Lomborg, 2001). International agreements have committed to reducing GHG emissions but have been consumed with difficulties as nation states battle to protect their own interests. The emission of GHG can be understood as an example of market failure (Stern, 2009, p. 11). Proposed solutions adopt an EM approach with a focus on target setting to be largely achieved through market-based approaches such as trading schemes and encouraging technological innovation.

President Obama hailed the 2015 Paris Agreement as a turning point for global action on climate change. However, the election of President Trump highlights the fragility of international agreements and the continued power of nation states. President Trump was explicit in his promise to prioritise American jobs and in his actions, including the appointment of a renowned climate change sceptic to the Environmental Protection Agency and withdrawal from the Paris Agreement, which threatens the progress made. In contrast, China has recognised the negative impact of economic growth on its own environment and has committed to a program to bring 'blue skies' back to Beijing, thereby taking the political advantage if it becomes a global leader on climate change.

The energy dilemma

The energy dilemma refers to the question of whether we can have 'secure, affordable, and equitable supplies of energy that are also environmentally benign' (Bradshaw, 2014, p. 1). The early environmental debates in the 1960s and 70s raised questions about our ability to sustain economic and population growth and identified the problems specifically surrounding energy. The two key concerns were the detrimental environmental impacts of resource extraction and production together with the long-term sustainability of relying on resources, particularly on fossil fuels (oil, gas and coal), for future energy needs (Meadows et al., 1972). These concerns provided the impetus for the debate around sustainability and further research into how much natural resources were left, with evidence proving the short-term 'doom and gloom' predictions incorrect. This took much heat out of the debate with one consequence being that the political aspect of the energy debate has been neglected (Hughes and Lipsey, 2013). However, worries remain about the longer term sustainability of fossil fuels, with current estimates suggesting production will peak in the next half century (Maggio and Cacciola, 2012).

It is also generally accepted that economic development leads to higher energy consumption and post 2000 the scientific community has provided more evidence of the negative environmental impact of not only energy extraction and production but also of energy consumption. In 2006, 83 per cent of global energy supply came from oil, coal and gas and the use of fossil fuels as an energy source makes a considerable contribution to GHG emissions a trend which will continue particularly in the light of growing energy demands from China and India (IEA, 2008). The link between energy, climate change and development may reignite the politics of energy debate.

Since 2000 the priorities for the energy policy have shifted as governments have moved from maintaining supply and controlling prices to addressing energy supply and demand concerns to meet their emission targets required by international climate change agreements such as the Kyoto Protocol. However, the challenges of dealing with environmental concerns are compounded when addressing the energy sector with its multiple objectives and market failures (Helm, 2005). Private energy production is largely in the hands of a few multinational corporations (including Exxon Mobil, Royal Dutch Shell and BP) and the market is dominated by a few powerful state actors (including the US, UAE and Kuwait) who regulate supply. The energy sector has also been guided by OPEC (Organisation of Petroleum Exporting Countries) which coordinates supply and thus price and the distribution of return on investment and on the consumer side, the International Energy Agency (IEA). National governments have been limited to looking towards how to regulate the market through the standard market instruments and attempt diplomacy to smooth cross-national relations (Hughes and Lipsey, 2013). The energy sector is also associated with high costs and long lifespan of projects which further constrain national political decision making. This past has produced variations in different countries in infrastructure provision and each country has its own institutional legacy which needs to be taken into account in any attempts to reduce GHG emissions (Helm, 2005).

Finally, consumers of energy also have conflicting objectives; most want low cost energy but there is increased recognition of the need for cleaner and sustainable energy sources and in the longer term higher prices would ensure energy security (Hughes and Lipsey, 2013). The characteristics of energy production and consumption mean that a wide range of actors have a stake in energy policy, from individuals and interest groups to governments and business with different objectives (Helm, 2005). There are problems of competing national interests and cross-national differences in energy policy together with the interests of energy firms themselves. Governments need to balance different goals of meeting climate change target agreements whilst protecting national interests by ensuring energy security (often managed through the private sector) and protecting jobs. In addition, there has been a longstanding tension between the nuclear industry and environmental groups, which has influenced government policy (Hughes and Lipsey, 2013). Energy supply and demand has become a political, and ideological, issue with governments aware that meeting climate change targets will require not only cooperation from energy companies but also subnational levels of government, businesses and citizens themselves.

The relationship between human development, energy and climate change is complex. The IPCC uses the Kaya Identity, which focuses on four elements – carbon intensity, energy intensity, GDP per capita and population – in its emission forecast scenarios. This helps explain why energy is so important in addressing climate change as governments' focus is primarily on how to influence energy policy (Bradshaw, 2014, pp. 19–20). The traditional nation state responses to delivering climate change obligations have been to use legislation to set emission targets and provide support for improvements in energy efficiency and the development of different energy sources. This has largely been done by using market-based initiatives to incentivise or control the direction of investment, to develop renewable sources of energy, namely solar and wind, and encourage consumers to change behaviour. However, private energy actors remain dominant and domestic measures which seek to influence energy demand and energy conservation have been resisted in some countries who are large energy producers such as the US (Hughes and Lipsey, 2013). Whilst there has been success in improving energy efficiency and some, albeit slow, growth in renewable energy, fossil fuels remain the primary energy source (Bradshaw, 2014, p. 55).

There are some signs of change within the energy sector. The IEA, which was formed in 1974 to help stop disruptions in energy supply, now claims a wider remit to ensure the reliable, affordable and clean energy for its members. Its annual *World Energy Outlook* reports have increasingly recognised the role of energy in contributing to climate change and the need for change to move away from fossil fuel sources to ensure the future of humankind; 'what is needed is nothing short of an energy revolution' (IEA, 2008, p. 37). The enormous growth in demand for oil, gas and coal from developing countries, such as China and India, has increased the concerns (IEA, 2008, 2016). China has itself acknowledged the environmental costs of its economic growth and has turned its attention to searching for cleaner forms of energy in the form of renewables and nuclear power. The 2016 IEA report examined the 'new era' opened up by the Paris Agreement and its projections to 2040 reflected the change to global renewable energy. However, the report also highlights that many people will still be left behind relying on basic solid biomass for cooking (IEA, 2016). However, the IEA has no formal policymaking powers and in contrast, OPEC maintains its defence of the interests of oil-producing members. Despite the pressures, the traditional governance of an energy system dominated by fossil fuel continues to prevail (Bradshaw, 2014, p. 189).

Governments now have an increased role in managing the energy sector, although the extent of this depends on nation state structures as to how much they can influence individual decision making on energy production and consumption. The number of actors involved has expanded as interest groups with stakes in renewable sources and those concerned with environmental impacts of fossil fuel have joined forces. Consumers also play a part as they are not just self-interested individuals but share concerns about the impact on the environment and can exert some pressure on governments and business. However, the key actors remain private companies and a handful of nation state producers and the conflict in interests continues to challenge energy policy. Persuading people to consume less energy, or pay more for sustainable sources, involves a multifaceted approach raising awareness of the environmental consequences and the need to mitigate and improve energy security. The multiple objectives of the energy sector remain and the challenge of how to convince private energy companies and nation states to act in the best interests of all before it is too late.

Conclusion

There have been many developments in global environmental politics over the last 50 years as the impacts of human development on the environment have been recognised. As our knowledge and understanding of complex ecosystems and our relationship with the natural environment have grown, many have recognised the enormity of the challenges we face. However, questions about the consequences and extent of our impact remain and we continue to search for ways to govern which will deliver satisfactory mechanisms to deal with the problems. Global environmental politics has driven, and been driven by, wider political developments. For politicians and business leaders, sustainable development resolves the question of whether growth needs to be limited, with the view that alleviating poverty and environmental degradation need to be tackled together. This requires a fundamental rethinking of the way in which global problems are addressed at every level of government. This rhetoric of sustainable development now dominates the international political arena.

Towards the end of the 20th century, consensus developed that climate change was a significant challenge for humankind. However, just as the severity of the problems was being acknowledged, the economic crisis emerged, which saw a return to economic priorities independent of the environment. The subsequent recession led many governments to revert to traditional economic models of behaviour. Climate change campaigners have continued to draw attention to an increasing body of evidence, keeping it on the political agenda. The impacts of rising temperatures are being felt ever more sharply and even some businesses, notably insurance companies, are seeing the costs of not acting. Paris COP21 (2015) might be seen as a turning point for agreement and action as all the powerful nation state actors committed to the agreement. However, the viability of such agreements remains in the hands of nation state actors.

The energy dilemma has become increasingly intertwined with international and nation state commitments to address climate change by agreeing limits to GHG emissions. However, the key actors for the energy sector, such as OPEC, multinational companies and nation state producers, remain largely focused on supply and return on investment. This makes implementation of agreements at the domestic level difficult as governments are constrained by what they can do to influence the change needed. The main approach is to encourage technological change through market-based instruments, such as the EU ETS, giving industry a central role. Supporting innovation to achieve these changes, such as developing renewable energy sources, requires significant investment. This has to come either from persuading business to invest or from public spending. Given these dilemmas, the governance structures surrounding the energy sector are still in need of improvement to address the complex environmental problems.

The argument that environmental and economic objectives can be achieved together underpins the evolution of Global Environmental Governance. International cooperation and agreements are key but the nature of global problems led to the emergence of the view that a new approach with new actors and different mechanisms were needed to address the problems. Some of this has been realised with new actors now part of the process from the inclusion of the scientific community and citizens who are encouraged to participate in making decisions about their own communities. The 'new actors' are largely economic, from the private sector, and the 'new mechanisms' are usually market-based initiatives, notably to incentivise the development of new technology. Yet much remains in the hands of nation state actors driving international agreements, with dynamics dominated by the power relations between them. There may be more actors but traditional ones remain powerful.

Global Environmental Governance has a normative aspect where it is presented as the answer to address the inadequacies of previous attempts to deal with global problems (Biermann and Pattberg, 2008; Pattberg and Zelli, 2015). However, the early debates around governance also raised concerns about the loss of nation state power to new actors across different spatial levels and problems arising from more fragmented and less transparent decision-making processes (Rhodes, 1997). These problems have been recognised within more recent debates as the increased range of actors may have led to some new initiatives but has also led to a more fragmented political environment. Nation states retain much power but they have devolved implementation to the private sector, which raises some questions about the authority, legitimacy and accountability of private actors. There is a view that such measures should complement not replace government regulations and enforcement (Dauvergne and Clapp, 2016). Whilst there have been changes, the question remains whether there really has been a move towards governance (from government). To what extent has this really happened? It is clear that the words 'sustainable development' appear across the political spectrum and since 2000 governance is increasingly referred to as a way to approach global problems. However, beyond this rhetoric it is not clear that much has changed in respect to delivering the outcomes of sustainable development.

Further reading

Baker, Susan (2006) *Sustainable Development* (Abingdon: Routledge).
Dauvergne, Peter (2012) 'Research trends in Global Environmental Politics', in Dauvergne, Peter (ed.) *Handbook of Global Environmental Politics*, 2nd ed. (Cheltenham: Edward Elgar).

Giddens, Anthony (2011) *The Politics of Climate Change*, 2nd ed. (Cambridge: Polity).

Mol, Arthur P.J., David Sonnenfeld and Gert Spaargaren (2009) *The Ecological Modernisation Reader: Environmental Reform in Theory and Practice* (London, Routledge).

Pattberg, Philipp H. and Zelli Fariborz (eds.) (2015) *Encyclopaedia of Global Environmental Governance* (Cheltenham: Edward Elgar).

Scoones, Ian (2016) 'The Politics of Sustainability and Development', *Annual Review Environmental Resources* 41, pp. 293–319.

Vatn, Arild (2015) 'Global Environmental Governance', in Martinez-Alier, Joan and Roldan Muradian Roldan (eds.) *Handbook of Ecological Economics* (Cheltenham: Edward Elgar), pp. 382–412.

Bibliography

Adger, William Neil and Andrew Jordan (eds.) (2009) *Governing Sustainability* (Cambridge: Cambridge University Press).

Baker, Susan (2006) *Sustainable Development* (Abingdon: Routledge).

Baker, Susan (2007) 'Sustainable development as Symbolic Commitment: Declaratory Politics and the Seductive Appeal of Ecological Modernisation in the European Union 16', *Environmental Politics* (2), pp. 297–317.

Baumol, William J. and Wallace E. Oates (1975) *The Theory of Environmental Policy* (Cambridge: Cambridge University Press).

Biermann, Frank, Norichika Kanie and Rakhyun E. Kim (2017) 'Global Governance by Goal-Setting: The Novel Approach of the UN Sustainable Development Goals', *Current Opinion in Environmental Sustainability* 26–7, pp. 26–31.

Biermann, Frank and Philipp Pattberg (2008) 'Global Environmental Governance: Taking Stock, Moving Forward', *Annual Review of Environment and Resources* 33, pp. 277–294.

Bradshaw, Michael (2014) *Global Energy Dilemmas* (Cambridge: Polity).

Carson, Rachel (1962) *Silent Spring* (London: Penguin).

Dauvergne, Peter and Jennifer Clapp (2016) 'Researching Global Environmental Politics in the 21st Century', *Global Environmental Politics* 16(1), pp. 1–12.

Dobson, Andrew (2007) *Green Political Thought*, 4th ed. (Abingdon: Routledge).

Ehrlich, Paul (1968) *The Population Bomb* (New York: Ballantine).

Finkelstein, Lawrence (1995) 'What is Global Governance?', *Global Governance* 1, pp. 367–372.

Giddens, Anthony (2011) *The Politics of Climate Change*, 2nd ed. (Cambridge: Polity).

Gore, Al (performer) David Guggenheim (director) (2006) *An Inconvenient Truth* (Los Angeles: Lawrence Bender Productions).

Gouldson, Andrew and Joseph Murphy (1996) 'Ecological Modernisation and the European Union', *Geoforum* 27(1), pp. 11–21.

Grosjean, Godefrey et al. (2016) 'After Monetary Policy, Climate Policy: Is Delegation the Key to EU ETS Reform', *Climate Policy* 16(1), pp. 1–25.

Hardin, Garrett (1968) 'The Tragedy of the Commons', *Science* 162(3859), pp. 1243–1248.

Helm, Dieter (2005) 'Climate-Change and Energy Policy', in Dieter Helm (eds.) *Climate-change Policy* (Oxford: Oxford University Press), pp. 322–329.

Hooghe, Liesbet and Gary Marks (2001) *Multi-Level Governance and European Integration* (Oxford: Rowman & Littlefield).

Houghton, John, Geoffrey Jenkins and James Ephraums (eds.) (1990) *Climate Change: IPCC Scientific Assessment* (Cambridge: Cambridge University Press).

Hughes, Llewelyn and Phillip Lipsey (2013) 'The Politics of Energy', *Annual Review of Political Science* 16, pp. 449–469.

Hulme, Mike (2009) 'On the Origin of "the Greenhouse effect": John Tyndall's 1859 Interrogation of Nature', *Royal Meteorological Society* 64(5), pp. 121–123.

International Energy Agency (2008) *World Energy Outlook* (Paris: OECD).

International Energy Agency (2016) *World Energy Outlook* (Paris: OECD).

International Union for Conservation of Nature and Natural Resources (1980) *World Conservation Strategy* (Gland, Switzerland: ICUN-UNEP-WWF).

Lomborg, Bjorn (2001) *The Skeptical Environmentalist* (Cambridge: Cambridge University Press).

Maggio, Gaetano and Gaetano Cacciola (2012) 'When Will Oil, Natural Gas, and Coal Peak?' *Fuel* (98), pp. 111–123.

Meadows, Donella, Dennis Meadows, Jørgen Randers and William Behrens III (1972) *The Limits to Growth* (London: Earth Island).

Millennium Ecosystem Assessment (2005) *Ecosystems and Human Well-Being: Synthesis* (Washington, DC: Island Press).

Mol, Arthur P.J. (1996) 'Ecological Modernisation and Institutional Reflexivity: Environmental Reform in the Late Modern Age', *Environmental Politics* 5(2), pp. 302–323.

Mol, Arthur P.J. and Janicke Martin (2009) 'The Origins and Theoretical Foundations of Ecological Modernisation Theory', in Arthur P.J. Mol, David A. Sonnenfield and Gert Spaargaren (eds.) *The Ecological Modernisation Reader* (London: Routledge).

Paterson, Matthew (2009) 'Global Governance for Sustainable Capitalism? The Political Economy of Global Environmental Governance' in William Neil Adger and Andrew Jordan (eds.) *Governing Sustainability* (Cambridge: Cambridge University Press), pp. 99–122.

Pearce, David (1993) *Blueprint: Measuring Sustainable Development 3* (London: Earthscan).

Pigou, Arthur C. (1920) *The Economics of Welfare* (London: Macmillan).

Rhodes, Rod A.W. (1997) *Understanding Governance* (Buckingham: Open University Press).

Rosenau, James N. (1992) 'Governance, Order, and Change in World Politics', in James N. Rosenau and Ernest-Otto Czempiel (eds.) *Governance without Governance: Order and Change in World Politics* (Cambridge: Cambridge University Press), pp. 1–29.

Stern, Nicholas (2006) *Stern Review on the Economics of Climate Change* (London: HM Government).

Stern, Nicholas (2009) *A Blueprint for a Safer Planet* (London: Bodley Head).

United Nations (1992) *Report of the United Nations Conference on Environment and Development* (New York: United Nations).

United Nations (2002) *Report of the World Summit on Sustainable Development* (New York: United Nations).WCED (1987) *Our Common Future* (Oxford: Oxford University Press).

World Bank (2012) *Inclusive Green Growth: The Pathway to Sustainable Development* (Washington, DC: The World Bank).

Chapter 18

Transnational politics of migration

From states to regimes and agents

Margit Fauser

FIGURE 18.1 NGO activists marching in support of migrants and refugees in Paris, France

The debate on the global migration and refugee 'crisis' (or 'crises') involves many issues: individuals who are fleeing war, violence, poverty, climate change, disaster and discrimination; labour migrants, refugees and unauthorised migrants; children and sometimes those left behind and in need of support from their migrant kin; and circumstances at sites of origin, transit and arrival and the dangers these migrants face, as well as the xenophobic reactions they elicit. Addressing the lack of a comprehensive response to these situations, the former United Nations (UN) Secretary-General Ban Ki-moon criticised the 'crisis of solidarity' displayed by the world community, emphasising that 'we urgently need countries to transcend their national interests and come together in a forceful, global response' (UNHCR, 2016). This has been taken up by the UN member states in their parallel negotiations of the two Global Compacts for Safe, Orderly and Regular Migration and on Refugees, designed to improve the situation for the world's 244 million international migrants and 60 million refugees and displaced persons.

Yet, despite its transboundary and transnational character, international migration is predominantly regarded as a national challenge. This is true of the policy responses that have long shown minimal international or multilateral cooperation (Betts, 2011b), as well as of the theoretical concepts in studies of migration. These concepts tend to take for granted the nation state as a container of social life, the sole regulator of mobility and the predominant unit of analysis – a perspective which has been criticised as methodological nationalism (Wimmer and Glick Schiller, 2003). More recent research has also considered the challenges of our interconnected world and is now focusing on the politics of migration that transcend national boundaries and the state. The regimes of mobility that bring together states, international arrangements and diverse actors, as well as the local and transnational struggles of migrants, have become the objects of vibrant research. These two streams of research are at the heart of this chapter and are addressed in the second and third sections, respectively. The first section explains what migration is and how it is defined, describing in some detail two more recent perspectives – the transnational turn and the mobility turn – that help us better understand contemporary migration. Finally, the concluding remarks briefly discuss the concepts and findings presented here and relate back to the unresolved tension between transnational phenomena and the world of nation states. This chapter focuses predominantly on Europe, which at present is the most attractive destination for international migrants (hosting 30 per cent, or 76 million, of the world's migrants), although Asia is now approaching this status, with 75 million migrants (UN, 2016). Many more movements across the world remain unaccounted for because they elude our current definitions.

Sedentarist concepts, contested mobilities

Much of the research on contemporary mobilities starts with the observation that migration is as old as humanity itself. For several millennia now, humans have engaged in short- and even long-distance movements, have crossed oceans and seas, have settled in distant territories or have led nomadic lives. In the second half of the 20th century, workers and their families, and later refugees and asylum seekers, were the predominant types of migrants (Castles, de Haas and Miller, 2014). Since the turn of the 21st century, students, high-skilled professionals, amenity seekers and mobile retirees, as well as business travellers and tourists, have joined these movements (Sheller and Urry, 2006). At the same time, some 244 million migrants worldwide represent about 3.2 per cent of the global population, a proportion similar to that of the 1960s (3.1 per cent) while the share had decreased over the following decades because the world population was growing faster than the absolute number of international migrants (Czaika and de Haas, 2015, p. 295).

It is therefore hardly surprising that scholars and others still disagree about whether sedentarism or mobility should be considered the norm. Whatever the conclusion, migration research has focused predominantly on human mobility from one place to another and, when it comes to international migration that involves the crossing of state borders, from one country to another. This focus is reflected in the current notion of migration. In early 20th century, Chicago sociologist Robert E. Park wrote, 'Migration is not, however, to be identified with mere movement. It is at the very least change of residence and the breaking of home ties' (Park, 1928, pp. 888–889). This view extends to the assumption that geographical relocation is accompanied by social and cultural reorientation, or assimilation. Today, the globally shared definition of 'international migrant' is someone who is living in a country other than his or her country of birth. To count someone as an international migrant, most statistics stipulate a minimum residency of one year. Those who stay outside their home country for a period of less than five years are considered 'temporary migrants', and sometimes a lower threshold of length of stay is applied. In this vein, many policy programs target either permanent emigration and resettlement (particularly in the US, Australia and Canada) or temporary migration and return, such as in the classical guest-worker schemes in Germany and other European countries (from the 1950s to the early 1970s) and the Bracero Program signed between the US and Mexico (1942–1964), as well as many other schemes in place around the world today (Castles et al., 2014).

Other programs designed to address the root causes and source regions of migration through international development aid are aimed at 'keeping people in their place' (Bakewell, 2007). Even in the context of the recent migration-development debate that welcomes migrants' monetary remittances, skills transfer and transnational networks, development agencies tend to adhere to this 'sedentarist' philosophy. Thus, from the perspectives of the immigration and emigration countries, and based on migration and international and development policies, and sometimes their study, migration is something to be stopped, controlled or at least tightly regulated, favouring settlement over mobility.

Two newer perspectives offer critiques of the sedentarist bias articulated in these predominating concepts. The first is the *transnational perspective* in migration research that emerged in the early 1990s. It emphasises a more dynamic and multidirectional understanding of migration and puts at its centre the continued role of migrants' homeland ties and, more generally, of cross-border interconnectivity (Glick Schiller et al., 1992; Faist et al., 2013).

Corresponding to the global flows of money, goods and ideas, this perspective considers the mobility of people within the framework of globalisation, which has been greatly facilitated by advances in communication and travel and has been shaped by increased global power asymmetries. In this context the monetary, skill and knowledge flows across state borders, as well as the exchange of ideas, emotions and information and of support and care, are crucial to the everyday experiences of those who left and those who stayed behind, of migrants and of non-migrants, across the world. This perspective shows that individuals and families, social groups, communities and organisations operate beyond the exclusive confines of sovereign nation states. Through these processes migrants are simultaneously connected to two or more places, societies and polities. Because they participate in and influence economic, political and cultural changes in more than one place, they are also influenced by the structural conditions and policy regulations on a variety of scales and in a variety of places, including the immigration and the emigration countries, regional spaces such as the European Union (EU) or the North American Free Trade Agreement (NAFTA), and other global arrangements.

The second perspective, the new *mobility paradigm*, suggests that the diversity of the current spatial movements be considered a constitutive element of contemporary global society. On the one hand, this new paradigm directs attention to movement, also meant as a critique of the social sciences that have been 'amobile' (Sheller and Urry, 2006, p. 208). Even migration research has generally considered resettlement to mean 'movement from one place to another rather than movement across borders' (Glick Schiller and Salazar, 2013, p. 185). Applying this perspective, scholars have contributed insights into the pathways and trajectories of migrating and being mobile – the forward, backward and onward movements that also put the notion of transit places as a clear-cut concept into question (Collyer, 2007; Schapendonk and Steel, 2014).

On the other hand, and perhaps more widely accepted, is the attention this new paradigm pays to the many different forms of spatial mobility, including the movement of asylum seekers, international students, terrorists, holidaymakers, tourists and backpackers, early retirees and lifestyle migrants, young mobile professionals, prostitutes, humanitarian aid personnel and soldiers (Sheller and Urry, 2006; Gill et al., 2011). Because of the various mobility regimes at work, and because of migrants' own practices and decisions, these flows or categories are not separate but are often interlocking, as will be shown in the next section. A critical approach to mobility suggests that the many different types of mobility should not simply be put into one single indistinguishable framework. Mobility scholars stress that mobility is not the same for everyone and that different forms of mobility and different categories of people are regulated through diverging regimes and are appreciated to varying degrees. In legal frameworks and in public discourse, an implicit, but often also explicit, distinction is made between the 'wanted' high-skilled mobile professional migrants and the 'unwanted' or 'unwelcome' low-skilled, poor or refugee migrants (Shamir, 2005; Sheller and Urry, 2006; Turner, 2007; Faist, 2013). Critical scholars therefore caution against normalising either mobility or stasis; rather, the social mechanisms of differentiation and inequality production that legitimise some movements and delegitimise others should be subjected to careful scrutiny (Faist, 2013).

Interlocking regimes of mobility

According to the notion of national sovereignty, it is the nation state that has the right and ability to control the spatial movement of people. In line with the Universal

Declaration of Human Rights that recognises people's right to leave and return to their own country, most nation states hardly regulate emigration but are greatly concerned with immigration. Yet, despite the transboundary and border-crossing nature of this phenomenon, a global institutional framework to regulate the mobility of people is much less in evidence in contrast to other fields that concern the mobility of money, goods and services (Koslowski, 2011a; Betts, 2011a). Increasingly, however, states are opting for international cooperation in this field. This situation has led to complex changes in the governance of mobilities, which in the eyes of many scholars have turned the state into 'an agent among others' (Tsianos and Karakayali, 2010, p. 376) and resulted in the now widely used notion of 'regime'.

Although migration researchers do not always offer a clear definition of the term, 'regime' generally refers to 'implicit or explicit principles, rules, norms and decision-making procedures' within specific issue areas to which actors, and particularly states, subscribe (see Betts, 2011c, p. 73; Koslowski, 2011b, p. 1). Some critical migration researchers further argue that, rather than investigating in binary terms how the state shapes migrants' trajectories and lives, 'regime' can describe a space for negotiation that involves multiple agents, specifically migrants (Tsianos and Karakayali, 2010).

From a mobility perspective it is important to acknowledge that there is not one but several regimes (Koslowski, 2011b; Glick Schiller and Salazar, 2013). Koslowski (2011b), for example, distinguishes the refuge, labour and travel regimes. If we include a view on migrants' settlement, one additional important issue area needs be considered – namely, the citizenship regime. It is in this issue area where globalisation and global norms have paved the way for some of the most profound changes in national societies. The concept of postnational membership recognises the rights that migrants have acquired outside the boundaries of the nation state. Having its sources in international human rights norms, postnational membership puts resident foreigners almost on a par with national citizens (Soysal, 1994). However, 'civic stratification' is the result of graduated national systems that allocate the degree to which migrants are entitled to residency and to access to employment and social support according to their legal status (Morris, 2003).

Therefore, nationally diverging systems of inequality of rights are in turn complicated by diverse international norms that further contribute to stratification. Whether an individual is a national citizen, is from a regional space that grants some membership rights (as does EU citizenship) or is a labour migrant, refugee or non-authorised resident makes a major difference when it comes to the availability of rights, entitlements and, thus, life chances. However, these categorisations by no means constitute a clear-cut hierarchy (Morris, 2003), and migrants can also move across these categories, as will be illustrated later.

The standards of protection for refugees are regulated relatively clearly. Most countries throughout the world participate in the international refugee regime based on the 1951 Refugee Convention and on the 1967 Protocol Relating to the Status of Refugees. The refugee regime sets basic rules that define who is a refugee – namely, a person fleeing persecution on the grounds of race, religion, nationality or membership in certain social or political groups – and the states' corresponding obligations. Thus, responsibility and status are regulated once a refugee has sought protection in the territory of a particular state. The process of burden-sharing is much less institutionalised when it comes to determining who is responsible for protecting refugees who reach the territories of other states (Betts, 2011c), especially considering that one fourth of the refugees worldwide are hosted in Africa by African states and that UNHCR burden-sharing is a crucial aspect that interplays with other issues such as international security, peace and development. Moreover, the chances of being granted refugee status vary greatly from country to country. Even within the EU, where efforts to harmonise asylum policies and procedures have been under way for more than a decade, recognition rates in general and for particular nationalities are considered to be the result of a hardly reliable 'lottery', which means, for example, that in 2014 the recognition rates for Somali asylum applicants were 96 per cent in Italy and 53 per cent in Germany while for Syrians it was 51 per cent in the former and 99 per cent in the latter country (ECRE, 2015).

With regard to labour migration, there is little global or international cooperation, and few global norms exist. The UN Convention on the Protection of the Rights of All Migrant Workers and Members of Their Families (MWC for short) has been ratified by no more than 44 states and, most importantly, not by the major labour-receiving countries (Martin, 2011). Similarly, the conventions on workers' rights of the International Labour Organisation (ILO) have been signed by only a small minority of countries. The General Agreement on Trade in Services (GATS) of the World Trade Organisation (WTO) affects some labour flows, specifically the short-term stays of high-skilled professionals and intra-company transfers. In some regional spaces, labour mobility is facilitated, most extensively within the EU, where there is free movement of workers. However, most regulations apply to EU citizens only. The European Blue Card provides some standards for skilled professionals from non-EU countries, but the migration of low-skilled workers is regulated by the EU member states, as elsewhere. Nevertheless, bilateral agreements, regional frameworks and global norms also address foreign workers' rights, such as non-discrimination or family reunion, which overlap the citizenship regime.

Regulations concerning travel have existed on a global scale for almost a century, especially through customary law and the standardisation of norms on passports meant to facilitate tourist and business travel (Koslowski, 2011c). This area has become highly securitised in recent decades. Organised crime, the increased concern over 'irregular migration' since the 1990s and terrorist attacks (particularly since 9/11) have aligned travel with security considerations. Concerns about border security have in fact resulted in the most far-reaching changes in the diversity of cross-border mobilities. New visa stipulations, readmission agreements with countries of origin, advanced surveillance technologies and biometric identification of passengers, an increase in the number of border guards, cooperation with travel companies through carrier liability, and the fight against people smuggling and human trafficking are some of the more recent measures pursued by national governments and in efforts towards regional and international cooperation, increasingly involving private actors such as air lines (Mau et al., 2012). These measures have reinforced and externalised state borders beyond their territory and their institutional apparatus. This is why most migration research discusses this area within the framework of the border (control) regime.

Institutional regulation, policy and discourse, as well as the agency of migrants, contribute to the interlocking of various forms and regimes of mobility, not least because 'contemporary migration often begins as tourism, study, or temporary work abroad' (Koslowski, 2011b, p. 3; Mau et al., 2012, p. 3). Many more and complex interconnections have important personal implications for opportunities for mobility and life chances. So far this section has only hinted at some of the linkages. We will now provide more detail concerning two specific aspects of such interlocking regimes: (1) the connections between labour migration and refugee migration and (2) the travel–refuge complex that emerges with border securitisation and the fight against 'irregular migration'.

Several newer notions stress the difficulties of clearly distinguishing between (voluntary) labour migrants and forced refugee migrants. 'Mixed migrations' emphasises that today the various types of migrants travel together on the same routes (see www.mixedmigrationhub.org). In addition, many flee not only in response to persecution but also because their state has failed to protect its citizens from human rights violations and deprivation, captured by the concept of 'survival migration' (Betts, 2013). Also, conflict-ridden countries are usually poorer states where for many people few prospects for finding work exist contributing to 'mixed motivations' for migration. Moreover, people make choices also under constrained conditions. Some may seek work abroad instead of becoming refugees, or those who come from a region at war may wish to migrate to a particular country because of job opportunities; this applies even to highly skilled professionals, as evidenced by ethnographic research on Sudanese professionals on their way to Europe through Turkey (Schapendonk and Steel, 2014, p. 264). In addition, transnational social networks make it possible for refugees to join and mix with settled labour migrant communities made up of people from the same region, religion or ethnonational identity.

In further examining the links between labour migrants and refugee migrants, it is important to note that economic migration can also lead to displacement and refugee movements, and vice versa (Nyberg-Sørensen et al., 2008). Take, for example, the Lampedusa in Hamburg group. The approximately 300 sub-Saharan Africans who had left their homes for a variety of reasons had worked in Libya for several years and then left for Italy in 2011, when the Libyan civil war broke out. Italy recognised them as refugees for humanitarian reasons and gave them residence and work permits for up to ten years. Yet, because there were no jobs available to them, the group continued its journey to Germany, now claiming that their permits must be accepted from one European country to another. Currently, most of them are staying in Hamburg without authorisation to either reside or work there (Hennig, 2015). Having moved from labour migrants to refugees, this situation now turns them into what are considered 'irregular migrants'. In this respect, mobility researchers have argued that displacement and mobility should be regarded as a series of departures and arrivals – that is, as a process rather than a one-time event (see e.g. Schuster, 2005, p. 760). In this process, individuals move across geographies and migration statuses, sometimes shifting back and forth between various places and statuses.

The second aspect of interlocking regimes we wish to discuss is the 'travel–refuge complex' (Betts, 2011c). In the course of the securitisation of migration that is emerging from the responses to terrorism, transnationally organised crime and the fight against 'irregular migration', the travel and border regime has greatly expanded beyond the territories and borders of individual Western states and regional spaces such as the EU. Measures that have deterred migrants from reaching these Western states include various instruments under 'remote control' (Zolberg, 1999), the enforcement of external border controls, carrier liability of travel agents and the involvement of both transit and origin countries in surveillance of the departures and re-admissions of nationals and transit migrants. These measures have affected the 'spontaneous-arrival asylum' procedure, the most important channel for refugee protection in European countries by means of which asylum claims are usually processed after the asylum seeker has already arrived within these territories.

Betts argues that this strategy has solved the dilemma faced by Western states wishing to limit new arrivals without strictly violating human rights norms, in that it allows these states to 'shift the regime' from refuge to travel, thereby also shifting the burden of refugee protection to the Southern states (Betts, 2011c, p. 85). These instruments greatly diminish the prospect of mobility for refugees and others who are displaced by conflict and poverty. Other groups, especially those with certain passports and visas, are less severely disturbed by such measures. Because intensified border controls tend to prolong the waiting time for all passengers, registered traveller programs (RTP) have been created to facilitate the movement of pre-screened individuals; RTP is currently suggested within the EU Smart Borders initiative and is already in place in the US and the UK, while in Germany the EasyPASS-RTP allows registered citizens from a few select countries to use an e-passport to get through automated border controls (Federal Police, 2017). In short, the different forms and regimes of mobility interlock because institutional regulations connect different issue areas in both intended and unintended ways, thereby resulting in very different outcomes for different categories of people. Simultaneously, migrants also move across places, regimes and statuses.

Local and transnational migrant activism

In the context of intensified securitisation and decreased channels for (legal) migration, the past decade has witnessed a rise in the visibility of migrant political activism (Tyler and Marciniak, 2013). Ignored for many decades at first, the political actions of migrants started to gain attention beginning in the mid-1980s as one element in the process of settlement, and migrants' cross-border involvement with their home country was generally regarded as detrimental to this process (Fauser, 2012). This view has changed somewhat, and a growing body of literature now documents the many local and transnational migrant networks, organisations and mobilisations that have emerged (Halm and Sezgin, 2013) and shows how migrants' struggles not only address the various regimes of mobility, citizenship, labour, refuge, travel and border but also relate to non-mobility issues such as development, democracy and peace or conflict. To different degrees these issues concern the governments and societies in immigration countries or in countries of origin or regional and international forums; and to varying degrees, such activity includes local action in the countries of arrival, in the homeland and through transnational networks that involve actors in several places (on the distinction between scope and place of activity, see Fauser, 2012). According to the typology proposed by Østergaard-Nielsen (2003), the following examples reflect migrants' immigrant politics, diaspora politics and development politics.

First, *im/migrant politics* addresses migrants' situations in immigration countries and sometimes also in transit countries and include mobilisations and other protest action through which migrants claim or realise a variety of rights related to social or cultural recognition, non-discrimination, voting rights, conditions at work or mobility and travel. Formal and informal migrant and migrant support organisations provide not only advocacy but also assistance and social services for social, legal and medical needs at arrival and in transit – tasks that are increasingly acknowledged and funded by national and international agencies and private donors. In mobilising against the existing parameters of the citizenship, labour or border regimes, two broad versions of migrant protest can be distinguished. One version, the integrationist approach, challenges the boundaries of citizenship and calls for inclusion. The other version, associated with the autonomy-of-migration approach, is more radical and tends to call into question the social, political and territorial closure that come out of the concept of citizenship and the corresponding logic of borders (Tyler and Marciniak, 2013).

Closer to the first version are many pro-regularisation movements that claim 'papers for all' and put pressure on governments to open exceptional regularisation procedures for 'irregular migrants', often with success (Fauser, 2012, Ch. 4). These initiatives often explicitly call for a concept of citizenship based on residence and not on nationality. In this vein, mobilisations in Spain (ibid.) and the Strangers into Citizens campaign in the UK (Tyler and Marciniak, 2013) have called for regularisation, naturalisation or social and voting rights regardless of legal status. In many countries and cities such mobilisations from migrant and pro-migrant groups are supported by trade unions, church-based groups, neighbourhood associations, solidarity networks, anti-racist groups and a variety of non-governmental organisations. Actors participating in pro-regularisation campaigns also use local and transnational actions to criticise the exploitation and vulnerability of migrant workers and call for their protection. For example, the European network RESPECT (Rights, Equality, Solidarity, Power, Europe, Cooperation Today) defends the rights of domestic workers, who in many cases are unauthorised migrant women. Together with other actors, such as WIEGO (Women in Informal Employment: Globalizing and Organizing), it has successfully put pressure on the ILO to adopt the Convention Concerning Decent Work for Domestic Workers (C189), which was eventually signed in 2011.

The more radical struggles are associated with the Sans-Papiers movement in France and protests in border zones and camps, such as the No Border Camp in Calais. These movements criticise the existence of border regimes more generally, along with a system of citizenship that defines who can move and who cannot (Tyler and Marciniak, 2013). Drawing on the concept of 'acts of citizenship' developed by Isin and Nielsen (2008), some scholars have described mobilisation and the protest actions of unauthorised migrants and refugees, as well as more subtle events and performances, as the means by which those who are at the margins or are excluded from status as granted by states transform themselves into political subjects, even in highly constrained situations.

Many of these activities take place in the country of immigration or in transit places, and they include wider transnational campaigns and networks. In addition, *transnational migrant politics* call on migrants' home country governments to protect their citizens against exploitation, discrimination and other forms of abuse. Through consular work and bilateral and multilateral negotiation, emigration states support migrants' social and economic rights and entitlements abroad. Over the past decade an increasing number of migrant organisations and networks have also surfaced as agents in the migration–development nexus. At this interface they also organise advocacy and services for emigration and return, as will be discussed later in relation to development politics.

The second type of migrant activism concerns (*transnational*) *diaspora politics*. Transnational migrant communities, now often called 'diasporas', play an important role in the everyday politics, local decision making, national elections and political parties, regime change, civil war and peace-building in their home countries across the world. Migrants often retain a strong sense of local membership and support their home communities with the money they earn in the immigration country. They continue to participate in local duties on collectively owned farming land, and some have even held political offices in cases as diverse as the famous California-based 'Tomato King' Andrés Bermúdez, who became a mayor in his hometown in Mexico (Bakker and Smith, 2003), and a Germany-based chief who rules in his village in Ghana and convenes his committee via mobile phone (Michels and Möhl, 2011). On the national scale, the ability to exercise extraterritorial voting rights has been expanded in many major migrant-sending countries such as Mexico and Turkey by allowing dual citizenship and facilitating voting from abroad. These transnational activities regularly elicit conflicting viewpoints in the debate on national sovereignty because, first, they bring the electoral campaigns of one country into the territory of another, and second, they bring a non-resident electorate to the political process of the country of origin without their being exposed to its decisions.

An even more contentious question remains – that is, whether diasporas contribute to peace or to conflict. Violent conflict leads to new flows of refugees but also often mobilises established (labour) migrant communities abroad who may feel the need to take sides. A widely cited study by Collier and Hoeffler (2002) has shown that diasporas have often fuelled or prolonged violent conflict in their homelands. This is exemplified by the established and recently displaced Croat populations in Germany, the US and elsewhere that have sent money and weapons to the fighters in the Yugoslavian Civil War (Ragazzi, 2009). However, other examples show that diasporas also contribute to conflict resolution, peace-building and democracy with financial support, political leadership and international and local lobbying (Lyons and Mandaville, 2011). Thus, transnational political action is interconnected with *local diaspora politics* that involves regional institutions or institutions, organisations and the public in the immigration country. Recent examples come from the many Arabic diaspora communities in Europe, Latin America and the US who mobilised in support of the revolutions in the Arab world, articulating claims on both host and home governments (see Journal of Immigrant and Refugee Studies, 2016).

Similarly, Kurdish local and EU-wide networks have lobbied national governments, especially the German government, and the EU to recognise and support their minority rights in Europe and in Turkey (Østergaard-Nielsen, 2003). Ashutosh

(2013) has used the case of the Tamil diaspora and their transnational acts of citizenship to illustrate the complexity of diasporic protest. Tamil protests in Toronto, London, Oslo, Chennai and many other places in 2009 called for a ceasefire agreement in the Sri Lankan Civil War and for the recognition of a separate Tamil state. The Tamils protested against their exclusion from the Sri Lankan government and the violence they suffered, as well as the lack of support from the Canadian government and the public, demanding that Canadian multicultural values be applied in Sri Lanka as well – a vision that was met with considerable criticism, not least because the Liberation Tigers of Tamil Eelam (LTTE), which supports Tamil separatism, is considered a terrorist organisation. At the same time, Tamil identity also refers to national belonging and a concrete territory, although invoked from afar. This example shows how diasporic activism may challenge the limits of home country and host country citizenship while simultaneously claiming recognition of transnational belonging.

Migrants also engage in *development politics*. The recent enthusiasm about the 'migration–development nexus' recognises migrants as agents of development who now receive considerable attention from researchers, policymakers and, especially, the development (aid) industry (Faist and Fauser, 2011). Individually and collectively, through hometown and village associations, migrants send remittances to families and home communities; support infrastructure projects, schools and hospitals; and invest in local businesses. Although in many parts of the world such development politics are not new to migratory processes, two related aspects are new: the enormous attention that goes along with financial and political support for this transnational engagement and the interconnectedness of development with the migration process. Migration itself has become part of the development policies and strategies in developing countries and in national and international development agencies.

A growing number of migrant organisations and networks now carry out local development projects and provide advocacy and services for migrants. Migrant organisations in Colombia, the Dominican Republic and Bangladesh are becoming increasingly professionalised in assisting and planning emigration, warning of the dangers of irregular migration and supporting return and re-integration. Their work ranges from fighting against migrant exploitation and for labour rights to providing pre-departure information and training, and it includes lobbying before the home government and through transnational networks with other actors across migrants' immigration countries (Fauser, 2012, Ch. 4; Crawford and Martin, 2014). 'Optimists' celebrate migrants' transnationalism as a way of democratising development beyond the state, whereas more critical observers consider the migration-for-development logic to be part of a neo-liberal political-economic project through which states channel mobilities and remittances for their own interests. This logic also reflects the powerful receiving states' interests in immigration control and serves as 'camouflage' for the deportation of irregular migrants and rejected refugees. As a baseline, it suggests that migration promotes development and will eventually end the root causes of migration, again favouring sedentarism (for a summary of the discussion, see Gamlen, 2014). In sum, the recent visibility of migrant activism in relation to the politics of im/migration and borders, diaspora and development challenges the congruence of state, territory and identity in local action and transnational space.

Conclusion

At the turn of the millennium, globalisation theorists were optimistic about the prospects of a borderless world and freedom of mobility for all. Globalisation was associated with increased interconnectedness that would transform the territorial and social boundaries of nation states. Mobility and transnational networks would lead to a decline in the importance of territorial nation states and their ability to control borders (see Mau et al., 2012) and were optimistically celebrated as pathways to global justice from below. Concepts such as global and postnational citizenship suggested the emergence of equal rights within a global human rights regime premised on universal personhood, and thus independent of national belonging and place. However, global terrorism, the global economic crisis and, more recently, the 'migration and refugee crisis' have heightened concerns about security, resources and identity that have always motivated closure (Mau et al., 2012). In this context, we observe a renewed emphasis on borders, ethnic boundaries and sedentarism (Glick Schiller and Salazar, 2013).

Many mobility scholars have therefore become sceptical if not pessimistic about the prospects for globalisation. Shamir (2005) argued that globalisation also produces closure through a principle of universal *dangerous* personhoods that he refers to as the 'paradigm of suspicion'. Similarly, Turner (2007) identified an 'immobility regime' as part of globalisation and perceived global risks that have become associated with the mobility of people. Various regimes of im/mobility converge, facilitating the movement of some categories of people and criminalising the movement of others (Glick Schiller and Salazar, 2013). In part, this occurs through states' regime shifting.

Yet, even if vigorously constrained, migrants will exercise their agency and will continue to shift places, statuses and regimes. At the same time, migrants' own local and transnational struggles challenge the sociopolitical and territorial boundaries of the state. Migrants protest against evidence of xenophobia and the exclusion and exploitation of non-citizens and of ethnic, racial, religious and other minorities. More radical actions also challenge the international system of states, citizenship and borders calling for the right to mobility. In the face of massive displacements, this situation is increasingly accompanied by demands for the right to stay and remain immobile (Anderson et al., 2009). In contrast, much diasporic activism creates or renews national identities and belonging from afar. These dynamics profoundly transform the state and society and the relationship between them, albeit not uniformly. Mobilities and transnational networks provide helpful prisms for analysing some of the most important challenges to global society.

Further reading

Andreas, Peter and Timothy Synder (eds.) (2000) *The Wall Around the West: State Borders and Immigration Controls in North America and Europe* (Lanham: Rowman and Littlefield).

Betts, Alexander (ed.) (2011) *Global Migration Governance* (Oxford: Oxford University Press).

Castles, Stephen, Hein de Haas and Mark J. Miller (2014) *The Age of Migration: International Population Movements in the Modern World*, 5th ed. (Houndmills: Palgrave Macmillan).

Citizenship Studies (2013) Special issue on 'Immigrant Protest', 17(2).

Faist, Thomas, Margit Fauser and Eveline Reisenauer (2013) *Transnational Migration* (Cambridge: Polity Press).

Kivisto, Peter (ed.) (2005) *Incorporating Diversity. Rethinking Assimilation in a Multicultural Age* (London and New York: Routledge).

Koslowski, Rey (ed.) (2011) *Global Mobility Regimes* (New York: Palgrave Macmillan).

Mezzadra, Sandro and Brett Neilson (2013) *Border as Method, or, the Multiplication of Labor.* (Durham: Duke University Press).

Østergaard-Nielsen, Eva (2003) *Transnational Politics: Turks and Kurds in Germany* (London: Routledge).

Soysal, Yasemin N. (1994) *Limits of Citizenship: Migrants and Postnational Membership in Europe* (Chicago: University of Chicago Press).

Bibliography

Anderson, Bridget, Nandita Sharma and Cynthia Wright (2009) 'Editorial: Why No Borders?', *Refuge* 26(2), pp. 5–18.

Ashutosh, Ishan (2013) 'Immigrant Protests in Toronto: Diaspora and Sri Lanka's Civil War', *Citizenship Studies* 17(2), pp. 197–210.

Bakewell, Oliver (2007) 'Keeping Them in Their Place: The Ambivalent Relationship Between Development and Migration in Africa', IMI Working Paper No. 8 (Oxford: International Migration Institute).

Bakker, Matt and Michael P. Smith (2003) 'El Rey del Tomate: Migrant Political Transnationalism and Democratization in Mexico', *Migraciones Internacionales* 2(1), pp. 59–83.

Betts, Alexander (ed.) (2011a) *Global Migration Governance* (Oxford: Oxford University Press).

Betts, Alexander (2011b) 'Introduction: Global Migration Governance' in Alexander Betts (ed.) *Global Migration Governance* (Oxford: Oxford University Press), pp. 1–33.

Betts, Alexander (2011c) 'The Refugee Regime and Issue-Linkage' in Rey Koslowski (ed.) *Global Mobility Regimes* (New York: Palgrave Macmillan), pp. 73–91.

Betts, Alexander (2013) *Survival Migration: Failed Governance and the Crisis of Displacement* (Ithaca: Cornell University Press).

Castles, Stephen, Hein de Haas and Mark J. Miller (2014) *The Age of Migration: International Population Movements in the Modern World*, 5th ed. (Houndmills: Palgrave Macmillan).

Collier, Paul and Anke Hoeffler (2002) 'Greed and Grievance in Civil War', CSAE Working Paper No. 2002–01 (Oxford: Centre for the Study of African Economies).

Collyer, Michael (2007) 'In-Between Places: Trans-Saharan Transit Migrants in Morocco and the Fragmented Journey to Europe', *Antipode* 39(4), pp. 668–690.

Crawford, David R. and Nina Martin (2014) 'The Transnational Project and Its Implications for Migrant Civil Society in Bangladesh', *Mobilities* 9(2), pp. 294–313.

Czaika, Mathias and Hein de Haas (2015) 'The Globalization of Migration. Has the World Become Migratory?', *International Migration Review* 48(2), pp. 283–323.

ECRE (2015) *Annual Report 2013/14. Mind the Gap. An NGO Perspective on Challenges to Accessing Protection in the Common European Asylum System* (Brussels: European Council on Refugees and Exiles).

Faist, Thomas (2013) 'The Mobility Turn: A New Paradigm for the Social Sciences?', *Ethnic and Racial Studies* 36(11), pp. 1637–1646.

Faist, Thomas and Margit Fauser (2011) 'The Migration – Development Nexus: Toward a Transnational Perspective' in Thomas Faist, Margit Fauser and Peter Kivisto (eds.) *The Migration – Development Nexus: A Transnational Perspective* (Houndmills: Palgrave Macmillan), pp. 1–26.

Faist, Thomas, Margit Fauser and Eveline Reisenauer (2013) *Transnational Migration* (Cambridge: Polity Press).

Fauser, Margit (2012) *Migrants and Cities: The Accommodation of Migrant Organizations in Europe* (London: Routledge).

Federal Police (2017) 'EasyPASS-RTP', Potsdam: Federal Police www.easypass.de/EasyPass/EN/EasyPASS-RTP/rtp_node.html (accessed February 20, 2017).

Gamlen, Alan (2014) 'The New Migration-and-Development Pessimism', *Progress in Human Geography* 38(4), pp. 581–597.

Gill, Nick, Javier Caletrío and Victoria Mason (2011) 'Introduction: Mobilities and Forced Migration', *Mobilities* 6(3), pp. 301–316.

Glick Schiller, Nina and Noel B. Salazar (2013) 'Regimes of Mobility Across the Globe', *Journal of Ethnic and Migration Studies* 39(2), pp. 183–200.

Glick Schiller, Nina, Linda Basch and Cristina Blanc-Szanton (1992) 'Transnationalism: A New Analytical Framework for Understanding Migration', *Annals of the New York Academy of Science* 645, pp. 1–24.

Halm, Dirk and Zeynep Sezgin (eds.) (2013) *Migration and Organized Civil Society: Rethinking National Policy* (New York: Routledge).

Hennig, Philipp (2015) *Was wurde aus den Lampedusa-Flüchtlingen?* (Hamburg: Norddeutscher Rundfunk), www.ndr.de/nachrichten/hamburg/Was-wurde-aus-den-Lampedusa-Fluechtlingen,lampedusa308.html (accessed February 20, 2017).

Isin, Engin F. and Greg M. Nielsen (eds.) (2008) *Acts of Citizenship* (London: Zed Books).

Journal of Immigrant and Refugee Studies (2016) Special Issue on 'Social Mobilization and Political Participation in the Diaspora During the "Arab Spring"', 14(3).

Koslowski, Rey (ed.) (2011a) *Global Mobility Regimes* (New York: Palgrave Macmillan).

Koslowski, Rey (2011b) 'Global Mobility Regimes: A Conceptual Framework' in Rey Koslowski (ed.) *Global Mobility Regimes* (New York: Palgrave Macmillan), pp. 1–25.

Koslowski, Rey (2011c) 'The International Travel Regime' in Rey Koslowski (ed.) *Global Mobility Regimes* (New York: Palgrave Macmillan), pp. 51–72.

Lyons, Terrence and Peter G. Mandaville (eds.) (2011) *Politics from Afar: Transnational Diasporas and Networks* (Oxford: Oxford University Press).

Martin, Susan F. (2011) 'International Cooperation on Migration and the UN System' in Rey Koslowski (ed.) *Global Mobility Regimes* (New York: Palgrave Macmillan), pp. 29–49.

Mau, Steffen, Heike Brabandt, Lena Laube and Christof Roos (2012) *Liberal States and the Freedom of Movement: Selective Borders, Unequal Mobility* (Houndmills: Palgrave Macmillan).

Michels, Arne and Stefan Möhl (2011) 'Chief Abroad: Transnational Chieftaincy and Village Organisation in Ghana' in Thomas Faist and Nadine Sieveking (eds.) *Unravelling Migrants as Transnational Agents of Development: Social Spaces in Between Ghana and Germany* (Münster: Lit), pp. 105–144.

Morris, Lydia (2003) 'Managing Contradiction: Civic Stratification and Migrants' Rights', *The International Migration Review* 37(1), pp. 74–100.

Nyberg-Sørensen, Ninna, Nicholas van Hear and Poul Engberg-Pedersen (2008) 'Migration, Development and Conflict: State-of-the-Art Overview' in Ninna Nyberg-Sørensen and Nicholas van Hear (eds.) *The Migration – Development Nexus* (Geneva: International Organization for Migration), pp. 5–50.

Østergaard-Nielsen, Eva (2003) *Transnational Politics: Turks and Kurds in Germany* (London: Routledge).

Park, Robert E. (1928) 'Human Migration and the Marginal Man', *American Journal of Sociology* 33(6), pp. 881–893.

Ragazzi, Francesco (2009) 'The Croation "Diaspora Politics" of the 1990s: Nationalism Unbound?' in Ulf Brunnbauer (ed.) *Transnational Societies, Transterritorial Politics*.

Migrations in the (Post-)Yugoslav Region 19th–21th Century (Munich: Oldenbourg), pp. 145–168.

Schapendonk, Joris and Griet Steel (2014) 'Following Migrant Trajectories: The Im/Mobility of Sub-Saharan Africans en Route to the European Union', *Annals of the Association of American Geographers* 104(2), pp. 262–270.

Schuster, Liza (2005) 'The Continuing Mobility of Migrants in Italy: Shifting Between Places and Statuses', *Journal of Ethnic and Migration Studies* 31(4), pp. 757–774.

Shamir, Ronen (2005) 'Without Borders? Notes on Globalization as a Mobility Regime', *Sociological Theory* 23(2), pp. 197–217.

Sheller, Mimi and John Urry (2006) 'The New Mobilities Paradigm', *Environment and Planning A* 38(2), pp. 207–226.

Soysal, Yasemin N. (1994) *Limits of Citizenship: Migrants and Postnational Membership in Europe* (Chicago: University of Chicago Press).

Tsianos, Vassilis and Serhat Karakayali (2010) 'Transnational Migration and the Emergence of the European Border Regime: An Ethnographic Analysis', *European Journal of Social Theory* 13(3), pp. 373–387.

Turner, Bryan S. (2007) 'The Enclave Society: Towards a Sociology of Immobility', *European Journal of Social Theory* 10(2), pp. 287–304.

Tyler, Imogen and Katarzyna Marciniak (2013) 'Immigrant Protest: An Introduction', *Citizenship Studies* 17(2), pp. 143–156.

UN (2016) *International Migration Report 2015. Highlights* (New York: United Nations).

UNHCR (2016) 'Secretary-General's Remarks at the Opening of the Executive Committee of the United Nations High Commissioner for Refugees', New York: United Nations Secretary-General, www.un.org/sg/en/content/sg/statement/2016-10-03/secretary-generals-remarks-opening-executive-committee-united (accessed February 20, 2017).

Wimmer, Andreas and Nina Glick Schiller (2003) 'Methodological Nationalism, the Social Sciences, and the Study of Migration: An Essay in Historical Epistemology', *International Migration Review* 37(3), pp. 576–610.

Zolberg, Aristide R. (1999) 'Matters of State: Theorizing Immigration Policy', in Charles Hirschman, Philip Kasinitz and Josh DeWind (eds.) *The Handbook of International Migration: The American Experience* (New York: The Russell Sage Foundation), pp. 71–93.

Chapter 19

Global poverty

Indrajit Roy

Global poverty is highly contested and politicised. It is an ill-structured and complex social problem able to be defined in different ways, the problem space changing with time and location, and the causal arguments being slippery and difficult to establish. Poverty definitions are not accounts of fact, but rather are fact-surrogates [which] are partial pictures drawn with the cognitive tools of particular disciplines. In the case of global poverty, the cognitive values of economics

FIGURE 19.1 Slums in the foreground of skyscrapers under construction in Mumbai, India

such as quantification, simplicity and measurability, just to name the most relevant, are clearly dominant.

(St Clair, 2006, pp. 58–59)

Can we and should we talk about global poverty? David Hulme (2015, p. 4) suggests that talking about global poverty entails a sensitivity that such deprivations cannot be understood at the local, community or even national level. Poverty must be conceptualised at the global level if one seeks seriously to understand it occurs. Action against poverty needs to be conceived of in global terms.

An important reason for considering 'global poverty' seriously stems from historical and political-economic analysis. This reasoning focuses on the ways in which the capitalist democracies of the Global North have been responsible for the global structures that create and maintain poverty across the Global South. Such structures originated in colonial exploitation and have been maintained in postcolonial contexts through trade regimes, rich country control over finance and technology, structural adjustment policies and military interventions. Recent arguments of scholars studying climate change have bolstered this line of reasoning. The concentration of global poverty in the postcolonial countries of sub-Saharan Africa and South Asia, as evidenced from the data presented in Table 19.1, provides empirical substance to this argument. The table presents a regional snapshot of the incidence of poverty. Although the two measures on which it is based are widely disparate, they point to an overwhelming concentration of poverty in the postcolonial countries of the Global South.

In this chapter, I direct attention to core themes in the study of global poverty. I first highlight the contentious perspectives on the measurement of poverty by discussing conceptualisations of absolute and relative poverty. Next, I discuss residualist and relational interpretations of the causes of poverty and ways of alleviating and reducing it. I then discuss the linkages between global poverty and global inequalities. On the one hand, I note the continuities in the concentration of poverty in the postcolonial countries of the Global South. On the other, I underscore the changes in the trajectories of poverty and inequality as spawned by economic and political changes in the emerging markets. I conclude by distilling the key observations on global poverty and outlining possible areas of further enquiry.

TABLE 19.1 Poverty headcounts, income and multidimensional poverty indices compared, 2012–15

Region	Income poverty (US$1.90 per day, 2011 PPP)	Multidimensional poverty index
East Asia and Pacific	7.2	7.1
Europe and Central Asia	2.1	2
Latin America and Caribbean	5.6	5.2
Middle East and North Africa	2.7 (2007)	20.7
South Asia	18.8	52.5
Sub-Saharan Africa	42.7	61.1
World	12.7	29.8

Measurement and identification: absolute versus relative poverty

Poverty is commonly thought of as the 'want of the necessities of life'. Most understandings of poverty are predicated on 'poverty lines', through which policymakers try to define the economic resources needed to meet an individual's minimum needs. Poverty lines determine the incomes or consumption levels below which it is estimated that a person is unable to access their minimum needs for survival and reproduction. Governments commonly establish poverty lines, based on a computation of the cost of a basic diet for an adult estimated at 2100 to 2300 calories per day plus the cost of a bundle of other essential commodities such as fuel, clothing and shelter. People whose consumption levels fall below this line are classified as poor, with many governments introducing further classifications of 'chronic poor', 'poorest of the poor' and 'ultra-poor'.

Such poverty lines could only be applied at the national level till 1990, when researchers at the World Bank devised a method for identifying a single poverty line. This involved manipulating national-level data so that it could achieve 'purchasing power parity' to adjust for differences in the commodities that money can buy in different countries. Initially, World Bank researchers set the global poverty line at US$1 a day to reflect the incomes required to sustain an adult individual at basic subsistence levels: people who lived on less than US$1 per day were considered to be living in poverty. In 2008, the line was revised upwards to US$1.25 a day. A further revision was made in 2015 when the poverty line was set at US$1.90 per day.

Conceptualising poverty in such narrow terms possesses an obvious attraction: it focuses attention of paramount human needs. After all, human beings cannot function effectively without sufficient food or incomes required to purchase food and other basic needs. However, many criticisms have been levelled against the absolute conceptualisation of poverty. Of these, the most potent are the arguments that emphasise the relational nature of human life. Since people are social actors, poverty needs to be defined in relation to other people living in the same society. People need incomes not merely to sustain and reproduce themselves but also to achieve social recognition and to avoid social exclusion. Such needs vary from society to society and could include access to mobile phones, owning a two-wheeled automobile and participation in the social life of the community.

For instance, the economist J.K. Galbraith (1958) argued that 'people are poverty-stricken when their income, even if adequate for survival, falls markedly behind that of their community'. In a similar vein, the sociologist Peter Townsend (1979) advanced the notion that 'individuals are in poverty when they lack the resources to obtain the types of diet, participate in the activities and have the living conditions and amenities which are customary, or are at least widely encouraged or approved, in the societies to which they belong'.

Such arguments have found institutional resonance in many countries of the Global North where official poverty lines are defined in relative, not absolute, terms (Lister, 2004). The governments of many European countries set the poverty line at 60 per cent of their national median income. Consequently, as a country's prosperity increases, so does its official poverty line. If poverty has to be reduced, then a perspective of relative poverty enjoins upon policymakers and politicians that they ensure that the country's growing income must be shared across populations. Most countries of the Global South, however, continue to use absolute measures of defining poverty and identifying the poor.

The trajectories of absolute poverty and relative poverty have diverged over the last two decades: across the globe and within most of its countries, absolute poverty has reduced but relative poverty has increased. Martin Ravallion and Shouaha Chen (2013) compute what they call 'a truly global poverty measure' which attempts to count both 'absolutely poor people' as well as 'relatively poor people'. In their work (also see Ravallion and Chen, 2011), the global poor refer to:

1   Those who cannot meet their basic needs in terms of a universal standard; and
2   Those who experience relative deprivation or social exclusion because their per capita income/consumption is low compared with average levels in their country.

According to their data, absolute poverty rates, or the proportion of population living under US$1.25 a day have declined in the Global South from approximately 40 per cent in 1990 to about 20 per cent in 2008. However, and this is a deeply sobering finding, relative poverty rates in the Global North as well as the Global South have *risen* during precisely this period. Poverty rates in the Global North have increased marginally from about 18 per cent to approximately 22 per cent. Relative poverty rates in the Global South have increased substantially from less than 10 per cent in 1990 to about 23 per cent in 2008. Chen and Ravallion's (2008) findings suggest that the 'truly global poverty rate' has declined from approximately 50 per cent in 1990 to about 42 per cent in 2008: the reduction of global poverty has clearly been hampered by the rise in relative poverty, making relative poverty among the most potent moral and political issues of our times.

Among the criticisms levelled against Chen and Ravallion have been that they ignore the human development dimension of poverty. In this context, Sabina Alkire and her colleagues (Alkire et al., 2014) have computed the multidimensional poverty index through which they assess severe deprivations in health, education and living standards at the individual level. The index comprises of ten weighted indicators: nutrition; child mortality; years of schooling; school attendance; access to cooking fuel; sanitation; potable water; electricity; quality of flooring; and household ownership of basic assets. Individuals deprived over three of these ten indicators are classified as 'MPI poor'. Readers will recall from Table 19.1 that subscribing to a multidimensional view of poverty challenges the overly optimistic narrative of poverty-reduction inhered in by income/consumption approaches to poverty. Although the direction of change for both income/consumption poverty and multidimensional poverty are similar (indicating in a decline in the proportion of the world's population since 1990), the rates of poverty indicated by the two measures are markedly different, with multidimensional indices conveying the very many challenges for policymakers in reducing poverty that lie ahead.

Explaining and understanding poverty: residual and relational interpretations

Additional to the debates over whether to subscribe to an absolute perspective towards identifying poverty or a relative one, scholars remain divided between analysing poverty as residual or relational. They answer the question: does poverty merely persist from the past or is it actively created by contemporary political and economic processes? Scholars taking a 'residual' view of poverty would have us believe that poverty is a residue of the past, an anachronism in the present, the result of incomplete transition from tradition to modernity, from backwardness to improvement, from arbitrary despotism to the rule of law, from a religious to a secularised society, from superstition to rationality, and from feudal serfdoms to capitalist democracy. As societies progress, they argue, the incidence of poverty diminishes. This is the optimistic prognosis of institutions such as the World Bank. As Table 19.2 indicates, World Bank data on poverty, based on an income-derived poverty line, suggests a steady decline in the incidence of poverty in almost every region of the globe.

By contrast, authors taking a 'relational' view point to the dynamic nature of poverty and the ways in which contemporary economic and political institutions exacerbate, if not produce, poverty. Far from being a relic of the past, poverty is a *product* of the 'transition' into capitalism and modernity. By alienating people from their means of production, capitalist development created winners and losers, and the losers swelled the ranks of the poor. Taking a relational view of poverty entails taking the lens of oppression, particularly exploitation and marginalisation, seriously.

The stakes of adhering to a relational or residual view of poverty are high. The two approaches lead to opposite conclusions about the nature of poverty and the relationship of the poor to contemporary economic and political institutions. The 'residualist' view of poverty – popular among prominent contemporary economists as well as national governments, actors in global civil society and multilateral financial institutions – entails enormous enthusiasm about the ameliorative possibilities of democracy and concomitant economic and political institutions. Advocates propose different combinations of aid, trade and human development interventions. On the other hand, the espousal of a relational view of poverty alerts scholars and practitioners alike to the perspective that the perpetration of poverty is *valuable* to members of certain social classes and that neither noble intentions nor robust policy might be sufficient to eliminate poverty. An appreciation of this view alerts analysts to questions of conflict that attend to attempts at poverty reduction: conflict over

TABLE 19.2 Trends in global and regional income poverty indicators; poverty line of US$1.90 a day (2011 PPP)

Region	Incidence of poverty within region		Share of global poverty	
	1990	2012	1990	2012
East Asia and Pacific	60.6	7.2	50.8	16.4
Europe and Central Asia	1.9	2.1	0.4	1.1
Latin America and Caribbean	17.8	5.6	4	3.8
Middle East and North Africa	6	2.7 (2007)	0.7	0.7 (2007)
South Asia	50.6	18.8	29.3	34.5
Sub-Saharan Africa	56.8	42.7	14.7	43.4
World	37.1	12.7		

redistributing resources and status, making meanings as well as setting agendas. Such analysis should sober the expectations that 'residualists' pin on democracy, capitalism and the alleged inclusiveness of concomitant institutions. They compel us to take seriously the concomitance of poverty and inequality.

Table 19.3 presents a summary of World Bank data to buttress the argument that in several countries the share of consumption/income of the bottom 10 per cent of the population *declined* during the period of high growth. While their absolute condition might have improved, their social position vis-à-vis the better-off sections of society worsened. The fortunes of the bottom 40 per cent of the population were similarly mixed.

Residualist themes: poverty as absence of growth or human development

Scholars who adopt a residualist approach to explaining the causes of poverty emphasise on the absence of economic growth and/or human development. In their analysis, they often emphasise the lack of economic growth as a major cause of poverty. Poverty is a residue of the past, which can only be alleviated and reduced by such measures as economic growth and political democracy. A spirited defence of this view is made by Surjit Bhalla (2002) who concludes that growth explains progress in poverty reduction. Likewise, Deepak Lal (2013) argues that market-led economic growth has massively reduced structural poverty through benefits 'trickling down'.

An excellent example of this approach is provided in the writings of William Easterly (2006, 2013), which are concerned with the prospects held by economic growth for poverty reduction. Poverty results from bad government spawned by the foreign aid and military interventions promoted by Western governments, Easterly tells us in his 2006 book *White Man's Burden*. Corruption, nepotism, dysfunctional regulations and red-tape, state-owned enterprises and excessive resource allocation to the public sector: together, these factors hinder economic growth. The reduction of poverty requires economic growth, which can be facilitated by free markets and free trade. In his more recent writings, Easterly (2013) extends this argument by directing attention to the possibilities of 'political and economic rights' in helping to reduce poverty.

Another example of the residualist approach to understanding the causes of poverty comes from the work of Jeffrey Sachs. Like Easterly, Sachs believes that economic growth is required to reduce poverty. Unlike Easterly, however, Sachs argues that the state has a major role to play. In his *The End of Poverty: How We Can Make it Happen in Our Lifetime*, Sachs (2005) makes the case for concerted public action in order to eradicate poverty in the short term and to connect poor people to market-based opportunities that will permit them to not only avoid poverty but also to steadily accumulate assets and improve their social and economic position. Because poor countries and poor people lack the finance and the technology needed for eradicating poverty, Sachs argues in favour of massive increase in foreign aid and financial transfers from richer to poorer countries, unlike Easterly who favours

TABLE 19.3 Changes in distribution of consumption or income among select consumption or income groups, select countries

Country name	Baseline year	% share of consumption or income for			Ratio of mean consumption or income per capita for bottom 40% to total population	Most recent year	% share of consumption or income for			Ratio of mean consumption or income per capita for bottom 40% to total population	Annualised growth in mean consumption or income per capita for bottom 40%	Annualised growth in mean consumption or income per capita for total population
		Bottom 10%	Bottom 40%	Top 10%			Bottom 10%	Bottom 40%	Top 10%			
Argentina	2007	1.2	12.4	34.9	0.307	2013	1.6	14.6	30.6	0.363	6.4	3.1
Brazil	2007	0.9	9.9	43.6	0.242	2013	1	10.9	41.8	0.274	6.9	4.5
China	2008	1.8	14.4	31.8		2010	1.7	14.4	30.0		7.2	7.9
Ethiopia	2004	4.1	22.5	25.6	0.556	2010	3.2	20.6	27.4	0.518	-1.5	-0.1
France	2007	3.1	20.6	26.3	0.516	2012	3.1	20.4	26.8	0.51	0.2	0.4
Germany	2006	2.5	19.3	25.5	0.505	2011	3.4	21.5	32.7	0.537	1.4	0.1
Greece	2007	2.2	18.5	26.2	0.469	2012	1.7	17.3	26.7	0.428	-10	-8.4
India	2004	3.8	20.8	28.3	0.535	2011	3.5	20	30	0.5	3.2	3.7
Indonesia	2008	3.6	20	27.8	0.391	2010	3.4	18.9	28.2	0.437		
Iran	2009	2.1	15.1	31.4	0.149	2013	2.9	17.9	29.1	0.18	3.1	-1.2
Mexico	2008	1.8	13.6	38.9	0.3	2012	1.9	13.7	38.9	0.312	1.1	-0.2
Nigeria	2003	2.1	16.1	29.8	0.391	2009	2	15.1	32.7	0.36	0.1	1.1
Pakistan	2004	3.8	21.5	28.4	0.529	2010	4.2	22.8	25.6	0.575	3.8	2.7
Philippines	2006	2.3	14.7	33.9	0.375	2012	2.5	15.4	33.4	0.385	1.1	0.4
Russia	2007	2.3	15.7	32.8	0.391	2012	2.3	8.2	32.2	0.402	5.9	5.3
South Africa	2006	1	7.3	54.3	0.178	2011	0.9	7.2	51.3	0.177	4.1	4.4
Tanzania	2007	2.5	16.9	31.9	0.417	2011	3.1	18.5	31	0.461	3.5	1.6
Turkey	2007	2.2	16.8	28.2	0.418	2012	2.2	16.3	30.5	0.411	4.3	4.8
Uganda	2009	2.3	15.7	36.4	0.387	2012	2.4	16.2	33.9	0.411	3.9	2.9
United Kingdom	2007	2.5	18.7	28	0.467	2012	2.9	19.8	24.7	0.49	-1.7	-2.8
United States	2007	1.3	15.2	30.7		2013	1.7	15.4	30.2		-0.2	-0.4
Vietnam	2004	2.9	18.2	29.1	0.42	2010	2.6	17.3	30.1	0.392	6.2	7.8

free markets and free trade unencumbered by governmental interference. Implicit in their differences is an agreement that growth reduces poverty.

A third example of the residualist approach to studying the causes of poverty can be seen from the works of Paul Collier. Collier's work is positioned between the pro-market and pro-trade arguments advanced by Easterly and the pro-state and pro-aid arguments advanced by Sachs. Even as he agrees with his economist-colleagues that lack of growth in poor countries is the proximate cause of poverty, Collier (2007) outlines four traps that keep poor people in poor countries poor: chronic conflict; resource curses; landlocked with bad neighbours; and bad governance in small countries. Collier argues that neither the market nor the state can help people facing these 'traps'. Rather, a dynamic set of instruments are required in order for countries interested in assisting what Collier calls 'The Bottom Billion'. These include such technocratic exercises as strengthening international laws and charters, reducing global corruption, fairer trade policies and better aid coordination but also such political measures as conflict prevention (including military interventions) and identifying and supporting progressive political reformers. How will these interventions help the poor? By facilitating economic growth, which – as many economists believe – is good for the poor.

Subscribing to residualist approach to understanding poverty is not confined to economists who espouse economic growth as a means of reducing poverty. In fact, this approach is implicit in the works of economists such as Amartya Sen, who have convincingly argued against an obsession with economic growth (1981) and who have enriched our understandings of poverty by pioneering the human development approach (1999). Sen's seminal contribution has been to argue that poverty is not so much about the lack of income as it is about the deprivation of capabilities, or what people value and have reason to value (Sen, 1999, p. 75). In a significant departure, Sen emphatically does not believe that economic growth alone can ameliorate poverty. Rather, he demonstrates that economic growth need not benefit the poor when its gains are not investing in such human development initiatives as education and health services that enhance people's quality of life. Instead of positing economic growth as a straightforward panacea for poverty, Sen insists that governments ought to direct attention to investments that not only promote economic growth but also human freedoms. Human freedoms are strengthened, in Sen's view, from the transition to political democracy. Inherent in Sen's conception of poverty is the notion that poverty is about absolute deprivations: the lack of schooling, the lack of health facilities and so on and so forth. With the emergence of democracy, these deprivations can and do disappear, since the force of public opinion makes governments responsive to concerns of citizens. Despite critical differences between his approach and those espoused by other economists, Sen's formulation too leads us to perceiving poverty as a 'residue' of the past which would progressively reduce and eventually be eliminated with public interventions in human development and the adoption of democracy by hitherto authoritarian governments.

Residualist understandings of poverty also inflect the work of such historically minded institutionalist scholars as Dani Rodrik, Daron Acemoglu and James Robinson, and Angus Deaton. Rodrik's (2007) analysis focuses on the possibilities of economic growth for poverty reduction. Acemoglu and Robinson (2012) too believe that economic growth is imperative for reducing poverty: distinguishing between extractive and inclusive institutions, they argue that the latter are better able to achieve economic growth and reduce poverty. Nevertheless, their criteria for identifying inclusive institutions is predicated upon the adoption of liberal economic and political arrangements, thereby suggesting their adherence to residualist understandings of poverty. A similar support for residualist interpretations is demonstrated in the analysis offered by Angus Deaton (2013). Deaton explains the ways in which the knowledge produced during the Enlightenment have transformed economic productivity and improved human health. The diffusion of Enlightenment knowledge has not taken place in poor countries because they lack, in his words, 'the institutions – government capacity, a functional legal and tax system, security of property rights, and traditions of trust – that are a necessary background for economic growth to take place' (Deaton, 2013, p. 234).

A residualist perspective hinges on a governmental understanding of poverty, making it the subject of intervention by states, markets, civil society or a combination thereof. As a governmental category, the normative constituency of poor people, or people living in poverty, has been the target of intervention by nation states, political parties, multilateral agencies, non-governmental organisations (NGOs) and increasingly even the corporate sector since 1990 (Wuyts, 2011). A multilateral financial institution such as the World Bank dreams of 'a world free of poverty'. World leaders, pursuing different ideological orientations, committed on 8 September 2000 at the United Nations General Assembly to halve the proportion of people living in 'extreme poverty' by endorsing the first of ten Millennium Development Goals (MDGs). Proponents of capitalism nod toward its poverty-reducing potential: an editorial in *The Economist* recently went so far as to suggest that capitalism could 'take a bow'[1] ostensibly because of its role in the massive reduction of global poverty (defined in World Bank terms) since 1990. The scholarly, journalistic and policy narratives converge on the understanding that poverty can be reduced, if not eliminated, by accelerating economic growth and/or political democracy.

Relational themes: poverty as oppression

A relational view of poverty enlivens analysts to the ways in which poverty is caused by the very processes that contribute to economic growth, the spread and deepening of capitalism (Mosse, 2010). This perspective draws on Marxian political-economic analysis and foregrounds unequal economic and social relations to argue that poverty is increasing, not decreasing. For example, Walden Bello (1999) argues that globalisation creates wealth for some but does this by dispossessing others. While this process makes some people very wealthy, it impoverishes a vast mass of people. Likewise, John Hillary (2013) argues that capitalism allows corporate elites to corner the wealth generated by economic growth, thereby preventing it from being shared with the majority of the world's population.

David Craig and Douglas Porter (2005) argue that the causes of poverty, understood as economic and social underdevelopment, can be traced back to the overarching dominance of liberalism in framing thinking and practice about the forms of governance and nature of institutions and policies that guide human progress.

Craig and Porter define liberalism as '[A] political ideology and form of governance that has hybridised over time, but generally emphasises the benefits of markets, the rule of universal law, the need for individual and especially property rights' (2005, p. 11).

Tracing the emergence of liberalism through early British colonialism in India in the 17th century right through the emergence of neo-liberalism in the 1970s and 1980s, Craig and Porter argue that liberalism maintains and creates poverty in many parts of the world by eschewing major redistribution and emphasising moral discipline and markets. Their perspective resonates with the searing indictment of liberal political and economic arrangements across the colonial world offered by Mike Davis (2000) in his provocative *Late Victorian Holocausts: El Niño Famines and the Making of the Third World*. Poverty is not merely a residue of the past waiting to be eliminated by the adoption of liberal economic and political arrangements: rather, it is made by the diffusion of precisely the liberal arrangements to which most 'residualist' analysts of poverty look for succor.

An even more radical perspective is offered by Benjamin Selwyn (2014), who focuses on economic inequalities, income distributions and financial flows. His conception of development is labour-centred, enabling him to investigate the class relations of worker exploitation in the 21st century. Indeed, Marxist scholars have conceptualised exploitation as the directly observable appropriation of the fruits of labour of one social group. They use the vocabulary of class in formulating their ideas of exploitation (Buchanan, 1982). Much of the literature on exploitation of labour relates to a context of formal employment in factories.[2] Some scholars distinguish exploitation from marginalisation, to direct attention to the 'people the system of labor cannot or will not use' (Young, 2005, p. 53). Formulations of marginalisation are important because they help analysts to recognise that people are consciously kept out of production systems and not inadvertently left out. They are not marginal to it, but marginal*ised* (Perlman, 1976). If the exploited contribute to the production process from the 'inside', the marginalised contribute to it from the 'outside'.

The neat analytic distinctions between exploitation and marginalisation blur considerably when confronted with the empirical reality of the fragmentation of labour and its dispersal across formal and informal employment in rural and urban areas throughout the world (Gooptu and Harriss-White, 2001; Breman, 1996; Bernstein, 2010; Veltmeyer, 2010). Unorganised workers, with casual contracts and precarious (often non-existent) social security – for example, construction workers, head-loaders and manual scavengers employed by public authorities – confront both exploitation as well as marginalisation. As do agricultural labourers, workers in brick kilns and small-scale garment-manufacturing units, and domestic help. Side by side, hawkers, vendors, masons, plumbers, weavers, potters and others in what governments and multilateral agencies such as the UN's International Labour Organisation (ILO) call 'self-employment' are excluded from formal political and economic institutions. Peasants owning marginal and small plots of land face similar exclusions, as do people engaged in animal husbandry and other activities allied with agriculture. Pastoralists, fisher-folk and people dependent on harvesting minor forest produce also share the same predicaments of exclusion, even though their specific vulnerabilities differ. As self-employed persons, they are not exploited in the domain of labour but in the domain of market and bureaucratic exchanges. Their marginalisation foments their exploitation which in turn marginalises them even further. Furthermore, it is not uncommon for marginalised populations to exploit labour, thereby resulting in the perpetuation of the exploitation-marginalisation complex (Panitch et al., 2001; Bernstein, 2010; Lerche, 2013).

Charles Tilly avers that the interlocked relations of exploitation and marginalisation are reproduced and stabilised by mechanisms that generate, and perpetuate, 'durable inequalities'. Central to the creation of these durable inequalities is 'opportunity-hoarding', or 'confining use of a value-producing resource to members of an *ingroup*' (Tilly, 1999, p. 366; emphasis added). Exploitation and marginalisation should therefore not be seen as individualised transactions but as unequal relations between social *groups*.

A consideration of the ways in which poor people are oppressed (Young, 2005) and the ways in which oppression is often conjugated (Bourgois, 1988) should not lead us to ignore their importance to the global political economy. Nearly three-quarters of the world's poor live in its middle income countries,[3] many of which are postcolonial states. They constitute the low-cost labour which powers economic growth and generates profit. It is this labour that produces the garments, mobiles, beverages and food consumed across the globe. Poor people in middle-income countries, many of which find pride of place in various lists of Emerging Market Economies, provide a range of cheap and casual labour to the rising global middle classes. These include domestic service, vegetable vending, pedalling trinkets, being electricians and plumbers in homes and offices, cleaning sewers and sweeping roads. Nevertheless, channels of oppression are not the only circuits through which they are included in the global economy. Social and economic entrepreneurs now emphasise political – economic inclusion. They suggest that poor people are a potentially useful market for mass produced goods and attractive credit services.[4] Their participation in electoral politics is enthusiastically solicited and genuinely considered to be a touchstone of legitimacy for political contestants in national politics. In this respect, Marxian authors are correct in suggesting that the poor are subjects of global capitalism,[5] oppressed by it but also included with its ambit as labourers and producers who fuel the engines of the global political economy. This argument can be further extended to insist that they are the subjects of internal colonialism,[6] a source of cheap labour and petty commodities, a market for mass-produced commodities and a field of investment for financial services and other social products. As targets of governmental and private philanthropic interventions which claim to educate, improve and even civilise them (Hindess, 1997), poor people epitomise the internal colonialism of contemporary states.

As subjects whose consent is sought through electoral mechanisms and entrepreneurial interventions, the inclusion of the poor into the global, national and local political economy synchronises with the oppression which they confront. The concomitance of inclusion and oppression points to a very specific kind of powerlessness that they experience. Such powerlessness stems from their inability to substantively influence the agenda of the political economy of which they are a part (Bachrach and Baratz, 1962). This quite specific understanding of powerlessness helps us to be wary of perceiving poor people as being either passive objects of oppression and slavery or gullible victims of false consciousness. As voters, consumers and labourers, the global poor are central to contemporary polit- ical economic projects epitomised by both capitalism and democracy. Although instances of brute force and stark slavery are not unheard of in capitalist democra- cies, mechanisms of social control cannot indefinitely rely on these tactics without, at some point, inviting public censure. If the strategy of direct coercion is unre- liable, the ability of postcolonial elites in middle-income countries – where the majority of the world's poor live – to create consent is limited due to the restricted hegemonic capacity of governments and the historic weakness of the bourgeoisie.[7] However, while poor people participate in the economy and the polity, they are rarely able to set the agenda of public discussion. They might benefit from specific governmental practices or philanthropic interventions. Their stark destitution and hunger may be ameliorated. But they have little substantive say in the formulation of agendas.

Espousing a relational approach enlivens scholars and analysts to the relations of oppression within which global poverty is embedded (Roy, forthcoming). Poor people witness myriad forms of oppression. Most often, they are its victims. How- ever, it is not uncommon for them to be participants as well as perpetrators.[8] They are exploited and marginalised by those better-off than themselves, people who may themselves be poor. Poor people belonging to certain social groups may be subjected to cultural imperialism by poor and non-poor alike of other social groups. They may be victims of violence as well as its perpetrators. They may be incorporated into broader structures of capitalist democracy as voters and consumers. But the situation of powerlessness, the inability to substantively set the agenda of their pol- ity marks the lives of poor people, and shapes their common political experience. Scholars adopting a relational view perceive poverty as a political problem perpe- trated by oppression.

Nevertheless, as a political category, poor people excite much less sympathy from states, multilateral agencies and NGOs. The possibility that impoverishment is the consequence of the oppressive social relations that underpin processes of economic growth is not one that these development bureaucracies are willing to consider very seriously. A content search of the World Bank's (2015) 221-page landmark report *Ending Poverty and Sharing Prosperity* does not contain the word 'oppression' or its derivatives even once. The few times the term 'exploitation' is used, the context is not the exploitation of people by other people. The term 'marginalisation' and cog- nate terms makes more of an appearance but in rather general terms. The political dimension of poverty, which stems from the social relations of oppression to which poor people are subject, is the subject of attention by only a few political parties, advocacy organisations and researchers across the globe.

Global poverty and global inequalities: changes and continuities

A relational approach to understanding poverty alerts scholars to the possibility that while transitions to capitalism and democracy may reduce and even eliminate extreme poverty, they do not imply the end of poverty per se. Indeed, as ever-higher numbers of countries globalise and adopt democratic institutions and capitalist economic systems, they are able to do little about containing inequality. The gains from globalisation are not evenly distributed, thereby exacerbating inequalities and generating global poverty.

Branco Milanovic (2016) ably demonstrates this unevenness by analysing percentage gain in income against original income of different ventiles/percentiles of global income distribution. As Table 19.4 reveals, the gains from globalisation are highest at about the middle tiers of the global income levels, particularly between the 40th and the 60th percentiles. The people inhabiting these percentiles are the rising middle classes of the Emerging Market Economies: China, Brazil, India, Mexico and South Africa. Milanovic suggests that members of these classes could be said to constitute the 'rising global middle classes'. Although their earnings in absolute terms may be less than the overwhelming majority of the people living in the (formerly) industrialised economies of the Global North. But the *growth* in their incomes outstrips all other income percentiles, including a very large number of the inhabitants of the Global North.

A look at Table 19.4 also shows the percentiles among whom the incomes have grown very little or barely at all. The gains from globalisation are lowest between the 80th and the 90th percentiles: the middle and working class inhabitants of the Global North. Although the table does not cover data after 2008, it would be reasonable to assume that it is these percentile groups that experienced absolute losses in their incomes after the crisis of 2008. Following Milanovic, these percentiles groups could be said to constitute the 'collapsing global middle classes'. In stark contrast with the experience of the middle and working classes of the Global North are the significant gains in the incomes of the top 1 per cent in these very same countries, exacerbating inequalities herein. Milanovic labels the top 1 per cent as the 'global plutocrats'.

Widening inequalities in the post-industrialised liberal democracies of the Global North have led some commentators to hold these trends as responsible for the emergence and flourishing of right-wing populism across Western Europe and the US (Blyth, 2016; Milanovic, 2016). The implication of their argument is that

TABLE 19.4 Relative gain in real per capita income by global income level, 1988–2008

Percentile of global income distribution	Cumulative % gain in real income	Percentile of global income distribution	Cumulative % gain in real income
100th (global top 1%)	65%	50th	69%
99th	28%	45th	68%
95th	18%	40th	68%
90th	7%	35th	60%
85th	5%	30th	51%
80th	0%	25th	48%
75th	29%	20th	41%
70th	60%	15th	40%
65th	65%	10th	39%
60th	70%	5th	15%
55th	77%		

Source: Adapted from Milanovic (2016, p. 11).

the growing number of poor people in these regions are alienated from the political and economic institutions of liberal democracy and have consequently turned to right-wing populism – exemplified by the electoral support for Donald Trump and the vote for Brexit. However, such a functionalist analysis is not borne out by the available evidence: support for right-wing populism spans class distinctions and there is little to suggest that poor people in the Global North are uniquely support- ive of such political tendencies. Such analyses are even less supported by evidence from such emerging economies as India, where the rising global middle classes have been among the most enthusiastic cheerleaders of such right-wing politicians as Narendra Modi.

Table 19.4 further reveals the changes in incomes among the poorer classes of the Global South. While the bottom ventile increased their incomes by a mere 15 per cent, those between the 10th and 30th percentiles saw a rise in their incomes by 39 to 51 per cent. Thus, even as low incomes remains concentrated among the post- colonial economies of the Global South, the growth in incomes among the bot- tom 30 percentiles since 1988 has contributed to reducing absolute poverty among them. Nevertheless, the growth in their incomes has fallen significantly behind those of the better-off within their countries (the global middle classes described earlier), spawning unprecedented levels of inequalities between different income percentiles and ventiles.

The varying fortunes of different percentile and ventile groups point to a quite specific feature of global inequality: layered onto the extant inequalities *between* countries are the widening inequalities *within* them. The conflicting trajectories of the global plutocrats and the collapsing global middle classes exemplify these inequalities within the ex-industrialised economies of the Global North. Likewise, the opposing trajectories of the rising global middle classes and the global poor demonstrate such inequalities within the postcolonial economies of the Global South, although the many variations in the trajectories among the different ven- tiles of the global poor considerably complicates the picture. These within-country inequalities are framed by considerable between-country inequalities: even as the incomes of the middles classes in the industrialised North collapse, they remain higher than the incomes of the rising global middle classes based in the postcolonial South.

Table 19.5 extends the data presented in Table 19.3 as well as nuances the broad strokes presented in Table 19.4. It directs attention to the changes in the share of the bottom 10 per cent in the consumption or income of their respective countries. The table notes a *decline* in this share the emerging market economies of Asia and Africa: however, the table also notes the reverse trend in the emerging market econ- omies of Latin America. If in China, India, Indonesia, Nigeria, South Africa and Vietnam the share of the bottom 10 per cent in the consumption/incomes of the national economies has dipped, the situation is quite the opposite in Argentina, Brazil and Mexico. Thus, the trajectories of the consumption/income trends of the global poor across the emerging economies are by no means uniform.

Table 19.5 allows us to appreciate the varying fortunes of the different income/ consumption deciles in the emerging markets, with some indications for the pos- sible coalitions and conflicts between them. In countries such as China, Iran and South Africa, the shares of the bottom 10 per cent and the top 10 per cent to the

TABLE 19.5 Changes in distribution of consumption or income among consumption or income groups, select emerging markets

Country name	Baseline year	% share of consumption or income among consumption or income for						Most recent year	% share of consumption or income for					
		Bottom 10%	Next 30%	Third 20%	Fourth 20%	Next 10%	Top 10%		Bottom 10%	Next 30%	Third 20%	Fourth 20%	Next 10%	Top 10%
Argentina	2007	1.2	11.2	14	22	16.7	34.9	2012	1.6	13	15.1	23	16.7	30.6
Brazil	2007	0.9	9	11.6	19	15.9	43.6	2013	1	9.9	12.4	19.3	15.6	41.8
China	2008	1.8	12.6	15	22.7	16.1	31.8	2010	1.7	12.7	15.3	23.2	17.1	30
Ethiopia	2004	4.1	18.4	16.9	21.4	13.6	25.6	2010	3.2	17.4	16.3	21.3	14.4	27.4
India	2004	3.8	17	15.8	21	14.1	28.3	2011	3.5	16.5	15.2	20.5	14.3	30
Indonesia	2008	3.6	16.4	15.9	21.5	14.8	27.8	2010	3.4	15.5	15.6	21.8	15.5	28.2
Iran	2009	2.1	13	14	22.2	17.3	31.4	2013	2.9	15	15.6	22	15.4	29.1
Mexico	2008	1.8	11.8	12.9	19.5	15.1	38.9	2012	1.9	11.8	12.8	19.5	15.1	38.9
Nigeria	2003	2.1	14	15.4	22.5	16.2	29.8	2009	2	13.1	14.4	21.6	16.2	32.7
Pakistan	2004	3.8	17.7	15.9	21	13.2	28.4	2010	4.2	18.6	16.5	21.3	13.8	25.6
Philippines	2006	2.3	12.4	13.5	21.3	16.6	33.9	2012	2.5	12.9	13.8	21.2	16.2	33.4
Russia	2007	2.3	13.4	14.2	21.2	16.1	32.8	2012	2.3	5.9	14.5	21.2	23.9	32.2
South Africa	2006	1	6.3	7.5	14.2	16.7	54.3	2011	0.9	6.3	8	15.9	17.6	51.3
Tanzania	2007	2.5	14.4	14.7	21.7	14.8	31.9	2011	3.1	15.4	15	20.7	14.8	31
Turkey	2007	2.2	14.6	15.9	22.7	16.4	28.2	2012	2.2	14.1	15.1	22	16.1	30.5
Uganda	2009	2.3	13.4	13.5	19.6	14.8	36.4	2012	2.4	13.8	14	20.4	15.5	33.9
Vietnam	2004	2.9	15.3	15.1	21.7	15.9	29.1	2010	2.6	14.7	14	20.7	17.9	30.1

national economies have both declined, while the shares of the intervening deciles have increased: if such trajectories continue, observers could expect to witness the coalescence of the top and bottom deciles against those in the middle. By contrast, the table suggests that in countries such as India, Indonesia, Nigeria, Turkey and Vietnam, the shares of the bottom 60 to 80 per cent to the respective national economies have declined while the shares of the top 20 per cent have increased: if these trends continue, we could expect to witness the coalition of the middle and bottom deciles against those at the top. Following exactly the opposite trajectory, Latin American emerging markets such as Argentina, Brazil and Mexico have witnessed an increase in the shares of the bottom 60 to 80 per cent to the respective national economies and a corresponding decline in the shares of the top 20 per cent: a continuation of such trends would suggest that the top two deciles are likely to attempt to reclaim the dominance which has been gradually eroded over the last decade. The collaborations and conflicts spawned by the varying trajectories of global poverty will emerge as key constituents of regional and national politics in the days to come.

Towards conclusions

I began this chapter by highlighting the importance of adopting the lens of global poverty because of the need to understand the structural, historical and political bases of deprivations. I then proceeded to emphasise the absolute and relative conceptualisations of poverty: whereas absolute formulations of poverty focus attention on paramount human needs, relative formulations remind us that human beings, including people in poverty, are embedded in their societal contexts and cannot be considered as entities sequestered from one another.

Subsequently, I highlighted contrasting interpretations of poverty by summarising residualist and relational explanations. Where residualist explanations prime analysts to believe that poverty is a residue of the past and will disappear with the flouring of capitalism and democracy, relational explanations urge scholars to be more sober and sombre in their conclusions. Poverty is the product of oppressive social relations: even as capitalism and democracy may erode certain forms of oppression, they create and entrench other forms of exploitation, marginalisation and cultural imperialism.

Finally, I noted the ways in which global poverty and global inequality enmeshed with one another. In this context, I specified the ways in which inequalities within countries nested within inequalities between the (ex-)industrialised countries of the Global North and the postcolonial nations of the Global South. Widening inequalities within the emerging market economies of Asia and Africa adds considerable complexity to our existing understandings of global poverty. However, specific trajectories of inequalities in different countries imply that no grand contradiction of the global poor against the global rich is likely to emerge. Rather, collaborations and contests between the poor, the rich and the classes in-between – refracted through the national politics of different countries – are likely to attend to the contemporary life of global poverty.

Notes

1 www.economist.com/news/leaders/21578665-nearly-1-billion-people-have-been-taken-out-extreme-poverty-20-years-world-should-aim
2 For useful studies, see Foster (1974), Stedman-Jones (1983) and Gallie (1984).
3 This fact is ably demonstrated by Summer (2012) and Alkire et al. (2014).
4 This is the suggestion of authors who write texts with titles such as the 'fortune at the bottom of the pyramid' (Prahlad, 2005).
5 See, for instance, Harriss-White (2005) and Panitch et al. (2001).
6 Variations of this argument have been advanced by Hechter (1977) and Gutiérrez (2004).
7 See Kaviraj (1988) for a Gramscian elaboration of this phenomenon in India.
8 This is a perspective to which such sensitive portrayals as in Scheper-Hughes (1992), Buur (2009), Bhatia (2005) and Kunnath (2012) direct our attention.

Further reading

Alkire, S., F.J. Maria, E.R. Paola, J. Foster, S. Seth, M.E. Santos, J.M. Roche, and P. Ballon. (2014) *Multidimensional Poverty Measurement and Analysis* (Oxford: Oxford University Press).
Bernstein, H. (1992) 'Poverty and the Poor', in B. Crow and H. Johnson (eds.) *Rural Livelihoods: Crises and Responses* (Oxford: Oxford University Press and Open University), pp. 13–26.
Collier, P. (2007) *The Bottom Billion: Why the Poorest Countries Are Failing and What Can Be Done About It* (Oxford: Oxford University Press).
Easterly, W. (2013) *The Tyranny of Experts: Economists, Dictators and the Forgotten Rights of the Poor* (New York: Basic Books).
Milanovic, B. (2016) *Global Inequality: A New Approach for the Age of Globalization* (Cambridge MA and London: Harvard University Press).
Pogge, T. (2008) *World Poverty and Human Rights: Cosmopolitan Responsibilities and Reforms* (Cambridge: Polity).
Ravallion, M. and S. Chen (2013) 'A Proposal for Truly Global Poverty Measures', *Global Policy* 4(3), pp. 258–265.
Roy, I. (2018) *Politics of the Poor: Negotiating Democracy in Contemporary India* (Cambridge: Cambridge University Press).
Sachs, J. (2005) *The End of Poverty: Economic Possibilities for Our Time* (New York: Penguin Press).
Sen, A. (1999) *Development as Freedom* (New York: Knopf).

Bibliography

Acemoglu, D. and J. Robinson (2012) *Why Nations Fail: The Origins of Power, Prosperity and Poverty* (London: Profile Books).
Alkire, S., F.J. Maria, E.R. Paola, J. Foster, S. Seth, M.E. Santos, J.M. Roche and P. Ballon (2014) *Multidimensional Poverty Measurement and Analysis* (Oxford: Oxford University Press).
Bachrach, P. and M. Baratz (1962) 'Two Faces of Power', *American Political Science Review* 56(04), pp. 947–952.
Bello, W. (1999) *Dark Victory: The United States, Structural Adjustment and Global Poverty* (London: Pluto Press).

Bernstein, H. (1992) 'Poverty and the Poor', in B. Crow and H. Johnson (eds.) *Rural Livelihoods: Crises and Responses* (Oxford: Oxford University Press and Open University), pp. 13–26.

Bernstein, H. (2010) *Class Dynamics of Agrarian Change* (Sterling, V.A.: Kumarian Press).

Bhalla, S. (2002) *Imagine There's No Country: Poverty, Inequality and Growth in the Era of Globalisation* (Washington, DC: Institute for International Economics).

Bhatia, B. (2005) 'The Naxalite Movement in Central Bihar', *Economic and Political Weekly* 40 (15), pp. 1536–1549.

Blyth, M. (2016) 'Global Trumpism: Why Trump's Victory Was 30 Years in the Making and Why It Won't Stop Here', *Foreign Affairs*, November 15.

Bourgois, P. (1988) 'Conjugated Oppression: Class and Ethnicity among Guaymi and Kuna Banana Workers', *American Ethnologist* 15(2), pp. 328–348.

Breman, J. (1996) *Footloose Labour: Working in India's Informal Economy* (Cambridge: Cambridge University Press).

Buchanan, A. (1982) *Marx and Justice: The Radical Critique of Liberalism* (Totowa, NJ: Rowman and Little).

Buur, L. (2009) 'The Horror of the Mob: The Violence of Imagination in South Africa', *Critique of Anthropology* 29(1), pp. 5–24.

Collier, P. (2007) *The Bottom Billion: Why the Poorest Countries Are Failing and What Can Be Done About It* (Oxford: Oxford University Press).

Craig, D. and D. Porter (2005) *Development Beyond Neoliberalism: The Poverty Reduction Paradigm* (London: Routledge).

Chen, M. and M. Ravallion (2008) 'The Developing World Is Poorer than We Thought, But No Less Successful in Its Fight Against Poverty', *Policy Research Working Paper 4703* (Washington DC: World Bank).

Davis, M. (2000) *Late Victorian Holocausts: El Niño Famines and the Making of the Third World* (London: Verso).

Deaton, A. (2013) *The Great Escape: Health, Wealth and the Origins of Inequality* (Princeton: Princeton University Press).

Easterly, W. (2006) *The White Man's Burden: Why the West's Efforts to Aid the Rest Have Done So Much Ill and So Little Good* (Oxford: Oxford University Press).

Easterly, W. (2013) *The Tyranny of Experts: Economists, Dictators and the Forgotten Rights of the Poor* (New York: Basic Books).

Foster, J. (1974) *Class Struggle and the Industrial Revolution: Early Industrial Capitalism in Three English Towns* (London: Weidenfield and Nicolson).

Galbraith, J.K. (1958) *The Affluent Society* (Boston: Houghton Miflin).

Gallie, D. (1984) *Social Inequality and Class Radicalism in Britain and France* (Cambridge: Cambridge University Press).

Gooptu, N. and B. Harriss-White (2001) 'Mapping India's World of Unorganised Labour', *Socialist Register* 37, pp. 89–118.

Gutiérrez, R.A. (2004) 'Internal Colonialism: An American Theory of Race', *Du Bois Review* 1(2), pp. 281–295.

Harriss-White, B. (2005) 'Poverty and Capitalism', *Economic and Political Weekly* 41(13), pp. 1241–1246.

Hechter, M. (1977). *Internal Colonialism: The Celtic Fringe in British National Development, 1536–1966* (California: University of California Press).

Hillary, J. (2013) *The Poverty of Capitalism: Economic Meltdown and the Struggle for What Comes Next* (London: Pluto Press).

Hindess, B. (1997) '*Politics and Governmentality*', *Economy and Society* 26(2), pp. 257–272.

Hulme, D. (2015) *Global Poverty: Global Governance and Poor People in the Post-2015 Era* (London and New York: Routledge).

Kaviraj, S. (1988) 'A Critique of the Passive Revolution', *Economic and Political Weekly* 23(45/47), pp. 2429–2444.

Kunnath, G. (2012) *Rebels from the Mud Houses: Dalits and the Making of the Maoist Revolution in Bihar* (Delhi: Orient Blackswan).

Lall, D. (2013) *Poverty and Progress: Realities and Myths about Global Poverty* (Washington, DC: Cato Institute).

Lerche, J. (2013) 'The Agrarian Question in Neoliberal India: Agrarian Transition Bypassed?' *Journal of Agrarian Change* 13(3), pp. 382–404.

Lister, R. (2004) *Poverty* (Cambridge: Polity Press).

Maddison, A. (2001) *The World Economy: A Millennial Perspective* (Paris: OECD).

Milanovic, B. (2016) *Global Inequality: A New Approach For the Age of Globalization* (Cambridge MA and London: Harvard University Press).

Mosse, D. (2010) 'A Relational Approach to Durable Poverty, Inequality and Power', *Journal of Development Studies* 46(7), pp. 1156–1178.

Panitch, L., C. Leys, G. Albo and D. Coates (2001) 'Preface to Issue on Working Classes: Global Realities', *Socialist Register* 37, pp. vii–xi.

Perlman, J. (1976) *The Myth of Marginality: Urban Poverty and Politics in Rio de Janeiro* (Berkeley: University of California Press).

Pogge, T. (2008) *World Poverty and Human Rights: Cosmopolitan Responsibilities and Reforms* (Cambridge: Polity).

Prahalad, C.K. (2005) *The Fortune at the Bottom of the Pyramid: Eradicating Poverty through Profits* (Wharton: Wharton Business School).

Ravallion, M. and M. Chen (2011) 'Weakly Relative Poverty', *Review of Economics and Statistics* 93(4), pp. 1251–1261.

Ravallion, M. and S. Chen (2013) 'A Proposal for Truly Global Poverty Measures', *Global Policy* 4(3), pp. 258–265.

Rodrik, D. (2007) *One Economics, Many Recipes: Globalization, Institutions and Economic Growth* (Princeton, NJ: Princeton University Press).

Sachs, J. (2005) *The End of Poverty: Economic Possibilities for Our Time* (New York: Penguin Press).

Scheper-Hughes, N. (1992) *Death Without Weeping: The Violence of Everyday Life in Brazil* (Berkeley: University of California Press).

Selwyn, B. (2014) *The Global Development Crisis* (Cambridge: Polity).

Sen, A. (1981) *Poverty and Famines* (Oxford: Oxford University Press).

Sen, A. (1999) *Development as Freedom* (New York: Knopf).

St. Clair (2006) 'Global Poverty: Co-production of Knowledge and Politics', *Global Social Policy* 6(1), pp. 57–77.

Stedman-Jones, G. (1983) *Languages of Class: Studies in English Working Class History* (Cambridge: Cambridge University Press).

Sumner, A. (2012) 'Where Do the World's Poor Live? A New Update', *IDS Working Paper* 393, pp. 1–27.

Tilly, C. (1999) *Durable Inequality* (Berkeley: University of California Press).

Townsend, P. (1979) *Poverty in the United Kingdom: A Study of Household Resources and Standards of Living* (Harmondsworth: Penguin).

Veltmeyer, H. (2010) *Imperialism, Crises and Class Struggle: The Verities of Capitalism* (Leiden: Brill Publishers).

Wolf, E. (1999) *Envisioning Power: Ideologies of Dominance and Crisis* (Chicago: University of Chicago Press).

World Bank (2015) *World Development Report: Mind Society and Behaviour* (World Bank).

Wuyts, M. (2011) 'The Working Poor: A Macro-perspective'. Valedictory Address (The Hague: Institute of Social Studies). Available at: http://www.iss.nl/fileadmin/ASSETS/iss/Documents/Academic_publications/MarcWwuyts_valedictory.pdf.

Young, I. (2005) 'The Five Faces of Oppression', in L. Heldke and P. O'Connor (eds.) *Oppression, Privilege and Resistance: Theoretical Perspectives on Racism, Sexism and Heterosexism* (McGraw-Hill Humanities Social), pp. 37–63.

Chapter 20

Failing states and statebuilding

Jutta Bakonyi

In the 1990s, state failure and statebuilding entered the vocabulary of international policy, development and academic forums, and think tanks. Both concepts were discussed, researched and advanced in reports, journals, policies and strategy papers. They populated databases and matrices, initiated research projects and culminated in the establishment of commissions, research centres, institutes and journals. With

FIGURE 20.1 United Nations aircraft at the airport of Mogadishu, Somalia

a combination of descriptive (failure) and prescriptive (building) features, these twin concepts are an example of the cooperation between academia and policy.

While both concepts emerged in tandem, they were further developed through collaborative conceptual-theoretical and political practice, critique and reflection upon this practice (Bueger and Bethke, 2014). They sparked scholarly works, guided a growing number of international interventions, and increasingly structured North–South relations. Recent statistics show that fragile states received 38 per cent of overseas development assistance (OECD, 2014, 24). The first part of this chapter discusses the rise of these twin concepts. It differentiates with Carment et al. (2010) two generations of the state failure/statebuilding discourse, and outlines how they were embedded in broader political and socio-economic developments. The second part points to theoretical and conceptual implications and questions the empirical utility of the state failure concept. The third and last section provides an overview of the main critiques. While it uses Cox's (1981) differentiation of problem-solving versus critical approaches, it also shows that the arguments of both camps often overlap. The chapter concludes with a summary of the critique and provides a short outlook into the currently evolving third generation of the failure concept.

Genealogy of state failure and statebuilding

Failing states, fragile states, collapsing, disintegrating and weak states – these characteristics are frequently, and often interchangeably, used to describe the decay of the political, and subsequently social and economic, order in a country, and to outline the implications this disruption has for international security. The concept gained prominence at the end of the Cold War. It was then embedded in a more general discussion on the future of the state in the context of globalisation (Strange, 1995), and the debate on new wars (Kaldor, 1999), which interpreted the increasing number of civil wars as an expression of a wider state crisis in the postcolonial world (also Gros, 1996). An influential early volume (Zartman, 1995) described state failure as a (increasingly violent) process that manifests itself in a downward spiral of institutional and societal disintegration. In the worst case, such as in Somalia, this can lead to the complete collapse of central authority, leaving behind deeply divided societies that are trapped in cycles of violence and humanitarian crisis.

Two types of interventions were swiftly designed, one to prevent weak or failing states from collapsing, the other to deal with the unruly outcomes of state failure. Prevention measures were integrated into the good governance agenda that dominated international development in the 1990s and aimed at enhancing the capacity and performance of state institutions (Scott, 2007). Simultaneously, peacekeeping was expanded into peace-making and peace-enforcement, and an increasing number of military interventions, among them also humanitarian interventions, were deployed to deal with violent conflicts (Doyle and Sambanis, 2006). Reflecting the dominant view that peace can only be achieved in democratic states with a functioning market-based economy, a view summarised as liberal peace (Richmond and Franks, 2011; Sabaratnam, 2011), the new generation of peacekeeping interventions promoted both democratisation and the establishment of a market-based economy. Humanitarian interventions initially aimed at providing aid to starving populations, but their mandate was, such as for example in Somalia, soon expanded to include peace- and statebuilding. In some cases, these interventions even took over governmental and administrative functions, such as in Bosnia-Herzegovina, Kosovo or East Timor.

The, at best, modest success of the first generation of international interventions led to the insight that political and economic liberalisation can only work on the basis of solid institutional frameworks (Ghani and Lockhart, 2008, pp. 152–153). The need to 'establish, reform and strengthen state institutions where these have been seriously eroded or are missing' (Rocha Menocal, 2011, p. 1719) was by the end of the 1990s summarised as statebuilding. Peacebuilding was by then increasingly subsumed to statebuilding (Paris, 2002; Call and Cousens, 2008; Chandler, 2010).

The rise of interventionist approaches in the 1990s required a redefinition of state sovereignty, the dominant principle in international relations. This was enabled by the discursive shift from national or state security to human security, which placed the individual at the centre of security considerations (Booth, 2007; Hoogensen and Stuvoy, 2006). The promotion of human security was followed by the responsibility to protect (R2P), which advocates the practical application of human security in the form of humanitarian interventions in failed states, that is states that are identified as either being too weak or unwilling to protect their own citizens (ICCS, 2001). The blurring of boundaries and the reconfiguration of the political and legal (Teitel, 2003), development and security fields at the end of the Cold War led to the closer alignment of foreign policy goals with development and humanitarian aid (Duffield, 2001; Hettne, 2010). This also laid the groundwork for the second generation of the state-failure debate and statebuilding practice.

While the first generation of state failure theory and practice interpreted failure mainly as domestic problems, at worst with regional implications (Yannis, 2002), the attacks of 9/11 changed this view. State failure was now (as reflected in this book) added to the list of global threats and brought to the forefront of international (security) politics. Failing states were denounced as 'breeding grounds' for international terrorism and were held responsible for unleashing dynamics that threatened international security, and with it the wealthy states in the Global North. State failure soon subsumed a variety of risks and threats, ranging from terrorism and organised crime, human trafficking and large scale migration, to global economic threats, infectious diseases and other health hazards. They were even seen as endangering American values and morals (Weinstein et al., 2004, p. 9). The power of the state failure concept lies in its ability to connect these threats with a broad range of other problems, such as poverty, institutional inefficiency, economic decline or corruption. The second generation of the state failure debate thus links discourses that were previously separated in the differentiated domains of development, defence, international law or foreign policy, and embeds them, or, as critical authors would claim, subordinates them conceptually and operationally into a security framework (Duffield, 2007).

Guided by the assumption that only effective and capable states are able to promote development and to counter security challenges, statebuilding became a priority in international politics, and was used to deal with the variety of problems and failures that were discursively connected in the state failure framework (Scott, 2007; Rocha Menocal, 2011). This discursive convergence found its operational equivalent in 3-D (defence, diplomacy, development) or 'whole government' approaches to statebuilding. These approaches aimed at the integration of previously disparate military, humanitarian, development, legal and political actions and resources (Collinson et al., 2010). The term failure was now broadened to fragility (Collinson et al., 2010, pp. 16–17; Manning and Trzeciak-Duval, 2010) taking account of the non-linear and gradual dynamics of state decay. State fragility implies different degrees of disintegration, while failure was left to characterise extreme cases of state collapse (Brinkerhoff, 2007, pp. 2–3). On the operational side, the term stabilisation gained prominence as an interventionist approach that offers more than mere peace-enforcement but falls short of wider statebuilding aims (Muggah, 2014, p. 1). Several countries established specialised departments, offices or tasks forces to facilitate interdepartmental cooperation in their attempt to promote stability and statebuilding. The UK, for example, set up the tri-departmental Post Conflict Reconstruction Unit in 2004 (in 2007 renamed the Stabilisation Unit) comprising the Ministry of Defence (MOD), Department for International Development (DFID) and the Foreign and Commonwealth Office (FCO). Another example is provided by the United Nations' establishment of a Peace Building Commission in 2005, which aims especially at enhancing cooperation between international and national state-builders. Other examples are the US Office on the Co-ordination for Reconstruction and Stabilisation (O/CRS),[1] established in 2004, or the Canadian Stabilisation and Reconstruction Task Force (START), established in 2005.

With the shift from failure to fragility, the narrow understanding of states as an embodiment of authority or as a set of core institutions, was broadened to include state-society relations (Brinkerhoff, 2007, p. 4; Rocha Menocal, 2011). The OECD (2013, p. 11), for example, identified states as fragile if they 'lack the ability to develop mutually constructive relations with society and . . . have a weak capacity to carry out basic governance functions'. Legitimacy received a central place in the second generation of state fragility/statebuilding debate, and the initial statebuilding focus on capacity and institution building was broadened, to include a wide range of activities that aimed at reshaping state-society relations. This was most prominently operationalised in the Provincial Reconstruction Teams (PRT) in Afghanistan. Beyond civil-military cooperation, the PRTs also used so called Quick Impact Projects as means to build the legitimacy of the state by 'providing immediately tangible benefits to the population – 'quick wins' – that underpin their confidence in the state and the political process that it represents' (SU n.d, p. 11; see also Gordon, 2014). The new statebuilding programs also promoted civil society engagement in statebuilding, and placed one focus on the 'empowerment' of citizens, here especially disadvantaged and minority groups. Civil society organisations and even citizens were expected to participate in the statebuilding exercise, and an increasing number of community-driven reconstruction initiatives were now designed to support the participation of citizens in the attempt to reconstruct institutions and to build states from the bottom up (Cliffe et al., 2003).

The interdepartmental cooperation, the stepwise approach from peace enforcement to stabilisation to statebuilding, and an increasing acknowledgement of local structures and actors further widened statebuilding practice. Interventions incorporated a broad number of activities combining security promotion with peace building and development, and including programs as diverse as the promotion of democratisation, institution building, bureaucracy promotion, support of rule of law, human rights and political participation, economic development, poverty reduction and welfare provision, and so on. However, while the practices of these interventions might not have changed significantly, their integration into the statebuilding framework provided them with new meaning (Chandler, 2010, p. 10).

Defining fragility: which states are fragile, and what exactly is failing?

The rise of the twin concepts of state failure/statebuilding is not matched by their conceptual coherence. A number of scholars have criticised the state failure/fragility concepts[2] for their lack of conceptual clarity and failure to provide empirical evidence (Hill, 2005; Hagmann and Hoehne, 2009; Patrick, 2007; Brinkerhoff, 2014). The broad variety of terms – failure, fragility, decay, collapse, weakness – already indicates conceptual ambiguity and challenges further theorising (Collinson et al., 2010, chap. 2). These labels have unclear or overlapping meanings, and are often used without specifying characteristics or criteria of failure or weakness (Scott, 2007). However, a minimalist understanding of failure can be carved out from the bulk of the state failure literature. The majority of authors seem to agree on three core functions of a state, among them the provision of security, the promotion of welfare (or basic needs) and a minimal degree of legitimacy and acceptance by the population. Accordingly, a state fails if it is unable to fulfil these core functions, and failure thus has the three features of authority failure (security gap); service entitlements failure (capacity gap); and legitimacy failure (legitimacy gap) (Milliken and Krause, 2002; Weinstein et al., 2004, pp. 14f; Stewart and Brown, 2009; Ghani and Lockhart, 2008). The Commission on Weak States and US National Security used such a minimalist understanding of failure, when it classified in 2004 around 50 to 60 countries as weak (Weinstein et al., 2004, p. 14).

Even if this minimalist understanding is accepted, the challenge remains to empirically identify if the core functions are fulfilled and to measure the degree of failure. A broad range of categories and indicators have been developed over the years to identify failure and measure the degree of weakness. The most prominent of these are the Political Instability Task Force (PITF)[3] and the Fund for Peace (FFP), which annually publish a Fragile States Index (until 2014 called Failed States Index). PITF provided a longitudinal assessment of state failure. With its intellectual roots in conflict studies, state failure was equated with chronic violence and civil conflict (Carment et al., 2010, p. 16) and failure identified in four violent phenomena: revolutionary wars, ethnic wars, genocide and politicide[4] and adverse regime change. Every subcategory integrated a broad variety of empirical cases. Under regime change, for example, the PITF listed the (violent) victory of Fidel Castro in Cuba in 1959, the coup in Chile 1973 or the killing of Liberia's president Samuel Doe in the war in Liberia in 1990. Similarly diverse phenomena were grouped together as ethnic or revolutionary wars, among the latter, for example, the Islamic Revolution in Iran from 1978 to 1979, the 'revolutionary movement in China' in 1989 and the war in Tajikistan (1992–8) (SFTF, 2002). If state failure, however, serves as catch-all category for different types of mass violence and crisis, its analytical value remains highly questionable.

The FFP's States Fragility Index relies on another, only partly overlapping, set of 12 indicators, among them six indicators related to political, four to social and two to economic developments. They comprise, for example, state legitimacy, security, public services, the rise of factionalised elites, refugee movements or economic decline. In its 2016 report, 71 countries were identified as being at risk of failure, albeit to varying degrees. Thirty-two countries received a high warning, 23 an alert, eight a high alert and another eight a very high alert (http://fsi.fundforpeace.org/). Other attempts to analytically and empirically grasp failure include the OECD-DAC database and its yearly published state failure report. It identified for example 51 countries as fragile in 2014. In 2016, the UK's Department for International Development provided a new list of 64 fragile countries and regions (DFID, 2016). The DFID list draws its data from other indices, but sub-divides degrees of high fragility (17 countries), moderate fragility (19) and low fragility (18). It additionally identifies neighbouring high fragility states (10), taking account of the risk of spill-over effects. The differences in numbers, indicators, matrices and typologies are symptomatic of the difficulty in defining failure and applying labels such as weak, fragile or failed to particular states (Putzel and Di John, 2012). Above all, they challenge the empirical validity and the analytical usefulness of the failure concept and confirm a general lack of theorisation.

The concept of failure/fragility nonetheless continues to guide statebuilding policies and to produce a wide set of prescriptions and interventions. Without a coherent conceptual basis, state failure runs the risk of being equated either with underdevelopment and poverty and/or with violence. While it is common sense that countries characterised by large-scale violence or civil war have a governance problem, most low-income countries are also likely to have difficulties fulfilling the criteria of stability and can thus be characterised as fragile. A proper differentiation between fragile states and developing countries is missing (Putzel and Di John, 2012). Patrick (2006) additionally criticised that many policymakers and some academics have taken the main assertion that state failure/fragility constitutes a major challenge for international security for granted, although little empirical evidence has been provided to underscore the connection and causal direction between weakness and security.

Some authors argue that the conceptual ambiguity of failure makes it especially attractive for policymakers and practitioners (Patrick, 2007; Brinkerhoff, 2014). Ambiguous and oversimplified concepts allow practitioners to apply one-size-fits-all approaches to countries with quite heterogeneous characteristics and problems and policymakers to obfuscate their own political interests (Patrick, 2007, p. 647). Such concepts additionally 'reduce the burden of information processing for decision makers in global governance organisations' (Brinkerhoff, 2014, p. 337).

Lack of conceptual coherence, doubt about the analytical utility of the concept, problems of empirical identification of failure and measurement of fragility, are complemented by problems of causality and the separation of causes and effects of failure. Brinkerhoff proposed to consider fragility as a 'wicked problem set', contested in its definition, ill-formulated and inherently complex, and comprising 'multiple interdependencies and causal connections' (Brinkerhoff, 2014, p. 334), as no matter which problems are identified, they 'can be viewed as a nested symptom of another problem' (Brinkerhoff, 2014, p. 333). In spite of the discomfort with the state failure concept, it continues to guide a large number of joint donor initiatives, for example, the New Deal for Engagement in Fragile States (2011), or the discussions around the post-2015 Sustainable Development Goals, in which fragility was identified as a major obstacle to reaching these goals. It often seems that governments, international organisations, NGOs or think tanks develop their own 'shopping lists' of failure, based more on prevailing ideologies or the will to intervene than on solid empirical (and preferably comparative) assessments. This, and the practice to export a particular model of the state, has raised suspicion that statebuilding is just a new way of promoting Western hegemony. The next section will outline some of these concerns.

Liberal statebuilding in crisis?

Both the concept of state failure and the practice of statebuilding are under critique. Cox's (1981) famous differentiation between problem-solving and critical approaches is applied in this section to differentiate between two strands of this critique. The observations of both strands overlap, but they provide different interpretations for the identified problems and often arrive at different conclusions. The problem-solving strand stems in large part from within the statebuilding circles, including applied academic and policy-relevant research. This strand accepts the main assumptions of state failure, but assesses shortcomings and reflects on lessons learnt in order to improve the identification of failure and the practice of statebuilding. The 'critical strand', in contrast, challenges the basic assumptions, especially the liberal peace framework in which statebuilding interventions are embedded. Critical authors emphasise the need to identify how knowledge production and statebuilding practice are embedded in relations of power, and to reveal the interests behind them. Critical approaches are highly sceptical of the benevolent rhetoric and criticise the search for technical solution to highly political problems.

Applied studies focus on the practice of statebuilding and technicalities of the interventions. Their main critique is framed in terms of aid effectiveness, and they regularly emphasise the absence of harmonised approaches and co-ordination among the vast range of statebuilding actors, the failure to jointly sequence interventions and the tendency to prioritise particular aspects of peace or statebuilding (such as institution building) to the detriment of others (such as legitimacy). They also criticise that programs are often not adapted to local conditions, and are dominated by international experts who do not engage in depth with local actors. Insufficient funding, different time-horizons of the donors, lack of long-term commitment and long-term planning, and limited flexibility due to bureaucratic hurdles are also regularly criticised (Paris and Sisk, 2009a; Paris, 2009; Lockhart and Ghani, 2009; Rubin, 2006; Manning and Trzeciak-Duval, 2010; Carment et al., 2010, pp. 156–157).

This critique found resonance in policy circles and among major donor countries. It was aggregated into lessons learned, and codified in policy recommendations and guidelines, among them most prominently the Principles for Good International Engagement in Fragile States (OECD, 2007), which were, in 2007, collectively adopted by the 30 OECD Development Assistance Countries (OECD-DAC). However, although considerable efforts of donors and international organisations to improve their practices were acknowledged, most of the targets were not met four years later when the OECD (2011) conducted a progress review. Harmonisation of policies was largely lacking, and information-sharing and co-ordination could not be sustained over a longer time frame. While the OECD interprets this mainly as a technical and organisational problem, Paris (2009) argues that co-ordination failure is caused by conflicting objectives, values and ideals of the intervenors. Additionally, the long list of issues to be tackled and the complex agenda of statebuilding is difficult, if not impossible, to be translated into practice. It was therefore suggested to reduce the objectives of statebuilding and to adapt objectives to the degree of failure. In many cases, for example, good governance might work better if objectives were reduced to enable at least 'good enough governance' (Grindle, 2007).

Another critique addresses the difficulty to actually implement policies and agreements that are developed at a central state level, or in headquarters of international organisations. Actors 'on the ground' have to deal with complex challenges on a daily basis, and their actions are often more shaped by the need to make fast decisions and to react to the ever-changing situation of conflict than by the implementation of a strategy developed in the main headquarters. Often, policy frames and statebuilding templates enter into conflict with local social rules and norms and the friction between them needs to be addressed by the state builders on the ground (Barnett and Zürcher, 2009; Millar et al., 2013). While the 'problem-solving camp' tries to improve communication and to speed-up (joint) operational responses, the 'critical camp' points to the fundamental problem of transferring ideas and models from one cultural context to another, a problem that social anthropology has elaborated as translation (Rottenburg, 2009, pp. 99–103).[5] Translation involves active agents, intermediaries or brokers (Sally Engle, 2006) who pick up a concept in one setting, strip it from its particular context, reinterpret it and place it in another setting where the model reacts with other, already available repertoires of meaning. While passing through the long chain of international development, concepts thus necessarily change their meaning and the translation outcome usually differs significantly from its 'original'. This observation stresses contingency and the emergent and unexpected outcome of social interactions (including discourses) and challenges the general ability to plan social transformations and thus to socially engineer societies and states.

Among the regularly repeated critique that overlap between the 'problem-solving' and the 'critical camp' is the failure to contextualise programs. Statebuilders, for example, continue to focus on central institution building instead of addressing state-society relations (OECD, 2011). While the focus on state-society relations would require a deeper engagement with local actors, statebuilders prefer to apply conventional development frameworks to fragile states, and rely on blueprints without alignment to local conditions or 'local ownership' (OECD, 2011). The bureaucratisation of development and the application of one-size-fits-all designs are not restricted to statebuilding but constitute a long-established critique in development and peacebuilding. The 'problem-solving camp' interprets this mainly as a technical problem, caused by the failure to develop or use adequate analytical tools, and to establish monitoring and evaluation mechanisms. The 'critical strand', in contrast, interprets this failure as systemic, as part of the contradictions and dilemmas of external interventions that aim at bettering societies they do not – and often do not even try to – understand. In the centre of the critical approach is the acknowledgement of the social relations that structure statebuilding and the enormous power differentials between the intervenors and the intervened upon.

This power gap, among others, is displayed in the taken-for-granted framework of liberal peace. Instead of discussing the type of state to be built or strengthened, intervenors rely on an idealised and de-historicised version of the Western state, ignore the violent and disruptive trajectory of European statebuilding, and use their superior power position in the global political economy to impose this idealised model, including its implicit norms and values, on less powerful, peripheral countries (Paris, 2002; Mallaby, 2002; Marquette and Beswick, 2011). The partnership and participatory rhetoric of the intervention is, in practice, often contrasted by the paternalistic and top-down behaviour of intervenors. They undermine locally driven peace- and statebuilding processes, and contribute to the bifurcation of social worlds, and the growing social distance and tensions between the intervenor and intervened upon (Chopra, 2000; Suhrke, 2009; Autesserre, 2010; Lemay-Hébert, 2011).

Another line of critique addresses the point that statebuilding does not really build states, but instead contributes to the establishment of a narrow circle of political authorities (Marquette and Beswick, 2011). These elites are usually closely aligned to the donors, have learned to juggle the jargon of international statebuilding and manipulate labels and buzzwords (such as fragility, local ownership, participation) while using international resources to their own personal or political advantage (Heiduk, 2014). Such forms of elite (and non-elite) capture and the fraudulent strategies and misuse of aid by local elites are identified by both camps. The 'problem-solvers' react by developing measures to enhance transparency and accountability of aid and to monitor its impact more tightly. The 'critical camp', instead, interprets these strategies as a result of the power relations that structure international interventions. Accordingly, development has created, and is placed in, a dual structure of power, in which the local side has become increasingly invisible for the external intervenor. Reflecting on their dependent position as aid receivers, southern actors have developed a broad repertoire of 'strategies of extraversion' (Bayart, 2009), that is practices intended to create and to capture 'a rent generated by dependency' (Bayart, 2000, p. 222).

The dual power structure also leads to the rise of local gatekeepers and intermediaries – in the case of statebuilding, the new state elites – who operate in the realm between the external donor and local receiver of aid, and use this in-between position to manipulate, direct and consume external resources and contacts. While this is characteristic of all external interventions, external statebuilding tends towards the erection of 'phantom states' (Chandler, 2006, pp. 192ff.), that is states that have lost any linkages to their population, but merely exist as nodes for external intervenors. Actors behind the façade of formal statehood (including 'phantom elites'), however, continue to define their own rules and order societies in a way that remains largely hidden from the external intervenors.

It is thus not a lack of local ownership – to use one of the contemporary buzz-words of international development – but the failure of the intervenors to understand how exactly locals own the statebuilding process. The (hidden) adaptation of intervention practices to local social rules, values and world views can be interpreted as re-appropriation of the state by local actors, as local resistance against external impositions, as frictions[6] between external and local actors, or simply (as problem-solvers tend to do) as misappropriation and diversion of international resources. The problem, however, remains. Externally built states often lack anchorage in their societies and fail to generate legitimacy.

Already the guiding assumptions that state weakness is accompanied by social disorder, that fragility equals weak governance, and that failure leads to social chaos are problematic. Several authors have shown that societies with weak formal state institutions tend to rely on strong informal networks and institutions and do not necessarily lack leadership but are characterised by a variety of social orders and forms of political authority (Reno, 2000; Bakonyi and Stuvoy, 2005; chapters in Bøås and Dunn, 2007). The ignorance of these actors and institutions was labelled as a main 'failure of the state failure debate' (Hagmann and Hoehne, 2009). Post-development studies have shown that such failures are not accidental but part of the Euro-centric imagination of the post-colonial world. Embedded in the modernisation ideology, post-colonial societies or states are conceptualised as transitional or incomplete, and can only be described negatively in terms of deficits, deficiencies and failures, that is by what they are not (developed for example) or what they do not have (functioning or strong states) (Chakrabarty, 2000, pp. 30–37; Hill, 2005). Scholars even lack the vocabulary to analyse and comprehend what post-colonial societies actually are and how they function. In the tradition of Michel Foucault (1980), who emphasised the nexus of knowledge and power, post-development studies interpret the identification of deficits in form of underdevelopment, weak statehood or fragility as a technique of power that links knowledge with interventions (Escobar, 1995). The mapping of fragile states thus produces them as objects to be intervened upon through peace-enforcement, stabilisation and statebuilding, and this has given rise to a previously unknown 'level of intrusion and degree of social engineering' (Duffield, 2002, p. 1052).

This critique links to another question of whether liberal peace is indeed suitable for societies with different political, cultural and religious heritages (Samuels and von Einsiedel, 2003; Paris and Sisk, 2009b, pp. 305–306). While parts of the problem-solving as well as 'critical camp' request in-depth, better and more serious engagement with local actors, one part of the 'critical camp' challenges exactly the 'moral framing of difference' and the consolidation of 'them' versus 'us' dichotomies (Duffield, 2002, p. 1050) that underlies these requests. The search for the local maintains an 'ontology of Otherness' (Sabaratnam, 2011), now displayed as difference between the liberal (Western) and non-liberal (post-colonial) subject, and justifies the subjection of the latter to betterment through capacity building and empowerment (Chandler, 2010). These interventions may be framed as attempts to save, develop or secure the (illiberal, non-rational, non-enlightened) 'Other', but they mainly legitimise external regulatory control. According to Duffield (2010) the main aim of these new interventionist frameworks is to police and contain informal and undocumented migration. Rather than overcoming poverty, these interventions are erecting new barriers that entrench the North–South divide, cement global structures of power and support the hegemony of the Global North. This hegemony, however, is exercised as denial of power and interest and instead reframed as a therapeutic attempt towards empowerment and capacity building (Chandler, 2006) and executed as administrative-technical tasks to ensure institutional efficiency, transparency and, above all, equity and participation.

Conclusion

This chapter traced the rise of the twin concepts of state failure and statebuilding, which were promoted by and further evolved in the cooperation between academia and policy. Although state failure is conceptually weak and built on shaky empirical foundations, it initiated a seemingly ever-increasing number of statebuilding initiatives. State failure (later fragility) connected debates and discourses that were previously divided into the fields of development, international politics, defence or law, and embedded them into a security framework. This had far-reaching practical consequences for the Global South. An increasing number of military interventions aimed at stabilising and rebuilding failed states, with ever-broadening goals, ranging from the promotion of democracy, rule of law, human rights and civil society to poverty reduction, security provision and institution building.

This chapter has also provided an overview of the main critique. While the 'problem-solving camp' aims to improve the identification of failure as well as the practice of statebuilding, critical approaches interpret statebuilding as a new form of global power politics. Increasingly, however, the 'problem-solving camp' seems to share doubts that social engineering is at all possible, emphasising the complex nature of interventions and their manifold uncontrollable and unintended consequences. This insight gave rise to the third generation of failure debate, which no longer focuses on states or state-society relations, and is also no longer confined to developing countries. Instead, it defines fragility as multidimensional and characterised by 'accumulation and combination of risks combined with insufficient capacity by the state, system and/or communities to manage it, absorb it or mitigate its consequences' (OECD, 2016, p. 6). Instead of producing lists of fragile states and designing programs to re-build them, the new approach aims at enhancing resilience, and thus at strengthening the ability of states, societies and people to cope with danger (World Bank, 2013). The fragility/resilience approach is already interpreted as a new and post-liberal form of governing complexity. The debate if resilience has the potential to move beyond modernist binaries and statist approaches, or if it is mainly a more sophisticated form of neo-liberal individualisation of responsibilities (Joseph, 2016) cannot be taken up here.

Notes

1 In 2011 this office was integrated into the US State Department's Bureau of Conflict and Stabilisation Operations.

2 For simplicity, the chapter sticks to the term 'failure', albeit 'fragility' became more prominent in the 2000s. Up to date, however, multiple terms with overlapping meanings circulate in academia and policy.

3 Previously called the State Failure Task Force (SFTF).

4 Genocide and politicide are defined in the SFTF report as 'sustained policies . . . that result in the deaths of a substantial portion of a communal or political group'. In genocides groups are victimized on basis of 'their communal (that is, ethnolinguistic or religious) characteristics', while in 'politicides, victims are defined primarily in terms of their political opposition to the regime or dominant groups' (SFTF, 2002, pp. 3–4).

5 Rottenburg builds on Actor Network Theory and their identification of translation as major mechanism in forming and maintaining social networks (Callon and Latour, 1981).

6 The metaphor of frictions was used by Tsing (2005) to explore the complex convergence of global-local interactions in the rainforests of Indonesia.

Further reading

Derick W. Brinkerhoff (ed.) *Governance in Post-Conflict Societies. Rebuilding Fragile States* (London/New York: Routledge).

Carment, David and Stewart Prest and Samy Yiagadeesen (2010) *Security, Development, and the Fragile State: Bridging the Gap Between Theory and Policy* (London/New York: Routledge).

Chandler, David (2006) *Empire in Denial: The Politics of State-Building* (London/Ann Arbor, MI: Pluto).

Chandler, David (2010) 'The Uncritical Critique of "liberal peace" ', *Review of International Studies* 36(S1), pp. 137–155.

Duffield, Mark (2001) *Global Governance and the New Wars. The Merging of Development and Security* (London/New York: Zed-Books).

Duffield, Mark (2007) *Development, Security and Unending War. Governing the World of Peoples* (Cambridge: Polity Press).

Ghani, Ashraf and Clare Lockhart (2008) *Fixing Failed States* (New York: Oxford University Press).

Muggah, Robert (ed.) *Stabilization Operations, Security and Development* (Abingdon/New York: Routledge).

Paris, Roland and Timothy D. Sisk (eds.) (2009) *Dilemmas of Statebuilding* (London/New York: Routledge).

Special Issue of: *Third World Quarterly* 2014, 35(2) Fragile States: A Political Concept.

Bibliography

Autesserre, Séverine (2010) *The Trouble with the Congo: Local Violence and the Failure of International Peacebuilding* (Cambridge: Cambridge University Press).

Bakonyi, Jutta and Kirsti Stuvoy (2005) 'Violence and Social Order Beyond the State: Somalia & Angola', *Review of African Political Economy* 104(5), pp. 359–382.

Barnett, Michael N. and Christoph Zürcher (2009) 'The Peacebuilder's Contract', in Roland Paris and Timothy D. Sisk (eds.) *The Dilemmas of Statebuilding. Confronting the Contradictions of Postwar Peace Operations* (London/New York: Routledge), pp. 23–59.

Bayart, Jean-Francois (2000) 'Africa in the World: A History of Extraversion', *African Affairs* 99(395), pp. 217–267.

Bayart, Jean-Francois (2009) *The State in Africa: The Politics of the Belly*, 2nd, revised ed. (Cambridge: Polity Press).

Bøås, Morten and Kevin C. Dunn (eds.) (2007) *African Guerrillas: Raging Against the Machine* (London: Lynee Rienner).

Booth, Ken (2007) *Theory of World Security* (Cambridge: Cambridge University Press).

Brinkerhoff, Derick W. (2007) 'Introduction – Governance Challenges in Fragile States: Re-establishing Security, Rebuilding Effectiveness, and Reconstituting Legitimacy', in Derick W. Brinkerhoff (ed.) *Governance in Post-Conflict Societies. Rebuilding Fragile States* (London/New York: Routledge), pp. 1–21.

Brinkerhoff, Derick W. (2014) 'State Fragility and Failure as Wicked Problems: Beyond Naming and Taming', *Third World Quarterly* 35(2), pp. 333–344.

Bueger, Christian and Felix Bethke (2014) 'Actor-Networking the 'failed state' – An Enquiry Into the Life of Concepts', *Journal of International Relations and Development* 17(1), pp. 30–60.

Call, Charles T. and Elizabeth M. Cousens (2008) 'Ending Wars and Building Peace: International Responses to War-Torn Societies', *International Studies Perspectives* 9(1), pp. 1–21.

Callon, Michel and Bruno Latour (1981) 'Unscrewing the Big Leviathan: How Actors Macro-Structure Reality and How Sociologists Help Them To Do So' in Karin Knorr-Cetina and Aaron V. Cicourel (eds.) *Advances in Social Theory and Methodology: Towards an Integration of Micro- and Macro-Sociologies* (Boston: Routledge and Kegan Paul), pp. 277–303.

Carment, David and Stewart Prest and Samy Yiagadeesen (2010) *Security, Development, and the Fragile State. Bridging the Gap Betwen Theory and Policy* (London/New York: Routledge).

Chakrabarty, Dipesh (2000) *Provincializing Europe: Postcolonial Thought and Historical Difference* (Princeton, NJ: Princeton University Press).

Chandler, David (2006) *Empire in Denial: The Politics of State-Building* (London/Ann Arbor, MI: Pluto).

Chandler, David (2006) 'Six Theses on Phantom States and Empire in Denial', www.david chandler.org/wp-content/uploads/ . . . /Six-Theses-on-Phantom-States.pdf (accessed June 7, 2017).

Chandler, David (2010) 'The Uncritical Critique of "liberal peace" ', *Review of International Studies* 36(S1), pp. 137–155.

Chandler, David (2010) *International Statebuilding: The Rise of Post-Liberal Governance* (London/New York: Routledge).

Chopra, J. (2000) 'The UN's Kingdom of East Timor', *Survival* 42(3), pp. 27–40.

Cliffe, Sarah, Scott Guggenheim and Markus Kostner (2003) *Community-Driven Reconstruction as an Instrument in War-to-Peace Transitions* (Washington, DC: World Bank), http://info.worldbank.org/etools/docs/library/35122/WP7final.pdf (accessed November 02, 2015).

Collinson, Sarah and Samir Elhawary and Robert Muggah (2010) 'States of Fragility: Stabilisation and its Implications for Humanitarian Action', www.odi.org/sites/odi.org.uk/files/odi-assets/publications-opinion-files/5978.pdf (accessed February 23, 2017).

Cox, Robert (1981) 'Social Forces, States and World Orders: Beyond International Relations Theory', *Millennium – Journal of International Studies* 10(2), pp. 126–155.

DFID, Department for International Development Aid (2016) 'Bilateral Development Review', Technical note, www.gov.uk/government/uploads/system/uploads/attachment_data/file/573890/Bilateral-Development_Review-technical-note-2016.pdf (accessed July 03, 2017).

Doyle, Michael and Nicholas Sambanis (2006) *Making War and Building Peace: United Nations Peace Operations* (Princeton: Princeton University Press).

Duffield, Mark (2001) *Global Governance and the New Wars. The Merging of Development and Security* (London; New York: Zed-Books).

Duffield, Mark (2002) 'Social Reconstruction and the Radicalization of Development: Aid as a Relation of Global Liberal Governance', *Development and Change* 33(5), pp. 1049–1071.

Duffield, Mark (2007) *Development, Security and Unending War. Governing the World of Peoples* (Cambridge: Polity Press).

Duffield, Mark (2010) 'The Liberal Way of Development and the Development – Security Impasse: Exploring the Global Life-Chance Divide', *Security Dialogue* 41(1), pp. 53–76.

Escobar, Arturo (1995) *Encountering Development: The Making and Unmaking of the Third World* (Princeton, N.J.: Princeton University Press).

Foucault, Michel (1980) *Power/Knowledge: Selected Interviews and Other Writings, 1972–1977* (New York: Vintage).

Ghani, Ashraf and Clare Lockhart (2008) *Fixing Failed States* (New York: Oxford University Press).

Gordon, Colin (2014) 'Afghanistan's Stabilization Program. Hope in a Dystopian Sea?' in Robert Muggah (ed.) *Stabilization Operations, Security and Development* (Abingdon; New York: Routledge), pp. 84–104.

Grindle, Merilee S. (2007) 'Good Enough Governance Revisited', *Development Policy Review* 25(5), pp. 533–574.

Gros, Jean-Germain (1996) 'Towards a Taxonomy of Failed States in the New World Order: Decaying Somalia, Liberia, Rwanda and Haiti', *Third World Quarterly* 17(3), pp. 455–471.

Hagmann, Tobias and Markus V. Hoehne (2009) 'Failures of the State Failure Debate: Evidence From the Somali Territories', *Journal of International Development* 21(1), pp. 42–57.

Heiduk, Felix (2014) 'State Disintegration and Power Politics in Post-Suharto Indonesia', *Third World Quarterly* 35(2), pp. 300–315.

Hettne, Bjoern (2010) 'Development and Security: Origins and Future', *Security Dialogue* 41(1), pp. 31–52.

Hill, Jonathan (2005) 'Beyond the Other? A Postcolonial Critique of the Failed State Thesis', *African Identities* 3(2), pp. 139–154.

Hoogensen, Gunhild and Kirsti Stuvoy (2006) 'Gender, Resistance and Human Security', *Security Dialogue* 37(2), pp. 207–228.

ICCS, International Commission on Intervention and State Sovereignty (2001) The Responsibility to Protect. Report of the International Commission on Intervention and State Sovereignty. Ottawa, https://web.archive.org/web/20070731161541/www.iciss-ciise.gc.ca/pdf/Commission-Report.pdf (accessed March 03, 2017).

Joseph, Jonathan (2016) 'Governing through Failure and Denial: The New Resilience Agenda', *Millennium* 44(3), pp. 370–390.

Kaldor, Mary (1999) *New and Old Wars: Organised Violence in a Global Era* (Cambridge: Polity Press).

Lemay-Hébert, Nicolas (2011) 'The Bifurcation of the Two Worlds: Assessing the Gap between Internationals and Locals in State-Building Processes', *Third World Quarterly* 32(10), pp. 1823–1841.

Lockhart, Clare and Ashraf Ghani (2009) *Fixing Failed States: A Framework for Rebuilding a Fractured World* (New York: Oxford University Press).

Mallaby, Sebastian (2002) 'The Reluctant Imperialist: Terrorism, Failed States, and the Case for American Empire', *Foreign Affairs* 81(2), pp. 2–7.

Manning, Richard and Alexandra Trzeciak-Duval (2010) 'Situations of Fragility and Conflict: Aid Policies and Beyond', *Conflict, Security & Development* 10(1), pp. 103–131.

Marquette, Heather and Danielle Beswick (2011) 'State Building, Security and Development: State Building as a New Development Paradigm?', *Third World Quarterly* 32(10), pp. 1703–1714.

Millar, Gearoid and Jaïr van der Lijn and Willemijn Verkoren (2013) 'Peacebuilding Plans and Local Reconfigurations: Frictions between Imported Processes and Indigenous Practices', *International Peacekeeping* 20(2), pp. 137–143.

Milliken, Jennifer and Keith Krause (2002) 'State Failure, State Collapse, and State Recon-struction: Concepts, Lessons and Strategies', *Development and Change* 33(5), pp. 753–774.

Muggah, Robert (2014) 'Introduction', in Robert Muggah (ed.) *Stabilization Operations, Security and Development* (Abingdon; New York: Routledge), pp. 1–14.

OECD, Organisation for Economic Development (2007) 'Principles for Good International Engagement in Fragile States & Situations', www.africa-platform.org/sites/default/files/resources/fragile_state_principles.pdf (accessed March 12, 2017).

OECD, Organisation for Economic Development (2011) 'Conflict and Fragility. International Engagement in Fragile States: Can't We Do better?' www.oecd.org/dac/conflict-fragility-resilience/docs/IEFS.pdf (accessed March 08, 2017).

OECD, Organisation for Economic Development (2013) 'Fragile States 2013. Resource Flows and Trends in a Shifting World'.

OECD, Organisation for Economic Development (2014) 'Fragile States 2014. Domestic Revenue Mobilisation in Fragile States', https://www.oecd.org/dac/governance-peace/conflictfragilityandresilience/docs/FSR-2014.pdf (accessed June 16, 2017).

OECD, Organisation for Economic Development (2016) *States of Fragility 2016. Highlights,* www.oecd.org/dac/conflict-fragility-resilience/docs/Fragile-States-highlights-2016.pdf (accessed June 12, 2017).

Paris, Roland (2002) 'International Peacebuilding and the "Mission Civilisatrice"', *Review of International Studies* 28(4), pp. 637–656.

Paris, Roland (2009) 'Understanding the "coordination problem" in Postwar Statebuilding', in Roland Paris and Timothy D. Sisk (eds.) *The Dilemmas of Statebuilding. Confronting the Contradictions of Postwar Peace Operations* (London/New York: Routledge), pp. 53–78.

Paris, Roland and Timothy D. Sisk (eds.) (2009a) *Dilemmas of Statebuilding* (London/New York: Routledge).

Paris, Roland and Timothy D. Sisk (2009b) 'Conclusion: Confronting the Contradictions', in Roland Paris and Timothy D. Sisk (eds.) *Dilemmas of Statebuilding* (London/New York: Routledge), pp. 304–314.

Patrick, Stewart (2006) 'Weak States and Global Threats: Assessing Evidence of "Spillovers"', www.cgdev.org/files/5539_file_WP_73.pdf (accessed March 15, 2017).

Patrick, Stewart (2007) '"Failed" States and Global Security: Empirical Questions and Policy Dilemmas', *International Studies Review* 9(4), pp. 644–662.

Putzel, James and Jonathan Di John (2012) *Meeting the Challenges of Crisis States.* London, www.lse.ac.uk/internationalDevelopment/research/crisisStates/download/finalreport/Meeting-the-Challenges-of-Crisis-States.pdf (accessed March 06, 2017).

Reno, William (2000) 'Shadow States and the Political Economy of Civil Wars', in Mats Berdal and David M. Malone (eds.) *Greed and Grievance. Economic Agendas in Civil Wars* (Boulder/London: Lynne Rienner), pp. 43–69.

Richmond, Oliver P. and Jason Franks (2011) *Liberal Peace Transitions: Between Statebuilding and Peacebuilding* (Edinburgh: Edinburgh University Press).

Rocha Menocal, Alina (2011) 'State Building for Peace: A New Paradigm for International Engagement in Post-conflict Fragile States?', *Third World Quarterly* 32(10), pp. 1715–1736.

Rottenburg, Richard (2009) *Far-Fetched Facts. A Parable of Development Aid* (Cambridge, MA: MIT Press).

Rubin, Barnett R. (2006) 'Peace Building and State-Building in Afghanistan: Constructing Sovereignty for Whose Security?', *Third World Quarterly* 27(1), pp. 175–185.

Sabaratnam, Meera (2011) 'The Liberal Peace? An Intellectual History of International Conflict Management, 1990–2010', in Susanna Campbell and David Chandler and Meera Sabaratnam (eds.) *A Liberal Peace? The Problems and Practices of Peacebuilding* (London: Zed Book), pp. 13–30.

Sally Engle, Merry (2006) 'Transnational Human Rights and Local Activism: Mapping the Middle', *American Anthropologist* 108(1), pp. 38–51.

Samuels, Kirsti and Sebastian von Einsiedel (2003) *The Future of UN State-Building: Strategic and Operational Challenges and the Legacy of Iraq.* New York, www.ipinst.org/wp-content/uploads/publications/future_of_un_state_building.pdf (accessed March 09, 2017).

Scott, Joey (2007) *Literature Review on State-Building*, www.gsdrc.org/docs/open/hd528.pdf (accessed February 22, 2017).

SFTF, State Failure Task Force (2002) *State Failure Task Force Report. Phase III Findings,* www.raulzelik.net/images/rztextarchiv/uniseminare/statefailure task force.pdf (accessed March 04, 2017).

Stewart, Frances and Graham Brown (2009) *Fragile States Oxford*, http://www3.qeh.ox.ac.uk/pdf/crisewps/workingpaper51.pdf (accessed March 03, 2017).

Strange, Susan (1995) 'The Defective State', *Daedalus* 124(2), pp. 55–74.

SU, Stabilisation Unit QIP Handbook (n.D) *Quick Impact Projects – QIP's Handbook.* London, http://ns2.amplifymedia.com/attachments/article/520/QIPs handbook[1].pdf (accessed March 06, 2017).

Suhrke, Astri (2009) 'The Dangers of a Tight Embrace: Externally Assisted Statebuilding in Afghanistan' in Roland Paris and Timothy D. Sisk (eds.) *The Dilemmas of Statebuilding. Confronting the Contradictions of Postwar Peace Operations* (London; New York: Routledge), pp. 227–251.

Teitel, Ruti G. (2003) 'Transitional Justice Genealogy', *Harvard Human Rights Journal* 16, pp. 69–94.

Tsing, Anna Lowenhaupt (2005) *Friction: An Ethnography of Global Connections* (Princeton: Princeton University Press).

Weinstein, Jeremy M. and John Edward Porter and Stuart E. Eizenstat (2004) *On the Brink: Weak States and US National Security. A Report of the Commission for Weak States and US National Security*, www.cgdev.org/doc/books/weakstates/Full_Report.pdf (accessed: March 04, 2017).

World Bank (2013) *Building Resilience: Integrating Climate and Disaster Risk into Development. Lessons from World Bank Group Experience.* Washington DC, http://documents.worldbank.org/curated/en/762871468148506173/pdf/826480WP0v10Bu0130Box37986200OUO090.pdf (accessed March 24, 2017).

Yannis, Alexandros (2002) 'State Collapse and its Implications for Peace – Building and Reconstruction', *Development and Change* 33(5), pp. 817–835.

Zartman, William I. (ed.) (1995) *Collapsed States. The Disintegration and Restoration of Legitimate Authority* (Boulder: Lynne Rienner).

Chapter 21

Soft and hard power

Annamarie Bindenagel Šehović

The distinction between so-called hard and soft power is at once superficial and penetrating. Hard power invokes force. Soft power whispers of persuasion. Hard power is not necessarily violence, though it is generally associated with force. *However, is it force when one state convinces another to act against its interests? Soft power evokes an idea of conviction, yet is it persuasion when economic straitjackets make all other theoretical policy options practically obsolete?* Richard Higgott

FIGURE 21.1 Two women check their smartphones in St Petersburg, Russia

refers to soft power as a 'notion', belying the lurking of hard power behind it. Indeed, hard and soft power are not always so easily separated.[1]

This chapter introduces hard and soft power as applied to national states. States continue to constitute the building blocks of the international system, and are conventionally understood to hold a legitimate monopoly over hard power as force. The chapter explores the origins of both hard and soft power, offering illustrative examples. Further, it analyses variations on the two as well as caveats which challenge their differentiation. Finally, the chapter introduces the idea of 'smart' power, also referred to as or 'collaborative' or contextual power, as another, more flexible lens and framework through which to analyse state power.

Conceptions of power lie at the heart of the study of international relations (IR). The discipline's four principal theoretical schools each view power, and its balance, differently. Realists envision a Hobbsian anarchy as the context within which states, and the sanctity of their borders, their territorial sovereignty, represent the highest ordering principles. This position arguably ceded its primacy to that of liberal institutionalism, over the course of the late 20th century. In this rendering, the institutions of the United Nations, conceived in the aftermath of World Wars I and II, constitute the central ordering mechanisms of the Liberal School. As the bifurcation of the Cold War gave way to the short-lived unipolarity of a seemingly ascendant Western society, as outlined in Francis Fukuyama's 1989 essay 'The End of History', the English School trumpeted the rise of a world society. This was underpinned by the consolidation of shared norms the Constructivists trace to the centrality of human rights[2] and their cousins, notably social, economic and cultural rights.[3]

Essentially, the development of each of these schools maps movement on a power spectrum from power 'over' to power 'with'. Describing the shift from vertical to horizontal power arrangements, Geoff Mulgan refers to 'connexity' (1998), Jessica Matthews to a power shift involving both state and non-state actors (NSAs) (1997) and Anne-Marie Slaughter to 'networks' (2011). Seeking to make clearer divisions, Joseph S. Nye had stepped into the fray in 1990 in an attempt to differentiate between what he called 'hard' and 'soft' power. The naming of the terms 'hard' and 'soft' power represents a further attempt to harness this change without negating the continued presence of hard power. The simple resonance and particular timing of this terminology is also, as articulated by Fukuyama, historically embedded in the end of the Cold War.

The Cold War arguably delineated the geopolitical world into two blocks, plus the so-called Third World.[4] This order was maintained, and contained, by the balance of hard-power, in the form of nuclear weapons, represented by the five recognised weapons' possessing states, the US, USSR (now Russia), China, France and the UK, which comprise the United Nation's Security Council (UNSC). Despite all of the geopolitical and governance shifts which have occurred in the interim, from the dissolution of the USSR to the decolonisation of Africa to the 'second-wave' of democracy at the juncture of 1989–90, this order has remained.[5]

All the while, soft power played a supportive role. On the one hand, it reinforced the Cold War order as each block propagated its ideals. On the other hand, it whittled away at it: so much so that with the fall of the Berlin Wall on 9 November 1989 and the end of the Cold War, the soft power of the West seemed to prevail over its hard power. The restrictive Second World succumbed to the freedoms – delivered via soft power and satellite TV – of the First World.

In naming 'hard' and 'soft' power, Nye thus gave a penetrating insight a superficial nomenclature (1990a). It is penetrating because hard and soft power can indeed be distinguished, in definition and in action. Nye defines 'hard power' as 'the use of coercion and payment' (Nye, 2009) and 'soft power' as 'the ability of a country to persuade others to do what it wants without force or coercion' (Nye, 1990b). But for all of the prowess of soft power, this end of the Cold War was couched in hard power: it is known that the Soviet, then Russian, arsenal of the Warsaw Pact did not match that of the West and of NATO (North Atlantic Treaty Organisation). Nonetheless, the narrative is of the prevailing of soft not hard power. The labels are used superficially everywhere: in state apparatuses to describe the military action and military efforts, for example, to 'win hearts and minds'; and from traditional to public diplomacy. Analysing their ongoing applicability to international relations is now necessary to understand the next phase of world order.

The current moment seems to be one of what Trine Flockhart[6] terms a 'multi-order' world (Flockhart, 2016). She argues that as opposed to multiple poles of power competing with one another within one global system, as in the bi-polarity between East and West during the Cold War and acting through the United Nations, a multi-order world is characterised not only by different power poles but by these competing within separate systems of which the United Nations constitutes only one. Others include the unwieldly G20,[7] IBSA,[8] the BRICS,[9] and the proliferating institutions of Asia, which boast the relatively power-less ASEAN,[10] and the centrifugal AIIB.[11] Approaching these shifts from a constructivist perspective, others have identified an increase in 'heteronomy': external rule that impacts agency (see Sending, 2017),[12] with reference both to state and individual scope of action: of power. Both descriptions emphasise a possible renegotiation and translocation of the post–World War II focus on peace and development and universal human rights' protection by states for their citizens. Towards what new organising principle, of what and between which multiple poles or orders, by whom and for whom, remains unclear.

Mary Kaldor highlights the failure of states to live up to objective dangers (2014). Those dangers may stem from the exertion of either hard and/or soft power. Perhaps no development showcases this as poignantly as does the rise in cyber (in)security. It is matched only by the inadequate abilities, legal as well as technological, and capabilities of states and citizens to respond. The threat is multidimensional, the product of both multiple orders and none.

On the one hand, the threat states themselves pose to the rights' of their citizens. On the other hand, the changing nature of the threats to peace and development – among them, climate change, pandemics, migration and cyber (in)security – threaten citizens and non-citizens as well as states themselves. These are accompanied by a rise in uncertainty with regard to the erstwhile accepted sanctity, not only of state sovereignty, but also of the human security within it. A simple delineation between hard and soft power comes up short. What is required at this juncture instead is 'smart power'. Smart power, which may also include 'collaborative' and contextual power, refers to 'the capacity of an actor to combine elements of hard power and soft power in ways that are mutually reinforcing such as that the actor's purposes are advanced effectively and efficiently' (Wilson, 2008).

In the remainder of this chapter I will first explore the concepts of hard and soft power. Second, I will spell out the critiques against such a binary vision, taking into account that states arguably need both hard and soft power. The current factious governance climate demarcated by concurrent trends in deceleration in economic growth, for instance, and acceleration, such as in the digitalisation of communication and automation, makes this especially clear. It can be argued that hard and soft power are vital to the articulation and protection of the norms and values, institutions and territories of states themselves. Yet, as briefly outlined earlier, these entities are themselves under pressure: where then can hard and soft power be deployed? Third and finally, the chapter will analyse the concept of 'smart' power and argue for its value as both political power and the IR discipline moves further into the 21st century.

Hard power

Hard power can on the one hand be reduced to coercive power. It is the power of one state to force another to act in a certain manner. In Nye's words, hard power is 'an ability to do things and control others, to get others to do what they otherwise would not' (1990, pp. 153–171). This definition equates hard power with resources; 'the possession of a population, territory, natural resources, economic size, military forces, and political stability'. While generally associated with military power that is not its only domain. Economic power is also a form of hard power.

In practise, however, no state has ever enjoyed an unadulterated monopoly of hard power. Stephen Krasner[13] identifies four dimensions of sovereignty, 'Westphalian, juridical, domestic and interdependence'. Westphalian sovereignty alludes to territorial integrity, and the ability to protect borders from external invasion;[14] juridical is legal recognition by other states;[15] domestic refers to internal policing, arguably including the provision of human security; and interdependence takes into account the ability of a state to control its border flow, including the transnational movement of people, goods and diseases. In this construct, inherited through Westphalian history and expanded throughout Europe and exported around the globe, the legitimate state alone can use military power to achieve its purposes. The first such purpose is to protect the integrity of the state's territorial borders. The second purpose is to provide for the human security of the population within those borders,[16] in order to:

1   Provide physical security to everyone living in its area of jurisdiction;
2   Build and maintain legitimate political institutions to implement government programs and sustain the whole;
3   Provide sound and consistent economic management; as well as
4   Create conditions for and providing mechanisms of social welfare to those who need them.[17]

Ultimately, hard power, wielded by a state, has as its mission the protection of borders and the provision of the external conditions under which any other form of power – security and sanctify of sovereignty of the state and of the conditions conducive of human security – are meant to flourish. However, given the interaction between internal and external forces in nearly all of these dimensions, it becomes clear that it is unrealistic to assume complete control, uncompromised sovereignty and unlimited recourse to the exercise of hard power.

In order to achieve its ends then, power requires influence on two planes. First, power if, when and where, it operates against the proclivities or interest of the actor upon whom it (power) is being exercised. Here hard power includes military apparatuses of air, land and naval force, as well as cyber. Highlighting the complexities of this further, juridical recourse against cyber (attacks) is limited, especially so long as the source of such an attack is untraceable and unknown.[18] This is because despite increased transnational exchange, including of components of power,[19] interdependence (sovereignty) and legal processes remain national. The sole exception here is NATO, with its ability to invoke Article V: wherein an attack on one is perceived to be an attack on all member states, requiring these to respond. Such a response includes military but also economic options. This highlights the role of economics as an element of hard power. Economic power is fuelled by demography, which in turn supports the military. Expansive and profitable industries were key to the military and economic success of the Western (capitalist) model over that of the Soviet Union at the culmination of the Cold War. Second, sanctioning key industries economically directly impacts on military power.

In an illustrative example, the long list of current conflicts alone – from the Crimea to the South China Sea, from the contested expansion of Daesh in Iraq and Syria to South Sudan – indicate that geography and its associated geopolitical significance are not an obsolete component of hard power ambition. Furthermore, Daesh's prolonged control over the Mosul Dam in 2016–17, whose floodwaters it could unleash to cause destruction, amply illustrates the continued role of geographic and territorial elements in the exercise of hard power: cutting off water to Aleppo and Damascus (latest events in December 2016 and January 2017, respectively) is evidence of a hard power tactic.

These examples illustrate that assertions of a one dimensional 'hard' power are misplaced. Resources, territorial, geographic and demographic, which create the fuel of military force, combined with economic incentives and sanctions to gain and gird power constitute the critical elements of hard power. When wedded to the complexities of (mis)communications, to unwinnable conventional stalemates, and cyber (warfare), the framework of conventional power will need to be adapted. This is because these powers are not neatly separable: particularly the space-less-ness of cyberpower showcases how economic and political incentives, from economic espionage[20] to electoral interference, skirt the definition of hard power. Indeed, the deployment of such hybrid forms of 'hard' power are better referred to as 'sharp' power: the exploitation and manipulation of ideas as well as cyber and military weapons to penetrate not only state boundaries but especially societies and social realities. It is the 'authoritarian determination to monopolize ideas, suppress alternative narratives, and exploit partner institutions' (Walker and Ludwig, 2017). Sharp power is a perversion of the power of meanings.

This leads to the second power through which a state can act upon to change the wishes, if not the interests, of the actor upon which it is being applied. This is what is simplistically described as 'soft' power – that of conviction.

Soft power

Soft power is conventionally equated with 'culture'. In international relations, however, soft power is a multifaceted tool strategically employed to garner not only goodwill but also tangible benefits for the 'national interest' of the state pursuing a particular agenda. Soft power, often in conjunction with hard power, thus serves an explicit purpose.

Soft power includes the allure of film culture as seen from Hollywood (US) to Bollywood (India) to Nollywood (Nigeria). These superficially but nonetheless reflect not only lifestyles but also ideals and ideas. Soft power is a dynamic power. It is its malleability that is the essence of soft power: it can be influenced and changed, both through external and internal influences. It 'is the ability to obtain preferred outcomes through attraction' (Nye, 2009). A fuller definition characterises soft power as 'the ability to affect others through the co-optive means of framing the agenda, persuading, and eliciting positive attraction in order to obtain preferred outcomes' (Nye, 2011, pp. 20–21).

The idea of soft power is not new as such. 'Political leaders and philosophizers have long understood the power of attractive ideas or the ability to set the political agenda and determine the framework of debate in a way that shapes others' preferences' (Nye, 1990, pp. 153–171). Soft power is projected through immigration policies and treaty agreements,[21] and propounded through cultural and educational exchanges, including Erasmus and Fulbright scholarships, Goethe Institutes and cultural diplomacy as practiced by (non-)diplomats. Soft power operates by convincing not coercing.

> America's greatest strength is not the example of our power but the power of our example. More than anything, it is our adherence to our values and our commitment to tolerance that sets us apart from other great powers.
>
> (Biden, 2016)

In order to work, soft power must be believable: 'Diplomacy and development can only be mutually reinforcing if the U.S. government also get its own house in order' (Clinton, 2010). Nye argues that 'nations must use soft power to develop networks and build institutions to address shared threats and challenges' (Nye, 2017). Even beyond official fora of global governance, soft power is seen in emulation of truth and reconciliation commissions (TRC), perhaps most famously by South Africa but also by Bolivia, Canada, Peru and others. Even in their failures, the discourse on a TRC is a form of soft-power.

The US has long held a special place in the exercise of soft power, having conceived and established and largely funded the 'basic architecture of the international order after the devastation of World War II' (Biden, 2016), working against that country's isolationist tendencies. By both sponsoring and adhering to such international rules, the US supported and expanded the role of soft power in maintaining the unprecedented peace in Europe – and by extension throughout much of the world. Where it fails to conform and comply, such as opting out of the International Criminal Court (ICC), the US undermines such soft power championship. Similarly, the current (2017) debate among some academic and policy elites regarding a possible German nuclear option in the wake of waning US support for NATO, threatens not only German rule-of-law as it would violate that country's signature of the Non-Proliferation Treaty (NPT), but also the more general principle of nuclear non-proliferation.

These examples illustrate that in the end, 'proof of power lies not in resources but in the ability to change the behaviour of states' (Nye, 2017), and beyond that, in the ability to influence the appropriateness of the behaviour of states. Perhaps the best proof of this has been the adherence of other states to this post–World War II order, without coercion. With regard to China, one of only five countries to hold a veto in the governing organ, the UN Security Council, it also accepts the jurisdiction of the World Trade Organisation (WTO) and the International Monetary Fund (IMF), while lobbying for more powerful voting rights in the latter. In addition, 'in 2015, Beijing joined with Washington in developing new norms for dealing with climate change and conflicts in cyberspace. On balance, China has tried not to overthrow the current order but rather to increase its influence within it' (Nye, 2017). Likewise, after hedging during the SARS outbreak of 2003, reaping it international condemnation, China chose to adhere to the International Health Regulations (IHRs) reporting requirements in the H5N1 and H7N9 crises, earning it international recognition and accolades. Thus soft power utilises persuasion, which can be backed by hard power.[22]

Operating as a facilitator of soft and hard power channels is diplomacy. Such diplomacy increasingly includes not only traditional, state-based diplomacy, but also economic, science and health diplomacy. While often juxtaposed as opposites, diplomacy is not the automatic counterweight of military power. In the words of Winston Churchill, 'diplomacy is the art of telling people to go to hell in such a way that they ask for directions', rendering it far more an instrument in the service of hard power as soft power in and of itself. Diplomacy does, however, rely on soft power: on communication and conviction. Yet it is also backed by coercive power – or the threat thereof. As such, diplomacy is not a pure embodiment of soft power, but much more a form of 'smart power'. It is diplomacy – increasingly specialised as 'public' or 'health' or 'science' diplomacy as well – that can bridge the gap between hard and soft power.

The resultant normative contributions of soft power are evidenced in the promulgation of human rights' agreements and accords, including the World Health Organisation's 'right to health' as evinced in the emerging Framework Convention on Global Health. Other such accounts are also the rise of the Global Health Security Agenda in the wake of the United Nation's Security Council votes to respond to first HIV and AIDS (2001) and Ebola Virus Disease (2014); as well as the Millennium Development Goals (MDGs, 2000) and the Sustainable Development Goals (SDGs, 2015). These agenda items are increasingly reflected in the high-level meetings of the United Nations, within the frameworks of the G7 and the G20, through forums of the IBSA and the BRICS, as well as at political-economic conventions such as at the World Economic Forum at Davos. As norms shift into action through International Health Regulations (IHRs) and similar norms, these soft power efforts become more effective. All of these examples operate in the state-centric structure outlined earlier. But a shift is occurring in the 'soft' power arena that might indicate a new systemic change.

For instance, science and technology (S&T) communities have emerged as catalysts of soft power. S&T, by inverting some of the hard power imbalances through an emphasis not only on 'capital-rich' but also on 'information-rich', can play an important role in elevating the soft power potential especially of otherwise poorer states (Nye, 1990). Luk Van Langehove points out that 'invisible colleges' of scientists 'across state-borders can contribute to building trust between nations or cultures'. He notes that through such interactions, science diplomacy can 'contribute to discovering technical solutions to political problems' (Van Langenhove, 2016, p. 18). S&T thereby contributes to the power of states, as well as interstate relations. Similar exchanges are occurring in the realms of climate and health diplomacy as well.

These 'newer' forms of diplomacy reflect on the one hand the increasing fragmentation of issue areas, and on the other hand, their interconnectivity. On the one hand, these continue to serve states. On the other, these aid the agendas and the agenda-setting among non-state-actors (NSAs). Soft power in the service of states reflects political values and foreign policies. At the same time, it also serves as a cultural export or allure beyond firm state control. Soft power in the service of NSAs can further particular agendas, such as human rights or access to medicines, but often relies upon states for their implementation. This reinforces the centrality of states to the current global order – despite the many challenges these confront. In order for soft power to succeed – for its allure to endure – it must be attractive.

That said, given the rising costs and stakes of hard power, soft power is of increasing value to state and NSAs alike. At the same time, soft power is itself multidirectional: translated and translocated locally and globally. This translatability and translocation of power represents a fundamental shift. It requires a new kind of 'smart power', a combination of hard and soft power seeded with contextual insight and persuasive force to set and streamline the global agenda for (human) security.

Beyond hard or soft power: smart power to catalytic power

At this stage, it should go without saying that successful states require hard as well as soft power capabilities.[23] The current moment beckons: the US re-evaluates its commitment to NATO, as the European Union and commentators in Germany review the Continent's conventional and nuclear arsenals, and as East Asia gears up for (re-)newed confrontation(s) between China and Japan and South Korea, and North Korea against all. The need to harness the insights of hard and soft power together is more apparent than ever.

Initial ideas, from connexity to collaboration to catalyst, can contribute to a new thinking on necessarily transnational power. Such a new conceptualisation must take into account the components of hard power and soft power, yielding perhaps a new 'smart power'.

Despite the short-lived triumph of soft power towards the turn of the last century, hard power remains a crucial and critical component of any analysis and practice of power. Hard power need not refer exclusively to military attack or invasion, or to economic sanctions (Nye, 2009), but can rather incorporate military deployment for a humanitarian initiative. One such example is of the international, including US and German, military involvement in the international response to the Ebola Virus Disease (EVD) outbreak in West Africa.

Yet hard power, unattached to communities and diplomacy, is not enough. Soft and softer power is also vital. 'If a state can make its power seem legitimate in the eyes of others, it will encounter less resistance to its wishes' (Nye, 1990, pp. 153–171). These wishes may then become the necessary responses to increasingly global problems by internationalised, networked communities. Seen through such a lens, hard and soft power essentially consist of the two poles of the three major facets of power: the power to 'command', to 'control agendas' and to 'shape preferences' (Nye, in Slaughter, 2011). Against the backdrop of competing world orders and the rising intensity of global problems and challenges, smart power emerges as a contextualised, collaborative imperative.

Wilson identifies such shifts on three panes of power: conceptualisation, institutional and political. The conceptual level refers to the post–World War II consensus of state dedication to the pursuit of peace and prosperity. The institutional level supports these assumptions through the administrative arrangements of the United Nations (UN), the European Union (EU), the Organisation for Security and Co-operation in Europe (OSCE) and the North Atlantic Treaty Organisation (NATO). The political level includes the negotiation of participation in power constructs on the part of both state and non-state actors. Strains, as outlined earlier, are emerging at each of these levels. He contends that such smart power combining elements of hard and soft power – and even pushing beyond their strictures is indispensable. He argues for a smart power as a 'national security imperative, driven both by long-term structural changes in international conditions and by short-term failures of the current administration' (Wilson, 2008).

While Wilson's vision continues to operate along the vertical dimension of Westphalian power, Slaughter offers another version of 'smart power'. Hers is a 'collaborative power'. Its three forms include: mobilisation, connection and adaptation (Slaughter, 2011). These are all powers along a horizontal plane, characterised by interconnections and interactions as in networks (Slaughter, 2004). So-called soft diplomacy is an example of such non-state, collaborative power. Taken together, they might produce a catalytic power that harnesses the incentives of hard power to the cooperative tendencies of soft power.

Soft diplomacy makes use of 'public diplomacy, broadcasting, exchange programs, development assistance, disaster relief, military-to-military contacts' (Nye, 2009). Incorporating both domestic and international aspects of soft and hard power into his overall calculation of power, US diplomat and historian George Kennan included America's mighty economic power, undergirded by 'globalization and the emergence of truly multinational corporations', in his assessment of tools of foreign policy.[24] Given the myriad challenges contemporary states face – from geographic and geological insecurities to food and health insecurity as well as climate-induced environmental change and (im)migration challenges – Kennan's analysis of a necessarily multi-dimensional smart power is persuasive.

The revival of soft diplomacy as smart power in international relations and its arrival in policy circles is evidenced especially in the field of global health: in the 'localisation' of the World Bank's partnership programs, in the conceptualisation of the Framework Convention on Tobacco Control (World Health Organization, 2003) as well as that of the promotion of the US President's Emergency Plan for AIDS Relief (PEPFAR) and the in-progress Framework Convention for Global Health (FCGH). Eric P. Goosby, who as US Global AIDS Coordinator from 2009–13, promoted and oversaw PEPFAR's second phase, regarded the program as soft diplomacy and smart power par excellence, aimed at 'leading with our hearts and minds' (Goosby, 2017). As such, 'smart power' (Wilson, 2008) can take into account the possibilities of employing hard power, for humanitarian purposes, for instance, while harnessing soft power in the form of research or development cooperation – as for medical trials. This was seen in the response to EVD.

> Diplomatic, international development and foreign policy trends are increasingly aligned with the theory of 'smart power' (Ferrero-Waldner, 2007): the strategic use of persuasion, capacity building and the projection of influence, in ways that are both cost-effective and have political and social legitimacy, based on an integrated strategy.
>
> (Kevany, 4)

Combining the worlds of state, business and society, soft diplomacy or smart power operates at an intersection between hard and soft power, between state and non-state actors (NSAs). It presents perhaps the glue between, and certainly highlights the necessity of linking, hard and soft power during what promises to be a new phase of contestation over geography, resources, values and allocations. How such smart power will be invoked and leveraged against a changing background of conceptual, institutional and political competition on the local and global levels will be a key challenge for specific sectors – including health and science – but also for scholars of international relations to identify, analyse and understand.

Conclusion

Global changes are challenging the bifurcation of 'hard' and 'soft' power. These changes include the rise of new institutions and NSAs noted earlier, as well as the increasing complexity of issue areas such as health and science, as well as communication and cyber technologies. Trine Flockhart identifies an emergent 'multi-order' world, a world where sharp and catalytic power will play an increasing role. In her rendering, such a world is characterised not by the bifurcation of the Cold War nor by the unipolar moment that appeared in its aftermath, but rather by a host of competing spheres each of them operating according to differing principles of power as reflected in their competing value structures, institutions and projections of both hard and soft power (Flockhart, 2016). How that same world chooses to adapt and respond at the intersection of powers and poles will define the course of the 21st century.

Some of the values in question include the human rights' based order familiar from the United Nations, and that of the community-centric Confucian; institutions such as the World Bank and the Asian Infrastructure Investment Bank (AIIB); and projections of power, including both to the NATO and Russian and Chinese military posturing in Eastern Europe and the Pacific, but also to the battles for 'hearts and minds' taking place face-to-face in space and time, and also in and through cyber-space. Amidst such seminal changes, states coercion or (imposition of) conviction may no longer work. In other words, when states upon whom coercion or conviction is being exercised shift their focus – from the definition of their values to that of their national interests to their priorities within these – they become less susceptible to such overtures, whether via hard or soft power.

Hard power continues to be associated with states, typically against other states. However, future research will be required to analyse the role of hard power invoked within states, as well as wielded by NSAs and other extra-state actors both internally and externally. Soft power refers to forces of persuasion and conviction, and increasingly includes not only traditional diplomacy, but also health and science diplomacy, whose remit stretches far beyond the borders of any state jurisdiction. Smart power marries the two: on the one hand with the purpose of furthering state influence and thus power, on the other hand with the aim of fostering (global) public goods.

As this chapter has striven to show, the distinctions between hard and soft and smart power are not set in stone. Nonetheless, it is useful to separate their key elements. This simplifies the study of 'power' in international relations, breaking it down into building blocks which can then be compared and contrasted, and perhaps most importantly, enabling the identification of changes and patterns and prognosis. As the conceptual, institutional and political spaces between state and NSAs are challenged and contested and constricts, the role of each of those powers and all three together will be key to the (re)making of the emergent international order.

Disclaimer

This chapter represents the author's view and does not necessarily reflect that of the project. She would like to especially thank the participants of the Diplomacy and Development workshop in Malta, 27–28 April 2017, for their valuable insights.

Notes

1 Presentation within the context of Horizon2020, EL-CSID, Diplomacy and Development conference, 27–28 April 2017, Malta.
2 United Nations (UN).
3 Economic and Social Council (ECOSOC).
4 The designation 'Third World' gave way to 'developing world", which in turn has given way to the 'Global South'. These terms stand in comparison and contrast to the 'First (and sometimes the communist/socialist "Second") World', the 'developed world' and the 'Global North'.
5 Although it is being tested in an unprecedented manner at the time of this writing.
6 Flockhart, Trine (2016) 'No One's World: The Coming Multi-Order World', *Contemporary Security Policy* 37(1).
7 Group of 20, whose ministers of various governmental sectors, including finance and foreign policy, increasingly meet to discuss, if not (yet) make, global policy.

8   A grouping of India, Brazil and South Africa. This has been particularly active in advancing the human 'right to health', also through access to medicines.
9   Brazil, Russia, India, China and South Africa: a political grouping more than a center of political or economic power.
10 Association of East Asian Nations. ASEAN does, however, coordinate the sharing of policy in the area of (human) security, and is even pioneering the sharing of health professionals. The latter is possibly the result of the 'viral sovereignty' crisis related to the sequencing of H5N1 in 2007, and Indonesia's refusal to participate without a guarantee of access to subsequently developed medicines to treat the epidemic.
11 Asian Infrastructure Investment Bank.
12 Sending, Ole Jacob at International Studies Association (ISA), Baltimore, US, 23 February 2017.
13 Krasner, Stephen (1999) *Sovereignty: Disorganized Hypocrisy* (Princeton, NJ: Princeton University Press).
14 This principle of non-violation has worked remarkably well, with the exception of territorial expansion in various resource wars (see 'Lebensraum' in World War II, for example). However, the ongoing territorial disputes in Kashmir, and Donbas in the Ukraine, to name but two examples, being met with inconsistent hard power response might yet indicate a (further) fraying of the principle (norm).
15 This is also required for membership into the United Nations. At times, such recognition is contested and incomplete: see Kosovo (1998), South Sudan (2011) and Crimea (disputed in 2014).
16 See also Hösle, Vittoria (2003) *Morals and Politics* (Notre Dame, IN: University of Notre Dame Press).
17 See Hösle, Vittorio (2003) *Morals and Politics* (Notre Dame, IN: University of Notre Dame Press).
18 The legal ramifications of this have yet to be tried: most states only recognize territorial attacks, leaving them powerless to respond to cyber (war).
19 These include military cooperation and exchange in particular, as well as economic transactions.
20 See 'Economic Espionage' definition by the Legal Information Institute, Cornell University Law School, with reference to the Economic Espionage Act of 1996 (EEA), www.law.cornell.edu/wex/economic_espionage (accessed March 13, 2017).
21 The US 'has some 60 treaty allies, and *The Economist* estimates that nearly 100 of the 150 largest countries lean toward it, while only 21 lean against it'.
22 See, for example, Fry, Michael Graham, Erik Goldstein and Richard Langhorne (eds.) (2002) *Guide to International Relations and Diplomacy* (New York: Continuum).
23 See also Nye, Joseph S. Jr (2005) *Soft Power: The Means to Success in World Politics* (New York: PublicAffairs).
24 Quoted in Jenkins, Brian Michael 'A Revanchist Russia Versus An Uncertain West: What Can Be Done?', via Marvin Zonis.

Further reading

Cooper, Robert (2004) 'Hard Power, Soft Power and the Goals of Diplomacy', in David Held and Mathias Koenig-Archibugi (eds.) *American Power in the 21st Century*, pp. 167–180.
Gray, Colin S. (2011) *Hard and Soft Power: The Utility of Military Force as an Instrument of Policy in the 21st Century* (Strategic Studies Institute).
Kearn, David W. (2011) 'The Hard Truths about Soft Power', *Journal of Political Power* 4(1).
Kevany, Sebastian (2014) 'Global Health Diplomacy, 'smart power,' and the New World Order', *Global Public Health* 9(7), pp. 787–807.
Nye, Joseph S., Jr. (1990) 'Soft Power', *Foreign Policy*, No. 80, Twentieth Anniversary (Autumn), pp. 153–171.

Nye, Joseph S., Jr. (2002) *The Paradox of American Power: Why the World's Only Superpower Can't Go It Alone* (New York: Oxford University Press).

Nye, Joseph S., Jr. (2009) 'Get Smart', *Foreign Affairs* (July/August).

Slaughter, Anne-Marie (2004) *Sovereignty and Power in a Networked World Order* (University of Pennsylvania Law), www.law.upenn.edu/live/files/1647-slaughter-annemarie-sovereignty-and-power-in-a (accessed May 3, 2017).

Womack, Brantly (2005) 'Dancing Along: A Hard Look at Soft Power', *The Asia-Pacific Journal, Japan Focus* 3(11) (November).

Bibliography

Ambos, K. and A. M. Poschadel (2013) 'Terrorists and Fair Trial: The Right to a Fair Trial for Alleged Terrorists Detained in Guantánamo Bay', *Utrecht Law Review* 9(4), pp. 109–126, doi:http://doi.org/10.18352/ulr.245.

Biden, Joseph R., Jr. (2016) 'Building on Success: Opportunities for the Next Administration', *Foreign Affairs* (September/October).

Border, Julian and Spencer Ackerman (2016) 'Russian Planes Dropped Bombs that Destroyed UN Aid Convoy, US Officials Say', *The Guardian* (21 September), https://www.theguardian.com/world/2016/sep/20/un-aid-convoy-attack-syria-us-russia (accessed March 13, 2017).

Castle, Alfred L. (1998) *Diplomatic Realism: William R. Castle Jr., and American Foreign Policy, 1919–1953* (Hawaii: University of Hawaii Press).

Chulov, Martin, Kareem Shaheen and Emma Graham-Harrison (2016) 'East Aleppo's Last Hospital Destroyed by Airstrikes', *The Observer* (19 November), www.theguardian.com/world/2016/nov/19/aleppo-hospitals-knocked-out-airstrikes (accessed March 13, 2017).

Clinton, Hillary Rodham (2010) 'Leading Through Civilian Power: Redefining American Diplomacy and Development', *Foreign Affairs* (November/December).

Ferrero-Waldner, Benita (2007) 'The European Union and the World: A Hard Look at Soft Power', Speech/07/576 (New York: Columbia University, 24 September).

Flockhart, Trine (2016) 'The Coming Multi-Order World', *Contemporary Security Policy* 37(1), pp. 3.30, http://dx.doi.org/10.1080/13523260.2016.1150053.

Fry, Michael Graham, Erik Goldstein and Richard Langhorne (eds.) (2002) *Guide to International Relations and Diplomacy* (New York: Continuum).

Goosby, Eric P. (2017) 'Leading with Our Hearts and Minds', *The Hill* (6 March).

International Commission on Intervention and State Sovereignty (ICISS) (2001) 'The Responsibility to Protect', International Development Research Centre (Canada).

The International Committee of the Red Cross (ICRC), www.icrc.org/en/war-and-law/treaties-customary-law/geneva-conventions (accessed February 7, 2017).

Kaldor, Mary (2014) 'Missing the Point on Hard and Soft Power?', *The Political Quarterly* 85(3) (July–September), pp. 373–377.

Kevany, Sebastian (2014) 'Global Health Diplomacy, "smart power", and the New World Order', *Global Public Health* 9(7), pp. 787–807.

Matthews, Jessica (1997) 'Power Shift', *Foreign Affairs* (January/February).

Mulgan, Geoff (1998) *Connexity: How to Live in a Connected World* (Brighton, MA: Harvard Business Review).

Nye, Joseph S., Jr. (1990a) *Bound to Lead: The Changing Nature of American Power* (New York: Basic Books).

Nye, Joseph S., Jr. (1990b) 'The Changing Nature of World Power', *Political Science Quarterly* 105(2).

Nye, Joseph S., Jr. (2009) 'Get Smart', *Foreign Affairs* (July/August).

Nye, Joseph S., Jr. (1990c) 'Soft Power', *Foreign Policy*, No. 80, Twentieth Anniversary (Autumn), pp. 153–171.

Nye, Joseph S., Jr (2005) *Soft Power: The Means to Success in World Politics* (New York: PublicAffairs).

Nye, Joseph (2011) *The Future of Power* (New York: PublicAffairs).

Nye, Joseph S. Jr. (2017) 'Will the Liberal Order Survive? The History of an Idea', *Foreign Affairs* (January/February).

Organisation for Security and Cooperation in Europe (OECD) (2016) 'Report on the 2016 U.S. Presidential Elections', www.osce.org/odihr/elections/usa/246356 (accessed February 7, 2017).

Sending, Ole Jacob (2017) 'Agency, Order, and Heteronomy', ERIS (3-2016), pp. 63–75, doi:https://doi.org/10.3224/eris.v3i3.27343.

Slaughter, Anne-Marie (2004) 'Sovereignty and Power in a Networked World Order' (University of Pennsylvania Law), www.law.upenn.edu/live/files/1647-slaughter-annemarie-sovereignty-and-power-in-a (accessed May 3, 2017).

Slaughter, Anne-Marie (2005) *A New World Order* (Princeton: Princeton University Press).

Slaughter, Anne-Marie (2011) 'A New Theory of the Foreign-Policy Frontier: Collaborative Power', *The Atlantic Monthly* (30 November).

Strohschneider, Peter (2016) 'The Importance of International Research Cooperation: Reflections from Germany' (12 January).

Van Langenhove, Luk (2016) 'Global Science Diplomacy as a New Tool for Global Governance', *Focir pensement* (United National University/Vrije Universiteit Brussel).

Walker, Christopher and Jessica Ludwig (2017) 'The Meaning of Sharp Power: How Authoritarian States Project Influence', *Foreign Affairs* (16 November).

Wilson, Ernest J. (2008) 'Hard Power, Soft Power, Smart Power', *The ANNALS of the American Academy of Political and Social Science* 616(1) (March), pp. 110–124, doi:https://doi.org/10.1177/0002716207312618.

World Health Organization (2003) 'Framework Convention on Tobacco Control', https://www.who.int/fctc/text_download/en/ (accessed June 14, 2019).

Chapter 22

The rise of religious fundamentalism

Dianne Kirby

Despite the widespread separation of religion from the ensemble of political institutions that constitute the modern national state and geopolitical system, religion never ceased playing a role in politics and in the constitution of the world order (Haynes, 2007). Certainly today it is clear that there was never anything inevitable about the inexorable forward march of secularism as the companion to modernisation, as many scholars once assumed. Religion, regardless of the secularising tendencies of the 19th century, always remained part of the 'dominant ideology'. No government has been able to ignore religion, albeit strategies toward and relationships with different religions vary considerably along a wide spectrum whereby the favoured enjoy protections and privileges, the feared persecution and oppression. True religious toleration remains an aspirational ideal everywhere.

Nor was religion discarded from state arsenals. Political leaders of all persuasions in the 20th century, no less than in previous centuries, sought to manipulate authoritative cultural and religious systems of belief and practice because they are proven powerful and potentially decisive determinants. The nexus between religion, politics and the global arena was reinforced in the Cold War era as each side proclaimed universal values and sought religious legitimation (Kirby, 2003). On a global level, the Cold War highlighted the extent to which secularist divisions between religion and politics were far from stable and frequently contested. Yet, whilst it would have been inconceivable to teach the history of the middle ages without reference to religion, the opposite was true for the last century, meaning that the significance, and indeed persistence, of religion in the modern era was insufficiently appreciated or understood. Throughout the Cold War, scholars neglected its religious dimension, failing thereby to identify significant developments which contributed to the rise of religious fundamentalism. Hence it could be argued that the proclaimed revival in religion in the post-war Cold War world reflected the revival of scholarly interest in religion invoked by consequential global events, not least 9/11, identified with religious fundamentalism.

The subsequent outpouring of literature devoted to fundamentalism revealed the inherent challenges confronting policymakers. Religion is supremely complex, deeply intertwined with other cultural and social forms and intricately implicated with the political. With multiple national sites and its transnational character, religion constitutes a very complex category for analysis. Religion is not a 'master variable' in international affairs, but one that acquires or loses salience in particular historical moments. At this moment in time it is a variable that matters. The world's sole remaining hegemon is subjected to the political influence attained by the American Christian Right, with its fundamentalist tendencies, in the Republican Party. At the same time, its military might and geo-political reach is challenged in strategically important regions by particularly virulent brands of militant fundamentalist Islam.

Fundamentalism is a global concern and states everywhere, great and small, have now to consider, if not confront, its messy particularity. Just as policymakers seem confounded by how to deal with fundamentalism, its very definition remains a matter of scholarly contention. The American Academy of Arts and Sciences initiated a project on 'fundamentalism', begun in 1988 and completed in 1995. A huge five volume study under the guidance of Martin E. Marty and R. Scott Appleby, it involved a host of distinguished academics (Marty and Appleby, 1991–1995). Yet no workable definition emerged, rather the suggestion that it should not be defined (Lustick, 1996, p. 26). It is, however, generally agreed that there are sufficient 'family resemblances' to identify fundamentalist or fundamentalist-like movements occurring in virtually every major religious tradition in many parts of the world, from the Americas to Southeast Asia.

Fundamentalists have traditionally preferred isolation and rejection of rather than engaging with their respective societies. Fundamentalism in its early phase is usually defensive, a retreat from the godless world into a self-contained community. Rather than an external enemy, fundamentalism usually begins as an internal struggle in which traditionalists confront their own co-religionists who they consider to have compromised the faith. In Lithuania in 1803, Rabbi Hayyim Volozhiner transformed traditional Jewish spirituality when he founded the Etz Hayyim *yeshiva*, meant to counter the threat of Hasidism. Hasidism was a mystical Jewish movement found in 18th century Poland. It rose in reaction against the rigid academicism of rabbinical Judaism.

Although the movement declined sharply in the 19th century, it too gave rise to fundamentalist communities. New *yeshivot* were established over the course of the century in other parts of Eastern Europe, where young men, separated from families and friends in quasi-monastic communities, were wholly immersed in Jewish scholarship as it was believed only the study of the Torah could prevent the extinction of true Judaism. The original retreat, however, has within it the potential for a counter-offensive. The *yeshiva*, an early example of embattled religiosity, became the defining institution of the ultra-Orthodox fundamentalism that would develop in the 20th century (Armstrong, 2000, pp. 109–111).

The extent to which fundamentalism is identified with resistance and oppositional movements is reflected by the way in which the term has been used in relation to a variety of disparate religious and politico-religious developments in various parts of the world. American Protestants were the first to use the term fundamentalist in the early decades of the 20th century at a time when people were seeking new ways to be religious. Fundamentalism was but one such attempt. American fundamentalists were intent on distinguishing themselves from 'liberal' Protestants and 'social gospellers'. Developed by Protestants, the 'Social Gospel' was an attempt to sacralise godless cities and factories by returning to the basic teachings of the Hebrew prophets and Christ, who had taught his followers to visit prisoners, clothe the naked and feed the hungry. Fundamentalists considered such 'basic teachings' a distortion of the faith. They emphasised the 'fundamentals' of Christian tradition, a literal interpretation of Scripture and adherence to specific core doctrines.

The term has since been applied to reform movements in other faiths, despite significant distinctions, different dynamics and diverse agendas. It remains, nonetheless, a useful label for movements that follow certain patterns as beleaguered forms of spirituality responding to a perceived crisis linked to modernity. Albeit regarded as inherently conservative and wedded to the past, fundamentalist ideas are essentially modern and highly innovative, manifesting as a set of strategies aimed at preserving their distinct identity, which is thought to be at risk. The modification of the retrieved fundamentals is intended to generate the religious intensity and commitment believed to have existed in the past. Fundamentalism is, therefore, a product of and yet hostile to modernity. Gilles Kepel points out how Christian fundamentalists seek not to modernise Christianity but to Christianize modernity, just as Islamic fundamentalist seek to Islamize it (1994, p. 66).

Fundamentalist rejection of valued features of modern society, including democracy, pluralism, religious toleration, free speech and the separation of the state from religion, is complicated by the perennial relationship between religion and lucre, God and Mammon, to which fundamentalist leaders and some of their followers are known to have succumbed. Certainly numerous fundamentalist movements are noted for their missionary work and welfare services, particularly in areas where states are unable or unwilling to meet the needs of the poor and dispossessed. Such activities are important means of winning hearts and minds and popular support and approval. But there are also instances of the misuse and misappropriation of funds. Even more disturbingly, Jessica Stern's research into the roots of terrorist psychology recounts how: 'What starts out as moral fervour becomes a sophisticated organisation. Grievance can end up as greed – for money, political power, or attention' (Stern, 2003, p. 282).

Attitudes toward, and very often the hypocrisy surrounding, sexual matters is another problematic complicating the study of fundamentalism. Several studies indicate that sex, or more precisely the control of female sexuality, features prominently in fundamentalisms. The promotion of 'family values' often conceals virulent homophobia and intolerance for gender diversity. Most shocking, however, in what are usually intra-societal disputes, is the use of violence and acts of terrorism, mostly against co-religionists and fellow citizens, which counters the compassionate ethic central to the faiths supposedly espoused.

A minority tendency in the modern world

Fundamentalism is a traditional and usually a minority feature of all religions. Its prominence, appeal and influence varies according to context and circumstances, both historically and contemporaneously. Religious phenomena do not occur in a vacuum. It is worth recalling Geoffrey Elton's observations on the Reformation:

'It will not do to treat the radical reformers as though only their theology mattered; neither the spread of their ideas nor the reaction of others can possibly be understood unless the secular discontent to which they give tongue is kept in mind' (1958). As with today's fundamentalists, Martin Luther was driven by a vision of 'true religion' and religious fanaticism (Hendrix, 2016). He too was aided by the IT revolution of his era, the movable type press invented only some 60 years earlier by Johannes Gutenberg (1398–1468) in around 1440. It was exploited by Luther for the circulation of all kinds of ideas, social and political as well as religious and theological.

The fundamentalist engagement with the modern world is a complex response to contemporary political processes and the implications of power as fundamentalists interact dynamically with their social and cultural surroundings. The emergence of a form of Buddhist fundamentalism in Sri Lanka, formerly Ceylon, can be traced back to the struggle against British rule, accompanied as it was by Christian missions, in the 19th century. In addition to the clergy's loss of royal patronage, their understanding of ultimate authority was challenged. Drawing myths from their chronicle of the founding of Buddhism in Ceylon, the *Mahavamsa*, they had some success in generating reform and revival. They lacked political clout, however, until mobilised by Solomon Bandaranaike and his Sri Lanka Freedom Party. Bandaranaike had sensed the groundswell of discontent once the political promises made at the time of independence began to evaporate and recognised the political potential of the fundamentalist movement that was gathering momentum through the activity of the Buddhist clergy. To gain power, Bandaranaike drew upon the fundamentalist sentiments of the Buddhist clergy and their leaders, proclaiming them the guardians of the faith who should do all possible to protect Buddhism against other encroachers, arousing feelings of ethnicity in the process, but winning the 1956 elections and achieving politico-nationalist ends (Taylor, 1987, pp. 138–155).

In the conclusion to the first volume in the fundamentalism project, Marty and Appleby point out that fundamentalists see themselves in conflict with enemies whose secularist policies and beliefs appear inimical to religion. Fearing annihilation, they seek to strengthen their identity through a selective retrieval of key doctrines and practices from the past. Fearing contamination from mainstream society can lead to withdrawal and the creation of a counterculture. Imbued with the pragmatic rationalism of modernity and guided by charismatic leaders, the selected fundamentals serve to construct an ideology that is also a plan of action that involves resistance to a decadent world and attempts to resacralise it. The struggle is for them a cosmic war between the forces of good and evil (Marty and Appleby, 1991, pp. 814–842).

The fundamentalist conviction that they are engaged in a Manichaean conflict between good and evil is particularly important because most treatments of fundamentalism stress the fundamentalist belief that they are fighting against secular modernity for their survival in a world that is inherently hostile to religion and neglect to look at the way in which the Cold War was presented by America, followed by its allies, as a cosmic struggle between good and evil, with of course the US positioned as the good and godly, the Soviet Union as the evil and godless. While some fundamentalists view the nation state as an alien Western invention, the emphasis on violence and polarisation are thoroughly statist. Mark Juergensmeyer, who substitutes the term 'religious nationalism' for fundamentalism, argues that the rise of secular nationalism in the 19th and 20th centuries constituted an assault on religion. The aim of religious nationalists was and is to re-link religion to the nation state, which was considered not only to have marginalised real religion but to have co-opted its key elements via the construct of 'civil religion' to legitimise the state's societal legitimacy (Juergensmeyer, 1993, p. 46).

States, large and small, have traditionally mobilised their religious resources to legitimise their own policies whilst demonising those of their enemies. Juergensmeyer sees nationalism and fundamentalism as complementary, each providing an overarching framework of moral order that commands ultimate loyalty. Above all, each has the ability to give moral sanction to martyrdom and violence. The labelling of opponents as enemies to be destroyed, their appropriation of truth and legitimacy, both reflect attitudes prevalent in America's Cold War administrations. In the post–Cold War era, George W. Bush famously inverted the sentiments of Al-Qaeda when he declared: 'Those who are not with us are against us'.

Islamic fundamentalism

For almost a century militant forms of piety were developing in the world religions. America pursued a dual policy of mobilising and promoting religious forces whilst it undermined and destroyed those of the Left. Left was, of course, broadly defined to include progressive movements and even liberal organisations, including religious ones. As a consequence the conditions were created in which the most conservative and, crucially, anti-communist religions achieved a momentum that would otherwise not have occurred. Most believers find fundamentalist convictions and demands unappealing. The Cold War context created a climate and conditions as well as opportunities and advantages that facilitated the rise of religious fundamentalism, particularly the Islamic variety given its location in areas of strategic interest to the US.

Addressing the recent history of Pakistan, Tariq Ali noted how by the 1950s an Islamist triangulation was in place that Washington regarded, and hence supported, as an essential ideological bulwark against communism and radical nationalism in the Muslim world. It comprised, first, of Wahhabism, described in July 2013 by the European Parliament in Strasbourg as the main source of Islamic terrorism. Secondly included was Maulana Abul Ala Maududi's Jamaat-e-Islami, founded as a counter to Mohammed Ali Jinnah's Muslim League. The latter was seen as misusing Islam to promote secular nationalism. Jinnah was an arrogant agnostic, contemptuous of all religious fundamentalisms. Worried by Gandhi's blatant use of Hindu religious imagery to awaken the countryside, he responded in kind with the Muslim League (Ali, 2002, p. 169). Thirdly included was the Muslim Brotherhood. Since its inception in Egypt in 1928, the Muslim Brotherhood has been the most prominent fundamentalist current in Sunni Islam. Founded by Hassan al-Banna as a movement for education and reform, it soon acquired a political dimension and subsequently developed its own armed and secret apparatus (Pargeter, 2013; Rosefsky Wickham, 2013; Barry Rubin, 2013). The Muslim Brotherhood, the flagship of fundamentalism in the Arab world, was a product of both religious and economic dissent

(Viorst, 2001, p. 53). It had served British imperialism and was similarly to serve the CIA (Amin, 2007, pp. 59, 7, 1–19). The Islamist triangle gave rise to the armed Sunni-Islamist groups that subsequently engaged in jihad against other Muslims as well as the US itself (Ali, 2002, pp. 176–177).

Cold War influences

Juergensmeyer, significantly, titled his book on fundamentalism *The New Cold War: Religious Nationalism Confronts the Secular State*. The first two Cold War presidents purposefully promoted a brand of civil religion that led to an atavistic representation of what was in essence a clash of two rival models of modernity. America presented the Cold War as a life and death struggle between the forces of good and evil, a struggle for the soul of the world. It was a crucial means of distinguishing and giving moral superiority to the American model of modernity over that offered by the Soviet Union. Religion endowed anti-communism with a pseudo-doctrinal status, strengthened and reinforced by the potency of religious themes, symbols and metaphors in American public discourse. It rested on two fundamental contentions: that communism was a supreme and unqualified evil, and that its purpose was world domination (Kirby, 2014, pp. 126–152). This form of 'absolutist' anti-communism resided at the heart of conservative religion and became an exceptionally potent weapon in the political warfare waged against the entire left, including other faith organisations and individuals with moderate, reform inclined tendencies.

The image of an aggressive, evil Soviet regime dedicated to world conquest – the godless Soviet bogey – became a crucial American Cold War asset (Kirby, 2013, pp. 491–530). At the same time, the nation moved toward a more direct identification with, if not embodiment of, religion itself. It was a deliberately orchestrated process by what Jonathan Herzog has aptly called the spiritual-industrial-complex. The result, as intended, was a top down domestic religious revival (Herzog, 2011). Mainstream clerical criticism of the way in which Christianity was instrumentalised in the service of secular forces led to the marginalisation of mainstream liberal churchmen who dared question American domestic and foreign policies. An opportunity was thereby created for American fundamentalist and evangelical Christians to forge a place for their own uncompromising brand of Christian anti-communism.

From the 1950s religion was an operational component of both American overt and covert enterprises in the international arena. The National Security Council (NSC) had a program to support the Orthodox Church and encourage resistance and subversion throughout the Soviet bloc. The NSC and Operations Coordinating Board (OCB) also looked to win support from Buddhist and Islamic leaders, which they feared were susceptible to the influence of Chinese communists. The support America and its allies accorded Islamic organisations throughout the Middle East is crucial to understanding how they were able to attain political power and popular support (Dreyfus, 2005; Zunes, 2003). Part of the legacy of the religious cold war was, as French scholar Olivier Roy cogently observed: 'Americans have never seen Islamism as an ideological enemy' (Beinin and Stork, 1996, p. 11). Indeed, Islam was deemed both a bulwark and a weapon against communism (Dreyfus, 2005). It was an attitude that was to have profound consequences with global repercussions. Many US diplomats viewed groups such as the Taliban as 'messianic do-gooders – like born-again Christians in the American Bible Belt' (Rashid, 2000, p. 176–177).

The event which most drew world attention to Islamic fundamentalism was the Iranian Revolution of 1979. Recently released documents show that America's religious cold war was a factor in the Ayatollah Khomeini's calculations. In November 1963 he sent a message to the US government explaining he was not opposed to an American presence in Iran, necessary as a counterbalance to Soviet influence, notably stressing 'his belief in close cooperation between Islam and other world religions, particularly Christendom'. When the Shah of Iran's regime was confronting collapse in 1979, President Carter feared a communist take-over and potential Soviet influence far more than that of a 'holy man' (Fattahi, 2016).

Khomeini wasted no time in eliminating all the Marxist groups that had supported the struggle against the Shah. It is worth noting that his regime was aided by the US, which, in recognition of the Islamic authorities' strident anti-communism, passed on the names of suspected Iranian leftists, resulting in the execution of hundreds of dissidents. From 1981 to 1986, the US secretly shipped arms to Iran's Islamic government, hoping to buy access to and influence on the Iranian military. Part of the clandestine arms transfers was channeled to anti-Soviet Afghan *mujahidin*, resistance fighters (Zunes, 2003, p. 69). Khomeini's antipathy toward communism extended to what he and others referred to as 'West-toxification' or 'Westomania', a consequence, he argued, of the insidious efforts of Western imperialists. Khomeini wanted to free Iran conceptually from Western ways of thinking (Juergensmeyer, 1993, p. 19). The early stages of the revolution witnessed a process of satanisation whereby Khomeini declared all of Iran's problems 'the work of America' owing to a conspiratorial network of US agents in all spheres, cultural and intellectual as well as political and economic.

Tim Aistrope coined the term 'Arab-Muslim paranoia narrative' in his examination of the view that Arab-Muslim resentment toward America was provoked by a conspiratorial perception of American power in the Middle East. Following 9/11 the connection between Arab-Muslim anti-Americanism and conspiracy theory became a matter of national security, as was particularly evident in numerous US government policy documents and initiatives advancing a War of Ideas strategy. Aimed at winning the 'hearts and minds' of Arab-Muslims, the main intent of the strategy was to deter criticism of American foreign policy and establish an image of America as benign and misunderstood. The Arab-Muslim paranoia narrative also deflected attention away from the substance of Arab-Muslim grievances towards their supposed cognitive or social-psychological pathologies. The War of Ideas framework, therefore, served to reinforce the concept of a civilisational confrontation between liberal democratic modernity and dysfunctional Arab-Muslims. It was in effect a structural hypocrisy. Imbued with racism, it exacerbated Arab-Muslim resentment as well as heightening distrust of US foreign policy (Aistrope, 2016, pp. 2–3).

Resentment and distrust were already in abundance from the dynamic of hypocrisy and double-dealing that marked American policies toward the Middle East during the Cold War. The lived experiences of Muslims encountering globalised modernity differed considerably from the terms deployed by the West, which implied positive outcomes. The West insisted it was delivering progress, but the impact on most Muslims was decidedly not progressive. Adding insult to injury, the 'backward' conditions emphasised by the West were at least partially a consequence of global modernity. Shameless Western claims regarding the promotion of democracy contrasted with the bitter reality whereby the West's alliance with Arab regimes worked to repress democracy.

With anti-communism the key criteria, the US cultivated the very conditions that facilitated the spread of fundamentalist Islam. In addition to itself allying with the most conservative representatives of Islam, American support, plus that of its allies in the region, most notably Saudi Arabia, helped create a situation in which otherwise unpopular and unrepresentative versions of Islam were able to secure a power and influence they otherwise would have been unlikely to attain. An ideological tendency with small and scattered numbers, out of power fundamentalist Islam had neither the aspiration of drawing strength from popular organisation nor the possibility of marshaling strength from any alternative source (Mamdani, 2004, pp. 129–130). From the early Cold War period, dispatches from US embassies reveal the extent to which Islam became a political football, leading to a situation fraught with potential danger. Nonetheless, policymakers, lacking understanding of Islam's complexity and power, continued to play the Islamic card. Too many remained wedded to the view that Third World nationalism was a Soviet tool and conservative Islam an ally to be used against presumed pro-Soviet nationalist leaders, such as Nasser in Egypt. The situation was exacerbated by the fact that America's Middle East allies shared assumptions that Islam would provide a local buffer against secular nationalism.

In addition, engagement with Islam meant dealing with often oppressive and corrupt Middle Eastern regimes that lacked popular support and for whom Islam was a useful tool. Conservative Arab regimes sheltered and aided militant Islamists (Abu-Amr, 1994, p. 17; Mishal and Sela, 2000, pp. 17–18). Hence, much of America's Middle East Cold War agenda was mediated through regimes and religious movements that would inevitably prioritise their own political agendas. These were naturally concerned with consolidating and/or extending their own power bases. US Cold War policies that eroded the left and progressive nationalism in the Middle East helped the rise of Islamic fundamentalism.

By removing what American officialdom regarded as their common foes on the Left, the US facilitated fundamentalist Islam's growing support throughout the region, albeit as a default option. US officials worried by the strength of the anti-Western sentiment harboured by some of their Islamist allies possibly drew some reassurance from thinking that the religious extremists lacked a popular base. Most Muslims rejected their ideology and their modes of operating. However, the weakening and discrediting of the Left in the Muslim world empowered fundamentalist Islam, making it the main ideological and organised means through which popular discontent and dissent could be expressed. The lack of progress and reform and the continuation of oppressive regimes allied with and supported by the West inflamed anti-Western sentiments. In the absence of secular left-liberal alternatives, this further galvanised support for the Islamists as the most ardent opposition to the status quo (Achcar, 2002).

American failure to learn from the Iranian revolution was demonstrated following the Soviet military intervention in Afghanistan. National Security Adviser Zbigniew Brzezinski saw an opportunity to export a composite ideology of nationalism and Islam to the Muslim majority Central Asian republics with a view to destroying the Soviet system (Dilip, 2002, p. 210). In pursuing the 'religious cold war', American presidents and officials gave insufficient attention to how the religious can and will transgress the boundaries between the sacred and profane to assert their own political, social and economic agendas. It was a lesson America had to confront on the home front as well as in the international arena.

Christian fundamentalism

The question of the emergence of America's 'religious right' is a matter of historiographical contention and likely to remain so for many years to come. Matthew Sutton persuasively argues that the antistatist ideology at the core of the modern religious right originated with the beginnings of fundamentalist political mobilisation, which 'developed among fundamentalists during the 1930s, parallel to and corresponding with the birth of modern liberalism' (Sutton, 2012, pp. 1052–1074). The Cold War provided a significant opening to the Christian Right, which had far less qualms about US foreign and domestic policies than their liberal mainstream counterparts. It also strengthened the fundamentalist tradition, more rigidly anti-communist than the evangelical.

American Christians held an array of often divergent views, including criticism of the capitalist system and the American way of life, meaning the religious had to be policed to ensure they did not deviate from America's Cold War consensus, built as it was on a religious foundation (Kirby, 2017, pp. 67–84). As early as 1949, the House Un-American Activities Committee (HUAC) claimed communism had infiltrated America's churches. It issued a pamphlet, *100 Things You Should Know About Communism and Religion* (Caute, 1973, p. 312). There was a cacophony of charges against liberal churchmen from informers within the American Communist Party. The most well known was Herbert Philbrick (Miller, 1990, p. 524). Philbrick warned the American public that 'The Communists Are After Your Church' (Philbrick, 1953, pp. 18–20, 92–95). FBI files reveal just how many churchgoers believed there was a communist campaign to subvert America's churches.

The most smeared and watched clergyman in America was the Reverend Martin Luther King Jr. The initial premise for investigating King and the Southern Christian Leadership Conference was communism, a charge widely used to damage and discredit civil rights activists, regarded as giving aid and comfort to 'enemy' propaganda that highlighted, especially in the developing world, American racism and mistreatment of its non-white citizens. The Cold War heightened divisions within American faith communities. Conservative evangelicals adhered to US nationalism and challenged the 'loyalty' of the liberal mainstream churches within which questions were raised about church-state relations and how to confront oppression, poverty and injustice when it derived from the policies of their own government.

The early Cold War world-view, induced by religious anti-communist rhetoric and underpinned by the threat of nuclear annihilation, reduced the distinctions separating secular and evangelical/fundamentalist America, facilitating a move from a tangential to a central subculture. Fundamentalists were thus able to construct a closer relational identity with the rest of America than had previously been the case, helping them assimilate into mainstream culture, which led to more political participation and subsequently a political power base (Lahr, 2007).

At leadership level by the 1960s, the bible-thumping, paranoid anti-communism, along with elements of bigotry and racism of the Old Christian Right, gave way to a 'secular sounding rights based discourse' carefully shaped to meet the needs of the New Christian Right (Hendershot, 2007, pp. 373–396). Today's Christian Right draws a distinct line between themselves and their predecessors. Protestant fundamentalism was initially a self-advertising label, a proudly worn epithet highlighting defence of the faith's fundamentals.

More recently the term fundamentalism has acquired unsavoury connotations and hence is no longer used as a badge of honour (Walker, 1987, p. 195–210). However, historian Heather Hendershot argues, 'The old extremists' language was softened, but many of their underlying ideas were intact in what had become mainstream conservatism' (Hendershot, 2007, p. 373–396). Conservative Christians, united by their anti-communism and ardent patriotism, especially the broad section emerging as the 'religious right', evangelicals, fundamentalists and conservative Catholics, remained convinced that they were engaged in an irrepressible conflict against an irreconcilable foe. The Cold War generated a momentum reflected in the election of Jimmy Carter, the nation's first born-again president. It was Ronald Reagan, however, who proved most adept at galvanising the legacy of the religious cold war, targeting conservative Christians for electoral support and securing office on a platform of tough talk with the 'Russians' accompanied by a massive arms build-up.

Fundamentalists were further politicised by the Think Tank revolution of the 1970s. Several think tanks, such as the Ethics and Public Policy Center, the Institute on Religion and Democracy, the Center on Religion and Society and the James Madison Foundation, had explicitly conservative religious platforms. They attacked the liberal Christian institutions they regarded as supportive of détente, influenced by liberation theology, supportive of Third World revolutionary movements, insufficiently critical of Soviet policies and 'soft' on communism. Progressive church leaders were targeted over foreign policy issues, especially US-Soviet relations, the arms race and Central America, by 'front groups' within several denominations established by the Institute on Religion and Democracy. With an agenda of discrediting and de-funding their targets, the conservative religious think tanks were themselves, very significantly, funded primarily from non-church sources, including major military contractors and well-known conservative foundations (Geyer, 1990, pp. 28–29). They were a key part of an aggressive corporate business assault on the mainline churches, 'largely indirect, covert and refracted through a variety of value-shaping institutions' (Geyer, 1997).[1]

An absolute verity of the Christian Right is that American influence is a force for good in the world, reinforced by traditional conceits, all of which were forefronted during the Cold War, such as the American Commonwealth as the new Israel, a Chosen People, a new promised Land, a redeemer nation. All helped sanction territorial expansion, moralistic foreign policies, cultural imperialism and unwarranted presumptions of innocence in world conflicts. All were verified in the eyes of the Christian Right when the Soviet bloc disintegrated, which they heralded as the 'triumph' of God's country over the godless Soviets and used to consolidate the link between Christian superiority and American exceptionalism, for them an essential feature of national identity. Very significantly, the disintegration of the Soviet bloc was also claimed as a victory by fundamentalist Islam, most notably Osama bin Laden. In both cases, the process served to reinforce the narrative of destiny and mission that now seemingly includes the pursuit of salvation in history and the apparent faith that redemptive violence can save the world (Gray, 2007).

According to Jason Stevens, in America the alignment of fundamentalism with the nation's foundational myths and global aspirations brought acceptance and respectability from people and policymakers, especially those who found the concept of lesser evil, with its attendant implications of sin and guilt, unpalatable and unacceptable. Salvation and regeneration were more appealing, particularly to civil religion adherents (Stevens, 2010, p. 63). America's distinctive civil religion has a millennialism at its core that subscribes to biblical visions of the final battle when good will triumph over evil. From this emerged the mainstreaming of forms of rapture theology, along with the conviction that evil must be destroyed. The conviction that evil cannot be redeemed led in turn to a popular belief in 'redemptive violence'.

Fundamentalist world views everywhere, with their combination of elevating disputes to the cosmic level and convictions concerning the purifying nature of violence, mean fundamentalist conflicts are more intractable and less responsive to negotiation. The Arab-Israeli conflict is but one example, with the religious Zionists of Gush Emunin, who oppose any return of Arab territory, and the Islamists of Hamas and Islamic Jihad, who oppose any accommodation with Israel. The precarious basis for a settlement is further diminished by Christian fundamentalist convictions based in part on a messianic theology that regards the ingathering of Jews to the Holy Land as a precursor to the second coming of Christ and hence support the distinct pro-Israel policies of successive American administrations.

American administration policies toward Israel are, however, based primarily on pragmatic considerations. Major US military and economic aid began after the 1967 war in which Israel demonstrated its strength. Israel has subsequently served US interests in the Middle East. Moreover, 'autocratic Arab governments, Islamic extremists, and others are blaming Israel, Zionism, or the Jews for their problems, leaving largely untouched the broader exploitative global economic system and their own elites who benefit from and help perpetuate such a system' (Zunes, 2003, p. 163). Rather than facilitating a peace process or bowing to fundamentalist Christian influence, America uses Israel to impose a Pax Americana. US support for Israel is one of the foremost reasons for Arab anger and is a favourite cause for Islamic extremists, leading to more martyrs and victims and thereby more recruits susceptible to fundamentalism.

Conclusion

Religion, whether or not of the fundamentalist variety, exists in and is part of the international as well as the regional or local order. Fundamentalists, whatever their criticism of the modern world, have had to respond to it and their responses reflect societal and political changes at a variety of sociopolitical levels. The alienation of some adherents, especially those with fundamentalist tendencies, certainly highlights the potential inherent in all religion to be a force for political dysfunction, subversive of wider societal values in the pursuit of its own agenda. Nonetheless, the dogmatism, irrationality and violence, encapsulated within a moral legitimising vision associated with minority tendencies in fundamentalist religion, can be seen as reflecting a global ethos in which secular fundamentalisms, foremost examples being market fundamentalism and imperialist fundamentalism, dominate (Kotz, 2002, pp. 64–79). Secular fundamentalisms derive from the neo-liberal project imposed on the world by the champions of global capitalism (Mirowski and Plehwe, 2009).

At its core neo-liberalism was a movement against non-capitalist political and intellectual forces, aimed at undermining the very possibility of socialism and destroying the enemies of liberal capitalism (Davies, 2016, pp. 121–134). The consequences for the developing world were profoundly damaging and further contributed to the despair and poverty that created the very conditions that permitted fundamentalist religion to flourish (Haar and Busuttil, 2003).

In addition, the ruthless means deployed to secure regimes sympathetic to Western policies, many of which were oppressive and undemocratic, used the mantle of religion to engage in 'state terrorism'. Unsurprisingly, this in turn generated terrorist responses that included religious terrorism (Ali, 2002). The present phase of what has been labelled 'punitive' neo-liberalism, characterised by irrational, vindictive varieties of policymaking, has as its religious fundamentalist counterpart ISIL, marked by its own extreme and counterproductive unreason. In stark contrast, other Islamic fundamentalist movements have opted into the electoral process, albeit possibly for non-democratic ends (Choueiri, 1996, pp. 20–21).

The evolution of fundamentalist religious movements from rejection of, to engagement with the wider world, has led to politicisation, and in some cases militarisation. It is a trajectory that raises questions about the present status and nature of these movements and whether they are now more politico-military than religious. Equally, as with other political ideologies, the role of faith has evolved and changed. For some it appears largely one of legitimisation. Certainly for other adherents to fundamentalism, secular modes and methods, politics and violence, possibly are a means of achieving messianic redemption.

In the final analysis of the journey made by fundamentalist religious movements, mindful of their differences and diversity and the ways in which each is impacted by their particular environment, some of the extreme forms in evidence today are in essence neo-fundamentalisms rather than religious fundamentalism in its original form. The future direction of fundamentalist religious movements will vary according to circumstances and context, including the capacity of Western policymakers to understand and respond to the complex and multifaceted challenges they now represent. Understanding the role of the West in the rise of religious fundamentalism, at home and abroad, is crucial.

Note

1 Alan Geyer meticulously detailed the attack on the mainstream liberal churches. Geyer's credentials were impeccable: a widely published Christian ethicist and ecumenical leader,

canon ethicist at the Washington National Cathedral, Professor of Political Ethics and Ecumenics at Wesley Theological Seminary in Washington, plus a former director of international relations for the United Church of Christ, based at the Church Center for the United Nations, and former editor of the *Christian Century* (1968–72).

Further reading

Antoun, Richard T. (2001) *Understanding Fundamentalism: Christian, Islamic and Jewish Movements* (New York: AltaMira Press).

Brink, Judy and Joan Mencher (1997) *Gender and Religious Fundamentalism: Cross-Culturally* (London: Routledge).

Choueiri, Youssef M. (2008) *Islamic Fundamentalism 3rd Edition: The Story of Islamist Movements* (New York: Continuum).

Hood, Ralph W., Peter C. Hill and W. Paul Williamson (2005) *The Psychology of Religious Fundamentalism* (Guilford: The Guilford Press).

Kepel, Gilles (1997) *Allah in the West: Islamic Movements in America and Europe* (Stanford, CA: Stanford University Press).

Marsden, George M. (1991) *Understanding Fundamentalism and Evangelicalism* (Grand Rapids, MI: Wm. B. Eerdmans Publishing Co).

Mawsilili, Ahmad (2013) *Moderate and Radical Islamic Fundamentalism: The Quest for Modernity, Legitimacy and the Islamic State* (Miami: University Press of Florida).

Ruthven, Malise (2007) *Fundamentalism: A Very Short Introduction* (Oxford: Oxford University Press).

Sarkar, Sumit (2002) *Beyond Nationalist Frames: Postmodernism, Hindu Fundamentalism, History* (Indianapolis: Indiana University Press).

Shahak, Israel (2004) *Jewish Fundamentalism in Israel* (London: Pluto Press).

Bibliography

Abu-Amr, Ziad (1994) *Islamic Fundamentalism in the West Bank and Gaza* (Bloomington: Indiana University Press).

Achcar, Gilbert (2002) *The Clash of Barbarisms: September 11 and the Making of the New World Disorder* (New York: Monthly Review Press).

Aistrope, Tim (2016) *Conspiracy Theory and American Foreign Policy* (Manchester: Manchester University Press).

Ali, Tariq (2002) *The Clash of Fundamentalisms: Crusades, Jihads and Modernity* (London: Verso).

Amin, Samir (2007) 'Political Islam in the Service of Imperialism', *Monthly Review* (December issue).

Armstrong, Karen (2000) *The Battle for God: A History of Fundamentalism* (New York: Ballantine Books).

Beinin, Joel and Joe Stork (1996) *Political Islam: Essays from the Middle East Report* (California/Oakland: University of California Press).

Caute, David (1973) *The Fellow-Travellers: A Postscript to the Enlightenment* (New York: Macmillan).

Choueiri, Youssef M. (1996) 'The Political Discourse of Contemporary Islamist Movements', in A. Sidahmed and A. Ehteshami (eds.) *Islamic Fundamentalism* (Boulder, CO: Westview Press).

Davies, William (2016) 'The New Neoliberalism', *New Left Review* (September/October issue).

Dilip, Hiro (2002) *War Without End: The Rise of Islamist Terrorism and Global Response* (New York: Routledge).

Dreyfus, Robert (2005) *Devil's Game: How the United States Helped Unleash Fundamentalist Islam* (New York: Metropolitan Books).

Elton, G.R. (1958) *Europe from Renaissance to Reformation* (Cambridge: Cambridge University Press).

Fattahi, Kambiz (2016) 'Two Weeks in January: America's Secret Engagement with Khomeini', 3 June, www.bbc.co.uk/news/world-us-canada-36431160.

Geyer, Alan (1990) *Christianity and the Super-Powers: Religion, Politics, and History in US-USSR Relations* (Nashville: Abingdon Press).

Geyer, A. (1997) *Ideology in America: Challenges to Faith* (Loiusville/Kentucky: Westminster John Knox Press).

Gray, John (2007) *Black Mass, Apocalyptic Religion and the Death of Utopia* (London: Allen Lane).

Haar, Gerrie ter and James J. Busuttil (eds.) (2003) *The Freedom to Do God's Will: Religious Fundamentalism and Social Change* (London: Routledge).

Haynes, Jeffrey (2007) *Introduction to International Relations and Religion* (London: Pearson Education Ltd.).

Hendershot, Heather (2007) 'God's Angriest Man: Carl McIntire, Cold War Fundamentalism, and Right-Wing Broadcasting', *American Quarterly* 59 (June issue), p. 2.

Hendrix, Scott H. (2016) *Martin Luther: Visionary Reformer* (Yale: Yale University Press).

Herzog, Jonathan P. (2011) *The Spiritual-Industrial Complex: America's Religious Battle Against Communism in the Early Cold War* (New York: Oxford University Press).

Juergensmeyer, Mark (1993) *The New Cold War: Religious Nationalism Confronts the Secular State* (Berkeley: University of California Press).

Kepel, Gilles (1994) *The Revenge of God* (Cambridge: Polity Press).

Kirby, Dianne (ed.) (2003) *Religion and the Cold War* (Basingstoke: Palgrave-Macmillan).

Kirby, D. (2013) 'The Religious Cold War', in Richard H. Immerman and Petra Goedde (eds.) *The Oxford Handbook of the Cold War* (New York: Oxford University Press).

Kirby, D. (2014) 'Christian anti-Communism', *Twentieth Century Communism*, Autumn, issue 7.

Kirby, D. (2017) 'J. Edgar Hoover, the FBI, and the Religious Cold War', in Sylvester A. Johnson and Steven Weitzman (eds.) *The FBI and Religion: Faith and National Security Before and After 9/11* (Oakland: University of California Press).

Kotz, David M. (2002) 'Globalization and Neoliberalism', *Rethinking Marxism* (12 Summer), p. 2.

Lahr, Angela (2007) *Millennial Dreams and Apocalyptic Nightmares: The Cold War Origins of Political Evangelicalism* (New York: Oxford University Press).

Lustick, Ian (1996) 'Fundamentalism, Politicised Religion and Pietism', *Middle East Studies Association Bulletin* 30.

Mamdani, Mahmood (2004) *Good Muslim, Bad Muslim* (New York: Harmony Books).

Marty, Martin E. and R. Scott Appleby (eds.) (1991–1995) *The Fundamentalism Project*, 5 volumes (Chicago: University of Chicago Press).

Miller, Robert Moats (1990) *Bishop G. Bromley Oxnam: Paladin of Liberal Protestantism* (Nashville: Abingdon Press).

Mirowski, Philip and Dieter Plehwe (eds.) (2009) *The Road from Mont Pelerin: The Making of the Neoliberal Thought Collective* (Harvard: Harvard University Press).

Mishal, Shaul and Avraham Sela (2000) *The Palestinian Hamas* (New York: Columbia University Press).

Pargeter, Alison (2013) *The Muslim Brotherhood: From Opposition to Power* (London: Saqi Books).

Philbrick, Herbert (1953) *Christian Herald* 76(April).

Rashid, Ahmed (2000) *Taliban, Militant Islam, Oil, and Fundamentalism in Central Asia* (New Haven: Yale University Press).

Rubin, Barry (ed.) (2013) *The Muslim Brotherhood: The Organisation and Policies of a Global Islamist Movement* (Princeton: Princeton University Press).

Stern, Jessica (2003) *Terror in the Name of God* (New York: HarperCollins Publishers).

Stevens, Jason (2010) *God-Fearing and Free: A Spiritual History of America's Cold War* (Harvard: Harvard University Press).

Sutton, Matthew Avery (2012) 'Was FDR the Anti-Christ? The Birth of Fundamentalist Anti-Liberalism in a Global Age', *Journal of American History* 98(4).

Taylor, Donald (1987) 'Incipient Fundamentalism: Religion and Politics among Sri Lankan Hindus in Britain', in Lionel Caplan (ed.) *Studies in Fundamentalism* (Basingstoke: Macmillan Press).

Viorst, Milton (2001) *In the Shadow of the Prophet* (New York: Westview Press).

Walker, Andrew (1987) 'Fundamentalism and Modernity: The Restoration Movement in Britain', in Lionel Caplan (ed.) *Studies in Religious Fundamentalism* (Basingstoke: Macmillan).

Wickham, Carrie Rosefsky (2013) *The Muslim Brotherhood: Evolution of an Islamist Movement* (Princeton: Princeton University Press).

Zunes, Stephen (2003) *Tinderbox: U.S. Middle East Policy and the Roots of Terrorism* (London: Zed Books).

Chapter 23

Human rights and the International Criminal Court

Yvonne McDermott

The International Criminal Court (ICC) was established in 1998, with the aim of ending impunity for the perpetrators of the most serious crimes of concern to the international community (ICC Statute, 1998, preamble). The ICC became

FIGURE 23.1 The International Criminal Court in The Hague, Netherlands

operational in 2002 and by today, 122 states are parties to the ICC Statute. Final judgments have been issued in cases arising from situations in Mali, the Democratic Republic of the Congo and the Central African Republic, and trials are ongoing for individuals alleged to have committed war crimes and/or crimes against humanity in Uganda, Côte d'Ivoire and the Democratic Republic of the Congo. A number of suspects remain at large.

This chapter seeks to situate the ICC as an institution within the machinery of the international human rights legal framework. In so doing, it notes that the ICC is not itself a human rights court but that it nevertheless bears an important role in the protection, development and interpretation of human rights. The first section examines the development of the ICC, and notes international criminal law's shared heritage with international human rights law, insofar as both bodies of law were developed in the aftermath of World War II. The second section of this chapter discusses the interplay between human rights and the International Criminal Court, in particular examining the role of human rights organisations in providing evidence for ICC trials, and human rights law's status as a source of law before the ICC. The third section analyses the impact of the ICC in developing, protecting and interpreting human rights. In setting out the four core crimes falling within the ICC's jurisdiction, it highlights that serious human rights violations can constitute international crimes. It also discusses the role of human rights in shaping the ICC's procedure and the right to a fair trial before the Court. In sum, this chapter demonstrates a symbiotic relationship between human rights and the ICC, in that human rights law bears an important influence over the law and practice of the ICC, while the ICC itself plays a role in the progressive development of human rights.

The development of the ICC and its character as a judicial institution

The parallel development of human rights and international criminal law

The founding international human rights legal instrument, the Universal Declaration on Human Rights (UDHR), was signed on 10 December 1948. The UDHR was clearly influenced by a recognition that the horrors suffered in World War II should never happen again; its preamble noted that 'disregard and contempt for human rights have resulted in barbarous acts which have outraged the conscience of mankind'. The UDHR, a non-binding instrument, led in turn to the twin binding international treaties of the International Covenant on Civil and Political Rights and the International Covenant on Economic, Social and Cultural Rights, both adopted in 1966. Since the adoption of these treaties, specialised UN treaties on human rights have been adopted; these include the Convention against Torture, the Convention on the Elimination of Discrimination against Women, the Convention on the Rights of the Child and the Convention on the Rights of Persons with Disabilities, amongst others.

Most commentators trace the birth of international criminal law to the Treaty of Versailles in 1919, which publicly arraigned Kaiser Wilhelm II and stated that he would be tried by 'a special tribunal' comprised of five judges, one from each of the following: the UK, US, France, Italy and Japan (Schabas, 2017, p. 3; Cryer et al., p. 116; Treaty of Versailles, Article 227). This intention was ultimately unfulfilled after the Kaiser fled to Holland, which refused to extradite him (Schabas, 2017, p. 3; Bassiouni, 1997, p. 14). In August 1945, the Allied Powers created the International Military Tribunal (IMT) at Nuremberg, which was followed in 1946 by the International Military Tribunal for the Far East at Tokyo. The IMT issued its judgment on 1 October 1946, and in December of that year, the principles of law in the Nuremberg Tribunal's Charter and its judgment were affirmed by the UN General Assembly, which asked the International Law Commission (ILC) to commence work on 'a general codification of offences against the peace and security of mankind, or of an International Criminal Code' (UNGA Resolution 95(I), 1946).

On 9 December 1948 (the day before the adoption of the UDHR), two significant developments in the creation of contemporary international criminal law emerged. First, the Genocide Convention was adopted, establishing an international crime of genocide that could be tried by domestic courts or 'such international penal tribunal as may have jurisdiction'. Relatedly, the General Assembly requested that the ILC begin work on the possibility of creating an international judicial body that could try international crimes (UNGA Resolution 280(III), 1948). Owing to Cold War politics, it would be 50 years before that permanent international criminal tribunal would be established. In the interim, two ad hoc international tribunals were created by the UN Security Council to prosecute those deemed most responsible for atrocities in the former Yugoslavia and Rwanda. Since 1998, international or 'internationalised' (i.e. hybrid creations of states' judicial systems with jurisdiction over international crimes and international judges) criminal tribunals have been established for Sierra Leone, Cambodia, East Timor, Lebanon and Kosovo, amongst others (Romano et al., 2004).

Thus, the development of both international criminal law and international human rights law share a heritage that can be traced back to the end of World War II. That influence continues today – some 50 years after the adoption of the UDHR, the ICC noted, in a strikingly similar preambular paragraph to the UDHR's equivalent quoted earlier, that 'during this century millions of children, women and men have been victims of unimaginable atrocities that deeply shock the conscience of humanity'. The growth of both bodies of law reflects the individualisation of international law, which had traditionally been the premise of states alone. As the International Criminal Tribunal for the Former Yugoslavia (ICTY) noted,

> the impetuous development and propagation in the international community of human rights doctrines . . . has brought about significant changes in international law, notably in the approach to problems besetting the world community. A State-sovereignty-oriented approach has been gradually supplanted by a human-being-oriented approach.
>
> (*Tadić*, 1995, § 97)

The ICC as a human rights institution

Unlike the ICTY and the International Criminal Tribunal for Rwanda (ICTR), the ICC does not have primacy over domestic courts. The ICTR and ICTY could demand that states defer to their jurisdiction and transfer defendants to stand trial before them, although they could choose to transfer cases of lower-level offenders to domestic jurisdictions if they were satisfied that the accused would receive a fair trial and would not be subject to the death penalty. Both the ICTY and ICTR could keep such transfers under review through trial monitoring, and demand that the domestic court transfer the accused back to the international tribunal if they were concerned that he or she was not receiving a fair trial or that there was a risk that the death penalty might be imposed (Gradoni, 2007). This monitoring role has now been passed to their successor institution, the Mechanism for the International Criminal Tribunals.

By contrast, under a principle known as complementarity, there is a preference that domestic trials be carried out for the crimes within the jurisdiction of the ICC. The ICC can only have jurisdiction over a case where a domestic state having jurisdiction over the same case is either unwilling or unable to put the accused on trial (El Zeidy, 2008; Kleffner, 2008).

In the Libya situation before the ICC, a debate arose as to whether the ICC could refuse to defer jurisdiction over two cases to Libya, where it seemed likely that the accused would be sentenced to the death penalty if convicted, and where there were doubts as to whether they could receive a fair trial. Libya argued that fair trial and death penalty considerations could not come into the Court's decision on jurisdiction, provided it was willing and able to put the accused on trial, because the ICC was not designed to act as a human rights court (*Gaddafi*, 2013, §§ 199–203).

Ultimately, the ICC determined that the Libyan state was unable to try Saif Gaddafi because he was in the hands of rebels in Zintan, but that, notwithstanding concerns about his lack of access to counsel, Libya was both willing and able to try its former intelligence chief, Abdullah Al Senussi (*Al Senussi*, 2014, §§ 169–198). That being said, as I have argued elsewhere, the *Al Senussi* judgment did seemingly leave the possibility open to accepting fair trial concerns in future complementarity challenges (McDermott, 2016, p. 161). The Chamber noted that the failure to provide Al Senussi with a lawyer in advance of trial would not be such an egregious violation that would render the proceedings incapable of providing justice. This suggests that egregious violations of the right to a fair trial, such as, perhaps, the use of evidence obtained by torture, could reach that threshold and could be considered by the ICC in future complementarity cases.

Thus, unlike the ICTY and ICTR, the ICC does not have the capacity to consider such issues as the right to a fair trial and the death penalty when deferring jurisdiction to domestic courts. This weakens its position as a court committed to protecting human rights, compared to the ad hoc tribunals. Nevertheless, the ICC has the capacity to develop human rights law through its jurisprudence on the core international crimes and on the right to a fair trial of persons facing trial before it, as shall now be demonstrated.

The interplay between human rights and the ICC

Human rights as a source of law before the ICC

Article 21(3) of the ICC Statute imposes an obligation on the Court to interpret its law in a manner that is consistent with international human rights law. The Appeals

Chamber in *Lubanga* determined that article 21(3) means that the interpretation as well as the application of the law is subject to internationally recognised human rights. The Chamber held that '[Article 21(3)] requires the exercise of the jurisdiction of the Court in accordance with internationally recognized human rights norms' (*Lubanga*, 2006, § 36).

This obligation has been expounded upon in discussions on substantive aspects of the law. The Court has relied on human rights law in finding that the recruitment of child soldiers by non-state armed groups constitutes a war crime (*Lubanga*, 2012, Separate and Dissenting Opinion of Judge Odio Benito, § 13). Procedural human rights standards were instructive in interpreting the defendant's right to be informed of the charges against him (*Lubanga*, 2012, Dissenting Opinion of Judge Fulford, § 20). Where applying a provision of the ICC Statute would effectively breach human rights law, the ICC has held that the Court's human rights obligations must prevail (*Katanga and Chui*, 2011, § 73). As a result of this provision, the case law of human rights tribunals has been extensive before the ICC (Zeegers, 2016).

The interplay between human rights organisations and the ICC

Given its temporal and geographic distance from the crimes upon which it adjudges, the ICC relies heavily on accounts of crimes gathered at the time the crimes were committed. It is perhaps unsurprising that a large number of such accounts come from human rights organisations, working on the ground in the affected regions. Such evidence is not without its deficiencies – in *Katanga*, the Trial Chamber noted that 'the preparation of a report on an investigation of human rights violations is not subject to the same criteria as those for a criminal investigation', given that the sources of the information therein are often (anonymous) hearsay or oral testimony, and are not subjected to rigorous scrutiny by the author of the report in a manner akin to cross-examination (*Katanga*, 2014, § 326). Similarly, in *Lubanga*, the Chamber received evidence that 'human rights and humanitarian organizations are lousy criminal investigators. They are not producing forensic evidence that can be used by a Prosecutor' (*Lubanga*, 2012, § 130).

On the other hand, the involvement of the Fédération Internationale des Ligues des Droits de l'Homme (FIDH) was crucial in the *Bemba* case. The FIDH had published a report in 2003 outlining crimes committed by Bemba's MLC troops in the Central African Republic. Bemba wrote to the FIDH's president, informing him that prosecutions would be undertaken for these crimes; the president, in turn, responded outlining some concerns on the sufficiency of those prosecutions, and encouraging Bemba to cooperate with the ICC (*Bemba*, 2016, §§ 607–611). This evidence was crucial in establishing the responsibility of Bemba as a commander over the MLC troops – having been made aware of the crimes, and having failed to adequately punish them, he bore responsibility under article 28 of the ICC Statute. One would hope that over time, and with the advent of technologies that can record events and testimony and store it securely on remote servers, human rights organisations will become even more adept at gathering reliable evidence in a manner that is useful to the ICC and other courts.

The role of the ICC in developing, interpreting and protecting human rights

Core crimes

The ICC currently has jurisdiction over the crimes of genocide, crimes against humanity and war crimes. It is likely that it will have jurisdiction over the crime of aggression at some time in the future, when two-thirds of states parties have ratified the amendments agreed at the ICC Review Conference at Kampala in 2010. Each of these crimes is closely related to human rights, and by adjudging upon them, the ICC, notwithstanding the fact that it is not formally part of the international human rights law framework, progressively develops human rights protection worldwide. It might be assumed that only breaches of civil and political rights (such as the right to life, right to be free from torture, right to a fair trial and right to liberty) fall under the ambit of international criminal law. However, as Evelyne Schmid has convincingly argued, breaches of economic, social and cultural rights may also constitute international crimes, in certain circumstances (Schmid, 2015).

Genocide

Genocide, often dubbed 'the crime of crimes', is the commission of one of five prohibited acts (killing, causing serious bodily or mental harm, inflicting conditions of life calculated to bring about destruction, imposing measures to prevent births, and forcible transfer of children) against a national, ethnic, racial or religious group with the intent to destroy that group (Schabas, 2009). Aside from a breach of the right to life implicit in the first of these acts, the other acts have clear human rights implications. In the situation relating to Darfur, Sudan, the Pre-Trial Chamber has issued a warrant of arrest against Sudanese President Omar al-Bashir for genocide under the form of serious bodily or mental harm, noting that acts of rape, torture and forced displacement (all themselves human rights violations) had been committed (*Bashir*, 2010, § 30). Al-Bashir was also charged with imposing conditions of life calculated to bring about the destruction of the group, with the ICC noting that displacement, destroying a group's means of survival, usurpation of land and denial of medical treatment could also be acts of genocide (*Bashir*, 2010, § 34).

War crimes

War crimes are serious violations of the laws of armed conflict, and are criminalised under article 8 of the ICC Statute for both international and non-international armed conflicts. The conduct that can constitute war crimes encompasses a broad range of human rights abuses, such as torture, murder, rape, pillage (thus denying victims' right to property) and the right to a fair trial. Article 8 also criminalises certain conduct such as causing widespread, severe and long-lasting damage to the environment; using certain types of weapons and methods of warfare; and launching attacks against buildings dedicated to religion, education, art, science or charitable purposes, historic monuments and hospitals. While these additional categories of war crimes do not explicitly link to a particular human right, their nexus to the human rights of those in affected territories is obvious. Environmental damage affects the right to health and the right to life; prohibited weapons can cause torture or inhumane treatment; and launching attacks against protected buildings and monuments impacts upon victims' right to freedom of belief, education, culture and health.

The ICC has not been afraid to extend the limits of the war crimes regime set down in the Statute to achieve greater protection for victims. Notably, a recent decision of the Appeals Chamber found that war crimes could be committed against fellow combatants from the same armed forces as the perpetrator. This runs contrary to conventional understandings and an ordinary reading of international humanitarian law, which seeks to protect certain categories of persons – civilians and those not directly taking part in hostilities, prisoners of war and wounded, sick and shipwrecked combatants. The Appeals Chamber noted the 'seemingly unprecedented nature' of its findings, and the fact that it was unaware of any previous case where the international humanitarian law regime was applied to victims from the same armed forces as the perpetrator (*Ntaganda*, 2017, §§ 60, 67).

Despite noting that Common Article 3 protects against inhumane treatment, '*requiring only that the persons were taking no active part in hostilities at the material time*' (*Ntaganda*, 2017, § 60; emphasis added), the Appeals Chamber found that there was no reason to believe that international humanitarian law 'suggests any limits on who may be victims' of war crimes under the jurisdiction of the ICC (*Ntaganda*, 2017, § 64). As such, it declined to enter into any discussion as to whether the victims were actively participating in hostilities at the time, finding that the requirement that the persons were taking no active part in hostilities does not exist (*Ntaganda*, 2017, § 69). This is a remarkable *volte-face* in the space of fewer than ten paragraphs of a decision. Moreover, while this decision has been hailed as 'an enormously important contribution to international criminal law' (Grey, 2017), it does raise issues on the right to a fair trial and the principle of *nullum crimen sine lege* in practice (McDermott, 2017). Ironically, while attempting to broaden the scope of the ICC's jurisdiction to cover the heinous crimes suffered by the victims (which are undoubtedly crimes under national law, and might arguably be better suited to domestic prosecution), the ICC could be breaching another human right – the right to a fair trial – itself.

Another interesting issue on the interplay between international criminal law and international human rights law arises when both bodies of law prohibit the same conduct, but each bears different jurisdictional or definitional issues. This arose in the case of *Kunarac* before the ICTY, where torture was prosecuted as a war crime. Under the Convention against Torture, torture is defined as:

> any act by which severe pain or suffering, whether physical or mental, is intentionally inflicted on a person for such purposes as obtaining from him or a third person information or a confession, punishing him for an act he or a third person has committed or is suspected of having committed, or intimidating or coercing him or a third person, or for any reason based on discrimination of any kind, when such pain or suffering is inflicted by or at the instigation of or with the consent or acquiescence of a public official or other person acting in an official capacity. It does not include pain or suffering arising only from, inherent in or incidental to lawful sanctions.

The problem for the prosecution in *Kunarac* was that the acts of torture committed were neither committed by or at the instigation of a public or state official, nor were they for the purposes of obtaining information or a confession, or similar. To circumvent this issue, the ICTY noted that the Convention against Torture was addressed to states to prevent acts of torture being committed by states, and it was for that reason that the definition in the Convention focused on individuals acting on behalf of the state or its organs in an official capacity (*Kunarac*, 2002, § 146). Thus, while international human rights law does act as an interpretative guide for certain war crimes, the ICC and other international criminal tribunals may see fit to derogate from the definitional limits set down in human rights, by examining the object and purpose of human rights statutes vis-à-vis international criminal law statutes.

Crimes against humanity

Crimes against humanity occur when certain acts are committed as part of a widespread or systematic attack against a civilian population. Article 7 of the ICC Statute enumerates 11 acts that constitute crimes against humanity when committed as part of such an attack. They are murder, torture, rape and other forms of sexual violence, enslavement, deportation, extermination, deprivation of liberty, enforced disappearances, apartheid, persecution and other inhumane acts of similar gravity. As with war crimes, the parallels between the underlying acts and human rights violations are clear. Some crimes against humanity, such as enforced disappearance and apartheid, are themselves subject to international treaties, but article 7 represents the first time that such violations have been defined as international crimes falling within the jurisdiction of an international criminal court (Schabas, 2016, pp. 202–206). Two specific crimes against humanity – persecution and other inhumane acts – are very closely linked to international human rights law and, as such, warrant further elucidation.

Persecution is defined as the intentional and severe denial, contrary to international law, of a fundamental right on the basis of political, racial, national, ethnic, cultural, religious, gender or other grounds that are recognised as impermissible under international law. In *Blé Goudé*, the Pre-Trial Chamber considered that rapes, murders and injuries committed by forces loyal to former Côte d'Ivoire President Laurent Gbagbo against perceived supporters of Alassane Ouattara in the wake of an election lost by Gbagbo could constitute acts of persecution. Interestingly, the Chamber found that the acts were committed not just on political grounds, but also on ethnic, national and religious grounds, as members of certain ethnic, national and religious groups were presumed to be Ouattara supporters and targeted on that basis (*Blé Goudé*, 2014, §§ 123–124). Persecution might also cover situations where the victims were denied the right to employment, to liberty, to a proper judicial process, or other fundamental rights as part of a discriminatory pattern of behaviour (Nilsson, 2011, p. 233).

The crime of 'other inhumane acts' constitutes conduct of a similar character to the enumerated acts constituting crimes against humanity, which intentionally cause great suffering or serious bodily injury or physical or mental health. One recent debate that has arisen in the jurisprudence of the ICC is whether the practice of forced marriage constitutes a separate crime against humanity, falling under other inhumane acts. Article 7 already includes slavery as a crime against humanity, and sexual slavery as a separate crime against humanity. Thus, the question arises as to whether a third form of criminalisation for the same conduct is necessary, or whether it would be preferable to prosecute forced marriage as either slavery or sexual slavery. In *Katanga*, the ICC preferred the latter approach, finding that the crime of sexual slavery adequately encompassed acts of forced marriage (*Katanga*, 2008, §§ 428–433). By contrast, the Chamber in *Ongwen* found that forced marriage may qualify as a separate crime against humanity under 'other inhumane acts', and that the practice differed from sexual slavery 'in terms of conduct, ensuing harm, and protected interests' (*Ongwen*, 2016, §§ 87–95). This example shows that the ICC's jurisprudence continues to evolve and develop to incorporate new interpretations of the law, in order to punish offenders for serious human rights violations. The creativity of international judges in interpreting the law has been widely discussed in the literature (Darcy and Powderly, 2010; Shahabuddeen, 2004).

Aggression

The Nuremberg and Tokyo Tribunals tried individuals for the crime of planning, preparing, initiating or waging a war of aggression, or a war in violation of international legal instruments. Since then, no international criminal tribunal has prosecuted a defendant for this crime. It was agreed at the drafting of the ICC Statute that the Court should exercise jurisdiction over the crime of aggression. However, the state parties negotiating the ICC Statute could not agree upon a definition of this crime. In particular, there was debate over the jurisdictional issues surrounding the crime, such as whether the prosecutor could launch an investigation acting *proprio motu* (on her own initiative) or on the basis of a referral by a state party. Because of these difficulties, no definition of aggression was included in the Statute upon its adoption in 1998. Instead, article 5(2) noted that the Court would exercise jurisdiction over the crime once a definition and provisions on the exercise of jurisdiction had been agreed in accordance with the review and amendment process set out in articles 121 and 123 of the Statute.

That agreement was ultimately reached at the ICC Review Conference in Kampala in 2010. There are two jurisdictional pre-conditions for the ICC's jurisdiction over this crime; first, 30 states must ratify the amendments (Palestine became the 30th state to ratify the amendments in June 2016), and, second, some time after 1 January 2017, a two-thirds majority of states parties must take a decision permitting the Court to exercise jurisdiction over the crime in the future.

What does the crime of aggression mean for the ICC's role in protecting human rights? Aggression has traditionally been seen as a state crime, with the victims being not individuals, but the state whose sovereignty, territorial integrity or political independence has been interfered with by the aggressor state. It is perhaps owing to this perception that high-profile human rights groups like Amnesty International and Human Rights Watch took a rather indifferent approach to the aggression amendments at the Kampala Review Conference (Schabas, 2012, p. 207). However, there is no question that acts of aggression between states can have a devastating impact on the human rights of citizens in affected territories, not least the right to life. A stand-alone right to peace was recognised by the UN General Assembly in 1984, noting that 'life without war serves as the primary international prerequisite for the material well-being, development and progress of countries, and for the full implementation of the rights and fundamental human freedoms proclaimed by the United Nations' (UNGA Resolution 39/11, 1984). If and when the ICC gains jurisdiction over this crime, it will bear a key role in developing the right to peace.

Procedure and the right to a fair trial

The most notable influence of human rights law over the ICC has been in the realm of international criminal procedure, and as regards the right to a fair trial in particular. The ICC borrows extensively from international human rights courts and instruments in determining the rights of the accused. For example, in *Ruto and Sang*, the prosecutor had challenged the Trial Chamber's decision permitting Kenya's Deputy President Ruto to be voluntarily absent from trial. The Appeals Chamber, in upholding the decision, held that the right of the accused to be present at trial could be voluntarily waived. It found support for this position in the case law of the European Court of Human Rights, ICTR case law, and the African Commission on Human and Peoples' Rights' Principles and Guidelines on the Right to a Fair Trial and Legal Assistance in Africa (*Ruto*, 2013, § 51). Human rights have also been relied upon extensively in decisions on equality of arms (*Lubanga*, 2008, Partly dissenting opinion of Judge Pikis, § 14), witness protection measures (*Katanga*, 2009, §§ 32–33), the right to be informed of the charges, and ensuring that trials are both expeditious and fair (*Katanga*, 2013, Dissenting Opinion of Judge Cuno Tarfusser, § 8; *Katanga*, 2010, Dissenting Opinion of Judge Erkki Kourula and Judge Ekaterina Trendafilova, § 42).

Not only does the ICC borrow extensively from human rights law, it also bears an illustrative function in demonstrating best practices to states, and providing an example of an international criminal procedure based on a mixed procedural model that is both closely modelled on, and bound to respect, international human rights standards. Amnesty International, in its most recent version of its *Fair Trial Manual*, relies on the standards of international criminal procedure in illustrating fair procedural standards. Thus, even though the Court refused to assume the role of a human rights court in examining the admissibility of the *Al-Senussi* case discussed in the second section, this does not mean that it seeks to derogate from human rights standards in developing its own procedural practice. Indeed, the Court declares in its public literature that '[i]n all of its activities, the ICC observes *the highest standards of fairness and due process*' (ICC, 2015, emphasis added).

Conclusion

The ICC, as the world's first permanent international criminal institution, plays an important role in the global legal framework for the promotion, protection and fulfillment of human rights, despite the fact that it is not, itself, a human rights court. Unlike the ad hoc tribunals that preceded it, the ICC does not have primacy of jurisdiction, and this means that it cannot deem a case admissible before it purely on the basis that the accused would not receive a fair trial in a domestic court. This, from the outside, appears to weaken the ICC's position as a cog in the machine of human rights protection.

However, the ICC is bound to interpret its law in a manner that is consistent with international human rights law, and human rights standards have had a significant bearing on the development of international criminal law before the ICC. Conversely, the ICC has been able to bring about progressive developments in the interpretation of its core crimes, all of which are closely linked to human rights. In this manner, international criminal tribunals have influenced the development of human rights and international law more broadly. The synergies between human rights and the ICC's legal framework are not limited to substantive legal issues. There is also evidence of an interplay between human rights and the ICC in procedural matters, especially in issues surrounding the accused's right to a fair trial, and in investigations, where human rights organisations play a not insignificant role in the collection and preservation of evidence. Thus, the relationship is mutually beneficial in that human rights law informs and shapes ICC law and procedure, and ICC practice in turn feeds into the development of human rights law.

It is apposite to end this chapter with a note of caution on expectations. As has been seen in this chapter, the ICC is but one Court, with jurisdiction over tightly defined crimes and an obligation to respect the presumption of innocence and try cases in accordance with the criminal standard of proof beyond reasonable doubt. It is sometimes expected to play a greater role in international politics, by ending conflicts, deterring future atrocities or forcing states to respect their human rights obligations, and is then found wanting against those unrealistic expectations. Despite the notable developments set out in this chapter, it is important to remember that the ICC is but one small part of a vast and often unwieldy machine of international justice, which comprises a range of bodies with different mandates, operational structures and powers. To quote the ICC prosecutor, in her recent statement on the situation in Libya:

> To those of you who express to my Office your fears and disappointments, as well as your hopes and aspirations for the future of a Libya grounded on the pillars of justice where gross human rights violations are distant memories of the past, your calls for action do not fall on deaf ears. . . . And while I am under no illusions that the International Criminal Court is a panacea – *it surely is not* – I, along with my team, are committed to playing our part.
>
> (ICC Prosecutor, 2017)

Ultimately, that is the best we can hope for with the ICC – that it will play its small part in the global march towards universal human rights, justice and the rule of law.

Further reading

Jones, Annika (2016) 'Insights Into an Emerging Relationship: Use of Human Rights Jurisprudence at the International Criminal Court' *Human Rights Law Review* 16(4), pp. 701–729.

Margueritte, Thomas (2010) 'International Criminal Law and Human Rights' in William A. Schabas and Nadia Bernaz (eds.) *Routledge Handbook of International Criminal Law* (Abingdon, UK: Routledge), pp. 435–452.

Mariniello, Triestino, and Paolo Lobba (eds.) (2017) *Judicial Dialogue on Human Rights: The Practice of International Criminal Tribunals* (Leiden: Brill/Nijhoff).

McDermott, Yvonne (2016) *Fairness in International Criminal Trials* (Oxford: Oxford University Press).

Schabas, William A. (2016) *The International Criminal Court: A Commentary on the Rome Statute*, 2nd ed. (Oxford: Oxford University Press).

Schabas, William A. (2017) *An Introduction to the International Criminal Court*, 5th ed. (Cambridge: Cambridge University Press).

Schmid, Evelyne (2015) *Taking Economic, Social, and Cultural Rights Seriously in International Criminal Law* (Cambridge: Cambridge University Press).

Shelton, Dinah (ed.) (2000) *International Crimes, Peace, and Human Rights: The Role of the International Criminal Court* (New York: Transnational Publishers).

Zeegers, Krit (2016) *International Criminal Tribunals and Human Rights Law* (The Hague: Springer).

Bibliography

Primary sources

International legal instruments

Agreement for the Prosecution and Punishment of the Major War Criminals of the European Axis, and Charter of the International Military Tribunal. London, 8 August 1945.

Convention Against Torture and Other Cruel, Inhuman or Degrading Treatment or Punishment, 1465 UNTS 85, 10 December 1984.

Convention on the Prevention and Punishment of the Crime of Genocide, 78 UNTS 227, 9 December 1948.

Treaty of Peace between the Allied and Associated Powers and Germany ('Treaty of Versailles') (1919) TS 4.

United Nations General Assembly Resolution 95(I), 11 December 1946.

United Nations General Assembly Resolution 280(III), 9 December 1948.

United Nations General Assembly Resolution 39/11, 12 November 1984.

Universal Declaration on Human Rights, General Assembly Resolution 217A (III), 10 December 1948.

Rome Statute of the International Criminal Court ('ICC Statute'), UN Doc. A/CONF.183/9, 17 July 1998.

Case law

International Criminal Court

Situation in the Democratic Republic of the Congo: Prosecutor v. Lubanga, Judgment on the Appeal of Mr. Thomas Lubanga Dyilo against the Decision on the Defence Challenge to the Jurisdiction of the Court Pursuant to Article 19(2) (a) of the Statute of 3 October 2006, Case No. ICC-01/04-01/06, ICC, Appeals Chamber, 14 December 2006.

Situation in the Democratic Republic of the Congo: Prosecutor v. Lubanga, Judgment on the Appeals of The Prosecutor and The Defence against Trial Chamber I's Decision on

Victims' Participation of 18 January 2008, Case No. ICC-01/04-01/06, ICC, Appeals Chamber, 11 July 2008.

Situation in the Democratic Republic of the Congo: Prosecutor v Katanga and Chui, Decision on the Confirmation of Charges, Case No. ICC-01/04-01/07, ICC, Pre-Trial Chamber I, 30 September 2008.

Situation in the Democratic Republic of the Congo: Prosecutor v Katanga and Chui, Decision on the Protection of Prosecution Witnesses 267 and 353 of 20 May 2009, Case No. ICC-01/04-01/07, ICC, Trial Chamber II, 28 May 2009.

Situation in Darfur, Sudan: Prosecutor v. Al Bashir, Second Decision on the Prosecution's Application for a Warrant of Arrest, Case No. ICC-02/05-01/09, ICC, Pre-Trial Chamber I, 12 July 2010.

Situation in the Democratic Republic of the Congo: Prosecutor v Katanga and Chui, Judgment on the Appeal of Mr Katanga Against the Decision of Trial Chamber II of 20 November 2009 Entitled "Decision on the Motion of the Defence for Germain Katanga for a Declaration on Unlawful Detention and Stay of Proceedings", Case No. ICC-01/04-01/07, ICC, Appeals Chamber, 28 July 2010.

Situation in the Democratic Republic of the Congo: Prosecutor v Katanga and Chui, Decision on an Amicus Curiae application and on the "Requête tendant à obtenir présentations des témoins DRC-D02-P-0350, DRC-D02-P-0236, DRC-D02-P-0228 aux autorités néerlandaises aux fins d'asile" (articles 68 and 93(7) of the Statute), Case No. ICC-01/04-1/07, ICC, Trial Chamber II, 9 June 2011.

Situation in the Democratic Republic of the Congo: Prosecutor v. Lubanga, Judgment pursuant to article 74 of the Statute, Case No. ICC-01/04-01/06, ICC, Trial Chamber I, 4 April 2012.

Situation in the Democratic Republic of the Congo: Prosecutor v Katanga and Chui, Judgment on the appeal of Mr Germain Katanga against the decision of Trial Chamber II of 21 November 2012 entitled 'Decision on the implementation of regulation 55 of the Regulations of the Court and severing the charges against the accused persons', Case No. ICC-01/04-01/07, ICC, Appeals Chamber, 27 March 2013.

Situation in Libya: Prosecutor v. Gaddafi and Al-Senussi, Decision on the admissibility of the case against Saif Al-Islam Gaddafi, Case No. ICC-01/11-01/11, ICC, Pre-Trial Chamber I, 31 May 2013.

Situation in Kenya: Prosecutor v. Ruto and Sang, Judgment on the appeal of the Prosecutor against the decision of Trial Chamber V(a) of 18 June 2013 entitled 'Decision on Mr Ruto's Request for Excusal from Continuous Presence at Trial', Case No. ICC-01/09-01/11, ICC, Appeals Chamber, 25 October 2013.

Situation in the Democratic Republic of the Congo: Prosecutor v. Katanga, Judgment pursuant to article 74 of the Statute, Case No. ICC-01/04-01/07, ICC, Trial Chamber II, 7 March 2014.

Situation in Libya: Prosecutor v. Gaddafi and Al-Senussi, Judgment on the appeal of Mr Abdullah Al-Senussi against the decision of Pre-Trial Chamber I of 11 October 2013 entitled 'Decision on the admissibility of the case against Abdullah Al-Senussi', Case No. ICC-01/11-01/11, ICC, Appeals Chamber, 24 July 2014.

Situation in Côte d'Ivoire: Prosecutor v. Blé Goudé, Decision on the confirmation of charges against Charles Blé Goudé, Case No. ICC-02/11-02/11, ICC, Pre-Trial Chamber I, 11 December 2014.

Situation in the Central African Republic: Prosecutor v. Bemba, Judgment pursuant to article 74 of the Statute, Case No. ICC-01/05-01/08, ICC, Trial Chamber III, 21 March 2016.

Situation in Uganda: Prosecutor v. Ongwen, Decision on the confirmation of charges against Dominic Ongwen, Case No. ICC-02/04-01/15, ICC, Pre-Trial Chamber II, 23 March 2016.

Situation in the Democratic Republic of the Congo: Prosecutor v. Nataganda, Judgment on the appeal of Mr Ntaganda against the 'Second decision on the Defence's challenge to the jurisdiction of the Court in respect of Counts 6 and 9', Case No. ICC-01/04-02/06, ICC, Appeals Chamber, 15 June 2017.

International Criminal Tribunal for the Former Yugoslavia

Prosecutor v. Tadić, Decision on the Defence Motion for Interlocutory Appeal on Jurisdiction, Case No. IT-94-1-AR72, ICTY, Appeals Chamber, 2 October 1995.
Prosecutor v. Kunarac, Kovac and Vukovic, Judgment, Case Nos. IT-96-23 & IT-96-23/1-A, ICTY, Appeals Chamber, 12 June 2002.

Official statements

ICC Prosecutor (2017) *Statement of ICC Prosecutor to the United Nations Security Council on the Situation in Libya*, 8 May 2017, www.icc-cpi.int/legalAidConsultations?name=17 0509-otp-stat-lib.

Secondary sources

Bassiouni, M. Cherif (1997) 'From Versailles to Rwanda in Seventy-Five Years: The Need to Establish a Permanent International Criminal Court', *Harvard Human Rights Journal* 10, pp. 11–62.
Cryer, Robert, Robert Friman, Darryl Robinson and Elizabeth Wilmshurst (2014) *An Introduction to International Criminal Law and Procedure*, 3rd ed. (Cambridge: Cambridge University Press).
Darcy, Shane and Joseph Powderly (eds.) (2010) *Judicial Creativity at the International Criminal Tribunals* (Oxford: Oxford University Press).
El Zeidy, Mohamed (2008) *The Principle of Complementarity in International Criminal Law* (Leiden/Boston: Martinus Nijhoff).
Gradoni, Lorenzo (2007) ' "You will Receive a Fair Trial Elsewhere": The Ad Hoc International Criminal Tribunals Acting as Human Rights Jurisdictions', *Netherlands International Law Review* 54(1), pp. 1–49.
Grey, Rosemary (2017) 'ICC Appeals Chamber Issues "Unprecedented" Decision on War Crimes of Rape and Sexual Slavery', *IntLawGrrls* (14 June 2017), https://ilg2. org/2017/06/14/icc-appeals-chamber-issues-unprecedented-decision-on-war-crimes-of-rape-and-sexual-slavery.
International Criminal Court (2015) *Reporting on the International Criminal Court: A Practical Guide for the Media*, www.icc-cpi.int/iccdocs/PIDS/publications/ICC_Guide_for%20 Journalists_EN.pdf.
Kleffner, Jann K. (2008) *Complementarity in the Rome Statute and National Criminal Jurisdictions* (Oxford: Oxford University Press).
McDermott, Yvonne (2016) *Fairness in International Criminal Trials* (Oxford: Oxford University Press).
McDermott, Yvonne (2017) 'ICC extends War Crimes of Rape and Sexual Slavery to Victims from Same Armed Forces as Perpetrator', *IntLawGrrls* (5 January 2017), https:// ilg2.org/2017/01/05/icc-extends-war-crimes-of-rape-and-sexual-slavery-to-victims-from-same-armed-forces-as-perpetrator/.
Nilsson, Jonas (2011) 'The Crime of Persecution in the ICTY Case Law', in Bert Swart, Alexander Zahar and Göran Sluiter (eds.) *The Legacy of the International Criminal Tribunal for the Former Yugoslavia* (Oxford: Oxford University Press), pp. 219–246.
Romano, Cesare P.R., André Nollkaemper, and Jann K. Kleffner (2004) *Internationalized Criminal Courts and Tribunals: Sierra Leone, East Timor, Kosovo, and Cambodia* (Oxford: Oxford University Press).
Schabas, William A. (2009) *Genocide in International Law: The Crime of Crimes*, 2nd ed. (Cambridge: Cambridge University Press).

Schabas, William A. (2012) *Unimaginable Atrocities* (Oxford: Oxford University Press).

Schabas, William A. (2016) *The International Criminal Court: A Commentary on the Rome Statute*, 2nd ed. (Oxford: Oxford University Press).

Schabas, William A. (2017) *An Introduction to the International Criminal Court*, 5th ed. (Cambridge: Cambridge University Press).

Schmid, Evelyne (2015) *Taking Economic, Social, and Cultural Rights Seriously in International Criminal Law* (Cambridge: Cambridge University Press).

Shahabuddeen, Mohamed (2004) 'Does the Principle of Legality Stand in the Way of the Progressive Development of the Law?' *Journal of International Criminal Justice* 2, pp. 1007–1017.

Chapter 24

The threat of transnational terrorism

Tobias Hof

Berlin, 19 December 2016: Anis Amri, a Tunisian, drove a truck into the Christmas market next to the Kaiser Wilhelm Memorial Church. He killed 12 people and injured 56 more. Amri was shot by Italian policemen outside Milan four days later. The Islamic State (IS) claimed responsibility for the incident and released a video of Amri pledging his allegiance to the group. This attack was just one in a series carried

FIGURE 24.1 Aftermath of a suicide bombing in Sehwan, Pakistan

out in the West in the name of IS. With deadly attacks like Paris in November 2015 and April 2017, Orlando in June 2016, Nice in July 2016, London in April and June 2017, Manchester in May 2017 or Barcelona in August 2017, IS has replaced Al-Qaeda, responsible for the 9/11 attacks in New York, as the most dangerous international terrorist organisation in the public consciousness.

The origins of IS go back to a smaller militant group, Jamaat al-Tawhid wal-Jihad, created under Abu Musab al-Zarqawi in 2000. After several setbacks and an uneasy alliance with Al-Qaeda in Iraq, the organisation successfully regrouped due to the chaos that followed the 2003 US invasion of Iraq and the outbreak of the Syrian Civil War in 2011. The group – now officially carrying the name Islamic State under its leader Abu Bakr al-Baghdadi – gained prominence in the summer of 2014 when it defeated the Iraq army and occupied strategic positions such as Mosul, Tikrit and Kirkuk. Though IS is now on the defensive, it once occupied vast areas of Iraq and Syria, possessed influence in Northern Africa and Yemen, and was the wealthiest terrorist group ever, controlling between six and eight million people. It also attracted several lone wolf terrorists and thousands of foreign fighters from Western countries, who joined IS to fight against the coalition armies.

While the public remains fixated on IS, other international terrorist groups still pose a serious threat: Al-Qaeda, weakened after the killing of Osama bin Laden on 2 May 2011, is still operative; Boko Haram, which pledged its allegiance to IS in 2015, is active in Nigeria; Al-Shabaab, a rival organisation to Al-Qaeda and IS, is based in Somalia; and far-right terrorist attacks – often considered domestic events though international ties exist – have increased over the last years (Lesperance, 2016, pp. 16–17).

In recent years scholars have produced an overwhelming number of studies dealing with the current terrorist threat and the reactions of nation states and the international community. This article can only offer a small glimpse into all the different aspects, problems and nuances of these topics. I would like to narrow my paper down to three main areas: First, I would like to give a brief overview about the present terrorism by focusing on IS and contextualising it within its wider history. Defining the threat is the first step to find more efficient methods of countering it (Penksa, 2005, p. 19). Second, I would like to address the current anti-terrorism measures through the lens of analysing the public discourse on terrorism. It is essential to examine the discourse, because it is used to justify certain counterterrorist tools. Finally, I would like to introduce historical examples of successful anti-terrorism policies into the current debate on how to counter the terrorism threat.

Conceptualising the current threat

Before we can assess the threat of international terrorism today, we should familiarise ourselves with the term itself. Few words in our language are used so often and so carelessly. Especially after 9/11 it has become a common phenomenon to use the term not to describe, but to stigmatise a certain event or group: When for instance 18-year-old David Sonboly killed nine people and later himself in Munich in the summer of 2016, some politicians were quick to tie this event to recent religious terrorist incidents in Europe without offering any proof (Linn and Liptak, 2016). Even after the police categorically dismissed any links between Sonboly and Islamic extremism, *TIME* magazine scolded the German law enforcement agencies for their 'rash' judgment: Was 'it equally obvious that he had no Islamist sympathies of any kind? . . . This early in the investigation, perhaps it would have been better to leave the preliminary conclusions at that' (Shuster, 2016).

Scholars have so far failed to offer a commonly accepted definition of terrorism that reflects its complex nature; some have even argued that the term is too difficult to define at all. Given that the term is so controversial, it is essential to clarify what definition is used in this article. I will adopt a definition put forward in 2004, which defines terrorism as 'a politically motivated tactic involving the threat or use of force or violence in which the pursuit of publicity plays a significant role' (Weinberg, Pedahzur and Hirsch-Hoefler, 2004, p. 786).

One reason why terrorism is hard to define is that its meaning has changed over time. To conceptualise this evolution, political scientist David Rapoport has developed his well-known wave theory of modern terrorism. According to him a wave 'is a cycle of activity in a given time period with expansion and contraction phases. Those activities occur in many countries, driven by a common predominant energy shaping the relationship of participating groups' (Rapoport, 2013, p. 283). The respective energy gives each wave its name. Rapoport determined four different waves of modern terrorism: the anarchist wave (1880s–1920s), the anti-colonial wave (1920s–1960s), the new left wave (1960s–2000) and the religious wave (1980s–2020s). Thus, by his definition we live today in the religious wave, which began with the Iranian revolution in 1979.

Since 9/11, however, and especially after the rise of IS, the phenomenon of lone wolf terrorism – or the 'leaderless resistance' – has become one of the most important trends in terrorism (Hoffmann, 2006, p. 271): Anders Behring Breivik (Norway, 2011), Dzhokhar and Tamerlan Tsarnaev (Boston, 2013), Mohamed L. Bouhlel (Nice, 2016), Omar Mateen (Orlando, 2016), Alexandre Bissonnette (Quebec, 2017) and Brenton Harrison Tarrant (Christchurch, 2019) are just a random selection of lone wolf actors. Most of these attackers either pledged their allegiance to jihadist terrorist groups or were adherents of Christian white supremacy. Some scholars struggle to place this development into Rapoport's wave theory and instead propose that terrorism is inspired by 'four different strains . . ., Nationalism, Socialism, Religious Extremism, and Social Exclusion' (Parker and Sitter, 2016, pp. 198–199). They are arguing that these strains have always been part of the history of terrorism.

Other scholars like Jeffrey Kaplan have been more reluctant to make a clear cut distinction between the terrorism of the late 20th century and a 'new' form of terrorism. Instead of proposing a 'fifth wave', they acknowledge that 'lone wolf and autonomous cell violence is as old as time itself' (Kaplan, 2014, p. 9); Gundolf Köhler (Munich, 1980) and Timothy McVeigh (Oklahoma City, 1995) are two examples that support this argument. Focusing on terrorist groups in Africa and on IS, Kaplan has developed his theory on 'tribalism' to capture the specifics of the current trend without neglecting the fact that religion remains the driving energy. According to him 'the Islamic State sees the battle in frankly eschatological (End of

Days) terms, giving them full confidence in ultimate victory, either as the defeat of the global forces arrayed against them, or by offering their lives as shahid (martyrs)' (Kaplan and Costa, 2015, p. 927). By declaring the end of time, a faithful follower of IS does not have to live according to the religious doctrine anymore. Thus, raping women and forceful conversion to Islam, usually forbidden, become acceptable tools to achieve the group's goals (Kaplan and Costa, 2015, pp. 931, 940).

When IS disseminates its apocalyptic message, they heavily rely on means of communication ranging from the internet and social media to conventional tools such as journals (Kaplan and Costa, 2015, pp. 938–939, 941–943). IS specifically targets individuals, many of whom are born outside the 'tribe', who often belong to a younger generation, and who feel marginalised by the society they live in. These individuals develop a 'malign aspirational tribalism' to become part of the imagined community of IS by either joining the group as foreign fighters or by executing a terrorist act. Since their action is legitimised as an essential pillar of the community's wider strategy, the 'leaderless resistance' is not as isolated as one might believe. Indeed we do have cases in which the lone wolf terrorist was in direct communication with members of IS (Joosse, 2017, p. 54; Kaplan and Costa, 2015, pp. 932–933). IS's message not only attracts individuals, but also helps to forge alliances with other terrorist groups. By May 2015, at least 33 groups pledged allegiance to IS (Kaplan and Costa, 2015, pp. 955–956). However, some scholars are more cautious and argue that there 'is a tendency of overestimating occurrences of terrorist alliances by mistaking instances of cooperation or public statement for the actual existence of an alliance' (Bacon, 2017, p. 79). Obvious obstacles such as rivalry, ideological differences and the fear of infiltration and betrayal have so far undermined any successful alliance (Bacon, 2017, p. 96; Lesperance, 2016, p. 19).

Kaplan's 'tribalism' theory offers useful insights into the propaganda methods of IS recruitment tactics and why they have such a huge appeal. However, as with all theories, it cannot fully account for the complexity of the current situation. First, since the summer of 2014 IS has occupied large areas of Iraq and Syria and has used guerrilla style tactics to harass the coalition forces, though these were supported by Western countries like the US, the UK and France. The control of a defined territory is often cited as a clear delineation between a guerrilla and a terrorist group, creating a categorisation issue when it comes to IS (Hoffman, 2006, p. 35). Whereas the theory of 'tribalism' might be helpful to capture the motivations behind some terrorist acts, it has its limits when analysing specific characteristics of IS, such as the guerrilla tactics or the establishment of a well-functioning state-apparatus in occupied areas. But can we then define IS as a purely terrorist organisation, even though the aforementioned definition captures parts of their tactics? Whereas terrorism expert Audrey Cronin has her doubts, other scholars demand a more thorough integration of terrorism studies within the scholarship on war, warfare and insurgency (Cronin, 2015; Martin and Weinberg, 2016, p 248).

Second, Kaplan's theory is based on the assumption that the leaders of IS 'are dead serious in their beliefs and actions', including – for example – the total destruction of cultural artefacts (Kaplan and Costa, 2015, pp. 934, 948–949). However, this overlooks the fact that the group is heavily involved in the traffic and sale of artefacts, only destroying those which they cannot transport or sell. At least in this regard, practical arrangements seem to trump religious fanaticism, which throws the 'dead seriousness' of the leaders of IS into question (Shabi, 2015). The idea of an imminent apocalypse also illustrates the problem of overstating the group's rhetoric. According to Kaplan, this worldview enables IS to commit atrocities that are officially forbidden under the rulings of the Quran. I argue, however, that an interpretation of the group's apocalypticism should additionally address its undeniably pragmatic – even cynical – side: over and over Muslim scholars and religious leaders have condemned IS and its affiliates as being against Muslims and the teachings of the Quran. This criticism, however, must fall on deaf ears when we acknowledge the significant role apocalypticism plays within the current teachings of IS. Furthermore, IS began as a politically motivated organisation committed to evicting the US forces and their collaborators from Iraq, toppling the regime in Baghdad and establishing a Sunni Islamic State under Sharia law. Over time, however, setbacks, shifting alliances, multiple reorganisations and new leadership led to an adjustment of these goals and the group 'managed to create a rhetoric suggesting it is an Allah-ordained caliphate' (Lansford and Holt, 2013, p. 1; Lesperance, 2016, p. 17). Analysing these changes, which are common for most terrorist organisations, and thoroughly scrutinising the group's propaganda can help us to better understand the threat IS still poses.

Third, the desire of people who feel excluded to belong to a 'tribe' is not new. Taking a look at the history of right-wing terrorism in Europe and North America we see a striking similarity: right-wing terrorists were – and still are – often individuals who felt threatened by the rest of society and betrayed by the state institutions (Sprinzak, 1995). Even though there are many differences between right-wing terrorists and people committing crimes in the name of IS, the desire to belong to an 'imagined community' – in the case of the former a racially defined 'true nation' – is not specific to jihadist terrorist groups. A comparative historical approach that transcends ideological/religious boundaries might further specify essential characteristics of the lone wolf phenomenon without overstating peculiarities that might apply only to certain groups or doctrines. It is worth mentioning that Rapoport also had trouble placing the right-wing terrorism of the 1970–80s within his wave theory, given that it cannot be fully understand as a mere reaction to a dominant wave as he suggested (Rapoport, 2016, p. 222).

And last but not least, do all individuals who carry out a terrorist act and pledge their allegiance to IS truly understand the group's message and want to belong to an 'imagined community'? Or are they driven by other motivations? To better grasp the various motives of so-called lone wolves we have to closely analyse their lives, their habits, their social interactions and environment, their living situations and many more possible influences. Such meticulous scrutiny helps to bring other motivations to light and mitigates the inclination to accept the simplest explanation – their allegiance pledges or the propaganda by IS – as the true one. Two examples from 2016 can illustrate the risk of jumping too quickly to conclusions and of taking IS's claims of responsibility at face value: the motives of Omar Mateen, who killed 49 people in a gay nightclub in Orlando on 12 June 2016, are still contested. Despite falsely bragging about his relationship to the Tsarnaev brothers and pledging his allegiance first to Hamas, then to IS, the target he picked and several testimonies could also point to a hate crime against the gay community (Goldman, 2016). Mohammad Daleel, who blew himself up in Ansbach in 2016 without any other casualties, did so after two failed suicide attempts and before his looming deportation to Bulgaria (Diehl and Sydow, 2016). Did these individuals really seek to belong to an 'imagined community'? Or were they looking for an excuse for antisocial behaviour or a way to obscure their true motives by pledging their allegiance to IS?

History has taught us that ideology is not always the driving force when it comes to committing crimes of an unimaginable scale. Instead, it is often used to justify the actions afterwards. But, why is this difference important? While it is true that the message coming from IS might radicalise people who feel marginalised and exhibit violent behaviour, there is little proof so far that their message attracts individuals within mainstream society. Understanding the motives of lone wolves and focusing on the reasons why they feel alienated might help to not only reduce the size of IS's recruitment pool, but also to create a more efficient reaction to this phenomenon in accordance to the rule of law.

Current responses to the terrorist threats

Over the years scholars have developed different models to classify anti-terrorism policies, with communicative and repressive strategies being the two most common categories. Communicative measures attempt to delegitimise the motives and aims of terrorist groups. They include social, economic and political reforms; anti-terrorism propaganda and psychological warfare; and negotiations between terrorists and governments as well as legislative initiatives to rehabilitate former terrorists. Repressive strategies centre on special anti-terrorism legislation; the use of security services, law enforcement units and the military; the formation and deployment of special anti-terror units and committees; and the creation of high security prisons. Taking into account the different levels and severity of repressive measures they are further subdivided into a criminal justice and a war model (Crelinsten, 2002).

Moreover, scholars have developed various guidelines for successfully implementing counterterrorism policies in a democracy. According to Peter Chalk every state response has to be appropriate and credible, limited in time and scope and under parliamentary control (Chalk, 1998, pp. 386–387). Peter Waldmann, a German sociologist, has a slightly different focus. He argues that any action against a potential threat has to be swift and repressive in order to isolate terrorists and to prevent any chance for them to regroup; anti-terrorism policies have to address the symbolic and communicative sphere of terrorism; terrorists should not receive a special status within the penal system; and finally, they should be offered individual ways out of the cycle of terrorist violence so that they can be reintegrated into society later (Waldmann, 2008, pp. 26–27). The ultimate goal of all these recommendations is to find a way to efficiently fight terrorism without violating the rule of law. If a state is unable to find a balance between these two pillars it risks undermining its own legitimacy and ultimately provoking a further radicalisation of political violence.

Since the attacks of 9/11 the reaction to terrorism has become overwhelmingly militarised. The American-led 'war on terror' in Afghanistan, the Iraq invasion in 2003, the fight against IS and US-led drone-warfare are the most obvious examples of this trend. But, the declaration of the state of emergency in France in

November 2015, which lasted until November 2017, and demands to utilise the German Bundeswehr against terrorists within the country are also symptoms of this trend. Special anti-terror legislations that restrict basic civil rights such as freedom of movement and violate the private sphere were introduced with little resistance in countries like the UK, the US and Germany (Dorle, 2016).

The slogan 'If you've got nothing to hide, you've got nothing to fear!' has seemingly trumped all fears about the establishment of an Orwellian surveillance state, with civil rights activists and some journalists being the only ones that are seriously alarmed by the gradual eroding of the rule of law (Prantl, 2008). A widespread feeling of constantly being under threat, coupled with the fear of living in a permanent emergency situation, allows the executive branch of government to push for more and more far reaching measures. This perception, however, is not so much warranted by facts, as it is by the public discourse on terrorism we encounter in the Western world.

This discourse operates on two different levels: first, the frequency of news and comments about terrorism, and second, the nature of these reports and statements. After the attacks in Paris, former CIA director Michael Morell published an article in *TIME* magazine with the title 'ISIS will strike America', while David Von Drehle was talking about a 'World War ISIS' (Morell, 2015; Von Drehle, 2015). Politicians such as Marine Le Pen in France and Donald Trump in the US constantly feed the image of being under siege by terrorist organisations. By exploiting the fear of the population they attempt to create a permanent state of emergency, which would allow the abolishment of civil rights for minority groups and the abuse of anti-terrorism legislation 'for purposes other than the fight against terrorism' (Pokalova, 2015, p. 492). In the case of Europe, the influx of migrants from the Middle East and North Africa has increased the fear that terrorists have infiltrated refugee groups. Again, politicians but also scholars oversimplify the complex situation by drawing misleading comparisons, for example, between the US and Sweden while neglecting the geographical dimension (Kaplan and Costa, 2015, pp. 945–946).

A closer look at recent incidents, however, reveals that this 'state of panic' – however understandable from an emotional point of view – is hardly factual: first, although we have experienced an increase in the frequency of terrorist attacks and fatalities, especially in 2016, the actual numbers are much lower than in the 1970–80s (Miller, 2016). Second, the indiscriminate nature of current terrorist acts is not a new phenomenon. Whereas separatist and left-wing terrorists usually targeted state officials, right-wing and nationalist terrorists considered these restraints counterproductive to their goal of spreading terror. Attacks carried out by right-wing terrorist groups in Italy and Germany or by loyalists in Northern Ireland exemplify this trend (Sprinzak, 1995). And third, most attacks have not been carried out by refugees and the number of refugees involved in terrorist activities is marginal in relation to the actual numbers of migrants fleeing war-torn Syria and Iraq (Funk and Parkes, 2016).

The public discourse – in the tradition of Samuel P. Huntington's *Clash of Civilization* – has also shifted towards the creation of a dangerous dichotomy between the 'West' and the 'Islamic World'. In their public addresses after the attacks in London (2007) and Paris (2015), politicians like Tony Blair, David Cameron and Francois Hollande vowed that the terrorists would not destroy the Western way of life, 'our way of life' (Cameron, 2015). After the Nice attack, Republican Newt Gingrich stated that 'Western civilization is in a war. We should frankly test every person here who is of a Muslim background and if they believe in sharia they should be deported' (Rappeport, 2016). In 2017 Donald Trump endorsed the use of torture, because we should 'fight fire with fire' (Merica, 2017), and enacted an executive order to ban refugees and migrants from seven countries from coming to the US. This order – labelled the 'Muslim Ban' by critics – targeted countries with a Muslim majority and would only allow an exception for people who belong to a religious minority in this country. It was challenged by several federal states and parts of the order were subsequently suspended due to concerns over its constitutionality. However, in 2018 the US Supreme Court upheld a modified version of the executive order with a 5–4 majority.

Calls for solidarity and emotional reactions after horrendous terrorist attacks are problematic but understandable at a time of shock and despair (Collins, 2004). However, when they become a commonly accepted part of the public discourse – as has been pointed out by numerous experts on counterterrorism – they complicate and even damage a successful fight against terrorism. Words have consequences and pose a serious problem in particular for Muslim communities in the West, which are already under constant pressure to distance themselves from attacks carried out by jihadist terrorists. Such demands may ultimately lead to the further radicalisation of Muslims and thus expand the potential recruiting pool for IS (Kaplan and Costa, 2015, p. 933). Moreover, equating Islam with terrorism also legitimises radical versions of counter-jihad movements such as Andres Breivik in Norway or the attack at mosques in Christchurch carried out by Tarrant. These lone wolf attackers accused their governments of not doing enough against illegal immigrants and 'Islamic terrorists' and thus embarked on their own crusade to 'save the West' (Koehler, 2017, pp. 253–254).

All these incidents are also examples of the double standards when reporting and commenting on terrorist acts. Attacks carried out by Christian white supremacists are more often treated as isolated hate crimes than as terrorist attacks. What makes it even more problematic for Muslims is the lack of sympathy and outcry on social media when these acts occur – the complete opposite can be seen after an IS inspired terrorist attack in the West. Although the show of solidarity is well meant, it fosters an image of 'us' versus 'them'. Taken together, Western states and societies are more likely to turn a blind eye towards the terrorist threat coming from far right Christian fanatics than towards jihadist terrorism (Koehler, 2017, p. 2). However, the peril from the far right is not a 'liberal conspiracy', but a symptom of an increasing nationalistic atmosphere in the Western world, legitimised by the rhetoric of leading politicians.

'Islamic terrorism' is the new bogeyman for Western governments and has replaced the Soviet Union of the Cold War era. That IS and other terrorists kill and rape innocent civilians of Christian and Islamic faith all over the world – on 16 February 2017 an attack in Pakistan killed at least 72 people – is often overlooked. The constructed dichotomy between 'Muslims' and the 'West' offers a convenient way to reduce the complex and intertwined challenges we face today – including terrorism and migration – into a simple, black and white picture. This oversimplification, however, might not only help IS in their recruitment efforts and increase far right-wing attacks. But it also leads to poorly thought out counterterrorist strategies that reflect the public discourse more than the actual threat. This can be seen in initial plans to contain IS in its area, mirroring the American containment policy of the Cold War era. However, given the group's goals and ideology this strategy was doomed from the start (Kaplan and Costa, 2015, p. 953).

The entire idea of declaring a war against terrorism – in itself problematic – was justified by the constant emphasis in public speeches that 'we are at war' (Hollande, 2015). The creation of high security prisons such as Abu Ghuraib and Guantanamo and the torture associated with them ultimately supported allegations that the Western allies would not treat Muslims as equals. While the torture scandals were utilised by terrorist groups for their recruitment propaganda, the prisons themselves offered inmates a chance to share radical ideas and form coalitions – they became 'universities for terrorism' (Lesperance, 2016, pp. 21–22).

Not surprisingly, IS hailed Donald Trump's election victory and the aforementioned order as a 'blessed ban', while terrorism experts were warning about the negative consequence (Dalgaard-Nielsen, Laisen and Wandorf, 2016, p. 708). Strategies that are based on general suspicions and not concrete evidence do not only violate the rule of law, but ultimately waste money and resources that are much needed in combatting terrorism. Secret services and law enforcement agencies are already struggling to protect an open society given cuts in federal funding. The Berlin attack in December 2016 is an example of what happens when law enforcement agencies do not have enough resources for a 24/7 surveillance of potential terrorists, so called Gefährder (Fürstenau, 2016).

Learning from the past?

The aforementioned statements should not be seen as a plea against anti-terrorism measures per se, but rather a call for a more nuanced and reflected strategy. There is no doubt that democratic states have an obligation to provide safety and security for their own people. A failure to do so would undermine their legitimacy and give rise to populist movements; however, a counterterrorist policy – as efficient it may appear – that substantially violates the rule of law also damages the democratic system it is supposed to protect. The current challenge is further aggravated by the migration crisis and the dilemma to find a balance between security and humanitarian concerns. Scholars have extensively addressed current issues such as better coordination and information sharing between secret services, a closer cooperation between EU member states, more funding and resources for law enforcement agencies and police training and the military campaigns in the Middle East and Africa.

In recent discussions, however, it is often forgotten that the question of how to counter a terrorist threat is not a new one. Especially in the 1970–80s, many European states were challenged by various terrorist groups ranging from nationalist-separatist to left-wing to right-wing organisations. Without ignoring the fundamental differences between past and current terrorism, it can be beneficial to review those anti-terrorist strategies and concepts previously implemented. Case studies from Northern Ireland, Germany and Italy can highlight obstacles and problems, but also successful policies in the fight against terrorism. Comparing these historical examples illustrates that two strategies in particular proved highly effective: information gathering and policies that reached out to potential sympathisers and to terrorists who wanted to abandon their organisation (Hof, 2015).

Accurate intelligence about a terrorist group is the essential precondition to countering it. Thus, intelligence work should not only focus on the prevention of future attacks, but also on compiling in-depth studies on the functionality, the structure, the aims and motives, the internal rivalries and the means of the groups in order to expose their weaknesses. There are three ways for the intelligence community to collect information: human intelligence, signal intelligence and open source intelligence. Furthermore, the cooperation between the intelligence community and relevant academic fields as well as international organisations is another asset when it comes to understanding and analysing the collected data. The area of intelligence gathering is, however, a slippery slope regarding possible violations of the rule of law.

The need and desire to collect as much data as possible might tempt lawmakers to enact very weak rules for surveillance operations and might be used to argue the use of torture. Better information gathering has already led to first results in the fight against IS: Knowledge about the internal workings of IS enabled the international community to target the group's wealth and supply lines and abandon the containment strategy in favour of a more focused counterattack against key positions of the group. Moreover, the increasing interest in foreign fighters or lone wolf attackers has led to a growing body of in-depth studies on these subjects. The nuanced picture that emerged addresses the social and educational background of these people in addition to their different motives why they join IS in the first place. These reasons range from a desire for adventure to religious zeal, from longing for personal power to re-assurance of their own masculinity (Pauly and Roberts, 2016, p. 165).

That social marginalisation can push people to join terrorist groups is not new: whether right- and left-wing or separatists, terrorists all felt to be outside society. This lack of belonging was shared by an even larger portion of the population who distrusted the state and the so-called elite. This environment helped the terrorists to thrive by providing hideouts as well as logistic, financial and moral support. After initially relying on repressive tactics that targeted not just terrorists, but suspected sympathisers, – Catholics in Northern Ireland or the left-wing scene in Germany and Italy – politicians and law enforcement agencies began to realise the importance of isolating the core group of terrorists from likely sympathisers. Reaching out to these communities and including them in the fight against terrorism became a new – and ultimately successful – strategy. Or, as Warren Chin states: 'If you cannot talk to terrorists or insurgents, then it is important to talk to the people who these groups claim to represent' (Chin, 2013, p. 210).

The UK government reformed the police force in Northern Ireland by abolishing the tarnished Royal Ulster Constabulary and inventing a new more integrated police force (Police Service of Northern Ireland) that included significantly more Catholics. London also cooperated with the Republic of Ireland in its counterterrorist efforts – a major milestone in the Northern Ireland Peace Process. In West Germany, the Ministry of the Interior conducted a year-long research project into the social and political reasons for left-wing terrorism. Bonn also abandoned controversial and indiscriminate strategies such as the Radikalenerlass – a law that could ban people who were suspected of radical political views from civil service.

In Italy, the government reached out to the left-wing milieu after the civil-war like situations of 1976–77 by enacting – often symbolic – reform laws. Most important, however, was the idea to reintegrate former members or supporters of terrorist groups into society by offering reduced sentences in return for their cooperation (*pentiti* law of 1982) – similar ideas were tested in Northern Ireland and Germany. Even though the morally questionable deal between states and terrorists caused a lot of criticism, it triggered in Italy a discussion as to whether sentences for terrorists who merely dissociated themselves from their former groups and repented their past independently of the crimes they had committed should be reduced. Unlike the *pentiti*, they were not required to testify against other people. Therefore, dissociation – implemented in 1987 – was more of a conflict resolution program than a counterterrorism tool, which proved to be very successful (Hof, 2015).

The key to the success of these anti-terrorism policies was a pragmatic and flexible double strategy and not just a single law. On the one hand, the repressive legislation facilitated police investigations and the work of the special units and of the police. On the other hand, a former enemy of the state was not to be excluded from society: a terrorist willing to abandon his former group was not a judicial persona non grata despite the martial rhetoric politicians often used. He did not stand outside the rule of law or society from a mere criminalistic point of view. This strategy, which constitutes the state's monopoly on the use of force as well as a conciliatory state – although it expects something in return – should be considered in the current discussion. Similar approaches might be useful in bridging the gap between the marginalised groups and the rest of society (Hof, 2013, p. 109).

Denmark and Sweden have already implemented a new policy for foreign fighters that mirrors the Italian laws from the 1980s and is not based on the general assumption that everyone who joined IS committed a criminal act. In an elaborate process law enforcement agencies attempt to separate foreign fighters who committed crimes from those who did not. The latter will be offered a spot in a re-socialisation program that aims to reintegrate them into society. A policy like this strengthens the image of an open society that welcomes all people and thus undermines the rhetoric of 'us' versus 'them' that is so essential to IS recruitment. Countering the IS narrative also includes more repressive measures such as closing down Quran schools in the West where radical Islamist thought is preached (Kaplan and Costa, 2015, pp. 946. 953–954).

However, it is equally important to change and adjust the divisive and xenophobic public discourse in the West. There are many different ways to achieve this and many politicians and social institutions are aware of them. We have to acknowledge publicly that not only 'Westerners' or 'Christians' are targets of terrorism and that it is only a small proportion of radical Islamists who commit attacks. Language, and with it the power to blame entire religious groups, needs to be applied more carefully than in the past. In this context, the media bears a huge responsibility. It is their duty to accurately report terrorist incidents and not to offer a platform for xenophobic rhetoric that is counterproductive to the security of the nation. The task is enormous: social media and the internet have been hijacked by fake news, and individuals intent on purposely spreading misinformation.

The attack on the mosque in Quebec, however, and the Munich shooting in the summer of 2016 are good examples when even the quality media quickly latches onto rumours without double-checking the facts (Backes et al., 2016). Creating a 'state of panic' is not only counterproductive for the investigations, but also plays into the strategy of the terrorist organisation; spreading terror, is, after all, the main goal of terrorism. Uncertainty and panic, coupled with the feeling that the state cannot guarantee the safety of its citizen can – as aforementioned – lead to right-wing terrorist attacks. Denying the danger of these groups, however, will ultimately also benefit the rhetoric of IS and other radical Islamic terrorist organisations.

Conclusion

Even though the Islamic State has faced major setbacks and lost its last significant terrority in the Middle East in March 2019, the threat this organisation and other jihadist organisations pose is not gone. The retreat of IS in Iraq and Syria might actually lead to more lone wolf attacks elsewhere, because the desire to join the fight as a foreign fighter might decrease (Europol, 2016). For years IS has benefitted from poorly thought out anti-terrorist measures, which relied heavily on a militarised answer, and an increasing xenophobic public discourse in the West that supports the IS narrative of 'us' versus 'them'. Exploiting this narrative, IS attracted many members of marginalised communities – especially in Western countries – who sought to become part of the 'imagined community' by committing terrorist acts. Changing the rhetoric and offering a more sober reflection and contextualisation of the current international terrorist threat within the wider history of modern terrorism is vital to the reduction of IS's recruitment base.

Successful counterterrorist efforts are based on in-depth studies and knowledge about the group's structure, aims, motives and behaviours and have to address not only the guerrilla tactics of groups like IS, but also the lone wolf phenomenon. More than ever it is necessary to reach out to marginalised groups within societies and therefore produce successful counter-narratives to the IS propaganda. Countries like Denmark and Sweden are at the forefront when it comes to offering former foreign fighters a way back into society. Such a strategy might not provide immediate results and is prone to criticism whenever a terrorist attack happens. Additionally, a wider strategy to reach out to marginalised communities must include social and economic reforms as well as reforms within the integration policy of the respective states to tackle possible reasons why individuals feel left behind in our societies. While this is a long process, an immediate adjustment of our rhetoric and closer integration of Muslim communities and countries in the fight against radical groups might be a solid first step (Pauly and Roberts, 2016, p. 176).

It will be never possible to completely prevent terrorist attacks in an open society. To suggest otherwise by promoting harsh anti-terrorism laws or promising increased security by closing national borders – when in fact many terrorists are home grown – is not only naive but dangerous to the ultimate legitimacy of democracies. Realising this and not spreading the illusion of 100 per cent security might help to reduce panic in the West when it comes to the threat of international terrorism.

Further reading

Baker-Beall, Christopher (2017) *The European Union's Fight Against Terrorism: Discourse, Policies, Identity* (Manchester: Manchester University Press).

Chenoweth, Erica, Richard English, Andreas Gofas and Stathis N. Kalyvas (eds) (2019) *The Oxford Handbook of Terrorism* (Oxford/New York: Oxford University Press).

Crenshaw, Martha (2011) *Explaining Terrorism: Causes, Processes, and Consequences* (London/New York: Routledge).

Crenshaw, Martha and Gary LaFree (2017) *Countering Terrorism* (Washington, DC: Brookings Institution Press).

Cronin, Audrey Kurth (2009) *How Terrorism Ends: Understanding the Decline and Demise of Terrorists Campaigns* (Princeton: Princeton University Press).

Hoffman, Bruce (2017) *Inside Terrorism*, 3rd ed. (New York: Columbia University Press).

Hoffman, Bruce and Fernando Reinares (2011) *The Evolution of the Global Terrorist Threat. From 9/11 to Osama bin Laden's Death* (New York: Columbia University Press).

Laqueur, Walter and Christopher Wall (2018) *The Future of Terrorism: ISIS, Al-Qaeda, and the Alt-right* (New York: Thomas Dunne Books, St. Martin's Press).

Law, Randall D. (ed.) (2014) *The Routledge History of Terrorism* (London/New York: Routledge).

Miller, Martin (2013) *The Foundations of Modern Terrorism: State, Society and the Dynamics of Political Violence* (Cambridge: Cambridge University Press).

Pfander, James E. (2017) *Constitutional Torts and the War on Terror* (New York: Oxford University Press).

Riedel, Bruce O. (2011) *Deadly Embrace: Pakistan, America, and the Future of the Global Jihad* (Washington, DC: Brookings Institution Press).

Silke, Andrew (2018) *Routledge Handbook of Terrorism and Counterterrorism* (London/New York: Routledge).

Bibliography

Backes, Thierry et al. (2016) 'Timeline der Panik', *Südddeutsche Zeitung*, http://sz.de/panik (accessed March 3, 2017).

Bacon, Tricia (2017) 'Hurdles to International Terrorist Alliances: Lessons From Al Qaeda's Experience', *Terrorism and Political Violence* 29(1), pp. 79–101.

Cameron, David (2015) *Prime Minister Statement on Paris Terrorist Attack*, 16 November 2015, www.gov.uk/government/news/prime-minister-statement-on-paris-terror-attack (accessed March 4, 2017).

Chalk, Peter (1998) 'The Response to Terrorism as a Threat to Liberal Democracy', *Australian Journal of Politics and History* 44(3), pp. 373–388.

Chin, Warren (2013) *Britain and the War on Terror: Policy, Strategy and Operations* (London/New York: Routledge).

Collins, Randall (2004) 'Rituals of Solidarity and Security in the Wake of Terrorist Attack', *Sociological Theory* 22(1), pp. 53–87.

Crelinsten, Ronald D. (2002) 'Analysing Terrorism and Counter-Terrorism: A Communication Model', *Terrorism and Political Violence* 14(2), pp. 77–122.

Cronin, Audrey Kurth (2015) 'ISIS Is Not a Terrorist Group', *Foreign Affairs* 94, pp. 87–98.

Dalgaard-Nielsen, Anja, Jesper Laisen and Charlotte Wandorf (2016) 'Visible Counterterrorism in Urban Spaces – Fear-Inducing or Not?' *Terrorism and Political Violence* 28(4), pp. 692–712.

Diehl, Jörg and Christoph Sydow (2016) 'Die Zwei Legenden des Mohammad Daleel', *Der Spiegel*, 27 July 2016, www.spiegel.de/politik/deutschland/ansbach-anschlag-die-zwei-legenden-des-mohammed-daleel-a-1104984.html (accessed March 3, 2017).

Dorle, Hellmuth (2016) *Counterterrorism and the State. Western Responses to 9/11* (Philadelphia: University of Pennsylvania Press).

Europol (2016) *Changes in Modus Operandi of Islamic State (IS) Revisited*, November 2016, www.europol.europa.eu/sites/default/files/documents/modus_operandi_is_revisited.pdf (accessed March 4, 2017).

Funk, Marco and Roderick Parkes (2016) 'Refugees Versus Terrorists', *EU Institute for Security Studies* (January 2016), www.iss.europa.eu/uploads/media/Alert_6_Refugees_versus_terrorists.pdf (accessed March 4, 2017).

Fürstenau, Marcel (2016) 'Berlin-Anschlag: Schwachstellen in der Gefahrenabwehr', *Die Deutsche Welle* (30 December 2016), www.dw.com/de/berlin-anschlag-schwachstellen-in-der-gefahrenabwehr/a-36955802 (accessed March 3, 2017).

Goldman, Adam (2016) 'FBI Has Found No Evidence that Orlando Shooter Targeted Pulse Because it was a Gay Club', *The Washington Post*, 16 July 2016, http://wapo.st/29U6xuE?tid=ss_mail (accessed March 3, 2017).

Hof, Tobias (2013) 'The Success of Italian Anti-Terrorism-Policy', in Jussi M. Hanhimäki and Bernhard Blumenau (eds.) *An International History of Terrorism. Western and Non-Western Experiences* (London/New York: Routledge), pp. 100–114.

Hof, Tobias (2015) ' "Anti-Terror-Gesetze" und Sicherheitskräfte. Bundesrepublik Deutschland, Italien und Großbritannien in den 1970er und frühen 1980er Jahren', in J. Hürter (ed.) *Terrorismusbekämpfung in Westeuropa: Demokratie und Sicherheit in den 1970er und 1980er Jahren* (Berlin Boston München: De Gruyter Oldenbourg), pp. 7–34.

Hoffman, Bruce (2006) *Inside Terrorism* (New York: Columbia University Press).

Hollande, François (2015) 'Speech by the President of the Republic Before a Joint Session of Parliament' (16 November 2015), www.diplomatie.gouv.fr/en/french-foreign-policy/defence-security/parisattacks-paris-terror-attacks-november-2015/article/speech-by-the-president-of-the-republic-before-a-joint-session-of-parliament (accessed March 3, 2017).

Joosse, Paul (2017) 'Leaderless Resistance and the Loneliness of Lone Wolves: Exploring the Rhetorical Dynamics of Lone Actor Violence', *Terrorism and Political Violence* 29(1), pp. 52–78.

Kaplan, Jeffrey, Heléne Lööw and Leena Malkki (2014) 'Introduction to the Special Issue on Lone Wolf and Autonomous Cell Terrorism', *Terrorism and Political Violence* 26(1), pp. 1–12.

Kaplan Jeffrey and Christopher P. Costa (2015) 'The Islamic State and the New Tribalism', *Terrorism and Political Violence* 27(5), pp. 926–969.

Koehler, Daniel (2017) *Right-Wing Terrorism in the 21st Century: The 'National Socialist Underground' and the History of Terror from the Far-Right in Germany* (New York: Routledge).

Lansford, Tom and David Holt (2013) 'Introduction: The Geography of the Islamic State', in Jack Covarrubias, Tom Lansford and Robert J. Pauly, Jr. (eds.) *The New Islamic State. Ideology, Religion and Violent Extremism in the 21st Century* (New York: Routledge), pp. 1–13.

Lesperance, Wayne F. Jr. (2016) 'The Rise of the Islamic State (IS)', in Jack Covarrubias, Tom Lansford and Robert J. Pauly, Jr. (eds.) *The New Islamic State. Ideology, Religion and Violent Extremism in the 21st Century* (New York: Routledge), pp. 15–27.

Lim, Naomi and Kevin Liptak (2016) 'Trump Offers Prayers in Low-Key Response to Munich Attack', *CNN* (22 July 2016), www.cnn.com/2016/07/22/politics/political-reaction-munich-shooting-donald-trump-hillary-clinton/ (accessed February 19, 2017).

Martin, Susanne and Leonard B. Weinberg (2016) 'Terrorism in an Era of Unconventional Warfare', *Terrorism and Political Violence* 28(2), pp. 236–253.

Merica, Dan (2017) 'Trump on Waterboarding: "We have to fight fire with fire" ', *CNN* (26 January 2017), www.cnn.com/2017/01/25/politics/donald-trump-waterboarding-torture/ (accessed February 19, 2017).

Miller, Erin (2016) 'Terrorism in Belgium and Western Europe; Attacks against Transportation Targets; Coordinated Terrorist Attacks', *Background Report*, START, College Park, www.start.umd.edu/pubs/START_BelgiumTransportationCoordinatedAttacks_Back groundReport_March2016.pdf (accessed March 4, 2017).

Morris, Loveday (2015) 'Islamic State Isn't Just Destroying Ancient Artifacts – It's Selling Them', *Washington Post* (8 June 2015), https://wpo.st/rGGf2 (accessed March 4, 2017).

Morell, Michael (2015) 'ISIS will Strike America', *Time Magazine* (30 November 2015/ 7 December 2015), http://time.com/magazine/us/4119944/november-30th-2015-vol-186-no-22-23-u-s/ (accessed May 9, 2019).

Parker, Tom and Nick Sitter (2016) 'The Four Horsemen of Terrorism: It's Not Waves, It's Strains', *Terrorism and Political Violence* 28(2), pp. 197–216.

Pauly, Robert J. Jr. and Kelly Roberts (2016) 'The European Response to IS', in Jack Covarrubias, Tom Lansford and Robert J. Pauly, Jr. (eds.) *The New Islamic State. Ideology, Religion and Violent Extremism in the 21st Century* (New York: Routledge), pp. 163–178.

Penksa, Susan E. (2005) 'Defining the Enemy: EU and US Threat Perceptions After 9/11', in H. Gärtner et al. (eds.) *European Security and Transatlantic Relations after 9/11 and the Iraq War* (London: Palgrave Macmillan), pp. 19–32.

Pokalova, Elena (2015) 'Legislative Responses to Terrorism: What Drives to Adopt New Counterterrorism Legislation', *Terrorism and Political Violence* 27(3), pp. 474–496.

Prantl, Heribert (2008) *Der Terrorist als Gesetzgeber. Wie man mit Angst Politik macht* (München: Droemer/Knaur).

Rappeport, Alan (2016) 'Newt Gingrich Echoes Donald Trump With Remarks on Muslims and Terrorism', *The New York Times* (15 July 2016), www.nytimes.com/2016/07/16/us/ politics/newt-gingrich-terrorism-muslims.html?_r=0 (accessed February 19, 2017).

Rapoport, David C. (2013) 'The Four Waves of Modern Terror. International Dimensions and Consequences', in Jussi M. Hanhimäki and Bernhard Blumenau (eds.) *An International History of Terrorism. Western and Non-Western Experiences* (London/New York: Routledge), pp. 282–310.

Rapoport, David C. (2016) 'It Is Waves, Not Strains', *Terrorism and Political Violence* 28(2), pp. 217–224.

Shabi, Rachel (2015) 'Looted in Syria – and Sold in London: The British Antiques Shops Dealing in Artefacts Smuggled by ISIS', *The Guardian* (3 July 2015), www.theguar dian.com/world/2015/jul/03/antiquities-looted-by-isis-end-up-in-london-shops (accessed March 3, 2017).

Shuster, Simon (2017) 'Why Germany – and the World – Is Arguing Over the Munich Shooter', *Time Magazine* (24 July 2016), http://time.com/4420817/munich-attack-terror-motivation/ (accessed March 3, 2017).

Sprinzak, Ehud (1995) 'Right-Wing Terrorism in a Comparative Perspective: The Case of Split Delegitimization', *Terrorism and Political Violence* 7(1), pp. 17–43.

Von Drehle, David (2015) 'World War ISIS', *Time Magazine* (30 November 2015/7 December 2015), http://time.com/magazine/us/4119944/november-30th-2015-vol-186-no-22-23-u-s/ (accessed May 9, 2019).

Waldmann, Peter (2008) 'Determinanten der Entstehung und Entwicklung terroristischer Organisationen', in Peter Waldmann (ed.) *Determinanten des Terrorismus* (Weilerswist: Velbrück Wissenschaft), pp. 11–28.

Weinberg, Leonard B., Ami Pedahzur and Hirsch-Hoefler, Sivan (2004) 'The Challenge of Conceptualizing Terrorism', *Terrorism and Political Violence* 16(4), pp. 777–794.

Chapter 25

Fighting corruption globally

A case of norm diffusion in international relations

Holger Moroff

Corruption has always been sanctioned by national laws. But when, how and why has it become a matter of concern for international relations and institutions like the OECD, World Bank, IMF and UN? What explains the diffusion of norms on the international stage? Three theories offer three distinct answers. Whereas realists would argue that the norms of strong, hegemonic powers are projected onto weaker ones, liberal and constructivist IR theories might see it as a process driven by economic interests and value changes, respectively. In the case of the internationalisation of anti-corruption norms and binding legal regimes I argue it is the combination of these explanations plus very active policy entrepreneurs that have shaped the process.

The US and the EU as policy entrepreneurs in anti-corruption

Domestic anti-corruption laws and policies have been ubiquitous throughout most countries for centuries. International anti-corruption policies are a US invention and were initiated through the Foreign Corrupt Practices Act (FCPA) of 1977, which sanctions the conduct of US companies abroad.[1] It is an example of an international policy through the extraterritorial effect of national law based on the citizenship principle or registration principal for companies. The other three kinds of international anti-corruption policies are (1) conditionality principles of aid providing donor countries or international financial institutions (IFIs, e.g. IMF, World Bank, regional development banks), (2) multilateral conventions to sanction corruption abroad, and (3) international policy advice programs by governments, international organisations and NGOs. To understand these policies, their approaches, and methods one needs to look at both their internal logic and the reasoning behind their justifications. This reasoning has changed over time and various actors have come to accept a common or similar global anti-corruption norm.

For the emergence of a multilateral anti-corruption regime the convergence of perceptions, norms and interests between the US and the EU was pivotal. This chapter focuses on the historical contexts of the discourses that gave rise to US and EU anti-corruption policies in the 1970s and 1990s. Economic aspects of creating a level playing field for international companies in a global marketplace seem to have dominated the interest-driven discourses during both decades. A norm-driven discourse became relevant only in the 1990s, shaped mainly by development and state building concerns. The skillfully negotiated combination of both discourses through the OECD, UN and IFIs with the help of NGOs like Transparency International made it possible to multilateralise the FCPA under US leadership and firmly establish anti-corruption policies in IFIs and IOs as well as mainstream it into all kinds of development, international investment and anti-crime policies. A facilitating factor has also been that legally binding 'hard law' regimes were limited to the technical, economic and legal aspects of clear cut quid pro quo corruption. That means corruption was narrowly defined as bribery with a strong focus on the low- and mid-level of the executive branch of government – that is, the administration responsible for implementing laws, regulations and awarding contracts. Developing and transition economies have consistently ranked low on the corruption perception index since its inception in 1995. The 20 least corrupt countries are exclusively advanced industrialised and service economies. This map sets the stage for the anti-corruption debates and strategies since the end of the Cold War.

Definition and theory

Political corruption is the illegitimate nexus between money and politics. Present day discourse seems to suggest that this transformation is more illegitimate the more its purpose is to further the material enrichment of both parties involved – the economic and the political one – to the detriment of the public coffers. Corruption for moral, political and ideological purposes receives less unequivocal condemnation. To escape a morally wrong situation, the concentration camp inmate's bribing of a guard is likely seen as legitimate.[2] Bribing governments in 'Third' World countries to stay in or switch to one of the two ideological camps during the East–West conflict was not only standard operating procedure, but deemed a legitimate Cold War tool of mutual containment.[3] Also, in a domestic context, corruption seems to be less abject if at least one party – usually the bribe giver – professes ideological and political rather than pecuniary motives. However, this is also the standard line of defence used by politicians who have received money illicitly.[4]

Political corruption is the illegitimate nexus between money and politics. However, what is deemed illegitimate and what becomes codified as illegal is subject to change over time and can vary substantially from one political system to the next. Opinions on what is illegitimate can vary among groups even within the same society. Even among liberal democracies, varying views on what is legal and illegal can be seen in their vastly differing laws on political and campaign finance. This is why the perceptions, and consequently definitions, of corruption by policy relevant actors are of prime importance to the analysis of evolving and converging international anti-corruption norms and policies. What is deemed corrupt, and what are perceived causes, consequences and moral implications? How these questions are answered by various actors is the key for understanding and reconstructing a new international policy field.

International anti-corruption norms and policy regimes are the historical product of an expert discourse among various relevant actors.[5] Reconstructing their reasoning, intentions and perceptions is thus a precondition for understanding the policies that evolved and their functional logic. This is a constructivist approach, assuming that corruption and anti-corruption is what states, international organisations, companies and NGOs make of it.[6] These are the actors who seem to have shaped the anti-corruption discourse most forcefully.

I proceed as follows. First, a brief comparative case study of two major international corruption scandals will serve to illustrate how the focus of attention has shifted since the 1970s. Second, the discourses on anti-corruption in the EU and the US will be compared in order to show how their partial convergence led to the establishment of the first multilateral anti-corruption regime – the 1999 OECD convention against bribery abroad. In a third step, the functional logic of various international anti-corruption instruments are analysed, revealing the thinking on corruption that lies behind them.

Similar cases in different times

This succinct diachronic comparison of two large-scale corruption cases aims at showing – in an exemplary way – how a channeling of focus to the output side of corruption and the bribe payer has facilitated an international norm convergence and norm diffusion. This, in turn, was a precondition for the multilateral internationalisation of anti-corruption regimes. Such legally binding 'hard law' conventions have been limited to the technical, economic and legal aspects of clear cut quid pro quo corruption – that is, bribery. The main focus has been at the low- to mid-level of the executive branch of government responsible for implementing laws and regulations, as well as awarding contracts.

The first international anti-corruption policy was put in place by the US in 1977. It was international through the extraterritorial reach of the Foreign Corrupt Practices Act as it punishes US companies (and those foreign ones listed on US stock exchanges) for corrupt actions undertaken in foreign countries. This was a response to the discoveries of massive corruption committed by more than 600 US companies abroad in the wake of the Watergate investigations (Rosenthal, 1989, p. 704). The case that received the greatest media attention was the Lockheed scandal. Lockheed had bribed numerous high ranking politicians in Japan, Italy, Belgium, Australia, the Netherlands and West Germany, among other things also in order to sell its overpriced and faulty aircraft – the Starfighter. Many of the politicians involved had to step down, like the Japanese Prime Minister Kakuei Tanaka.[7] The media and judicial focus rested almost exclusively on the implicated politicians through home grown domestic scandals and judicial proceedings in the targeted countries ensued.

This focus has changed considerably with the largest known case of bribery abroad in the first decade of the 21st century – the Siemens scandal (Graeff, Schroder and Wolf, 2009). Even though more than 1.8 billion euros were paid in bribes to foreign officials – including high ranking elected politicians – most of the media coverage and legal action has focused not on the recipients of these bribes, but on the company who doled them out. No case of high level political casualties concerning the then current office holders has been recorded yet.[8] Whereas the Lockheed scandal focused almost exclusively on bribes paid to democratic governments of the advanced industrialised West, the Siemens scandal focused mainly on developing and transition countries.[9]

The justification for prosecutions and motives of scandals have changed considerably from 1970s to 2009 and beyond. Whereas Watergate sparked a deep domestic legitimacy crisis in the US, Lockheed was mainly seen as having tarnished the international reputation of the leader of the Western world. These considerations play virtually no role in the scandal of the Siemens case. It is almost exclusively discussed under market, development and good governance aspects by pointing out that bribery distorts the level playing field of fair market competition, thus hindering the development of targeted societies through inefficient resource allocations and fostering bad governance. None of these issues were ever of great concern during the Lockheed scandal. What has changed? At the time of the Lockheed scandal, the politicians and recipients of bribes were in the limelight. In the more recent Siemens case, the company that paid the politicians was scandalised and prosecuted in its home country, Germany, and by the US Department of Justice, which could claim jurisdiction since Siemens also listed its stocks in the US.[10] We thus see a transatlantic prosecution of Siemens for bribery it committed throughout the world but not inside Germany or the US.

Whereas Lockheed and many other foreign bribery scandals of the 1970s and 80s were covered in the political section of the quality press, Siemens and most other corruption scandals since the mid-1990s have been treated in the business section of the broad sheets. These are signs that – despite the heightened media, as well as judicial and scientific interest in corruption – the phenomenon and its scandalisation have become depoliticised.

Despite all technical, legal and methodological sophistication no common answer as to what constitutes a legitimate nexus between money and politics has yet been found.[11] Though international anti-corruption regimes suggest they have done so by focusing only on the illegitimate direct quid pro quo of bribery. This quid pro quo and a corrupt intent is hard to prove on the input side, the legislative and election side of politics, which is why the focus rests almost exclusively on the output and administrative side of politics.

Converging norms for different reasons in the US and the EU

The focus on the topic of output corruption – that is, on payments for awarding public contracts, as well as on bending the implementation of rules, laws and guidelines – means that issues concerning payments for influencing the rule, law and guideline making – that is, the input side of politics – are carefully avoided by international anti-corruption regimes and for the most part also by anti-corruption NGOs and the media. That has meant sidelining expenses for lobbying, including party and campaign finance, political action committees and super PACs, revolving door practices, influence peddling, parachuting business experts into ministries and everything that became known as cultivating the political landscape in general.[12] The input side is not really addressed because it cannot be regulated by technical, hard and fast rules. This is because there is no unified theory of democracy and representation that could tell the experts what the common good is and how it is generated. Is it the sum of all forces of self-interested individuals and collectivities in society on whose behalf politicians act like lawyers and delegates; and if so, how could this sum of forces be objectively measured?[13] Or are politicians fiduciaries who – with the help of experts and the epistemic community – understand what is best for all and thus act as trustees of the common good?[14] Since the vast subject of how to regulate corruption on the input side of politics is quite controversial within and among Western democracies, a common norm could not emerge. Such a norm should clearly state where legitimate lobbying stops and corruption starts.

Historically, the anti-corruption discourse in Western Europe has indeed mostly focused on the technical and narrow output side of politics, on the bribery of judges, civil servants and the public administration (Moroff, 2004, p. 89). Also, in communist Eastern Europe, corruption was never thought of as systemic, but rather as deviant behaviour of single individuals inside the bureaucracy. Low- to mid-level apparatchiks were targets of anti-corruption crack downs with the occasional high level leader, for whose disposition a good pretext was needed or to showcase how ostensibly serious the leadership takes anti-corruption. Thus, it seems that focusing on the technical output side of corruption within the new international anti-corruption regimes would take up historically rooted norms, perceptions and approaches of European countries.

One can trace these perceptions not only to European feudalism and absolutism but to its etatism at large, which was mainly a response to bloody religious and ethnic wars, popular upheavals, revolutions and nationalism – especially after World War II. All have contributed to an etatist society-state relationship in which the government and the state-sustaining elites usually mistrust 'the people'. The raison d'état claims a higher cause (the stability of a country and foreign threats) which then might also justify lower means such as corruption abroad or at home.

This contrasts sharply with the domestic US discourse on corruption and anti-corruption. The general mistrust of (big) government[15] is a pervasive and deeply rooted phenomenon of American political culture which can be traced back to its constitutional debates that focused, to a large extent, on questions of how to avoid input corruption and the abuse of power. Many of the Federalist Papers are dedicated to the question of how to protect 'the people' from an arbitrary government, and not how to protect the government from an erratic and arbitrary people (joining in Robespierre's reign of terror or electing dictators like Mussolini or Hitler). Hence, awareness of political corruption is also historically focused on the input side and might explain the long standing debates on lobbying, party and campaign finance, and the very detailed system of rules and regulations as well as the extensive public monitoring of lobbying activities in the US.[16] Such an attitude spills also over into the political campaigns where virtually all candidates who run for public office run an anti-Washington campaign, claiming to root out insider ways of influence peddling, pork barreling and log rolling. Analogous anti-Paris, anti-London or anti-Berlin campaigns seem rather unthinkable and somewhat ridiculous for France, the UK or Germany. Even though the more recent populist parties paint themselves in such colours. However, in the US's efforts to multilateralise the FCPA, issues of input side corruption and lobbying that are so hotly debated inside the US were carefully avoided.[17] This further underlines that only around a narrow, business oriented approach a consensus could be built. It also hints at the strong lobbying of American business to be put on equal footing with their foreign competitors.

Nevertheless, the discourse on international anti-corruption regimes in the US and the EU converged during the 1990s, even though each side had different reasons to arrive at such a common norm. First, a closer look at the US side is warranted, since the discourse on international anti-corruption started a decade earlier in the US than in Europe and it was the main governmental driving force behind the push for internationalisation.

The US side

In the 1970s economic crises in the wake of the Vietnam War, Lyndon Johnson's Great Society, the end of the Bretton Woods system, the oil price shocks, as well as the numerous corruption cases at home and abroad weakened US political and economic leadership of the West. The Lockheed scandal damaged America's image significantly as it was a case of grand systematic corruption on the highest political levels in allied countries. To restore its reputation, the US came up with a symbolically strong international anti-corruption measure – the FCPA. It was adopted unanimously by Congress and was neither conceived of as a development policy – which would indirectly strengthen good governance and the rule of law abroad – nor was it seen as a measure to foster fair market competition, as military contracts were rarely put out to open and transparent tender. The FCPA's rationale was indeed one of avoiding market distortions and misleading information about a companies' competitiveness for potential investors, i.e. stockholders. This is also the reason why the Security and Exchange Commission (SEC) was charged with overseeing the FCPA and given investigatory power as well as the right to levy substantial fines on violators. In 1988, the provisions were weakened somewhat (Sheffet, 1995) and during the first two decades of its existence there were only a handful of successful prosecutions with minor financial fines (Cohen, 2008, p. 1253; Windsor and Getz, 1999, p. 432).

Everything changed with the end of the Cold War and its anticipated consequences in the early 1990s. Meddling in internal political affairs was off limits for international institutions like the UN, but also for IFIs such as the World Bank and the IMF. Only since the mid-1990s could they discuss issues of corruption or good governance, introducing new forms of conditionality and sanctions in the late 1990s (Marquette, 2004). They were conceived of as supporting developing and transition countries in setting up functioning market economies and democracies, as well as preventing failed states from turning into hotbeds of organised international crime. The World Bank's definition of 'state capture' as the highest level of pervasive corruption coincides with many features of failed states. However, this discourse was predated by another often neglected discourse in the US.

Three factors played a prominent role here. First, the importance of private direct foreign investments grew rapidly worldwide and in 1993, for the first time, they were greater than the combined governmental development aid in Third World and transformation countries (Elliott, 1997, p. 204).[18] Second, the new transformation countries in Eastern Europe, China and various countries on the threshold of industrialisation were viewed as the 'big emerging markets' (US Department of Commerce, 1995). Third, the greatest need and opportunity for foreign investments was expected in the infrastructure sectors of these countries. They were called the 'big emerging sectors'. Those were highly regulated and contracts usually awarded by governments or governmental agencies. Many of these countries were also viewed as corruption prone, which has been borne out by all subsequent CPI rankings (see Figure 25.1). US businesses feared they might lose out to their European and Asian competitors over these contracts, ostensibly since they were legally prohibited from paying bribes abroad. However, whether it truly prevented them from doing so is difficult to ascertain. Thus, they lobbied the US administration to push for an internationalisation of the FCPA, and the US trade secretary recommended that the government should work towards establishing a level playing field for all globally active companies. In 1995, he presented a report to the US Senate in which the CIA estimated that US companies lost contracts worth some US$50 billion to competitors from other industrialised countries because they had bribed decision makers in the 'big emerging markets' of the 'big emerging countries' (Elliott, 2002, p. 935).

This report introduces another group of actors in the quest for establishing an international anti-corruption norm – the intelligence services. They could hope to employ their formidable 'monitoring' and investigatory tools. This toolbox needed to find new problems to solve since the Soviet threat had disappeared.[19] Robert Gates, then director of the CIA, stated that 'the most senior policymakers of the government clearly see that many of the most important challenges and opportunities through and beyond the end of this decade are in the international economic arena' (quoted in Groll, 2014). Although Gates said that the CIA would 'not do commercial spying', the agency could 'be helpful on economic intelligence, by identifying foreign governments that are involved in unfair practices . . . where they are colluding with businesses in their country to the disadvantage of the U.S.' (quoted in DeConcini, 1994, p. 40). During a meeting of the Senate Select Intelligence Committee in 1992, discussing the issue with top US corporate executives and intelligence experts, the former CIA director Stansfield Turner said: 'If we spy for military security, why shouldn't we spy for economic security?' (quoted in Groll, 2014). But it was only later in the 1990s that the long-serving CIA Director James Woolsey admitted freely to US services using the Echelon surveillance system to 'spy on friends and allies' because their companies had been involved in corrupt and unfair business practices abroad to the detriment of US companies (Woolsey, 2000, p. 10). Subsequent revelations about the NSA activities point to the possibility of industrial and economic espionage, further buttressing this often-neglected actor and yielding corroborative evidence for their proactive stance as a policy entrepreneur (Office of the Director of National Intelligence, 2009).

FIGURE 25.1 Corruption Perceptions Index 2016

Source: Transparency International (2017), licensed under CC BY-ND-4.0.

The first US attempt at internationalising the FCPA was undertaken within its own Western hemisphere of influence. In 1996, the Organization of American States adopted the first international anti-corruption convention (Manfroni, 1997). At the same time the topic was put onto the active agenda of the OECD by the Clinton administration.

The EU side

The discourse of creating a level playing field was nothing new on the other side of the Atlantic, but it focused first on the inside of the EU and only later on the EU neighbourhood and further afield. Since the Single European Act of 1985, creating and extending such a level playing field inside the EU was called the common market project. A free internal market for goods, businesses, capital and labour was to be completed during the 1990s with the introduction of a common currency, the euro, in 1999. Deepening the EU's internal market brought with it more cross border investments and capital movement. Fear that cross border crime could also increase triggered three response patterns that became linked to the international fight against corruption. In 1991, the EU put in place its first laws against money laundering (EU Council Directive, 1991) which is not only important in fighting organised crime but also in identifying slush funds and black money used for bribery. It is also no coincidence that the OECD Task Force on Money Laundering was the precursor to the OECD Financial Action Task Force that negotiated and now monitors its anti-bribery convention (Heidenheimer and Moroff, 2002, p. 956; Moroff, 2005, p. 455). A further measure was to protect the financial interests of the EU against fraud and corruption (EU Council Regulation, 1995). Finally, cross border bribery inside the EU was made a criminal offence (EU Convention, 1997). Such was the spectrum of the EU's new internal anti-corruption discourse.

On the outside, the EU's assistance programs for the Eastern transformation countries, especially the post-communist EU candidate countries, emphasised domestic anti-corruption and good governance efforts inside these countries (Frisch, 1999). The anti-corruption and money laundering policies for the whole of Europe were mainly shaped by the Council of Europe through its 1996 action program and its civil and criminal law convention of 1999. Of course, if the EU demands good governance in its neighbourhood and for its candidate countries, this triggers an echo effect. The outsiders will ask whether the insiders comply with their own demands. If the EU and its member states didn't want to be accused of hypocrisy and double standards, they also had to undertake credible anti-corruption measures – a special case of rhetorical entrapment (Schimmelfennig, 2001).[20]

Beyond that, many highly scandalised corruption cases in the wake of the privatisation processes in Eastern Europe, but also the repercussions of the *mani pulite* scandal in Italy – which transformed a whole party landscape during the early 1990s (Koff, 2002) – and the threat thereof by the CDU party finance scandal in Germany at the end of decade did not only heighten the attention afforded to corruption of Europeans and their media, but also changed the formerly hesitant stances of European governments on international anti-corruption measures (Heidenheimer and Moroff, 2002, p. 950).

Negotiated norm convergence and diffusion

The mid-1990s saw a new rapprochement between the EU and the US that resulted in the New Transatlantic Agenda (NTA) in 1995. Trade integration was deepest between these two blocs worldwide (Windsor and Getz, 1999, p. 422) and much talk focused on working towards a Transatlantic Free Trade Area comprised of NAFTA and the EU. Among the 150 policy items of the NTA, a special emphasis on fair business practices can be made out easily: 'We will combat corruption and bribery by implementing the 1994 OECD Recommendations on Bribery in International Transactions' (US-EU, 1995). The Transatlantic Business Dialogue issued a statement in 1998 in which it 'stresses the urgent need for early ratification of the OECD Convention on Criminalizing Bribery of Foreign Officials' (TABD, 1998). At the May 1998 US–EU summit, a Transatlantic Economic Partnership was established that aimed at both multilateral action through the WTO and bilateral action to reduce trade, investment and non-tariff market barriers (Windsor and Getz, 1999, p. 417). EU–US cooperation to combat bribery of public officials mainly targeted the development countries and 'big emerging markets' outside the transatlantic community, aiming for a level playing field among themselves and their companies.

Both the EU (and its member states) and US thinking on the importance of anti-corruption policies for economic and political purposes changed and converged for different reasons during the 1990s. That is why US efforts in the OECD fell on fertile ground on the other side of the Atlantic. Suspicions that the US might want to gain a trade advantage by using its unrivaled intelligence power were no longer harboured openly. Although, during the negotiation of the OECD convention, some delegates of small countries stressed that large countries and especially those with lots of political and military clout like the US had other means to pressure foreign governments into awarding contracts to their companies (Heidenheimer and Moroff, 2002).

Instrumental logics

Only a narrow definition and a focus on output-side corruption could bring about convergence towards a common, hard and fast anti-corruption norm that would spread globally. The functional logic of various anti-corruption policy instruments is revealing of the actors' reasoning. Table 25.1 provides a brief and exemplary overview of the most important international anti-corruption regimes, highlighting various target groups and how their corrupt practices are sanctioned. Its chronology also shows how the formerly (business) interest-driven discourse was complemented by a norm-driven one in the 1990s. The only mechanism not discussed previously is the SEC's administration of the FCPA. Its official raison d'être is protecting shareholders. Historically, the stock market has been of much greater importance for company capitalisations in the US than in Europe with its stronger reliance on banks. In the US, the importance of high transparency and accounting standards is stressed so that stockholders and buyers can evaluate a company's performance more accurately before making their investment decisions.[21] This explains why the

SEC could investigate an Italian company for bribing Italian officials. From the Italian company's point of view this is bribing domestic public office holders, but since their stock was listed in the US, its authorities considered it bribing of foreign officials. It distorted the books and had the company look more profitable without disclosing the higher risks of losing business which was gained only by bribery. The correct assessment of the company's performance and prospects was thus distorted. The heavy fines multinational companies had to pay under the FCPA since 2007 has contributed the delisting of their stocks from US exchanges (more than 60 since 2011, prominent among them Daimler in 2010 after it paid a US$181 million fine) or not listing them in the US in the first place, like Siemens medical equipment division in 2018.[22]

All those legally binding conventions and changes in development-aid policies during the 1990s are predicated on the new-found consensus between the US, Western Europe and Japan (Heidenheimer and Moroff, 2002). However, none of the large emerging economies have signed on to or followed through on any of the hard law conventions against bribery abroad. Whereas the FCPA and the OECD

TABLE 25.1 Chronology of major international anti-corruption efforts

Organisations	Instruments/functional logic	Target groups
1977 SEC (Security and Exchange Commission administers the FCPA)	Logic of protecting stockholders, instrument of accounting and transparency standards, strong financial sanctions	All companies whose stocks are traded in the US
1979 International Chamber of Commerce	Voluntary self-regulation of companies through good corporate governance codes	Multinational companies
1992 Transparency International	Mobilising national and international public Blaming and shaming Advocacy scholarship/policy advice	Corrupt actors, governments, companies, international organisations
1996 World Bank/IMF	Conditionality for loans Policy advice	Development and transformation countries
1999 Council of Europe	Criminal convention plus civil law convention (hard law) and strong compliance system through peer review monitoring, goes beyond OECD provisions	Member states of the Council of Europe, bracketing industrial, transition and development countries
1999 OECD	Binding criminal law convention (hard law), sanctioning bribe payer side Internationalising the FCPA Compliance through soft instruments such as reporting, monitoring, peer review, bench marking, best practices	Companies of OECD countries and some additional ones (though not China, India, Brazil and Russia)
2001 UN	Soft law declarations (Global Compact), not enforceable	Same as preceding, with special focus on failed states (India and China have ratified)

convention can be viewed as mainly US inspired, the Council of Europe conventions and the EU's legal acts are more genuine European efforts, reflecting its concerns about the integrity of the EU budget, distortions in the common market, and stable politico-economic systems in the Eastern transformation countries. Especially the latter focus turned the Council of Europe convention into more far reaching documents that somewhat widened the narrow, bribery focused approach of the other instruments. The organisations, their instruments and targets demonstrate that an international consensus on what constitutes corruption could only be found by defining it very narrowly as the as bribery of public officials. Who is considered a public official – officials of political parties, candidates for elected public offices, managers in partially state owned companies – remains controversial, as does everything connected to influencing the input side of governance, and law making, namely 'legitimate' lobbying, party, and campaign finance.

Conclusions

It was the aim of this analysis to treat global anti-corruption policy like any other public policy by reconstructing the various interests, reasonings and justifications behind it. This is not the most common approach for analysing 'anti-policies' – that is, policies against 'bad' things. They are mostly studied by evaluating their goal attainment through measuring the effectiveness of their policy instruments, or the degree of harm is assessed by establishing correlations with other 'bad' things. Instead, I tried to take those studies into account as examples of how actors and scholars came to think about corruption and anti-corruption and thus identifying an expert discourse that focused mainly on corruption in international business transactions, on the output side of politics, using technical skills (legal, economic, political) in constructing a new mechanics of anti-corruption policies.

The following observations for the policy formation and transformation have been made: First, a necessary precondition for establishing this international regime is a broad consensus on norms between the US and the EU (including its most significant member states) which is supported by a dominant epistemic community (that agrees on the harmfulness/dysfunctionality of corruption) and disseminated by norm entrepreneurs who are not suspected of serving other interests (NGOs like TI). In a second step, platform organisations of the international state system (IFIs, OECD, UN) have to take on board this new consensus and push for policy responses. Third, a hegemonic state actor like the US can serve as a driving force and use the catalyst functions of international organisations as well as the blaming and shaming power of NGOs, such as TI, in order to bring other more reluctant states in line, thus bringing about a new regime. As soon as the new norms are supported and actively advocated by NGOs, IOs and several powerful countries, a domino effect sets in which continually raises the pressure for those countries that want to stay out of this consensus and its policy regime.[23]

The goal convergence of establishing an international anti-corruption regime has been based on a convergence of perceptions and interests on both sides of the Atlantic and beyond. Whereas the US pushed for an internationalisation of its FCPA because it expected large contracts in the 'big emerging sectors' of the 'big emerging markets' in the 1990s, the EU's deepening common market and its Eastern enlargement fostered anti-corruption policies that straddled the borders of EU member states, candidates and neighbourhood countries. These converging perceptions and interests were then taken up and initially woven together by the OECD.

A clear-cut causal relationship that triggered the internationalisation cannot be established because three potential driving forces changed in parallel. First, values and norms changed through a new focus of the epistemic community and NGOs on the harmful consequences of corruption. Second, international organisations changed in the wake of the end of the Cold War, so that they could now address matters of good governance and countries' internal affairs that were off limits before. Third, the international system changed from a bi-polar to a multi-polar one in which a new consensus on both political and economic models became dominant. However, the illegitimate nexus between money and politics – beyond the technical quid pro quo of bribery at the output side of politics – has not been clearly defined yet and will remain elusive as long as political systems change; that is, as long as there will be no end to history.

Notes

1   The UK had a Commonwealth anti-corruption provision dating back to 1915 and West Germany had 1958 anti-corruption law, sanctioning the bribery of NATO officials as well as some bilateral agreements pertaining to foreign customs officials at border crossings. None of them had the global reach of an international regime (Moroff 2005, p. 478).

2   Such an extreme example seems fairly clear cut; however, contriving rationalisations of being wronged in one way or doing good in another is a common human strategy for self-justification.

3   The focus on 'Third' World countries and, since the end of the East–West conflict, also on the former 'Second' World and transformation countries, seems to suggest a continuity of international targets – first for corruption and now for anti-corruption by hegemonic powers.

4   Thus Helmut Kohl, former chancellor of Germany, stressed repeatedly that the illegal donations he received had benefited exclusively his party, the CDU, and were not used for self-enrichment.

5   As such, any norm of deviation presupposes or generates an implicit knowledge of what the right norm and behaviour is. It is thus part of a normalisation process (Foucault, 1979). Any 'anti-discourse' can also be read as delineating the borders of a norm from the outside.

6   To paraphrase and adapt Alexander Wendt's (1992) dictum, 'Sovereignty is what states make of it'.

7   He died just before the court could hand down a four-year prison sentence.

8   The fact that the late Nigerian dictator Sani Abacha and the former Argentinean President Carlos Menem are implicated in the Siemens bribery scheme underlines that it does not affect current power holders, and especially none in any country that could be considered a great or middle power in international relations.

9   Even though some of the 'less developed' EU members like Greece, Portugal and Bulgaria were also targeted.

10 Siemens cooperated extensively with the German authorities mainly in order to limit the heavy fines and penalties that were to be expected from the US side (Cohen et al., 2008, p. 1264).

11 Most salient examples of this contested nexus are the Citizens United ruling and the *McCutchen* ruling of the US Supreme Court in 2010 and 2014, respectively.

12 'Kultivierung der politischen Landschaft' (cultivating the political landscape) was the description used by Eberhardt von Brauchitsch who sponsored all parties in the German parliament on behalf of the Flick concern (von Brauchitsch, 2001).

13 The pluralists would argue that the common good is the resultant of all interest vectors in society (Fraenkel, 1964). Then the only 'social responsibility' of individuals, companies and political parties is to seek their self interest of maximizing profits or votes (Friedman, 1970). The 'common good' then is the equilibrium of all those forces, one of which is economic power expressed through the medium of money.

14 One particularly well-developed theory of generating the volonté générale versus volonté de tous can be seen in Habermas' concept of deliberative democracy. This process involves all concerned with and affected by a political decision, presupposing some common norms and a common standard of rationality a consensus can be reached on the basis of the 'better arguments' (Habermas, 1992).

15 Even though it is much smaller than in most EU member states measured by the public share of BIP.

16 This does not mean that there is necessarily less input side corruption in the US, maybe even the contrary. It just sketches the different focus of domestic corruption discourses.

17 Senator John McCain's bid for the presidential nomination in 2000 was lost by a slight margin to George W. Bush with one of McCain's main themes being campaign finance reform, lobbying and corruption as symbolized in the McCain-Feingold bill (Moroff, 2002).

18 Since development aid was also part of the bloc competition during the Cold War, which explains its relative decline afterwards.

19 This is in full accordance with the garbage can model (Seibel, 1992, p. 135), in which solutions search for problems, as well as with the model of bureaucratic politics in international relations (Allison and Zelikow, 1999).

20 Eva Heidbreder (2011) shows a rather weak echo effect for the political Copenhagen criteria for EU candidate countries. This is especially true for minority rights where some old members like France and Greece have never signed the relevant Council of Europe conventions but required all candidate countries to do so.

21 For that reason, the 2002 Sarbanes-Oxley Act also focuses on higher accounting standards for companies after Enron and WorldCom were brought down by undetected fraud. This is another example of the 'Americanisation' of international commercial law, since all major European and Japanese companies trading their stocks in the US must comply with this act as well as with the FCPA.

22 This led the New York City Bar, under the auspices of Jay Clayton (since 2017 chairman of the SEC), to recommend less stringent enforcements and penalties for violating the FCPA (Committee on International Business Transaction of the NYC Bar, 2011, 21).

23 Finnemore and Sikkink (1998, p. 895) refer to this process as a norm cascade, a concept developed by Cass Sunstein. Of course, important countries like India and China have not joined the binding regimes yet, but they do not seem to object to its underlying norms, as signified by their ratification of the UN convention.

Further reading

Buchanan, Bruce and Lisa Hill (2014) *An Intellectual History of Political Corruption* (London/New York: Palgrave Macmillan).

Cockroft, Laurence and Anne-Christine Wegener (2017) *Unmasked: Corruption in the West* (New York: I.B. Tauris & Co Ltd).

Heidenheimer, Arnold J. and Michael Johnston (eds.) (2002) *Political Corruption. Concepts & Contexts*, 3rd ed. (New Brunswick: Transaction Publishers).

Heywood, Paul M. (2015) *Routledge Handbook of Political Corruption* (London/New York: Routledge).

Hough, Dan (2013) *Corruption, Anti-Corruption and Governance* (London/New York: Palgrave Macmillan).

Johnston, Michael (2012) *Syndromes of Corruption: Wealth, Power, and Democracy*, 2nd ed. (Cambridge: Cambridge University Press).

Moroff, Holger and Diana Schmidt-Pfister (eds.) (2017) *Fighting Corruption in Eastern Europe. A multilevel perspective*, 2nd ed. (London/New York: Routledge).

Bibliography

Allison, Graham and Philip Zelikow (1999) *Essence of Decision: Explaining the Cuban Missile Crisis*, 2nd ed. (New York/London: Longman).

Berger, Peter and Thomas Luckmann (1972) *The Social Construction of Reality* (Harmondsworth: Penguin).

Brauchtisch, Eberhard von (2001) *Der Preis Des Schweigens* (Berlin: Ullstein).

Cohen, Joel M., Michael P. Holland, and Adam P. Wolf (2008) 'Under the FCPA, Who Is a Foreign Official Anyway?', *The Business Lawyer* 63, pp. 1243–1274.

DeConcini, Dennis (1994) 'The Role of U.S. Intelligence in Promoting Economic Interests', *Journal of International Affairs*, 48(1), pp. 39–57.

Della Porta, Donatella and Alberto Vannucci (1999) *Corrupt Exchanges* (New York: Aldine de Gruyter).

Elliott, Kimberly Ann (2002) 'Corruption as an International Policy Problem' in Arnold J. Heidenheimer and Michael Johnston (eds.) *Political Corruption. Concepts & Contexts*, 3rd ed. (New Brunswick/London: Transaction Publishers), pp. 925–941.

Elliott, Kimberly Ann (ed.) (1997) *Corruption and the Global Economy* (Washington, DC: Peterson Institute).

EU Commission (2003) 'Framework Decision Criminalizing Corruption in the Private Sector', *Official Journal L* (No.192/54) (31 July 2003).

EU Convention (1997) 'Convention on the Fight against Corruption Involving Officials of the European Communities or Officials of Member States of the European Union', *Official Journal C* (No.195/01) (25 June 1997).

EU Council (1991) 'Directive 91/308 on Prevention of the Use of the Financial System for the Purpose of Money Laundering', *Official Journal L* (No.166) (28 June 1991).

EU Council (1995) 'Regulation 95/2988 on the Protection of the Communities' Financial Interests', *Official Journal L* (No. 312) (23 December 1995).

Finnemore, Martha and Kathryn Sikkink (1998) 'International Norm Dynamics and Political Change', *International Organization* 52, pp. 887–917.

Foucault, Michel (1979) *Discipline and Punish: The Birth of the Prison* (London: Vintage Books).

Fraenkel, Ernst (1964) *Deutschland und die westlichen Demokratien* (Stuttgart: Deutsche Verlags-Anstalt).

Friedman, Milton (1970) 'The Social Responsibility of Business Is to Increase Its Profits', *The New York Times Magazine* (13 September 1970).

Frisch, Dieter (1999) 'Fighting Corruption: What remains to be done at EU level', *TI Working Paper*, Transparency International, November 1999, www.transparency.de (accessed 2016).

Graeff, Peter, Karenina Schroder, and Sebastian Wolf (eds.) (2009) *Der Korruptionsfall Siemens* (Baden-Baden: Nomos).

Groll, Elias (2014) 'How much Economic Espionage is too Much?' *Foreign Policy*, May 19, https://foreignpolicy.com/2014/05/19/how-much-economic-espionage-is-too-much/

Habermas, Jürgen (1992) *Faktizität und Geltung: Beiträge zur Diskurstheorie des Rechts und des demokratischen Rechtsstaats* (Frankfurt a.M: Suhrkamp).

Heidbreder, Eva (2011) *The Impact of Expansion on European Union Institutions: The Eastern Touch on Brussels* (New York: Palgrave Macmillan).

Heidenheimer, Arnold J. and Holger Moroff (2002) 'Controlling Business Payoffs to Foreign Officials: The 1998 OECD Anti-Bribery Convention' in Arnold J. Heidenheimer and Michael Johnston (eds.) *Political Corruption. Concepts & Contexts*, 3rd ed. (New Brunswick/London: Transaction Publishers), pp. 943–959.

Kober, Stanley (1992) 'The CIA as Economic Spy: The Misuse of U.S. Intelligence After the Cold War', *Cato Policy Analysis* (185).

Koff, Stephen P. (2002). *Italy: From the 1st to the 2nd Republic* (Abingdon: Routledge).

Kohlberg, Lawrence (1981) *The Philosophy of Moral Development* (San Francisco: Harper & Row).

Krasner, Stephen D. (ed.) (1983) *International Regimes* (Ithaca: Cornell University Press).

Kratochwil, Friedrich (1989) *Rules, Norms, and Decisions: On the Conditions of Practical and Legal Reasoning in International Relations and Domestic Affairs* (New York: Cambridge University Press).

Manfroni, Carlos A. (1997) *La Convención Interamericana Contra la Corrupción* (Buenos Aires).

Marquette, Heather (2004) 'The Creeping Politicisation of the World Bank: The Case of Corruption', *Political Studies* 52, pp. 413–430.

Merton, Robert K. (1995) 'The Thomas Theorem and the Matthew Effect', *Social Forces* 74, pp. 379–424.

Moroff, Holger (2002) 'American and German Fundraising Fiascos and Their Aftermath' in Arnold J. Heidenheimer and Michael Johnston (eds.) *Political Corruption. Concepts & Contexts*, 3rd ed. (New Brunswick/London: Transaction Publishers), pp. 689–712.

Moroff, Holger (2004) 'A Polychromatic Turn in Corruption Research?' *Crime, Law, and Social Change* 42, pp. 83–97.

Moroff, Holger (2005) 'Internationalisierung von Anti-Korruptionsregimen' in Ulrich Alemann (ed.) *Dimensionen Politischer Korruption. Beiträge zum Stand der Internationalen Forschung PVS-Sonderheft 35* (Wiesbaden: VS Verlag für Sozialwissenschaften), pp. 444–477.

Office of the Director of National Intelligence (2009) 'Quadrennial Intelligence Community Review – Final Report April 2009' (Washington, DC) (accessed 2019 at: https://theintercept .com/document/2014/09/05/quadrennial-intelligence-review-final-report-2009/

Rittberger, Volker (ed.) (1993) *Regime Theory and International Relations* (Oxford: Clarendon Press).

Rosenthal, Michael (1989) 'An American Attempt to Control International Corruption' in Arnold J. Heidenheimer, Michael Johnston, and Victor T. LeVine (eds.) *Political Corruption*, 2nd ed. (New Brunswick: Transaction Publishers) pp. 701–715.

Schimmelfennig, Frank (2001) 'The Community Trap: Liberal Norms, Rhetorical Action, and the Eastern Enlargement of the European Union', *International Organization* 55(1) (Winter 2001), pp. 47–80.

Seibel, Wolfgang (1992) 'Das Mülleimermodell in der Verwaltungspraxis – oder: Wie Lösungen sich ihre Probleme suchen' in Arthur Benz and Wolfgang Seibel (eds.) *Zwischen Kooperation und Korruption: Abweichendes Verhalten in der Verwaltung* (Baden-Baden: Nomos), pp. 135–173.

Sheffet, Mary Jane (1995) 'The Foreign Corrupt Practices Act and the Omnibus Trade and Competitiveness Act of 1988: Did They Change Corporate Behavior?', *Journal of Public Policy and Marketing* 14, pp. 290–300.

Transatlantic Business Dialogue (1998) 'Charlotte Statement of Conclusions', www.trans atlanticbusiness.org/storage/tabd/documents/charlotteconferencereport1oct98.pdf (accessed 2016).

U.S. Department of Commerce (1995) *The Big Emerging Markets: 1996 Outlook and Sourcebook* (Washington, DC: Bernan Press).

US-EU (1995) 'Joint Action Plan' (3 December 1995), www.eurunion.org/partner/actplan .htm (accessed 2017).

Walters, William (2008) 'Anti-Policy and Anti-Politics: Critical Reflections on Certain Schemes to Govern Bad Things', *European Journal of Cultural Studies* 11, pp. 267–288.

Wendt, Alexander (1992) 'Anarchy Is What States Make of It: The Social Construction of Power Politics', *International Organization* 46, pp. 391–425.

Windsor, Duane and Kathleen A. Getz (1999) 'Regional Market Integration and the Development of Global Norms for Enterprise Conduct', *Business and Society* 38, pp. 415–449.

Woolsey, James (2000) 'Eure Unternehmen arbeiten mit Bestechung', *Die Zeit* (30 March 2000), p. 10.

Chapter 26

Nuclear proliferation and international stability

Jonas Schneider

The question of how the number of states possessing a nuclear arsenal impacts international stability has long been a major concern for scholars, pundits and policymakers working on global security. Many of these experts have worried that new nuclear-armed nations would exert a destabilising effect on regional and global

FIGURE 26.1 India test fires a long-range nuclear-capable Agni-5 missile from Wheeler Island, India

order. For example, in the 1960s, officials from numerous countries shared a deep apprehension that the Chinese bomb or a West German 'finger on the nuclear trigger' would gravely endanger Asian and European security, respectively (see Gavin, 2004/05; Popp et al., 2016). In the 1990s, many experts viewed the revelation of Iraq's secret nuclear weapons program, North Korea's efforts to get the bomb, as well as India and Pakistan's nuclear tests as unmistakable signs that the spread of nuclear weapons was becoming the defining threat to global security during the dawning post–Cold War era (Bracken, 1999; Tanter, 1999). In recent years, more than a few scholars have warned that Iran's pursuit of the bomb may, by accident or design, trigger a military conflict with Israel that could even escalate to nuclear war (Kahl et al., 2012, pp. 28–30; Kroenig, 2014a, pp. 140–146).

Other analysts have sounded a much less alarmist tone, however. Some scholars even suggested that an Iranian bomb held great potential for stabilising an unbalanced and volatile Middle East (Waltz, 2012). Closer to the mainstream of Western strategic discourse, various experts have argued that despite the risks of proliferation, nuclear weapons, and the deterrent they provide should get (more) credit for contributing, in combination with other factors, to what has been labelled 'the Long Peace' among the great powers since 1945 (Gaddis, 1999, p. 268–271; Gavin, 2012a, p. 164; Acton 2010, pp. 16–17). Still others have contended that because nuclear proliferation is such a rare phenomenon, and since robust nonproliferation measures tend to be disruptive, the *net* destabilising effect of new nuclear countries is quite small and, therefore, manageable (Mueller 2010, pp. 95–99; Hymans 2013, pp. 293–296).

The question of whether nuclear proliferation has stabilising or destabilising effects is not just fascinating for scholars of the nuclear age, but also highly consequential for practical policy issues. For in order to debate the merits of particular policy choices – such as preventive military strikes against nuclear facilities, grand bargains with potential proliferators or complete nuclear disarmament – we need to understand first how the spread of nuclear weapons impacts regional and global security.

The chapter proceeds in three steps. The first section provides the foundation for the other parts by summarising what we know about empirical patterns of proliferation and the utility of nuclear weapons for statecraft. The second section then engages the literature on the consequences of proliferation, focusing in particular on how proliferation has influenced international stability. The final section explores whether some states have been more affected than others, and what measures these states have taken to prevent proliferation, or at least mitigate its negative consequences.

Patterns of nuclear proliferation and the utility of nuclear weapons

Nuclear proliferation is commonly defined as the spread of nuclear weapons to states that did not previously have them. Within a broader conceptual framework that is rarely used by scholars, yet popular in the arms control community, this diffusion of nuclear weapons to additional states is labelled *horizontal* proliferation.

It is conceptually accompanied by the notion of *vertical* proliferation, which refers to qualitative improvements and increases in the number of nuclear weapons in the stockpiles of existing nuclear weapon states. In accordance with the typical usage of the term in the scholarly debate, this chapter focuses only on how the horizontal proliferation of nuclear weapons affects international stability.

One important empirical pattern that has shaped how nuclear proliferation is understood concerns the way in which nuclear weapons have spread. The word 'spread' appears to suggest that the established nuclear powers have provided other interested nations with (at least a few) operational nuclear warheads. Yet such transfers have never been undertaken. Certainly, states that sought nuclear weapons have often received significant assistance from other nations (Schofield, 2014; Fuhrmann, 2012), sometimes in the form of highly sensitive technologies (Kroenig, 2010). Nonetheless, since all these transfers remained well below the weapons threshold, nations seeking nuclear weapons always had to build them indigenously. Hence, in reality, the spread of nuclear weapons has meant that merely the *ambition* to possess a nuclear arsenal has spread to additional states, each of which then had to pursue that goal primarily through indigenous efforts.

Importantly, since a state's national efforts to turn its desire for nuclear weapons into reality naturally span several (and sometimes many) years, nuclear proliferation must be conceived of as a process, as opposed to just a single step (Meyer, 1986). This point is reinforced by the fact that 29 out of 39 states that have embarked upon that path (Müller and Schmidt, 2010, p. 157; Mikoyan, 2012; Santoro, 2017) have not acquired a nuclear arsenal. Hence, a lot of nuclear proliferation activity has been undertaken by nations that did not ultimately become nuclear weapon states. Three patterns explain this situation.

First, owing not just to the technological, but also the institutional and managerial challenges of the task, some nations simply failed in their efforts to build the bomb (Hymans, 2012; Braut-Hegghammer, 2016). Second, a few countries have chosen a nuclear 'hedging' strategy, intentionally confining their efforts to developing the technological capability to build an arsenal quickly while refraining from exercising that option (Narang, 2016–17, p. 134). Third, several states have undertaken a 'nuclear reversal', abandoning their nuclear weapons activities before developing nuclear explosive devices (Müller and Schmidt, 2010).

Given that every case of nuclear proliferation should be understood as a process, scholars distinguish different phases along that path, with the majority using a model encompassing three sequential steps: the exploration, pursuit and acquisition of nuclear weapons (Bleek, 2017; Singh and Way, 2004). Within that framework, nations *exploring* nuclear weapons give serious consideration to an arsenal. For example, political leaders might debate the need for a nuclear deterrent, officials may conduct feasibility studies, or the state hedges by developing its nuclear infrastructure. The *pursuit* of nuclear weapons then necessarily involves the binding top-down decision to build the bomb, and it includes all actions aimed at implementing that order.

Finally, nuclear *acquisition* turns a country into a nuclear weapon state. Traditionally, a nation's first nuclear test has been the indicator of its acquisition of nuclear weapons. However, if a state chooses – as South Africa did – to refrain from testing, it 'acquires' nuclear weapons by inducting the untested nuclear warheads into its military arsenal (Hymans, 2010b). Distinguishing between acquisition, on the one hand,

and exploration and pursuit on the other, is crucial for fully grasping the impact of proliferation on international stability because a state's proliferation behaviour may influence the regional or global order well before it acquires the bomb.

States have sought nuclear weapons for different reasons (Hymans, 2010a; Sagan, 2011; Debs and Monteiro, 2017). Yet according to one influential typology, each of the numerous causes of proliferation that scholars have identified can be linked to one of three broader motivations (or 'models'): the quest for security, the narrow self-interests of domestic political actors, or the pursuit of national self-esteem through compliance with influential global norms (Sagan, 1996/97, 2001). Among the causes of proliferation that can be subsumed under the 'security model', scholars have paid most attention to rivals possessing a nuclear arsenal or enjoying superiority in conventional weaponry (Betts, 1977; Thayer, 1995; Monteiro and Debs, 2014).

Drivers of proliferation reflecting the 'domestic politics model' include powerful inward-looking domestic coalitions thriving on conflict and economic isolation (Solingen, 2007). Of importance are also parochial efforts of key state bureaucracies to enhance their organisational status and influence through nuclear programs (Walsh, 2001). Lastly, within the rubric of the 'norms model', scholars have found political leaders who hold oppositional-nationalist views of their nation's identity (Hymans, 2006) and elites championing pro-bomb 'myths' (Lavoy, 1993) to be key factors that push states toward nuclear weapons.

Although the notion, or 'myth', that possessing a nuclear arsenal provides states with numerous politico-military benefits has been influential, the utility of nuclear weapons as tools of statecraft has sometimes been overstated. Certainly, they *can* make for a powerful deterrent: a posture that not just allows for, but envisions the first use of nuclear weapons early in a conflict has been shown to effectively deter other countries from launching military attacks against nuclear powers (Narang, 2013). Moreover, recent research suggests that nuclear weapons may offer states greater independence from patrons and improve their capability to resist pressure from opponents, bolster their junior allies and pursue conventional aggression (Bell, 2015).

On the other hand, nuclear arsenals have often been credited with providing possessors with vast coercive leverage, enabling them to employ stronger threats to extract concessions in crisis bargaining. Thus, nuclear weapons have also been regarded as tools of compellence (Betts, 1987; Beardsley and Asal, 2009; Kroenig, 2013). However, recent scholarship has presented persuasive evidence that nuclear weapons have not conferred noteworthy coercive leverage since nuclear compellent threats typically lack credibility (Sechser and Fuhrmann, 2013, 2017). Nonetheless, because many policymakers have long believed nuclear compellence to be feasible, this belief has naturally influenced how the spread of nuclear weapons has affected international stability in practice (Trachtenberg, 1991; Sechser and Fuhrmann, 2017, pp. 132–231).

The effects of nuclear proliferation on international stability

The literature on the consequences of nuclear proliferation is vast (see Lavoy, 1995 Gartzke and Kroenig, 2016). For decades this debate was mostly theoretical, with scholars employing deductive reasoning and drawing on empirical evidence merely to illustrate their ideas. The early contributions also had a narrow focus, debating primarily nuclear arsenal safety and whether *other* nations would initiate *full-scale war* (defined as sustained combat resulting in a minimum of 1000 battle-related fatalities) against states pursuing or possessing a nuclear arsenal.

More recent research has been able to overcome these shortcomings. As new methods and archival sources have become available, scholars have shifted toward testing the received wisdom systematically against the historical record. Many of these works have also adopted a wider focus, including *low-level* military conflict and behavioural changes on the part of new *nuclear powers*. These studies have greatly improved our understanding of how proliferation influences global stability. The emerging picture, however, is also more complex.

The established theories

The abstract debate over whether more proliferation will make war more or less likely has ushered in a divide among nuclear scholars in which 'proliferation optimists' have been pitted against 'proliferation pessimists' (see Busch, 2001). Although this discussion has involved a great many voices on both sides, the by now classic exchanges between Kenneth Waltz and Scott Sagan (Sagan and Waltz, 1995, 2003, 2012) best epitomise the nuclear optimism-pessimism debate.

Both Waltz and Sagan base their arguments about the strategic effects of proliferation on deductive claims about the requirements of stable nuclear deterrence. Representing the optimists, Waltz presumes that *all* new nuclear powers will build survivable nuclear forces – which can withstand an enemy's first strike – and effectively guard their nuclear arsenal against accidental or unauthorised use because they have vast incentives, and will find it technically easy, to do so. Under these conditions, adversaries will be deterred from aggression since they must fear nuclear retaliation. Moreover, in case a military crisis still erupts, cooler heads will prevail because the risk of nuclear escalation induces caution on all sides. Accordingly, as nuclear weapons spread, both the number and intensity of military conflicts will decrease and international stability will be enhanced. In fact, when it comes to proliferation, according to this theory, 'more may be better' (Waltz, 1995).

Notably, Sagan's proliferation pessimism does not dispute that nuclear deterrence *can* be a stabilising force in world politics. In contrast to Waltz, however, he is sceptical whether *new* nuclear nations – most of whom he sees as having only weak civilian control of the military – will meet the requirements of stable nuclear deterrence. In particular, Sagan contends that owing to the parochial interests and organisational biases of militaries, such new nuclear powers are unlikely to build survivable nuclear forces and develop adequate nuclear safety measures. As a result, whether by accident or design, nuclear deterrence is bound to fail someday. In addition, the same biases make these states prone to conduct preventive strikes against their rivals' nascent nuclear programs, thwarting the emergence of *mutual* deterrence. Hence, far from fostering stability, more proliferation is a recipe for disaster (Sagan, 1995).

Situated between these extremes of atomic peace and inadvertent nuclear catastrophe, a few theoretical works have made the case for a more nuanced impact of nuclear proliferation on different levels of military conflict. In this vein, scholarship on the 'stability-instability paradox' claims that as nuclear weapons dampen the prospects of all-out nuclear war, they ratchet up conflict at the conventional level (Snyder, 1965). Specifically, the paradox argues that the *more* robust and stable mutual deterrence becomes at the nuclear level, the *greater* the tendency of nuclear powers to wage high-intensity conventional violence will be because neither side fears escalation to strategic nuclear war (see Jervis, 1984). As a result, the spread of nuclear weapons may not lead to all-out nuclear war, yet still exacerbate conventional conflict.

Empirical research on nuclear deterrence stability

The deductive arguments at the heart of these classic works on deterrence have come under pressure as recent scholarship has engaged in rigorous theory testing. Admirably, these empirical analyses did not shy away from scrutinising the few claims on which proliferation optimists and pessimists have been able to agree. This effort in particular has led to surprising findings. For instance, in contrast to both Waltz and Sagan, innovative work by Narang (2013) suggests that a nuclear posture of 'assured retaliation' (which relies on survivable nuclear forces to retaliate against strategic targets, such as major cities) does not provide nations with substantial deterrent power beyond their conventional deterrents.

Against this backdrop, it is no longer startling that nations adopting an assured retaliation posture have suffered significant deterrence failures. For instance, the respective assured retaliation postures of China and India deterred neither the Soviet Union from initiating substantial fighting in the Ussuri River Crisis in 1969, nor Pakistan from launching the Kargil War in 1999. Likewise, Israel's assured retaliation posture (since 1991) failed to deter serious military conflict even against non-nuclear opponents.

More generally, Narang's important study is able to show empirically that different nuclear postures, defined as ways to operationalise a nuclear arsenal, generate differential deterrent power. All regional nuclear powers – global powers face different constraints – have adopted one of three postures (Narang, 2014). While assured retaliation postures do not provide meaningful deterrent benefits, a 'catalytic posture' (which uses alerting one's nuclear forces to trigger diplomatic intervention by a third party, such as the US) seems to make for an even *weaker* deterrent. It has failed repeatedly to deter even high-intensity conflict. For example, Israel's (until 1991) catalytic posture did not stop Egypt and Syria from launching a full-scale war against it in 1973.

Notably, a posture of 'asymmetric escalation' (which envisions using nuclear weapons first and early in a conflict to repel invading forces) was found to offer *by far* the greatest increase in deterrent power both over existing conventional forces and compared to the other nuclear postures. Against non-nuclear aggressors, asymmetric escalation postures seem to have successfully deterred conflict at both high and low levels of intensity, and nuclear challengers, too, have never dared to go beyond a war of words (Narang, 2013).

What is good for deterrence, however, might not necessarily also be good for stability. In fact, postures of asymmetric escalation have long been deemed destabilising (in crisis settings) and aggressive, far more so than the other postures (Gavin, 2012a; Sagan, 2009). In terms of international stability, then, there seems to be no nuclear posture 'silver bullet', but only thorny and messy tradeoffs: the one posture that apparently deters all military conflict – asymmetric escalation – often comes at the prize of heightened international tensions and increased risks of crisis instability. North Korea's recent shift toward an asymmetric escalation posture (Fisher, 2017) is a case in point, because this posture necessarily entails the current fast expansion of Pyongyang's nuclear arsenal and the first-use threats that many observers find terrifying. On the other hand, less threatening postures are prone to deterrence failures. Overall, then, Narang's findings suggest that the spread of nuclear arsenals to additional states might ratchet up international tensions at best, and fail to deter full-scale conventional war at worst. In any case, the proliferation optimists' case for stable nuclear peace seems tenuous.

Faith in the broad deterrent benefits of nuclear weapons is further undermined by the findings in the recent work by Bell and Miller (2015). Their work has resolved a number of methodological problems that had afflicted earlier studies. According to their research, two nuclear-armed countries are not less likely to fight a *full-scale war* than two non-nuclear nations. This surprising finding represents a serious challenge to the central claim of proliferation optimists. To be fair, however, Bell and Miller did not find an increased probability for full-scale war between nuclear weapon states, either. Hence, their results also undercut a major element of the theory of proliferation pessimism. This neutral overall impact dovetails nicely, however, with research suggesting that military technologies in general make war neither more nor less likely (Lieber, 2005).

Focusing on *lower levels of conflict*, Bell and Miller's work improves upon earlier studies by controlling for the confounding influence of pre-nuclear bilateral conflict. This change in research design allows them to isolate the effect of nuclear acquisition on conflict between nuclear-armed states. Under these conditions, their analysis suggests that countries that are locked in a relationship of mutual nuclear deterrence are *not* more likely than non-nuclear powers to experience low-level military conflict (Bell and Miller, 2015). This finding is significant because it seems to show that the stability-instability paradox lacks broad empirical support. As far as mutual nuclear deterrence is concerned, then, more nuclear powers do not mean *additional* instability.

One aspect of nuclear deterrence that the aforementioned studies did not examine is the influence on stability of *extended* nuclear deterrence. This was the practice under which the US, the Soviet Union and the UK provided 'nuclear umbrellas' to deter aggression against allies. According to Fuhrmann and Sechser (2014), these formal nuclear alliance commitments have been effective deterrents: the respective allies have been much less likely to be targeted in violent militarised disputes than junior allies in non-nuclear alliances. In this regard, then, nuclear acquisition by the US, the Soviet Union and the UK seems to have reduced international conflict.

As with regional powers, however, what is good for deterrence does not always enhance stability. For example, precisely because the US has struggled to make its extended deterrent threats credible (Gavin, 2012a, pp. 149–150; Trachtenberg, 2002), it resorted to aggressive nuclear policies – such as counterforce targeting, a first-use doctrine, foreign-deployed nuclear weapons and the quest for a preventive nuclear first-strike capability – that have threatened strategic stability (Long and Green, 2015; Lieber and Press, 2006). The net effect of extended deterrence has thus been mixed: It has deterred the *outbreak* of violence while increasing the *risks* of conflict.

Empirical research on the effects of pursuing the bomb

The empirical works reviewed earlier have focused on the stability of deterrence once a nation, or two rivaling states, have acquired a nuclear arsenal. As every instance of nuclear proliferation must be conceived of as a process, however, a country's efforts to get nuclear weapons could affect international stability long before it crosses the acquisition threshold.

Recent scholarship has paid particular attention to such effects of nuclear weapons *pursuit*. For example, Fuhrmann and Kreps (2010) have identified no less than 50 occasions during the 20th century where states considered attacking or actually attacked the nuclear facilities of another nation in an effort to *prevent* a nuclear arsenal. The Israeli bombing of the Osirak reactor in Iraq in 1981 is only the best-known of those cases. Another spectacular attack occurred in 2007, when Israel's air force obliterated an alleged nuclear reactor in Syria (Spector and Cohen, 2008). In recent years, military strikes against Iran's nuclear facilities were vividly debated in Israel and the US (Kahl et al., 2012).

The question of how these cases of preventive war considerations have affected international stability, however, requires a nuanced answer. The sheer number of more than 50 cases suggests a markedly destabilising influence. Yet as critics have pointed out, in the end only 12 strike plans were carried out, and just four attacks occurred independently of wider wars that would have been fought even if the attacked state had not had a nuclear program. Moreover, none of the four counter-proliferation strikes precipitated retaliatory attacks or escalated to a wider conflict (Cohen, 2016, pp. 427–430).

Even with these less than worst-case outcomes, however, preventive war considerations against proliferators are still destabilising. First, the use of force is by definition a risky and disruptive action. Second, the Osirak bombing demonstrated that military strikes might prompt reactions that turn a vague nuclear ambition into a determined weapons pursuit, thus sowing the seeds for more conflict down the road (Braut-Hegghammer, 2011). Finally, merely contemplating attacks may still have destabilising effects. As the struggle over Iran's nuclear program prior to 2013 showed, explicit threats of counterproliferation strikes or public advocacy of 'military options' can be sufficient to increase tensions and undermine regional security (Kreps and Pasha, 2012).

Besides the risk of inviting preventive strikes against its nuclear infrastructure, a state's pursuit of nuclear weapons might also exacerbate military disputes that have no direct bearing on the nuclear issue. For example, according to quantitative research by Sobek et al. (2012), the closer a nation gets to acquiring nuclear weapons, the greater the risk that it will be targeted in militarised conflicts – both over its nuclear program and otherwise. In these authors' theory, rivals view a nation's acquisition of a nuclear arsenal as a threshold that will irreversibly alter the bargaining dynamic to their own detriment. For that reason, a country's efforts *toward* acquiring the bomb give its rivals vast incentives to pursue, with military force if necessary, favourable conclusions to *any* unresolved disputes before the balance of power between the two sides shifts drastically. As a result, the path to proliferation is often paved with violent conflict. Recent research by Narang (2016–17, pp. 113–116), which revisited that question, yet confined the analysis to nations that eventually acquired a nuclear arsenal, confirms that states experience increasing militarised conflict as they draw closer to nuclear acquisition.

The dynamics identified by these quantitative studies have received additional empirical support from recent qualitative works. For example, historical research by Trachtenberg (1999) and Gavin (2012a, pp. 57–74) revealed that West Germany's nuclear weapons ambitions played a key role in Khrushchev's decision in 1958 to initiate the Second Berlin Crisis. Likewise, Pakistan's decisive moves toward nuclear acquisition motivated Indian military leaders to provoke the Brasstacks Crisis of 1986–1987, which brought the South Asian rivals perilously close to full-scale war (Chengappa, 2000, pp. 322–323). Overall, even the mere pursuit of nuclear weapons seems to exacerbate conflict and trigger violence, thus undermining global stability well before nuclear acquisition.

Empirical research on the behaviour of nuclear powers

Nuclear proliferation affects international politics not just because *other states* react to their rivals' pursuit and acquisition of nuclear weapons with destabilising countermeasures. The spread of nuclear weapons also impinges on international stability because the acquisition of a nuclear arsenal can change the foreign policy behaviour of new nuclear powers.

In this respect, several empirical studies suggest that states adopt bolder policies after acquiring nuclear weapons. For example, quantitative work by Horowitz (2009) shows that, compared to non-nuclear nations and their own non-nuclear past, new nuclear powers exhibit a much greater propensity to reciprocate in interstate disputes. Notably, however, Horowitz finds that this effect washes out over time, which suggests that increasing experience with being a nuclear-armed power exerts a restraining influence on states' conflict propensity.

This conclusion was strengthened by statistical work by Gartzke (2010) that examined whether new nuclear nations were also more likely to *initiate*, rather than reciprocate, militarised disputes. According to his analysis, newly nuclear powers are prone to initiate military conflict, but after a few years become just as likely to start disputes as they were before acquiring a nuclear arsenal. New evidence from case studies of Soviet, Chinese and North Korean dispute behaviour in their post-acquisition periods likewise suggests a sudden appetite for greater risk-taking that diminishes over time (Cohen, 2016, pp. 435–436; Carlin and Jervis, 2015).

Interesting work by Bell and Miller (2015) has further enriched this picture of a heightened conflict propensity of nuclear-armed nations. Focusing on relationships between nuclear and non-nuclear powers, they find that such dyads experience more low-level conflict than relationships between two non-nuclear nations, and that responsibility for initiating these conflicts typically rests with the nuclear-armed state.

Notably, their analysis also reveals that these disputes that nuclear powers initiate mostly target states with whom the nuclear-armed state did not have previous conflicts. Besides, these new non-nuclear opponents are not more powerful conventional-armed countries. These two latter findings are important: That nuclear nations do not start fights with *more powerful* non-nuclear countries runs counter to the widely-shared concern that new nuclear powers will use their nuclear weapons as a shield behind which they engage in conventional aggression against stronger non-nuclear enemies (Kroenig, 2014a; Van Crefeld, 1993). Moreover, the finding that nuclear powers initiate disputes with *new* opponents, rather than old enemies, appears to support the recently-proposed idea (Bell, 2016) that nuclear acquisition might lead states to expand their foreign policy interests.

Recent qualitative research has added further nuance to our knowledge of how states' foreign policies can change after they acquire a nuclear arsenal. In a valuable conceptual contribution, Bell (2015) distinguishes six different foreign policy responses to nuclear acquisition. Most important for the question considered here, two of these behavioural shifts of new nuclear powers have immediate destabilising effects for the international environment: Besides an *expansion* of a nation's foreign policy interests as outlined earlier, nuclear acquisition may also lead a state to engage in more intense *aggression* against opponents with whom it had previous conflict.

Subsequent research has detailed the conditions under which new nuclear powers adopt these courses of action. Bell (2016) has argued that only those few new nuclear states who face severe territorial threats, such as Pakistan, opt for aggression, using their nuclear weapons as shields to deter nuclear and extensive conventional retaliation. Similarly drawing on Pakistan's increased conflict propensity following its nuclear acquisition, Kapur's (2007) research suggests that it is the rare combination of revisionist ambitions and conventional inferiority that leads new nuclear powers to pursue aggressive military policies toward their rivals. Importantly, while they offer different explanations, the two studies concur that aggression is a fairly unlikely effect of nuclear acquisition.

Meanwhile, according to Bell (2016), new nuclear states undertake an expansion of their foreign policy interests if their territory is not threatened *and* their relative material power is rising. Historically, such expansions have been more common than aggression: upon acquiring nuclear weapons, the US, South Africa, Israel and the Soviet Union all initiated several militarised disputes targeting states with whom they had no previous conflict (Bell and Miller, 2015: online appendix). Despite the mostly low intensity of these disputes, such expansive conflict behaviour can hardly be considered stabilising. Overall, then, new nuclear states seem to have a moderately destabilising influence on world politics: they initiate new disputes and take greater risks. At the same time, however, acquiring nuclear weapons rarely facilitates severe aggression.

Reconsidering nuclear accidents and nuclear terrorism

The notion that the spread of nuclear weapons would someday lead to tragic nuclear accidents or even nuclear terrorism has long been among proliferation pessimists' foremost concerns. However, as reliable datasets on all (attempted) nuclear terrorism plots and on nuclear safety incidents in all nuclear states and proliferators have proved elusive, empirical scholarship has not kept pace with theoretical work. Hence, research has been limited to deductive analyses, buttressed by empirical illustrations. Even so, the more sophisticated of those studies have called the pessimists' claims into question.

For instance, Cohen (2016, pp. 432–434) revealed that the vast majority of the gravest nuclear accidents that Sagan (1993, p. 9) points to as support for his logic occurred during global crises in 1962 or 1973, when leaders sought to leverage their nuclear arsenals for coercive bargaining. It was, in other words, not organisational pathologies that raised the specter of accidental nuclear war, as Sagan holds, but rather the deliberate attempts at nuclear compellence. These accidents, then, represent the actual 'effects' of nuclear compellence: while the compellent threats did not affect the trajectory of either crises (Sechser and Fuhrmann, 2017, pp. 207, 220–224), they led to precarious nuclear safety incidents.

Other critics have rightly pointed out that, seven decades into the nuclear age, the fact – however fortunate it is – that the world has still not experienced a catastrophic fatal nuclear accident should give proliferation pessimists pause (Sechser, 2013, pp. 184–186). Obviously, the bounded rationality of such organisations alone does not make tragic nuclear accidents nearly as likely as the pessimists contend. Their fear, hence, seems to be overstated.

The same must probably be said about nuclear terrorism. Determinate predictions that a terrorist attack involving nuclear weapons was bound to occur soon (Allison, 2004, p. 15; Graham, 2008, p. VI) have come and gone without anything happening. Sceptical experts have argued that this outcome is not surprising at all, given the formidable practical obstacles such a terrorist scheme would encounter (Levi, 2009). Moreover, to the extent that fissile materials from nuclear weapons can now be traced back to specific state arsenals, the idea that a nuclear power could willingly share its arsenal with terrorists and hope to remain anonymous has been challenged as lacking plausibility (Lieber and Press, 2013).

Nuclear proliferation and other states' influence: differential effects

Both the classic proliferation optimism-pessimism debate and the recent empirical scholarship have studied the spread of nuclear weapons largely through a systemic lens: they have focused on how further nuclear proliferation affects *international* stability. For the world as a whole, as we have seen, the effects of proliferation must be described as (only) moderately destabilising.

Crucially, however, these moderate overall effects are distributed unequally across states in the international system. As Kroenig's work (2009, 2010, 2014b) stresses, states that are capable of projecting conventional military power over long distances are most affected by the consequences of further proliferation, regardless of whether their rivals or allies build the bombs. If rivals get nuclear weapons, then such power-projecting states lose their ability to coerce and invade these rivals. If junior allies acquire an arsenal, power-projecting states lose sway over the ally's policies because they can no longer manipulate its military dependence. In contrast, states with little or no power-projection capability are affected by proliferation only if it occurs in their own region, but have little to lose from proliferation in other parts of the world because they did not have the capability to intervene in far-away countries in the first place and do not extend security guarantees to nations in other regions.

Given these differential effects, it is no surprise that regional military powers like France, West Germany and China have often refused to sacrifice economic benefits to prevent proliferation (Kroenig, 2014b; Müller, 1990), whereas nonproliferation has been at the forefront of US grand strategy throughout the nuclear age (Gavin, 2015). Equipped with the strongest conventional forces and the ambition to make its influence felt in every corner of the globe, the US has had the most to lose from the spread of nuclear arsenals: rivals with nuclear weapons might be better able to resist pressure from Washington, bolster other US adversaries or engage in aggression against the US or its allies and partners, while nuclear-armed allies may act more independently of, or even thwart, American interests (Bell, 2016).

Facing such daunting scenarios, the US has consistently opposed proliferation by foes and friends alike. To prevent others from building nuclear weapons, Washington has wielded all tools of US statecraft, ranging from security guarantees (Gavin, 2015), vigorous bilateral diplomacy (Schneider, 2016; Miller, 2014a) and mandatory US sanctions (Miller, 2014b) to collective technology denial (Burr, 2014) and even sustained collusion with its chief adversary, the Soviet Union (Coe and Vaynman, 2015). Remarkably, when these preventive efforts failed, the US more than once cut secret deals committing the new nuclear power to forgo nuclear testing so as to avoid, at least, triggering further proliferation (Miller and Rabinowitz, 2015).

Today, virtually every policymaker, official and pundit in the US intuitively opposes the spread of nuclear weapons as extremely dangerous, no matter where it occurs (Carus, 2016; Gavin, 2012b). The same can be said about many officials and experts from states that are US allies or close partners (Gibbons, 2015; Schwartz, 2014). Yet as we have seen, such alarmist appraisals are not borne out by the empirical record about how nuclear weapons have influenced *international* stability, but appear to be a consequence of the differential effects of proliferation. Thus, these excessively concerned voices do not abstract themselves from the specific policy interests of their states (Betts, 2001, pp. 64–65): They see an international order underwritten by US military primacy and American political leadership as preferable to any alternative.

Every official who shares that outlook must view proliferation as a major threat because it sharply limits Washington's global influence and undermines the US-led international security order. Scholars, however, should be transparent about the fact that this appraisal is coloured by specific policy preferences. In contrast, an equidistant assessment of the available scholarship on nuclear proliferation can only conclude that, for the world as a whole, the spread of nuclear weapons appears to be destabilising, but only moderately so.

Further reading

Bell, M. (2015) 'Beyond Emboldenment: How Acquiring Nuclear Weapons Can Change Foreign Policy', *International Security* 40(1) (Summer 2015), pp. 87–119.

Bell, M. and N. Miller (2015) 'Questioning the Effect of Nuclear Weapons on Conflict', *Journal of Conflict Resolution* 59(1) (February 2015), pp. 74–92.

Gavin, F. (2012) *Nuclear Statecraft: History and Strategy in America's Atomic Age* (Ithaca, NY: Cornell University Press).

Horowitz, M. (2009) 'The Spread of Nuclear Weapons and International Conflict: Does Experience Matter?', *Journal of Conflict Resolution* 53(2) (April 2009), pp. 234–257.

Kroenig, M. (2009) 'Beyond Optimism and Pessimism: The Differential Effect of Nuclear Proliferation', Harvard Kennedy School, Working Paper No. 2009–14.

Levi, M. (2009) *On Nuclear Terrorism* (Cambridge, MA: Harvard University Press).

Mueller, J. (2010) *Atomic Obsession: Nuclear Alarmism from Hiroshima to Al-Qaeda* (Oxford, UK: Oxford University Press).

Narang, V. (2013) 'What Does It Take to Deter? Regional Power Nuclear Postures and International Conflict', *Journal of Conflict Resolution* 57(3) (June 2013), pp. 478–508.

Sagan, S. and K. Waltz (2012) *The Spread of Nuclear Weapons: An Enduring Debate* (New York: W.W. Norton).

Sechser, T. and M. Fuhrmann (2017) *Nuclear Weapons and Coercive Diplomacy* (Cambridge, UK: Cambridge University Press).

Bibliography

Acton, J. (2010) 'U.S. Allies and the Politics of Abolishing Nuclear Weapons', in S. Sagan et al., *Shared Responsibilities for Nuclear Disarmament: A Global Debate* (Cambridge, MA: American Academy of Arts and Sciences).

Allison, G. (2004) *Nuclear Terrorism: The Ultimate Preventable Catastrophe* (New York: Times Books).

Beardsley, K. and V. Asal (2009) 'Winning with the Bomb', *Journal of Conflict Resolution* 53(2) (April 2009), pp. 278–301.

Bell, M. (2015) 'Beyond Emboldenment: How Acquiring Nuclear Weapons Can Change Foreign Policy', *International Security* 40(1) (Summer 2015), pp. 87–119.

Bell, M. (2016) 'What Do Nuclear Weapons Offer States? A Theory of State Foreign Policy Response to Nuclear Acquisition', Massachusetts Institute of Technology, March 7, 2016, https://papers.ssrn.com/sol3/papers.cfm? abstract_id=2566293 (accessed March 23, 2017).

Bell, M. and N. Miller (2015) 'Questioning the Effect of Nuclear Weapons on Conflict', *Journal of Conflict Resolution* 59(1) (February 2015), pp. 74–92.

Betts, R. (1977) 'Paranoids, Pygmies, Pariahs, and Nonproliferation', *Foreign Policy* (26) (Spring 1977), pp. 157–183.

Betts, R. (1987) *Nuclear Blackmail and Nuclear Balance* (Washington, DC: Brookings Institution Press).

Betts, R. (2001) 'Universal Deterrence or Conceptual Collapse? Liberal Pessimism and Utopian Realism', in V. Utgoff (ed.) *The Coming Crisis: Nuclear Proliferation, U.S. Interests, and World Order* (Cambridge, MA: MIT Press), pp. 51–85.

Bleek, P. (2017) *When Did (and Didn't) States Proliferate? Chronicling the Spread of Nuclear Weapons* (Cambridge, MA: Project on Managing the Atom, Belfer Center for Science and International Affairs, Harvard Kennedy School and the James Martin Center for Nonproliferation Studies, Middlebury Institute of International Studies, Monterey, CA).

Bracken, P. (1999) *Fire in the East: The Rise of Asian Military Power and the Second Nuclear Age* (New York: HarperCollins).

Braut-Hegghammer, M. (2011) 'Revisiting Osirak: Preventive Attacks and Nuclear Proliferation Risks', *International Security* 36(1) (Summer 2011), pp. 101–132.

Braut-Hegghammer, M. (2016) *Unclear Physics: Why Iraq and Libya Failed to Build Nuclear Weapons* (Ithaca, NY: Cornell University Press).

Burr, W. (2014) 'A Scheme of "Control": The United States and the Origins of the Nuclear Suppliers Group, 1974–1976', *International History Review* 36(2) (April 2014), pp. 252–276.

Busch, N. (2001) *Assessing the Optimism-Pessimism Debate: Nuclear Proliferation, Nuclear Risks, and Theories of State Action* (PhD dissertation, University of Toronto).

Carlin, R. and R. Jervis (2015) *Nuclear North Korea: How Will It Behave?* (Washington, DC: U.S.-Korea Institute/School of Advanced International Studies, Johns' Hopkins University).

Carus, S. (2016) 'Why U.S. Policymakers Who Love the Bomb Don't Think "More Is Better"', in H. Sokolski (ed.) *Should We Let the Bomb Spread?* (Carlisle, PA: U.S. Army War College), pp. 28–61.

Chengappa, R. (2000) *Weapons of Peace: The Secret History of India's Quest to Be a Nuclear Power* (New Delhi: HarperCollins Publishers).

Coe, A. and J. Vaynman (2015) 'Collusion and the Nuclear Nonproliferation Regime', *Journal of Politics* 77(4) (October 2015), pp. 983–997.

Cohen, M. (2016) 'How Nuclear Proliferation Causes Conflict: The Case for Optimistic Pessimism', *Nonproliferation Review* 23(3–4) (September 2016), pp. 425–442.

Debs, A. and N. Monteiro (2017) 'Conflict and Cooperation on Nuclear Nonproliferation', *Annual Review of Political Science* 20, pp. 331–349.

Fisher, M. (2017) 'The North Korea Paradox: Why There Are No Good Options on Nuclear Arms', *New York Times*, April 17, 2017, www.nytimes.com/2017/04/17/world/asia/north-korea-nuclear-weapons-missiles-sanctions.html (accessed April 18, 2017).

Fuhrmann, M. (2012) *Atomic Assistance: How 'Atoms for Peace' Programs Cause Nuclear Insecurity* (Ithaca, NY: Cornell University Press).

Fuhrmann, M. and S. Kreps (2010) 'Targeting Nuclear Programs in War and Peace: A Quantitative Empirical Analysis, 1941–2000', *Journal of Conflict Resolution* 54(6) (December 2010), pp. 831–859.

Fuhrmann, M. and T. Sechser (2014) 'Signaling Alliance Commitments: Hand-Tying and Sunk Costs in Extended Nuclear Deterrence', *American Journal of Political Science* 58(4) (October 2014), pp. 919–935.

Gaddis, J. (1999) 'Conclusion', in J. Gaddis, P. Gordon, and E. May (eds.) *Cold War Statesmen Confront the Bomb: Nuclear Diplomacy since 1945* (Oxford, UK: Oxford University Press), pp. 260–271.

Gartzke, E. (2010) 'Nuclear Proliferation Dynamics and Conventional Conflict', University of California San Diego, May 1, 2010, http://pages.ucsd. edu/~egartzke/papers/nuketime_05032010.pdf (accessed March 22, 2017).

Gartzke, E. and M. Kroenig (2016) 'Nukes with Numbers: Empirical Research on the Consequences of Nuclear Weapons for International Conflict', *Annual Review of Political Science* 19, pp. 397–412.

Gavin, F. (2015) 'Strategies of Inhibition: U.S. Grand Strategy, the Nuclear Revolution, and Nonproliferation', *International Security* 40(1) (Summer 2015), pp. 9–46.

Gavin, F. (2012a) *Nuclear Statecraft: History and Strategy in America's Atomic Age* (Ithaca, NY: Cornell University Press).

Gavin, F. (2012b) 'Politics, History, and the Ivory Tower-Policy Gap in the Nuclear Proliferation Debate', *Journal of Strategic Studies* 35(4), pp. 573–600.

Gavin, F. (2004/05) 'Blasts from the Past: Proliferation Lessons from the 1960s', *International Security* 29(3) (Winter 2004/05), pp. 100–135.

Gibbons, R. (2015) 'Baruch to Barack: Hegemony and the Politics of the Nuclear Nonproliferation Regime', Georgetown University, Working Paper.

Graham, B. (2008) *World at Risk: The Report of the Commission on the Prevention of WMD Proliferation and Terrorism* (New York: Vintage).

Horowitz, M. (2009) 'The Spread of Nuclear Weapons and International Conflict: Does Experience Matter?', *Journal of Conflict Resolution* 53(2) (April 2009), pp. 234–257.

Hymans, J. (2006) *The Psychology of Nuclear Proliferation: Identity, Emotions, and Foreign Policy* (Cambridge, UK: Cambridge University Press).

Hymans, J. (2010a) 'The Study of Nuclear Proliferation and Nonproliferation: Toward a New Consensus?', in W. Potter and G. Mukhatzhanova (eds.) *Forecasting Nuclear Proliferation in the 21st Century, Vol. 1: The Role of Theory* (Stanford, CA: Stanford University Press).

Hymans, J. (2010b) 'When Does a State Become a "Nuclear Weapon State"? An Exercise in Measurement Validation', *Nonproliferation Review* 17(1) (March 2010), pp. 161–180.

Hymans, J. (2012) *Achieving Nuclear Ambitions: Scientists, Politicians, and Proliferation* (Cambridge, UK: Cambridge University Press).

Hymans, J. (2013) 'The Threat of Nuclear Proliferation: Perception and Reality', *Ethics and International Affairs* 27(3) (September 2013), pp. 281–298.

Jervis, R. (1984) *The Illogic of American Nuclear Strategy* (Ithaca, NY: Cornell University Press).

Kahl, C., M. Dalton, and M. Irvine (2012) *Risk and Rivalry: Iran, Israel, and the Bomb* (Washington, DC: Center for a New American Security).

Kapur, P. (2007) *Dangerous Deterrent: Nuclear Weapons Proliferation and Conflict in South Asia* (Stanford, CA: Stanford University Press).

Kreps, S. and Z. Pasha (2012) 'Threats for Peace? The Domestic Distributional Effects of Military Threats', in E. Solingen (ed.) *Sanctions, Statecraft, and Nuclear Proliferation* (Cambridge, UK: Cambridge University Press), pp. 174–208.

Kroenig, M. (2009) 'Beyond Optimism and Pessimism: The Differential Effect of Nuclear Proliferation', Harvard Kennedy School, Working Paper No. 2009–14.

Kroenig, M. (2010) *Exporting the Bomb: Technology Transfer and the Spread of Nuclear Weapons* (Ithaca, NY: Cornell University Press).

Kroenig, M. (2013) 'Nuclear Superiority and the Balance of Resolve: Explaining Nuclear Crisis Outcomes', *International Organization* 67(1) (Winter 2013), pp. 141–171.

Kroenig, M. (2014a) *A Time to Attack: The Looming Iranian Nuclear Threat* (New York: Palgrave Macmillan).

Kroenig, M. (2014b) 'Force or Friendship? Explaining Great Power Nonproliferation Policy', *Security Studies* 23(1) (Fall 2014), pp. 1–32.

Lavoy, P. (1993) 'Nuclear Myths and the Causes of Nuclear Proliferation', *Security Studies* 2(3–4) (Spring/Summer 1993), pp. 192–212.

Lavoy, P. (1995) 'The Strategic Consequences of Nuclear Proliferation: A Review Essay', *Security Studies* 4(4) (Summer 1995), pp. 695–753.

Levi, M. (2009) *On Nuclear Terrorism* (Cambridge, MA: Harvard University Press).

Lieber, K. (2005) *War and the Engineers: The Primacy of Politics over Technology* (Ithaca, NY: Cornell University Press).

Lieber, K. and D. Press (2006) 'The End of MAD? The Nuclear Dimension of U.S. Primacy', *International Security* 30(4) (Spring 2006), pp. 7–44.

Lieber, K. and D. Press (2013) 'Why States Won't Give Nuclear Weapons to Terrorists', *International Security* 38(1) (Summer 2013), pp. 80–104.

Long, A. and B. Green (2015) 'Stalking the Secure Second Strike: Intelligence, Counterforce, and Nuclear Strategy', *Journal of Strategic Studies* 38(1–2), pp. 38–73.

Meyer, S. (1986) *The Dynamics of Nuclear Proliferation* (Chicago, IL: University of Chicago Press).

Mikoyan, S. (2012) *The Soviet Cuban Missile Crisis: Castro, Mikoyan, Kennedy, Khrushchev, and the Missiles of November*, ed. S. Savranskaya (Washington, DC: Woodrow Wilson Center Press).

Miller, N. (2014a) 'Nuclear Dominoes: A Self-Defeating Prophecy?', *Security Studies* 23(1) (Fall 2014), pp. 33–73.

Miller, N. (2014b) 'The Secret Success of Nonproliferation Sanctions', *International Organization* 68(4) (October 2014), pp. 913–944.

Miller, N. and O. Rabinowitz (2015) 'Keeping the Bombs in the Basement: U.S. Nonproliferation Policy toward Israel, South Africa, and Pakistan', *International Security* 40(1) (Summer 2015), pp. 47–86.

Monteiro, N. and A. Debs (2014) 'The Strategic Logic of Nuclear Proliferation', *International Security* 39(2) (Fall 2014), pp. 7–51.

Müller, H. (1990) *After the Scandals: West German Nonproliferation Policy* (Frankfurt: Peace Research Institute Frankfurt).

Müller, H. and A. Schmidt (2010) 'The Little-Known Story of Deproliferation: Why States Give Up Nuclear Weapons Activities', in W. Potter and G. Mukhatzhanova (eds.) *Forecasting Nuclear Proliferation in the 21st Century, Vol. 1: The Role of Theory* (Stanford, CA: Stanford University Press), pp. 124–158.

Mueller, J. (2010) *Atomic Obsession: Nuclear Alarmism from Hiroshima to Al-Qaeda* (Oxford, UK: Oxford University Press).

Narang, V. (2013) 'What Does It Take to Deter? Regional Power Nuclear Postures and International Conflict', *Journal of Conflict Resolution* 57(3) (June 2013), pp. 478–508.

Narang, V. (2014) *Nuclear Strategy in the Modern Era: Regional Powers and International Conflict* (Princeton, NJ: Princeton University Press).

Narang, V. (2016–17) 'Strategies of Nuclear Proliferation: How States Pursue the Bomb', *International Security* 41(3) (Winter 2016–17), pp. 110–150.

Popp, R., L. Horovitz, and A. Wenger (2016) *Negotiating the Nuclear Non-Proliferation Treaty: Origins of the Nuclear Order* (London: Routledge).

Sagan, S. (1993) *The Limits of Safety: Organizations, Accidents, and Nuclear Weapons* (Princeton, NJ: Princeton University Press).

Sagan, S. (1995) 'More Will Be Worse', in S. Sagan and K. Waltz (eds.) *The Spread of Nuclear Weapons: A Debate* (New York: W.W. Norton), pp. 46–87.

Sagan, S. (1996/97) 'Why Do States Build Nuclear Weapons? Three Models in Search of a Bomb', *International Security* 21(3) (Winter 1996/97), pp. 54–86.

Sagan, S. (2001) 'Rethinking the Causes of Nuclear Proliferation: Three Models in Search of a Bomb', in V. Utgoff (ed.) *The Coming Crisis: Nuclear Proliferation, U.S. Interests, and World Order* (Cambridge, MA: MIT Press), pp. 17–50.

Sagan, S. (2009) 'The Case for No-First Use', *Survival* 51(3) (June/July 2009), pp. 163–182.

Sagan, S. (2011) 'The Causes of Nuclear Weapons Proliferation', *Annual Review of Political Science* 14, pp. 225–244.

Sagan, S. and K. Waltz (1995) *The Spread of Nuclear Weapons: A Debate* (New York: W.W. Norton).

Sagan, S. and K. Waltz (2003) *The Spread of Nuclear Weapons: A Debate Renewed* (New York: W.W. Norton).

Sagan, S. and K. Waltz (2012) *The Spread of Nuclear Weapons: An Enduring Debate* (New York: W.W. Norton).

Santoro, D. (2017) *Myanmar: A Nonproliferation Success Story* (Canberra: Australian Strategic Policy Institute).

Schneider, J. (2016) *Amerikanische Allianzen und nukleare Nichtverbreitung: Die Beendigung von Kernwaffenaktivitäten bei Allianzpartnern der USA* (Baden-Baden: Nomos).

Schofield, J. (2014) *Strategic Nuclear Sharing* (London: Palgrave Macmillan).

Schwartz, L. (2014) 'How Supportive of the Nonproliferation Regime Are the United States and Its Allies? U.S. Security Guarantees and the Free Rider Problem', in J. Fields (ed.) *State Behavior and the Nuclear Nonproliferation Regime* (Athens, GA: The University of Georgia Press).

Sechser, T. (2013) 'Should the United States and the International Community Aggressively Pursue Nuclear Nonproliferation Policies?' in P. Haas and J. Hird (eds.) *Controversies in Globalization: Contending Approaches to International Relations*, 2nd ed. (Washington, DC: CQ Press), pp. 177–188.

Sechser, T. and M. Fuhrmann (2013) 'Crisis Bargaining and Nuclear Blackmail', *International Organization* 67(1) (Winter 2013), pp. 173–195.

Sechser, T. and M. Fuhrmann (2017) *Nuclear Weapons and Coercive Diplomacy* (Cambridge, UK: Cambridge University Press).

Singh, S. and C. Way (2004) 'The Correlates of Nuclear Proliferation: A Quantitative Test', *Journal of Conflict Resolution* 48(6) (December 2004), pp. 859–885.

Snyder, G. (1965) 'The Balance of Power and the Balance of Terror', in P. Seabury (ed.) *Balance of Power* (San Francisco, CA: Chandler).

Sobek, D., D. Foster and S. Robison (2012) 'Conventional Wisdom? The Effect of Nuclear Proliferation on Armed Conflict, 1945–2001', *International Studies Quarterly* 56(1) (March 2012), pp. 149–162.

Solingen, E. (2007) *Nuclear Logics: Contrasting Paths in East Asia and the Middle East* (Princeton, NJ: Princeton University Press).

Spector, L. and A. Cohen (2008) 'Israel's Airstrike on Syria's Reactor: Implications for the Nonproliferation Regime', *Arms Control Today* 38(6) (July/August 2008), pp. 15–21.

Tanter, R. (1999) *Rogue Regimes: Terrorism and Proliferation* (New York: St. Martin's Press).

Thayer, B. (1995) 'The Causes of Nuclear Proliferation and the Utility of the Nuclear Nonproliferation Regime', *Security Studies* 4(3) (Spring 1995), pp. 463–519.

Trachtenberg, M. (1991) *History and Strategy* (Princeton, NJ: Princeton University Press).

Trachtenberg, M. (1999) *A Constructed Peace: The Making of the European Settlement, 1945–1963* (Princeton, NJ: Princeton University Press).

Trachtenberg, M. (2002) 'Waltzing to Armageddon?', *The National Interest* (36) (Fall 2002), pp. 144–152.

Van Crefeld, M. (1993) *Nuclear Proliferation and the Future of Conflict* (New York: Free Press).

Walsh, J. (2001) *Bombs Unbuilt: Power, Ideas, and Institutions in International Politics* (PhD dissertation, Massachusetts Institute of Technology).

Waltz, K. (1995) 'More May Be Better', in S. Sagan and K. Waltz (eds.) *The Spread of Nuclear Weapons: A Debate* (New York: W.W. Norton), pp. 3–45.

Waltz, K. (2012) 'Why Iran Should Get the Bomb: Nuclear Balancing Would Mean Stability', *Foreign Affairs* 91(4) (July/August 2012), pp. 2–5.

Index